CAPITALISM AND SOCIALISM
ON TRIAL

CAPITALISM AND SOCIALISM ON TRIAL

by

FRITZ STERNBERG

Translated by

EDWARD FITZGERALD

LONDON
VICTOR GOLLANCZ LTD
1951

PRINTED IN GREAT BRITAIN BY RICHARD CLAY AND COMPANY, LTD.,
BUNGAY, SUFFOLK.

PREFACE

THE WORK WHICH culminated in this book was spread over a period of almost thirty years.

In 1923 I began work on a book which was entitled "Der Imperialismus" ("Imperialism"), and which was published in German by the Malik Verlag in Berlin, and was never translated into English.

Many of the basic ideas of the present book were already adumbrated in that book. Some of them were developed further in the following years and set out chiefly in two subsequently published books, "Der Niedergang des Deutschen Kapitalismus" ("The Decline of German Capitalism"), which was published in German by Rowohlt in Berlin and was also never translated into English, and "The Coming Crisis", which was published in English in London and New York in 1947–48.

The actual writing of this book began in 1946, and was completed in the summer of 1950.

FRITZ STERNBERG.

New York, 1950.

CONTENTS

PART ONE

The Rise of Capitalism

7

PART TWO

The Epoch of the First World War

PART FOUR

The Second World War

DIAGRAMS

THE RISE OF CAPITALISM

CHAPTER ONE

CAPITALISM CONQUERS THE WORLD

THE BEGINNINGS OF the capitalist economic system go back for several centuries, but compared with the vigour it showed during the past hundred years its development before that was relatively slow.

When Karl Marx and Friedrich Engels wrote "The Manifesto of the Communist Party"—that is to say, about the middle of the nineteenth century—capitalism was dominant only in England; the United States was still a colonial country in which the agricultural population far outnumbered the industrial; in Europe the beginnings of capitalism were confined to the west—in Germany, for instance, pre-capitalist forms of production were still dominant; Russia and Japan were still feudal States; and there were relatively few points on the Asiatic coastline which were in contact with those occidental countries in which capitalist development had begun.

To say that at that time perhaps 10 per cent of the world's population were engaged in capitalist production is probably an optimistic estimate.

However, it was about this time that capitalist expansion and the development of capitalist productive forces began to increase at a rate which put all previous developments well into the shade.

CAPITALISM BECOMES THE DOMINANT FORM OF PRODUCTION

Capitalist development had taken several hundred years to arrive at a stage at which perhaps 10 per cent of the world's population produced along capitalist lines, but within the two-thirds of a century which followed—approximately from the middle of the nineteenth century up to the outbreak of the first world war—capitalism became the dominant form of production not merely in one country, England, but all over the world, until perhaps between 25 and 30 per cent of the world's population were producing along capitalist lines, whilst in Great Britain, the United States, Germany and Western Europe in general capitalism held practically a monopoly of production. At the same time capitalist development had made considerable progress in Russia and Japan, although the remnants of feudalism still existed, whilst in the other Asiatic countries the pre-capitalist forms of production had been definitely undermined.

In this whole period the development of the productive forces under capitalism went side by side with a tremendous expansion into areas which had not previously produced within the framework of the capitalist economic system—for instance, into areas which still had to be settled.

This expansion took place in four main forms:

1. In countries like Great Britain, where capitalism was already well developed, the destruction of pre-capitalist forms of production proceeded rapidly, so that capitalism soon became the only prevailing form of production, whilst in those countries in which capitalism had developed rather later—for instance, the European countries, and especially those in Western and Central Europe—it rapidly became the dominant form of production. This was true in particular of Germany.

2. Capitalism penetrated into countries which had scarcely any industrial development around the year 1850, but which, as they developed their capitalist systems, retained their political independence—for instance, Russia and Japan.

3. Capitalist forms of production also penetrated into areas which were unable to maintain their political independence and which became the colonial areas of the imperialist (chiefly European) powers—for instance, large tracts of Asia and Africa. Thus in these areas the interests of the imperialist "motherlands" decided whether, and to what extent, they should be capitalistically developed and industrialized.

4. At that time capitalism also developed in sparsely populated areas, particularly in the United States, but also in Canada and the other "White" settlement colonies; that is to say, in countries where there were no considerable feudal and pre-capitalist vestiges for capitalism first to destroy.

In all these four spheres of capitalist development much greater and much more rapid progress took place in the period from around 1850 to the outbreak of the first world war in 1914 than ever before —or since. The basis of capitalism extended in an unprecedented fashion. At the beginning of this big period of development capitalism was an island in a pre-capitalist world, but at its end it had become the dominant form of production for almost one-third of the world's population, and, further, it completely controlled, both economically and politically, those areas in which pre-capitalist methods of production still prevailed.

However, even at the end of this big period of capitalist expansion the majority of the world's population still did not produce under capitalist conditions. Capitalism embraced the vast majority of the population of Great Britain, the United States and the western parts of the continent of Europe, but even at this peak point of its development, pre-capitalist—chiefly feudalist—forms of production still dominated in Eastern Europe, Asia and Africa. In this period of capitalist expansion, in which capitalism demonstrated its economic superiority over pre-capitalist methods of production, it was generally assumed that the advance of capitalism would continue, until in the end the majority of the world's population would be living and producing under capitalist conditions.

This did not come about.

Long before this objective was even approximately reached, tendencies began to make themselves felt which led to a slowing down of capitalist expansion, and ultimately put an end to it. In Part Three of this book we shall discuss the reasons for this.

THE RISE OF INDUSTRIAL PRODUCTION

The period of capitalist expansion was at the same time the period of economic progress in all spheres, and it was reflected in particular in the growth of industrial production.

The Rise of Industrial Production *
(1913 = 100)

Year.	Germany.	Great Britain.	France.	Russia.	Italy.	U.S.A.	Whole World.
1860	14	34	26	8	—	8	14
1870	18	44	34	13	17	11	19
1880	25	53	43	17	23	17	26
1890	40	62	56	27	40	39	43
1900	65	79	66	61	56	54	60
1910	89	85	89	84	99	89	88
1913	100	100	100	100	100	100	100

* These figures are taken from the Quarterly Reports of the German Business Research Institute issued in a special number entitled: "Tendencies of German and World Industrial Production", Berlin, 1933, p. 18. The methods of investigation adopted by this Institute differ in certain respects from the methods of others, but the difference is not material for us, because we are interested only in the general tendency of industrial development in the period, and that is not in dispute.

The above figures indicate that between 1860 and 1913 world industrial production as a whole increased rather more than sevenfold, whilst between 1870 and 1913 it increased fivefold.

This gigantic increase in world industrial production is one of the decisive features of the whole period, and it continued to dominate the scene up to the outbreak of the first world war. Each succeeding decade showed a very considerable increase, and it cannot be overemphasized that the variations from decade to decade, and the variations from country to country, took place on the basis of a tremendous development not only in the world as a whole, but also in each separate industrial country.†

Within the general framework of this gigantic progress that of the individual countries varied very considerably. Those European countries which were industrially farther ahead in 1860 did not register the same percentage increase; for instance, industrial production in Great Britain increased "only" threefold, whilst in France it increased "only" fourfold; as compared with Germany,

† The source previously quoted writes (p. 13) concerning the variations from decade to decade in Germany:

"The rate of increase, which varied between 4 and 5 per cent in the years 1866–1872, was not quite 3 per cent in the years 1872–1890, whilst in the years 1890–1913 increases of between 4 and 5 per cent annually were again obtained."

where it increased more than sevenfold, and the United States, where it increased more than twelvefold.

Variations in the progress of industrial production between 1860 and 1913 brought about fundamental changes in the order of importance of the leading industrial countries.

1860.	1870.	1880.	1890.	1900.
Gt. Britain	Gt. Britain	U.S.A.	U.S.A.	U.S.A.
France	U.S.A.	Gt. Britain	Gt. Britain	Germany
U.S.A.	France	Germany	Germany	Gt. Britain
Germany	Germany	France	France	France

By 1880 Great Britain had lost first place in industrial production to the United States, whilst France had been overtaken by Germany. In 1900 Great Britain was outstripped by Germany and fell to third place.

Another important tendency made itself felt in this period: whilst there was a tremendous increase in absolute figures for industrial production, Europe's share in the whole steadily decreased.

Regional Distribution of World Industrial Production [1]*
(Percentages of total world production)

	Europe.	North America.†	Elsewhere.
1860 . . .	75	22	3
1913 . . .	53	42	5

† The figure for North America for 1860 is a rough estimate, whilst the figure for "Elsewhere" for the same year is based on the returns for thirty-eight countries.

The following picture shows the changes:

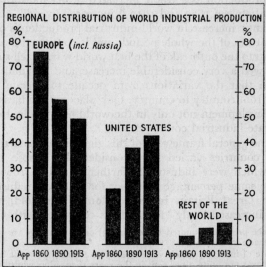

REGIONAL DISTRIBUTION OF WORLD INDUSTRIAL PRODUCTION

* Such figures refer to the original sources as listed on pp. 577–584 et seq.

The sevenfold increase in world production in this period was far greater than the increase of population which took place concurrently in the big industrial countries, and far greater than the increase in the number of workers engaged in industrial production. The increase in industrial production led to a tremendous development of large-scale industrial organization, and in some countries such organization was introduced for the first time. In the first decades of the nineteenth century capitalism had developed chiefly the light industries, textiles and foodstuffs, whilst the so-called heavy industries—iron and steel, iron-ore and coal-mining—were still in an embryonic stage. This was one of the many indications that the capitalist mode of production had still to go through the decisive stage of its development. It was only in the period we are considering that a phenomenal development of the heavy industries took place.

For instance, in the years 1855–1859 the production of pig-iron in the four leading industrial countries—Great Britain, the United States, France and Germany—amounted to 5·1 million tons only, but by the years 1910–1913 it had increased to 57·1 million tons, whilst their production of steel rose from 0·06 million tons in the year 1857 to 53·6 million tons in the years 1910–1913, and their production of coal increased from 86 million tons in the years 1855–1859 to 1,023·7 million tons in 1913.

These figures show that the growth of heavy industry in this period was very much greater than that of industry as a whole. This tremendous growth of the heavy industries created the basis for the enormous extension of the railways and for the great production of machinery which are characteristic of large-scale industrial development.

At the same time it must be emphasized that the general increase of industrial production in this period was so tremendous that apart from the creation and/or development of the means of transport and the development of heavy industry, etc., the production of the light industries also increased, though to a lesser extent. But here, too, production increased to a greater extent than the number of workers engaged in it. Thus not only was the productive apparatus extended, but also the production of consumer-goods per head of the population.

It should be borne in mind that this parallel growth is not a necessary phenomenon. The creation of a powerful industrial productive apparatus might well have unfavourably affected the development of the light industries, with the result that the production of consumer-goods increased only in accordance with the growth of the population, or perhaps not even to that extent. This was the case later in the Soviet Union, where the forced develop-

23

ment of heavy industry took place in part at the expense of production in the light industries and at the expense of the living standards of the masses of the people.

Capitalist development in Europe and the United States proceeded along different lines. It tremendously increased the production of heavy industry, whilst at the same time it quite considerably increased the production of the light industries producing consumer-goods.

How tremendous the growth of the productive apparatus was can be seen, amongst other things, from the fact that the production of the means of production—i.e. of so-called capital-goods—increased far more rapidly than the production of consumer-goods, until in the more advanced industrial countries the former entirely outstripped the latter. The following diagram, which shows the development in Germany in this period, is typical of the development all over the world:

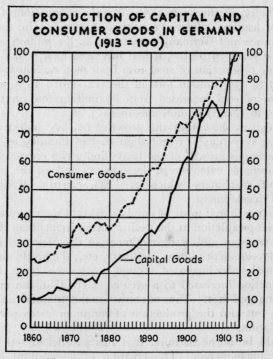

PRODUCTION OF CAPITAL AND CONSUMER GOODS IN GERMANY (1913 = 100)

THE GROWTH OF URBANIZATION

Parallel with the increase of industrial production there was a great growth in population in the capitalist countries and an increasing concentration of the population in the towns. The following are the figures for the United States:

24

Population of the United States [2]

Year.	United States (total population).	Urban.*	Rural.
1850 . .	23,191,876	3,543,716	19,648,160
1870 . .	38,558,371	9,902,361	28,656,010
1890 . .	62,947,714	22,106,265	40,841,449
1910 . .	91,972,266	41,998,932	49,973,334
1920 . .	105,710,620	54,157,973	51,552,647
1930 . .	122,775,046	68,954,823	53,820,223
1940 . .	131,669,275	74,423,702	57,245,573

* Urban population for the purposes of the above figures is taken to mean "the population living in incorporated places having 2,500 inhabitants or more".

In the period before the outbreak of the first world war the rural population in the United States was greater than the urban population because the opening up of America in the second half of the nineteenth century had resulted in the creation of millions of new farms. In Europe the process of urbanization had begun much earlier, not only in Great Britain, whose development can be regarded as exceptional in this respect, but elsewhere also, and particularly in Germany. In 1875, 26 million people in Germany were living in rural communities of up to a maximum population of 2,000, whilst 14 millions lived in small and medium-sized towns with a population ranging between 2,000 and 100,000, and 2·7 million people lived in big towns each with a population of over 100,000. By 1900 the corresponding figures were: 25·7 millions, 21·5 millions and 9·1 millions. The rural population of Germany in 1875 represented 60·9 per cent of the total population, but by 1900 it represented only 45·6 per cent, so that the urban population of Germany outnumbered the rural population considerably earlier than was the case in the United States.

This process of urbanization is only another aspect of the steady decline in importance of agriculture within the framework of world capitalist development. The figures of the agricultural population fell parallel with a decline in the agricultural percentage of production and the agricultural share of the national income.

THE RISE IN NATIONAL INCOME AND WAGES

We have seen that in the period under discussion there was a tremendous increase of industrial production as a whole, which varied only as between the individual capitalist countries. Another aspect of the same process was the equally tremendous increase in the national incomes of the countries concerned. And as the general increase in production was far greater than the increase in the population in the same period, there was also a rise in the *average income* per head of the population.

The biggest increase in the national income in this period took place in the United States, because parallel with the increase in productivity went a particularly great increase in population, thanks to mass immigration.

United States of America *

Year.	National income, in milliard dollars.†	Real national income at 1925–1934 prices.	Working population, in millions.	Real income per head of working population.
1850	2·38	6·06	7,697	787
1870	7·18	12·40	12,930	959
1890	12·00	27·20	23,320	1,259
1913	33·70	52·50	39,300	1,333

* In order not to clutter up the book with too many statistics, we are confining ourselves to the figures given by Colin Clark on the general tendency in his book "The Conditions of Economic Progress", Macmillan, London 1940.
† Milliard equals billion in the United States.

These figures show that with a more than eightfold increase in the national income the income per head of the working population rose by considerably more than half, and in reality the increase was even greater than these average figures show. In this period American immigration figures were tremendously high. Now, the conditions from which the vast majority of these immigrants had come were much inferior to those they found awaiting them in their new home. Once there, they started off with what were very low wages for the U.S.A., but nevertheless these wages gave them a much higher standard of living than the one they had left behind. However, even though they earned far more than they had earned before, their U.S. earnings depressed the general average.

What was the analogous development in Great Britain and in the leading capitalist countries on the European mainland?

Great Britain.		France.‡		Germany.[3]	
Year.	National income produced per head of the working population in pounds per annum at 1930 prices.	Year.	Income per head of the working population in francs at 1925–1934 prices.	Year.	Income per head of the working population in marks at 1925–1934 prices.
1860–1869	116·2	1850–1859	6,760	1854	1,520
1877–1885	141·7	1870–1879	10,580	1877–1885	2,600
1894–1903	175·8	1880–1889	11,420	1894–1903	2,914
1904–1910	182·3	1890–1899	13,000	1904–1910	2,999
1911–1913	195·4	1900–1909	14,420	1911–1913	3,116

‡ Alsace and Lorraine are not included in the above figures for France for the years 1871–1909.

Thus we see that the same phenomenon was operating everywhere, though with variations: there was a tremendous increase in national income and at the same time a rise in average individual income which ranged between 75 and 100 per cent.

Now of course the "average income" could also increase if the rich got richer and richer and the poor grew poorer and poorer—if "the accumulation of capital" on the one hand was matched by an "accumulation of misery" on the other. In other words, the "average income" could increase, whilst at the same time the broad masses of the people, and the working class in particular, grew more and more impoverished. But, in fact, this did not happen.

In this period—that is to say from the time when Marx was writing his "Manifesto of the Communist Party" up to the outbreak of the first world war—national incomes increased, but not at the expense of increasing misery for the working people, or even with a mere maintenance of their standards. On the contrary, wages increased considerably in all industrial countries. We do not propose to enter here into the reasons which made these wage increases possible within the framework of the capitalist system of production, but merely to quote figures to show that it was, in fact, so.

If we take the level of real wages in 1913 as 100,[4] then wages in Great Britain stood at 57 in 1850, but by 1855 they had risen to 63, and further increases, with setbacks, followed until the end of the century: 1860, 64; 1865, 67; 1870, 70; 1875, 89; 1880, 81; 1885, 82; 1890, 90; 1895, 88 and 1900, 100.

Wage levels rose in France in the same period in much the same fashion. Taking their level in 1900 as 100, it was 59.5 in 1850. It then rose steadily to the end of the century as follows: 1860, 63; 1870, 69; 1880, 74.5; 1890, 89.5 and 1900, 100. Thus both in Great Britain and France wage levels rose from under 60 around the middle of the nineteenth century to 100 at the end of it.

Thus, as these figures show, this period of capitalist progress brought about a considerable rise in real wages for the working people in all leading industrial countries.

Wages rose from decade to decade throughout the second half of the nineteenth century. Certainly there were considerable variations as between one group of workers and the other, but the decisive point is that such variations as did occur did so on the basis of a general improvement of living standards both for skilled and unskilled workers. Certainly also there were big differences between one country and another, and we know that standards of living did, and do, vary as between country and country; but the fact is that even allowing for such differences there was a quite general improvement in the living standards of working people in all industrial countries.

27

With the rapid increase of industrial production the numbers of workers engaged in industry also steadily increased. Figures are available for the United States from the middle of the nineteenth century:

Manufactures *

Census year.	Number of establishments.	Wage-earners (annual average).
1849	123,025	957,059
1859	140,433	1,311,246
1869	252,148	2,053,996
1879	253,852	2,737,595
1889	355,405	4,251,535
1899	512,191	5,306,143
1899 †	204,750	4,501,919
1904	213,444	5,181,660
1909	264,826	6,262,242
1914	261,193	6,613,189

* Factories and hand and neighbourhood industries.
† Factories with a production of over $5,000 annually.

The tendency for a steady growth in the numbers of workers employed in industry in this period is clearly visible. With the tremendous increase of production the number of industrial workers and their relative importance also increased. Their numbers grew less than the increase in production because the productivity per worker also rose, but the increase in industrial production was so tremendous that it brought about an absolute increase in the number of workers employed and a growth of their relative importance in the total population.

The figures for Germany give us the following picture:

Year.	Number of workers.[5]
1875 ‡	3,517,800
1895	6,471,500
1907	9,350,100

‡ For the year 1875 workers and clerical employees are combined.

This growth in the number of industrial workers took place not only in Germany and the United States, but also in the rest of the capitalist world.

With the increase of industrial production and national incomes the size of each country's domestic market increased. But that was not all, and the expansion of capitalism all over the world was accompanied by a tremendous increase in foreign trade.

THE GROWTH OF WORLD TRADE

It is estimated [6] that in 1851 the countries of the world imported goods to the value of £336 million and exported goods to the value of

£305 million. The order of importance in world trading at that time was as follows:

(In millions of pounds)

European countries.			Non-European countries.		
	Imports.	Exports.		Imports.	Exports.
Gt. Britain .	100	70	U.S.A. . .	39	32
France . .	45	56	India . .	12	20
Hamburg .	22	20	Brazil . .	6·5	5·5
Bavaria . .	0·8	1·2	Cuba . .	5·7	5·6
Holland . .	22	18	China . .	2	5
Belgium . .	16	15	Canada .	4	3
Russia . .	14	14	Java . .	2	5
Sardinia .	9	6·5	Egypt . .	2·5	2
Papal States .	1·5	1·2	N.S. Wales .	1·5	1·8
Spain . .	6	5	New Zealand .	0·6	0·5
Denmark .	5·5	3·5	Ceylon . .	1·2	1·5
Sweden . .	2·3	2·5	Mauritius .	1·2	1·2
Portugal .	2·5	1·6	South Africa .	1·1	0·5
Greece . .	1	0·8			

In order to give the reader some idea of how little developed world trade was in the middle of the nineteenth century—i.e., before the tremendous surge of development we have already noted —be it observed that sixty years later, in 1913, the value of Germany's exports totalled 544 million pounds and her imports 580 million pounds. In other words, the foreign trade of one of the big industrial countries in 1913 was greater than the total foreign trade of the world around 1850.

From 1850 up to 1913 there was a tremendous growth in world trade. The following are the figures from 1851 on, reckoned in pounds, first of all at the prices prevailing in each particular year, and secondly in 1929 prices:

World Trade [7]

(in millions of pounds)

Year.	Current prices.	Reckoned in 1929 prices.
1851	641	997
1860	1,428	1,903
1865	1,742	1,861
1874–1875	2,709	3,310
1880	3,024	4,230
1885	3,056	4,980
1886–1890	3,350	5,650
1892–1896	3,852	6,890
1900	4,025	6,610
1905	4,955	7,960
1910	6,430	9,050
1913	7,840	10,710

These figures show that between 1850 and the end of the nineteenth century world trade increased sixfold; and from the beginning of the twentieth century up to 1913—the last normal year before the outbreak of the first world war—there was a further increase of approximately two-thirds. The total increase from the time the "Manifesto of the Communist Party" was written up to the outbreak of the first world war was approximately 1,000 per cent.

Naturally, this increase did not take place as a steady uninterrupted process. During crisis periods foreign trade experienced setbacks, but these were temporary only, and very often they affected only the value of world trade and not its volume,* and made no difference to the general tendency of development, which was one of tremendous growth.

CAPITALISM IN THE FULL TIDE OF DEVELOPMENT

On the basis of his analysis of various social systems, Marx came to the conclusion that ". . . a social system never goes under before it has developed all the productive forces of which it is capable".

Now, if we accept Marx's own dictum, it is perfectly clear that capitalism in Marx's day was not, or at least not yet, condemned to go under. It was precisely in the period after the publication of "The Manifesto of the Communist Party", and after the publication of "Das Kapital", that a development of the productive forces took place which was unprecedented not only in the history of capitalism, but in the history of any previous social system. The quantitative development of capitalism in the period of several hundred years up to 1850 is relatively insignificant when we compare it with the quantitative development which took place between 1850 and the outbreak of the first world war.

COLONIAL IMPOVERISHMENT

However, all this undeniable economic progress of capitalism is only one side of the picture. Even in this period of rapid capitalist development, progress did not take place all over the world equally. On the contrary, as against the tremendous progress in the capitalist centres—in what are known as the "mother countries", though their real role was anything but "motherly"—there was little or even no progress, and sometimes even a decline, in those countries which they had turned into their colonies or which were otherwise more or less politically, economically and financially dependent on their decisions.

* Vladimir Voitinsky, "The Social Consequences of the Economic Depression", Geneva, 1936. See also text on p. 281.

Later we shall analyse the functional reactions between this tremendous development in the capitalist centres and the conquest of colonial and semi-colonial countries. For the moment we propose to present a few facts which will help to create an over-all picture of the capitalist process instead of the distorted picture which results from dealing with these capitalist centres only.

Capitalist progress brought about a considerable growth in the national incomes of the capitalist centres, but no approximate increase in the national incomes of the colonial and semi-colonial countries, not even an improvement beginning at a very much lower level. On the contrary, the gap between the capitalist metropolitan centres and their colonial and semi-colonial dependencies increased quite considerably precisely in this great period of progress. Colin Clark has made an interesting attempt to represent this gap in figures. Of course, only estimates are possible, because there are no exact statistics available concerning income in the colonial empires. However, there are many indications which suggest that his estimates are not far from the truth.

Colin Clark translates incomes into so-called International Units, or I.U's, in order to have a valid criterion for international comparisons.* In the period on which his calculations are based the population of the world was approximately 2,095 millions.† He then proceeds to group the population of the world according to its average income per head, with the following results:

Income per head in I.U's.	Millions of the Population.
Over 1,250	139
1,000 to 1,250	65
700 to 1,000	18
600 to 700	130
500 to 600	39
400 to 500	72
300 to 400	451
200 to 300	68
Under 200	1,113
	2,095

The incomes above 600 I.U's were in the capitalist metropolitan centres and in the world's four leading industrial countries—the United States, Great Britain, France and Germany—in particular.

The incomes below 200 I.U's were in those areas which were the objects of imperialist expansion, and they were "enjoyed" by the peoples of the colonial and semi-colonial areas of the imperialist

* An International Unit is defined as the amount of goods and services which one dollar would purchase in the United States over the average of the period 1925–1934, and all data are reduced to this standard.

† The figure is not much different from that for the last few years before the first world war, and the differences in national incomes also approximate to this period.

Powers. These people numbered 1,113 million and represented *more than half the population of the world.*

According to Colin Clark, the four leading industrial countries had national incomes totalling 119 milliard International Units: 65·6 for the United States, 21·9 for Great Britain, 19 for Germany and Austria and 12·5 for France.

In the same period the figures were China 22·7, British India 15, and the Dutch East Indies 2·6. Thus although China has a population approximately ten times as great as that of Britain, her national income is approximately the same.

Living standards for more than half the world's population amounted to only between one-fifth and one-tenth of the living standards in the capitalist metropolitan centres.

If these miserable standards of living in the colonial and semi-colonial countries could be explained away by saying that they were so low because capitalist industrial development began later in these countries, then perhaps the fiction of progress all over the world might still be maintained. But they cannot.

The speed of capitalist imperialist progress was based to some extent on the exploitation of the colonial and semi-colonial peoples, and in consequence the gap in the standards of living between the two groups was made still wider. Further, capitalist development in the metropolitan centres was accelerated to some extent by the fact that industrial development in the colonial and semi-colonial countries was prevented, or deliberately slowed down when it could not be prevented altogether.

Thus it was not that industrial development began later in the colonial and semi-colonial countries, but that it was quite deliberately suppressed and hampered by a whole series of measures.

Consider, for instance, what Professor Buchanan [8] writes about India:

"Here was a country with all the crude elements on which manufacturing depends, yet during more than a century it has imported factory-made goods in large quantities and has developed only a few of the simplest industries for which machinery and organization have been highly perfected in other countries. With abundant supplies of raw cotton, raw jute, easily-mined coal, easily-mined and exceptionally high-grade ores; with a redundant population often starving because of lack of profitable employment; with a hoard of gold and silver second perhaps to that of no other country in the world . . . with an excellent market within her own borders and near at hand in which others were selling great quantities of manufactures; with all these advantages India, after a century, was supporting only about 2 per cent of her population by factory industry."

Whilst world industrial production was constantly breaking its own records, industrial production in India—that is to say in a country whose population was about as large as that of all the leading capitalist metropolitan centres put together—was about the same absolute volume as that of Australia, with a population of only seven millions.

This low level of industrial production was not specifically Indian: it was typical of all the colonial and semi-colonial countries—for instance, the total industrial production of a vast country like China before the first world war was approximately the same as that of Belgium.*

Thus even at the height of its forward drive the capitalist system of production was not altogether progressive. It was progressive in the United States and in the European capitalist countries, and it was progressive in those countries which succeeded in retaining their political independence whilst at the same time experiencing some degree of expansion, but it was not progressive in Asia and Africa—in short, it was not progressive in any of those areas which were the objects of capitalist imperialist expansion.

CHAPTER TWO

EUROPEAN EXPANSION AND IMPERIALISM

THE TREMENDOUS ADVANCE of capitalism in the period before the first world war, embracing all sectors of the capitalist economic system—production and foreign trade, profits, wages and national incomes—was accompanied—later we shall see that the proper word is "facilitated" or "made possible"—by an outward extension of the capitalist productive system to an extent unequalled either before or since in the history of capitalism.

The extension of the capitalist sphere of operations was, of course, not a new factor. From the moment that capitalism began to develop in Europe in the womb of feudalism it expanded. It expanded at the expense of pre-capitalist production forms; it began to compete with the independent artisans and to drive them out of existence, thanks to its improved methods of production; it began to increase the proportion of agricultural production which was sold on the markets, and to reduce the proportion which was consumed before it reached the markets.

Capitalism is a dynamic system of production. From the moment it began to develop, this characteristic had a two-fold effect. First

---

* "In industrial production it is smaller than Belgium." John King Fairbank in "The United States and China", Cambridge, Mass., 1948, p. 10.

of all, it set up a ceaseless process of technical development which continually revolutionized its own methods of production and increased the productivity of labour. And, secondly, it expanded in all directions; it enlarged the sphere of capitalist production by destroying former pre-capitalist groups and forms of production, and countries which formerly produced by pre-capitalist methods or drawing them into its own sphere. The history of capitalist development can be written only if both processes are analysed.

The process of the development of capitalism from handicraft to the small factory, and on to larger and larger undertakings, culminating in the giant corporations of our own day, and the process of technical revolution in its various phases, have been described again and again, and precisely because this analysis has been so stressed, whilst the factor of outward expansion has been neglected or not treated with the proper importance, a distorted picture of capitalist development has arisen.

The outward expansion of capitalism did not merely extend the field of capitalist activities, but it represented a decisive factor for the capitalist system as such in this period. As later chapters will show, it exercised a decisive functional influence on the whole process of capitalist development; it determined the historical framework in which that process developed.

Although the inner development of capitalism from the small factory, in which the owner was at the same time the manager, to the giant corporations of our own day, which have no individual proprietors, is very important indeed, a description which confined itself to this development would be more like a photo of capitalism than an analysis, because an analysis requires that the historical factors which made this inner capitalist development possible in the first place should also be described.

For this reason, the analysis of this outward expansion will, for the moment, occupy the centre of our attention.

THE THREE FORMS OF EUROPEAN EXPANSION

The outward expansion of capitalism took place at first within those countries in which the capitalist mode of production was developing. If there should seem to be a paradox here, it is more apparent than real. At the beginning of the period of tremendous capitalist activity this process was already several centuries old; it was now enormously accelerated. In Great Britain—or England as it was generally known then—it started up earlier than elsewhere. England was the country in which capitalism was most highly developed, and it then became the country in which the destruction of pre-capitalist forms of production was most thorough. In this period capitalism in England was not merely dominant, it was practically the only system.

This outward extension of capitalism within its own country began only at a later date on the Continent, and it took generations before the process had developed as far in Germany and western Europe in general as it had in England.

It must also be stressed, as a matter of fundamental importance, that this process of capitalist development and capitalist expansion at home not only started later on the continent than in England, but also that it proceeded under different conditions. In consequence, the development in England can be regarded as classic only with considerable qualifications.

Certainly, as far as the transition from a society of handicraftsmen and artisans via small factories to great capitalist undertakings is concerned, England was a "classic" capitalist country, and to that extent a similar development took place in approximately the last quarter of the nineteenth century on the continent.

But in two essential points the English development was not at all "classic".

1. Precisely because England was the first country in which large-scale capitalist industry developed, and was therefore able to occupy a dominating position on the world market, she allowed her agriculture to decline to an extent to which there was subsequently no parallel on the continent. At that time England found it more advantageous to purchase the greater part of the foodstuffs she needed in exchange for her manufactured goods, rather than grow them herself. In this way England became the only great power in the world whose agricultural population represented less than 10 per cent of her total population.

2. England's capitalist development proceeded with particular rapidity towards the end of the eighteenth century, and it established itself firmly in the Napoleonic Wars, at a time when there was economic stagnation in Europe. At that time England had already built herself an empire, and she proceeded to develop it strongly. It was an empire whose extent could not be compared with the empires of the European States. On the basis of this exceptionally early capitalist industrial development—with an unusually small agricultural sector and an unusually large empire—the development of English capitalism certainly became classic in some respects for Europe, but at the same time it had specific characteristics which were never repeated subsequently anywhere in the world.

CAPITALIST EXPANSION INTO AREAS WHICH MAINTAINED THEIR POLITICAL INDEPENDENCE

Parallel with the advance of the capitalist mode of production in England went an extension of English capitalism beyond its own frontiers. The superiority of large-scale industrial production over handicraft production was demonstrated throughout the world. It

35

offered a strong incentive to numerous other countries to develop in the same direction. England assisted this development, particularly on the European continent. She not only exported her own industrial goods, but also her capital. In this way continental industrial development was greatly facilitated, because it was financed not only with continental capital, but also with English capital. For instance, a considerable sector of the continental railway network was not only built with English steel, but was also largely financed by English capital investments.

With this process a second phase of capitalist expansion began: expansion into countries which retained their political independence —for instance, an expansion of English capitalism into Germany. With the extension of the basis of capitalism, this form of capitalist expansion made enormous progress; from England to Europe, then later from England and the more developed continental countries to Austria-Hungary, Russia and Japan, and then from the continent on a tremendous scale to the United States.

This capitalist expansion into sovereign States—which retained their sovereignty—such as Russia and Japan, in which pre-capitalist production forms dominated right up into the period of the first world war, went parallel with a further extension of the capitalist mode of production at home—not in the sense that it established a practical monopoly, as in England, but that it became more and more the dominant form, as in Germany and Western Europe in general. At first there were differences in the extent of capitalist development between England on the one hand and, say, Germany on the other, but these differences gradually became less until, as far as any difference still existed, it was possible to say more or less accurately that continental industrial backwardness was due only to the fact that England had gone ahead first and established an advantage for herself, but it was an advantage which Germany, for instance, was subsequently to neutralize.

Now, apart from this type of expansion into politically independent and sovereign States, which remained so despite the expansion, and were therefore in a position to decide their own economic future for themselves despite foreign capital investments, there was another kind of capitalist expansion.

IMPERIALIST EXPANSION

Unlike capitalist expansion into countries whose political independence was not endangered even in the period of their industrial backwardness, imperialism is characterized by capitalist expansion into areas which it dominates politically and turns into colonies of the capitalist metropolitan centres. In addition to this direct and open establishment of political domination, it also extends its power by turning certain countries into semi-sovereign, politically de-

36

pendent areas. Of course, the conquest of colonial territory did not begin in the period we are discussing; England had conquered India, and Holland had carved out her colonial empire in the East long before. This colonial drive, which was largely European, reached a certain culminating point in the nineteenth century with an extension of colonialism in Asia and a particularly strong drive from Europe into Africa in the last quarter of the century.

Commencing with the year 1876, the following table shows the growth of colonialism in Asia and Africa up to the end of the nineteenth century:

Colonial Possessions in Asia and Africa [1]

	1876.		1900.		*Increase or decrease.*	
	Sq. km.	Population, in thousands.	Sq. km.	Population, in thousands.	Sq. km.	Population, in thousands.
ASIA .	22,772,900	291,495	25,012,700	390,636	2,239,800	99,141
Gt. Britain .	3,765,400	241,835	5,224,400	301,495	1,459,000	59,660
Holland . .	1,520,600	24,170	1,520,600	37,494	—	13,324
France . .	160,000	2,683	664,200	18,073	504,200	15,390
Spain . .	296,300	6,000	—	—	296,300	6,000
Portugal . .	19,900	849	19,900	810	—	39
Germany. .	—	—	500	84	500	84
Russia . .	17,010,700	15,956	17,286,800	25,045	276,100	9,087
U.S.A. . .	—	—	296,300	7,635	296,300	7,635
AFRICA .	3,218,700	11,425	26,950,900	123,349	23,732,200	111,924
Gt. Britain .	706,900	2,331	9,201,200	53,097	8,494,300	50,766
Belgian Congo .	—	—	2,382,800	19,000	2,382,800	19,000
France . .	700,000	2,875	10,211,200	31,518	9,511,200	28,643
Spain . .	9,800	319	220,300	673	210,500	354
Portugal . .	1,802,000	5,900	2,073,200	6,865	271,200	965
Italy . .	—	—	510,000	731	510,000	731
Germany. .	—	—	2,352,200	11,465	2,352,200	11,465

These figures show that in the last quarter of the nineteenth century the territorial extent of colonial possessions in Asia and Africa increased by more than 50 per cent, and that the population of the colonial possessions then numbered over 500 millions. The imperialist drive, however, did not confine itself to territories which became direct colonies, and industrial, financial and military superiority was exercised in order to reduce a whole series of other countries to semi-colonial dependencies, and in this way to deprive them of the decisive levers of power which would have enabled them to decide their own future.

If we consider that throughout this whole period China, for example, was not a completely sovereign State, but was more or less a semi-colonial country dominated by a number of imperialist countries, then we realize that at the end of this period of imperialist expansion, at the culminating point of the imperialist drive, *more than half the total population of the world were the objects of colonial or semi-colonial exploitation on the part of the capitalist metropolitan centres.*

They were, be it noted in particular, exploited by *capitalist* States;

that is to say, their relations to these States were not the same as the relations of the former colonial empires to their "motherlands". Ancient Rome also had an empire; but, as Rome did not live under a dynamic industrial economy, her relations to her colonies were very one-sided: the colonies were exploited directly; they were plundered; they had to pay tribute, chiefly in the form of foodstuffs, to Rome. This simple type of relationship required no fundamental change in the economic structure of the colonies after their conquest by Rome. The old forms of production could, and very often did, remain unchanged.

MARKETS DEVELOP IN THE COLONIES

Under a capitalist economic system the situation is very different. Certainly, the colonies are directly exploited and plundered, and at the beginning of modern colonial dominance this was the main aspect of relations between the capitalist metropolitan centres and their colonies.

However, with the increasing industrialization of the capitalist metropolitan centres and the increasing domination of the capitalist mode of production, the relationship between them and their colonies changed. The latter were no longer merely countries which were compelled by force to pay tribute to the metropolitan centres, and the relationship between the two began to adapt itself more and more to the exigencies of capitalism and to become less simple and one-sided. The colonial countries no longer had merely to supply; they developed at the same time into markets to which the goods produced in the metropolitan centres were exported.

Precisely because capitalism is such a dynamic mode of production, and because under the pressure of competition it constantly revolutionizes its own productive technique, increases the productivity of labour and increases production as a whole, it is constantly faced with the problem of finding additional markets for its production.

Amongst other things, this was a function of imperialist expansion, and it was harnessed into the pursuit of this aim. In fact in this period of imperialist expansion a steadily growing stream of commodities flowed from the metropolitan centres into the colonies. For instance, the English textile industry, which first demonstrated its productive superiority by putting English textile handicraftsmen out of business, then began to export its products all over the world. India, in particular, became a market for English textile products. But not only for such products; it also became a market for English heavy industry. Railways were built and—a circumstance which is not unimportant—in absolute figures India soon had more railways even than England herself, and this at a time when the building of railways in England had more or less ended. By 1890 England had

38

built approximately 17,000 miles of railways in India, or just about the length of the English railway system. But from 1890 to 1911 the Indian railway network was approximately doubled, and there were about 33,000 miles of railways, whilst in the same period the increase in England was only a little over 300 miles.

The Function of Capital Exports

Thus in this phase of imperialist expansion big markets were opened up in the colonies over a long period for the textile and heavy industrial products of the metropolitan capitalist centres. The increasing sales of such exports in the colonies did not have to wait until such time as the process of colonization had gone so far that sufficient foodstuffs and raw materials could be sold by the colonies on other markets to enable them to pay for their imports from the capitalist metropolitan centres, because at the same time the latter began to export capital on a big scale, and this helped to bridge the transitional period. It was not Indian capital accumulation, for instance, which financed the building of India's railways, but English capital. England did not wait with her exports of all the materials necessary for building India's railways until such time as India was in a position to export sufficient goods of her own to pay for these materials, and their export was largely financed by English capital exports. To this extent, therefore, the export of capital to colonial areas accelerates economic development there in the same way as does capitalist expansion into politically independent countries.

The Changing Colonial Social Structure

Now the fact that markets for the industrial products of the metropolitan capitalist centres must be opened up, and are, in fact, opened up in the colonial empires, necessarily brings about a fundamental change in the economic and social position of the colonial countries.

Asiatic peasants, who produce for themselves more or less all they require, do not represent a market for the products of industrial capitalism any more than the peasants of Europe did under feudalism. Therefore, up to a point, imperialism sets out to destroy the independent peasant economy and a great part of native handicraft.

When it thus destroyed certain pre-capitalist forms of production in the colonial areas, capitalist imperialism did no more than it had already done generations, or even centuries, before in its own country. With this difference. In the metropolitan capitalist centres it was an indigenous form of capitalism which developed on the basis of the destruction of pre-capitalist, in part feudal, forms of production. It was an indigenous capitalist class which organized manufacture and, later, factories, and by competition forced handicraft

39

out of existence. But at first there was no native capitalist class in the colonial empires, and no native factories either. There were at first no towns to become the centres of growing industrial activity. At the beginning of this new imperialist expansion there were no such things, and imperialism had no interest in creating them.

MARX AND COLONIAL INDUSTRIAL DEVELOPMENT

Imperialism did not bring about a form of economic development in the colonial areas analogous to economic developments in the capitalist metropolitan centres. The course of world development was not that the older industrial countries penetrated into industrially backward colonial countries, whereupon, after a longer or shorter period, these one-time backward countries developed to the same industrial level as the older capitalist countries. History did not develop as Karl Marx imagined when, on August 8th, 1853—almost a century ago—he wrote an article in the *New York Daily Tribune* entitled "The Future Results of British Rule in India", in which he said:

> "I know, of course, that the only reason for the desire of the English millocracy to bless the Indians with railways is to take out the cotton and other raw materials its factories need at a cheap price. But once machinery has been introduced into the transport system of a country which possesses iron and steel it is no longer possible to prevent that country from producing its own. It is impossible to maintain a railway network in a country of such vast dimensions without at the same time introducing all those industrial processes which are necessary to satisfy the direct and current requirements of railway traffic, and from this the use of machinery develops branches of industry which are not directly connected with the railways. In this way the railway system in India will, in fact, be the forerunner of a modern industrial system." [2]

That is not what happened. It did not happen in the period of imperialist expansion in which Marx was writing, and it did not happen in the period of imperialist stagnation between the two world wars. England did build a great railway network in India, but she had no intention of allowing it to become "the forerunner of a modern industrial system". The reasons are obvious enough.

The British in India were out to open up markets for the products of their own industry, and for this reason they did not encourage the development of a native industrial system. On the contrary, they used all their political, financial and economic power to prevent any such development, or, where this proved impossible, to slow it down as far as possible.

In order to achieve its aim of retaining India as a market for British industrial goods, British imperialism pursued an economic policy in India which, as far as any native industrial development was concerned, bore marked parasitic characteristics.

This policy of preventing, or at least retarding, any large-scale native industrial development did not apply only to British India; it was a policy which was pursued by all European imperialisms in their colonial empires and in the semi-colonial areas as well. Whilst the British imperialists hypocritically sought to gloss over the absence of any native industrial development in their colonial empire, the French were much more frank. For instance, Charles Robequain [3] writes:

> "The free development of industry has never been allowed in any colony; even the possibility of such development was long considered paradoxical, almost inconceivable, by the mother country. Indo-China is no exception to this rule."

In the preface to the first volume of "Das Kapital" Karl Marx wrote:

> "The industrially developed country only shows the less-developed country the picture of its own future."

With certain modifications, that was true of the attitude of England towards Germany and Western Europe in general in the second half of the nineteenth century; it was not true of England in relation to India, and it was not true of European imperialism in relation to the countries of Asia and Africa. If Marx had formulated his sentence rather differently—for instance: "The imperialistically developed country only shows the less-developed country the picture of its own future"—then his error and the reasons for it would have been quite clear. Throughout the whole century the imperialistically developed country did not show the less-developed country the picture of its future development. On the contrary, the imperialist countries adopted a policy which prevented the colonial countries from going the same way as they had gone—the way of capitalist countries.

The importance of this fact for the subsequent development of capitalism and for the future of world history can hardly be exaggerated. We shall meet it again and again in all stages of our investigations. It was not only of decisive importance for the past century, but it is of fundamental importance for future developments.

Apart from economic reasons—the desire to obtain a preferential position for their own industries—there were important political reasons why the imperialist countries sought to prevent the industrial development of the colonies, or to slow down that development where it proved impossible to prevent it altogether. The colonial countries were separated from their "mother" lands by thousands of miles of land and sea, and the Europeans in the colonies represented

41

only a negligible minority of the population. In India, for example, the census of 1931 showed that there were only 168,000 Britishers in the whole country, or roughly one Britisher to 2,000 Indians. However, this handful of Britishers controlled the key positions in the administration and they held military, political and economic power.

Much the same situation existed in the French and Dutch colonies.

How this small group of Europeans, so far away from their own countries and without any large European armies in the colonies to support them, could maintain their dominant position became their main problem.

It is clear that the development of strong native industries would have led to the rise of a native employing and capitalist class; with the support of the native working class it would then have organized a struggle for national emancipation from European imperialism. It is clear, therefore, that not only economic but also political reasons were behind the attempts of the imperialists to prevent, or, if that proved impossible, to slow down industrial development in the colonial countries.

Imperialism and Feudalism Join Hands

At the same time it also became necessary for the imperialists to look around for reliable allies among the colonial population. Now, the only social strata where such allies could be found was amongst the old feudal ruling classes, and therefore imperialism began to support these elements, and where they had begun to decline it even encouraged their resuscitation.

This policy was adopted very early on in India, and towards the end of the eighteenth century a new class of landlords was created with the so-called Permanent Land Settlement under Lord Cornwallis.

In a speech delivered during his term of office as Governor-General of India, Lord William Bentinck referred quite openly to the alliance formed by British imperialism with the, in part, newly resuscitated feudal class in India:

"If security was wanting against extensive popular tumult or revolution, I should say that the Permanent Settlement, though a failure in many other respects and in its most important essentials, has this great advantage at least of having created a vast body of rich landed proprietors deeply interested in the continuance of the British dominion and having complete control over the mass of the people." [4]

Such alliances were not confined to British India; they were concluded in the other colonies of the British Empire and in the colonial

42

empires of the other imperialist Powers as well. In this respect the observations of Professor Robequain,[5] who is not a socialist or even an anti-imperialist, concerning French Indo-China are very interesting:

> "The rural population has felt the consequences of European intervention in still another way. . . . In Tonkin large estates have come into existence since the French occupation, and as a result many small owners have now become tenant farmers."

Following the example of British imperialism in India, French imperialism encouraged agrarian feudalism in Indo-China at the expense of the small farmers.

This feudal upper class, which to some extent already existed and which to some extent was newly revived by European imperialism, became the chief ally of European colonial imperialism. The result was a politically very important phenomenon—namely, that the same capitalism which developed in Europe in a struggle against feudalism, which it partly destroyed, and whose influence it in any case very greatly reduced, now supported feudalism in its colonial empire, and in many instances actually developed it anew, and it did so because the feudal elements and their satellites, the usurers and tax officials, represented its only important political allies.

Now, this alliance between European imperialism and colonial feudalism had certain important economic results. It greatly slowed down industrial and economic development in general in the colonial empires.

The maintenance and, in some cases, the strengthening of agrarian feudalism meant that the standards of living of the overwhelming majority of the population of the colonial countries remained extremely low, whilst their income was only a fraction of that enjoyed by the peoples of the big industrial countries. In consequence, the domestic market for new industries was naturally very restricted, and because of the maintenance of agrarian feudalism the possibilities of improvement were very slender.

Further, so long as agrarian feudalism continued to exist it gave the native moneyed elements the possibility of plundering the millions engaged in agriculture, and loan capital in particular brought in usurious rates of interest. So long as conditions were favourable for this kind of usury, native owners of capital had very little interest in founding industrial undertakings, to which there was always a certain amount of risk attached, and whose rates of profit were not so high as the usurious rates of interest on loans.

It is very interesting to note that when certain English writers sought to explain away the backwardness of industrial development in India they always pointed out how difficult it was to interest native owners of capital in the idea of founding industrial undertakings,* whilst omitting to mention the real connections between the usurious rates of interest obtained on loans by native moneyed elements, thanks to the maintenance of agrarian feudalism, and their unwillingness to take risks and accept a lower return on their capital by investing in industry.

Because European imperialism desired to maintain its industrial advantage on the colonial markets, and therefore prevented or slowed down the development of native industry as far as possible, and because, in its desire to obtain reliable allies in its colonial empires, it supported the reactionary agrarian feudal elements, the course of development in the colonial countries was fundamentally different from that in the imperialist countries.

It was this juxtaposition of economic and political factors which brought about the result which we described at the end of Chapter One—namely, that in a period in which capitalism in Europe was tremendously developing the productive forces, it slowed down their development, and even sought to stop it altogether, in the colonial countries. Thus whilst capitalism was still a progressive force in Europe, it was already parasitic when it appeared in the colonial countries as imperialism.

The Era of Double Imperialist Expansion

In Part Three of this book we shall show in some detail how this parasitic policy led to stagnation in the colonial countries, even in a period when their industrial development had made very little progress, and how therefore the repercussions on the metropolitan countries declined in strength comparatively early.

In the period up to the outbreak of the first world war the colonial countries experienced more or less all the horrible accompaniments of the early years of capitalist development without, however, sharing in its subsequent progress, whereas in this same period of imperialist development the favourable results still greatly outweighed the unfavourable as far as the metropolitan countries were concerned.

We must bear in mind that this was a period of double imperialist expansion. First of all, this was the period in which markets were opened up and developed in the already conquered colonial countries, and secondly, it was also a period of new imperialist expansion, when new colonial and semi-colonial spheres of influence were added to the old. The imperialist colonial drive in the colonial empires, which exported foodstuffs and raw materials to pay for the imports of industrial products from the metropolitan centres, con-

* "There is a scarcity of capital for industrial purposes in India and this is partly due to competition from other forms of investment. The main body of Indian investors still prefer to invest in real property, ornaments and jewellery, moneylending, trade and Government securities rather than in industry, in which many serious losses have been incurred." G. E. Hubbard, "Eastern Industrialization and its Effects on the West", O.U.P., London 1935, p. 257.

tributed very considerably to the tremendous growth of world trade in this period. At the same time the repercussions of imperialism on world trade were far greater than indicated in the figures for trading between the metropolitan centres and the colonial empires, because this form of expansion, for example, much encouraged the growth of trade between the European metropolitan centres themselves.

In that period it was the European industrial countries which were the prime movers in the tremendous process of imperialist expansion. Japanese imperialism was still in its infancy, whilst imperialist expansion played only a very small role for the U.S.A.

Liberal capitalism was dominant in European countries. The State exercised very little direct influence on economic affairs, and the State economic sector itself was still very small. Far from being shaken, capitalism was still definitely on the upgrade, and so there was no tendency towards a planned economy even in the metropolitan countries. Naturally, it was the economic and political structure at home which determined the imperialist methods abroad, and as there was no question of any planned economy at home, so there was no attempt at economic planning in the colonial countries. Thus little or no effort was made to co-ordinate systematically developments in the metropolitan centres and those in their colonies such as characterized the subsequent policy of Japanese imperialism.

To a very considerable extent colonial empires had already been carved out before the opening of the nineteenth century—that is to say, at a time before the development of modern industrial capitalism—but it was not until the second half of the nineteenth century that they began to assume their main function as exporters of foodstuffs and raw materials to the metropolitan centres and as markets for the industrial products of the latter.

Thus imperialist expansion proceeded parallel with the whole process of capitalist expansion: *capitalist progress and imperialist expansion coincided.*

It is a cardinal error to suppose that imperialist expansion began only at the end of the nineteenth century. It was not imperialist expansion which began then, but the aggravation of foreign-political tension as a consequence of imperialist expansion, and that had begun generations earlier. Thus imperialist expansion took place in various phases of capitalist development in Europe. It also took place on the basis of varied capitalist social organisms, with the result that there were important differences in imperialist methods and imperialist aims. This is a point with which we shall deal in greater detail later, when we compare the different imperialist policies of Great Britain and Japan.

A whole series of misunderstandings and errors in the analysis of imperialism have arisen because investigations have been confined to the imperialist policy of one particular country in one particular

45

phase of capitalism development, and the conclusions drawn have been generalized as applying to imperialism as a whole. Obviously such an inadequate method necessarily led to over-hasty generalizations and false conclusions.

In England capitalism very early became the dominant mode of production, and British imperialist expansion set in comparatively early too. The big European States—France, and then Germany—followed later. When England was building up her great colonial empire she was already the most highly developed industrial country in the world; but in the period of her further imperialist expansion she lost this advantage, and it is a matter of importance for subsequent capitalist and imperialist development that industrially Great Britain fell behind Germany and the United States, two big Powers which had no colonial empires in which they enjoyed a privileged economic position.

Imperialism not the Same as Monopoly Capitalism

It is important to note that both Great Britain and France had more or less completed the building up of their colonial empires at a time when there was hardly any question of monopolist concentration in their domestic economies.

Imperialism has been described by some writers [6] as a phase of monopoly capitalism, but that is incorrect. In fact it was really only in Germany that there was any parallel development between monopolist concentration on the one hand and the imperialist drive on the other. Rudolf Hilferding's book "Das Finanzkapital" is illuminating in many respects, but it is robbed of a part of its value precisely by the fact that he identifies imperialism in Germany in a particular phase of capitalism with imperialism as a whole.

The imperialist drive of Great Britain and France began decades before there was any considerable monopolist concentration. On the other hand, of course, monopolist concentration was already predominant in the United States before the question of imperialist expansion began to play any noteworthy role there. Monopolist concentration in the United States went hand in hand with the capitalist conquest of the American continent.

Imperialism and Surplus Profit

Imperialist expansion was experienced by countries in which at this period free competition prevailed and in which the State exercised no decisive influence on economic affairs. The impelling force behind the individual capitalist groups which carried out this imperialist expansion was the hope of bigger profits than they could obtain at home. This hope was largely fulfilled. For a very long period the raw materials obtained from the colonial empires were sold at a high rate of profit. Thanks to the extremely low standards

46

of living which prevailed generally in the colonial countries, the working people there could be excessively exploited. When the industrial products of the metropolitan centres came on to the market in the colonial countries they had no competition from other capitalist undertakings, but only from small handicraft producers whose production technique was very backward, and therefore, despite the fact that a surplus profit was earned on their sale, it was still possible to undercut the native producers. Thus the motive behind the economic drive of individual capitalist groups into the colonial and semi-colonial areas was the same as the motive for economic activity at home: the desire to obtain the highest possible rate of profit.

But the question of the economic interests of those particular capitalist groups which were the prime movers in imperialist expansion is only the first point of our analysis.

We have seen in this chapter that imperialist expansion brought about a fundamental change in the social structure of the colonial countries. But there was more to it than that: it also had important repercussions on the economic system, and on the whole social and political structure of the capitalist metropolitan centres as well. Of course, the prime movers in the imperialist drive had no such thought in their minds; they acted as they did in the hope of a higher rate of profit than they could obtain at home, and they were well content when their hopes were realized. But quite apart from their motives and the extent to which their hopes were fulfilled, the fact remains that one of the results of the imperialist drive was a decisive change in the social structure of Europe. The question now arises: how did, in fact, imperialism, and the whole expansion which took place in this period, affect European society?

Let us first of all investigate its effects on a phenomenon which is one of the most important factors in the functioning of the capitalist system as a whole, the phenomenon of economic crisis.

CHAPTER THREE

THE CRISES DURING THE RISE OF CAPITALISM

In no period of capitalist development did the growth of the productive forces, no matter how tremendous it may have been, take place in an uninterrupted process. For instance, if we draw a curve to represent the development of capitalist industrial production in the nineteenth century, we shall see that the curve does not rise all the time, and this is true not only of world production as a whole, but also of production in the individual capitalist countries. In fact the upward curve is frequently interrupted. We see that here and there it even declines, remains stagnant for a while and only continues its upward course after a more or less long period of quiescence. But then it goes on *far above* the level of production at which the rising curve was interrupted.

In other words, the forward march of capitalism was interrupted again and again by economic crises.

The capitalist system of production is different from all previous systems of production, in that it does not merely produce goods, but commodities—that is to say, goods which must be sold on a market at a price which includes the normal rate of profit.

Now, the main aim of capitalism is to find a profitable market for a steadily growing mass of commodities. The contradictions of the capitalist mode of production show themselves in the solution, or in the failure to find a solution, for this problem of markets. The finding of a favourable solution spells prosperity; the failure to find such a solution means crisis.

CRISES OF OVER-PRODUCTION

Economic crisis resulting from the failure to find a profitable market for a constantly growing mass of commodities belongs specifically to the capitalist mode of production. Crises were known in pre-capitalist societies, but then their causes were exactly the opposite of those which produce crises in capitalist society.

Let us make the matter clearer with the help of two diagrams, each of which consists of two parts, one of which represents production and the other consumption. Crises in pre-capitalist societies were brought about when production lagged behind consumption— or, better perhaps, demand—and was no longer in a position to satisfy consumer requirements, whatever the reason for this may have been. Perhaps large tracts of country had been devastated by war; perhaps the harvests had failed; perhaps, as was often the case in Oriental countries, the all-important irrigation works had been allowed to deteriorate.

A Pre-capitalist Crisis

PRODUCTION	Deficit of Production in the Crisis
CONSUMPTION	

Thus economic crisis in pre-capitalist societies consisted in a deficit in production (as indicated in the above diagram). The result was, of course, great misery amongst poor people. However, such a crisis was not accompanied, as capitalist economic crises are, by the

48

presence of warehouses crammed full of goods which cannot be put on the market as commodities and bring in a profit. In those days there was an absolute deficit of the necessities of life. In normal periods production and consumption cancelled each other out in all pre-capitalist societies.

But under capitalism economic crisis is characterized by diametrically opposite factors. The specific problem of capitalist production is not the danger of a deficit in production, but the danger of over-production and declining consumption.

A Capitalist Crisis

PRODUCTION	Over-production in the Crisis
CONSUMPTION	Declining Consumption in the Crisis

What is the reason for this constantly recurring gap between the development of production on the one hand and the development of consumption on the other under capitalism?

CAPITALIST AND SOCIALIST EXPLANATIONS

Many answers have been given to this question, but when all possible variations have been taken into account, they have resolved themselves during the past century into two main explanations: that of the capitalist school and that of the socialist school. Generally speaking, the latter regards economic crisis as a phenomenon inseparably connected with the capitalist system and its social order, one that shakes it to the core, and one which will finally threaten its very existence. The former school, on the other hand, argues on the basis of certain specific phenomena that each crisis is no more than an "interruption" or "disturbance", and very often an avoidable one at that, and in particular it denies that economic crises must inevitably grow more and more severe until their severity undermines the very existence of the capitalist system.

In support of its arguments the capitalist school was able to point out that although there were repeated crises throughout the century of capitalist rise, they declined in violence in the second half of the nineteenth century; that, in any case, they had been surmounted fairly easily; and that, above all, and in direct contradiction to the prophecies of Karl Marx, they had not seriously threatened the existence of the capitalist system at any time during that period.

"Already it has been proved empirically that the sort of crises which Marx and Engels had exclusively in mind, i.e. the recessions which follow a period of economic prosperity have not increased but decreased in violence. The capitalist economic system never remotely experienced such a boom as it did from the middle of the nineties up to the close of the century, and nevertheless the recession which began in 1900 (the first for 25 years!) was milder than ever before." [1]

.   .   .   .

Karl Marx, the founder of most modern socialist theories, believed that the capitalist social system, which presupposes limited consumption by the workers and the great masses of the people in general, was in the last resort itself responsible for the crises. He declared that the disposal of commodities under capitalism was limited by "consumption power on the basis of antagonistic conditions of distribution which reduce the consumption of the great masses of society to a minimum which varies only between more or less narrow limits". [2]

Thus, according to Marx, crises are due to the fact that capitalism must continually increase its production whilst at the same time the consumption of the masses of the common people cannot increase proportionately because it is kept within "more or less narrow limits" by the class stratification of capitalist society. With some justification, therefore, we can say up to a point that according to Marx and the socialist theory, under-consumption on the part of the masses of the people is the cause of economic crises, and that this cause cannot be removed within the framework of capitalist society.

Now, the actual process in which this under-consumption on the part of the masses of the people expresses itself is a very complicated one. Capitalist society produces not only what are known as consumer goods, but also what are known as producer, or capital goods. The more highly developed the capitalist system of production, the greater the proportion of capital goods in its total production, and this is true both absolutely and relatively. There is no difficulty in disposing of those consumer goods which the workers can buy with their wages or which the capitalists need for their personal consumption. And at first there is no difficulty in disposing of those capital goods which have been produced in order to extend production—i.e. machinery, etc.—because the capitalists create their own market for them.

Now, as the market for these capital goods expands, so also does the market for consumer goods, because more workers are required for this expansion of production, and with their wages they increase the demand for consumer goods. Thus as long as this period of expansion continues the whole market problem is readily soluble. But sooner or later a time comes when the new factories have been built and the process of expanding the productive apparatus has reached its end. At this point the workers who were engaged in building the

50

new factories and extending the old ones are dismissed. As they no longer draw wages, they are not in a position to purchase the same quantity of consumer goods as they did when they were in work, and to that extent the demand for consumer goods—i.e. the consumption of society—decreases. But although consumption has now begun to decline, the production of consumer goods continues to increase as a result of the preceding expansion of productive capacity.

In other words, a gap opens up, and this gap affects the economic system as a whole. Capital goods are latent consumer goods. As soon as there are indications of a decline in the sale of consumer goods, investments in capital goods decline in sympathy, with the result that production in this sector of the economic system falls. The result is crisis.

A crisis thus follows on a period of expansion, on an extension of production, on a period of prosperity. However, an economic crisis is a sickness of the body economic which embodies elements of its own cure. During the course of the crisis a part of production is put out of operation by financial failures. The crisis thus creates new productive levels and new price levels, thereby making new expansion possible.

In "The Manifesto of the Communist Party" written in 1848, Karl Marx and Friedrich Engels declared:

> "How does the bourgeoisie overcome crises? On the one hand by the enforced destruction of a mass of productive forces; and on the other by the conquest of new markets and the more thorough exploitation of the old ones."

Thus far, therefore, we have noted certain factors which explain why crises come about in capitalist society, and why progress does not go in a straight line, but is constantly interrupted by crises.

However, this is not enough to help us answer the question of how deeply the capitalist system is shaken by the economic crises, and, in particular, general observations are not sufficient to help us answer the question of whether and why there are tendencies in the capitalist system towards the intensification of the economic crises, and thus towards the progressive undermining of capitalist society.

Under the impression of the economic crises which took place in the second quarter of the nineteenth century in England, Marx assumed that the general tendency was towards an intensification of the crises, although, in fact, he never took up a clear and definite attitude in the matter. In the Inaugural Address of the International Working Men's Association [12] he wrote:

> "In all European countries it has now become a truth clearly visible for every unprejudiced observer and denied only by those who have an interest in preventing its recognition, that no per-

fecting of machinery, no application of science to production, no improvement in transport, no new colonies, no emigration, no opening up of new markets, no free trade, and not all these things put together, can eliminate the misery of the working masses from the world, and that, rather, on the present false basis, *every further development of the productive forces of labour must inevitably deepen social differences and intensify social contradictions.*" [3] *

In this passage Marx stresses the fact that, apart from inner capitalist development proper, the perfection of techniques and the effects of the application of science to production, the historical framework in which capitalist development takes place and experiences its crises is of enormous importance.

Later on we shall investigate this historical framework in greater detail. The mere fact that in the second quarter of the nineteenth century the crises were so violent did not necessarily mean that subsequent crises must also be violent. Similarly, the mere fact that the crises in the second half of the nineteenth century were not so violent did not mean that this lesser violence was now the "normal" condition and that future crises would be equally mild. The decisive question remained open: was it immanent in the development of the capitalist mode of production that the crises should be mere interruptions in a period of tremendous progress, or were the reasons for this phenomenon of an external character? Was, for instance, the historical environment in which capitalist development took place at the time the real cause? To formulate the question differently: was there an essential connection between the magnitude and the depth of the crises on the one hand and the tremendous expansion of capitalism in this period on the other?

Before we attempt to answer this question we must return once again to the description of the historical framework of the crises in the second quarter of the nineteenth century. Its investigation will help us to understand the later period up to the outbreak of the first world war.

Economic Crises in the Period of Primarily Domestic Capitalist Development

In Chapter One, when we analysed the various phases of capitalist expansion, we made a distinction between capitalist expansion at home together with the destruction of pre-capitalist forms of production, and capitalist expansion abroad. Expansion at home naturally came first; but that, of course, does not mean that capitalist expansion abroad waited until capitalism at home was already absolutely dominant; on the contrary, it set in at a much earlier stage.

The first question we have to ask ourselves is why were the crises

* Italics mine.—F. S.

in the second quarter of the nineteenth century in England so violent? Capitalism in England had developed earlier than on the continent, and in consequence it reached a dominating position in England earlier than it did on the continent. Thus the second quarter of the nineteenth century was characterized by the fact that English capitalism made great progress in England itself and at the same time destroyed the pre-capitalist forms of production. Now, in these decades in which domestic capitalist expansion occupied the foreground, English capitalism was much more shaken by crises than it was later on—much more, for instance, than in the period from 1850 up to the outbreak of the first world war.

We must now ask ourselves why this was so, why in these historical circumstances the gap between English production and English consumption was so great and the crises so much more violent than was the case later, when English capitalism was already engaged in its victorious drive all over the world?

There is no dispute about the fact that the crises were very much more violent in this period. When Marx and Engels regarded the crises in particular as a decisive indication that the capitalist system was being shaken to the core, it was these crises in the second quarter of the nineteenth century which formed the basis of their conclusions. Now, why were these crises so violent? Why was the great increase of productivity not accompanied by a great increase in consumption and, therefore, by a rise in general living standards; why, instead, was it accompanied by enormous unemployment and increasing misery for the working class or, in the best case, wage stability?

With regard to the wage situation, if we take the level of real wages as 100 in 1913, then in 1820 it was only 59. In 1825 it was still 59; by 1830 it had dropped a point to 58, and by 1835 it had dropped a further point to 57. By 1840 it had risen again to 59, only to drop to 57 in 1845 and to remain at that level until 1850. Thus real wages were two points lower in 1850 than they had been even in 1820.*

Mass Unemployment

The descriptions of the economic crises of that period, with their mass unemployment, are reminiscent of the world economic crisis which broke out in 1929, rather than of the crises which followed that period in the years from 1850 up to the outbreak of the first world war.

Unfortunately there are no exact statistics available concerning unemployment at the time, "so that we are not in a position to say

* The above figures are taken from Dr. Carl Tyszka's book "Löhne und Lebenskosten in Westeuropa im 19. Jahrhundert", Schriften des Vereins fur Sozial-Politik, Munich, 1914, No. 145, Part III, p. 99, "Wage Movements in Great Britain during the Nineteenth Century", and also from Arthur L. Bowley's book "Wages in the United Kingdom in the Nineteenth Century", C.U.P., 1900, p. 126.

just how great unemployment was in those days, or how long it lasted. However, logical conclusions based on many individual items of information indicate that at times between 30 and 50 per cent of all textile workers were either fully unemployed or working short time, that such periods of unemployment and short-time work lasted for years, and that in certain less lengthy periods of acute crisis those percentages were even greatly exceeded." [4]

The following trade-union statistics for the employment of iron-moulders in England, Ireland and Wales are available:

Percentage of Unemployed Organized Iron-founders of England, Ireland and Wales [5]

Year.					Year.				
1837	.	.	.	12·4	1844	.	.	.	5·1
1838	.	.	.	10·5	1845	.	.	.	3·9
1839	.	.	.	11·1	1846	.	.	.	19·3
1840	.	.	.	14·8	1847	.	.	.	15·7
1841	.	.	.	18·5	1848	.	.	.	33·4
1842	.	.	.	11	1849	.	.	.	22·3
1843	.	.	.	7·4	1850	.	.	.	13·8

These figures indicate that there was considerable unemployment in England not only in the crisis years, but throughout the whole period. From 1837 to 1842 unemployment in this branch was never lower than 10·5 per cent, and rose in 1841 to 18·5 per cent. In the years 1846–1850 it was never lower than 13·8 per cent, varied around 20 per cent in these four years, and reached no less than 33·4 per cent in 1848.

MARX ON THE DEVELOPMENT OF THE ENGLISH COTTON INDUSTRY

Karl Marx writes as follows concerning the situation of the most important industry in England in this period, the cotton industry:

"The fate of the factory worker can best be seen by a rapid glance at the development of the English cotton industry. . . .

"1815 to 1821 depressed; 1822 to 1823 prosperous; 1824 repeal of the Combination Laws, general and widespread extension of factories; 1825 crisis; 1826 great misery and riots amongst the cotton workers; 1827 slight improvement; 1828 great increase in the number of steam looms and in exports; 1829 exports, particularly to India, greater than in all earlier years; 1830 glutted markets and great distress; 1831 to 1833 continued depression; trade with Eastern Asia (India and China) freed from the monopoly of the East Indian Company; 1834 considerable growth in the number of factories and the use of machinery; shortage of hands; the new Poor Law encourages the migration of rural workers into the factory districts; children brought in large num-

54

bers from the rural areas into the factory districts—a white-slave trade; 1835 great prosperity, but the handloom cotton weavers were starving; 1836 still great prosperity; 1837 and 1838 depression; 1839 recovery; 1840 great depression, riots, troops called out; 1841 and 1842 factory workers suffered terribly; 1842 factory owners locked out their operatives to enforce the repeal of the Corn Law, thousands of workers streamed into Yorkshire, driven back by the troops, their leaders brought to trial in Lancaster; 1843 great misery; 1844 recovery; 1845 great prosperity; 1846 at first prosperity continues but then signs of a recession; repeal of the Corn Laws; 1847 crisis, general lowering of wages by 10 per cent and more to mark the introduction of 'the big loaf'; 1848 continued depression, Manchester under military protection; 1849 recovery; 1850 prosperity; 1851 fall in commodity prices, low wages, frequent strikes." [6]

Not only were the economic crises which arose in this period particularly violent, not only did they shake the whole fabric of English society more rudely than the crises which subsequently followed in the second half of the nineteenth century up to the outbreak of the first world war, but throughout the whole period, and not only during the crises, the situation of large sections of the English working class was extremely bad and their mood violently discontented. This was the period of Friedrich Engels' famous book "The Condition of the Working Class in England", which so impressively, and on the whole so accurately, described the misery of the working people.

"The description given by Engels agrees with the evidence of other contemporaries. As an example we cannot do better than quote D. Tuckett, a bourgeois economist of the forties who is an upholder of Free Trade and is by no means inclined to take a gloomy view of the picture: 'The following description is an impartial and accurate one of the present situation of that section of the population of Great Britain which lives by working in the manufacturing industries. When trade is normal about a third of the population lives in terrible poverty and on the verge of starvation. A second third, perhaps even more, earns little more than the ordinary rural worker. Only one-third receive wages which allow them a fairly reasonable standard of life and a little comfort.' " [7]

The horrifying situation of the English working class in this period was accompanied by a tremendous accumulation of wealth in the hands of the possessing classes.

"An increase of the national wealth is by no means always accompanied by an improvement in the situation of the working

55

class. The best proof of this is offered by what happened in England in the first half of the nineteenth century when, together with the advance of industry and the enrichment of the upper classes of the population, there was progressive impoverishment for the lower classes and a lowering of wages for the greater part of the working class." [8]

Now, if the accumulation and concentration of capital increase on the one hand, whilst the impoverishment of the masses of the people increases on the other, whilst at the same time the crises become more and more violent and mass unemployment becomes a permanent social phenomenon, then it seems a logical conclusion that such a society must collapse, and Friedrich Engels [9] wrote:

"This is the reason for the deep resentment of the whole working class from Glasgow to London against the rich by whom they are systematically exploited and then left callously to their fate, resentment which must sooner or later—one can almost calculate the time—culminate in revolution, a revolution which will make the French Revolution . . . look like child's play."

The revolution did not come. It did not come then, and it did not come at any time during the lives of Marx and Engels. On the contrary, around the middle of the nineteenth century a great period of capitalist progress opened up and this time it was accompanied by a considerable improvement in real wages—i.e. by a rise in working-class standards of living.

Both Marx and Engels lived for quite a long time after this period, but neither of them was ever able to free himself completely from the impressions received and the conclusions drawn in the second quarter of the nineteenth century. Despite all the qualifications made in later formulations, Marx never freed himself from the tendency to generalize on the basis of capitalist development in England in the second quarter of the nineteenth century and to draw fundamental conclusions from the course of development in that particular period to the future development not only of English but of world capitalism.

Now, in fact, the development of English capitalism in this period was determined by quite specific conditions which were not typical for capitalist development as a whole and which were confined to this one particular period of development in England. When we investigate these specific conditions in detail we shall discover why the crises of that period were so violent, why the situation of the working class was so desperate, why unemployment was so high, why the accumulation of capital on the one hand was accompanied by an accumulation of misery on the other, and why, above all, the subsequent development of capitalism considerably diminished social antagonism.

Why Unemployment was so Great

Unemployment was so great at that time as a result of two factors which were confined to that specific period. Both in the second quarter of the nineteenth century as well as in its second half, English capitalism extended the field of its operations, but in the second quarter this expansion was primarily at the expense of pre-capitalist forms of production at home, which were destroyed in the process. In the second half of the century, on the other hand, the main factor in the process of expansion was the increasing drive of English capitalism beyond its own frontiers. Now, we must ask, how did it come about that capitalist expansion at home brought about such an unfavourable situation for the English working class and created such mass misery and high unemployment?

The increase of unemployment brought about by the advance of capitalism, by the modernization of its production technique, was certainly not responsible, because this so-called "technological" unemployment existed in the second half of the century also, though then it could comparatively easily be cancelled out. So if it was not technological unemployment which was responsible, what were the factors which caused unemployment to rise to such heights? If it was not the unemployment created by the capitalist process itself, then it must have been a series of other factors.

It was caused by unemployment which was over and above technological unemployment—unemployment which was due to the glutting of the labour market by:

(1) the often compulsory migration of the rural population into the towns; and (2) the fact that hundreds of thousands of handicraftsmen were put out of business by capitalist competition, lost their social basis and their middle-class position and were turned into wage-workers.

Both these processes reached their culminating point precisely in that period which preceded the publication of "The Manifesto of the Communist Party".

The Rural Migration into the Towns

"Up to the twenties of the nineteenth century the rural population of England increased. According to Porter, the number of families engaged in agriculture in Great Britain rose from 895,998 in 1811 to 978,656 in 1821. Thus despite the enclosure of common land, the turning of small holdings into large farms, the clearing of the estates and the compulsory eviction of smallholders to make way for grazing land, the agrarian revolution of which Arnold Toynbee speaks had not yet gone far enough in the first couple of decades of the nineteenth century to drive the rural population into the towns. But from the twenties onward there was not a single

57

census which did not show an absolute diminution of the numbers of people engaged in agriculture in Great Britain." [10]

Parallel with the great migration from the rural into the industrial districts went a large-scale process of destruction which devastated the ranks of the handicraftsmen.

"As far as the interests of the working masses were concerned, the 'most revolutionary' period was not in the last decades of the eighteenth and the first decades of the nineteenth centuries (the period in which 'the industrial revolution' is usually placed), but in the second quarter of the nineteenth century when machinery ruthlessly displaced the hand-loom weavers. The close of the eighteenth century was marked by technical inventions which were to bring about a fundamental transformation in the world economic system. However, these inventions were not put to practical use immediately. Judged by the number of persons engaged in it, one of the most important branches of the manufacturing industry was weaving, but machinery was introduced here only considerably later. Up to the thirties of the nineteenth century the number of hand-loom weavers hardly decreased at all. According to the figures of a Parliamentary Commission appointed to inquire into their conditions in the years 1834–1835, the total number of hand-loom weavers at that time was about a million. After that machinery rapidly began to displace them and by the end of the fifties there were practically no hand-loom weavers left at all in the English cotton industry." [11]

These two factors—the large-scale migration from the rural areas into the towns, and the execution wreaked amongst the handicraftsmen by the introduction of machinery—were contributory to the widespread misery suffered by the English working class in the period to which Marx and Engels constantly referred, and to the high level of unemployment, which was as high in times of crisis as it was in the crisis years of the twentieth century after the first world war.

However—and this point must be stressed—these two factors did not operate to the same extent in all periods of capitalist development; they were specific factors which operated in England in the period in which English capitalism had not yet become the only mode of production and was still engaged in destroying pre-capitalist productive forms. Thus these two factors were specific for the end phase of the clash between the two economic systems in England: the pre-capitalist, feudal, handicraft system of production and the large-scale industrial capitalist system.

In this period in England there was a tremendous industrial reserve army, and its existence greatly depressed working-class stan-
58

dards of living. However, the fact that this was so then did not mean that it must always be so under capitalism. As a result of industrial concentration itself there is a strong tendency for the creation of unemployment, but in that period it was supplemented by the two other factors we have mentioned. In later phases of capitalist development, however, the importance of these two factors greatly declined.

The factor of industrial concentration had important consequences for the situation of the working class in the whole period and for the crises which took place in it. The productivity of labour in England, which was the leading industrial country of that period, rose tremendously, and with it, of course, the volume of production. The question of finding markets for this greatly increased volume of production naturally arose at once. Now, because the situation of the working class in England was very bad at the time, because its purchasing power was declining (even when it increased it did so only within very narrow limits), the domestic market in England did not increase proportionately to the expanded market needs of English industry.

INCREASED EXPORTS NO FULL SOLUTION

The result was that the typical crisis gap began to develop, and English industry therefore began to look outside England for markets to close it. The whole period is then marked by a drive on the part of English capitalism to open up new markets overseas.

But there were limits to the extent to which this drive could be successful, and those limits were set in the specific, historical conditions in which English capitalism operated within the framework of the nascent world economic system. They can be summarized by saying that English industry set out to open up new markets abroad at a time when there was not yet really a world market in existence; at a time, that is, when, generally speaking, pre-capitalist production forms still dominated in Europe, and the European States were trying to develop their own industries against the competition of the more highly-developed English industries by erecting high tariff walls around their own markets.*

* "The extent to which English industry was hampered by European tariffs can be seen from the fact that in the forties England exported less to France than to Holland (the average annual export of British products to France was valued at 2·5 million pounds, whilst that to Holland was valued at 3 million pounds), and less to Spain than to Portugal (0·5 million as compared with a million pounds). International trade streamed into the restricted channels open to it, and between neighbouring countries which could have represented excellent markets for each other there was very little trade. The European market was not in a position to absorb the ever-increasing volume of English products. All that remained to English industry was to open up those markets which were available: the British colonies and the non-European countries in general. And this was true in particular of the most important branch of English industry, cotton manufacture, which accounted for almost half the total exports." [12]

In other words, English industry, which faced growing market difficulties at home owing to the impoverishment of the English working class and the high level of unemployment, found that the situation on the world market was also not favourable to its market requirements, because in this early period of capitalist development the world market extended only irregularly and spasmodically.

That is why the crises in this period were so severe.

These specific conditions which existed in England at that time were never subsequently repeated anywhere in the world. Capitalist development began later on the continent than in England. The continental industries were therefore not first on the world market, and they had to fight for their place there against English industries which were superior to them, at least in the beginning. Precisely because they had lagged behind England in their industrial development, and because they therefore appeared on the world market at a later date with the products of their export industries, they found the world market already in existence and in a phase of almost continual growth. At the same time these continental countries did not dream of allowing their agriculture to be ruined by overseas competition, and they therefore protected it against foreign competition by high tariff walls. Thus the agricultural sector remained greater in all continental countries than it was in England.

Of course, in the period of continental capitalist development there was also a migration on a large scale from the rural areas into the industrial areas, but it was not concentrated into such a short space of time, and therefore it did not exercise the same deplorable effects on the labour markets.

In this period the United States was still a colonial country, and throughout this whole period she suffered from an acute shortage of labour power instead of mass unemployment. And as at this time the United States and the countries of Europe were not so advanced as England in their industrial development, handicraft in these countries had not been destroyed by capitalist competition to the same extent as in England. Thus we see that the two specific factors which contributed so greatly to mass unemployment in England did not operate to anything like the same extent in Europe and in the United States.

CRISES IN THE PERIOD OF IMPERIALIST EXPANSION

The analysis of capitalist development in the first half of the nineteenth century shows England the undisputed leader of the world and responsible for about half its total industrial production. From the middle of the nineteenth century the picture began to change rapidly, until in the eighties Great Britain was overtaken by the United States, and in the nineties by Germany.

Any investigation of the phenomenon of economic crisis up to the middle of the nineteenth century was necessarily confined to England. In any investigation of capitalist development from the middle of the nineteenth century onwards England still plays an important role, of course, but she no longer occupies the centre of the stage.

Labour Market Conditions Favourable for a Long Time

Like previous periods, the period from the middle of the nineteenth century up to the outbreak of the first world war was characterized by a clash of the two economic systems: the former feudal, handicraft system, in which agricultural production and the agricultural population predominated, and the modern, large-scale industrial system of capitalism. But whereas in the first half of the nineteenth century the clash between the two systems and the destruction of pre-capitalist production forms took place in England itself, in the second half of the century, and not only for England but also, somewhat later, for the big industrial countries of the continent, it took place largely outside the frontiers.

The main question we have to answer now is how did it come about that this new clash between the old and the new economic systems had such totally different effects on the labour market, on the living standards of the working people, on economic crises and on the social body as a whole?

First of all it must be pointed out that once capitalism has become the dominant economic form in any particular country, the two supplementary factors which we have seen creating a vast reserve army of labour diminish in importance and finally disappear altogether. Of course, there was still a migration from the rural areas to the town in the second half of the nineteenth century, and there were still handicraftsmen being put out of business by capitalist competition, but most of the handicraftsmen who had managed to survive into that period continued to do so. Therefore, first of all in England, and later on the continent, there was materially only one factor which tended to increase unemployment, and that was a factor stressed by Ricardo long before—the factor of industrial concentration, the increased use of machinery, or, in other words, the fact that fewer workers were employed per capital unit.

Let there be no misunderstanding on this point; it is a factor which operates more or less in all phases of capitalist development. It operated at the time when capitalism was engaged in destroying pre-capitalist production forms at home; it operated when capitalism was driving beyond its own frontiers; it operated in the period of imperialist expansion; and it operated in the period between the two world wars. It is a factor which permanently encourages increased unemployment, and it produces unemployment unless its effects are compensated and cancelled out by other factors. Now, in the first half of the nineteenth century this permanent factor was supplemented in England by the two other factors which we have previously analysed; the mass migration from the rural areas into the towns, and the rapid destruction of handicraft and the reduction of those engaged in it to the status of wage-workers. But in the second half of the nineteenth century it was no longer supplemented to any great extent by these two factors, and its effects were therefore more easily compensated for.

EMIGRATION RELIEVED THE PRESSURE ON THE LABOUR MARKET

In addition, the new forms of capitalist expansion which began to operate created two new factors which at first tended to relieve the pressure on the labour market in the capitalist countries, and therefore to that extent improved the situation of the working class.

The first of these factors was the emigration of masses of workers to overseas countries, and in particular to the United States. Of course, there had been emigration to the United States even in the first half of the nineteenth century, and to some extent it had also relieved the pressure on the labour market at home, but from the middle of the nineteenth century on emigration increased enormously. For instance, in the ten years from 1850 to 1860 the number of emigrants was greater than it had been in the whole of the previous thirty years, as the following figures taken from the "Statistical Abstract of the United States" (1942, p. 129) show:

Immigration into the United States

1821–1830 .	143,439
1831–1840 .	599,125
1841–1850 .	1,713,251
1820–1850 .	2,455,815
1851–1860 .	2,598,214

And in the decades from 1870 up to the outbreak of the first world war emigration to the United States was, with certain variations, much greater than in the decade 1850–1860.

Thus the expansion of U.S. capitalism in its own country not only created favourable conditions on the U.S. labour market, but at the same time it improved conditions on the European labour markets. It opened up an important channel through which the European reserve labour armies could pour away, and it diminished social antagonisms not only in the United States, but also in Europe.

What was true in this respect of the United States was also true, though to a lesser degree, of the "white" British Dominions beyond the seas, and they, too, offered an outlet to European labour-power and European capital.

But apart from this capitalist expansion into areas which had previously been only sparsely populated, the other forms of capitalist expansion also had important repercussions on the labour market in the capitalist industrial countries.

62

We have previously made a distinction between two forms of capitalist expansion: the one into areas which nevertheless retained their sovereignty and political independence—such as Germany, Austria-Hungary, Russia and Japan. In the first phase of their industrial development such backward countries represented a supplementary market for the export industries of the more developed industrial countries, and as their development was encouraged by capital exports, this market extended fairly rapidly. As one example amongst many: in the comparatively short period from the beginning of the twentieth century up to the outbreak of the first world war Russian foreign trade doubled. In 1900 Russian imports were valued at 626.4 million roubles and exports at 716.4 million roubles, but in 1913 imports were 1,374 million roubles and exports 1,520 million roubles. Russia's share in world trade was then approximately 3·5 per cent, and was very little smaller than her share in world production.

What was true of her foreign trade and her exchange with industrial Europe was also true in the same way for the other industrially backward countries: they afforded growing markets for the industries of the capitalist metropolitan centres. In this way the expansion of capitalism beyond its own frontiers had an important effect on the labour markets in the more developed capitalist countries: the export industries were able to employ increasing numbers of workers. Naturally, this development could not go on indefinitely.

Germany, for instance, was at first an important market for the English export industries, but she then rapidly became a big industrial country in her own right and began to expand economically beyond her own frontiers. But in this period—i.e. more or less at the beginning of the second half of the nineteenth century—the capitalist mode of production was dominant for only about one-tenth of the world's population, so that capitalism found a tremendous area open to its expansionist drives. At the same time the fact that the capitalist basis of this expansion was steadily extending did not play such a decisive role as long as one country after the other was still being drawn into the capitalist sphere. Thus capitalist expansion into countries which retained their political independence created growing labour markets over a long period before counter tendencies, produced by the fact that some of them became embittered competitors, began to exercise their effect.

Apart from this form of expansion, the whole period was characterized by vigorous imperialist expansion—i.e. by expansion into areas in which the metropolitan capitalist centres were able to determine the course of development in accordance with their own imperialist interests. The imperialist powers opened up markets in these countries just as they did in those countries which succeeded in retaining their own sovereignty and political independence; but in the colonial countries they also did their best at the same time to prevent these countries from developing into competitors.

IMPERIALISM AND THE LABOUR MARKET

It is now important for us to discover what effect this imperialist drive had on the labour market in the metropolitan capitalist centres, what effect it had on the gap between the growing volume of production on the one hand and the development of consumption on the other, and what effect it had on those factors which are decisive for the problem of economic crisis.

Let us examine this process on the basis of England's imperialist drive in India. It is here that we can see quite clearly why this form of English capitalist expansion produced effects which were diametrically opposed to those produced by the domestic expansion of English capitalism.

The textile industry was dominant in England in the beginning, and it played the leading role in the opening up of new markets in India. Similarly, just as the English textile industry had destroyed pre-capitalist forms of production at home, so it now destroyed them in India also. It destroyed hand-weaving, and it also largely destroyed the part-time industrial activity of the Indian village. The process was ruthless and brutal. Karl Marx, who had already described the misery of the English cotton operatives during the period when hand-weaving was being destroyed in England, also quotes the famous words of an English Governor-General of India on the effects of English mechanized textile competition in the years 1834–1835:

"The misery hardly finds a parallel in the history of commerce. The bones of the cotton weavers are bleaching the plains of India." [13]

There was a certain similarity between the process of destroying the independent weavers in England and that which took place subsequently in India. However, in England the former hand-weavers became industrial workers, and thus increased the pressure on the labour market at home, and this was one of the reasons for the existence of mass unemployment at the time. The situation in India was quite different, primarily because the English did their utmost to prevent the rise of a native Indian textile industry on a large-scale capitalist basis. Pandit Nehru [14] describes what happened:

"The Indian textile industry collapsed, affecting vast numbers of weavers and artisans. The process was rapid in Bengal and Bihar; elsewhere it spread gradually with the expansion of British rule and the building of railways. It continued throughout the nineteenth century, breaking up other old industries also: shipbuilding, metalwork, glass, paper and many other crafts.

"To some extent this was inevitable as the older manufacturing

64

came into conflict with the new industrial technique. But it was hastened by political and economic pressure, and no attempt was made to apply the new technique to India. Indeed, every attempt was made to prevent this happening, and thus the economic development of India was arrested and the growth of new industry prevented. Machinery could not be imported into India. A vacuum was created in India which could only be filled by British goods, and which led also to rapidly increasing unemployment and poverty. The classic type of modern colonial economy was built up, India becoming an agricultural colony of industrial England, supplying raw materials and providing markets for England's industrial goods.

"The liquidation of the artisan class led to unemployment on a prodigious scale. What were all these scores of millions, who had so far been engaged in industry and manufacture, to do now? Where were they to go? Their old occupations were no longer open to them; the way to new ones was barred. They could die, of course; that way of escape from an intolerable situation is always open. They did die, in tens of millions. . . .

"But still vast numbers of them remained, and these increased from year to year as British policy affected remoter areas of the country and created more unemployment. All these hordes of artisans and craftsmen had no jobs, no work, and all their ancient skill was useless. They drifted to the land, for the land was still there. But the land was fully occupied, and could not possibly absorb them profitably. So they became a burden on the land, and the burden grew; and with it grew the poverty of the country, and the standard of living fell to incredibly low levels. This compulsory back-to-the-land movement of artisans and craftsmen led to an ever-growing disproportion between agriculture and industry; agriculture became more and more the sole business of the people because of the lack of occupations and wealth-producing activities.

"India became progressively ruralized. In every progressive country there has been, during the past century, a shift of population from agriculture to industry, from village to town; in India this process was reversed as a result of British policy. The figures are instructive and significant. In the middle of the nineteenth century about 55 per cent of the population is said to have been dependent on agriculture; recently the proportion so dependent was estimated at 74 per cent."

Thus the drive of British capitalism into India did not at first lead to the rise of any large-scale native industry or to the development of a native industrial working class.

India's feudal-handicraft society was shaken to its foundations, but at the same time English imperialism prevented the rise of a native large-scale industry such as had developed in England itself, in Europe and, later, in the United States. It did this at a time when it was already beginning to destroy the means of life of the Indian hand-weavers by the competition of its own textile industry. It was this period to which Marx refers in Volume One of "Das Kapital". But this policy was continued in the years that followed, in the whole period from the middle of the nineteenth century up to the outbreak of the first world war. Throughout this period England did her utmost to prevent the development of a large-scale native industry in India, and when it proved impossible to prevent it altogether she did her best to slow down that development—with the result that right up to the outbreak of the first world war large-scale industry in India remained negligible.

What were the effects of this drive of English capitalism out into the world—a drive subsequently emulated by capitalism in other countries—with its opening up of markets for its own domestic production and its prevention of any large-scale industrial development and the rise of a native working class in the colonial and semi-colonial countries? First of all this new clash between modern capitalist production methods and pre-capitalist production forms abroad improved the situation on the labour market in the metropolitan capitalist centres, and in consequence it was much easier to cancel out the tendency of new machinery to cause unemployment.

Let us assume that in a particular period the number of workers engaged in the English textile industry was 300,000, and let us further assume that with the increased introduction of machinery to raise the productivity of labour the same total product could be produced by 250,000 workers. This would mean that machinery had made 50,000 textile workers redundant. However, if at the same time Empire markets offered scope for a greatly increased volume of textile products, and not only for a short transitional period but for generations (because, as we have seen, large-scale textile production in the Empire was deliberately prevented), so that English textile sales doubled, then there would be work not for 250,000 English textile workers, or even for 300,000, but for twice 250,000. In other words, despite the increased introduction of machinery, the total number of workers employed in the English textile industry would increase by 200,000. That was typical of what happened not only in England but in all other capitalist metropolitan centres in the period of imperialist expansion.

INCREASING EMPLOYMENT CHARACTERIZES IMPERIALIST
EXPANSION

The clash of capitalism with pre-capitalist production forms, as far as it took place in the shape of imperialist expansion, greatly improved the situation on the labour market for the working class in the more highly developed capitalist countries.

Thus the fact that no industrial working class arose in India and in the British Empire in general, or in any other of the colonial and semi-colonial countries, decisively affected the condition of the English working class and of the working class in all other capitalist countries. But, as Nehru [15] writes:

"The cost in human suffering was paid . . . and paid in full by others, particularly by the people of India, both by famine and death and vast unemployment. It may be said that a great part of the costs of transition to industrialism in western Europe were paid for by India, China and the other colonial countries whose economy was dominated by the European powers."

Let us sum up. In this period when capitalism clashed with pre-capitalist production forms, and when new countries were opened up, there were three factors which favourably affected the situation on the labour market for the working class in the metropolitan capitalist centres:

1. Large-scale emigration to the United States and to other overseas countries.

2. Capitalist expansion into countries which nevertheless succeeded in retaining their political sovereignty; and

3. Imperialist expansion into areas inhabited by half the population of the world, an expansion which opened up new markets for the industries of the metropolitan capitalist centres without at the same time leading to the development of native large-scale industries with their own working classes.

If we add at the same time that the two factors which formerly led to increased pressure on the labour market—the migration from the rural areas into the towns and the destruction of handicraft at home— became much less important in this period, we can easily see why the situation on the labour market in the capitalist metropolitan centres was so favourable in this period of capitalist and imperialist expansion. The number of workers employed in industry increased in all big industrial countries. Whereas formerly in England there had been tremendous unemployment in periods of acute crisis, and permanent unemployment throughout all phases of the business cycle, in the period we are now discussing unemployment was very greatly reduced during the years of prosperity, and even in the years of crisis it never remotely reached the level of the crisis years of the second quarter of the nineteenth century.

The comparatively favourable situation of the labour market, which continued—and this is a point whose importance can hardly be over-estimated—not merely for a few years, or for a decade or two, but throughout the whole period of vigorous capitalist–imperialist expansion, had a decisive effect on wages and working-class standards of living, and thereby on marketing and crisis problems.

In this second half of the nineteenth century the ceaseless revolutionizing of technique increased the productivity of labour, and this took place at a time when the organization of the working class into trade unions was not very far advanced. However, this time, as distinct from what happened in the second quarter of the nineteenth century, the increase in the productivity of labour did not result in growing unemployment, but, on the contrary, produced a comparatively favourable situation on the labour market, and sometimes even a shortage of labour. The result was that employers were compelled to increase wages.

Thus capitalist expansion, which led to a tremendous extension of markets abroad, was one of the main factors which created a situation in which the increasing productivity of labour was accompanied by rising profits *and* rising wages. Wages rose not merely for a few years, or even for a few decades, but for whole generations, and this was true not only of England, but of all big industrial countries. This process was further encouraged by the fact that capitalist expansion into under-developed areas, and particularly imperialist expansion, often produced higher rates of profit than the average.

Now, the fact that employment increased by many millions from decade to decade, whilst at the same time real wages rose, resulted in a tremendous growth in the home markets of all industrial countries. For example, if the sum of wages increased by between 50 and 100 per cent in the second half of the nineteenth century, then the capitalists were obviously in a position to make huge investments for home industry, because they were quite certain that the growing production would find a big market ready to absorb it. Now, as the industries working for the home market, both the capital and consumer-goods industries, found their markets growing, and could therefore expand without fear, the total number of workers employed in them also increased.

Thus capitalist–imperialist expansion first had direct effects on the export industries of the capitalist metropolitan centres. But even more important than these direct effects were the indirect ones: by improving the situation on the labour market, by increasing the number of employed workers and by increasing their real wages it contributed tremendously and continuously to an extension of the home market for industrial goods.

SECONDARY EFFECTS

The very important effects of capitalist–imperialist expansion beyond the frontiers, directly on the export industries and indirectly on the industries working for the home market, were naturally not confined to those countries which already possessed colonial empires, such as Great Britain, France and Holland, but extended to all big industrial countries. There were two reasons for this.

First of all, apart from direct imperialist expansion—i.e. expansion into colonial countries, or into countries which subsequently became colonial—there was also expansion into countries which succeeded in maintaining their political sovereignty, or whose political sovereignty was not materially restricted. The whole of industrial Europe, and in particular Germany, whose colonial possessions were negligible, took part in this expansion. In the last decades of the nineteenth century and at the beginning of the twentieth, German capitalism expanded more and more to the east and south-east of Europe, and reinforced this process with capital exports.

Secondly, there was a big increase in inter-European trade precisely because this was a period of such tremendous expansion. For instance, in this period Great Britain enjoyed a growing revenue from her so-called invisible exports, and in particular from her investments all over the world. As a result of these tremendous revenues Great Britain was in a position to finance increasing import surpluses, and to a very large extent these import surpluses came from Europe. Thus those European countries which had no colonial empires, and which were therefore not directly imperialist Powers, also enjoyed a share in the favourable economic effects of imperialist expansion, because it was the latter in particular which allowed Great Britain to finance such a big import surplus from Europe in this period.*

To argue therefore, as some people do, that imperialist expansion was not decisive for European development as a whole because many European countries had either no colonial empires, or only negligible ones, misses the cardinal point of the whole situation. This argument also overlooks the fact of European capitalist expansion into industrially under-developed countries which nevertheless retained their political independence, a form of expansion in which Germany played a particularly important role.

It is no doubt true that the surplus profits enjoyed by the big imperialist powers from their direct imperialist expansion were very great, and certainly their world political position was much strengthened by their colonial possessions—the aggravation of foreign-political conflicts before the first world war was primarily due to the fact that the distribution of colonial possessions became less and less

* When, after the second world war—that is to say, in a period when imperialism was declining—Great Britain's revenues from invisible exports were greatly reduced, and she was therefore compelled to cut down her imports to more or less the size of her exports—that is to say, when she was no longer in a position to finance a surplus of imports in her trade with Europe—the fact that previously European countries had profited indirectly from Great Britain's favourable imperialist balance was made abundantly clear to those countries.

appropriate to existing power relations—but the fact remains that the favourable effects of imperialist expansion were not confined to those countries which had large colonial possessions, but affected industrial Europe as a whole.

THE ECONOMIC CRISES BECOME LESS VIOLENT

In all phases of its development, capitalism has been faced with the problem of finding additional markets for its constantly increasing production, but in the nineteenth century, and in the twentieth century up to the outbreak of the first world war, it had to find them in a world in which the capitalist mode of production was not yet dominant everywhere, a world therefore which offered capitalism a possibility of greatly increasing its sphere of operations. Capitalist expansion as a whole, and the imperialist expansion which took place within its general framework, played a decisive role in the opening up of new markets. In this connection it must be stressed again that the real extension of markets cannot be estimated from the growing figures for foreign trade alone.

The volume of foreign trade certainly increased tremendously— and it increased constantly. As price variations are particularly great where exports are concerned, world foreign-trade statistics based only on prices do not give an adequate picture. The constancy of the increase in foreign trade is shown much more clearly in statistics based on its volume.

The Volume of World Trade [16]

(1913 = 100)

Year.	Total.	Manufactures.	Primary products.
		(Percentage of 1913.)	
1876–1880 . .	31·6	32·2	31·2
1881–1885 . .	38·8	40	38
1886–1890 . .	44·8	45·2	44·5
1891–1895 . .	49·3	45·9	51·4
1896–1900 . .	55·6	48	60·3
1901–1905 . .	67·9	63·2	70·7
1906–1910 . .	81·2	78	83·1
1911–1913 . .	96·5	95·7	97
1913 . . .	100	100	100

Allowing for all temporary variations in the rate of growth, the over-riding fact is that there was a continual increase in the volume of foreign trade throughout the entire period. And this fact is clearer to us to-day than it was to contemporaries. The volume of foreign trade in 1913 being represented by 100, it had increased only to 107·4 by 1936–1938. For manufactures it was only 92·2 [17] in those years, or below the 1913 level. 1950 hardly reached the level of 1936–1938, so that, in other words, from 1913 to 1950 world trade was more or less stagnant.

But apart from the tremendous increase in the volume of foreign trade in the period under review on the basis of capitalist and imperialist expansion, capitalism also found greatly increased markets at home, thanks to the comparatively favourable situation on the labour market, the increase in the number of employed workers and the rise in real wages—thanks, in other words, to the fact that in this period of expansion both profits *and* wages increased.

This double increase of markets, the growth of export markets and the growth of home markets, was the decisive factor which gave the economic crises of the period their unusual character—a character not experienced either before or since. It is not necessary to deal in any detail with the individual crises which took place in this period. Different as they were from each other in many respects, they all had one thing in common: they were comparatively short interruptions in a constant and vigorous advance of capitalism. This was true not only of foreign trade, but also of world capitalist production as a whole and of production in the individual big industrial countries. The essential characteristic of this whole period is not only that world production increased so considerably, but also that such setbacks as occurred, even in the most violent of the crises of this period, were not very great.

In analysing the production curves of the leading industrial countries of the day—Great Britain, Germany and America—Joseph A. Schumpeter [18] could justly write with regard to the development of production in this period:

"The broad fact of great steadiness in long-term increase . . . remains, both in the sense of rough constancy of the gradient of the trend and in the sense of what, merely by way of formulating a visual impression, we may term the general dominance of trend over fluctuations. . . . In no country does 1873 look very catastrophic. In America 1884 produced almost no fall at all. The crisis of the early nineties shows, for Germany, only an inconsiderable dent. In the long English series it happens only twice that absolute fall outlasts two years. In the case of Germany, this occurred only in 1868, 1869 and 1870; in America also but once."

This gigantic forward development of world trade and world production within the framework of the capitalist system, which was interrupted only slightly by the outbreak of economic crises, applied only to this epoch of capitalism under the specifically prevailing conditions of expansion and imperialism. It did not apply to England in the period before, and it did not apply to world capitalism in the period between the two world wars.

Those writers who failed to analyse the historical conditions under which the advance of the capitalist mode of production took place were usually satisfied with the explanation that the crises in this period were so very much less violent because capitalism had already emerged from its infancy and had overcome its teething troubles. Further to this explanation they also believed that, subject to certain inner changes, the capitalist system had since created a basis on which production could continue to rise steadily together with increasing labour productivity, growing employment, and a related growth of profits and wages and of the national income as a whole.

The subsequent development of the capitalist system in the period between the two world wars amply demonstrated the erroneousness of these assumptions. When capitalist expansion as a whole, and with it imperialist expansion, ceased, the character of the economic crises changed fundamentally. Rosa Luxemburg had foreseen this long before. When towards the end of the nineteenth century German social-democratic circles were discussing to what extent the amelioration of the economic crises over a long period refuted the views of Marx, she pointed out in the first edition of her book "Social Reform or Revolution":

"When we examine the present economic situation we must certainly admit that we have not yet entered that phase of full capitalist maturity which is presupposed by Marx's theory of periodical crises. The world market is still in a stage of expansion. Thus, although on the one hand we have left behind those sudden impetuous openings-up of new areas to capitalist economy which took place from time to time up to the seventies, and with them the earlier, so-to-speak, youthful crises of capitalism, we have not yet advanced to that degree of development, including the full expansion of the world market, which would produce periodic collisions between the productive forces and the limits of the market, or, in other words, the real economic crises of fully-developed capitalism. . . . Once the world market is more or less fully expanded so that it can no longer be suddenly extended, then the ceaseless growth in the productivity of labour will sooner or later produce those periodic collisions between the productive forces and the limits of the market which will become more and more violent and acute by repetition."

Those lines were written in 1898. Their accuracy was dramatically confirmed by capitalist development between the two world wars, and in particular by the world economic crisis which began in 1929.

THE CRISES NOT AT REGULAR INTERVALS

When we bear in mind the decisive influence of external expansion on all those factors which determine the related problems of markets and economic crisis, it is clear enough why crises do not take place at regular intervals. The effect of expansion as a whole was not confined to facilitating the liquidation of crises once they had broken out —for instance, by offering new possibilities of investment—but it affected development as a whole; it affected the markets in every phase of the business cycle because it was a contributory factor to the development of exports, profits, employment, wages and home markets.

Even if we were to assume—and experience offers no opportunity for testing the hypothesis, because capitalism was never the only prevailing mode of production and never will be—that there are certain forces immanent in the capitalist mode of production which make for the outbreak of economic crises at regular intervals, past experience has shown clearly that there is no regularity in the outward expansion of capitalist production. No regularity existed in this respect at any time up to the first world war. Periods of vigorous expansion alternated with periods in which expansion was slow. Outward capitalist expansion never stood in any fixed relation to the development of capitalist production. Because this was so, and because the direct and indirect effects of outward capitalist expansion on all the factors which determine economic crises were so very great, it is quite clear that there could be no regularity in the outbreak of crises. This was true of capitalism at that time; it is true of capitalism to-day; and it will be true of capitalism in the future. In fact, the whole idea that there could be any regular periodicity about the outbreak of economic crises springs from the erroneous belief that the laws of capitalist development can be analysed purely on the basis of the capitalist metropolitan centres, and without taking the decisive factor of outward expansion into consideration. The fact is that no effective analyses can be made without taking into consideration the passive objects of capitalist–imperialist expansion.

IMPERIALISM AND ECONOMIC CRISIS

Capitalist expansion, and, within its framework, imperialist expansion in particular, had decisive effects on the development of the whole capitalist system, including the very important result of greatly diminishing the severity of the economic crises. This development can be fully understood only when the relation between imperialist expansion and economic crises in this phase of capitalist development is taken into account.

Capitalist expansion and, within its framework, imperialist expansion were not something which came about in addition to—so to speak, on top of—a capitalism system which was already functioning very well without it; capitalist expansion and imperialism were the decisive factors which resulted in the smooth working of the capitalist system in this period, above all because they gave a great impetus to

73

both home and foreign trade. A standstill in capitalist expansion in this period, including a standstill, or even a decline, of imperialist expansion, would have had tremendous repercussions on the capitalist system as a whole. Later on, between the two world wars, the world was to see in practice just what those repercussions were. Thus a decline of imperialism would not have meant merely the loss of surplus profits for various capitalist groups, but also a tremendous intensification of the economic crises even in that period.

Therefore if we are to obtain a complete picture of its all-important effects on the capitalist metropolitan centres, imperialism must be analysed on three levels.

The first approach is to discover why certain capitalist groups showed such a great interest in imperialist expansion and in the subsequent maintenance of colonialism. The answer to this is quite simple; it was the urge to obtain profits greater than they could hope to obtain at home, and to win positions for themselves in the colonies which could not be won at home. In this connection James Mill rightly refers to the colonial empires as "a vast system of outdoor relief for the upper classes".

The second approach is to discover how it came about that these capitalist groups which profited directly from imperialist expansion wielded such power that they were able to influence the foreign policy of capitalist States at the time in their interests. J. A. Hobson gives us the answer to this question in his book on imperialism,[19] and he shows how, although they were never all-powerful, yet, together with certain militarist circles, they were able to guide foreign policy in a direction favourable to their interests.

The third approach is to find out what were the effects of imperialist expansion, within the framework of the general outward expansion of capitalism, on the whole social and political structure of the capitalist metropolitan centres.

Only if we combine our analysis in this way shall we be able to understand the full scope and intensity of the impelling force which urged capitalism to its enormous imperialist drive. If the analysis were limited to the first two methods of approach it would certainly show that imperialism was a matter of great importance, but it would not suggest that it was of decisive importance for the functioning of the capitalist system as a whole. And if that had not been so, then a movement against imperialism could have been opened up within the framework of the capitalist system with some prospect of success. Hobson's argument that the whole direct volume of imperialist profits—although relatively high—was not so great as the military costs imperialism involved, owing to the intensification of foreign-political antagonisms, would have won the day and had practical results. Under his slogan that imperialist surplus profits were less than the military expenditure they involved, an anti-imperialist movement could then have developed; but, in fact, there was no such effective anti-imperialist movement in the capitalist countries, and only the socialists were staunch opponents of imperialism.

Why was there no social group strong enough to oppose the imperialist drive in this period? The simple explanation is that imperialism exercised a decisive effect on the capitalist economic system as a whole, on the problem of markets and the problem of crises, and on class stratification in general.

Hobson's equation is therefore wrong. The juxtaposition of imperialist surplus profits on the one hand and increased military expenditure on the other is an over-simplification. It assumes that the capitalist system would have worked very well at the time without imperialism. In fact a standstill or decline of imperialism would have led to economic crises of the extent and violence of that of 1929. Thus the real equation is very different: imperialist surplus profits did not stand alone on the one side against increased military expenditure on the other, but side by side with imperialist surplus profits went the ameliorating effect of imperialism on the whole process which made for economic crises. Small wonder, therefore, that capitalism chose imperialism as the better and easier solution!

To a certain extent Hobson [19] was himself aware of this point, and it is therefore as well to quote his own words in order to stress the real alternatives:

"By far the most important economic factor in imperialism is its influence on investments. . . . It is not too much to say that the modern foreign policy of Great Britain has been primarily a struggle for profitable markets of investment. . . ." But not only for Great Britain. "In the early nineties Germany was suffering severely from what is called a glut of capital and of manufacturing power: she had to have new markets; her consuls all over the world were 'hustling' for trade; trading settlements were forced upon Asia Minor; in East and West Africa, in China and elsewhere the German Empire was impelled to a policy of colonization and protectorates as outlets for German commercial energy.

"Every improvement of methods of production, every concentration of ownership and control, seems to accentuate the tendency. As one nation after another enters the machine economy and adopts advanced industrial methods, it becomes more difficult for its manufacturers, merchants and financiers to dispose profitably of their economic resources, and they are tempted more and more to use their governments in order to secure for their particular use some distant undeveloped country by annexation and protection.

"The process, we may be told, is inevitable, and so it seems upon a superficial inspection. Everywhere appear excessive powers of production, excessive capital in search of investment. It is admitted by all businessmen that the growth of the powers of production in their country exceeds the growth in consumption, that more goods can be produced than can be sold at a profit, and that more capital exists than can find remunerative investment.

"It is this economic condition of affairs that forms the taproot of imperialism." [20]

Now Hobson did not think this development inevitable, and he gave the alternative as follows:

"If the consuming public in this country raised its standard of consumption to keep pace with every rise of productive powers there could be no excess of goods or capital clamorous to use imperialism in order to find markets; foreign trade would indeed exist, but there would be no difficulty in exchanging a small surplus of our manufactures for the food and raw materials we annually absorb, and all the savings that we made could find employment, if we chose, in home industries." [21]

A few pages later on he writes even more clearly:

"Thus we reach the conclusion that imperialism is the endeavour of the great controllers of industry to broaden the channel for the flow of their surplus wealth by seeking foreign markets and foreign investments to take off the goods and capital they cannot sell or use at home.

"The fallacy of the supposed inevitability of imperial expansion as a necessary outlet for progressive industry is now manifest. It is not industrial progress that demands the opening up of new markets and areas of investment, but maldistribution of consuming power which prevents the absorption of commodities and capital within the country." [22]

Hobson is right inasmuch as the existence of a satisfactory relationship between production and consumption at home would abolish the need for imperialist expansion. He is also right when he says:

"A completely socialist State which kept good books and presented regular balance sheets of expenditure and assets would soon discard imperialism." [23]

But what he failed to estimate at its true value was the difficulty European capitalist society would have experienced at that time in finding an acceptable alternative to imperialism, because the suitable alternative is not liberalism. Liberalism had proved itself unable to bring about a capitalist development anywhere in which production and consumption were attuned to each other at home. The liberal capitalist State whose motto was *"laissez-faire"* was not capable of performing this task. What was required was a State planned-economy with the definite object of increasing the consuming power of the masses of the people, and in this way steadily extending the home market without intensifying economic crisis and without an imperialist drive beyond the frontiers. But there was no such State in existence at that time, and the imperialist drive took place precisely in a period in which the State exercised relatively little influence on economic affairs. Further, there was no highly-organized and politically conscious working class to struggle for influence in the State in order to secure the adoption of such a programme. In addition, a by-product of imperialism, not only in England, but elsewhere, was a very considerable improvement in the situation of the working class at home. The result was that the alternatives as they appeared to Hobson—imperialist and reactionary forces on the one hand, and the battle for liberal principles on the other—did not fit the facts of the situation as it existed at the time.

With a certain over-simplification we could formulate the problem as follows: but for imperialism, European capitalism in its then form would have developed in a fashion which would have led inevitably to much more violent economic crises.

But instead European capitalism experienced a great phase of expansion in which imperialism played a decisive role, and the result was such a diminution of crisis severity that crises did little more at that time than affect the surface of economic affairs, without fundamentally shaking the social structure.

The alternative to this result achieved by imperialism, which involved a diminution of social antagonisms, would have been a fundamental change in the distribution of political power in the State and, in consequence, a change in the economic structure fundamental enough to bring production and consumption into line with each other.

But there were no social forces at the time strong enough to bring about this great change in capitalist society, and in part this was precisely due to the fact that imperialist expansion had resulted in a big change in class stratification and in the social structure, and to some extent this change cut the ground from under the feet of the anti-imperialist, incidentally mainly socialist, forces.

We shall deal with this point again in Chapter Five when we discuss the general class stratification of society in the period of capitalist expansion. First of all, however, we must analyse that particular form of capitalism whose expansion in this period was relatively little affected by imperialism—namely, United States capitalism.

CHAPTER FOUR

U.S. CAPITALISM CONQUERS ITS OWN LAND

IT IS TRUE of world capitalism as a whole that in the second half of the nineteenth century it entered on a period of progress unparalleled in its history. The volume of production and the productivity of labour in this period increased to an unprecedented extent. And this is true in particular of capitalism in the United States. In this period of rapid progress on the part of world capitalism as a whole, progress in the United States throughout the century was far greater than in any other capitalist country.

THE U.S.A. FROM MARX'S BIRTH TO THE NOVEMBER REVOLUTION

From the birth of Karl Marx in 1818 to the Russian Revolution in 1917 was practically a century. In 1818 the population of the United States was less than ten millions, or not much bigger than the present population of New York and about a third of the population of France at the time. But when Karl Marx began to write "The Manifesto of the Communist Party", just before the middle of the nineteenth century, the population of the United States had already more than doubled, and was then over twenty millions, or greater than the population of Great Britain. However, at that time, and even on into the seventies, the agricultural population was dominant in the United States, so that into the third quarter of the nineteenth century Great Britain was still indisputably the leading capitalist country in the world. When Marx published the first volume of "Das Kapital", British capitalism was still dominant in the world, and the result was that he dealt with U.S. capitalism only in passing, regarding it as a kind of side-show, which had its own specific characteristics, perhaps, but characteristics which would gradually disappear. U.S. capitalism therefore played no important role in Marx's treatment of the development of world capitalism.

But when Marx died in the eighties, U.S. capitalism had caught up with British industrial production, and then passed it for good and all, to make the United States equally indisputably the leading industrial Power in the world, even at this comparatively early stage in capitalist development.

The rapid capitalist industrial development in the United States was no passing trend, and it continued, more rapidly than anywhere else in the world, until in 1910 the U.S.A. had a population of 92 millions—i.e. greater than that of Great Britain and France combined.

The first world war resulted in a considerable drop in European production and an increase in U.S. production, until by the time of the Russian Revolution the United States produced almost as much as the whole of Europe.

Thus although Great Britain was in the lead when Marx wrote "The Manifesto of the Communist Party", and also his monumental work "Das Kapital", this was no longer the case towards the end of the nineteenth century and in the first years of the twentieth century up to the first world war, though it needed the experiences and repercussions of that war to make the importance of the United States for the development of world capitalism dramatically clear.

To-day it is a matter of course to regard the United States as the centre of world capitalism, and any analysis of its future development must begin with America. However, it should never be forgotten that this was not true of the nineteenth century as a whole, and that it was only towards the end of the century that the United States became the leading industrial capitalist power in the world. It was for this reason that we first analysed developments in Europe, and in Great Britain in particular, and dealt with the capitalist and imperialist expansion of the European States, because this was the decisive factor for a very long period of capitalist development.

U.S. development in the nineteenth century and up to the first world war is remarkable not only for the fact that this great farming land outstripped all others in capitalist development and rapidly took the lead in world capitalism, but also because U.S. development in decisive points differed fundamentally from European development. On the whole U.S. expansion remained within its own national frontiers. It represented primarily a conquest of its own vast territory, which up to then had been largely empty. In consequence the population of the United States could grow from approximately five millions in 1800 to 92 millions in 1910—a rate of growth which was not remotely approached in any other country in the world.

In our analysis of the development of European capitalism we had to draw a distinction between the phase in which it, too, expanded at home and destroyed the pre-capitalist production forms, and the phase in which it expanded beyond its own frontiers, (a) into countries which remained politically independent, and (b) in the form of imperialism, into colonial and semi-colonial areas which made up the empires of the various metropolitan capitalist centres and were under their economic and political control. American development in the nineteenth century did not experience these two separate phases.

U.S. capitalism did not break into a system of feudalism to undermine it and destroy it in part, as European capitalism did; it expanded instead into areas which had previously hardly been settled at all. Again, unlike the European metropolitan centres, it did not extend materially beyond its own frontiers in the second half of the

79

nineteenth century, but continued to expand within its own territory, pushing forward its own frontiers continually. In Europe the fact that capitalism was the centre of a gigantic periphery which was economically, and often politically, controlled by the European metropolitan centres was of decisive importance for the development of the economic crises and for class stratification as a whole. Whereas in America the development of economic crises and class stratification was decisively affected by the tremendous expansion which took place at home.

THE U.S. LABOUR MARKET

In Great Britain the clash between the capitalist mode of production and pre-capitalist production forms in the second quarter of the nineteenth century created two supplementary factors which depressed the situation on the labour market—namely, the, in part, enforced migration from the rural areas into the industrial districts, and the destruction of the old handicraft system by capitalist competition. The result was chronic unemployment and misery on the one hand and the stagnation of the home market or, in the best case, a slowing down of its development, on the other. However, in the United States in this period such supplementary factors adversely affecting the situation on the labour market did not exist to any material extent. There were no big feudal landowners in the United States to drive their tenants into the towns, and there were not the hundreds of thousands of handicraftsmen who had been put out of business by capitalist competition.

Thus in the United States, unlike Great Britain, the situation on the labour market was favourable. For the time being there was only one factor which tended to affect conditions on the labour market adversely, and that was technical progress as such, the introduction of new machinery. However, it was easily possible to cancel out the effect of this factor. As we have seen, in Europe it was the *outward* expansion of capitalism in all the forms we have previously described which decisively improved the situation on the labour market in the capitalist metropolitan centres; in the United States the same favourable effect was obtained by the expansion of capitalism within its own national frontiers, by the conquest of the American continent.

This expansion was so tremendous that for a century it absorbed not only all the labour forces the American continent could provide, but also masses of immigrants from Europe. Emigration from Europe to the United States developed on a scale unprecedented in the history of capitalism. From the final years of the nineteenth century up to the outbreak of the first world war it continued to increase.

The following figures clearly show not only the growth of immigration into the United States from the middle of the nineteenth century up to the year 1910, but also its share in the growth of the population:

Census year.	Population as reported by the census (millions).	Increase over preceding census (millions).	Immigration in the preceding decade. (millions).	Immigration as a percentage of population increase.
1850	23·2	6·1	1·7	27·9
1860	31·4	8·3	2·6	31·3
1870	39·8	8·4	2·3	27·4
1880	50·2	10·3	2·8	27·2
1890	62·9	12·8	5·2	40·6
1900	76	13	3·7	28·5
1910	92	16	8·8	55

THE GROWTH OF U.S. AGRICULTURE

One thing the United States had in common with Europe in its capitalist development was that the relative importance of agriculture steadily declined. But whereas in Europe the growth of the agricultural population was very slow, or there was no growth at all, or there was even a decline, there was a considerable absolute increase in the arable area and in the farming population in the United States right up into the last years before the outbreak of the first world war. From 1850 to 1910 farmland in the United States increased from 294 million acres to 879 million acres, and in the same period the number of farms increased from decade to decade:

(In 1,000's)

Year.	Number of farms.[2]
1850	1,449
1860	2,044
1870	2,660
1880	4,009
1890	4,565
1900	5,737
1910	6,362

This very considerable growth in agriculture and, parallel with it, the opening up of new areas on the American continent, was not without its effect on the labour market. On the whole, in this century the structure of the United States was colonial. There was no unemployment, but a recurrent shortage of man-power.

The relations between town and country in the United States had not yet become one-sided; the rural areas were not constantly sending their surplus population into the towns. Of course, there was already a certain migration from the countryside to the towns, but in addition there was a migration from the towns to the newly-opened-up areas. There was a migration from the districts which had been settled earlier on into these newly-opened-up districts.

There was no need for any great numbers of industrial workers to migrate; it was enough that potential industrial workers had this vent. As Louis Hacker writes in his book "The Triumph of American Capitalism":

". . . if industrial workers in America did not migrate westward to become free farmers, certainly *potential* workers did. In other words, these small farmers of New York, New England, the British Isles, Germany and Scandinavia who began to fill up first the old North West and then the prairie States would have been converted easily into industrial workers—as were the small farmers and agricultural labourers of England and Germany who stayed behind—if they had not had the opportunities to continue farming under more satisfactory conditions. These opportunities were to be found in the American West, certainly throughout the whole of the nineteenth century and, in considerable measure, up to the end of the World War."

INNER U.S. EXPANSION UP TO THE FIRST WORLD WAR

How long did the United States retain this largely colonial structure with its constantly recurring shortage of labour and its consequent favourable effect on the situation of the labour market?

When Karl Marx wrote "Das Kapital" he was well aware of the existence of this exceptional situation on the U.S. labour market, and he pointed out in the final chapter of the first volume that there could be no question of any industrial reserve armies in a country with such a colonial structure. However, he believed that the U.S. would soon lose this privileged position.

"On the one hand, the vast and ceaseless stream of human beings pouring into America year after year leaves a viscous sediment behind it in the eastern States of the American Union; for the flood of emigration from Europe throws men on the American labour market more rapidly than the current of emigration from the eastern States to the western can carry them onward. On the other hand, the American civil war has left a colossal national debt behind it, with the consequent increased pressure of taxation, the creation of a financial aristocracy of the meanest kind, the handing over of an enormous proportion of the public lands to speculative companies for exploitation by means of railways, mines, etc.—in a word, the centralization of capital at a headlong pace. The great republic is no longer the promised land for immigrants. Capitalist production is advancing there with giant strides, although wages have not yet been forced down to the European level, and the wage workers are not yet so dependent there as they are in Europe." [3]

Beyond all question, Marx completely misjudged the time element. From Europe's standpoint the United States continued to be the tremendous immigration country right up to the period of the first world war. And even from the standpoint of the United States itself one can say that this gigantic expansion within her own territory lasted more or less up to the same point.

It is too superficial a view to declare that the limits of this expansion were reached at the end of the nineteenth century because by that time there was no more "free land" available. That may be legally true, but it is not true economically and sociologically. From the end of the nineteenth century up to 1910 the number of farmers in America and the number of farm hands employed by them increased absolutely to quite a considerable extent.

The limits of this expansion were gradually reached round about the period of the first world war. It was only after this war that a development began in the United States which had opened up in Europe long before—namely, that the agricultural sector declined not only relatively, but that in absolute figures there was also a decline of the agricultural population.

The development of the railways shows very clearly how great this internal expansion of American capitalism still was even in the first decade of the twentieth century. In 1900 the United States had 193,000 miles of railways. By 1910 the figure had grown to 240,000 miles, whilst in 1914 it was still higher—namely, 252,000 miles. In other words, from the beginning of the twentieth century up to the first world war the American railway network had increased by about 59,000 miles, so that in this comparatively short period new lines were built three times as long as the whole railway network in Great Britain, and about as long as the combined railway networks of Great Britain and Germany.

Thus, as we have seen, the internal expansion of American capitalism created a safety-vent which prevented the over-burdening of the labour market right up to the last years before the outbreak of the first world war. But it did more than that.

THE DEVELOPMENT OF AMERICA'S HOME MARKET

In the previous chapter we saw that the nineteenth-century expansion of European capitalism beyond its own frontiers in the form of imperialism, accelerated by capital exports, opened by new markets for the export industries of the capitalist metropolitan centres, favourably influenced the situation on the labour market in those centres, increased the number of employed workers and increased their wages, with the result that home markets were also much strengthened. Now, the result which was obtained in Europe by outward capitalist expansion and imperialism in the nineteenth century was obtained to an even greater degree by American capitalism as the result of an inner expansion within its own territory. This conquest of the American continent for capitalism, including the building of a vast network of railways and the establishment of millions of new farms, demanded a tremendous amount of capital, just as the triumphant progress of European capitalism over the world had done. Thus in this period the question was not where to find possibilities of investment for capital, but where to find the capital for the gigantic investment possibilities which opened up.

American capital alone was not sufficient, and there was a considerable flow of European capital to the United States—for instance, a great part of the U.S. railways were built with European capital. As Louis M. Hacker points out in his book "The United States since 1865", of the 3,330 million dollars worth of American securities held abroad at the end of the nineteenth century, the greater part was made up of railway stocks and bonds. In England the total held was 2,500 million; in Holland, 240 million; in Germany, 200 million; in Switzerland, 75 million; and in France, 50 million.

Thus the situation then was very different from what it became after the first world war. At that time the United States was an import land for capital. From 1850 up into the seventies the United States had considerable import surpluses, and they were financed with European capital exports. Although from the seventies on U.S. exports were greater than U.S. imports, the U.S. balance of payments was still passive, and this was made possible by further capital imports from Europe.

One effect of this constant extension of the frontiers of capitalist expansion and the increasing volume of capital investments it demanded was naturally the growth of home markets for industry in the newly-opened-up areas. This was an analogous phenomenon to the growth of markets for Europe's exporting industries as a result of the drive of European capitalism beyond its own frontiers.

The Rise of Wages

Now, this enlargement of markets for U.S. industries took place at a time when, for reasons which we have already analysed, the situation on the labour market was comparatively favourable to working people. The growth of markets for U.S. industry which resulted from the continual extension of the frontiers of capitalist expansion and which made high profits possible, was therefore combined with a rising trend of wages and an increase in employment. Just as was previously the case in the European capitalist countries, the increase of the productivity of labour in the United States was accompanied by an increase in wages: not because an increase in the productivity of labour necessarily brings about an increase of wages, but because the situation on the labour market compelled the industrial capitalists to pay higher wages.

84

Wages in the United States therefore rose, and they rose in this period higher than they had risen in Europe, because the continued extension of the frontiers of internal capitalist expansion in the United States was not a temporary phenomenon, but one which went on for generations and continued to exercise a beneficent influence on the labour market.*

This very considerable increase in wages was one of the main incentives for the large-scale introduction of machinery and for the constant improvement of productive technique. Machinery introduced in this way saved labour power which was more than twice as highly paid as labour power, say, in Germany. The result was that

* In his book "Warum gibt es in den Vereinigten Staaten keinen Sozialismus?" Werner Sombart has published some interesting comparative figures for this period: In 1900 average annual wages were paid in Germany and the United States as follows:

Industrial groups.	Germany.	United States.
	(Both columns in marks.)	
Clothing industry . . .	621·4	1,323 to 2,276·4
Glass manufacture . . .	724·9	2,156·6
Ceramics	772·2	1,701
Brick manufacture . . .	556·2	1,482·6
Iron and steel industries . .	792·5 to 1,014·2	1,642·2 to 3,074·4
Chemical manufactures . .	929·4	2,060·6
Textile industry . . .	506 to 776·5	1,129·8 to 2,192·4
Paper-making industry . .	714·4 to 765·9	1,318·8 to 2,087·4
Leather trades	894·8	1,436·4 to 1,822·8
Timber trades	698 to 821	1,417 to 1,801·8
Milling	743	2,007·6
Sugar manufacture . . .	596	2,045·4 to 2,326·8
Tobacco manufacture . .	541	1,024·8 to 1,663·2
Printing trades	893·7	1,747·2 to 2,234·4

Sombart comments on these figures as follows:

"Although each separate figure is open to objection, and in particular every comparison between German and American figures, nevertheless, in my opinion, from the strictly statistical point of view, these figures give us on the whole a quite accurate picture of the situation. For one thing there is the conformity of figures deriving from different sources. On the basis of the statistical material at our disposal I think it can safely be said that *money wages in the United States are between two and three times as high as they are in Germany.* They are at least twice as high, because not one of the comparisons reveals a lesser difference. On the other hand, there are numerous cases in which American wages are seen to be three times as high as the corresponding German wages, whilst in some cases—though these are probably not typical—they are even four times as high. The manufacture of sugar and the cigar-making trade, for example, if we take Baden as a point of comparison. If we compare German wages on an average in the tobacco trade, we find that they are one-third to one-half the level of corresponding American wages. We can perhaps sum up in this way: American wages (excluding the South, perhaps) are 100 per cent higher than wages in the best-paid parts of Germany (in the West), and certainly between 150 and 200 per cent higher than German wages in the poorly-paid districts (Eastern Germany and parts of the South)."

many machines were profitable in the United States which would not have been profitable in Germany and in Europe in general.

In addition, in America—unlike the situation in Europe—a country the size of a continent represented one homogeneous economic area, and thus a market for U.S. industry. Further, so far as the supply of raw materials was concerned, the United States was in an exceptionally favourable position. To sum up, the favourable position on the labour market, which resulted in higher wages on the one hand and a great improvement in industrial technique on the other; the harnessing of a vast country to the needs of the economic system; and the favourable raw-material supply position, all combined to raise the productivity of labour in the United States far above that in Europe.

Europe needed the export trade; Europe needed an imperialist drive beyond its own frontiers in order to provide a greater degree of employment in the export industries, thereby raising wages and increasing the purchasing power of the home markets. For the United States in this period of expansion the process was much simpler. There was no necessity for any expansion beyond the frontiers. The area available was so great that the frontiers of expansion could be pushed continually farther. As a result of European expansion the exporting industries grew rapidly. The analogous process in the United States was the "exporting" of commodities from the already developed areas into the areas which were in process of development. In Europe wages rose and the number of workers in employment increased because of growing export business. In the United States the process was twofold: wages and employment increased in the districts which were already industrially developed and also in the districts which were being opened up and industrialized for the first time. In Europe there was a fundamental functional relation between capitalist expansion, the imperialist drive and the growth of home markets. As far as the United States was concerned this same functional relationship existed within its own frontiers.

The Relative Decline of U.S. Foreign Trade

In Europe in this period in which capitalism expanded vigorously beyond the frontiers foreign trade increased in relation to production as a whole, and we shall see later that the subsequent development of European capitalism was decisively affected by its close integration with economic areas beyond its own frontiers. In the United States, on the other hand, the development in this respect was almost diametrically opposite in direction. At the beginning of American large-scale industrial development foreign capital streamed into the country, and at this time the U.S. economic system was more closely linked up with foreign economies than at any subsequent period. The more industrial production developed in the United States, and
86

the closer it came in total volume to British production—which it soon overtook—the smaller became the volume of U.S. foreign trade in relation to production as a whole.

"In 1850 nearly 20 per cent of the commodities (exclusive of services) consumed in the United States came from abroad; in 1880 it was something over 10 per cent; in 1937 it was only 6 per cent." [4]

Thus, whilst in the second half of the nineteenth century up to the first world war—during its vigorous advance over the world—European capitalism developed its foreign trade relatively more than its production as a whole, the contrary was true of the United States: during its expansion within its own frontiers, and whilst building up its own agriculture and industry, the United States reduced the relative volume of its foreign trade by comparison with its production as a whole. And when the United States had completely opened up its own great country, its foreign trade in relation to its production as a whole was much smaller than that of Great Britain, France, or Germany.

Economic Crises in the Period of Progress

U.S. capitalist expansion within its own frontiers, with its favourable effect on the labour market, its twofold increase of markets by greater business activity in the already developed areas and by considerably increasing wages and employment, had much the same effect on the U.S. economic system as the expansion of European capitalism, plus imperialism, had on the economic system of the European metropolitan centres. It also had similar effects on the character of U.S. economic crises in this period. What we have already said about the economic crises in Europe from the fifties up to the first world war applies equally to the United States. Allowing for all differences in details—and they were often quite considerable—they had this one thing in common: they did not shake the capitalist economic system to the core; they did not threaten its continued existence; and they did not provoke the creation of big and influential movements aiming at a fundamental transformation of the social system.

In fact it is characteristic of the whole period—unlike the period of crisis which began in 1929, about which Moulton observes in his book "Controlling Factors": "For the first time in industrial history the powers of government were extensively invoked to stem the tide of depression and to stimulate recovery"—that even during times of depression there was no influential move to secure the intervention of the State in economic affairs in order to help the economic system out of the crisis. In short, the circumstance that economic crises in this period did not fundamentally threaten the existence of the capitalist mode of production was as true of the United States as it was of Europe. Despite the great differences in form between capitalist expansion in the United States and in Europe, the two were similar in this respect.

The Fundamental Differences between U.S. and European Capitalist Expansion

But in other and very important respects there were fundamental differences owing to the fact that capitalist expansion in Europe and the United States developed along dissimilar lines.

The tremendous expansion of European capitalism went largely beyond its own frontiers. From the middle of the nineteenth century up to the first world war, European capitalism became the industrial centre for Eurasia. It was, so to speak, a factory centre which, unlike the United States, was unable to produce raw materials at home in the great quantities it required, which was also compelled to import great quantities of foodstuffs, and which had a volume of production which was excessive for its own population, i.e. the population of the capitalist metropolitan centres. It produced too much machinery and too many capital goods. In other words, it was a factory centre which could utilize its productive capacity to the full only if it was in a position to export a large quantity. Thus Europe's economic and social structure depended on the maintenance of close economic relations with peripheral areas outside its own frontiers—more than that, it depended on the continued expansion of those areas under its control, i.e. the colonial empires. Any fundamental upheaval in these areas therefore would necessarily have important repercussions on Europe's economic and social system.

But capitalist expansion in the United States took place largely within its own frontiers, and therefore such expansion as did take place beyond the frontiers was not of very great importance. Further, the United States produced by far the greater part of the raw materials it needed within its own frontiers, and it also produced its own foodstuffs. In fact, it produced so much food and raw materials that, unlike the European capitalist countries, by far the greater part of its exports in this period were made up of these commodities. In the years 1871–1875 the export of raw materials, food and manufactured foodstuffs represented 80 per cent of all U.S. exports, and even in the years 1910–1914 they represented a good 53 per cent of the total.

The proportion of finished goods and of the products of heavy industry in the total of U.S. exports certainly increased, but total exports remained small in comparison with production as a whole. And—a very important point—the United States was never in a position in which it was compelled to export its industrial production in order to pay for imports of foodstuffs and raw materials. Unlike

Europe, the United States did not carve itself out an empire in this period, and it did not become the factory centre of a largely imperialist-controlled area outside its own frontiers. The expansion of U.S. capitalism was in no way dependent on any such empire, and therefore it is not at all surprising that when great changes took place in the colonial empires of Europe, because imperialist expansion ceased and imperialism then began to decline, U.S. capitalism was not directly affected.

IMPERIALIST EXPANSION UNIMPORTANT FOR U.S. CAPITALISM

It is quite true, of course, that U.S. capitalism experienced a certain imperialist expansion in the years immediately preceding the first world war, but its importance for the U.S. economic system as a whole was practically negligible and certainly not to be compared, even remotely, with the importance of the Eurasian continent for the economies of the European capitalist metropolitan centres. As far as the economic system and social structure of the United States were concerned, this imperialist expansion was nothing but a sideshow. Behind it was the great economic power of one or two big monopolies which were already strong enough to exercise an influence on U.S. foreign policy.

Hobson was wrong when he assumed that as far as Great Britain was concerned the abandonment of imperialism would adversely affect only the profit interests of certain capitalist groups, and he overlooked the decisive effect of imperialist expansion on economic crises, on the state of the market and on the whole class stratification of British society. But Hobson would have been right if he had drawn the same conclusion with regard to U.S. imperialism in this period. Its direct repercussions affected only a very narrow sector of the U.S. economic system, and its indirect effects were not much more important. Not only was U.S. imperialist expansion of very little moment for the U.S. economic system and social structure, but it hardly interfered with the imperialist expansion of the European capitalist countries. Incidentally, this was one of the reasons why in the beginning the United States was not directly affected by the aggravation of foreign-political antagonisms which came about as a result of Europe's imperialist expansion and finally led to the outbreak of the first world war.

In this period U.S. capitalism was engaged in opening up its own vast territories, and only towards the end of this process did it engage to some extent in imperialist expansion, though even then it was of no very great account. The United States had gone through a bloody civil war before it became one united whole, but the civil war was over at a time when the country was still largely agricultural. The gigantic industrial advance of the United States took place later, and thus the process was not hampered and slowed down, as it was in Europe, by internal frontiers, customs barriers and so on.

This process in which the United States opened up its own vast territories for capitalism was unique. There is no parallel in the whole history of the capitalist mode of production for such a tremendous advance of industrial development and concentration within national frontiers. It permitted millions of Americans to migrate westward and at the same time it permitted tens of millions of working people in Europe to enter the United States.

The End of Internal Expansion Coincided with the End of European Expansion

This process of opening up American territory was approximately at an end by the outbreak of the first world war. Its conclusion coincided more or less with the time when the capitalist expansion of the European metropolitan centres beyond their frontiers began to grow more difficult, when their imperialist drive met with ever-increasing resistance. This historical coincidence was not necessary and inevitable. The process of opening up American territory might well have been concluded at a time when Europe's imperialist drive still had great possibilities of development. It might also have come about that Europe's imperialist drive reached its limits and began to decline at a time when the opening up of American territory by U.S. capitalism was not yet at an end. However, the historical coincidence did, in fact, take place: the process of opening up America to capitalism came to an end approximately at the same time as the imperialist drive of the European metropolitan centres reached its limits.

By this time the United States had become the strongest capitalist social organism and the biggest industrial producer in the world. The productivity of labour was greater there than anywhere else, and so were profits, wages and the national income. And this development had taken place in the United States itself whilst at the same time the direct political and economic control of other countries by the U.S.A. had not played any material role in the process.

Now, if the unique feature of U.S. capitalist expansion—i.e. its conquest of its own vast territories without the aid of imperialist expansion—is overlooked, or not estimated at its true value, then it is natural enough that Americans, of all people, should begin to believe that—provided it is not interfered with—the capitalist mode of production can tremendously develop the productive forces as a matter of course, and that it is quite a "natural" thing under capitalism that the productivity of labour should increase *together* with a rise in profits, wages and employment.

So long as this progress continued, and so long as its results were so dramatically obvious, it is not surprising that few people asked to what extent it was all due to the unique historical conditions in which it took place, and to what extent, with a change in these unique historical conditions, the factors which had brought it about might also change.

Such disquieting questions were made even less likely by the fact that the great progress achieved in this period—which was much greater in the United States than in Europe—had led to a class stratification in which the overwhelming majority of the population approved of the capitalist system—if they gave the problem even a moment's thought.

CHAPTER FIVE

CLASS STRATIFICATION AND THE RISE OF CAPITALISM

IT WAS ONE of Marx's fundamental assumptions that the process of capitalist development would necessarily greatly simplify class stratification, that it would polarize society and split it into two hostile camps. This polarization of society, coupled with the intensification of economic crises, the increase of unemployment and mass misery, represented the decisive factors which would undermine capitalism and finally lead to the triumph of socialism.

Over a century ago, at a time when capitalism was still in its infancy, and when it was just beginning to build the first railways, Marx and Engels wrote in "The Manifesto of the Communist Party":

> "Our epoch, the epoch of the bourgeoisie, possesses, however, this distinctive feature: it has simplified classs antagonisms. Society as a whole is more and more splitting up into two great hostile camps, into two great classes directly facing each other— bourgeoisie and proletariat. . . . The lower strata of the middle class—the small industrialists, merchants, and rentiers generally, the handicraftsmen and peasants—all these sink gradually into the proletariat. . . ." [1]

Why should this simplification of class stratification take place? Marx tells us why in "Das Kapital". It is the result of capitalist concentration, which Marx assumed would embrace both industry and agriculture. His opinions on the point are often quoted by both his followers and his opponents. We are quoting them again here because they show clearly the difference between the class stratification by Marx and the class stratification which actually came about in the epoch of capitalist expansion and imperialism. After describing the earlier stages of capitalist development, Marx wrote:

"As soon as this process of transformation has sufficiently disintegrated the old society, has decomposed it through and through; as soon as the workers have been turned into proletarians, and their working conditions into capital, as soon as the capitalist mode of production can stand on its own feet—then the further socialization of labour, and the further transformation of the land and of the other means of production into socially utilized (that is to say, communal) means of production, which implies the further expropriation of private owners, takes on a new form. What has now to be expropriated is no longer the workman working on his own account, but the capitalist who exploits many workmen.

"This expropriation is brought about by the operation of the immanent laws of capitalist production, by the centralization of capital. One capitalist wipes out many of his fellow capitalists. Parallel with such centralization, and with the expropriation of many capitalists by the few, the co-operative form of the labour process develops to an ever-increasing degree; with this we find a growing tendency to the purposeful application of science to the improvement of technique; the land is more methodically cultivated; the instruments of labour tend to assume forms which are utilizable only in combined effort; the means of production are economized through being used only by joint, by social labour. All the peoples of the world are drawn into the network of the world market, and therefore the capitalist regime tends to assume an international character. Whilst there is a progressive diminution in the number of capitalist magnates (who usurp and monopolize all the advantages of this process of transformation) there is a corresponding increase in the mass of poverty, oppression, enslavement, degeneration and exploitation, but at the same time there is a steady intensification of working-class anger, the anger of a class which grows ever more numerous, and is disciplined, unified and organized by the very mechanism of the capitalist mode of production. . . .

"The transformation of scattered private property based on individual labour into capitalist property is, of course, a far more protracted process, a far more violent and difficult process, than the transformation of capitalist private property (already in actual fact based upon a social method of production) into social property. In the former case we are concerned with the expropriation of the mass of the people by a few usurpers; in the latter case we are concerned with the expropriation of a few usurpers by the mass of the people." [2]

A good forty years after the publication of "The Manifesto of the Communist Party", and after Marx's death, but whilst his friend and collaborator, Friedrich Engels, was still alive, the German Social

Democrats adopted the famous "Erfurter Programme", which declared:

"The economic development of bourgeois society leads naturally and inevitably to the ruin of the small undertaking, whose basis is the private property of the worker in his means of production. It separates the worker from the means of production and turns him into a propertyless proletarian, whilst at the same time the means of production become the monopoly of a comparatively small number of capitalists and large landed proprietors.

"Hand in hand with this monopolization of the means of production goes the squeezing out of the scattered small undertakings by giant large-scale undertakings, the development of the tool into the machine, and a tremendous growth in the productivity of human labour power. But all the advantages of this transformation are monopolized by the capitalists and large landed proprietors. For the proletariat and the sinking middle classes—petty-bourgeois and peasants—it means growing economic insecurity, misery, oppression, slavery, humiliation and exploitation.

"The number of proletarians increases, the reserve armies of labour grow, the antagonism between the exploiters and the exploited intensifies, the class struggle between the bourgeoisie and the proletariat grows fiercer, and divides modern society into the two hostile camps which are characteristic of all industrial countries."

As a result of these views concerning the polarization of society into two hostile camps, Marx and the socialists expected the downfall of the capitalist mode of production and its socialist transformation even in the second half of the nineteenth century.

Reality did not conform to their beliefs. The expected polarization of society into two big hostile camps did not come about either in Europe or America. What actually did arise was a much more complicated situation.

In important points Marx was right: once capitalism had destroyed the pre-capitalist forms of production, thanks to the superiority of its own methods of production, the competitive struggle under capitalism went on, and led to an increasing industrial concentration, until in the end a few undertakings—the "giant corporations" in the United States—were responsible for, or controlled, the greater part of industrial production. Marx was also right when he assumed that this process would bring about fundamental and decisive changes in the structure of capitalist society. He prophesied their coming generations before they materialized. In the period when he wrote "The Manifesto" and later "Das Kapital" the process of industrial concentration was only just beginning. In the United States, where even in the seventies the agricultural population was preponderant, the independent farmers, handicraftsmen and small undertakings gave American society its characteristic features. In Germany at that time the situation was very little different. In 1875 46 per cent [3] of industry, trade and transport was in the hands of small independent businesses, and in agriculture the independent holdings were in a large majority. Thus in German society the independent small and medium-sized undertakings were still dominant.

However, the continuation of capitalist development fundamentally changed this social stratification, because the process of industrial concentration put the independent small undertakings out of business and at the same time greatly increased the number of wage workers and employees, and also because in all capitalist countries, though in varying degrees, the proportion of the agricultural population to the population as a whole progressively declined.

Marx was wrong when he assumed that in this same period there would be a process of concentration in agriculture analogous to the process of concentration in industry. This did not take place, but as the process of industrial concentration did make great strides, whilst the proportion of the agricultural population to the population as a whole steadily declined, capitalist development in this period turned a society which had formerly been marked by the preponderance of independent elements into a society in which henceforth wage workers and employees were in the majority.

The following figures show the situation in the United States in the period before the first world war:

Social-Economic Grouping of Gainfully-Employed Persons (14 *and over in* 1910) [4]

Social Economic Group.	Number.	Percentage.
Proprietors, managers and officials . .	8,579,458	23
Farmers (owners and tenants) . .	(6,132,368)	16·5
Wholesale and retail dealers . . .	(1,245,801)	3·3
Other proprietors, managers and officials.	(1,201,289)	3·2
Professional persons	1,632,185	4·4
Clerks and kindred workers . . .	3,804,474	10·2
Skilled workers and foremen . . .	4,363,984	11·7
Semi-skilled workers	5,489,315	14·7
Unskilled workers	13,401,944	36

Thus even before the first world war, after a period of tremendous industrial concentration, workers and employees accounted for almost three-quarters of the total population of the United States.

The development in Germany was very similar. An occupational census taken after the first world war, in 1925, showed that the figure for independent undertakings, etc., had fallen to less than one-fifth of the whole, or 17·3 per cent, whilst the number of workers and employees had risen to 66·2 per cent of the whole.*

Thus the spread of capitalism and industrialism in the leading capitalist States brought about a complete change in social stratification.

From the fifties of the nineteenth century, when Karl Marx wrote "Das Kapital", until the first world war a radical process of social transformation had been proceeding. The independent middle classes in town and country no longer gave society its characteristic structure. They had become a minority, and represented no more than about one-fifth of the total population, and the general tendency was towards a still further reduction.

The face of capitalist society to-day is more and more determined by the existence of a few giant undertakings on the one hand—undertakings which control whole branches of industry—and masses of dependent wage-workers and employees on the other, who now represent the overwhelming majority of the population. It is a tribute to the far-sighted genius of Marx that at a time when the independent elements were still in a great majority in society he prophesied this process of concentration and its effects.†

The process of concentration, which was not confined to the period of capitalist progress, but which continued even after the first world war, brought about a complete change in the social structure of the leading industrial countries; it brought about a decisive transformation of their class stratification. To that extent Marx was right—but only to that extent, because the process did not lead, as he had prophesied, to a polarization of society. It was not true that the

* The German statistics are not directly comparable with those for America because the former include a category of family members assisting in the business and representing 17 per cent of the population. These were chiefly women who helped their husbands in agriculture.

† Marx also foresaw that what had formerly been a natural unification of the owner of capital and the manager of an undertaking in one person would cease to exist in the further development of capitalism, and that a clear line would be drawn between the two. At a time when joint-stock companies (the "corporations" in the United States) were still in their infancy, Marx foresaw that their subsequent development would influence the structure of capitalism itself and represent a factor making for its disintegration. In Volume III of "Das Kapital" he makes the following observations concerning "The Formation of Joint-Stock Companies":

"1. A tremendous extension of the scale of production and of undertakings which would be impossible for individual capital owners;

"2. Capital, which as such is based on a social mode of production and presupposes a social concentration of the means of production and of labour power, now directly receives the form of social capital (the capital of directly associated individuals) as against private capital, and its undertakings appears as social undertakings as against private undertakings. It represents the abolition of capital as private property within the framework of the capitalist mode of production itself;

"3. The really active capitalists are changed into mere directors, administrators of the capital of others, and the owners of capital are changed into mere owners, mere money capitalists."

whole of society split into two hostile camps, or that "the lower strata of the middle class sink gradually into the proletariat". It was not true that this process meant "growing economic insecurity, misery, oppression, slavery, humiliation and exploitation" for the working people.

It would be truer, though an over-simplification, to say that in this period of capitalist expansion and imperialist drive the working people tended to become more and more middle class, quite apart from the fact that the destruction of certain middle-class strata (which took place, and will always take place, as the result of the capitalist mode of production) does not exhaust the effects of the process of concentration, because at the same time this process constantly creates new middle-class strata.

The Changing Social Outlook of the Working Class

In earlier chapters we have seen how it came about that in the period in which U.S. capitalism opened up America's own vast territory by leaps and bounds and European capitalism carried out its successful imperialist drive all over the world, the situation on the labour market developed so favourably for the working class, and that the great increase in the productivity of labour was accompanied by a considerable rise in the living standards of both the American and European working classes.

Apart from the ever-growing process of industrial concentration, it was this generation-long rise in real wages which was the decisive factor in determining the social stratification of the capitalist metropolitan centres in this period.

For working people the prospect of ever being independent grew more and more remote in this period with every decade of industrial concentration. But although their hopes in this respect steadily vanished, at least their income increased and their living standards rose. The great majority of the working people, not only in the United States but also in the leading industrial countries of Europe, obtained a standard of living from the fifties to the end of the nineteenth century which was often higher than that formerly enjoyed by the independent middle classes at the beginning of that period of development. The process of industrial concentration was not accompanied by any analogous concentration of income. On the contrary, it was accompanied by a general increase in the wages of the working class as a whole, i.e. not only of the skilled workers, but also of the semi-skilled and unskilled.

This was the decisive factor which lengthened the life of capitalism and made the capitalist elements in this period so supremely confident, so absolutely certain that their system was made to last. Precisely in the period in which Marx was writing his great work, real wages increased very considerably, particularly in England, and it is therefore not surprising that although he spent the second half of his life in England, writing his great book there and taking the development of capitalism there as the basis for it, he was never to see "Das Kapital" translated into English and published.

This general rise in real wages greatly undermined the strength of the socialists in this period. In countries where no strong socialist movement already existed none developed. In countries where such a movement already existed it continued to exist, but its character steadily changed. The Socialist Parties still favoured a total transformation of the capitalist mode of production on paper, but in reality they gradually became parties which worked for social reforms within the framework of capitalist society. This great rise in real wages was already effective when Marx and Engels were completing their life's work. They were unable to ignore its existence altogether, but they refused to recognize its full significance.

This had important consequences for the future development of the socialist movement in Europe and for the development of socialist ideas. In this period Marxism became the main socialist stream of thought in Europe because it closely combined theory and practice, enabled progressive elements in the working class to understand capitalism and the position of the working class in capitalist society, and helped them in their economic and political agitation.

But in the same period in which Marxism became of primary importance for the European working class their conditions of life and, above all, the general trend of their development were not in the least in accordance with the laws of capitalism as analysed by Marx. It thus became necessary to explain why these laws were not operating, or not fully operating, in this period; to find out whether the laws were wrong, or whether perhaps they had been temporarily suspended for a certain historical period or for a certain country. Marx and Engels made no attempt to do this, and the result was that, as Marxism continued to spread, dissension arose in the socialist movement. On the one hand there were those who uncritically accepted Marx's views even when they were obviously at variance with facts, and on the other hand there were those who marshalled all the facts which seemed to refute Marx's analysis, without bothering themselves very much about their fundamental causes.

The question of the wage trends is of decisive importance not only for the development of capitalism, but also for the development of the socialist movement. It determined the attitude of the socialists in the period of the first world war, and it determined Lenin's views which led to the disruption of the politically organized working-class movement.

In previous chapters we have analysed the reasons for this very considerable rise in real wages, a trend which continued not merely for a short time but for generations, and with this analysis we thus indirectly criticized the attitude of Marx and Engels. However, the

D

matter is important enough to follow up our analysis with a direct criticism. We have already dealt with Marx's views on the United States. He regarded it as a country whose inner colonial structure ameliorated social antagonisms. In Marx's day the United States was not yet the industrial centre of the world, but Engels was still alive when it was already the leading industrial country in the world, with a volume of production which far outstripped that of Great Britain, and with wage levels which steadily continued to rise. Engels made no attempt to give any systematic explanation for this phenomenon, but in an article published in the London *Commonwealth* on March 1st, 1885, he did at least deal with developments in Great Britain. He regarded this article as so important that he subsequently added it as a preface to his famous book "The Situation of the Working Class in England". Forty years previously he had assumed that a continued deterioration of the living conditions of the workers in England would finally lead to a social revolution.

Now, of course, he had to admit that he had been mistaken. And this is how he did it:

> "The truth is this: as long as England's industrial monopoly lasted the English working class enjoyed a certain share in its advantages. The advantages were very unequally distributed amongst them; the privileged minority pocketed the major share, but even the broad masses had a share at least now and again. And that is the reason why there has been no socialism in England since the disappearance of Owenism. With the collapse of England's industrial monopoly the English working class will lose this privileged position. Quite generally, not excluding the privileged and dominant minority, it will one day be brought down to the same level as that of foreign workers. And that is the reason why there will once again be socialism in England."

These observations of Engels are open to criticism from various angles.

First of all, they do not provide an adequate explanation of why the position of the English working class improved so very considerably in the second half of the nineteenth century. Engels tells us that so long as England's industrial monopoly lasted the working class would have a share in its advantages—would, thus, obtain some share of the surplus profits enjoyed by the capitalists. But why? The mere fact that capitalists enjoy surplus profits does not necessarily mean that their workers receive higher wages, and no one knew that better than Engels himself, as his own famous work shows. There were periods when English capitalists made enormous profits and yet at the same time the condition of the working class was deteriorating. For instance, Marx writes in Vol. I of "Das Kapital":

"In the period from 1799 to 1815 the rising prices of foodstuffs in England brought about a nominal increase in wages, but real wages, as expressed in foodstuffs, actually fell. . . . However, thanks to the increased intensity of labour and a compulsory lengthening of working time, surplus value increased both absolutely and relatively. This was the period in which the reckless lengthening of the working day became an established custom, the period which was characterized in particular by the rapid increase of capital on the one hand and pauperism on the other."

Even in the period which Engels himself describes—in the twenties, and thirties of the nineteenth century—England had a tremendous industrial advantage over all competitors and English industry produced more than the industry of all the rest of the world, and yet it was precisely in this period that the English working class suffered the greatest misery.

In the first decades of the second half of the nineteenth century, too, English capitalism was still in an advantageous position compared with the less-developed capitalism of the continent, though certainly its advantage was then no longer so decisive as it had been in the first half of the nineteenth century. But when we find that this same period, though less advantageous, nevertheless saw a rising standard of living for working people, we are forced to the conclusion that new factors must have been operating. One of these factors, which Engels made no attempt to analyse, was the much more favourable position on the labour market.

Thus the explanation provided by Engels is seen to be inadequate. But even the facts themselves are not rightly judged by him. He writes: "The privileged minority pocketed the major share, but even the broad masses had a share at least now and again". He makes no attempt to give us a real analysis of English wages at the time. But what does such an analysis reveal? It certainly shows that there were considerable variations in real wages as between one group of workers and another—for example, between the wages of skilled workers and those of unskilled workers, and that these differences were often greater than the analogous differences on the continent; but, allowing for this, it shows also that the general trend of all wages was upward; that the real wages of the English working class as a whole were increasing. It is thus quite wrong to say, as Engels does, that "even the broad masses had a share at least now and again". The truth is that for many decades the real wages, and thus the living standards, of the great masses of the English working class steadily improved.

Engels was unable to bring himself to correct his earlier errors completely.

Further, when Marx declared that the special circumstances which had favoured the position of the American workers would soon come to an end, and that they would then find themselves depressed to the continental European level, Engels went on to say the same thing about the English working class. Thus Marx and Engels believed that certain exceptional circumstances had operated in both countries to prevent the accumulation of capital on the one hand resulting in an accumulation of misery on the other, and they also believed that these exceptional circumstances would soon disappear.

In reality, however, the situation of the working class throughout the capitalist world had changed. The factors which favoured the working people of England and the United States were not confined to those two countries; they operated also, though to a lesser degree, in favour of working people in the more developed capitalist countries of Europe, with the result that from the middle of the nineteenth century on real wages there rose very considerably. This was the case in France, Germany, Western Europe in general, and Scandinavia. Thus the situation did not develop as Engels had prophesied; the English working class was not depressed after a certain period to the level of the workers in Europe. What happened was that the condition of the working people in Europe improved because real wages rose for the reasons we have already analysed, and living standards rose with them. Allowing once again for differences, this favourable development applied to the whole working class in the more developed European countries; and it lasted not for a short period, but for generations.

We shall see later that the observations of Engels which we have quoted led to a completely false estimate of the situation in the period of the first world war, when the capitalist countries stood the shock of war far better than most socialists expected. The reason for this was precisely because real wages in the capitalist centre of the world had steadily risen for a protracted period and the stability of capitalism had thus been consolidated.*

Occasionally Engels himself seemed to be aware that the improvement in living standards was not confined to a small section of the working class, and in a letter written to Marx dated October 7th, 1858, he declares:

"The English proletariat is in fact becoming more and more bourgeois, so that it looks as though this most bourgeois of all

* The fact that in the highly-developed capitalist centres not only certain privileged groups of working people, but the working class as a whole enjoyed higher wages and a better standard of living was confirmed many years later, a long time after the end of the first world war, from a somewhat unexpected source. When Bucharin was still the undisputed leading theoretician of the Russian Communist Party and of the Communist International, he declared at the Sixth Congress of the latter organization in 1928: [5]

"When we examine the picture as a whole we observe a number of, so to speak, 'aristocratic' countries which, *conditionally speaking*, have *an aristocracy of labour*, that is to say, a proletariat whose living conditions are above the level of those in which the world proletariat lives."

nations will end up by having a bourgeois aristocracy and a bourgeois proletariat as well as a bourgeoisie."

This tendency was correctly observed, but the point which must be stressed is that it applied not only to the English working class, but also to the working class of all European countries, and it was one of the results of the great period of capitalist and imperialist expansion.

Such "bourgeois" workers also developed in the United States on the basis of capitalist expansion there, but, unlike the workers of other countries, these new American workers had never regarded themselves as "proletarians". Thus "bourgeois" workers existed in the United States, but not as the result of any imperialist expansion. The "bourgeois" workers of Europe, on the other hand, grew up in a period of tremendous capitalist expansion and imperialist exploitation.

FUNCTIONAL RELATION BETWEEN "BOURGEOIS" DEVELOPMENT OF THE WORKING CLASS AND CAPITALIST EXPANSION

At the same time hundreds of millions of people in the colonial and semi-colonial countries had a standard of living far below that of the European workers. It was not only the workers of these colonial and semi-colonial countries—who were often "free" only in name—who lived in conditions far inferior to those prevailing in Europe, but 90 per cent of the whole population of the colonial and semi-colonial countries; in other words, the majority of the population of the world. It was, in fact, the relationship between the metropolitan capitalist centres and the colonial and semi-colonial countries which represented one of the most important factors which made the working classes of the European countries so "bourgeois".

From this it follows that it is impossible to deal satisfactorily with the class stratification in the capitalist metropolitan centres alone and without regard to the situation in the colonial and semi-colonial countries. To confine our investigations to the former would be to provide a photograph of conditions, perhaps, but not an adequate analysis. A real picture of the situation can be obtained only if the class stratification in the metropolitan capitalist centres, and the development of their workers into "bourgeois" workers, are examined in their functional relationship with those countries which were the object of imperialist exploitation in this period, because it was precisely this exploitation which turned the workers of Europe into "bourgeois".

We cannot satisfactorily analyse the position in England's towns in this period if we ignore the position in India's towns. We cannot adequately analyse the class stratification of the capitalist centres in Europe without at the same time analysing developments in China, the Dutch East Indies and also in Eastern Europe, because the capitalist metropolitan countries were more and more becoming the industrial centre of this vast outer area. Similarly, any analysis of this colonial and semi-colonial periphery must be closely related to a description of the class stratification in the metropolitan centres. Only then can we hope to obtain a really scientific analysis of the whole problem.

Working-class Percentage of the Total Population Ceases to Grow

Now, we have seen that in this period the real wages of the working classes rose, that their living standards improved, and that in consequence their outlook became more and more middle class, or "bourgeois". But that was not all. Marx believed that a strong tendency towards the increase of the working-class percentage of the total population would be maintained. Now, this also was not the case: the previous tendency in this direction began to weaken progressively even at that time.

When Marx was writing, at the time of "The Manifesto" and "Das Kapital", and even up to the time of his death, the number of workers in the capitalist centres had steadily increased. The destruction of feudalism and of the part-time handicraft activities of the peasants had driven millions of former peasants and farm labourers into the towns, where they became workers in the rapidly expanding capitalist industries. The numbers of workers were also increased by the fact that numerous artisans and handicraftsmen were driven out of business by the capitalist competition of nascent large-scale industry.

Thus when Marx was at work there was a particularly big increase in the number of workers in the highly developed capitalist countries, and it was both absolute and relative. But in the period after the death of Marx up to the outbreak of the first world war the situation changed.

The number of workers continued to increase from year to year in absolute figures; it increased by millions, but it no longer increased relatively everywhere. In fact, in the last decades before the first world war the relative increase of the working-class percentage in the total population ceased, and in some places there was even a slight decline. The particular development in Germany is shown clearly in the diagram on p. 103.

Thus we can see a steady decline in the relative figure for people engaged in independent businesses, but the process is not accompanied by both an absolute and a relative increase in the number of dependent wage-workers. That took place only up to the year 1895, but from 1895 to 1907 there was a decline of the working-class percentage in relation to the total working population.

What was true of Germany was also true on an international

scale. The working-class percentage stabilized itself at round about 50 per cent; in England it was rather more, in France and Germany it was rather less.

In other words, although the tendency towards the destruction of independent existences continued in this period, their relative decline in the total labour force was no longer accompanied by a corresponding growth in the numbers of the working class. In consequence, the process of polarizing society into two opposing camps was slowed down.

There were a whole series of factors which operated in this direc-

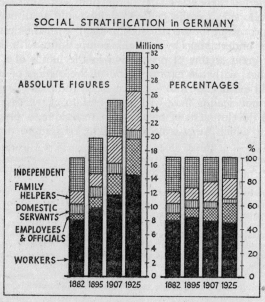

tion at the time. As they are quite well known and as they have often been described, it is sufficient to enumerate them summarily here.

No Agricultural Concentration but Decline in the Relative Importance of Agriculture

The destruction of independent existences was not a process which applied equally to all sectors of the economic system. The destruction of independent existences in industry, or, better, in the towns, took place on the basis of capitalist concentration together with a tremendous increase both in the numbers of those engaged in industry and of those living in the towns.

The situation in the rural areas was quite different: there was no destruction to any material extent of small and medium-sized agricultural undertakings by large-scale agricultural undertakings throughout this whole period. Thus where the number of independent existences in agriculture declined, the circumstance was part of a whole process of decline—partly relative and partly absolute—of agriculture within the general framework of capitalist economy.

In world capitalism as a whole small and medium-sized undertakings maintained themselves in agriculture, and this was a circumstance whose importance for the general development, not only in this period, but also in the period between the two world wars, and even after, can hardly be over-estimated.*

In this period there was no development in agriculture, even in the highly developed capitalist centres, which could at all be compared with the process of industrial concentration, with the destruction of the smaller undertakings by capitalist competition, with the concentration of great sectors of production in the hands of a few giant undertakings, with the expropriation of the owners of small businesses and their decline into the ranks of the industrial working class.

We are not dealing here with the question of whether, with the continued development of science and technique, a phase will be possible in which large-scale undertakings begin to dominate in

---

* The weakness of Marx's analysis of agriculture was that it was undertaken on the assumption that the capitalist mode of production was dominant. In volume III of "Das Kapital" [6] in the introduction to an analysis of ground rent Marx wrote:

"The analysis of landed property in its various historical forms lies beyond the scope of this work. We shall occupy ourselves with it only to the extent that a part of the surplus value produced by capital goes into the pockets of landed proprietors. Thus we assume that agriculture, like manufacture, is dominated by the capitalist mode of production, that is to say that it is carried on by capitalists who differ from other capitalists in the first place only in that their capital, and the wage-labour set in motion by this capital, is invested in a different element. As far as we are concerned the leaseholder produces wheat in the same way as the manufacturer produces yarn or machinery. The assumption that the capitalist mode of production has taken over control of agriculture involves the further assumption that it controls all spheres of production and the whole of bourgeois society. . . .

"If the capitalist mode of production assumes the expropriation of the workers from their conditions of labour it also assumes in agriculture the expropriation of the rural workers from the land and their subordination to a capitalist who carries on agriculture for profit. For this development therefore it is a totally invalid objection to recall that other forms of landed property and agriculture have existed or still exist."

Marx analysed industrial production on the assumption that the capitalist mode of production existed alone, but that was, of course, not true in the period in which he was writing, but in the century after the publication of "The Manifesto" the general trend of development was towards an increase of the capitalist industrial sector, a steady growth in the percentage of the people who produced in the capitalist centres under capitalist conditions, so that more and more people were drawn into the capitalist orbit.

But this was true only to a very much lesser degree of agriculture, and thus the abstraction which Marx adopted in "Das Kapital" of regarding agriculture as though it produced under purely capitalist conditions was much more daring than the same assumption was for industry, and it makes sense only if the transitional phases between this abstract scheme and the actually existing historical process are analysed.

agriculture as well as in industry and to put the smaller farms, etc., out of business by large-scale competition. For us it is enough to recognize that up to the present this development has not come about, that there has been no agricultural concentration analogous to industrial concentration in the social environment in which the class struggles of the past hundred years have been fought out.*

The fact is that in this very important sector of the economic system conditions have on the whole tended to remain stable in that respect, and this is a circumstance which has also contributed greatly to slowing down the tendency for society to split up into two hostile camps.

That there has, in fact, been no concentration in agriculture on any scale comparable with that of industry can be seen from the following statistics relating to Germany: [17]

Number and Extent of Agricultural Holdings in the Years 1882, 1895 *and* 1907, *Listed according to Size*

Group.	Number of holdings.			Total of arable land (in hectares).		
	1822.	1895.	1907.	1882.	1895.	1907.
Hectares : †						
Below 2 . .	3,061,831	3,236,367	3,378,509	1,825,938	1,804,444	1,713,311
2 to 5 . .	981,407	1,016,318	1,006,277	3,190,203	3,285,984	3,304,878
5 to 20 . .	926,605	998,804	1,065,539	9,158,398	9,721,875	10,421,564
20 to 100 .	281,570	281,767	262,191	9,908,170	9,869,837	9,322,103
Over 100 .	24,991	25,061	23,566	7,786,263	7,831,801	7,055,018

Group.	Per hundred holdings.			Per hundred hectares of arable land.		
	1882.	1895.	1907.	1882.	1895.	1907.
Hectares : †						
Below 2 . .	58·03	58·23	58·9	5·73	5·56	5·44
2 to 5 . .	18·6	18·28	17·54	10·01	10·11	10·38
5 to 20 . .	17·56	17·97	18·58	28·74	29·9	32·74
20 to 100 .	5·34	5·07	4·57	31·09	30·35	29·28
Over 100 .	0·74	0·45	0·41	24·43	24·08	22·16

† The holdings under two hectares consist chiefly of allotments which are spare-time tilled and which do not fully maintain their holders.

The above figures show that the changes were of very little importance, and that where they took place at all they were to the

* After the first world war the number of farms in the United States which consisted of 1,000 acres or more increased, whilst their share of the total area of arable land increased even more. From 1920 to 1940 the number of farms of 1,000 acres or more increased from 67,405 to 100,331, or from 1 per cent of all farms to 1·6 per cent. In the same period their share of the arable land increased from 23·1 per cent in 1920 to 34·4 per cent in 1940.[18] But even in the United States, where this development has proceeded farthest, there is still no question of putting the smaller and medium-sized farms out of business by capitalist competition.

"All things considered, the scale of agricultural operations in general appears to have undergone little change since the turn of the century. The number of producing units remains very large compared with most branches of manufacturing or mining." [19]

disadvantage of the large-scale holdings. There was no question of any destruction of the smaller holdings by large-scale competition. In addition, it must be pointed out that those large-scale holdings which did exist in Germany in that period were by no means run on modern scientific lines, and that most of them were survivors from the feudal era and had to be kept going with subsidies.

The continued existence of the small and medium-sized holdings in agriculture even in the more highly developed capitalist States represented a decisive factor in the class stratification of society in this period.

At the same time, however, it must be pointed out that the importance of the agricultural sector has declined steadily in world capitalism as a whole. Within this general trend of development there were important differences, so that the share of the agricultural sectors in the various leading capitalist countries varied greatly and still does vary. At the same time there were further important differences because, despite the relative decline which took place on an international scale, some countries showed a considerable increase in the absolute figures, and the actual time at which not only a relative but an absolute decline took place in the agricultural population was different in the various capitalist countries. But allowing for all these differences, the main trend was clear and indisputable: there was a general decline of the agricultural sector in all capitalist centres.

In the United States in 1850, for example, the agricultural sector accounted for two-thirds of the total population or 63·7 per cent, and in 1870 it still accounted for the majority of the population, or 53 per cent; but in the years immediately preceding the first world war it accounted for less than one-third, or 31 per cent, and in 1940 it accounted for less than a fifth, or 17·6 per cent.

The general trend in the European industrial countries was the same. A series of factors led to this steady decrease in the agricultural sectors in the highly developed capitalist countries.

1. In this period the productivity of labour increased, and this was the case in agriculture as well, though the rate of increase was not so great as in industry. However, this increase in the productivity of agricultural labour by no means fully accounted for the tremendous decline in the agricultural sector.

2. In addition, industry affected agriculture in two ways. It destroyed to a very great extent the part-time productive activities of the agricultural population, and it provided them with a considerable part of the products which they formerly made for themselves. In other words, a considerable part of the labour which had formerly been performed in the rural areas was now transferred to the towns, where it was henceforth performed by large-scale industry. Thus part of the migration from the rural areas to the towns consisted of

men and women who followed their lost occupations into the industrial areas. In the same way a considerable part of the increase in female labour was due to the fact that industry deprived women of much of the part-time work they had been accustomed to do at home, and women therefore began to work directly in industry.

Industry also influenced agriculture in that it provided agricultural implements and machinery of all kinds and raw materials such as artificial fertilizers, and thus helped to increase the productivity of labour. In other words, a growing part of the labour used in agriculture was indirectly performed by industry.

3. In addition, the decline of the agricultural sector was caused in part by increasing imports of agricultural produce. To that extent, of course, there was no decline of the agricultural sector on an international scale, but only a shifting of the point of production, and this often came about because industrially backward countries and countries which had become colonies of the capitalist industrial centres provided—sometimes were compelled to provide—the latter with agricultural produce.

This was true in particular of England, and the great decline in the agricultural population there was made possible because the country largely imported its foodstuffs. It was also true to some extent of Germany, because in this period agricultural self-sufficiency ceased and an increasing percentage of agricultural products was imported. In the last few years before the first world war about a quarter of the total agricultural produce consumed in Germany was imported from abroad.

Farmers the Main Contingent amongst Independent Occupations

The fact that the small and medium-sized undertakings in agriculture were not shattered, whereas in industry they declined relatively, and absolutely in many places, had one very important consequence. When the total number of independent undertakings in the capitalist countries is broken down into its component parts, we find that almost everywhere—Great Britain is the one exception because the decline of the agricultural sector there was quite unusually thorough—farmers and peasants represent the main contingent. This was, above all, the case in the United States because the destruction of the independent industrial small-scale undertakings was very thorough there and the concentration of production into giant industrial undertakings was more definite.

In the year 1910 there were 8,579,000 "proprietors, managers and officials", and amongst them were no fewer than 6,132,000 farmers. At that time this category represented 23 per cent of the total population of the United States, and 16·5 per cent were farmers. Even in 1940—by which time there had been a further sharp decline of the agricultural sector and a decline of this independent category—farmers still accounted for 10·1 per cent out of a total of 17·8 per cent for this category.

Industrial concentration did not proceed so far in Germany as it did in the United States, but even in Germany the number of independent existences was greater in agriculture than in industry and handicraft. In 1925 there were 2,202,900 independent operators in agriculture, as against 1,785,100 in industry and handicraft, and the former represented approximately 40 per cent of the total number of independent existences in Germany, although the agricultural population represented only a good fifth of the population as a whole.

Thus farmers and peasants represented the main contingent amongst the independent existences under capitalism not only at the beginning of capitalist development, but in all subsequent stages of that development, including the final decades before the first world war and the period between the two world wars.

FATE OF THE INDEPENDENT URBAN MIDDLE STRATA

Compared with the comparatively slow development experienced by agriculture in the capitalist countries, the development in the towns proceeded by leaps and bounds. However, it cannot be said that the general trend was definitely in the direction of the destruction of the urban middle strata as a whole. In fact in some cases the destruction of the middle strata in one sphere was accompanied by the creation of new middle strata in others. In industry the process of abolishing these middle strata proceeded rapidly. After having destroyed pre-capitalist production forms, capitalism went on to an increased process of concentration, together with the destruction of the smaller undertakings which were already capitalist but which were not sufficiently productive.*

The concentration of industry increased, and it is still increasing. The proportion of industrial production turned out in large and giant undertakings is growing, and new industries are often founded directly on a large-scale industrial basis. And in this respect the process of destroying the independent strata is very much more thorough than the statistics on the point would seem to indicate, because it is often in the interests of big capital to leave certain of the independent strata in existence on paper, although in reality they are completely dependent economically and socially on the big undertakings.

However, despite this growing power in the hands of the big

---

* Joseph A. Schumpeter rightly declares in his book " Kapitalismus, Sozialismus und Demokratie":

"What (capitalism) did to the pre-capitalist strata it now proceeded to do—and with the same mechanism of competition—to the lower strata of capitalist industry. In this respect Marx, of course, gets full marks."

undertakings, which account for an ever-increasing proportion of production, small undertakings were not entirely destroyed even in industry. In this period of a steady increase of production as a whole the proportion due to the large-scale undertakings increased both relatively and absolutely, but although on the one hand many small undertakings were destroyed, many more were created on the other, precisely on the basis of this industrial expansion, and thus we see that although the tendency towards the destruction of the smaller independent undertakings continues, it does not result in their complete abolition.

CLASS STRATIFICATION AND THE "TERTIARY" INDUSTRIES

Much more important for the question of class stratification, however, is the fact that in this period of expansion, with growing production, growing national income, growing profits and growing wages—in other words, a rise in standards of living for the whole population of the United States and of the European capitalist countries—that sector of the economic system which Colin Clark has termed "tertiary industries" also grew very considerably. With this term he describes that production which, unlike the production of agriculture and industry, is not tangible, and it refers in general to trade, transport, public administration, services of all kinds, hotels, restaurants and so on.*

In the period from 1850 until 1910 the development of employment in the United States, according to its general categories, was as follows:

U.S.A. Percentages of Working Population [10]

Year.	Agriculture, forestry and fishing.	Mining.	Manufacture and building.	Trade, transport and communications.	Domestic, personal and professional.
1850	64·8	1·2	16·4	5·4	12·2
1860	60·2	1·6	18·3	7·4	12·4
1870	53·8	1·4	21·2	10·4	13·1
1880	49·4	1·5	24	12·2	12·8
1890	42·6	1·7	25·6	15·7	14·4
1900	37·4	2	27	18·7	14·8
1910	31·9	2·6	28·4	21·3	15·8

The decline in the agricultural sector was accompanied by an increase in the industrial sector, but the latter increase was much less

* "For convenience in international comparisons production may be defined as primary, secondary and tertiary. Under the first-named we include agricultural and pastoral production, fishing, forestry and hunting. Mining is more properly included with secondary production, covering manufacture, building construction and public works, gas and electricity supply. Tertiary production is defined by difference as consisting of all other economic activities the principal of which are distribution, transport, public administration, domestic service and all other activities producing a non-material output." [11]

than the decrease in agriculture, so that agriculture and industry together accounted for a steadily decreasing percentage of the total population: 82·4 per cent in 1850, but only 62·9 per cent in 1910.

This tendency, which naturally differed in degree, was valid for all highly industrialized countries. It applied not only to the United States, but also to the big industrial countries of Europe. For our purposes it is very important to note that the tendency to concentration in the tertiary industries in this period was by no means so strong as in industry generally, so that in this sector there was a constant creation of new "independent existences", and thus even in the towns the process of destroying the independent strata was by no means so definite, and by no means in full accord with the process of destruction in industry itself.

This was true for a great part of tertiary production, and particularly for trade.

For world capitalism in this period the section of the population living on trade increased greatly and rapidly, with the result that its relative importance in the economic system as a whole increased. This was a natural consequence of capitalist development. The more capitalism dominated production at home, the more it secured a monopoly of production, the more it destroyed production for the direct use of the producer and turned production into commodities for the market, the greater became that section of the economic system which existed for the purpose of bringing the commodities from the producer to the consumer—namely, trade.

The tendency to concentration in trade, so far as it existed at all, was much less powerful than in industry itself. In other words, here the smaller and medium-sized undertakings continued to be of very great importance. Unlike industry, there were few new fields in trade which lent themselves to exploitation from the beginning on the basis of intense concentration. Machinery, for example, played a much smaller role in trade than it did in industry. Further, the main business of trade was in consumer goods, in production for personal use—that is to say, in a sphere in which concentration in industry itself was not so far advanced as in other spheres.

In the industrial sector the number of smaller undertakings increased only very slowly, if at all, and in some countries there was an absolute diminution, but there was no question of any such stagnation in the growth of the small and medium-sized undertakings engaged in trading in this period. On the contrary, there was a very considerable absolute increase in the numbers of small and medium-sized undertakings engaged in trade in all countries, and this phenomenon existed not only in times of depression and stagnation, when the increase was particularly great for the time being, but it was a general trend.

The figures for Germany are typical of the general trend in all the leading capitalist countries. The number of undertakings engaged in trade in 1875 was 529,000; by 1895 it had increased to 777,500; and by 1907 it was no less than 1,097,800. Thus in this period the number of such undertakings almost doubled, whilst at the same time the process of concentration in industry was so powerful that the number of undertakings decreased from 2,334,000 in 1875 to 2,084,000 in 1907.

Apart from this quite considerable survival of independent existences, the tendency towards social polarization was still further weakened by the fact that the decline in the number of independent existences was not reflected in a simple proportionate increase in the number of wage-workers, and that new middle strata were formed (and they were formed particularly rapidly precisely in large-scale industry), strata which increased far more rapidly than did the working class throughout the whole period; these strata were the employees and professional persons.

Occupational statistics for the United States show a considerable increase in the number of employees even in the period before the world war, when they represented more than 10 per cent of the total labour force. Incidentally, this strong tendency towards an increase in the numbers of employees did not apply to this period only, but continued to operate subsequently both in the United States and Europe. In the United States the percentage of employees in the total labour force rose from approximately 10 per cent in 1910 to 17·2 per cent in 1940.

The tendency towards an increase operated with equal force in Germany and in the whole of Europe. In the period from 1895 to 1907 independent existences in industry and mining increased by 2·52 per cent; the number of workers increased by 44·28 per cent; whilst the number of employees increased by no less than 160 per cent. This great increase in the numbers of employees in the United States, Germany and the whole of Europe was not a passing phenomenon; it applied not only to this period, but also to subsequent periods, including the time between the two world wars and the periods of capitalist stagnation and depression.

However, with the process of increased capitalist concentration and the growing power and influence of a few industrial magnates over industry as a whole, this mass of employees had less and less chance of one day being independent. The category of employees became just as much a permanent phenomenon as the category of wage-workers, and to that extent there is some justification for the term which arose to describe the new category: the white-collar proletariat. This was particularly true because the salaries of these employees were not much, if at all, greater than the wages of skilled workers.

Now it was a matter of great significance for the struggle between capital and labour that the millions of employees, at least in this period, did not regard themselves as in the same class as workers, and that, in fact, they did their best to stress in every possible way what they regarded as the differences between them. This was even true of countries in which there was a strong and class-conscious working class with definitely socialist aims. And it was still true in a period when capitalism was no longer generally regarded as the only possible mode of production—namely, in the time between the two world wars.

How little these employees felt themselves to be workers, and how anxious they were to stress their supposed position as the new middle strata in society, can be seen from the way in which they organized themselves. In Germany between the two world wars, for instance, there was not one association of employees, but several. From our standpoint it is important to note that whilst a section of these employees joined organizations which were similar to those of the workers and set themselves socialist aims, other sections joined organizations which just as definitely approved of the capitalist mode of production. The way in which the employees differed from the workers in this respect was typical. The following figures show the organizational groupings of workers and employees respectively.

Organizations.	Workers.	Employees.
Socialist Unions . . .	4,415,700 or 81·3%	415,300 or 27·2%
Christian-National Unions .	720,050 or 13·3%	454,900 or 29·8%
Liberal-National Unions .	202,450 or 3·5%	340,600 or 22·3%
Syndicalist and Communist Unions	49,800 or 0·9%	—
Economic-Collaboration Unions	—	65,000 or 4·3%
Independent Unions . .	20,200 or 0·4%	241,800 or 15·8%
Religious Unions . .	24,500 or 0·4%	10,000 or 0·6%

The overwhelming majority of organized workers, or 81·3 per cent, were members of the socialist unions—that is to say, of unions whose final aim was to bring about a socialist mode of production—but only just over a quarter, or 27·2 per cent, of the clerical employees were organized in such unions. The overwhelming majority of them were organized in various associations which rejected socialism.

Our analysis has now shown us that the continued process of capitalist concentration in industry in this period led to a very complicated class stratification. There was no question of any simple polarization of society into two hostile camps. In this period of vigorous expansion accompanied by a strong imperialist drive, society, in which at one time independent existences had been in the majority, now consisted of an overwhelming majority of dependent wage-workers and employees. But simultaneously real wages in this society rose between 50 and 100 per cent as compared with earlier times, and the workers had a higher standard of living than that of the former middle strata. At the same time independent small and medium-sized holdings survived in agriculture or changed only very gradually, and the so-called tertiary industries developed and constantly created new independent existences. And finally, new middle strata of employees, officials and professional men were created, and these strata not only showed a considerable absolute increase, but their numbers grew more rapidly than those of the workers, so that they represented an increasing percentage of the population as a whole.

The result of this process was that although the workers, whose numbers had previously increased both absolutely and relatively, continued to increase absolutely in numbers, they hardly increased at all relatively, whilst in some countries their relative strength even declined. In other words, in the highly-developed capitalist countries the process of industrial concentration was no longer accompanied by a continued increase in the relative strength of the working class, and the numerical strength of this class stabilized itself on a level which was hardly more than 50 per cent of the population as a whole. Not only had the workers shown a tendency to become more middle class in their outlook, but the actual middle strata had shown an astonishing stability: losses on the one hand had been made good by gains on the other.

The New Middle Strata Highly Susceptible to Crises

However, a fundamental change had taken place in the social structure of these middle strata. The middle strata which had existed before the opening up of the great process of industrial development and capitalist concentration, and which had represented the majority of the population up to the seventies—the farmers of the United States and the peasants of Europe, and the artisans and handicraftsmen of both continents—had been largely outside the framework of capitalist production. In the period when large-scale industry was just beginning to develop a considerable section of the peasantry were hardly connected with market economy at all. To a very great extent they consumed their own produce, and were therefore not so affected by disturbances in the purely capitalist sector of production. The same was true of the artisans and craftsmen.

Thus at that time production under capitalist conditions represented only a small sector of the whole economic system, and when an analysis is made of the crises which took place in this period it must not be forgotten that crises in the capitalist sector of the economic system were by no means identical with crises in the economic system as a whole.

However, it was in this period that a fundamental change began to take place. Agriculture as a whole in the capitalist countries was drawn more and more into the capitalist process, and a growing percentage of agricultural production came on to the market, whilst at the same time farmers, etc., became more and more dependent on the products of capitalist industry. Thus the self-sufficing peasants progressively became small agricultural units producing for the capitalist market.

On the other hand, the independent handicraftsmen had almost disappeared. Small undertakings in industry became more and more dependent on the big undertakings, and were thus more and more closely integrated with the capitalist process as a whole.

The "tertiary" industries were also closely bound up with the general trend of capitalist economy, and they often represented a sort of barometer of the business cycle.

With the development of industrial concentration many millions of employees were just as much threatened with unemployment as the wage-workers themselves.

In other words, the former middle strata had shown a certain immunity to the effects of economic crises, and that was particularly important in another respect: they represented a sector in capitalist society which showed a certain stability in times of crisis, and therefore represented a factor which made it easier for capitalism to overcome its crises.

But the new middle strata, from the agricultural small units to the proprietors of restaurants and petrol pumps, employees and professional men, enjoyed no such crisis immunity; they were just as susceptible to all the effects of economic crisis as the other sectors of capitalist economy, in fact more so.

Now, at first the fact there was no longer any sector in capitalist society which was immune to the effects of economic crises, once this fundamental change had taken place in the social structure of the middle strata, was not so noticeable, because precisely in this period the expansion of capitalism and the imperialist drive had resulted in a great diminution of the severity of the crises, so that when they did break out, the new middle strata were also not very seriously affected. For instance, in this period unemployment amongst employees was very low. However, as soon as the imperialist drive came to an end the effects of economic crises were greatly intensified, and then the change in the social structure of the middle strata made itself clearly felt.

On the other hand, as long as the period of capitalist expansion and imperialist drive continued, a class stratification was brought about in the highly-developed capitalist countries which did not, on the whole, intensify social antagonism, but, on the contrary, tended to diminish it.

It must never be forgotten that this diminution of social antagonisms stood in direct functional relation to the process of imperialist expansion; it therefore represented only one side of the picture. This side was continually stressed and the other side was forgotten, or mentioned only in passing as something of little importance.

Even so, this rosy and harmonious view of the period was valid only when the countries which were the objects of capitalist and imperialist exploitation were conveniently left out of account. Only very few people, relatively speaking, actually saw what was happening in those far-off countries, and therefore it was comparatively easy for most people to "forget", or even to know nothing whatever about it. In this way the idea arose that the progress being made in the capitalist countries of Europe was independent of capitalist expansion beyond the frontiers—i.e. imperialism. Not only was it easy to believe this, but millions of people had every reason to want to believe it, because a real analysis of the functional relationships would have revealed the brittleness of the social basis on which their very existence rested. The fact that so many people had every interest in believing in this illusion was the chief reason for the degeneration of economic science in this period.

Economic science dealt exclusively with a capitalist economic system functioning under conditions of free competition. It did not bother to analyse the clash of the capitalist system with the other systems it destroyed or undermined. When the colonies and the empires had to be mentioned, economists spoke about free trade and investments. Now free trade presumes the existence of equal partners with equal bargaining rights, but this was not in the least the relationship between the capitalist metropolitan centres and their empires. Economic science assumed the existence of free workers, but in the colonial areas their "freedom" was fictitious. It also assumed the decline of feudalism, but in the empires there was often an alliance between imperialism and feudalism which helped the latter to survive and even to consolidate itself.

If capitalist and imperialist expansion had produced only the direct results we have seen—the increase of surplus profits and a certain encouragement of foreign trade—then the "overlooking" of the greater part of humanity would not have been quite so dangerous and the sources of error in the analysis of the highly-developed capitalist countries would not have been so great. But, in fact, capitalist and imperialist expansion had decisive effects on the functioning of the capitalist system as a whole, on the business cycle, on the labour market, on wages, and on the entire structure of class stratification. Thus any "overlooking" of this important factor necessarily deprived any analysis of a very great part of its value, and, in fact, most of the economic writing of this period suffers precisely from this weakness.

And it was not only in this period. Although developments between the two world wars clearly demonstrated the functional relationship between imperialism, economic crises and social stratification, books about the business cycle were still being written in which the word "imperialism" was never even mentioned. For instance, books were written purporting to analyse British society, and yet they ignored the functional relationship between class stratification at home and that in the Empire.

But a theory which ignores capitalist and imperialist expansion, which takes no account of the alliance between imperialism and feudalism, or of the struggle for national liberation in the colonial countries—a theory which, in other words, thinks it can confine itself to capitalist development and class stratification in the metropolitan centres, is so far removed from the whole complex of decisive facts that it cannot be termed a theory at all; it turns out to be little more than a superficial presentation of certain facts which are in any case not of much value, because they are carefully abstracted from the historical environment which is the decisive condition for their proper ordering in any analysis of the total development of capitalist production.

DIFFERENCES IN U.S. AND EUROPEAN CLASS STRATIFICATION

In the period up to the outbreak of the first world war the development of class stratification in the United States and in the European capitalist countries was similar in important respects. The big differences which subsequently developed set in after the first world war.

However, despite the important similarities in this earlier period, there were, even then, certain differences, and we propose to summarize them briefly here in order to facilitate the understanding of our analysis of the subsequent period.

U.S. capitalism had no feudal system to destroy in its own country, as European capitalism had had. Now, the destruction of the feudal system was not altogether identical with the destruction of the political and social influence of the former feudal strata. In Germany feudal remnants remained particularly strong, and the former feudal magnates continued to play an important role in German ruling circles, and exercised an influence on policy. But even in England, where the destruction or transformation of feudalism had begun much earlier, the old feudal elements continued to exercise a big political influence.

In America, on the other hand, capitalist development began in what was largely an economic vacuum, and U.S. leading circles numbered very few individuals from earlier feudal epochs in their ranks; capitalist elements were absolutely dominant.

This predominance of the purely capitalist upper strata was still further encouraged by the fact that in this early period the United

States needed no army in times of peace, or at least nothing comparable with the armies of Europe, and amongst the immigrants were many men who had left their own countries on account of their hostility to the militarist ideology which prevailed there.

Unlike Europe, but in this respect like England, the U.S. ruling stratum was formed without any considerable militarist admixture, and it remained without it right up to the period of the first world war, because up to then the United States had been protected from all aggression by two mighty oceans and by its own undisputed leadership on the American continent, and it therefore had no reason to take part in the armament race which was already proceeding in Europe.

This capitalist upper stratum in the United States controlled a productive apparatus which, like the productive apparatus of capitalist Europe, was subject to a process of industrial concentration—except that it was much more intense than anywhere else in the world.

The circumstance that U.S. industry had a home market which was so large that it was a continent rather than a land, and the further circumstance that the constant migration to the undeveloped areas of the west strengthened the position of labour on the market and caused a steady rise in wages, facilitated the development of industries producing for mass sales, and concentration was particularly marked in these industries.

Earlier on we gave a table showing the position of the big industrial countries in their relations to each other from decade to decade, according to the volume of industrial production. In the period before the first world war this table was also in approximate accordance with the development of industrial concentration: the United States was in the lead—a very strong lead—then came Germany, with Great Britain in third place, followed by France.

Thus U.S. society was characterized on the one hand by the fact that the process of industrial concentration had gone much farther in America than in Europe, and on the other by the fact that not only did wages steadily rise, but, because it was possible to put back the frontiers of capitalist expansion farther and farther, and because the increase in the productivity of labour had been so great, they were far above the level of wages in the European capitalist countries, including Great Britain.

Now, in Europe there was, as we have seen, a functional relationship between the rise in wages and the imperialist drive beyond the frontiers, but this was not the case with regard to the rise in U.S. wages. It was the expansion of U.S. capitalism within its own territorial frontiers which provided the necessary conditions for this rise in wages.

Another point of difference between the United States and Europe was that whereas in Europe the working class was relatively homogeneous, there were greater and more obvious differences between one stratum of workers and the other in the U.S.A. than anywhere else. For one thing, immigrant workers played a big role in the development of U.S. capitalism, and therefore the economic, social, national and religious differences which existed in the heterogeneous working class of America were so enormous that they were not really comparable with analogous differences in the ranks of the British, German and French working classes.

The "Fourth Estate" in Europe—the working class of the metropolitan centres—was paralleled outside the frontiers by what might be called a "Fifth Estate", namely, the great majority of the peasants of Eurasia, of the colonial and semi-colonial countries. Now, in the United States there was a "Fourth Estate" made up of English-speaking workers to the manner born, and a vast "Fifth Estate" consisting of the American negroes and of the newly arrived foreign-born workers, the great majority of whom did not speak English, or spoke it very badly, and most of whom—particularly in the last decades before the first world war—came from countries in which general living standards, and their own in particular, were far below American standards.

These very considerable differences within the American working class were of great significance for the class stratification of the country as a whole. The middle-class outlook of the American-born workers had been fostered by the fact that their own standards of living had risen so high, and this outlook was naturally still further encouraged by the presence of many millions of foreign-born workers, whose standards, though higher than they had been in Europe, were still considerably lower than their own. The aim of these newly immigrated workers was, generally speaking, not to bring about any transformation of American society, but to raise their own standards to those of the American-born workers, and this direct and immediate aim was thoroughly feasible; in fact millions of immigrant workers progressively achieved it, if not for themselves, then for their children.

Thus the fact that large sections of this "Fifth Estate" gradually rose into the "Fourth Estate", that in this period of great progress the American working class became, economically considered, middle class, and that the American upper class—being much less influenced by feudal and militarist elements—was never such a closed group as it tended to be in European countries, gave the American social structure a much greater degree of elasticity. The comparative rigidity of class stratification which existed in Europe did not exist in the United States—at least, it did not exist in this period. Thus the fact that the frontiers of U.S. capitalist expansion could be extended farther and farther in this period not only provided a vent for labour and prevented the overcrowding of the labour market, but, with all its direct and indirect results, it also greatly facilitated the rise from one social stratum into the next higher.

CLASS STRATIFICATION OUTSIDE THE CAPITALIST COUNTRIES

The state of class stratification in the countries outside the capitalist metropolitan centres was very different indeed at this period from what it was in capitalist Europe and the United States. In addition, it varied considerably as between those countries which succeeded in maintaining their political independence and those which lost it and became wholly subject to capitalist imperialist exploitation.

Russia was one of the countries which maintained its political independence. Capitalist development in Russia set in much later, but it did so to a marked degree in the last decades of the nineteenth century and at the beginning of the twentieth up to the outbreak of the first world war. To a great extent this capitalist development was financed by foreign investments, and it took place in a country which was still largely under a feudal system. Thus before the first world war Russian society was very different from capitalist society in Europe and the United States. At the apex of the Russian social pyramid were the feudal aristocracy, the military caste and the Tsarist bureaucracy, and, to a certain extent, the relatively weak capitalist elements. At the bottom of the pyramid, forming its broad base, were the overwhelming majority of the rural population, some of them rural labourers, some of them peasants who owned so little land that it was not enough to sustain them, and they had to work in addition for the "masters". In the lower levels of the pyramid were also the industrial workers, whose living standards up to the first world war were probably even below that of the workers in England in the early days of capitalist development as described by Engels in his famous book. These industrial workers were concentrated in large-scale undertakings to a much greater degree than was the case in Europe, because Russian capitalism had started up much later than capitalism in England and Western Europe, and because, being financed largely by foreign capital, it began its life at a higher stage of production than had been the case there. Now, as feudalism was still so strong in Russia, and as capitalist development was so greatly dependent on foreign capital, there was no opportunity for any strong urban middle strata to develop, and social antagonisms were very acute in this period.

CLASS STRATIFICATION IN THE COLONIAL EMPIRES

At that time class stratification in Russia occupied a position somewhere between the social structure in the more developed countries of capitalism and that in the countries which made up the colonial empires of those countries and represented the primary objects of capitalist imperialist exploitation. In Russia in this period, however, there was at least a general tendency in the same direction as that taken generations earlier by the more developed capitalist countries of Europe. In the colonial countries this tendency had been crippled from the start. At the head of their social pyramid were the representatives of foreign imperialism, and beside them the old feudal ruling cliques. As in Russia, the agricultural population was in the overwhelming majority, but whereas in Russia there was a certain tendency towards the strengthening of the urban and industrial centre, in the colonial countries the preponderance of agriculture remained, and there was even a strengthening of the agricultural sector not only absolutely, but relatively. The development of industrialism in the colonial countries did not proceed at the expense of feudalism, but feudalism was maintained, and even deliberately strengthened. At the same time the conditions of the labourers on the plantations were not much different from slavery, and much worse than those existing in Russia.

In Russia there was to some extent a co-ordinated industrial development, a development of both heavy industry and the manufacturing industries. There was nothing of the sort in the colonial countries. Their industries developed without any co-ordination, and, in particular, the production of raw materials bore no relation to their own requirements, but was determined solely by the trading needs of the capitalist metropolitan centres. In this period Russia enjoyed a growing volume of trade with a number of other countries, whereas colonial countries usually traded only with the country which controlled them as part of its empire, or with countries which required raw materials. Trade between the colonial countries of Asia and Africa themselves was usually very restricted.

Thus capitalist development and industrial concentration in this period were not accompanied in the colonial countries which were the objects of imperialist exploitation by the creation of a large-scale industrial working class, by an improvement in working-class living standards, or by the development of any considerable middle stratum in the towns; instead the representatives of foreign imperialism stood at the head of the social pyramid, and by their side were the old feudal landlords, whilst the basis of the pyramid was made up of the overwhelming majority of those engaged in agriculture, and the industrial and plantation workers whose living standards were even lower than those of the Russian workers. Such bourgeois middle strata as did exist between these two poles of colonial society were in a negligible minority.

From this it followed first of all that European imperialist dominance, precisely because it was a parasitic dominance for the colonial economic system, had to be maintained chiefly by force, and could be maintained only so long as the imperialist powers were in control of the decisive instruments of power. And secondly it followed that when the imperialist drive came to an end, when the period of imperialist decline set in and the colonial countries began to regain their political independence, a fundamental process of social transformation became necessary both in the metropolitan capitalist centres and in the countries which had formerly been the objects of their capitalist imperialist exploitation.

The former colonial countries, whose economic system under imperialist exploitation had developed without proper reference to their own needs, which had been linked up with the world markets only by the production of certain raw materials which the highly-developed capitalist countries required, and in which the agrarian revolution had been delayed, now naturally needed a complete social transformation in order to develop an economic and social structure in accordance with the requirements of their own populations.

But the decisive consequences of this process were not confined to the former colonial countries, and, as Part Three of this book will show in greater detail, the decline of imperialism had important consequences for the metropolitan capitalist countries in which the rise of imperialism had fundamentally affected the social structure and the nature and intensity of the economic crises. The fact that the whole transformation process of European capitalism took place under such unique historical conditions is of almost inestimable significance.

Just as the rise of European capitalism can be understood only in conjunction with an analysis of imperialist expansion, so the present transformation process can be understood only if it is borne in mind that this transformation is not an inner one, but that it is taking place in a definite historical environment, in which the former wide-scale imperialist relationships are being more and more dismantled and in which therefore the repercussions in the metropolitan States of what happens in the colonies are growing less and less, so that, apart from the purely inner social transformation, a transformation of the productive apparatus is necessary in accordance with the changed historical conditions.

Such questions had naturally not arisen when capitalism was still developing, and a tremendous process of expansion was taking place. Imperialism was still pressing forward vigorously, even though the limits of European imperialist expansion were already beginning to make themselves felt in the end phase of the process.

CHAPTER SIX

IMPERIALIST EXPANSION LED TO WAR

Up to the present we have drawn a distinction between the expansion of United States capitalism within its own territorial limits and the expansion of European capitalism along imperialist lines beyond its own territorial frontiers. As far as the general trends of capitalist development as a whole in this period were analysed, that distinction was enough, but only to that extent.

The United States was one country—a country as big as a continent. However, there was not one united Europe, but a large number of separate States, and they did not start the process of capitalist development at the same time, and once the process had begun, the speed of development varied very greatly between the various countries. In particular there was a great difference in the speed of industrial development as between the two great Powers of Europe—Great Britain and Germany.

Now, Germany's capitalist industrial development was particularly rapid in a period in which, as far as imperialism was concerned, the world was almost completely divided up, and in which there was therefore very little opportunity for new imperialist drives.

Thus there was a powerful capitalist industrial development in Germany which had no adequate imperialist vent. This dilemma led to a progressive aggravation of foreign-political antagonisms and became the decisive factor which led to the outbreak of the first world war.

We must therefore supplement our analysis of European capitalist development as a whole in this period with a particular analysis of British and German development, whereby we can confine ourselves to discussing those factors essentially connected with the difference in the rate of development of the two countries.

Great Britain was the leading industrial country in the world not only at the very beginning of the industrial revolution but for a long time afterwards: even in the seventies, at the time of the Franco-Prussian War, the production of Britain's heavy industries and of the cotton industry was greater than that of the rest of the world combined. From 1870 to 1874 [1] Britain produced an annual average of 6·4 million tons of pig-iron. In the three other capitalist countries which were most highly developed in this period—the United States, Germany and France—the total annual production of pig-iron was 5·2 million tons. Thus Great Britain produced 55 per cent of the total production of pig-iron of the four leading industrial countries of the day. In the same period Britain's coal production was 120·7 million tons, which represented 57 per cent of the total coal production of these same four countries. And with 35·9 million spindles, Great Britain owned 69 per cent of the total in these four countries. At this time the production of steel was still relatively unimportant, but with an annual average of 0·9 million tons in the years 1875–1879 Great Britain's production represented 41 per cent of world production. Germany produced 0·4 million tons, or 18 per cent; France produced 0·3 million tons, or 14 per cent, whilst the United States produced 0·6 million tons, or 27 per cent.

Thanks to this preponderant position in industrial production, British capitalists were able to export their commodities not only to their own colonial empire, which they completely dominated, but also to countries which had retained their political independence—for instance, Western Europe, including Germany. In this way the first railways in Europe were built with British assistance, whilst the first textile machinery set up in France and Germany came from England. Thus the countries of Europe played a considerable role in the British export trade, and even up to the time of the Franco-Prussian War they bought about half Great Britain's total exports.

But in the final third of the nineteenth century, and still more so in the first decade of the twentieth century, the picture began to change rapidly.

First of all, Great Britain's dominant position on all the important fields of industrial production was broken. Great Britain's own production continued to increase, but at a much slower rate than that of the rest of the world, with the result that her share in world production steadily declined. It was in this period that Great Britain was industrially outstripped, first by the United States and then by Germany.

Secondly, the more other countries strengthened their own process of industrialization the less they bought from Great Britain, with the result that their importance for Britain's export trade diminished, whilst that of the industrially backward countries increased. But here in particular Britain's foreign trade came more and more into competition with the foreign trade of the new capitalist Power, Germany, and German competition was often successful.

The following tables show us the development of production in two most important industries.

Coal Production from 1875–1879 to 1913 [2]

Year.	Gt. Britain.		Germany.		United States.		France.		Total.
	Million tons.	Per cent.	Million tons.	Per cent.	Million tons.	Per cent.	Million tons.	Per cent.	Million tons.
1875–1879	133·3	55	38·4	16	52·2	22	16·3	7	240·2
1900–1904	226·8	35	110·7	17	281	43	31·8	5	650·3
1913 .	287·4	28	187·1	18	508·9	50	39·4	4	1,022·8

Number of Cotton Spindles 1875–1879 *to* 1910–11 [3]

Year.	Gt. Britain.		Germany.		U.S.A.		France.		Brit. India.		Total.
	Millions.	Per cent.	Millions.	Per cent.	Millions.	Per cent.	Millions.	Per cent.	Millions.	Per cent.	Millions.
1875–1879	39	67	4·8	8	10·4	18	3·8	7	—	—	58
1900–1904	46·4	53	8·5	10	21·4	25	5·9	7	5	6	87·2
1910–1911	56·3	52	10·5	10	28·8	27	6·8	6	6·1	6	108·5

The general trend is unmistakable. Great Britain was steadily losing her leading industrial position in the world.

It was in this period that the production of steel became so important for the total economy of the industrial countries, and here the development is striking.

The Production of Steel 1875–1879 *to* 1913 [4]

Year.	Gt. Britain.		Germany.		France.		U.S.A.		Total.
	Million tons.	Per cent.	Million tons.	Per cent.	Million tons.	Per cent.	Million tons.	Per cent.	Million tons.
1875–1879	0·9	41	0·4	18	0·3	14	0·6	27	2·2
1885–1889	3	41	1·1	15	0·5	7	2·3	38	6·9
1890–1894	3·2	29	2·8	25	0·8	7	4·3	39	11·1
1900–1904	4·9	18	7·3	27	1·7	6	13·4	49	27·3
1913	7·6	13	17·3	29	4·6	8	31·3	51	60·8

In the nineties Great Britain was outstripped in the production of steel by Germany, and German production continued to develop so strongly that in the period immediately prior to the first world war Germany produced twice as much steel as Great Britain and more than Great Britain and France combined.

Even before the first world war the United States produced more steel than the rest of the world, but this was not a very serious threat to Great Britain's position at the time, because most of U.S. production was used at home, and very little was exported overseas.

The situation with regard to Germany was different. Not only had Germany outstripped Great Britain in industrial production as a whole, but in this same period Germany had begun to develop increasingly beyond her own frontiers.

With this we have arrived at the decisive factor which aggravated foreign-political antagonisms—namely, the increasing competition between British and German industries.

GERMANY'S GROWING EXPORTS ENDANGER BRITAIN'S FOREIGN TRADE

The importance of the industrial countries for Britain's foreign trade continued to decline. Whilst in 1871 they still bought 44 per cent of Britain's total exports, that percentage had fallen to 30 in 1900 and to 20 in 1913.[5]

On the other hand, the export of Britain's industrial commodities to industrially backward countries had increased proportionally, until shortly before the first world war they accounted for 80 per cent of all her export trade.

A fact of cardinal importance for what follows is that Great Britain needed to export these goods; she was more dependent on exports than any other country in the world. The reason for this was that precisely in the period of her undisputed industrial hegemony she had allowed her agriculture to go largely to ruin, so that subsequently she had to import not only raw materials for her industries—in this respect she was in the same position as other European countries— but also the greater part of her foodstuffs. France and Germany were differently situated; they had not allowed their agriculture to decline to the same extent, and were much less dependent on food imports.

Now, in this situation Great Britain found her export trade more and more threatened by Germany, whose industrial production was growing much more rapidly, and this was true to an even greater extent of her industrial export trade. Germany had just ended the phase of her own internal capitalist development, and her exports increased more rapidly than her own industrial production.

"From 1872 to 1913 German industrial exports increased by almost 900 per cent as compared with a total increase of industrial production of 400 per cent." [6]

Both Great Britain and Germany increased their exports, but the following figures indicate how much more rapid the process was in Germany:

British and German Exports of Capital and Consumer Goods [7]

Country.	Capital goods.		Consumer goods.	
	1880.	1913.	1880.	1913.
Great Britain . . .	100	300	100	189
Germany	100	850	100	275

The trend for capital goods in general applies in particular to iron and steel. On an annual average in the years 1880–1884 Great Britain's exports of iron and steel were valued at 27·6 million pounds and represented about two and a half times more than Germany's corresponding exports, which were valued at 11·5 million pounds. But on an annual average in the years 1909–1913 Germany's exports of iron and steel were valued at 41·7 million pounds, or not far short of Great Britain's corresponding exports, which were valued at 45·6 million pounds.

From the beginning of the twentieth century up to 1913 Germany had doubled her export trade and almost caught up with Great Britain, and the important point was that outside the British Empire Germany's export trade had considerably outstripped Great Britain's.

125

A growing volume of Britain's exports went to empire countries. In the years 1871–1875 the proportion exported to the Empire had been rather less than a quarter, or 23 per cent, but in the years 1909–1913 the proportion had risen to 37 per cent. Within the Empire, of course, Great Britain enjoyed a position of tremendous advantage against all competitors. For instance, in the final years before the first world war she exported goods to the value of £240 million to Empire countries, whereas Germany's exports in the same period to the same countries amounted to only a tenth of that figure.

Within a few decades Great Britain had lost her leading industrial position in the world. She had been overtaken not only by the United States—which did not matter so much, as the United States was still busily engaged in opening up its own territory—but also by Germany. Thus Great Britain was no longer the one and only factory centre for an enormous agrarian Hinterland, but she had to cope with vigorous German export drives, which, outside the British Empire, where conditions were more or less equal for the two competitors, deprived her of very many markets.

SIGNS OF STAGNATION IN BRITAIN'S ECONOMY

British capitalism continued to grow on many fields, but its growth was no longer so striking as it had been in previous periods. The following figures afford ample proof that the rate of development was slowing down and that signs of stagnation were beginning to make themselves felt:

Material Progress in the United Kingdom in Relation to the Population [8]

Period.	Coal production per capita.		Pig-iron production per capita.		Shipping tonnage.		Cotton consumption per capita.		Wool consumption per capita.	
	tons.	Per cent.	cwt.	Per cent.	1,000 BRT.	Per cent.	lb.	Per cent.	lb.	Per cent.
1855–1864	2·62	50·2	2·7	62·8	9·72	47·7	28·1	70	—	—
1865–1874	3·59	68·8	3·6	83·7	13·52	66·4	33·5	83·5	10·4	84·2
1875–1884	4·21	80·6	4·2	97·7	15·99	78·5	38·6	96·3	10·25	83
1885–1894	4·62	88·5	4	93	16·68	81·9	40·6	101·2	11·85	96
1895–1904	5·22	100	4·30	100	20·36	100	40·1	100	12·35	100
1905–1913	5·89	112·8	4·34	100·9	21·49	105·5	42·2	105·2	12·56	101·7

Period.	Real wages.	Real income per capita in 1913 prices.		Food consumption.	Housing (in Scotland).
	Per cent.	Pounds sterling.	Per cent.	Per cent.	Per cent.
1855–1864	60·1	26	56·6	71·3	79·9
1865–1874	67·1	29·6	63·8	76·8	84·7
1875–1884	76·6	34·1	74·3	85·7	90·6
1885–1894	90·7	40	87·1	90·9	95·4
1895–1904	100	45·9	100	100	100
1905–1913	100	46·9	102·2	101·7	103·9

As can be seen, production was still increasing, and so was foreign trade, but the rate of increase had diminished. In many cases production increased only as the population increased, and not *per capita*. Real wages, which in the half-century from 1850 to 1900 had risen from 60 to 100, did not increase any further in the first years of the twentieth century up to the outbreak of the world war. According to some statistics they even decreased. In the same period the volume of unemployment in Britain was very much greater than in earlier years. Up to the opening of the twentieth century the British working class still felt that its interests would be best guarded under capitalism, and workers had therefore voted either Liberal or Tory, with a preference in favour of the former, but in 1900 they founded a political party of their own, which was known first as the Labour Representation Committee and became the present Labour Party in 1906. At the General Election in that year twenty-nine Labour M.P.'s were returned to the House of Commons.

To sum up, we can say that at the beginning of the twentieth century up to the first world war the continued advance of British capitalism was threatened, but not its very existence. It was to take decades of violent convulsions, economic crisis, stagnation and two world wars, together with the loss of a great part of the British Empire, to threaten the very existence of British capitalism.

However, even at that time British capitalism had more to fear than a mere slowing down in the rate of its progress; it had to fear a positive decline and the weakening of its whole world position. It had to fear that German capitalism would not only continue its economic expansion, but that it would undermine Britain's world position altogether.

A Powerful Industrial State without an Empire

Germany, which had become the leading industrial country in Europe, had no empire. German capitalism had developed later than its British counterpart. British capitalism had two tremendous advantages: Great Britain was the first country to develop capitalist industry, and she was the commanding centre of a great empire. When Britain's position in other markets was threatened she countered by strengthening her economic and financial bonds with the various parts of her empire.

Germany outstripped Great Britain and became the most powerful industrial country after the United States. Having rapidly completed the capitalist transformation at home and industrialized her own territory, Germany then began to increase her exports at a great rate. She had become a capital-exporting country later than either Great Britain or France, but in the last years before the first world war her total capital investments abroad amounted to between 1,250 and 1,750 million pounds.

But whilst British and French capitalisms both possessed colonial empires which were of great economic advantage to them, Germany had nothing comparable. German capitalism had not only been late in developing, but it had appeared at a time when the outside world had been more or less completely divided up between the imperialist powers.

Germany's colonial empire was negligible in size. Germany's total trade with her colonies in the years before the first world war amounted to no more than 5 million pounds, or less than 1 per cent of her total export trade. At the same time Germany's capital exports to her colonies were hardly of much greater importance than her trade with them. A Reichstag memorandum of 1906–1907 estimated the capital investments of the German Government in the colonies at 3·5 million pounds, whilst private capital investments were estimated at about 15 million pounds.[9]

In other words, at a time when Germany's total capital exports were estimated at between 1,250 and 1,750 million pounds, the total capital exports from Germany to her colonies amounted to only about 18 million pounds, or a little over 1 per cent of the total. At the same time British capital investments in the Empire amounted to approximately 1,750 million pounds or about half her total capital investments abroad.

With this we have laid bare the decisive source of the imperialist antagonisms which finally led to the outbreak of the first world war. In the heart of Europe a country had grown up to be the leading industrial country of the whole continent, including Great Britain; the speed of her industrial development and the rate at which she increased her foreign trade were much quicker than corresponding developments in the older industrial countries; and this country entered into competition for the world markets at a time when the formerly unclaimed areas had already become the colonial and semi-colonial territories of the older industrial countries—which were now her keen rivals.

Certainly, Germany had also profited to some extent from the general process of capitalist expansion, and, favoured in particular by her geographical position, she also profited extensively from expansion into the industrially backward areas of Eastern Europe. In addition, all the secondary effects of imperialist expansion we have already mentioned benefited her too. However, all this was not enough, and Germany hankered after the direct surplus profits of imperialist expansion, and sought to strengthen her foreign-political position as her competitors had strengthened theirs through their colonial possessions, by opening up an imperialist drive of her own.

Under conditions of free competition Germany was already able to compete successfully on the world markets, but a great part of the world was already closed to any direct German expansion, and for this reason, too, she found it impossible to build up a big empire of her own.

Unfavourable Geographic Position of German Imperialism

Unlike the geographical situation of Great Britain, France, the United States, Russia and Japan, Germany's geographical situation was very unfavourable in her phase of imperialist expansion. A glance at the map is sufficient to make this abundantly clear. Great Britain was in a position to guard her colonial possessions with her navy. The distances involved were certainly very great, but at the same time Britain's command of the sea was sufficient to guarantee that any attacks could be effectively repulsed. France had the greater part of her colonial possessions comparatively near at hand in North Africa, and as long as the Entente Cordiale held good the remainder in Indo-China were also safe. The direction of Japan's imperialist drive was obvious. The objects of her expansion lay near at hand on the Asiatic mainland.

Germany was very differently situated; not only were there no favourable communications between her colonies, but other powers lay across her own line of communication with them. Theoretically there were two possibilities for Germany to build herself up an empire. The first was to create a colonial block, or some economically suitable sphere of influence, somewhere or other in the world, whether in South America, Asia or Africa. But once obtained, such a block or sphere of influence would have to be defended, and this would require a powerful German fleet and—a point not to be forgotten—strong naval bases strategically placed. Some writers have suggested, with an almost incredible indifference to the close relationship between economics and politics, that the first world war did not break out for economic reasons and as the result of an increasingly bitter trade war between Germany and Great Britain, but because the Germans insisted on building up a powerful fleet which represented a threat to British security.

But the German navy was not an end in itself; it did not come into being as the result of a militaristic or dynastic whim, merely from a desire to have a big fleet because Great Britain had one; it was built for a very cogent economic reason. It was to facilitate the expansion of German capitalism along imperialist lines and to give Germany the advantages which were already enjoyed by the other imperialist powers. Now, a strong fleet is nothing without strong strategic bases, and German imperialist circles were well aware, long before the first world war, that these would be unobtainable without an armed clash with Great Britain. When the war finally did break out, the direction of Germany's annexationist drive was quite in accordance with these plans. German control of the coast of Flanders and the strengthening of the German fleet were to be the guarantees that an overseas colonial block under German control could be successfully defended against any other imperialism, and against British imperialism in particular.

The second possibility for the creation of a German empire, or a corresponding sphere of influence, was via the overland route across Austria-Hungary and the Balkan States to Turkey; the famous Berlin–Baghdad line, which was to ensure the safety of communications between Germany and the area in which a very considerable part of her foreign capital exports were invested. Before the first world war a preliminary condition for the success of this project was an understanding between Austria-Hungary and the Balkan Slavs. Later, during the first world war, the famous line actually came into existence temporarily, but for its permanent existence it presupposed a successful issue of the war for Germany.

Germany's foreign policy before the first world war was marked by persistent attempts to drive first in one direction and then in the other as opportunity afforded. But every such drive aroused the liveliest apprehensions in Great Britain, who felt that her own world position was being threatened. It was already bad enough for British capitalism that Germany was winning markets for her industries outside the British Empire at Britain's expense.

If, in addition, Germany succeeded in giving her great industrial and economic progress an appropriate foreign-political expression; if she succeeded in building up a powerful empire and at the same time a fleet strong enough to check Britain's attempts to thwart her growth, then clearly Britain's own world position would be gravely threatened.

But the threat would have been very little, if at all, less serious if German capitalism had succeeded in creating an undisputed field of expansion in Europe itself, even if this sphere were given some harmless title and not called an empire. Germany was already strong, but then she would be absolutely dominant in Europe.

Great Britain had always pursued the famous "Balance of Power" policy, whose aim was to prevent the dominance of any single country in Europe. But the hard fact was that Germany was already much stronger than France, and, together with Austria-Hungary, which was economically and politically dependent on Germany, she was stronger than any possible European coalition against her. There was a very real danger that if Germany were allowed to continue her imperialist expansion in Eastern and South-Eastern Europe, the block of which she was the leader would become so very much stronger than any other possible European coalition that further resistance would become hopeless.

Thus Great Britain felt herself just as much threatened by Germany's imperialist expansion within Europe, and for this reason she supported the Balkan Slavs and the Russians in their opposition to Germany and Austria-Hungary. The result was that every further attempt on the part of Germany to expand her sphere of influence even in Europe met with increasingly strong resistance.

IMPERIAL POSSESSIONS AT VARIANCE WITH CHANGED RELATIONS OF ECONOMIC STRENGTH

The distribution of imperial possessions as it existed before the first world war was no longer in accordance with the changed economic strengths of the various imperialist countries. When Great Britain was still the undisputed industrial leader of the world, the relationship had been more or less appropriate. But that meant going back to the seventies of the nineteenth century. In the first years of the twentieth century up to the first world war the relationship between imperial possessions and economic strength was completely lop-sided.

Great Britain had lost her industrial predominance, even in Europe, to Germany, but this change in the relation of economic and industrial strength had found no reflection in the division of imperial possessions. Thus there was a dangerous hiatus between the new economic strengths of the big powers and the extent of their respective imperialist empires and spheres of influence. And this lack of proportion became worse rather than better, because whilst the world was already more or less completely divided up between the various colonial powers, Germany's industrial development proceeded at a greater rate than that of her rivals, with the result that the dangerous gap widened.

In this situation the two most powerful industrial countries in Europe—Great Britain and Germany—became the leaders of two hostile blocks, and the foreign-political tension increased. The continuation of German imperialist expansion increased the danger of war, particularly as Germany naturally did her utmost to change the existing foreign-political situation and to bring it into closer relation with economic strength on the one hand and the possibilities of imperialist expansion on the other.

To sum up, the greater speed of German industrial development as compared with the older European industrial countries, which already owned big imperial possessions, gave rise to those factors which finally led to the outbreak of the first world war.

Any attempt to present particular actions on the part of any particular power in any particular period as being responsible for the outbreak of war means overlooking the decisive factors which led to the war, or, at least, attaching insufficient importance to them, or deliberately glossing over them, but it is often done because the apologists of the capitalist system are unwilling to admit that capitalism itself in its phase of imperialist expansion inevitably led to war.

The decisive factor was the discrepancy between the speeds of capitalist development in the two leading European great powers, Great Britain and Germany, and the discrepancy between their possibilities of imperialist expansion. This *necessarily* led to a growing aggravation of the antagonisms between the two great powers and, finally, to war.

However, Great Britain and Germany were not alone in the world, were not even alone in Europe. The first world war was therefore not exclusively a clash between these two countries, in which capitalism had become almost the only system of production. We must not forget that at this time hardly a third of the total population of the world lived in countries which were directly dominated by capitalism, that the leading capitalist countries needed allies in war, and that side by side with the main imperialist antagonism there were a series of other enmities and antagonisms.

Some writers have contended that the first world war was not really an imperialist war at all, and have pointed out, for example, that Serbia fought the war as a struggle for national independence against the oppression of Austria-Hungary, and that Russia entered the war to provide a vent for internal social tension and, in particular, to ward off the threatening agrarian revolution.

These points are not without foundation; but, then, the fact that other influences were at work to bring about the war, apart from purely imperialist reasons, was due to the circumstance that capitalism was not the dominant mode of production in the world and certainly not the only mode of production. In the two systems of alliances there were countries on each side in which capitalism was not yet the dominant mode of production, and they played a very important role. On the one side there was Austria-Hungary, and on the other there was Tsarist Russia. Thus the causes of the war were not exclusively capitalist and imperialist; some of them were of a nature to interest particularly those countries which were not exclusively capitalist and which were, in part at least, pre-capitalist feudal States.

If anyone says that the first world war was not *purely* an imperialist war, then that is quite true—as true as the fact that the world at that time did not consist only of capitalist imperialist States.

However, capitalism was already the dominant mode of production in the chief countries engaged in the conflict; the imperialist drive was so important for capitalism in this period that within the general framework of the factors which led to the war the most important factor was the expansionist drive of German imperialism, backed up by Austria-Hungary, and the resistance offered by the Entente to the aggressive expansionist drive of the new German imperialism to secure a redistribution of the world.

Thus in order to understand fully the causes which led to the first world war we must, above all, acquaint ourselves with the intensity of the factors which caused imperialist expansion.

In this period the European capitalist States made no attempt to resolve the contradictions immanent in the capitalist system by a radical inner transformation of that system, but by a tremendous expansion, and, within the framework of that expansion, an imperialist drive beyond the frontiers.

Thus imperialism played a decisive role in the whole economic and social development of capitalism; it was equally important for its effects on the crises as for its effects on the general social stratification.

The imperialist drive was therefore of great intensity, with the result that its consequences, which finally led to the first world war, were of corresponding vigour and intensity.

With the first world war a new epoch opened up in the history not only of Europe but of all mankind.

The previous century—the century of tremendous capitalist expansion from the Napoleonic wars, from Waterloo to Sarajevo—knew no wars which exercised any decisive influence on capitalist development. Most of the wars which took place in this hundred years were fought away from the capitalist centres. The Franco-Prussian war was an exception in this respect, but it did not last long, and it represented only a temporary interruption in the main line of capitalist progress.

With the first world war decisive changes in the nature of war made themselves felt; so much so that this war represented a real turning point in the development of capitalism itself.

Thus beginning with the first world war the analysis of the nature of war, with all its direct and indirect repercussions, with all its devastation and upheavals, becomes an integral part of the general analysis of capitalism and its social and political system.

THE EPOCH OF THE FIRST WORLD WAR

ON THE EVE OF THE FIRST WORLD WAR

THE RAPID PROGRESS of capitalism in Germany which made her
into the strongest industrial country in the Old World, and the constant attempts of German imperialism to build itself up a position in
the world in accordance with its economic and industrial strength,
completely upset the old balance of power in Europe.

For a long historical period the continental European powers had
been more or less equal in strength, which meant that the balance of
power was in England's hands; a comparatively moderate exercise
of her strength was sufficient to tip the balance in one direction or the
other, according to her interests. But the rise of capitalist imperialist
Germany upset this most convenient state of affairs for England.
Germany was now stronger than England and stronger than France,
and as her capitalist industrialist development proceeded, the gap
grew larger and larger and the old balance of power more and more
illusory. At this period the Central Powers under German leadership
were far stronger than any possible continental coalition against
them, as was clearly proved when the first world war did break
out.

Thus England found herself threatened by Germany's imperialist
expansion not only in Europe but also as a world imperialist power.
Great Britain's answer to the threat to her world position was to
strengthen her fleet; her answer to the threat to her position in
Europe was the creation of the Entente Cordiale—an alliance subsequently to be joined by Tsarist Russia—with a view to creating a
block which should be at least as strong militarily as the Central
Powers.

THE ENTENTE CORDIALE

Great Britain found France a very willing ally. France had been
defeated in the Franco-Prussian War at a time when the population
of Germany was only between four and five millions more than that of
France, and when Germany was only at the beginning of her subsequent enormous industrial development. With her defeat in the war
of 1870–1871 France lost her leading position in Europe.

France certainly succeeded in building herself up a big colonial
empire in the period after the Franco-Prussian War, but her industrial development had become relatively slow, so that even with the
resources of her empire she was still far from being a match for Germany. From decade to decade the industrial and military gap
between the two powers grew wider and wider in Germany's favour.

137

There were strong groups in the French Republic which were hotly in favour of a war of revenge to wipe out the defeat of 1870–1871. Marx's warning * was seen to be well founded: when Germany continued to wage the war as a war of conquest after the French collapse, and annexed Alsace-Lorraine, a great abyss opened up between the two nations and brought grist to the mill of both the French and German militarists and reactionaries.

Even apart from the political groups who hankered after a war of revenge, the solid majority of the French bourgeoisie was in favour of the alliance with Great Britain. The reason for this was clear enough. France had lost the leadership in Europe, but she was still a great power. But if Germany succeeded in creating a big sphere of influence for herself in Eastern and South-Eastern Europe, and the German block thus became still more powerful, then France saw herself threatened with degradation to the rank of a second-class power. In addition, Germany continued to strengthen her army to bring her purely military strength more into accordance with her growing population.

The French knew that their army was the only serious opponent of the German army on the continent, and so when the German imperialist drive continued and threatened France's colonial empire in North Africa, thereby still further aggravating foreign-political antagonisms, the French answered in two ways.

1. The three-year period of military service was introduced in peace-time in order to cancel out to some extent the weakness of France's man-power potential and to create an army which would be numerically almost as strong as the German army, at least in the first stages of a possible conflict.

2. An alliance was concluded with Tsarist Russia, whose population was more than twice as big as that of Germany, and at the same time a great deal of French capital—about a quarter of France's total foreign investments—was invested in Russia. Much of it was not used for strictly commercial purposes, but to finance the construction of strategic railways to facilitate a Russian mobilization and thereby increase Russia's military power.

RUSSIA'S FOREIGN POLICY AND INTERNAL DIFFICULTIES

The object of Great Britain and of France was the defence of empire, the defence of their positions in Europe and in the world. In neither country were inner social stresses sufficiently strong to

---

* "If the German working class allows the present war to lose its strictly defensive character and to degenerate into a war against the French people, then either victory or defeat will be ominous. All the misfortunes which Germany suffered after the so-called Wars of Liberation will return again with increased violence." Karl Marx in his First Address to the General Council on the Franco-Prussian War. It was written whilst the war was still in progress and the French Second Empire was collapsing under the first German victories.[1]

strengthen the hand of the war party or to represent a real problem. The situation in Tsarist Russia was very different.

In Asia Japanese imperialism found its drive into the Asiatic continent hampered by the opposition of Tsarist Russia. A decade before the outbreak of the first world war Japan had defeated Russia in the war of 1904–1905 because the brutal regime of feudal oppression exercised by a corrupt ruling class in Russia over the masses of the people made it impossible to deploy Russia's real strength.

The Russian defeat had led to revolutionary risings in 1905, to organized revolutionary movements on the part of the workers in the towns and to agrarian revolts of the peasant masses in the rural areas. The two movements were not co-ordinated, and Tsarism succeeded in suppressing first one and then the other, but its victory did nothing to remove the causes which had given birth to them, and social antagonisms smouldered on under the surface ready to burst into flames again at the first favourable opportunity.

In this situation the aggravation of foreign-political tension offered a welcome outlet. Russian Tsarism found an opportunity of turning the attention of the masses of the people away from the struggle to overthrow feudalism. In this it was greatly assisted by Russian nationalism and Pan-Slavism, because in its attempts to drive through the heart of Europe and through the Balkans to open up the Berlin–Baghdad line, German imperialism encountered vigorous opposition from the South Slavs—Serbs, as they were then known, and Yugoslavs as they later became—who resisted Austro-Hungarian expansion and looked to the great "Slav brother", Tsarist Russia, for support.

The Growth of Imperialist Antagonism

Such was the situation in Europe on the eve of the first world war. The tension did not increase steadily; sometimes there were even signs of a *détente* and the situation seemed to ease. However, considered as a whole, it was a period of increasing menace. It therefore does not help us very much to understand what actually happened when some writers point out that the conflict between Austria-Hungary on the one hand and Servia on the other, which provided the immediate occasion for the outbreak of the first world war, could have been resolved. Of course that particular conflict could have been resolved, just as each individual conflict could have been resolved. But the point is that each individual conflict was only one aspect of a whole complex of antagonisms, and the main antagonism was the one between the big imperialist powers, and that had its roots in the fact that the world had already been carved up between the big powers and that the resultant distribution was not in even approximate accordance with the real relation of forces. Thus the whole period was fraught with terrible danger; at the time the

139

situation was compared to a powder-barrel with trains in all directions. Each match that flared up might separately have been extinguished without necessarily leading to the final explosion, but that did nothing to alter the fact that the incendiary material was heaped up everywhere, and would remain so as long as the fundamental capitalist imperialist antagonism continued to exist.

THE INCREASE OF MILITARY EXPENDITURE

In the last years before the conflict finally came to a head the growth of foreign-political tension was reflected in what was, for the circumstances of that time, a very considerable increase in military expenditure on all sides. Germany strengthened her army and her fleet. Great Britain replied by strengthening her fleet. France replied by introducing the three-year period of military service, and Russia replied by speeding up her preparations for mobilization. All this naturally resulted in a great increase of armament and quasi-armament expenditure.

Now, this steady increase in military expenditure in Europe took place in a period of economic prosperity, and in this respect the situation was very different from what it was to be in the period which led up to the second world war. The chronic mass unemployment which was characteristic of the years after 1929 was absent then. The productive organisms of the day were not working at only two-thirds or perhaps three-quarters of their capacity, but they were all busy producing peace-time goods, whilst unemployment was at a very low level, with the one exception of Great Britain, but even there it was nothing like what it was to become in the years after 1921.

In other words, in the period before the first world war military expenditure was a clear and direct burden on the economic organism. Every additional million spent on military preparedness did not help, as it did later, to revive an economic system suffering from depression. On the contrary, every million expended in this way hampered the production of goods for peace-time use.

Every new recruit to the army or navy, and every man who had to serve a year longer than usual in the army, reduced the number of productive workers.

MILITARY EXPENDITURE NOT PARTICULARLY BURDENSOME

However, despite all this, the burden of military expenditure was not very great by comparison with the increase in national incomes. Nevertheless the socialists carried on their struggle against imperialism and against the threatening danger of war primarily as a struggle against the growing military expenditure, which, according to them, imposed an intolerable burden on the peoples. For instance, in his famous preface to "The Civil War in France" which was published shortly before his death in 1895 Engels writes:

"It (the great revolution in the technique of modern warfare) forced up the taxes to impossible heights owing to the costs of military expenditure, which increased in geometrical progression, and thus drove the poorer classes of the people into the arms of socialism."

That was a gross exaggeration, and in consequence socialist propaganda based on it met with little success. The masses of the people did not feel that the burden of military expenditure was particularly onerous, and any realistic analysis will confirm their feeling. Military expenditure in 1913 was certainly greater than it had been in 1900, and the rate of increase had been quite considerable. However, it was still relatively small by comparison with national incomes as a whole, and even by comparison with the rate of increase of national incomes. For instance, if we compare military expenditure in Great Britain and in Germany in this period with the figures for national income in both countries, we find—particularly in comparison with the period preceding the second world war—that the former represented only a very small percentage of the latter.

Hohenzollern Germany was regarded as definitely militaristic, and in the years which immediately preceded the first world war she greatly increased her military budget, which reached its culminating point in peace-time with what was then (1913) the huge sum of 100 million pounds, inclusive of naval expenditure. But even then it represented only rather less than 4 per cent of the total national income, which was then no less than 2,500 million pounds.

In other words, although military expenditure increased considerably, and although there may have been individual years in which it increased as much as, if not more than, the increase in production, years in which it was perhaps big enough to prevent a rise in standards of living, or even to lower them a little, that was not typical of the period as a whole, and the truth is that British, French and German workers enjoyed higher living standards in the period immediately preceding the outbreak of the first world war than they had enjoyed in the decades which went before—despite the growth in military expenditure. The increased sums spent on armaments accounted for only a fraction of the increased productivity of labour, which reflected itself in a rise in general living standards. In those days there was no such thing anywhere as what we now know as a war economy existing in times of peace, and thus socialist propaganda against the burden of military expenditure was singularly ineffective.

With this we have arrived at a decisive point in our investigations, at a fundamental factor in the world situation as a whole. It is a point which was hardly recognized at the time, and one whose importance is not even now fully appreciated.

141

The period of capitalist imperialist development which culminated in the outbreak of the first world war was not characterized
—as many socialists, including Lenin and Rosa Luxemburg, thought
—by a simultaneous increase of both social and foreign-political tension. At the same time the situation was not so rosy as it was painted
not only by the apologists of capitalism but also by certain right-
wing socialist leaders—for instance, Eduard Bernstein in Germany,
who believed that capitalism had reached "maturity" and had, by its
own efforts, succeeded in reducing its inner social tensions, and that
only the power lust of certain feudal militarist and armament cliques
threatened to lead to war.

The truth was that the period immediately before the first world
war was marked by a lessening of social tension and by a rise in
living standards for all sections of the population in the highly-
developed imperialist States, though this had been brought about by
capitalist and imperialist expansion all over the world, and this expansion necessarily aggravated foreign-political antagonisms and
finally led to war.

It was characteristic of this pre-war period that there was no
simultaneous intensification of social tension and of foreign-political
tension. And the fact that all classes—the ruling capitalist class and
the working class—were so wrong in their estimate of the situation
was due to their failure to recognize the functional relation between
imperialist expansion on the one hand and the temporary lessening of
inner social tension on the other, or to appreciate its full significance
in the general relation of social forces.

No Fear of Social Revolution

In this stage of capitalist development, despite the process of industrial concentration, the middle strata succeeded on the whole in
maintaining their position, whilst in part they even consolidated and
extended it; the living standards of millions of workers improved or,
in the worst case, as in Great Britain, they maintained themselves
after a long period of improvement, with the result that a middle-
class outlook was widespread amongst the workers; and—unlike the
period which led up to the second world war—there was a considerable degree of social stability in all the leading European industrial
countries.

In consequence—and here once again it is in direct contrast to the
situation before the second world war—the fear of social upheavals,
of socialist revolutions, played no very important role in the development of those systems of alliances under which the first world war was
subsequently fought.

When Hohenzollern Germany made her military and foreign-political preparations for the first world war she did so unhampered by any fear of social revolution at home, and she was encouraged in this by the fact that in the period which led up to the war the great majority of Germany's workers and their social-democratic leaders had on the whole turned away from the revolutionary wing of the socialist movement and tended to support the Right wing, which favoured the improvement of the situation of the working class by reforms within the framework of capitalist society.

In Great Britain and France the question of a social revolution at home did not even exist. The only interest of the leaders of those two countries was to build up a block which would be stronger than that of their enemies, the Central Powers. They did not even consider the possibility that if they did succeed in defeating Germany social-revolutionary movements might arise in the defeated country and spread all over Europe. The situation between the two world wars was very different, and this was particularly true of France. At that time the French Right was horrified at the possibility of social revolution as the result of a new war, and that was one of the most important factors which contributed to its defeatist policy both before and during the second world war.

Fixed Alliances before the First World War

Before the outbreak of the first world war the constellation was already reasonably clear. The rapid progress of German industrial development and the increasing aggressiveness of Germany's imperialist drive had upset the balance of power and drawn a clear dividing line between the older industrial countries, which had already more or less carved up the world between them, and Germany and her allies, whose share in the colonial spoils was infinitesimal. Thus, once again, in sharp contrast to the period which led up to the second world war, there were settled alliances in existence long before the outbreak of the war.

It is true that the attitude of one or two of the less important powers—for instance, Italy, Roumania and Turkey—was still ambiguous, but this was of no great consequence in view of the existence of the Entente Cordiale and the Franco-Russian alliance on the one hand and the alliance between Germany and Austria-Hungary on the other.

Despite all these clear preparations, when war did come it came as a surprise, even as a shock, to the masses of the peoples of Europe. But there was no surprise to anyone in the general line-up of the belligerent powers.

The ruling classes in the leading industrial countries of Europe entered the first world war without any fear of a socialist revolution as the upshot, and it is perfectly true that there was no such revolution

143

either in defeated Germany or in the victorious Entente countries. To that extent, therefore, their confidence was well founded.

However, they also entered the war without the least idea of what it meant, without suspecting that it represented the conclusion of a long period of vigorous capitalist expansion, without realizing that the war opened up a new period of social transformation, a process which it also greatly accelerated.

They failed to appreciate these things because, as we have already seen, they refused to recognize the functional relation between capitalist expansion and imperialism on the one hand and rising living standards and the amelioration of crisis severity on the other, and they were therefore unable to recognize the *historical conditions* which were responsible for the temporary decline of social tension.

THE RULING CLASSES ENTERED THE FIRST WORLD WAR IN TERMS OF PREVIOUS CONFLICTS

Further, they under-estimated the effects of the war itself. When they entered the first world war they did not realize what they were beginning; they had no idea of the forces they were unleashing—a point which we shall deal with in greater detail later in our observations on the changing nature of war.

When the first world war broke out, almost a century had passed since the end of the Napoleonic Wars. Those wars had involved the whole of Europe, but it had been a Europe in which there were no big industries. In the hundred years succeeding those wars there had been many others, but with one exception—the Franco-Prussian War of 1870–1871—they had all been fought out far away from the capitalist metropolitan centres.

This one exception—the Franco-Prussian War—differed in many respects from the first world war.

1. It was fought between two European powers only.

2. It was a war which did not last very long (after about a year its outcome was already clear).

3. In comparison with the first world war only a small percentage of the able-bodied population of the belligerent countries was involved, and economic life was not profoundly affected, mainly because both in France and Germany the agricultural population still outnumbered the urban population. The German General Staff had made careful military preparations for the war, but neither side had made any economic preparations, and neither side bothered its head much about the possible economic consequences of the war.

It was not necessary that they should. The war was decisive for the relation of forces in continental Europe and it established Germany's hegemony, but economically considered it was nothing but a temporary interruption of a period of gigantic capitalist expansion which involved the whole of Europe.

Hohenzollern Germany entered the first world war with the idea that it would proceed more or less along the lines of the Franco-Prussian War of 1870–1871, except, of course, that, in view of the Franco-Russian alliance, it knew that this time it would be a war on two fronts; but for this eventuality it had drawn up the famous Schlieffen Plan. Germany's leaders still believed that a quick decision could be obtained. When Wilhelm II announced, "We shall all be home again for Christmas", he really believed it, and so did his generals.

Generals usually know very little about the waging of coming wars, and this is true in particular of a military caste which was victorious in the previous war. Germany had been victorious in the Franco-Prussian War, and now her military leaders made all their preparations with a repetition of that war in mind.

Naturally, the general advance of industrial technique had also produced improvements in weapons of war, but that was about the full extent of Germany's preparations for a modern war. The outlook of her leaders had remained exclusively military, and they had not the faintest idea that the tremendous changes which had come about in European society in the meantime as a result of large-scale industrial development had fundamentally changed the nature of war.

They did not realize that war would now be largely a war of factories and industries; they did not realize that in the current phase of capitalism a war would necessarily be a "total" war; they did not realize that, unlike the Napoleonic Wars and the Franco-Prussian War, the new war would leave no sector of economic life and no sector of the population undisturbed.

Germany's military budget had been greatly increased, but the expenditure was used exclusively for military purposes, to increase the man-power and improve the equipment of the army and navy, and so on. There was no question of any general increase in armaments production. As for economic preparations, there were none at all. They had not even made any attempt to analyse their economic situation and recognize their weaknesses.

One of the reasons for this lack of economic preparation for war was that the leaders of all countries were convinced that the war could not last for any length of time.

Secretary of State Helfferich,[2] a leading German statesman at the beginning of the war, wrote:

"I do not think there is anyone in Germany who could honestly say that from the beginning he reckoned with such a long war and with such a painful isolation of Germany from all her sources of foreign supplies, an isolation which became more and more complete as the war proceeded. The opinion that modern warfare could not last long prevailed in both military and economic circles. This view was supported by the terrible destructive powers of modern weapons, which seemed to hold out a hope of quick decisions. And then there was the vast withdrawal of labour power from industry on the basis of general conscription, whose effects on the economic system have been compared with those of a general strike. And the costs of the conflict, which far exceeded the sums with which financiers and economists had been accustomed to reckon. And finally there was the idea that human reason would not allow the peoples of Europe to fight to the end of their physical and moral resources, would not allow the devastation of their economic and cultural riches, would not allow them to indulge in mutual destruction."

No Economic General Staff or Economic Preparations

The first world war was prepared militarily, but not economically. No attempt had been made to form an economic general staff, though, as the "Reichsarchiv" wrote in its history of the war: [3]

"Suggestions had been made for the creation of an economic general staff on more than one occasion, but Secretary of State Delbrück was not in favour of the idea. On December 28th, 1912, he wrote to the Reich's Chancellor informing him that he was unable to see any practical use in the proposal that an economic general staff should be set up, but this did not prevent him from writing later [4] that it was difficult to understand why the preparations for economic mobilization had been carried on with such dilatoriness before 1912. The Reich's Chancellor, Bethmann-Hollweg,[5] himself describes it as a indisputable omission that Germany did not store up great quantities of grain, fodder and raw materials for the event of war."

This is a very important point.

That Germany failed to set up an economic general staff, and that she failed to make preparations for an industrial mobilization to match her military mobilization, can be explained by the fact that such measures were outside the general run of ideas on the subject of war at the time. The experiences of "total" warfare were necessary to impress on people that preparations for war must extend far beyond those of a purely military nature.

At the same time every responsible person in Germany knew that the country no longer produced all the foodstuffs it needed and that, apart from foodstuffs, it had to import numerous industrial raw materials. It was also quite clear to everyone that the British fleet alone was stronger than the German, and that the combined Franco-British fleet was stronger still. People also knew perfectly well that a very large quantity of the foodstuffs and raw materials Germany imported came from overseas sources,

It should therefore have been fairly obvious that in the event of a war with Great Britain Germany's overseas supplies of foodstuffs and raw materials would be endangered, and that therefore one of the important preparations for such a war must be to reduce Germany's vulnerability in this respect as much as possible.

But in reality no such conclusions were drawn and nothing at all was done in the matter. Clemens von Delbrück, who was Germany's Secretary of State for the Interior when the war broke out, describes in his book [6] how in the last week of July 1914 he tried to buy certain stores of grain lying in Rotterdam on behalf of the Reich. He approached the Secretary of the Treasury with a request for a credit of five million marks for the purpose, and the reply he received was:

> "I am not in a position to comply with your wishes. There is going to be no war, and if I grant you a credit of five million marks to buy the grain we shall have to sell it later at a loss to the Treasury. Apart from that it would increase the already very great difficulties I am experiencing in drawing up the 1915 budget."

Thus for Germany the war was such an exclusively military affair that in the last week of peace a highly-placed minister could lightly reject a suggestion from a responsible quarter for the improvement of Germany's food supplies.

In the same way Germany entered the war without having made the slightest attempt to safeguard and husband her raw-materials supplies. It was only after hostilities had already begun that discussions took place between Walter Rathenau and Germany's generals (August 8th and 9th, 1914) with a view to rationing the use of Germany's raw-material resources.

Shortly before the outbreak of war leading officials of the Reich rejected a proposal for the establishment of a Central Raw-Materials Board, on the ground that the War Ministry had agreements with civilian contractors for the supply of all the weapons and munitions it needed and that the contracts specified penalties for non-observance.

However, in all fairness it should be pointed out that German military circles were not quite so short-sighted, and they replied: "Unfortunately we can't shoot with contracts, and now preparations must be made to ensure that we can shoot."

In dealing with the lack of economic preparations for the first world war we have confined our remarks to Germany, because Germany was in the weakest position in this respect, and one might therefore reasonably have expected her ruling classes to grasp the situation better than the others and to take the necessary steps.

The situation in the Entente countries was very much the same, and

147

there is little to add to the general picture. They, too, had restricted their preparations exclusively to those of a military nature, whilst Great Britain had lagged far behind even in this, and had done little more than strengthen her fleet; it was only during the war that she set about creating an army as well. Measures for industrial mobilization were not even discussed.

Thus it is true of both sides that they went into the war without any real idea of what sort of war it was going to be; neither side had the faintest idea that the war would bring about any decisive changes. In reality they had loosed a war which shook their social system to the core, and that was true of both victors and vanquished.

On the other hand the fact that they were ignorant of what they had let themselves in for, and had therefore made no adequate preparations, greatly contributed to their relative social stability when they entered the war.

We have already seen that despite the rapid growth in military expenditure in the last few years before the outbreak of war it was still small in relation to the total national incomes of the big industrial countries. This relative insignificance of military expenditure was due to the fact that war preparations were exclusively of a military nature; that there was no economic general staff preparing for war side by side with the military general staff; and that even in the period immediately preceding the outbreak of the war there was no large-scale armaments or war economy already in existence.

If the ruling classes had had a more or less accurate idea of the real character of the first world war, and if they had then prepared for such a war—and not for the one they imagined—they would have had to build up a large-scale war economy before the outbreak of war, and this would in all probability have resulted in an aggravation of social antagonisms and a very much stronger opposition to the war.

It is one of the many ironies of world history that the lack of adequate preparation for the first world war on both sides owing to the erroneous views generally held concerning its nature, contributed to the social stability of the leading capitalist industrial countries. Incidentally, during the course of the war this social stability was seen to be very much stronger than socialists had believed.

Socialists Underestimated Capitalist Strength

It was not the first time in history that in a period of decline and at the beginning of a period of transformation the ruling classes had shown themselves unable to appreciate their own true position and to realize that their decline had begun.

The first world war opened up the period of capitalist decline, and played an important role in it, but although it introduced this period of decline, it did not end it. The ruling classes in all the capitalist countries of Europe entered the war fully conscious of their foreign-political differences, but without appreciating that the settlement of these differences by force in a total war would shake the capitalist system to its very foundations. They entered the war as subjects of the process; they ended it as objects. Once the process had begun they were no longer in a position to control it.

However, the capitalist system in Europe had been greatly strengthened precisely by the long period of tremendous expansion which preceded the first world war, and its social stability was there-fore very considerable. The result was that, although it received a series of very hard blows during the course of the war, it succeeded in surviving it, against all the hopes, expectations and considered beliefs of the socialist leaders.

A characteristic feature of the first world war was thus that both the ruling classes and the ruled (the working class in particular) mis-judged the situation. The war itself and the upshot of the war were not in accordance with their expectations. In fact, as far as the socialist movement was concerned, the first world war opened up a very critical period in which the international organizations of the working class collapsed; it was a period of crisis for the socialist working-class movement and for the socialist idea itself. The first world war mercilessly exposed the inadequacy of the socialist analysis. It showed that it had not been in accordance with the past and demonstrated its bankruptcy in face of the present. It also showed clearly the necessity for a new general analysis capable both of adequately interpreting the past and of indicating action for the future.

To sum up, we have seen that the decisive characteristic of approximately half a century prior to the first world war was the tre-mendous development of capitalism, and within its framework the advance of imperialism over the world; and we have seen that this led to a decline of social antagonisms which would otherwise have in-creasingly threatened the existence of the capitalist system.

The general situation prior to the first world war was character-ized by the inevitable aggravation of foreign-political antagonisms as a result of imperialist expansion, but also by a decline of social ten-sion at home, with the result that the social stability of the highly-developed capitalist countries in particular increased.

There was no party, and not even a group within a party, in the European working-class movement at the time which clearly under-stood these essential relations.

Of course, "the facts" as such were not overlooked. For instance, the "Revisionists"—so called because they set out to revise the Marxist theory in accordance with these "facts"—wrote volumes analysing the obvious strengthening of social stability under capitalism. But although they saw the "facts", they were unable to offer any satisfactory explanation of just why existing reality had turned out to be so different from Marx's prophecies. The Revisionists, and most other people, neglected the functional relationship between the tremendous expansion of capitalism and, within its framework, the advance of imperialism over the world, together with its repercussions on the whole economic system of the leading industrial countries, and therefore they were unable to put forward an analysis which squared with all the facts. The Revisionists contented themselves with superficial explanations which were, when they were not quite wrong, totally inadequate. They declared, for example, that the transition of capitalism from free competition to cartels, trusts and monopolies had diminished the violence of economic crises because these monopolies, etc., were in a position to "regulate" the market, and they explained the improved living standards of the working class by the increased strength of the trade unions.

Now, if what this Right wing of the working class believed was true—that is to say, if steady social progress was to be expected within the framework of the capitalist mode of production—and if political democracy could gradually be developed into social democracy as well, then obviously imperialism, increasing foreign-political antagonisms and the growing burden of military expenditure, were all really anachronisms to be explained solely by the influence of the last remnants of feudal and reactionary elements. Believing this, these socialists opposed the increase of military expenditure and fought against certain imperialist actions, but they did not realize that, in the particular phase of capitalism in which they lived, capitalist expansion beyond the frontiers, imperialism, growing military expenditure and increasing foreign-political tension were an inseparable whole.

Now, the Left wing of the working-class movement, whose leaders did recognize the functional relation between capitalism and imperialism, and the consequent danger of war, believed, with Rosa Luxemburg, that social antagonisms were intensifying in the imperialist phase of capitalism, or, with Lenin (a point we shall discuss in greater detail later on), that imperialism improved the living standards of only a minority of the working class: the so-called aristocracy of labour. They refused to see that the repercussions of this outward expansion of capitalism had raised living standards for the whole of the working class in the highly-developed industrial countries, and had done so not for a short time only, but for years, even whole generations, in succession. The result of this blindness was that the Left wing of the working-class movement believed that if a world war did break out it would end comparatively swiftly in the overthrow of capitalism.

These ideas were reflected in two important historical documents:

150

the one, written at the beginning of the nineties, by Friedrich Engels, and the other the famous Basle resolution of the Second International.

Engels on the Coming War

We propose to quote at length from the article written by Engels because, with its truths and its errors, it formed the basis for the attitude of the Left wing of the European working-class movement to the world situation before the first world war.

First of all let us quote Engels on German Social Democracy's chances of carrying out its programme in times of peace, because this will help us to see his prophecies concerning the coming war in their right perspective. After having given figures concerning the increasing parliamentary poll of German Social Democracy in the eighties, he writes:

> "To-day one out of every five soldiers is a socialist; in a few years from now one soldier in every three will be a socialist, and by 1900 approximately the army, which formerly represented the Prussian element in the country, will have a majority of socialists. That is coming about as inevitably as the decrees of fate. The Berlin government sees it coming just as well as we do, but it can do nothing to stop it. The army is slipping out of its hands."

And his conclusion is:

> "In short, peace will see the victory of the German Social-Democratic Party in about ten years from now." [7]

But will peace be maintained that long? Engels asks, and he answers:

> "The foregoing applies only provided that Germany is allowed to pursue her economic and political development in peace. The outbreak of war would alter everything. And war can break out from one day to the next. Everyone knows what 'war' means to-day: France and Russia on one side, and Germany and Austria, and perhaps Italy, on the other."

He then discusses the consequences of such a war:

> "If war comes nevertheless then at least one thing is certain: this war, which would lock between fifteen and twenty million armed men in murderous combat and devastate Europe as it has never been devastated before, would either bring about the immediate victory of socialism or it would upset the old order of things from top to bottom and leave behind such a heap of ruins that the old capitalist society would be more impossible than ever, and the social revolution, though postponed for ten or fifteen years, would

151

then inevitably be victorious after an even more rapid and thorough development." [8]

More than half a century has now passed since Engels wrote those words, and it was almost a quarter of a century afterwards that the first world war actually did break out.

Engels realized much more clearly than all the generals and their governments, although they played the leading role in the world drama, that such a war would be a real turning-point in world history. He also saw clearly that such a war would be what it subsequently became the fashion to call a "total war". He realized, too, that any comparison with the Franco-Prussian War of 1870–1871 was totally misleading. He saw clearly that such a war would open up a new epoch in the history of the world. He also foresaw the constellation of alliances in which the war would be fought. He prophesied the tremendous devastation the war would cause. And he realized that the alliance of the French Republic with Tsarist Russia against Germany would cause the German working class to fight for Germany, because naturally they would quite properly regard even semi-absolutist Hohenzollern Germany as a much more progressive State than Tsarist Russia.

"In view of the fact that a Russian victory over Germany would mean the crushing of German socialism what would be the duty of German socialists when faced with such a danger? Should they remain passive and allow the threat to take its course? Should they abandon the position for which they had accepted responsibility in the eyes of the whole world proletariat?

"Not at all. In the interests of the European revolution they are under an obligation to defend the positions they have won, and not to capitulate either to the enemy at home or to the enemy abroad. And they can only do this if they fight against Russia to the last, and against all Russia's allies whoever they may be. If the French Republic places itself in the service of His Majesty the Tsar, absolute monarch of all the Russians, then the German socialists would regretfully take up arms against it—regretfully, but decidedly." [9]

Engels' views on the character of the war and on all the military and politico-military questions arising out of it were almost prophetic. The errors in his estimate of the future were based on the erroneous view of capitalist development he had taken over from Marx.

It is true that the social-democratic poll in the German elections continued to grow, but the progress was by no means up to the expectations of Engels. There were two reasons for this. First of all, the German working class, like the working classes in all other big capitalist countries, did not increase its numerical strength at the same speed as before. The point arrived at which, although the absolute figures continued to grow, the relative strength of the working class in the population as a whole remained more or less stationary. In Germany that took place at a point at which the working class did not represent the majority of the population. And secondly, the tendency, which had made itself felt in Great Britain in previous decades, towards an increase in the wages of the working class as a whole now made itself strongly felt in Germany, and continued to do so more and more noticeably from the nineties up to the outbreak of the first world war. This greatly increased the stability of German and world capitalism. Engels' expectation of a socialist victory before the first world war was therefore made illusory, and the same was true of his views of the consequences of that war.

The victory of socialism did not come with the first world war because there was no class in the industrial countries of Europe which fought for it with all its energies; and it did not come ten or fifteen years later. Instead the capitalist system revealed itself to be much stronger than socialists had thought, and although it was badly shaken, it was still strong enough to survive the period between the two world wars.

This wrong estimate of the nearness of capitalist collapse, of the nearness of socialist victory, was held by the Left wing of the European working-class movement right into the years which immediately preceded the first world war. It was believed that as imperialism had resulted in an aggravation of both foreign-political antagonisms and social antagonisms at home, the socialist elements in the working class would be strong enough to take advantage of war, if it came, to bring about the overthrow of capitalism.

The Basle Manifesto

The congress of the Second International, which took place in Basle in 1912, adopted a manifesto which laid down the attitude of the socialist parties of Europe to war. It declares:

"Should the outbreak of war threaten, then the working classes and their parliamentary representatives in the countries concerned must do everything possible, supported by the co-ordinating activity of the International Bureau, to prevent its outbreak by whatever means they consider most effective, which will naturally vary according to the intensification of the class struggle and the intensification of the general political situation.

"Should war nevertheless break out, it is their duty to work for its speediest possible conclusion, and to strive with all their energy to take advantage of the political and economic crisis brought about by the war to arouse the people and thus accelerate the abolition of capitalist class rule."

These passages literally reaffirm the principles which had already been adopted at the International Socialist Congress in Stuttgart in 1907.

In the years which lay between the Stuttgart and Basle congresses foreign-political tension in Europe had greatly increased, and the danger of war had become more menacing, and so in its justification of the policy it proposed the Basle Manifesto declared:

"The happenings of recent times have more than ever imposed an obligation on the proletariat to concentrate all its force and energy on its joint systematic actions. On the one hand armament madness has increased the already very high cost of living and thus intensified class antagonisms and caused invincible indignation amongst the working class. The workers wish to set limits to this system of disturbance and waste. On the other hand, the constantly recurring threats of war are becoming more and more provocative. . . .

"By jointly entering the struggle against imperialism, whereby each section of the International opposed its own government with the resistance of the proletariat and mobilized public opinion at home against all war-mongering, a grand co-operation of the workers of all countries was obtained which has already done much to save the threatened peace of the world. The fear of the ruling classes of a proletarian revolution as the result of a world war has proved to be an important guarantee of peace. . . .

"The Congress declares that the whole Socialist International is united with regard to these principles of foreign policy. It appeals to the workers of all countries to oppose capitalist imperialism with the power of international proletarian solidarity. It warns the ruling classes of all countries against still further intensifying the mass misery caused by the capitalist mode of production by indulging in warlike actions. It categorically demands peace. The governments should not forget that in the present situation of Europe and having regard to the mood of the working class, they cannot unleash war without danger to themselves. Let them remember that the Franco-Prussian War produced the revolutionary outbreak of the Commune, and that the Russo-Japanese War set the revolutionary forces of the peoples of the Russian Empire into movement. Let them remember that the military and naval armaments race has tremendously intensified class conflicts in England and on the continent and brought about huge strikes. It would be lunacy for the governments not to realize that the mere thought of such a monstrous thing as a world war must arouse the indignation and anger of the working class."

As a result of our analysis we have already seen where the Basle Manifesto of the Socialist International went wrong and misjudged the situation in the capitalist metropolitan countries and the attitude of the working class.

First of all, it was not true to say that "the fear of the ruling classes of a proletarian revolution as the result of a world war has proved an important guarantee of peace". The truth was that there was no fear of social revolutionary developments at that period (unlike the period before the second world war), and so it could affect neither foreign politics nor the formation of alliances.

And secondly, it was also not true to say that "the military and naval armaments race has tremendously intensified class conflicts in England and on the continent. . . ." The truth was that as armaments affected only the purely military sphere and there was no war economy in peace-time, the general trend in this period was towards an improvement in working-class living standards, even though here and there the trend had shown signs of coming to an end.

Further, it was not true that the war, when it did come, still further intensified "the mass misery caused by the capitalist mode of production", though it did depress working-class living standards below the relatively high level they had reached in previous generations of steady improvement, which was a very different thing.

In consequence the first world war did not lead to social revolutionary actions on any dangerous scale in the big European industrial countries, and that was true of both the victors and the vanquished.

CHAPTER TWO

THE COURSE OF THE FIRST WORLD WAR

THE FIRST THING to be said about what has come to be known as the first world war is that it was not really a world war at all. It began as a purely European war, and although Japan declared war on the Central Powers, she took no part in any of the decisive military operations. Even when the United States entered the war it still remained essentially a European war in which the United States tipped the scales of conflict in favour of one of the European belligerent groups.

For the German general staff the chief military enemy was France, because at the beginning of the war France alone had an army which could be compared with the German in leadership, cadres and equipment.

The Russian army was big in numbers, but it was very backward in relation to the demands of modern warfare, and that was the natural consequence of the fact that the agricultural population in Tsarist Russia outnumbered the urban population by more than four to one, that in absolute figures Russian heavy industry did not produce even a quarter of Germany's total, and that the *per capita* industrial production of Tsarist Russia was hardly a tenth of that of Germany.

GERMANY SOUGHT A LIGHTNING DECISION

In this war on two fronts Germany's strategy aimed at obtaining the quickest possible decision on the Western Front by a vast concentration of her resources there, whilst, together with Austria-Hungary, remaining on the defensive in the East.

A decisive victory on the Western Front would have meant that Germany had won the war, because Tsarist Russia could never have hoped to oppose a German invasion effectively once Germany found herself able to transfer her main concentration to the East.

On the other hand, a decisive German victory on the Eastern Front would not have brought about a decision, and the Western Powers might still have been victorious even if Germany had to fight a war on one front only after a victory in the East.

There was another reason why the German general staff decided to seek a quick decision in the West, and that was the military unpreparedness of Great Britain. All the countries of continental Europe which took part in the war—the Germans, the French, the Russians, the Austrians and Hungarians—had had compulsory military service for generations. Thus they had millions of trained men at their immediate disposal and cadres for the rapid training of millions more, so from the outset they were able to put big land armies into the field. There had never been general compulsory military service in Great Britain. Her wars had all been fought far away from her own shores. She had the most powerful fleet in the world, but she had no army of any size. She had never needed a large army for her imperialist conquests because the military strength of the countries she had conquered had been weak in consequence of their industrial backwardness. Comparatively small military forces had been sufficient to conquer them in the first place and hold them in subjection subsequently. And these small forces had been readily obtainable by the voluntary system. And at that time Great Britain's island position made her impregnable, so she needed no large forces to defend her frontiers. The result was that when Great Britain entered the war she did so not only in a state of unpreparedness from the armament and industrial standpoint—in which she was no worse off than all the other belligerents—but also in a state of unpreparedness from a purely military standpoint.

Thus at the beginning of the war Germany was not opposed by a large Anglo-French military combination, but only by the French army supported by a small British expeditionary force amounting to a few divisions. Had the military strength of Great Britain and

France at the beginning of the war been in accordance with their industrial potential, then Germany would have had no chance whatever of obtaining a decisive military victory, because the combined populations of Britain and France were bigger than the population of Germany, whilst their combined industrial production was also bigger than that of Germany. Thus Germany's chances of victory were based precisely on the fact that the military strength of the Western Allies at the outbreak of the war was much farther below their industrial strength than was the case with Germany.

Germany's aim was therefore to win a decisive victory whilst France was still fighting practically alone. Germany had to take advantage of the earlier military mobilization of her forces and win a decisive victory before large British forces appeared on the continent. The fact that Germany would not subsequently be able to defeat Great Britain on her own territory was not decisive. Once France was defeated the whole power on the continent would fall into German hands.

Germany defeated France in the war of 1870–1871, which was a war on one front only. This time the plans of the German general staff were laid for a war on two fronts, but from the first day of the new war the overwhelming majority of Germany's resources in manpower and armaments were concentrated on the Western Front, and —unlike the second world war—they remained so during the whole campaign. There was not a single day throughout the whole war when this was not so.

Germany's advantage in man-power over France, which had been only four millions in 1870, was now approximately 25 millions, and the fact that Germany deployed a few army corps on the Eastern Front to deal with the Russians made very little difference to her numerical superiority on the Western Front in the early part of the war before big British armies appeared on the continent. Even the introduction of the three-year service period by the French reduced the disparity only for a while and did not abolish it entirely.

Germany's Failure to make Economic and Industrial Preparations Robbed Her of Victory

Thus the Germans could not have been held off indefinitely but for the fact that the French were assisted by a circumstance which was not accidental, but which was deeply rooted in the whole situation of the capitalist economic system at the time—namely, the inadequate state of German armaments production and the lack of industrial war preparations.

We have already dealt with this point elsewhere, and a few supplementary observations are all that is necessary here.

The Franco-Prussian War was not prepared for by any great increase in the production of armaments, and that was not necessary.

157

The Prussian armies had all the arms and ammunition they required for the first decisive battles, and subsequently German industry provided the necessary supplies without much difficulty. German military operations in that war were never hampered by any inability of the industries producing arms and ammunition to provide supplies. Armament requirements in war were not very great in those days, with the result that even during the course of the Franco-Prussian War the German economic system carried on very much as usual. In this war Frederick the Great's axiom, "The peaceable citizens should not even notice the fact that the nation is at war" was more or less a fact.

Now, when Germany entered the first world war the situation was very different from that which existed when the second world war broke out: a great crisis hardly overcome and a war economy already in operation. Instead she entered the first world war after a long period of economic progress in which her production had steadily risen, and without any very great volume of unemployment. The German State had not intervened in all phases of the economic process for years before the outbreak of the war, as was the case at the time of the second world war. The German State had to create the organization of war industry in accordance with the demands of this first total industrial war as the war proceeded—and at first the whole thing was very improvised. Germany had made such inadequate preparations for the transition from peace to war that despite the fact that millions of men were called up, unemployment increased in the first few months of the war, because many building operations ceased and the textile factories reduced production and there was, as yet, no possibility of putting the unemployed building and textile workers into other jobs.

This absolute unpreparedness for war production naturally applied not only to Germany; it applied to all the belligerent powers. *But the decisive point was that the unpreparedness hit Germany fatally because Germany was the aggressor.* Germany needed swift victory if she was to be victorious at all. Her armies therefore needed a tremendous superiority in armaments for their decisive drive against France, and they needed it not only for the first three or four weeks of the war, but until decisive victory had been achieved, however long that might take. But the German armies had adequate supplies of arms and ammunition only for the first weeks of the war. If they had won decisive successes in this period, then perhaps Germany's industrial unpreparedness would not have mattered so much.

They certainly did win important successes in the first weeks of the war. They over-ran Belgium and they drove deep into France—but then came the defeat on the Marne. That defeat proved decisive precisely because it took place at a time when the German armies were beginning to feel a shortage of arms and ammunition. Ger-
158

many's drive was held up until her industries had adapted themselves to war-time requirements and were able to supply the German armies with all they needed for the continued and continuous waging of modern warfare. But in this pause the Western Front was stabilized. France also re-organized her economic system for total war, and the big change began in Great Britain. Thus the advantage of an earlier military mobilization, which Germany had enjoyed at first, was largely lost, and the element of surprise no longer played the same role. Germany's only hope of victory on the Western Front was now pinned to the deployment of a tremendous man-power and armament superiority.

She never succeeded in obtaining it. Thus the phase of lightning war and the hope of lightning victory ended in the first weeks of the war.

The winter of 1914–1915 set in and no decison had been obtained. At the same time every passing day gradually changed the relation of forces to Germany's disadvantage as the British proceeded to narrow the very wide gap between their industrial strength and their immediate military strength. In addition, the French army was not broken in the first world war; it continued to offer resistance in the field, and so the British had not first to carry out a precarious and difficult invasion of the continental mainland before they could bring their power to bear. At no time during the first world war were the Germans in a position to interfere materially with the transporting of British men and materials to France.

The answer of the German general staff to this new situation was twofold. Once it was realized that the war, unlike the Franco-Prussian conflict, was going to be a long one, all Germany's resources were mobilized for total war. Industry was concentrated on war production and every possible able-bodied man was called up for military service. During the first world war Germany had no fewer than 13 million men under arms—that is to say about one man in five of the total population and about one man to 2·5 men in the male population as a whole.

GERMANY TURNS TO THE EAST FOR VICTORY

But Germany's re-organization for total war did not give her a sufficient advantage on the Western Front because, of course, the Western Powers did exactly the same thing. In this situation there seemed only one way open to Germany to obtain the superiority she needed on the Western Front, and that was first to knock the Russians out of the war, and thus turn it into a one-front war in the West.

There were fundamental differences between the waging of the first world war and the waging of the second. During the second world war Nazi Germany had the advantage of a one-front conflict

159

for the greater part of the war. The fatal dangers of a war on two fronts were always present in the minds of Germany's generals, and at first even Hitler shared their fears, with the result that all Germany's diplomatic and other political preparations for war were directed towards preventing the development of an East–West war on two fronts.

During the second world war the Germans fought a one-front war until 1944, and once the Anglo-Saxon forces had landed successfully and the war on two fronts began in earnest Germany soon collapsed. The two-front campaign in the second world war lasted only for about a year.

The situation in the first world war was quite different: it was a two-front war from the start, and this circumstance contributed to Germany's inability to secure decisive victories on the Western Front. There was only a minority of Germany's forces on the Eastern Front at any time—never more than a third and usually less than that—but because the Germans were never very much stronger than the Western Powers, the fact that they had to defend themselves against the Russians in the East was sufficient to prevent their ever securing the decisive superiority they needed in the West. So when the German lightning war plans bogged down on the Western Front in the autumn of 1914, the German High Command turned its attention to the East in an attempt to knock the Russians out of the war.

On the Eastern Front the Germans immediately won tremendous successes, and they administered such severe punishment to the Russian armies that never again throughout the course of the war was German territory remotely threatened by the Russians. However, despite a series of terrible defeats, Russia's armed forces still remained in the field. Germany's victories against Russia in 1915 did not win her the much-coveted one-front war, and thus her situation on the Western Front was not materially improved by them.

On the other hand, the armies of the Western Powers were unable to win any decisive victories against the Germans. Armies faced each other there whose industrial backing was more or less equally strong. Only a very great superiority in men and munitions offered any hope of achieving decisive victories, and in 1915 and 1916 neither side had any such superiority.

Thus those two years passed without either side being able to obtain a decisive victory. The losses on both sides were terrible. In every year of the first world war, for instance, France lost more men than she did throughout the whole of the second world war. Great Britain's losses on the Western Front were also several times greater than her total losses throughout the second world war.

But the longer the war lasted the more difficult Germany's military and economic situation became. There were two main reasons for this.

160

First of all there was the fact that she had made no adequate preparations for such a war, either with regard to food or raw-materials supplies. For instance, in 1916 Germany's food situation was still more or less tolerable, but in the two last years of the war it deteriorated rapidly owing to her inability to break Britain's naval blockade. The population went hungry, and the result was that the productivity of labour began to decline. But even at the front the food situation deteriorated, and the discrepancy between the feeding of Germany's soldiers and those of the Western Powers became greater and greater.

Secondly, U.S. exports to the Western Powers greatly increased, and, as the latter controlled the seas, despite the unrestricted submarine warfare waged by Germany, they were able to increase their imports from overseas, and thus their strength, whilst Germany's imports were very greatly reduced. That meant that both the civilian populations and the armies of the Western Powers were better fed than those of Germany and her allies. It also meant that the former could supplement their own production of war materials by overseas supplies. And finally it meant that, as the imports of consumer goods were very great, a smaller proportion of the working population of Great Britain and France was needed to produce these goods at home, with the result that a proportionately larger percentage of their man-power could be used in the armed forces and in the munitions factories.

Thus the whole situation changed gradually, if slowly, and at first almost unnoticeably, in favour of the Western Powers.

The comparatively stable position on the Western Front, where the Western Powers gradually began to obtain the upper hand, but not decisively enough to bring victory, was affected in 1917 by two events.

GERMANY GETS HER ONE-FRONT WAR BUT THE U.S.A. INTERVENES

Tsarism, which had gone into the war with a badly shaken social system, was unable to survive the series of heavy defeats inflicted on the Russian armies by the Germans. The first revolution broke out in March 1917, and Tsarism was already so discredited that it had hardly any defenders left at all. This, however, did not mean the end of the war. The elements which now came to the top attempted to continue the war under democratic slogans, and the Brussilov offensive was launched. The Germans had little difficulty in bringing it to a standstill.

Now, the fact that the March Revolution did not bring peace to the Russian people was one of the most important factors for the subsequent successful seizure of power by the Bolshevists. The Germans did not obtain their one-front war in 1915 or 1916, when it might have proved effective, but only after the seizure of power in Russia by the Bolshevists in November 1917.

F

The last year of the second world war was the only year in which Germany had to fight on two fronts; the last year of the first world war was the only year on which she was able to fight on one front only. But the developments on the Eastern Front which brought relief to Germany came too late to be decisive. It was no longer possible for Germany to obtain material superiority on the Western Front. On the contrary, even during the one-front phase of the campaign the superiority of the Western Allies became more and more marked.

In 1917 the United States entered the war against Germany. U.S. industrial strength was greater than Germany's even without British and French industry, and it was now bent more and more to the aid of the Entente Powers, whose combined resources had already been approximately as great as Germany's. Once this situation had been reached it became only a matter of time before the superiority of the Western Allies was so great that it encompassed Germany's final defeat.

The German High Command had made two fatal errors. First of all it had concentrated its preparations for war exclusively on purely military mobilization, whilst neglecting industrial and economic mobilization. It paid for its error with the loss of all hope of a lightning victory on the Western Front in the first phase of the war. Great though Germany's preliminary military successes were, they were not decisive, and stalemate followed.

Secondly, it under-estimated the gigantic armaments potential of the United States. It argued that as the United States had already been providing the Entente Powers with munitions, food and raw materials, the U.S. entry into the war would not materially increase those supplies. At the same time it hoped that unrestricted submarine warfare would open up a vital chink in the armour of the Entente Powers. Its calculation was wrong and its hope was illusory. The unrestricted submarine campaign certainly met with considerable preliminary successes, but they were not decisive, and once the United States was in the war the volume of supplies to the Entente Powers increased tremendously, and, in addition, strong and well-equipped U.S. armies appeared on the Western Front and greatly raised the morale of the British and French forces, which had been fighting for years without much hope of obtaining a decision. Now they knew that every day would increase their own strength, whilst their enemies had very little left to throw into the battle against them.

Germany's High Command * launched a last great offensive in March 1918 with the object of gaining a decision before the Ameri-

* Hindenburg and Ludendorff were Germany's High Command at this time, and the High Command was not only the military leadership of Germany but also the political leadership. The still semi-feudal militarist character of Germany at this time was reflected in the fact that political decisions were taken not by parliament, but by the military leadership.

162

cans appeared in any strength on the Western Front. Once again considerable preliminary successes were obtained, but they were not decisive, and the offensive was brought to a standstill. The German army was now completely exhausted and without reserves, whilst the armies of the Western Allies grew daily in strength.

Now, the German High Command had launched this offensive without abandoning its imperialist policy or its imperialist war aims, whereas the majority of Germany's parliament was already opposed to a policy of imperialist annexations and in favour of a peace without annexations and without indemnities.

Let us suppose that after the November Revolution had put Russia out of the war Germany had approached the Entente in somewhat the following terms: "Here we are firmly established deep in French territory. Up to the present you have not succeeded in driving us out. Now that we can withdraw our troops from the Russian front we shall naturally be much stronger, and you will therefore have even less chance of defeating us. So why go on? We are prepared to make peace on the basis of the *status quo ante bellum*. If you refuse to agree we shall, of course, fight on. You will then have to fight hard for every inch of ground and you will also have to explain to your own people why you insist on continuing to wage a useless war which is costing the lives of considerably more than a thousand British and French soldiers a day."

It is possible that such a German policy might have averted total German defeat, but the German High Command, the German ruling classes, were not capable of pursuing such a common-sense policy. Instead they dictated the imperialist robber treaty of Brest-Litovsk in the east, and launched the hopeless offensive of March 1918 in the west. And when the offensive bogged down, Ludendorff lost his head and suddenly informed the flabbergasted civil government of Germany that it must ask for an armistice within twenty-four hours or the German front would collapse.

THE U.S.A. IN THE FIRST WORLD WAR

With the first world war, and in the war itself, the relationship between the United States and Europe underwent a fundamental change. America's entry into the war decisively changed the relation of industrial strength between the combatants and, in consequence, the relation of military strength. Without the United States the industrial strength of Great Britain and France on the one hand and of Germany and her allies on the other was at least comparable, but with the United States the relation of strength changed to approximately 3 : 1 against Germany. With this the prospect of a German military victory became hopeless. The fact that Germany under-estimated the industrial strength of the United States, and her ability to translate it into military power, brought about Germany's defeat in the first world war. It was a mistake which Hitler was later to repeat.

The United States turned the scales in favour of an Entente victory in the first world war, but it is important to note that this did not turn defeat into victory, but stalemate into victory. Even before the effective entry of the United States into the war Germany was unable to obtain a decisive victory on the Western Front, and the relation of forces there was indecisive. Thus a late and comparatively small expenditure of U.S. resources was sufficient to bring about a military decision, and the United States had no very great strategic tasks to perform. The situation was very different in the second world war.

America's role in the first phase of the war was that of supplier to the Entente Powers, and she provided food, raw materials, arms and munitions. Once America had entered the war she not only sent still bigger supplies, but she arrived in France with a million men. There was only one front she had to supply, and that was in France; there was only one danger, and that was Germany. There were no very great social and political problems to resolve in this war because the capitalist system on both sides of the front was still comparatively stable. There were no great world problems to be solved either. It was, after all, primarily a European war, and not really a world war.

When we analysed the factors which led to the outbreak of the first world war—the growth of foreign-political antagonisms between the leading European countries—we confined ourselves to Europe. The United States played little or no role in the general relation of forces before the first world war. Capitalist expansion in the United States took place largely within the country itself, and there were few points of friction with the imperialist interests of other countries. The United States therefore did not enter the war until towards the end, and then she was drawn in as the logical development of the supply situation. The Entente Powers held undisputed command of the sea, and thus America's supplies could go only to them.

The United States was not faced with the alternatives: war on the side of Germany or war on the side of the Entente Powers. The only alternatives she was faced with were: support of the Entente Powers whilst remaining outside the war, or support of the Entente Powers to the point of taking a direct part in the war. The U.S. Government decided on the latter alternative, and in entering the war it cast the die against the Central Powers.

The U.S.A. brought about the decision without feeling the burden of war very heavily. For the U.S.A. the war was more a sort of colonial undertaking on a rather bigger scale than usual. It resulted in an increase of U.S. production, and it demanded only a comparatively small man-power effort, an effort which was not only relatively but also absolutely far less than that of any other single big power engaged in the war. United States casualties were also very low. With a population already more than twice as big as the population of France, the United States lost 50,000 dead against total French deaths of 1,400,000. In other words, for one American who was killed twenty-eight Frenchmen died. However, although it was far from being a total war for the United States, whose war effort was very small by comparison with the enormous resources of her social organism, her intervention was enough to turn the scales decisively.

U.S. intervention was the harbinger of a fundamental change in the world political relation of forces. Throughout the greater part of the nineteenth century the European big powers were more or less equally balanced, and the strong position of Britain in the world was partly due to the fact that she was in a position to tip the balance in one direction or the other. Then the exceptionally rapid and vigorous capitalist industrial development of Germany upset the balance for good and all.

The first world war showed that Germany in alliance with Austria-Hungary was stronger than France allied with Russia, and just about as strong as France and Russia in alliance with Great Britain. This lack of a balance of power in Europe, together with Great Britain's inability to turn the scales decisively against Germany even with full-scale intervention, was not confined to the period of the first world war. It continued to exist after the victorious conclusion of the war for the Western Powers, and it was further complicated by a great intensification of all social antagonisms.

APPENDIX TO CHAPTER TWO

The Role of Coal, Iron and Steel

It is, of course, an over-simplification, but it is very interesting to treat the history of military developments during the first world war in relation to the production of the most important raw materials for the waging of war, coal, iron and steel.

Marx wrote that the history of large-scale landed property represented the secret history of India. In the same way, one might almost say that the volume of coal, iron and steel production represented the secret history of the first world war.

Frederick the Great once pronounced the famous axiom that God was on the side of the big battalions. In the first world war, under conditions of highly-developed industrialism, this axiom might have been adapted to mean that God was on the side of the battalions which were supported by the greatest volume of coal, iron and steel production.

Ferdinand Friedensberg,[1] a German economic expert, wrote:

"If we examine the strength of the two camps as a reflection of their capacity to produce coal, iron and steel, taking the production figures for the last few years before the outbreak of war, instead of, as usual, on the basis of population figures, territorial extent and armaments, then we see that the inequality which is so marked on all other fields is here very considerably less. A total coal production of 331 million tons on the part of the Central Powers was countered by a total of 394 million tons on the part of the Entente Powers. . . .

"The situation was considerably more favourable for the Central Powers with regard to the production of iron and steel. Blast furnace capacity and pig-iron production were level at 22 million tons each. . . . In the production of steel the Central Powers even enjoyed an advantage: 21 million tons against 19 million tons."

Thus before the outbreak of the first world war the steel production of the belligerent camps was more or less equal, but after the first German victories the heavy-industrial situation changed in Germany's favour, and Friedensberg continues:

"The first phase of the war resulted in a considerable strengthening of the position of the Central Powers. The swift German offensives in both arenas of war brought the coal and iron-producing districts of South-West Poland, Belgium and North-West France, which, from a strategic viewpoint, were unfavourably placed near the frontiers, almost entirely into German hands. . . .

"The industries in the occupied areas did not remain in full production, however, and when they were subsequently worked under the occupation authorities they reached nothing like their former level of production. . . . But even if we set the increased production which was added to the Central Powers at no more than fifty per cent of normal, the first six weeks of the war had brought about an important change in the relation of forces with regard to the production of coal and iron."[2]

Coal and Iron Production of the Belligerent Powers

(in million tons)

	August 1st, 1914.		September, 15th, 1914.	
	Central Powers.	Entente Powers.	Central Powers.	Entente Powers.
Coal . . .	331	394	355	346
Pig-iron . .	22	22	25	16
Steel . . .	21	19	24	13

Thus, thanks to their preliminary victories, the Central Powers had won a certain heavy-industrial advantage over the Entente Powers but it was not big enough to guarantee any decisive victory on the Western Front. Just as they had made no preparations before the war for the gigantic production of armaments which the prosecution of the war was seen to require, so they had also made no arrangements to harness the industries in the occupied areas to the German war machine. For this reason they were able to make no progress on the Western Front in 1915. But every day on which they failed to make any progress was a day nearer their final defeat, because not only was Great Britain's very considerable industrial strength rapidly being turned into military strength, but America's vast industrial resources were also being used, and to an ever-increasing extent, on the side of the Entente Powers. Growing U.S. exports made it possible to raise French iron and steel production above the pre-war level as early as 1916. And whilst Germany's iron and steel production declined during the course of the war, the entry of the United States created an overwhelming heavy-industrial superiority against the Central Powers, as can be seen from the following figures given by Friedensberg for 1917:

Coal and Iron Production of the Belligerent Powers

(in million tons)

	Central Powers.	Western Powers.
Coal	340	851
Pig-iron . . .	15	50
Steel	16	58

CHAPTER THREE

EFFECTS OF THE FIRST WORLD WAR ON EUROPEAN CAPITALISM

EUROPEAN CAPITALISM WAS shaken to the core by the first world war. The European capitalist States entered the war after a period of great progress which had lasted for generations and with a social system which was on the whole quite stable. At the end of the war the capitalist system still survived, but it had been so deeply shaken that never again could it confidently regard its continued existence as the natural condition for future development.

Before the outbreak of the war all economic and political struggles in Europe had been fought out within the framework of the capitalist

167

system. After the war that period in European history, that period in the history of capitalism, was seen to be at an end for good. Henceforth all economic and political struggles were fought out in a system which was already greatly undermined and extremely vulnerable, and often they threatened the existence of the system itself and sought to bring about its fundamental transformation, though for decades they led to no decisive results.

The first world war represented a decisive turning point in the history of Europe in general and in the history of European capitalism in particular. The war itself was not alone directly responsible for bringing this state of affairs about; it was rather that its tremendous direct and indirect repercussions strengthened and accentuated a trend in this direction which already existed independent of the war.

THE STATE AND WAR ECONOMY

It was also not the economic changes which came about as an inevitable consequence of the war that led to this permanent and fundamental change in the capitalist system, but as these changes, the result of war economy, have often been stressed beyond their real importance, it is necessary for us to treat them in some detail.

For the first time in the history of modern capitalism, the war brought about a fundamental change in the relationship between the State and the economic system. Because the war was waged as a total war, and because no sector of the economic system was left untouched in this war of industries and factories, the power of the State was tremendously increased for the duration of the conflict.

This great extension of the powers of the State did not take place uniformly everywhere. For instance, it was greater in Germany, which was cut off from overseas supplies by the blockade, than it was in the Entente countries, and it was greater in the latter countries than it was in the United States. But the general trend was the same everywhere.

The reason for this general trend was very simple: in all the belligerent countries—with the exception of the United States, where production increased—diminished productive organisms were expected to produce more and more war materials, although the most productive categories of workers had been largely called up for military service. The result was that in all the belligerent countries— once again with the exception of the United States—the picture, with differences in degree, was that of a typical deficit economy. There were production shortages, raw materials shortages and labour shortages. In this situation the State was compelled to intervene to determine just what should be produced, in what quantities it should be produced and in what order of priority, and also to determine what should not be produced at all.

The State, and the State alone, had sufficient power and authority to "plan" the country's war economy and to guide and control it in accordance with that plan. But in order to do so it was essential that the State should also control the production of raw material, and in war-time that meant practically a hundred per cent control of foreign trade. And as the shortage of labour was another serious factor, the State had to control the labour market as well. The places of the millions of men who had been called up had to be filled somehow, and such labour power as was still available had to be used at the point best suited to the exigencies of war.

The longer the war lasted the greater became the shortage of certain consumer goods, and in particular foodstuffs. Thus, in the interests of the prosecution of the war, maximum prices had to be introduced and a system of rationing organized to guarantee the working people, and quite generally those at lower-income levels, a certain minimum of foodstuffs purchasable with their wages.

The generation which lived through the second world war is very familiar with that sort of State intervention, but in the first world war it was all new. None of the belligerent States had entered the war with any organization for a planned war economy, and the first measures which were taken in this direction were improvised, until finally a systematic and total organization developed.

During the first world war, and particularly in Central Europe, people talked of "War Socialism", of a "Socialism of consumption". They confused the planned economy organized for prosecuting the war with a socialist planned economy. But what existed during the first world war was not a socialist planned economy but a planned war economy—something very different—and it existed within the general framework of capitalist society. That is why the capitalists, and in particular the large-scale capitalists, were easily able to co-operate in a planned war economy. The State, which now controlled production, guaranteed them a market for their products and an exceptionally high rate of profit at the same time. In addition, the process of industrial concentration was greatly stepped up during the war, and in consequence the power and influence of the leading capitalist groups were increased.

All other considerations took a back seat for "big business" by comparison with this strengthening of its position. The fact that the economic power of the State had increased so greatly was not regarded as at all decisive, particularly as it was thought to be a war-time measure only. In fact, on the whole big business was right in its estimate of the situation. The first world war did not change the great capitalist industrial countries of Europe from a system of more or less liberal capitalism to one in which the State sector was tremendously increased. The intervention of the State in economic affairs was at its height during the war; after the war there was a general dismantling of the war-time apparatus of State control. Although the State sector remained greater between the two world wars than it had been in the period leading up to the first world war, the immediate result of the arrival of peace was its very considerable reduction.

The tremendous growth of State intervention in economic affairs which took place during the first world war demonstrated how erroneous it is to believe that any strengthening of the State sector, that any State planned economy, is a progressive step. The States during the first world war were not socially neutral bodies; they were capitalist States. Thus the growth of the State sector in the economic system during the war had nothing whatever to do with progress. The sole object of this State intervention was to facilitate the prosecution of the war to a victorious conclusion, and it took place in a form which did not endanger the continued existence of the capitalist system. At that same time it strengthened the position of big business because it inevitably stepped up the process of industrial concentration.

The utter military defeat of Germany and her allies made it possible to dismantle the war economy which had been built up during the war, and to dismantle it rapidly and thoroughly.

The general relation of world forces from the military standpoint after the first world war was comparatively stable, primarily because the economic and political systems of the victorious countries were not so very different from each other and because the great process of transformation in Europe and Asia was only just beginning. The situation after the second world war, with the United States on the one hand and the Soviet Union on the other, was very different. Thus after the first world war, war economy was followed by a normal peace-time economy; the second world war was followed by a sort of armistice or truce economy. Because a peace-time economy followed the first world war, and the military and armaments sector was rapidly and vigorously dismantled, very little remained of the State sector.*

The war economy which had been built up in Europe during the first world war was rapidly dismantled after the war, but the process was even more speedy and thorough in the United States, where, in any case, its extent had been incomparably smaller than in Europe.

Thus if the war economy which was built up during the course of the first world war had no very permanent and material effects on the capitalist system in Europe, the question which arises is what did,

---

* Although its effects in the period after the war were not very great, they were to play a considerable role later on. It was precisely the experience of industrial unpreparedness before the first world war, and the experiences of war economy during the war, which formed the basis for the greater part of the war-preparation economy, or, as they called it, "*Wehrwirtschaft*", which the Nazis built up in Germany before the second world war, thereby enormously increasing the purely military and armaments sector in times of peace.

in fact, so greatly shake the capitalist system in Europe as a result of the first world war?

The First World War Closed the Period of Capitalist Progress in Europe

The arena of hostilities was Europe, and the war was prosecuted with all possible energy and the exertion of all possible forces only by the European powers engaged in it. However, up to the outbreak of the first world war Europe had been the capitalist and industrial centre of the world, and so when its position was very greatly shaken as a result of the war, the direct and indirect repercussions were felt far beyond the frontiers of Europe, a point with which we shall deal in much more detail later on.

It is a matter of course that the considerable weakening of Europe as a result of the war automatically strengthened the position of the non-European great powers, the United States and Japan, and the international production index for the war and post-war periods, which shows a tremendous drop in European production and a big rise in production in the United States and in Japan, accurately reflects this change in the relation of world forces.

The first world war, being primarily a European war, did not represent a decisive turning point in the development of the non-European big powers, Japan and the United States. But for Europe it ended the period of capitalist expansion and capitalist progress. It also ended the period in which European capitalism had been the heart of world capitalism, and opened up a period of fundamental transformation for European capitalism.

However, this transformation did not follow the scheme of a general decline of European capitalism, after a period of uninterrupted progress, leading to a new social order with the rise of socialism. The process of transformation led to years of stagnation in the industrial countries of Europe, during which the socialist forces were not strong enough to take advantage of the stagnation and temporary decline of capitalism to bring about a socialist transformation.

The first world war also produced a revolution, but not in any of the big European industrial centres. It brought about the November Revolution in Russia, whose tremendous dynamic power was due in particular to the fact that Russia had not yet experienced her agrarian revolution against feudalism—a revolution which had long been concluded in industrial Europe.

Because no socialist transformation came about in any of the industrialized countries of Europe as a result of the first world war, the spark of the Russian November Revolution did not cause any sympathetic conflagration elsewhere; the Russian Revolution remained isolated, and in this way a new type of State grew up on the outskirts of the former capitalist centre of the world, a new type of State which was neither capitalist nor socialist.

THE UNIFORM CAPITALIST TREND OF WORLD DEVELOPMENT INTERRUPTED

One of the most important results of the first world war was that the uniformity of world industrial development, which up to that time had been more or less capitalistic, was interrupted.

Up to the outbreak of the first world war, from the industrial revolution on throughout the whole of the nineteenth century, there had been a comparatively uniform trend in world development and a long period of tremendous capitalist industrial progress. The various countries had entered into this process of development at different times. Great Britain had started first, before Germany and the United States, and Germany had come in before Eastern Europe, and so on. At the same time the rate of development was not uniform everywhere; it varied from country to country. However, despite these differences, the general trend was on the whole uniform, a victorious advance of capitalism, which won control of one country after the other, whereby the number of people living and working under capitalist methods of production increased far more rapidly than the total population of the world.

The first world war interrupted this general trend, though in the United States and Japan capitalist progress and expansion continued comparatively unchanged during the war and after it.

For industrial Europe, however, the first world war was a turning point, inasmuch as capitalist progress and expansion had now come to an end, and, in addition, a new State had been created in Russia, which not only broke away from the capitalist periphery, but henceforth sought to influence that periphery in its own interests.

For the moment we propose to deal primarily with the effects of the first world war on industrial Europe and on Russia, leaving the changed position of the United States in the world until later.

The profound disturbance suffered by the capitalist system in Europe was naturally not brought about by one cause, but by a series of causes and their cumulative effects. Some of these causes were directly connected with the war; others were merely accelerated and accentuated by the war.

The fact that the war took place, that it could take place at all, shook capitalism to the core, and at the same time it shook the confidence of the majority of the population of Europe in the capitalist system. Doubts as to the value of the capitalist system now extended beyond the ranks of the socialist working class, which, of course, had always opposed the capitalist social order on principle. It was not necessary to agree with the socialist argument that foreign-political antagonism resulting from capitalist imperialist ex-

172

pansion was the real cause of the war—i.e. that capitalism as such, as a certain definite economic and social system, was responsible for the war—but the fact remained that capitalism, which was the dominating mode of production in industrial Europe, had been unable to prevent the war, and that the war itself had become more and more a war precisely between the highly-developed capitalist countries.

The hundreds of millions of people who lived in Europe had grown up in a long period of capitalist progress which had lasted for generations and created a whole way of life. The life which they had previously known had been a life of peace and progress. They had regarded peace as identical with progress, and, consciously or unconsciously, peace, progress and capitalism had been a natural trinity in their minds.

Because peace had lasted so long within the framework of a certain social system, it was tempting to conclude—particularly as such a conclusion reflected the wishes and hopes of almost everyone—that it was this social system, with its specific structure and its specific mode of production, which had led to peace and guaranteed its preservation.

And then war came, after all. For the overwhelming majority of Europeans it was totally unexpected; it was the sort of thing that ought never to have happened. And when it came it was not of short duration, but longer than any war had been for over a century. It was not only long, it was also extremely costly in blood and riches, and it affected every sphere of human life. The fact of war alone destroyed all ideas of the inevitability and naturalness of progress. The fact of war alone destroyed all ideas of security, all idea of any "plans for the future". If the countries of Europe could wage war against each other for years, and a total war at that, in which hundreds of millions of people were involved and all personal lives wrenched out of their usual course, what was the use of making plans for the future at all? And because all this could happen whilst the capitalist system was absolutely dominant in Europe, that system itself was gravely weakened in men's eyes.

The terrible devastation caused by the first world war undermined and shook the belief of large numbers of people in the capitalist system, and they ceased to identify it as a matter of course with human progress. Thus the fact of war in itself represented a psychological turning point in Europe.

But although the war shook people profoundly they refused to recognize its inseparable relationship with the social system under which they lived. The result was that scores of various explanations were gratefully welcomed, despite their superficiality, because they sought the cause of the war in this or that specific factor which could have been avoided or eliminated, and therefore made it possible to believe that the first total war in Europe would be the last.

But the war had so deeply affected Europe that its whole existence was changed. From now on the people of Europe knew war as a terrible reality in all their actions, their thoughts and their imaginings.

War was a fact. It was no longer possible to believe that war was impossible under capitalism. War and capitalism were therefore not mutually exclusive terms. They were not so at present, and perhaps they would not be in the future either.

A long period of peace lasting for generations, and a new period of economic progress, would have been necessary to exorcise this terrible experience from people's minds. But there was no such period of progress after the war, and the new upheavals which took place between the two world wars found the millions of people who lived in industrial Europe in a state of mind which no longer permitted them to identify capitalism with peace and progress, as they had formerly quite naturally done.

Intellectually the first world war also represented a turning point for the peoples of Europe. Despite all national differences, the progress of capitalism in the industrial countries of Europe had created conditions for broader and broader sections of the population which caused their way of life to approximate more and more closely. At the same time it had encouraged a wider and wider intellectual exchange between the peoples, not only in science and technique, but also in literature and art. Despite the continued existence of national differences, the consciousness of a joint European culture grew steadily.

The first world war interrupted this development. Nationalism and chauvinism received a tremendous fillip from the war, and they destroyed the developing tendencies towards a European cultural and intellectual international.

Thus the first world war was also a milestone in European intellectual and cultural degeneration, which subsequently offered such a fruitful field for the growth of Fascism and National Socialism, which were by no means the first act in the drama.

THE WAR SHATTERED THE IDEA OF THE INEVITABILITY OF SOCIALISM

The first world war not only destroyed the comforting idea that capitalism was identical with progress, but it also destroyed the idea amongst the socialist workers that socialism must inevitably follow on capitalism. Before the war millions of workers in Europe had grown up in socialist ideas, and they were quite convinced that at some time or other in the future the transition from capitalism to socialism was inevitable, that socialism was the next phase in human history. The leading socialists of Europe were not agreed amongst themselves as to whether the process would be short or long, or whether it would take place along evolutionary or revolutionary lines; but despite their differences they were all convinced that in the end socialism would be victorious, and it was just this unshakeable belief in the ultimate victory of socialism which had given the socialist movement a good deal of its strength.

The first world war put an end to this comfortable conviction. It had broken out, and the socialists had not been strong enough to prevent it breaking out; as it proceeded the forces of socialism did not grow markedly very much stronger; and when it ended the socialists had no decisive say in the manner of its ending.

The war showed European socialists very clearly that they were not so strong as they had supposed. But it did more than that: it destroyed the idea that socialism must inevitably follow capitalism, and that world history offered no alternative, for if such a war were possible under capitalism, and if the elements opposed to capitalism found it impossible to prevent, then clearly other wars could follow, in which case a declining and doomed capitalism need not necessarily imply a rising socialism and an ultimate socialist victory; it might well mean that the decline of capitalism would lead through new wars to barbarism.

In the famous article he wrote in the nineties, from which we have already quoted several times, Friedrich Engels assumed that, whatever the details of the process, a world war would lead to socialism; but when the first world war actually came it destroyed the belief in the minds of many socialists that socialism was an inevitable necessity.

Leading socialists warned the socialist masses that the alternative to capitalism was not necessarily socialism, and that there was a real possibility that that alternative might be a phase of barbarism. For instance, Rosa Luxemburg [1] wrote:

"The characteristic of imperialism as the last stage of the capitalist struggle for world dominance is not merely the exceptional vigour and extent of the expansion, but—and this is the specific sign that the circle of development is closing—the recoil of the decisive struggle for expansion from those areas which represent its objects to the countries in which it originated. Imperialism thus takes the catastrophe as a form of existence from the outskirts of capitalist development back to its starting point. After having threatened the existence and the culture of all the non-capitalist peoples of Asia, Africa, America and Australia with endless convulsions and mass destruction for four hundred years, capitalist expansion now plunges the people of Europe into a series of catastrophes *which can end only in the decline of culture or a transition to a socialist mode of production.*"

In the passage which I have italicized, Rosa Luxemburg's views are in agreement with Lenin's, and on April 10th, 1917, he wrote:

"Capitalism, which has now developed into imperialism, inevitably produced the imperialist war. The war has brought the whole of humanity to the verge of the abyss and threatens to destroy human culture." [2]

Developments after the first world war showed very clearly that capitalist decline was not necessarily synonymous with the rise of socialism, and they revealed the existence of strong tendencies to barbarism. They showed that capitalist decline could well be the decline of society as a whole, including the working class. Thus our further analysis can be properly understood only if the idea is abandoned that capitalist decline and capitalist collapse on the one hand must necessarily mean the rise of socialism on the other.

The war, which demonstrated the falsity of any such conclusion, was thus a turning point for the whole of Europe; it was one of the decisive milestones of modern history. The whole of bourgeois society was shaken to the core by a recognition of the fact that the previous, matter-of-course, identification of capitalism with progress had been so overwhelmingly disproved by the course of development that even to talk about it again was absurd. And as this was the case, the generation which grew up during the first world war felt itself separated by a great chasm from the pre-war generations which had grown up in a long period of capitalist progress and had come to regard such progress as the natural course of things.

The socialist working class, of course, had never accepted this identification of capitalism with progress; on the contrary, they had always stressed its profound abuses, its reactionary characteristics and its immanent contradictions. But they, too, had been guilty of an error of judgement; they had always believed that there was a certain inevitable synchronism between capitalist decline and capitalist collapse on the one hand and socialist progress towards a new and more progressive order of society on the other. They had always assumed that the convulsions suffered by capitalism, and the fact that capitalism was not identical with progress, would facilitate the process of transformation from capitalism to socialism.

They now had to recognize that they, too, had been mistaken, that the decline of the capitalist system did not necessarily mean the rise of new progressive forces, and that, in fact, the socialist workers and their organizations were also involved in the convulsions and in the process of decline, that they represented a part of it.

Thus the first world war destroyed not only the bourgeois illusion which identified capitalism with progress, but it also and just as mercilessly destroyed the socialist illusion that the decline and collapse of capitalism on the one hand necessarily meant the rise of socialism on the other.

The war marked a phase in the destruction of bourgeois illusions concerning capitalist progress, and thus undermined the bourgeois way of life, but it did the same for socialist illusions and socialist

176

organizations, in so far as their object was an international socialist transformation of capitalist society.

The War Reduced European Production by more than One Third

In addition to the destruction of these deeply-rooted bourgeois and socialist illusions, the first world war had very important direct effects on the state of industrial production in all the belligerent countries of Europe.

Unlike the period which led up to the second world war, the period which preceded the first knew no very great reserves of idle machinery and labour power immediately available to supplement production in war-time. On the contrary, all European countries entered the first world war at a time when their productive organisms were almost fully engaged in turning out peace-time commodities. In other words, they entered the war after a long period of prosperity, and not, as was the case at the time of the second world war, after a period of unresolved crisis and in a period of "war economy" in peace-time. The European powers waged the war for over four years with all their energies and all their reserves. At the end of it the drop in production was unexampled in the history of capitalism.

The reasons for this were quite clear: in what was a war of industries and factories, an ever-growing proportion of production was naturally used for purely military purposes, whilst at the same time millions of men in the best years of their lives were withdrawn from production to serve in the armed forces. The fact that almost 50 per cent of production as a whole was devoted to the prosecution of the war resulted in a corresponding reduction in the output of consumer goods. But the thing went still farther: in normal times a considerable part of production was used for investments, partly to replace worn-out or obsolescent machinery, and partly to instal new machinery to extend production still farther. During the war the European capitalist powers naturally had very little opportunity for making new investments, and even the necessary replacements of worn-out and obsolescent machinery suffered because all resources were concentrated on the production of munitions. The investments in munitions for the prosecution of the war, most of which quite literally vanished into thin air, were so great that there was no adequate replacement of old machinery during the war, with the result that investments became a minus quantity. As it was impossible to keep the productive apparatus in proper trim without adequate investments, industrial production declined year after year in all the industrial countries of Europe during the war. At the same time the transport apparatus also rapidly deteriorated. Agriculture suffered as well, because on the one hand it was unable to obtain the necessary machinery, fertilizers and transport, and, on the other hand, millions of farmers, peasants and land-workers were called up for military service.

It must be remembered that this decline of production during the first world war took place although the industrial countries of Europe were not themselves battlefields. Great Britain and Germany were never fought over, and even France only in part. In other words, that decline of production came about although the first world war was not fought as a war against towns and industrial centres. At the end of the war the towns and industrial centres were still intact and the factories and their machinery were still there. But they were impoverished and exhausted to a degree never before experienced.

By 1919 the industrial production of all the European belligerent countries had fallen by more than a third. None of the previous economic crises through which capitalism had passed had led to anything like such a fall in production. European capitalism had experienced long periods of depression in which production had not increased. It had experienced comparatively short periods of crisis in which production had dropped sharply, but it had hardly ever dropped by more than 20 per cent.

In the early days of capitalism, when the capitalist sector represented only a comparatively small part of production, it occasionally suffered heavy set-backs, but the economic system as a whole had not been so deeply affected, because a considerable part of production was still carried on outside the sphere affected by the workings of capitalist crisis, and therefore went on operating without being very much affected by the crisis. However, by the time of the first world war capitalist industrial production was dominant in the leading European countries, and so the decline affected the economic system as a whole.

In Britain and France the decline of production in the first world war was greater even than in the subsequent, never fully liquidated, economic crisis of 1929, when British production declined by 18 per cent and French production by a good 25 per cent.

Industrial production declined so much during the first world war because the devastation caused by the war and the direct and indirect effects of the war made it impossible to produce as much as before.

Here was the fundamental difference between the decline in production during the war and the decline of production as the result of economic crisis. The characteristic feature of the latter is precisely that more could be produced, but is not produced because no profitable market outlet can be found for the increase in production. In the latter case production declines whilst factories stand idle and the productive apparatus is not utilized to the full, and at the same

178

time there is a tremendous volume of unemployment. In this case the decline of production is a corollary of over-production.

In the first world war the situation was just the opposite. As in the crises in the pre-capitalist period, in the days of antiquity and during the middle ages, the fall in production was a crisis of under-production, and not a modern capitalist crisis of over-production. After the first world war industrial Europe produced one-third less commodities than usual because it was physically unable to produce any more.

That was a heavy blow for the capitalist system, and when the great economic crisis of 1929 broke out millions of people in Europe were already sceptical of the capitalist system as a whole, and a contributory cause of this was the fact that, ten years before, the first world war had resulted in a tremendous decrease in production.

Europe would perhaps have been able to overcome this shock if the first world war had been followed by a period of capitalist progress like the period which preceded it, but this possibility was now influenced by a factor which was to make its mark not only on the period between the two world wars, but even in the second post-war period—namely, the changed position of Europe in the general economic and political relation of world forces.

Europe's Position as Centre of the Capitalist World Undermined

During the course of the nineteenth century Great Britain, and later Western Europe, became the industrial centre of the world. A gigantic period of capitalist expansion made them into the factory-centre of the world, and, in particular, of the Eurasian continent. After the second world war it was perfectly clear how greatly this position of industrial Europe was shaken as a result of the political repercussions of a war which had brought about revolutionary changes in Asia and Eastern Europe.

However, it must not be thought that this weakening of Europe's position was brought about in the first place by the second world war. It was, in reality, the outcome of a very long process extending over many years, and the first world war, with all its direct and indirect repercussions, was no more than the first big milestone in it.

Let us investigate certain of the decisive points.

1. Europe's Position in the Colonial Empires.

In the first world war Europe was the battlefield, and Asia and Africa were not directly involved. The victors in the first world war retained their colonial empires. Germany, the vanquished, lost hers, though it was not a very large one. However, the prestige of Europe had already been greatly undermined amongst the coloured peoples of Asia and Africa. For one thing, it was undermined because these

179

peoples—Indian and African soldiers fought in the British and French armies—saw the soldiers of the European imperialist powers mutually slaughtering each other. It was further undermined by the fact that these peoples felt for the first time that they were badly needed by their European masters, not merely their man-power, but also, as in the case of British India, their economic power. It was therefore no accident that movements developed in many parts of the European colonial empires for national independence. Although at first they met with no decisive successes, they nevertheless helped to undermine the position of the European imperialist powers, and they prepared the ground for the great revolutionary changes which were to take place in the period of the second world war.

However, after the first world war the victorious European powers still retained their colonial possessions and were able to renew economic relations with them. But the utmost they could do was to keep what they already had, and their prestige had been greatly damaged by the war. Any extension of their position was quite out of the question.

But precisely an extension was necessary if the position as a whole was to be maintained, because elsewhere there was a noticeable decline.

2. European Expansion in Russia Halted.

Later on we shall investigate to what extent the changes in the social structure of Russia as a result of the November Revolution affected her economic relations with the capitalist world. For our purpose at the moment it is important to note that in the period of the November Revolution and in the subsequent years of the civil war Russia's foreign trade sank away practically to nothing. The following figures [3] show us the trend of development from 1913 up to 1920:

Russia's Foreign Trade
(in millions of 1913 roubles)

Year.	Exports.	Imports.
1913	1,520·1	1,374
1914	835	1,109
1915	274	870
1916	237	862
1917	137	802
1918	7·5	61·1
1919	0·1	3
1920	1·4	28·7

The figures require very little comment. European capitalism lost one of its best markets. The exchange of Europe's industrial products with the agrarian produce and raw materials of Russia had been a very valuable source of profit for Europe.

180

Thus in this respect the war had not merely stopped expansion, but had brought about a great decline. Even later, when the Soviet power was safely established, Russia's foreign trade with the capitalist world never again reached the level of Tsarist days.

3. *Tendencies to Stagnation in Eastern Europe.*

The situation was different with regard to Europe's economic relations with Eastern and South-Eastern Europe, including all the countries which lay between Germany and Russia. At that time the Soviet Union was by no means as strong as she subsequently became when she emerged as a victor from the second world war. In the first world war the Russian armies had been defeated and broken up by the Germans, and after the war Russia was in the throes of civil war. In consequence Russian expansionist tendencies were weak, and the Red Army drive after the war was brought up short before Warsaw. Hungary, it is true, experienced a red dictatorship, but only for a few months.

Thus the sphere of influence of the Soviet Union was confined to a part of the former territories of Tsarist Russia, and the capitalist mode of production continued to prevail in all the countries between Germany and Russia.

Even so, there had been a noticeable change. In the period before the first world war there had been considerable capitalist expansion in the countries formerly ruled by the Austro-Hungarian monarchy. The break-up of Austria-Hungary as a result of the first world war, and the establishment of a group of smaller States, slowed down the rate of this expansion and even in some of them stopped it almost entirely. We shall see later on that the period of stagnation was not confined to the immediate post-war period, but that in the whole following period there was never any capitalist progress in most of these countries at all comparable to that of the pre-war period.

4. *European Countries as Exporters of Capital.*

In the long years before the first world war the leading capitalist countries of Europe were capital exporters to the whole world, and in this period their foreign investments grew tremendously.

The first world war put an end to this process.

During the course of the war itself Europe as a whole lost a very great deal of its capitalist investments abroad. It emerged from the war not only with a much weakened productive apparatus, but also with a greatly reduced volume of foreign investments, and, of course, its revenues from these investments also declined. But—what was still more important—there was no adequate process of recovery: Europe had become so weak that the sum of her capital investments abroad never again reached the level of 1913, the last year before the outbreak of war, and in no subsequent year did her new capitalist exports reach the volume of pre-war capital exports.

Europe as a whole, greatly weakened by the first total war in modern history, by the loss of millions of lives—which hit the industrial countries particularly hard because their birth-rates had constantly been declining—by a decline in production bigger than anything experienced previously, even during the worst economic crises, saw her position in the colonies still more or less intact outwardly but gravely undermined, saw Russia turning her back on the capitalist world, saw her progress in Eastern and South-Eastern Europe halted, or at least slowed down, and saw her position as the leading exporter of capital to the rest of the world profoundly shaken.

Thus, as a result of the first world war, Europe lost her position as the capitalist centre of the world.

THE U.S.A. TAKES EUROPE'S PLACE

Up to the outbreak of the first world war Europe had provided the necessary basis for any analysis of world capitalism and world capitalist development, though even in the years immediately preceding the war this had no longer been completely true. Even before the first world war the United States had experienced a tremendous period of progress, stronger and more rapid than in Europe, but rather more than half the total industrial production of the world had still been concentrated in Europe. It was the war which accelerated the decline of European industrial production and made the trend of development abundantly clear. In a world in which it no longer expanded greatly, it was forced to share its world position; it did not lose it altogether, but it was no longer alone. A new power had come dramatically to the fore: the United States.

At the beginning of large-scale industrial production in the middle of the nineteenth century about half of the total industrial production of the world had been concentrated in Great Britain, but in the meantime industrial supremacy had shifted to the United States, and the process was greatly accelerated by the first world war.

SOCIAL POLARIZATION BEGINS IN EUROPE

When we analysed the fundamental difference between capitalist expansion, which had been largely imperialist, in Europe and capitalist expansion in the United States, which took place largely within U.S. territory, we pointed out that there had been considerable variations in the position of the individual European capitalist countries within the framework of this imperialist drive. Now, what was true of the period before the war was equally true of the period after, when the effects of the war began to make themselves felt.

With the changed relation of industrial Europe towards the rest of the world there were important differences between the victor and the vanquished countries, and there were even bigger differences in the development of the social structure of the various countries.

In this respect the first world war produced fundamental changes as compared with previous capitalist development. To sum up its effects we can say that it greatly accentuated the tendencies towards a polarization of European society. However—and this was to be of some considerable importance for the future—this process varied very considerably as between country and country.

Let us recall certain of our conclusions in Part One. Industrial concentration in the period before the first world war was accompanied by tremendous capitalist progress, including an increase in production as a whole, a strengthening of both home and foreign markets, the creation of new social middle strata, a rise in real wages and an improvement in general living standards.

The Social Structure of Agriculture in Industrial Europe

The process of industrial concentration in the European capitalist countries which preceded the first world war was not accompanied by a similar process in European agriculture, and agricultural property relations and working conditions did not change very much even in the more highly developed capitalist countries.

The social structure of agriculture in the European industrial countries did not change much during the first world war—or the second. In fact, throughout all the economic and political storms of this long period it showed a surprising degree of stability.

After the first world war there were approximately as many agricultural units in industrial Europe as there had been before. The peasants survived the war comparatively well. With certain exceptions, the war was not fought out on the land, and during the war the peasants retained their peace-time middle-strata income.

The war stressed the importance of agricultural production in the belligerent countries, gave the peasants a heightened consciousness of their own importance in society and made them reliable supporters of the capitalist system. Precisely because there was no process of agricultural concentration in Europe throughout this whole period, including the first world war, which was at all comparable with the process of concentration in industry—in contradiction to the prophecies of Karl Marx—and because social tension in agriculture did not materially increase, not even during or after the war, the process of social transformation in Europe was not accompanied and reinforced, as it was in Russia, by an agrarian revolution. On the contrary, the social transformation took place in Europe at a time when the masses of the peasantry were largely in the conservative and even reactionary camp. Thus on the whole this process of social transformation took place against the will of the peasants.

Now, whilst the social structure of agriculture remained largely stable, the situation in industry was very different.

The process of industrial concentration was not held up by the war; on the contrary, it was accelerated. The war demanded the mobilization of great armies of millions of men in the most productive years of their lives, and they were lost to production; at the same time the population had to be provided with at least a minimum of consumer goods; all the war material required had to be produced as well; and constant efforts had to be made to outstrip the enemy. All this could be done only if production were concentrated in the most up-to-date factories, etc., where what man-power was available could be used to the very best advantage. For this reason the process of concentration went faster in the first and second world wars than in peace-time.

The process of industrial concentration need not, in itself, lead to a polarization of society, and we have already seen that in the period before the first world war the great expansion of capitalism and the extension of capitalist production gave rise to counter-factors in Europe.

For instance, in Germany in the years from 1875 to 1907 the H.P. capacity used in industry and handicraft increased from 950,000 to 2,808,000. Of course, this development was accompanied by a big process of industrial concentration, but in the same period German capitalism expanded so greatly, and its production increased so much, that the number of undertakings hardly changed in all those thirty years. There were 2,334,000 undertakings in industry and handicraft in 1875 and 2,251,000 in 1907.[4]

In the first world war the accelerated process of industrial concentration was accompanied by a drop of more than one-third in industrial production as a whole. The greatly reduced productive apparatus of the European industrial countries produced that lesser volume of production in larger production units. That necessarily meant the destruction and liquidation of many smaller units, and the middle strata, which lost a part of their social basis in this fashion, found no appropriate place for themselves elsewhere.

Now, the war led not only to an acceleration of the process of industrial concentration, but also to a considerable degree of impoverishment. It was waged by all the European powers engaged in it with the total use of all their economic resources, and none of them had any considerable reserves of productive capacity or labour power to draw upon. All the European belligerent powers without exception were considerably poorer at the end of the war, and that was true both of victors and vanquished, although it took some time for people to realize the full extent of that impoverishment. The factories, the machinery, the railways, and in general the whole productive mechanism, had been profoundly affected, and agriculture had not been immune. Although pre-war production was reached again in the middle of the twenties, this did not mean that pre-war living standards had again been reached, because a large proportion of the increased production had to be used to make good the direct and indirect damage done by the war to the productive apparatus.

The war resulted directly in great impoverishment for the economic body as a whole, and there was a strong tendency towards a polarization of European society in general, partly because the possessing classes, particularly in continental Europe, did their best to shift the burden of this impoverishment—in other words, the real costs of the war—and place it as far as possible on the shoulders of the lower middle strata and of the working class.

During the war itself this tendency towards social polarization was not so keenly felt, and that was primarily because people realized that production had to be concentrated as far as possible in large-scale undertakings in order to outstrip the enemy. People realized that, in war, production as a whole necessarily declined, and all the disagreeable consequences were blamed on to the war, with the idea that once peace came again everything would soon return to normal, that once peace-time production got into swing the old relation of classes would be restored.

People were all the more willing to believe this because, as far as money was concerned, the process of polarization did not make itself so readily felt. The money income of the middle strata and of the working class increased during the war. It was true that there was not a great deal to buy with this extra money, but that, once again, was put down to the war and its consequences. When the war was over, it was believed, there would no longer be any shortage of commodities, and then the "too high" prices would drop back to normal and the real income of the middle strata and the real wages of the working class would rise again until peace-time levels had been reached.

Inflation Ruined the Urban Middle Strata

As far as the people of continental Europe were concerned, these comforting thoughts proved to be a complete illusion. During the war the "money veil" hid the real situation and concealed the full extent of the impoverishment and devastation brought about by the war. That veil was now torn down.

In France and Germany the war had been financed almost exclusively by the floating of loans. The Germans hoped that after the war the Entente Powers would pay the costs of the war; France hoped that, on the contrary, the Central Powers would pay the piper. They were both mistaken.

When the war did finally end both countries found themselves with a productive apparatus which was no longer able to produce as much as before the war, and with a gigantic burden of debt. Germany's debt was three times as great as her total annual national income before the war. In both countries, therefore, the process of inflation which had begun during the war went on into the peace, though in varying degrees. And with it went the great drama of social polarization in Europe which had begun with the enormous process of industrial concentration during the war.

Germany's enemies did not pay her war debt; it was largely paid by the German workers, who had earned high wages before the war, and by the German middle strata, who had lost the greater part of their savings during the war, and who now found their income paid out in steadily depreciating currency, so that their annual earnings represented only a fraction of what they had been in peace-time. Incidentally, we shall deal with this process in greater detail in Part Three.

As Germany did not pay France's war debts, as expected, the depreciation of the French franc continued rapidly, with the result that the French middle strata and the French working class lost a great deal of their savings, and at the same time their real income diminished as a result of the continued inflation, even though the process never reached the astronomic dimensions it assumed in Germany.

Now, all this meant that whereas in the years before the first world war the process of industrial concentration in the highly developed capitalist centres was accompanied by an increase in working-class living standards to such an extent that large sections of the working class began to live on a middle-class scale, and at the same time by a relative stability in the situation of the urban middle strata, the process of industrial concentration which went on in continental Europe during the first world war and immediately afterwards was accompanied by a great impoverishment of the middle strata and the working class and by a steep reduction in their living standards, not only during the war itself, but in the post-war years as well.

Thus the tendency towards a decline of social antagonisms was abruptly halted by the first world war, by the accelerated process of industrial concentration it brought with it, and by the inflation. The result was that when the world economic crisis broke out in 1929 it engulfed a continental Europe whose social organism was no longer remotely so stable as it had been before the first world war, and which was far less stable than Great Britain's not to mention America's.

What was the difference between developments in Great Britain in this period and those in the industrial countries of continental Europe?

Britain's Greater Social Stability

Social stability throughout this period was stronger in Great Britain than in any of the continental countries. Despite certain tendencies to economic stagnation, Great Britain entered the war as the richest country in Europe. At the same time the social stability of her middle strata was strengthened by the possession of a large empire, whilst, on the whole, the real wages of British workers were higher than those in continental countries. Great Britain and France emerged as victors from the first world war, but, unlike France, British territory had not been devastated, and therefore British industry suffered only indirectly. Before the first world war the total of Britain's foreign investments was about as great as the foreign investments of France and Germany put together. Unlike France, who lost a very considerable part of her foreign investments during the war, and unlike Germany, who lost them practically all, Britain emerged from the war with the bulk of her foreign investments intact. She could thus face the difficult post-war period as a country still rich and still in possession of a large empire.

Once again unlike France and Germany, Great Britain had financed a very considerable proportion of her war expenditure by taxation instead of by loans, and, in addition, she had not reckoned, even during the war, and certainly not after the war, that "the enemy would pay for it all". Great Britain was therefore the only great power in the Old World in which there was no inflation to any material extent either during the war itself or in the post-war years. In consequence, the end of the war saw her middle strata and her working class still largely in possession of their savings. Thus there was no excessive inflation to intensify social antagonisms in Great Britain as there was in both France and Germany.

. . . . . .

The profound disturbances suffered by European capitalism as a whole as a result of the first world war were so great that it was never able to recover from them fully. But during the war, and in the years after the war, the real extent of these disturbances was at first not felt, and therefore not realized. It took a long time for people in Europe to recognize that Europe had lost her former position as the industrial and imperialist centre of the world. It was quite obvious, of course, that Europe's production, and therefore her living standards, had sunk considerably, but that was put down entirely to the war, and it was assumed that in peace-time capitalism would be in a position to repair the ravages fairly quickly. The social changes which had been brought about during the war were regarded in much the same way: as a passing phase entirely due to the war. Peace, it was felt, would bring about a return to "normality".

In addition, as the same classes were still in the saddle at the end of the war, there was no political vacuum, and the political institutions of the victors were not disturbed. There were no revolutions in the victorious countries either during the war or after; there were not even any serious tendencies in that direction. It therefore took years of experience before it began to be generally recognized that a return to the situation which had existed before the war, which was regarded as capitalist "normality", was impossible, and that a fundamental process of transformation had begun.

The situation was very different for Germany and her Austro-Hungarian ally. As a result of military defeat, the old powers lost control of the State, and a political vacuum did arise. On the territory of the former Austro-Hungarian Empire, in which the nationality struggles had endangered the unity of the working-class movement even before the war and greatly weakened its powers of action, this vacuum was soon filled by the establishment of a series of new, so-called succession States.

No Serious Movement for Social Transformation in Germany

The socialist working-class movement was much stronger in Germany before the first world war than in any other country. It was already a consciously political movement at the time of the Franco-Prussian War in 1870. The leaders of that movement came out openly in determined opposition to Bismarck and the ruling classes when the latter continued the war after the collapse of the French Second Empire, and they denounced the annexation of Alsace-Lorraine. The German Social Democratic Party continued to grow rapidly up to the outbreak of the first world war. It was the strongest socialist party not only in Europe, but in the world, and in 1912, at the last general election which took place in Germany before the outbreak of war, almost a third of the electorate voted social democratic. Because the power and influence of reactionary military and feudal junker groups were stronger in Germany than in the other Western European States, the opposition of Social Democracy to the Hohenzollern State was very much more vigorous than the opposition of the working-class parties in the other countries of Western Europe to their governments.

However, working-class living standards had improved under German capitalism too, and, reflecting the exceptionally rapid rate of German industrial development in the last decades before the first world war, wages in Germany had risen so much that there was no longer a very great difference between German and British working-class living standards. For this reason, the opposition on principle to capitalism as such in Germany was no longer so strong. Why fight on principle against a system which had shown that it could considerably improve working-class living standards? And that not only for certain categories of workers, but for the working class as a whole, and not for a few years, but for generations. It was, in fact, primarily this steady upward movement in working-class living standards which persuaded the German social-democratic deputies of the Reichstag,

188

despite all their opposition to the reactionary, feudal characteristics of the Hohenzollern regime, to vote for the war credits.

The war itself brought heavier burdens and greater sacrifices for Germany than it did for the Entente Powers. In relation to her population Germany suffered heavier casualties in both dead and wounded, and the living standards of her people sank lower. However, the upheaval brought about by the war was still not sufficient to unleash any powerful actions against the war. The ranks of German Social Democracy split over the war issue, and a growing minority voted against the war credits, a minority which consisted not only of convinced revolutionary socialists like Liebknecht, but also of pacifists—men like Eduard Bernstein, for example. But the overwhelming majority of the German workers were opposed to any anti-war action during the war. The German workers contented themselves with expressing their opposition to their ruling classes by joining with the Liberals and the Catholic Centre Party in voting for a motion in the Reichstag, against the will of the German Government and the German High Command, for peace without annexations and without indemnities. The majority of German Social Democracy was in favour of such a peace, but together with the so-called Independents, who voted in the Reichstag against war credits, they refused to engage in any direct anti-war action.

Lenin's appeal to turn the imperialist war into a civil war for the overthrow of capitalism was not taken seriously by any influential group in Germany, and therefore the war ended only when the German High Command came to the conclusion that it was not in a position to wage it any longer. Thus the war was ended, as it had been begun, from above, and not from below, and in this respect the situation in Germany was totally different from that in Russia. When the war came to an end the German Army was still fighting everywhere on enemy soil. The war was already over when the Hohenzollern regime collapsed. The two socialist parties (the old Social Democratic Party and the "Independent Socialist" breakaway) came to office as a result of that collapse. Thus the socialist parties in Germany did not come to power as the result of a struggle against a bourgeois regime which desired to continue the war, but as the successors of a regime which had already ended the war.

If after the collapse of the Hohenzollern regime in Germany, and after the desperate situation at the front had become generally known, a German Kerensky government had been formed of bourgeois elements which had tried to continue the war, then it is quite possible that the socialists would have seized power under the slogan of an immediate cessation of hostilities, and that then big sections of the German working class, having won peace in a struggle against a purely bourgeois government, would have demanded a socialist transformation of the capitalist society.

But the situation in Germany was nothing like that. In Russia the slogan "Peace!" had won over millions of soldiers to the cause of the Bolshevists, although those millions were not Bolshevists at all. But such a slogan would have had no meaning in Germany because the war was already over. And, unlike Russia, Germany was no longer a feudal State. There were certainly feudal remnants in Germany, but there was not the slightest sign of any agrarian revolution. The German peasants already had their land, and they were in a position to live on it. Thus the second powerful Bolshevist slogan, "The Land to the Peasants!" had no meaning in Germany either, because the peasants had done fairly well for themselves during the war.

A fundamental social transformation in Germany would have been possible only if advantage had been taken of the collapse of the previous political system in what was the biggest industrial power in Europe to carry through a programme of socialization on a scale big enough to eject the capitalist ruling groups from their decisive economic positions. But the great majority of the German working class, which alone could have carried through such a programme against all opposition and against all sabotage, was not in the least prepared for, nor did it really desire any such action.

Certainly, a large section of the German working class had socialist traditions and had always voted social democratic at the elections. Certainly, this section of the German working class—unlike the workers of the United States—was socialist in that it rejected the capitalist mode of production on principle and hoped that one day it would be replaced by socialism. But even for these German workers the bringing about of socialism was not an immediate task, but rather a task for some future generation. Before the war the majority of them had assumed, together with their leaders, that their living standards could be greatly improved within the framework of capitalism, and, as we have seen, up to a point they were right. They went into the first world war holding these views, and they had not been cured of them at its end.

What they expected of the immediate future was a further period of reforms which would extend their political rights, and social reforms which would improve their wages and working conditions. It is typical of the attitude of the great masses of the German working class that even in the last year of the war the question of the continuation of the monarchy or its abolition was not one which worried them very much; they began to discuss it only after President Wilson's famous Fourteen Points had been published in the autumn of 1918.

The Socialists had no Programme of Action

The majority of the German working class, and their leaders as well, were caught napping by the political and military collapse. The

Social Democrats came to power not after a struggle for power, like the Bolshevists, but because the collapse of the old political order had left a vacuum which they were the only ones capable of filling. Thus they came to power with no idea of the enormous possibilities which that power gave them, and with no clear idea of what to do with it now they had got it. In short, they came to power without a programme.

Of course, the Social Democratic Party had an official programme; it was the famous Erfurt Programme, which had been decisively influenced by Marx and Engels, and that programme contained a section which purported to show why capitalism must lead to socialism. It also contained a list of demands which Social Democracy wished the existing State to carry into execution. But it had no section dealing with the practical action of Social Democracy, once it was in power, to organize and accelerate the process of transformation from a capitalist society to a socialist society.

There was no such thing in 1891, when the Social Democratic Party adopted the Erfurt Programme. The gap was not filled during the period of the first world war, and it was still painfully obvious when the Hohenzollern regime collapsed and the socialists actually did come to power.

The fact that there was no such programme was not by any means an accidental omission. A programme of action for the transformation of capitalism to socialism can be drawn up only when the question of power is real rather than academic. But that had never been the case in Germany or anywhere else in the whole of industrial Europe. Despite certain socialist slogans and socialist hopes, when the first world war broke out, capitalism was seen to be so stable that there was no real question of any socialist transformation of society; the idea was a fond dream, and not an immediate task of the living generation.

The result was that when the social democrats came to power they did a very great deal to liquidate the feudal remnants in Germany (though they did not complete the job) and to develop a political democracy along the lines familiar in the other countries of Western Europe, but they made no serious attempt to bring about any fundamental transformation of capitalism, and Germany remained a capitalist State.

It is thus wrong to talk as though a revolution took place in Germany in 1918. In consequence of the military defeat, the Hohenzollern regime collapsed; that is all.

There was no revolution in Germany, and there was no revolution in any other country in which capitalism was the dominant note of production.

The capitalist mode of production was preserved in Germany, but, as a result of the lost war and the subsequent Treaty of Versailles, it continued to exist under conditions which rapidly aggravated both social antagonisms at home and political tension abroad.

German militarism was defeated and German imperialism was overthrown. Germany was declared solely responsible for the outbreak of the first world war by the Entente Powers, and an attempt was made to hold her down for good and all. German imperialism had an empire, though it was a very small one. This empire was taken away and Germany was deprived of all her colonial possessions. Before the war growing capital exports had reinforced Germany's export industries. During the course of the war Germany lost a considerable part of those investments, and the Versailles Treaty deprived her of the rest. More than that, by the reparations payments imposed on her she was to remain a debtor country for an indefinite future.

German imperialism had made its expansion possible by utilizing Germany's military strength; the Western Allies therefore decreed that her army should be reduced to 100,000 men and her navy to a mere token force. Apart from her imperialist overseas drive, Germany had sought to obtain a sphere of expansion in Eastern and South-Eastern Europe. That was now automatically made very much more difficult by the collapse of the old Austro-Hungarian Empire and the rise of a group of independent succession States. In addition the so-called Little Entente, which consisted in part of remnants of the old Austro-Hungarian Empire, was created and bound to the Western Powers, and to France in particular, by a military alliance.

Now, if German imperialism had been merely the consequence of Germany's feudal past, and made possible by the fact that she had not brought her struggle against feudalism to an end, then everything might have been well. German militarism and German imperialism both lay shattered. France was now militarily stronger than the rest of Europe put together, and Great Britain's world position was no longer threatened by a rising Germany.

It began to look as though only the ruling classes in the vanquished countries had been wrong when they thought that by their victory they could re-shape the imperialist map of the world after they had successfully re-shaped the economic map in the previous decades, and that the ruling classes in the victorious countries had been more realistic. They had entered the first world war without any fear of a socialist revolution, and there had, in fact, been no socialist revolution as a result of the war. They had entered the war to defend their colonial empires, and they had succeeded in doing so. At least, it looked like it, because those empires were still in existence—they were even larger than before, because the colonial possessions of the vanquished powers had been added to them. They had entered the war to prevent any alteration of the imperialist map to the detriment of their interests, and now their only enemy, imperialist Germany, had been utterly defeated.

Certainly, the victorious powers had had to pay a heavy price for their victory, but the defeated countries were now expected to pay back a good deal of it in reparations. Before the outbreak of the first world war the capitalist world had lived in peace, but German militarism and imperialism had destroyed that peace—so went the argument. Germany was the sole guilty party, and now that she had been taught a lesson, and prevented from doing further harm, the way was open for a new long period of peace and prosperity.

It is easy enough to-day to laugh at the preposterous naivete of the beliefs, the ideas, the hopes and the illusions of those days, but it is of more practical importance to recognize their source. There were three main reasons for them.

1. The belief that within the framework of the capitalist system in its then form a German State could have existed without imperialist expansion.

2. The failure to recognize just how profound were the disturbances which the war had brought about for the capitalist system in Europe as a whole, both for the victors and the vanquished—we have already analysed this point.

3. The failure to recognize that quite apart from the profound disturbances caused by the war, European capitalism had already entered into a new phase of development—a phase which was marked by the slowing down of outward expansion—that the first world war itself represented a turning point, that it concluded the historical period of rapid and widespread expansion beyond the frontiers, and that although it was certainly one of the factors which contributed to bringing this process to an end, it was not by any means the only one, a point which is dealt with in Part III.

With regard to the first point, the causes of Germany's imperialist expansion had not been abolished, and the result was that a tremendously dangerous degree of tension continued to exist in Central Europe.

It was not a feudal Hohenzollern whim which had driven German capitalism in a certain historic phase of its development towards imperialist expansion, but the operation of irresistible economic forces.

German imperialism was not an accidental affair. Its dynamic strength was not vested in the fact that Germany had a strong army and a long militarist tradition, and it could therefore not be swept away merely by the defeat and destruction of that army. There were only two ways of getting rid of it: one was by the complete destruction of Germany as a politically independent State, and the other was by the fundamental transformation of her social structure. But the first world war brought neither of these solutions. Germany remained a sovereign, politically independent State, and at the same time—with certain political and social reforms—she remained a capitalist State. The result was that the source of the dangerous tension which had led to war in the first place was not liquidated, but continued to exist.

At first, of course, this was not very evident, because, like the Entente powers, Germany needed some time to repair the damage done by the war and to raise her production to pre-war levels again. But once she had reached this level of production again it gradually became evident that the Versailles "solution" was not a solution at all, and that the operation of foreign-political antagonisms had merely been suspended for a while, and that they would sooner or later break out again with still more murderous intensity.*

In the period of its imperialist expansion German capitalism had advanced at a much greater rate than the other big imperialist countries of Europe. Its defeat in the first world war ended this period of vigorous imperialist expansion, and—a fundamental point —it ended it without any socialist transformation of German society.

The upshot of the first world war destroyed the hopes of Germany's imperialists and capitalists, and it seemed at first to justify the hopes of the ruling classes in the Entente countries. But this, as we know now, was an illusion.

At the same time, however, it also destroyed Lenin's hopes of a German socialist revolution, and of a revolution in any other of the leading European industrial countries.

* It was, of course, no accident that the conviction in the Entente countries of Germany's sole guilt was so deeply rooted. First of all, it is always a good thing for the ruling classes to persuade their people that the other side is solely responsible for the trouble. But, in addition to this, there was a much more important factor: if German militarism and imperialism represented the sole cause of the war, then this was at the same time a verdict of "not guilty" for capitalism as a system. And if capitalism as such had not been responsible for the war, then there was no reason why, once Germany had been utterly defeated, there should not be another long period of peace under capitalism. As far as Germany herself was concerned, all that was necessary to make German militarism appear responsible was to stress the connection between Germany's former semi-feudal political and military structure and her imperialist expansionism, and to gloss over the much more fundamental connection between German capitalism as such and imperialist expansionism. After that Hobson's solution, the abandonment of imperialism—incidentally, a solution which the Entente powers never even dreamed of adopting themselves —could be made to appear as a practical policy for German capitalism. If the peoples could thus be persuaded that the capitalist system as such had little to do with the causes of the first world war, and that the responsibility rested on remnants of earlier social forms—which had been particularly strong in Hohenzollern Germany—then a good deal had been won on the ideological field for the continued existence of the capitalist system. And this was of very great importance, precisely because the disturbances suffered by European capitalism as a result of the war had been so profound.

CHAPTER FOUR

LENIN AND THE NOVEMBER REVOLUTION

Lenin, the leader of the Russian November Revolution, held erroneous views concerning the European working class and their willingness to undertake socialist revolutionary action in the period of the first world war.

Lenin was the real creator of the November Revolution. As David Schub [1] rightly says:

> "Lenin might well have said: 'I created the Bolshevik Party. I was the brain of the November Revolution. Several times when our power seemed about to crumble, I saved it by bold improvisation, by signing an unpopular peace in 1918, by introducing the NEP in 1921. . . .' Lenin could rightfully have said all this, but he never did, for no dictator in history was less vain. In fact he was repelled by all attempts on the part of the men around him to set him on a pedestal."

It was of decisive importance for the future fate of the Russian Revolution just how capitalism was developing in the same period in Europe. At the same time it was of great importance just how the leader of the Russian Revolution summed up European capitalist developments and the attitude of the European working class.

Thus before we go on to discuss the November Revolution itself, we must discover and analyse Lenin's attitude to the situation of capitalism in the European metropolitan countries and to the policy of the socialist working-class parties in Europe.

For Lenin the November Revolution was not an isolated event limited to Russia. It was not something to be kept within the frontiers of Russia. Lenin was profoundly convinced that the war would lead to a world socialist revolution. What had happened in Russia was only a beginning. However, for him a socialist revolution was essentially bound up with a certain degree of maturity and development on the part of capitalist industrialism. For him therefore a real socialist revolution was possible only in industrial Europe, or, at least, in one of the leading industrial countries of Europe. A Russian revolution accompanied by a socialist revolution in industrial Europe might therefore have some reasonable prospect, as part of this revolution, of springing over certain capitalist stages of development.

In other words, if a socialist revolution came about in Europe, then it would no longer be necessary for Russia to pass through all the phases of capitalist development through which the older capitalist countries of Europe had necessarily passed. In alliance with a

195

socialist Europe, Russia could attempt to develop socialist forms of production straight away, without first having developed all the usual capitalist forms.

Thus Lenin's idea was that the Russian Revolution should coincide with·a socialist revolution in Europe, though of course it need not necessarily take place in the same month, or even in the same year. If the specific conditions which existed in Russia allowed it, the Russian Revolution could become a precursor of the socialist revolution in Europe. But for Lenin the decisive significance of the Russian Revolution was that it would be a part of the general socialist revolution which he expected as a result of the first world war. So fixed was this view in his mind that a few months after the victory of the November Revolution, on January 24th, 1918, he declared bluntly: "The final victory of socialism in one country alone is impossible". But he added optimistically: "And now we observe that the socialist revolution is maturing all over the world daily, even hourly".

In the same speech he mentioned the view of Marx and Engels that the victory of socialism in the world would come about by "the French starting the work and the Germans finishing it". And he concluded by observing:

> "Things have come about rather differently to what Marx and Engels expected. The honourable role of being the advance guard of the international socialist revolution has fallen to us, the exploited Russian working class, and we can now see quite clearly how far the development of the revolution will go. The Russians have started the work, the Germans, the French and the British will finish it, and socialism will be victorious." [2]

Thus for Lenin the Russians were just the advance guard; their example was to be followed by the workers of the more highly developed countries. At the time of the Russian November Revolution, and in the months which followed it, he was quite convinced that without a socialist revolution in Europe, or at least in one or other of the advanced industrial countries of Europe, the Russian Revolution would not be able to maintain itself, and in his famous speech to the Seventh Congress of the Russian Communist Party on March 7th, 1918,[3] he declared:

> "If we measure things along world historical lines then there cannot be the slightest doubt about the fact that our revolution would be a hopeless undertaking if it remained alone, if there were no revolutionary movement in other countries. If we, the Bolshevist Party, have taken up the task alone, we have done so in the conviction that the revolution in other countries is maturing, that in the last resort—and not right at the beginning—the international

socialist revolution will break out, despite all the difficulties which we shall have to face, despite all the defeats which we shall suffer, for the revolution is on the march. It will mature fully, because it is maturing now. Our salvation from all our difficulties—and I repeat it again—is the European revolution."

In particular, in Lenin's view, the Russian Revolution was bound up with the German, and in the same speech he declared:

"It is an absolute truth that without the German revolution we shall go under. Perhaps not in Petrograd, perhaps not in Moscow, but in Vladivostock, or in other far-off places to which we shall perhaps have to withdraw, places farther away perhaps than the distance between Petrograd and Moscow, but in any case, and despite all conceivable developments, we shall go under unless the German revolution comes."

He still remained convinced that the first world war would unleash a series of revolutions, and on June 27th, 1918, more than six months after the November Revolution, he declared in his report on the general situation to the Fourth Conference of the Labour Unions and Factory Councils of Moscow:

"Capitalism has led to such a profound and painful collapse that it is now clear to everyone that without a series of difficult and bloody revolutions, of which the Russian Revolution is only the first, only the beginning, the present war will not come to an end."[4]

Thus when Lenin organized and carried out the November Revolution in Russia he did it as part of the world socialist revolution, as a forerunner of the socialist revolution in industrial Europe, or at least in one of the leading industrial countries of Europe.

In other words, Lenin organized and carried out the November Revolution with totally erroneous views on the situation of European capitalism and on its powers of resistance. Lenin's whole life had only one aim, to organize a successful revolution in Russia, but to him, as a staunch internationalist, the revolution in Russia and the revolution in Europe were one and indivisible.

Thus for him the first world war would *necessarily* lead to a socialist revolution in Europe. And the temptation to arrive at this necessary conclusion was so great that he unconsciously made himself a totally false picture of the real situation in industrial Europe and of the real attitude of the European working class, and he put forward that picture as reality again and again.

It is of the utmost importance for us to investigate his views, not only because they were the views of the man who made the Russian Revolution, but because in the upshot they became a factor of primary importance in the struggle between the communists and the socialists which followed.

In the preface of his famous book "The State and Revolution", [5] written after the March Revolution in Russia, Lenin declared:

> "This whole revolution can be understood only as a link in the chain of proletarian socialist revolutions brought about by the imperialist war."

The obvious fact that the overwhelming majority of the working classes in the industrial countries of Europe had supported their own countries during the war was not enough to shake his convictions. It was a heavy blow for him when he learned that on August 4th, 1914, all the social-democratic deputies in the German Reichstag had voted for the war credits. At first the news had seemed quite incredible and he had put it down as an invention of the German propaganda machine.

> "The German Social Democrats, including such fiery anti-militarists as Karl Liebknecht, confounded both Lenin and Zinoviev by voting in favour of the first war credits. When Lenin picked up the Berlin 'Vorwärts' he refused to believe the news.
>
> " 'It is impossible,' he cried out. 'This copy is certainly a forgery. The bourgeois German canaille must have published a special number.' " [6]

But he finally had to believe that it was the truth, and not a German propagandist lie. And he had to realize that what was true of Germany was true of all the other capitalist industrial countries of Europe as well.

But if the workers of all the leading industrial countries of Europe had obviously not the slightest intention of exploiting the war to bring about the overthrow of the capitalist system, thus creating the preliminary conditions for a revolutionary socialist situation, what made Lenin expect them to nevertheless?

He was perfectly well aware that a socialist revolution in any of the capitalist countries of Europe would not stand a chance unless it had the majority of the working class behind it. And when all the socialist parties of Europe refused with one accord to undertake any action against the war such as he recommended, and when instead the overwhelming majority of them placed themselves behind their own capitalist governments, Lenin was in a quandary with his belief in the certainty of a socialist revolution in industrial Europe. He resolved it by declaring that the "corrupt" social-democratic leaders were one thing and the broad masses of the workers another altogether. According to him, these "corrupt" leaders had betrayed socialism and the working class, and therefore the next task was to separate the masses of workers from their treacherous leaders.

He was sure that the masses of the workers would show themselves susceptible to socialist revolutionary slogans. Once they could be separated from their leaders the preliminary conditions for a socialist revolution would be created, because, of course, as he believed, the majority of the workers were in favour of a socialist revolution.

The question now arises: what were the reasons which led the social-democratic leaders to betray socialism and the interests of the overwhelming majority of the working class as, according to Lenin, they did? Lenin has told us in an article written in 1915, and entitled "The Collapse of the International",[7] in which he takes over the ideas developed by Engels and criticized by us:

> "The period of imperialism is the distribution of the world amongst the 'great' and privileged nations, by whom all other nations are oppressed. Scraps of the booty enjoyed by the privileged as a result of this oppression undoubtedly fall to the lot of certain sections of the petty-bourgeoisie and of the aristocracy and bureaucracy of the working class."

Now, how great was the section of the working class which, according to Lenin, received these "scraps of booty"? He has never given us any exact information on the point, but he writes in this same article:

> ". . . these sections, which represent an infinitesimal minority of the proletariat and the working masses."

Such was the situation, according to him, before the outbreak of the first world war, and the fact that "scraps of the booty" fell to the lot of "an infinitesimal minority of the proletariat"—he later called this minority "the aristocracy of labour"—was sufficient reason in his opinion for the rise of the so-called "Revisionist" movement, for the opportunism of the socialist leaders of the working class in the industrial countries of Europe.

Now, during the war this revisionist, opportunist policy of the socialist leaders was continued and took on a new meaning. Lenin writes:

> "Opportunism meant the sacrifice of the fundamental interests of the masses of the workers in favour of the temporary interests of an infinitesimal minority of the workers, or, in other words, the alliance of a section of the working class with the bourgeoisie against the mass of the proletariat. War lends this alliance a particularly obvious and compelling character. Opportunism arose in the course of decades, thanks to the specific characteristics of that epoch of capitalist development, in which a privileged working-class stratum enjoyed a comparatively peaceful and cultured existence which turned them into 'bourgeois', enjoyed certain

199

scraps from the profits of their own national capitalists, and were thus isolated from the misery and sufferings and the revolutionary feelings of the oppressed and impoverished masses. The imperialist war is the direct continuation and completion of this state of affairs because it is a war around the privileges of the great powers, for a re-distribution of the colonies amongst them, and for dominance over other nations. To defend and consolidate their privileged position as an 'upper stratum' of the petty-bourgeoisie or the aristocracy (and bureaucracy) of the working class is the natural continuation of the petty-bourgeois opportunist hopes and the appropriate policy to follow during a war—this is the economic basis of the social imperialism of our day."

Lenin held these views not only during the war and the period of the November Revolution, but also in the subsequent years. In a preface dated July 6th, 1920, to his book "Imperialism, the Highest Stage of Capitalism",[8] which was published during the war, Lenin, after having pointed out that imperialism meant big profits, declared:

"It is clear that with such gigantic extra profits (because the capitalists pocket these profits over and above the profits they squeeze out of the workers of their 'own' country) it is possible to bribe the working-class leaders and an upper stratum of labour aristocracy. And, in fact, they are bribed by the capitalists of the 'progressive' countries, bribed in a thousand and one ways, directly, indirectly, overtly and covertly.

"This stratum of 'bourgeois' workers, or 'aristocracy of labour', totally petty-bourgeois in their incomes, in their way of life and in their whole outlook, is the chief support of the Second International, and in our day the social (not military) chief support of the bourgeoisie, for they are the real agents of the bourgeoisie within the working-class movement, the Labour Lieutenants of the capitalist class, the real vessels of reformism and chauvinism. In the civil war between the proletariat and the bourgeoisie they inevitably—and in no small numbers—take the side of the latter, take the side of 'Versailles' against the Communards.

"Without first having understood the economic roots of this phenomenon, and without appreciating its political and social significance, it is impossible to take even one step towards the solution of the practical tasks of the communist movement and the coming social revolution.

"Imperialism is the eve of the social revolution of the proletariat. That has been confirmed on a world scale since 1917."

Thus according to Lenin the leaders of the social democratic parties were revisionist and opportunist before the war, social chauvinists during the war, and the agents of the bourgeoisie within the working-class movement after the war. They were bribed by the capitalists with "scraps of the booty", and this was made possible by the "extra profits" which resulted from imperialism. They represented an aristocracy of labour, an infinitesimal minority of the working class.

All this, Lenin decided, afforded an opportunity during the war of working to separate the overwhelming majority of the workers from their leaders. It was this which made Lenin reckon with the possibility of the outbreak and success of a socialist revolution in the capitalist countries of Europe.

Our own investigations have already shown us how fundamentally false Lenin's views were. It is simply not true that in the period before the world war only an infinitesimal minority of the working class, a sort of aristocracy of labour, enjoyed higher standards of living. The truth is that the living standards of the whole working class in all the big industrial countries of Europe improved. Of course, there were differences in living standards between one section of the workers and the other, but the important point is that those differences existed within a general trend of improvement for the working class as a whole. There was no exception to this in any industrial country in Europe. It is highly interesting to note that although Lenin publishes a great deal of statistics in his book on imperialism, a striking omission is any table dealing with the movement of the real wages of the industrial workers in the big industrial countries of Europe in the decades which led up to the world war. It is equally interesting to note that the Programme of the Bolshevists and the Programme of the Communist International both remain silent on the point when they do not try to gloss over the question.

It was because Lenin refused to see that the overwhelming majority of the workers enjoyed great improvements in their living standards in the period before the first world war that he was able to imagine such a gaping abyss between the leaders of the working class and the so-called aristocracy of labour on the one hand and the broad masses of the working class on the other, although such a chasm did not exist anywhere in industrial Europe.

Precisely the fact that the epoch of imperialism brought about a decline of social antagonism in the capitalist imperialist countries, and not an intensification, as Lenin imagined, was the reason why reformism—or social chauvinism, as Lenin later called it—was not supported, not merely by a so-called aristocracy of labour, but by the overwhelming majority of the working class. And the result of this was that it proved absolutely impossible for Lenin and his followers to separate the great majority of the workers from their leaders either during the war or after.

When Lenin, from his refuge in Switzerland, assisted in the organization of international conferences of the more radical elements in the working-class movement first at Zimmerwald and then at Kienthal, it became quite obvious that as far as delegates attended from the industrial countries of Europe they enjoyed no very great backing from the workers of those countries. As that was undoubtedly the case, and as the majority of the socialist working class supported their old leaders, even the tremendous and bloody sacrifices of the first world war were not sufficient to make the masses of the workers revolutionary. But as the majority of the workers were not revolutionary and did not become revolutionary, no socialist revolution had any chance in any of the big industrial countries of Europe.

Unfortunately the obvious fact that the necessary conditions for a social revolution were absent simply did not exist for Lenin. It just could not exist for him because it would have undermined the tremendous vigour with which he set about organizing the November Revolution in Russia.

It is a matter of cardinal importance to recognize that whereas no one in Western Europe realized the full significance of the November Revolution, the prime mover in that revolution, during that revolution and to the end of his days, was totally wrong in matters of decisive importance concerning the situation in capitalist Europe, and that he regarded the Russian Revolution as part and parcel of a world socialist revolution which did not come and, by the nature of things, could not come.

Lenin had already formed the main body of his ideas on imperialism and the so-called aristocracy of labour before the outbreak of the first world war. He developed them during the war, but he did not modify or qualify them, although all the events of the war, from the approval of war credits at the beginning of the war right up to the end of the war and on into the post-war period, flatly contradicted his views and his expectations. It was on the basis of these erroneous ideas that he organized the Communist International in order, as he thought, to separate the broad masses of the workers from their leaders and from the aristocracy of labour, which in his view had been corrupted by "scraps" from the extra profits of imperialism. It was Lenin's totally wrong estimate of the situation in the industrial countries of Europe which led him to split the international working-class movement.

Contrary to Lenin's expectations, the November Revolution in Russia remained isolated, because the conditions for a socialist revolution were not present in Europe. Contrary to the expectations of everyone in Western Europe—and contrary to Lenin's own expectations—the Bolshevists succeeded in maintaining themselves in power despite the isolation of their revolution.

The fact that they succeeded in remaining in power, and the fact that they remained isolated, caused the November Revolution to develop in a direction which neither Lenin nor anyone else foresaw.

Lenin organized the November Revolution in Russia at a time when, although European capitalism had been badly shaken, no effective attempt had been made to bring about a radical transformation of capitalist society.

It was the first time in modern history that a war begun "from above" had been ended "from below"—against the will of the ruling classes and, naturally, against the will of Tsarist Russia's allies in the first world war.

And for the first time since the days of the French Revolution an oppressed class rose in revolution and was victorious, thereby releasing a tremendous source of energy.

Four main factors contributed to the victory of the Bolshevists and to their maintenance of power.

1. When the heavy defeats suffered by the Russian arms in the war led to the March Revolution and the overthrow of Tsarism, the new government did not conclude a separate peace with Germany, but attempted to continue the war. From the very beginning of the war Russian soil had been the scene of hostilities. Russia had had to make great sacrifices; she had suffered the heaviest casualties, and the already low living standards of her people had sunk steadily lower and lower. In consequence the longing of the masses of the Russian people for peace was particularly intense. The overthrow of Tsarism was a reflection of this tremendous desire of the people for peace, and of their conviction that they could not hope for peace as long as Tsarism was in power.

When the war continued even after the March Revolution and the Brussilov offensive bogged down in huge further losses, the parties which had been in favour of the continuation of the war rapidly lost the support of the masses of the people, and the Bolshevists, who were only a small party at the time of the March Revolution, as rapidly gained ground, because the great masses of the people felt that whatever else the Bolshevists might do if they got to power, at least they would make peace.

2. Russia was the only big power in Europe in whose territory feudalism was still dominant at the outbreak of war. In 1905 Tsarism had managed to defeat the agrarian revolution, but all the agrarian reforms which had been rather reluctantly and half-heartedly introduced since then had not solved the burning agrarian question or satisfied the hunger of the poor peasants and rural labourers for land. Thus Tsarist Russia entered the first world war with a latent agrarian revolution within it. When Tsarism was overthrown in March 1917 the cry for land arose louder than ever, because now the backbone of landed reaction was broken. The peasants were promised the land after the March Revolution, but no effective steps were taken to give it to them. First of all they were to

203

join in the continued prosecution of the war on the side of the Entente and wait patiently for their land until victory had been won.

The Russian army consisted primarily of peasants and rural labourers, and these men had more interest in the liquidation of feudalism and large-scale landed property and the distribution of the land amongst the peasants and labourers than they had in the continuation of a war which meant very little to them. After the March Revolution they began to get anxious lest if they remained at the front the land would be divided up in their absence and they would go short or get nothing. The result was that they deserted in masses and flooded back to their homes in order to guard their rights when the distribution came.

Now, the Programme of the Bolshevists proposed the expropriation of large-scale landed property, but after that the land was to be socialized, and not divided up in small parcels amongst the individual peasants and landless labourers. But when the Bolshevists realized the tremendous energies which had been released in the rural areas, and the vigour with which the poor peasants and labourers were carrying through the agrarian revolution, which for them was identical with taking the land for themselves, the Bolshevists supported them.

It was these millions of peasants and landless labourers, who had obtained land as a result of the revolution, who subsequently provided the main contingents to the Red Army which defended the revolution so successfully against the counter-revolutionary forces supported by foreign intervention. They fought fiercely for the revolution, not because they were Bolshevists, but because they feared that the defeat of the Bolshevists and the victory of the counter-revolution would mean that they would lose their land again.

3. Thus the Bolshevists, whose sole organized support came from a small section of the working class, won millions of supporters because they were in favour of a separate peace, because they proposed the liquidation of feudalism, and because they supported the immediate distribution of the land amongst the peasants. In addition, for the time being their enemies had been greatly weakened. Tsarism was so corrupt and it had been so profoundly shaken by its military defeats that the feudal elements which were its chief support were unable to summon up any effective resistance. Unlike the capitalist countries of Europe, Russia had no very strong capitalist class, so that when the masses, who wanted peace and land, flocked to the Bolshevists after the March Revolution, the latter had not first to carry out a revolution against the Russian capitalists and their supporters, because they hardly existed; all they had to do was to fill up a political vacuum. The result was that the actual November Revo-

lution, the seizure of power by the Bolshevists, was carried through without very much bloodshed.

4. Once the Bolshevists had been victorious circumstances favoured their retention of power. The November Revolution took place long before the end of the first world war. The year which followed the revolution was a year of bitter fighting on the Western Front, a year in which the Germans drew the greater part of their forces away from the Eastern Front to throw them in for the final decision against the western powers, who were forced to fight desperately to contain the German March offensive. Nevertheless, the year ended with the utter military defeat of Hohenzollern Germany. Thus although the Western Powers did intervene against the Bolshevist Revolution, their intervention was on a very small scale compared with what it might have been had their main military strength not been fully engaged elsewhere.

If the western powers and the central powers had concluded a peace without annexations and without indemnities at the time of the November Revolution, or if the Germans had been victorious—then the intervention against the revolution in Russia would in all probability have taken place on such a scale that it would have overthrown the revolution. But the revolution took place at a time when the European big powers were still locked in bitter combat, and when the war was over Soviet Russia had a defeated Germany as her nearest important neighbour. These were the decisive factors which made it possible for the Bolshevists to retain power.

THE REVOLUTION VICTORIOUS IN THE MOST BACKWARD COUNTRY IN EUROPE

The victory of the November Revolution in Russia led to a radical transformation of Russian society and of the Russian State. The former ruling classes not only lost their political and economic power, but, in so far as they were unsuccessful in getting out of the country, they were to a great extent physically liquidated. The rich landed proprietors lost their land; the capitalists lost their factories; and all foreign capital in the country was confiscated. The new State not only directed and controlled production, but it took possession of the factories, the means of transport and the banks.

Thus the new State held all the commanding positions in the economic system, but it did so in an industrially backward, largely agricultural country. The revolution was victorious in a country whose *per capita* industrial production in the years before the first world war had been one-tenth of Germany's, a country in which the rural population outnumbered the urban population by four or five to one—that is to say in a country in which the numerical relation of the agricultural and urban populations was approximately on a par with the situation in industrial Europe in the year 1800.

When Marx and his followers spoke of the coming socialist revolution they always envisaged it as taking place in the capitalist industrial centre of the world and sending out its radiations into the rest of the world. For instance, writing to Kautzky on November 12th, 1882, and dealing with the phases of a socialist transformation and with the colonies of the imperialist powers, Friedrich Engels [9] declared:

"Once Europe and North America are reorganized they will represent such a colossal power and such an example that the semi-civilized countries will automatically be drawn into their orbit. Economic circumstances alone will bring this about. What social and political phases these countries will then go through until they also become socialist it is difficult to say to-day; we can only set up rather academic hypotheses. Only one thing is certain: the victorious proletariat could not attempt to force good fortune on another people without undermining the basis of its own victory."

Incidentally, the last passage is particularly interesting to-day because it shows very clearly the fundamental difference between the views of Marx and Engels on this point and the current practice of Soviet expansionism.

Marx and Engels expected the socialist transformation to take place in countries in which the industrial workers—the real instrument of socialist revolutionary transformation—represented the majority of the population. But Russia, the country in which the revolution did take place, was not the industrial heart of Europe, and the Russian workers represented only a small minority of the total population.

THE DICTATORSHIP OF THE PROLETARIAT ACCORDING TO MARX

The result of this was that developments in Russia after the revolution were quite different from those expected by Marx and his followers. Precisely because the working class in Russia represented only a small minority of the population at the time of the revolution and in its subsequent phases, the Bolshevists were compelled to break with the principles which had guided Marx in his analysis of the social revolution.

Marx had assumed that the social revolution would take place in an industrial centre in which the working class would represent the "overwhelming" majority of the population on account of the previous "proletarization" of society. He then further assumed that with the victory of the revolution the resistance of the former ruling classes would not have been completely broken, and that therefore a dictatorship of the proletariat would be necessary during a certain transitional period to defend the socialist victory against any counter-revolutionary action on the part of the former ruling classes.

206

Now, for Marx the dictatorship of the proletariat was a transitional phase only—and this is a point of great importance—because, after all, the social revolution was in the interests of the overwhelming majority of the population, and he assumed that before long socialism would effectively demonstrate its superiority over capitalism as a mode of production.

In Russia the November Revolution expropriated the former ruling classes. The landowners lost their land and the capitalists lost their factories. The revolution socialized the main means of production. To this end the Bolshevists used terrorist methods, and they declared that the state of affairs created in this way was the dictatorship of the proletariat which Marx had envisaged. But in reality, from the first stages of the November Revolution on, the terror in Russia was not a proletarian dictatorship as Marx had envisaged it; it was a terror under the dictatorship of the Bolshevist Party, which represented only a section even of the workers.

Precisely because Russia was an industrially backward country, and because therefore a *socialist revolution* was out of the question, a part of the working class, particularly those workers who followed the Menshevists, was opposed to Lenin's policy, and therefore the revolutionary terror waged by Lenin was directed against them as well.

A long and difficult struggle against Tsarism had succeeded in obtaining certain democratic liberties, a certain amount of freedom for the press, for political parties and other organizations, and a certain modicum of individual liberty. And after the March Revolution, though only for a few months, Russia had become one of the freest countries in the world, with freedom of the press, freedom of speech and freedom of organization and assembly. But at the very start of the November Revolution all the liberties won by the March Revolution were abolished, and even all the minor liberties which had been wrested previously from Tsarism in years of hard struggle.

In short, the November Revolution established not the dictatorship of the proletariat but the dictatorship of a political party, the Bolshevist Party.

The November Revolution brought about the most tremendous transformation in Russia for centuries. The old ruling classes were overthrown so thoroughly that every attempt to regain their positions failed miserably. With this the November Revolution released immense energies which had been dormant in the Russian people during the long period of Tsarist oppression, and they now found an outlet and an articulate expression.

Thus on the one hand the November Revolution was a powerful dynamic and progressive force, and as the struggle against feudalism and semi-slavery in the world is not completely at an end even today, it still to some extent remains so.

However, these energies were released in a country whose people had been oppressed for centuries by Tsarism, and who therefore did not know, and could not know, what personal and political freedom really meant.

The Bolshevists did not attempt to guide the people in the direction of personal and political liberty, but to reconcile them with the dictatorship of the Bolshevist Party, and, if this were not entirely successful, then to direct and control them.

The dictatorship of the Bolshevist Party in Russia, which was never a dictatorship of the majority of the Russian people and, in view of the social structure of the country, could not be, was naturally excused in the first place by the plea that it was necessary for the carrying out of the revolutionary transformation and for the suppression of the former ruling classes and all counter-revolutionary elements in general. And as, in fact, the anti-revolutionary elements in Russia, at first supported by the former allies of Tsarist Russia, had to be defeated, the dictatorship was supported in its first stage by numerous socialist and progressive elements which were not Bolshevist or in complete agreement with the Bolshevists.

Once the attempts at intervention and counter-revolution had been defeated, the continuation of the Bolshevist dictatorship was excused by the necessity of preserving the gains of the November Revolution until such time as the socialist revolution was victorious in one of the more highly developed countries of capitalist Europe.

That socialist revolution outside Russia never came about, and the Bolshevist dictatorship remained.

In its subsequent phases the Bolshevist dictatorship, called the dictatorship of the proletariat, had only the name in common with the dictatorship of the proletariat as understood by Marx. In the Soviet Union, as Russia was subsequently called, it was the dictatorship of a political party in a country in which, at the beginning of the revolution, the workers represented only a very small minority of the total population, and in which even to-day, approximately thirty-four years later, they still do not represent the majority of the population. It was a country which was, and still is, industrially backward by comparison with its neighbours, and which therefore first had to build up industry to a dominant place in the economic system.

Although the bolshevist dictatorship in Russia had, as we have said, only the name in common with Marx's ideas, the Bolshevists continued to insist that their attitude was based on Marx's ideas, and they continued to use Marxist terminology. They did this first of all because most of them had had a Marxist training and had gone through the war as Marxists, though with all their utterly erroneous views on the historical situation and on the position of world capitalism; secondly because they were naturally not anxious to expose their own errors; and thirdly because Marxism is still a living force amongst wide sections of the European working class, and therefore by presenting themselves as the real successors of Marx they hoped to strengthen their own influence over these workers.

However, because from the very beginning of the November Revolution they used Marxist terminology for conceptions which were not Marxist at all, they actually contributed to the degeneration of that science of economics which Marx's genius had done so much to develop, and they did a great deal to misrepresent and falsify the real state of affairs in Russia both then and now.

No Marxist analysis of the Russian revolution, of the Russian State and of Russian society has ever been published under the Bolshevist regime in Russia.

The November Revolution broke up the most reactionary State in Europe. The revolution destroyed that State and replaced it by a State of a new type, a State whose real character and content cannot be satisfactorily identified in a sentence or two.

Capitalism was destroyed, destroyed once and for all, in a country which was the least capitalist of all European States. Capitalism never returned in Russia, but its place was not taken by socialism. Lenin was quite well aware of this, and he repeatedly explained why it was so, and why, in fact, anything else had been impossible.

The tremendous transformation of the social and economic system in Russia took place in a country which was culturally and industrially very backward, and which always had, throughout the process of transformation, more highly developed industrial countries at its frontiers. Up to the present day the Soviet Union has not succeeded in fully overcoming the heritage of slavery and industrial backwardness left behind by Tsarism.

The result was that both progressive and reactionary trends went to make up the new State. It is useless to give it a name which is not applicable. It is misleading to stress one aspect of Soviet development at the expense of another. It is not only useless and misleading, but it is dangerous, because a wrong picture of Russia would, in view of her enormous importance for the world as a whole, give us a wrong picture of the world situation and its general trends.

What we must do is to analyse objectively both the reactionary and progressive factors in Russian development from the days of the November Revolution up to the present time, and then we shall be able to see the real Russia, instead of a phantom built up of hopes, fears and emotions, and to give her her rightful place in the general constellation of world forces.

THE NEW CONSTELLATION OF FORCES AFTER THE FIRST WORLD WAR

Let us sum up the result of our investigations so far. The first world war ended with the victory of the Entente Powers over the Central Powers, a victory brought about by the intervention of the United States. Germany suffered total military defeat and the

Hohenzollern regime collapsed. The old Austro-Hungarian monarchy also collapsed. For the moment Germany's imperialist drive into Eastern and South-Eastern Europe and beyond the seas was brought to a stop. At the same time Germany retained her political sovereignty and continued to exist as an independent capitalist State. The victory of the Western Powers was accompanied by the preservation of the capitalist system both amongst the victors and the vanquished countries throughout industrial Europe.

The war showed the working class that capitalism was stronger than they had thought, that they really had no international organization, and that their possibilities of carrying out any independent action were much more restricted than they had previously assumed.

But although capitalism had demonstrated that, after a tremendous period of expansion, it was much stronger than Lenin and the Bolshevists, and many socialists in the industrial countries of Europe, had thought, it had nevertheless received very heavy blows as a result of the war.

1. In a world in which capitalism was dominant, a terrible war, the worst ever, had nevertheless been possible, and it had been fought out primarily between the leading industrial countries of Europe.

2. The war was waged by the industrial countries of Europe with all their resources and all their reserves, whilst non-European countries, and the United States in particular, had been much less involved. In consequence, Europe had begun to lose her position as the capitalist centre of the world.

3. During the war, with its millions of dead, production fell by over a third, and in consequence social antagonisms began to grow, and quite naturally, this process was strongest amongst the vanquished.

Thus the first world war brought European capitalism its most shattering disturbance ever. The first world war also brought the overthrow of Tsarism. The November Revolution was victorious, and it led to the creation of a new type of State, the Soviet Union.

European capitalism, already badly shaken, now no longer had a clearly reactionary State, Russian Tsarism, on its eastern frontier, but a new type of State which was neither capitalist nor socialist, a State which despite its reactionary tendencies also contained extremely powerful progressive elements.

And, on the other hand, to the west it had American capitalism, which had emerged from the first world war enjoying a very much stronger position than before.

In addition to these changes in the relation of forces as between the various big industrial countries, there was a new factor which fundamentally affected the position of world capitalism as a whole.

We have already touched briefly on this point in the last chapter of Part One of this book, when we discussed the reasons which had led to an intensification of foreign-political tension between the European great powers in the period before the outbreak of the first world war. It was the tendency for external capitalist expansion to slow down. And during the war that tendency increased until, in fact, capitalist expansion ceased altogether.

During the war itself this tendency did not make itself felt, and even in the post-war period it was at first not clearly visible, because the great decline in industrial production which had taken place during the war offered an adequate outlet for an extension of production without the need of any outward expansion.

But once that gap had been filled this new factor dominated the whole of subsequent development up to the second world war. Now that we have arrived at an analysis of the period between the two world wars we must deal centrally with this new problem, together with the decisive changes brought about by the war itself.

PART THREE

THE PERIOD OF CAPITALIST STAGNA-
TION BETWEEN THE TWO WORLD
WARS

CHAPTER ONE

CAPITALIST EXPANSION COMES TO A STOP

STAGNATION OF WORLD TRADE

THE FIRST WORLD war concluded an extended period through-out which capitalist progress was never interrupted for very long. That was not so clear to the generation which experienced it, but it is clear enough to-day.

After that war the situation was fundamentally different. Despite temporary and quite considerable advances, the period between the two world wars was, on the whole, a period of stagnation, depression and crisis.

This was true of Europe for the period as a whole. It was true of the United States, whose development had never been fully syn-chronized with that of Europe, from 1929 on.

The development of world trade was symptomatic of the funda-mental difference between the period which led up to the first world war and the period which followed it and led up to the second world war.

Before the first world war, world trade increased constantly; sometimes the rate of increase was rapid, sometimes it was slow, but the general tendency remained the same.

The situation between the two world wars was totally different. World trade varied in this period. After the end of the war, in the twenties, it rose at first, but during the world crisis which broke out in 1929 it dropped more rapidly and farther than it had ever done in previous periods of crisis. The general picture in the whole period between the two world wars was one of stagnation.

Taking 1913 as 100, world trade in 1876–1880 represented only 31·6, and by 1896–1900 it had grown to 55·6. In the comparatively short period from 1900 to 1913 it had thus almost doubled. The situation in the period between the two world wars was very different, as the following table shows:

The Volume of World Trade[1]

(1913 = 100)

Year.	Total volume.	Manufactures.	Primary products.
		(Percentages of 1913 level.)	
1921–1925 .	82·3	76·6	85·8
1926–1930 .	110·1	103·4	114·1
1931–1935 .	95·3	73·5	107·2
1936–1938 .	107·4	92·2	116·6

The reason for this different trend of world trade between the two world wars was, apart from the effects of the first world war, the fact that capitalist development now proceeded in a different historical environment.

The tendency of capitalist development in the period between the two world wars was characterized on the whole by a halt in the process of external capitalist expansion. This was the decisive factor which caused this latter period to differ from the period of capitalist expansion which preceded the first world war. With certain variations, this halt continued throughout the whole period after the first world war, in the immediate post-war period up to the outbreak of the world economic crisis in 1929, during that crisis and in the subsequent years up to the outbreak of the second world war.

We must now analyse this factor in order to create a basis on which we can investigate the whole period between the two world wars.

For a new wave of capitalist expansion in the period between the two world wars, with similar effects to those brought about in the century before the first world war, world capitalism would have had to expand to a much greater extent than ever before. A very simple consideration will show us that this is the case. In the middle of the nineteenth century the proportion of the population of the world producing under capitalist conditions was estimated at about 10 per cent. A degree of expansion sufficient to enlarge this capitalist core of the world by one-tenth would therefore have meant drawing in just one further per cent of the total population of the world into the capitalist orbit.

But, at the time after the great period of capitalist progress, about 30 per cent of the total population of the world produced under capitalist conditions of the first world war. Now, in order to secure the same effects in the period after the first world war as those brought about by the inclusion of a further 1 per cent of the population of the world in 1850, approximately 3 per cent of the population of the world would have had to be drawn into capitalist production.

In other words, in view of the very great growth of the capitalist core of the world, a very much more considerable degree of expansion would have been necessary to produce the results obtained by capitalist expansion in the years before the first world war.

To come to the point at once, there was no such very much greater degree of capitalist expansion; there was not even the same degree of expansion as there had been in former years—in fact, on the whole, expansion came to a halt, and here and there there was even a certain decline.

Why was this?

1. The process in which capitalism had become the dominant and almost the only mode of production in the capitalist metropolitan

countries had already come more or less to a conclusion in the years immediately preceding the first world war. Pre-capitalist forms of production had ceased to be of any very great importance, first in Great Britain and then in Germany. As there was little further possibility of such capitalist expansion at home, an increased volume of expansion beyond the frontiers would have been necessary to redress the balance. In fact, the development tended in the other direction.

2. The November Revolution in Tsarist Russia expropriated not only Russia's capitalists, but also all foreign investments in Russia and repudiated all foreign loans. Of the 35 milliard gold dollars worth of capital invested abroad by the European capitalist States, 3·5 milliard gold dollars worth was invested in Tsarist Russia. Thus with the Russian revolution the European capitalist countries lost about 10 per cent of their total capital invested abroad. But that was not all; far more important was the change which came about in Russia's economic relations to the capitalist world.

In the last decade before the outbreak of the first world war Russia's total foreign trade had increased considerably, and, thanks to their trade with Russia, Europe's export industries had been able to increase their sales and also the number of workers they employed.

The November Revolution put an end to this favourable development. During the civil war which followed the revolution, Russia practically ceased to exist as a market for Europe's exports. But even later on, when Russia's foreign trade began to recover to some extent, Soviet Russia never played the same role for the industrial countries of Europe as Tsarist Russia had played before the first world war. In no single year from 1919 to 1939 did Russia's import figures again reach pre-war levels.

As far as European capitalism was concerned, therefore, the victory of the November Revolution resulted not only in slowing down capitalist expansion, but it even reduced the size of a market for European goods which had previously steadily extended.

3. The first world war brought about a halt in capitalist expansion in Eastern Europe. In the whole period which led up to the first world war there had been a steady expansion of capitalist industry into Eastern Europe. This expansion was carried out chiefly by capitalist Germany, which found it to some extent a substitute for the lack of an adequate colonial empire, but also to a certain extent by the industrially more developed territories of the old Austro-Hungarian monarchy.

The upshot of the first world war led to the breaking up of the old Austro-Hungarian monarchy and the rise of a series of smaller succession States. The rise of these new States between the Soviet Union and Germany greatly slowed down capitalist industrial development in these areas. This was true of the territories which had formerly made up the old Austro-Hungarian monarchy, and of all the other Eastern European countries. The new Austria, with a total population of less than 7 millions, could never again hope to experience any real economic progress.

The same was true of Hungary. In the period before the first world war the industrial production of Hungary increased by approximately 8 per cent annually. In the period which followed the war it increased by no more than about 1 per cent annually.[2]

The experience of the new State of Czechoslovakia was somewhat similar:

"On the whole, the great industrial legacy inherited from Austria could not be maintained at its former level. The industries of the Bohemian countries had been built up for supplying the markets of a wide empire, and they had, in addition, created a large export trade. After the dismemberment of Austria-Hungary most of these industries suffered heavy losses. . . .

"Our study examines the economic development in the new States by means of copious statistical material. It shows that all the efforts to foster, by an extreme protectionism, either the rapid increase of agricultural production or that of industrial output had only a very limited success. Increases of production were smaller than the progress under the former conditions of free trade within the Austro-Hungarian Customs Union. . . . The pre-war amount of income was scarcely ever reached in any country—not even at the peak of the fallacious boom of the late twenties. In the subsequent years the national income everywhere fell rapidly to unprecedented depths, far below the pre-war level, and then recovered only slowly. It can be said that twenty or more years after the outbreak of the Great War the national income per head was everywhere much smaller than before." [3]

In the period in which the United States more or less concluded the conquest of its own vast territory, and developed industrially— amongst other reasons, because its development was not hindered by any customs barriers—more quickly than the much smaller economic units represented by the European capitalist countries, and in the period in which a new social system began to develop in Russia on territory which represented about one-sixth of the surface of the world, there was no tendency towards greater unity in Europe, whilst in the East there was even a strong tendency to "Balkanization"—to the creation of small States cut off from each other by formidable customs barriers.

That represented practically the end of any expansion on the part of Europe's highly developed industrial countries into these areas, though the capitalist system there continued in existence. After the overthrow of the Hungarian Soviet Republic in 1919, capitalism was no longer threatened in these areas at any time between the two world wars. But the rate of expansion which had existed in the century before the first world war no longer existed.

Expansion to Non-European Countries Came to a Stop

Before the first world war industrial and capitalist Europe greatly accelerated industrial development in two non-European countries, Japan and the United States.

Japan took only a formal part in the first world war, and, unlike the European belligerent powers, she suffered practically no losses. Far from being damaged during the war, her productive apparatus was strengthened. During the war she had made large profits from her exports to the Entente countries, and had finished up with an export surplus of about three milliard yen, as an exporter of capital instead of a debtor country, though in this respect her progress had not been comparable with that of the United States.

Like the rest of Asia, Japan in the first stages of her industrial development had been an important sphere of investment for European capital. At that time Japan had belonged to a certain extent to Europe's semi-capitalist periphery, and in 1900 no less than 45·5 [4] per cent of Japan's total imports had come from Europe. As Japan pursued her own industrial development, Europe's share in her imports fell in the years before the first world war to 26·6 per cent (in 1914), or to rather more than a quarter.

This decline of Europe's share in Japan's imports was continued in the period between the two world wars, and in no year in that period did Europe's share reach the pre-war percentage; even in the most favourable years it was still less than one-fifth; in 1925 it was 17·4 per cent, and in 1929 18·9 per cent. Thanks to the general increase in Japan's foreign trade, the absolute figures for European imports remained more or less the same despite their relative decline, but Japan was certainly not an expanding market for Europe.

We have seen that once the capitalist centre of the world had grown from 10 to approximately 30 per cent of the world's total population, an exceptionally heavy drive into the semi-capitalist and non-capitalist periphery would have been necessary to obtain analogous results to those obtained from the middle of the nineteenth century on up to the outbreak of the first world war for a considerably smaller effort.

The development in Japan clearly illustrates our point. Japan became less and less a field for European capitalist expansion, and, as a result, the older capitalist countries had to find some substitute for the lost ground. But at the same time Japan herself became an active participant in the imperialist drive, and in this way, too, she restricted the possibilities of expansion of the older imperialist States.

And what was true of Japan on a small scale was true on a giant, world-historical scale, of the United States.

In order to avoid all misunderstanding, we must point out that for the moment we are dealing with these developments exclusively from a European angle; later we shall deal with them from the American standpoint.

Accelerated by the first world war, a fundamental change had taken place in the world situation of the United States. Formerly the United States had played a great role for Europe as a land of immigration, whilst offering an excellent field of investment for European capital and a steadily growing market for European industrial production.

The situation changed for Europe, even before the outbreak of the world economic crisis in 1929, when the United States drastically changed its immigration laws, and henceforth took only a small fraction of the mass of immigrants it had received in the previous years. Now, in so far as the European industrial countries had been dependent in this respect on America, this meant that the factors which had helped to reduce unemployment greatly diminished in effectiveness and soon ceased to operate at all. It is important to note that this cutting down of immigration applied not only to the United States, but to the American continent as a whole. For example, immigration figures for Canada and the Argentine, even in the period before the 1929 economic crisis, were far below the level of the pre-war years. Thus America as a whole represented a greatly reduced vent for surplus European labour.

At the same time the role of America as a market for the industrial products of the European capitalist countries also greatly declined. The United States had developed from an agricultural country into an industrial country, and then to the leading industrial country in the world. Naturally, the character of its foreign trade also changed. European industrial goods now found a much less ready market in the United States than they had done before the first world war, and the same was true of European capital investments, because the United States had also now become the world's biggest exporter of capital.

In other words, not only did America cease to be a suitable sphere for the expansionist drive of European capitalism beyond its own frontiers, but she herself became a power, and a very big and growing power, interested in foreign markets on her own account. Thus U.S. developments doubly accentuated Europe's difficulties in this period. America was no longer a country open to European immigrants, European industrial goods and European capital, and things were made worse by the fact that she began to appear more and more on the markets of the world as a powerful competitor.

It was the trend of U.S. developments which played the chief role in hampering the extension of the European capitalist centre in this period.

STAGNATION IN THE COLONIAL EMPIRES

In Part One of this book we saw why the process of industrialization and the development of capitalism in the colonial empires of the imperialist States had made only very modest progress.

Thus, from the technical quantitative standpoint it would seem that there were great possibilities for a new wave of expansion, for a new powerful drive of the capitalist mode of production beyond the frontiers of the capitalist metropolitan States.

If the expansion of capitalism into areas which were not fully opened up had had such important repercussions on the capitalist metropolitan centres in the past, then the obvious solution was to continue that expansion.

More than half the total population of the world lived in Asia. There were almost twice as many people living there as in the industrial capitalist centres. In this period Asia was more or less an object of exploitation for the capitalist imperialist metropolitan States, which held all the decisive military, political, economic and financial positions in their hands.

If the Asiatic countries had merely been industrially backward, then capitalist expansion would have operated there as it did in the industrially backward countries which retained their political independence, and nothing would have been more likely than a new wave of progress in the period between the two world wars. Yet nothing of the sort occurred.

The methods of imperialist expansion in the period before the first world war provide the key to the riddle of why there was stagnation in the period between the two world wars in numerous colonial areas.

STAGNATION IN INDIA

Although there were considerable differences in the colonial methods of the European capitalist powers, the basic factors which led to stagnation were all very similar. We have already seen that, against the expectations of Karl Marx, the British did not dream of carrying out any co-ordinated industrialization of India. They had no interest in any such thing in the period before the first world war, and they had no interest in it in the period between the two world wars. Even before the first world war the British had lost their position as the leading industrial power in the world. They therefore sought to organize India as a great market for their industrial goods, and not as a competitor. With the exception of certain branches of industry, they deliberately hampered any total industrialization of India before the first world war. And even during that war industrial development in India was very small in relation to the size of the country and its population. This industrial stagnation continued on the whole in the period between the two world wars. It was precisely the position of advantage which Great Britain had enjoyed so long in her colonial empire which contributed to keeping British industry backward as compared with such modern industrial powers as the United States and Germany. At the same time this relative industrial backwardness of Great Britain was one of the reasons why she continued to hamper any systematic industrialization of India.

Only the industrialization of India on a big scale, together with a very considerable improvement in the living standards of her huge population, could have created new markets. We have already seen that the building of India's railways and the destruction of millions of handicraft undertakings at first provided British export industries with growing markets.

But by the time the first world war broke out the building of India's railway system was more or less completed. The Indian railway network, which totalled about 40,000 miles, was naturally not very large by comparison with that of the U.S.A., but it was big enough for India, which, with her population of 350 million, produced hardly more industrial goods than Australia. Thus when the Indian railway network was first built, growing markets had been created for Great Britain's export industries for a very long period. Stagnation now set in because there was a general stagnation in industrial development in India.

Industrial development in India in this period was so hampered that, according to the census of 1931, the number of Indians engaged in industrial pursuits had fallen from 17·7 millions to 15·3 millions. At the same time the proportion engaged in agriculture rose from 61 per cent in 1891 to 73 per cent in 1921. In 1931 it was still 65·6 per cent, and more than in 1891. The proportion of industrial workers to the total population fell from 5·5 per cent in 1911 to 4·9 per cent in 1921, and to 4·3 per cent in 1931.*

It is quite natural that this stagnation in India's industrial and economic development was reflected in foreign trade figures. Up to 1913 the volume of India's foreign trade had steadily increased, but after that the situation changed. Indian imports in 1913 amounted to 1,833 million rupees. By 1929 they had risen only to 2,408 million rupees. Indian exports in 1913 amounted to 2,442 million rupees. By 1929 they had risen only to 3,108 million rupees. Thus nominally India's foreign trade had increased by about one-third in this period, but, in fact, this increase was purely on paper, because the

---

* Industrial workers in this connection does not mean workers engaged in large-scale factories only, but includes also workers employed in small workshops using no mechanical power. In factories within the meaning of the Factory Act there were only 1·7 million workers in 1931, and even in 1939 the total number of such factories was only 10,466.

wholesale-trade index in Bombay and Calcutta in 1929 showed that prices were then about 50 per cent higher than in 1913.

Thus in actual volume India's foreign trade in this period which preceded the outbreak of the world economic crisis was no greater than it had been in 1913. In other words, India no longer performed her function of providing a growing market for the industrial goods of European imperialism, though the existing market had been more or less maintained.

European imperialist methods can be seen clearly in this artificial hampering of industrial development in the colonies. That was true of India, and it was also true of the colonial empires of all the other imperialist powers.

The situation reflected itself very clearly in the foreign trade of the colonial countries.

The development of industrialization in all the European colonial empires was so backward that the export of manufactured articles from the various colonial countries remained at a very low level.

In overseas territories belonging to the Netherlands the export of manufactured articles in the year 1928 amounted to only 2 per cent of the total exports, and remained at this level in 1935 and 1937, while the import of manufactured articles for the same territories amounted to 60 per cent of the total imports in 1928, fell to 55 per cent in 1935, and rose again to 60 per cent in 1937.[5]

In French overseas territories the export of manufactured articles in the years 1928–1937 varied between 2 and 4 per cent of the total exports, while in the same period imports of manufactured articles varied between 71 and 74 per cent of the total imports.[6]

It was not only in the colonial countries of the European capitalist States that industrial development was very slow in this period; the same thing applied to the other Asiatic countries in which pre-capitalist forms of production still prevailed. China was not a colony of any one particular imperialism, and she retained a certain limited sovereignty. Her population embraced about one-fifth of the total population of the world. Quite clearly tremendous possibilities were present here, and if, despite the halt in industrial development in the colonial empires, a process of industrialization had gone on in China, say at more or less Russian tempo, world capitalism would have found a gigantic market to help it out of its difficulties.

The tremendous possibilities were not taken advantage of.

China re-entered world history not as a sovereign State, like Japan, and not as a colony of an imperialist power, like India, but as a semi-colonial area squabbled over by a number of imperialist countries, primarily Great Britain and Japan, and to a lesser degree Germany, France and the United States. Of course, none of these countries aimed at an organized industrialization of China, or wished to raise the living standards of her people; their interests were purely capitalist: markets for their industrial production, sources of raw materials, and high profits by the use of cheap Chinese labour. Such industry as did develop in China was largely in foreign hands.

"The extent of foreign control over China's economy before July 1937 may be illustrated by the following facts. Foreign controlled coal mines supplied almost half of China's total annual production of some 20 million tons. Most of the iron ore mining in China was controlled by Japanese capital and practically the entire output was earmarked for export to Japan. Out of a total of 5,032,700 cotton spindles in China, the Chinese controlled 2,627,700, the Japanese 2,183,600, and the British 221,300. With regard to cotton looms the figures were: Chinese 25,100, Japanese 30,800, and British 4,000. Foreign interests controlled more than two-thirds of all the steam tonnage engaged in Chinese shipping. China's 6,705 miles of railway had been built almost entirely with foreign capital." [7]

In this period the imperialist powers had not the slightest interest in the creation of a strong central Chinese government; quite the contrary, they felt that such a government would threaten their own position in the country. In this period, therefore, China remained a semi-colonial country, and, in particular, a reactionary parasitic landlord class remained in being and represented, as always, a great obstacle in the path of any systematic development of industrialism.

It should be remembered that this stagnation of industrial development set in on a very much lower level even than that of British India. This can be seen in particular from the fact that China's railway network—the essential condition for any systematic industrialization—remained totally inadequate, and in the thirties it was still only about 6,000 miles, or hardly one-seventh the size of that of India.* Thus it is not surprising that in absolute figures China's industrial production was less than that of Belgium.

Only if this extraordinarily low level of Chinese industrial de-

* "After 1911 the combination of war-lord rivalry, foreign absorption in the world war, and the international bankers consortium, which tended to act as a brake on the investment of both Japanese and other foreign capital, all contributed to the retardation of railroad development. By 1926 the total mileage in China, including Manchuria, was only 7,683, and by 1935 it was still below 10,000 miles. . . .
"The main lesson in the history of Chinese railroad construction is its retardation by an unfavourable social environment in general and, specifically, by lack of capital for investment. The provincial gentry demanded control over railroad construction before the revolution of 1911. But although projects were put forward in fourteen provinces, they were unable to mobilize the requisite capital for actual construction. After the National Government came to power its programme also suffered a stalemate because of the nationalist aversion to foreign financial control and the foreign hesitation to invest without more definite security."
"The United States and China", by John King Fairbank, American Foreign Policy Library, Harvard University Press, Cambridge, Mass., U.S.A., 1948. Pp. 226–227.

velopment is kept in mind will it be possible to appreciate fully the trend in the years between the two world wars.

From 1885 up to the end of the century China's foreign trade had doubled in volume, and it increased at more or less the same rate from 1900 until the outbreak of the first world war.[8]

The following table shows us its development up to the outbreak of the world economic crisis.

China's Foreign Trade
(in millions of Haykwan Taels)

	1913.	1921.	1925.	1929.
Imports . .	570·2	906·1	947·9	1,265·8
Exports . .	403·3	601·3	776·4	1,015·7

There was thus a very considerable increase in the value of China's foreign trade in this period: but, in fact, the increase in actual volume was by no means so great, because there had been a considerable rise in prices. It must also be remembered that the commencing point was very low—much lower even than was the case in India. Despite the increase after the first world war, China's share of world trade amounted to 2·13 per cent in 1929, although China had a population which represented about 20 per cent of the total population of the world.

In relation to world trade and world production, the increase in China's foreign trade, most of which was with Japan and the United States, was infinitesimal.

The result was that in this period world capitalism did not find markets in China important enough to make good the losses suffered elsewhere.

THE ALLIANCE OF IMPERIALISM AND FEUDALISM

We have already seen that one of the reasons for industrial stagnation in the colonial empires of the European powers was that, seeking to consolidate their position without the expenditure of any very great military effort, they allied themselves with the old feudal ruling cliques, which are, and always were, the sworn enemies of any systematic process of industrialization. This imperialist alliance with reactionary feudalism dates back to before the first world war, and it continued in existence after that war, and in the period which led up to the second world war.

The result of the first world war did not seriously threaten the rule of the imperialist powers in their colonial territories, but nevertheless their position had certainly been shaken, and, in particular, the national-revolutionary movements had increased in strength. This was naturally one more reason for the imperialist powers to consolidate their alliance with feudalism, with the reactionary landlord groups. Certain tendencies in British India in the period between the two world wars were typical of the general situation. The following are the census figures for India in 1921 and 1931:

(In millions)

	1921.	1931.
Non-cultivating landlords	3·7	4·1
Cultivators (owners and tenants)	74·6	65·5
Agricultural labourers	21·7	33·5

As a result of the stagnation of industrial development in India the living standards of the great majority of Indians remained appallingly low, and the British therefore sought to improve them to some extent by the introduction of certain agrarian reforms. However, their alliance with the Indian feudal strata seemed to them of such importance for the maintenance of their power that no reforms affecting landed property were allowed to threaten the basis of the feudal system which they had helped to preserve and consolidate, and therefore the report of a Royal Commission on Agriculture in India in 1928 declares: "It will not be within the scope of the Commission's duties to make recommendations regarding the existing systems of land ownership and tenancy". And so, because the alliance of imperialism with feudalism in India remained, the economic life in one of the most important areas of European colonial imperialism continued to stagnate, despite one or two isolated attempts at progress. So long as India remained an imperialist colony and so long as Great Britain supported the reactionary feudal strata in India in order to preserve her own position with a minimum of effort, there was no hope of any fundamental change.

It was therefore only logical and inevitable that the Indian promoters of the so-called Bombay Plan, which was drawn up during the second world war—themselves anti-socialists and the representatives of industrial capitalist development in India—should regard India's political independence as an absolutely necessary condition for any systematic industrialization of the country.

The alliance between imperialism and feudalism was not confined to India; it extended to all the colonial areas throughout Asia, and to China as well. Wherever imperialist powers intervened they supported the reactionary feudal landlord cliques, and what was true of India was true also of China: without a fundamental agrarian reform there was no possibility of any real progress in the industrialization of the country.

There was no such agrarian reform in the colonial areas of Asia or in China in the period between the two world wars, and there could not be under the rule of European colonial imperialism, because that rule was based on an alliance with the reactionary feudal strata who represented the chief obstacle to reform.

Thus in this period there was stagnation in two ways:

1. Unlike the period before the first world war, there was no quantitative expansion of European colonial imperialism. That phase was past for good and all.

2. European imperialism found no compensation for the end of quantitative expansion in an increased rate of development in its colonial empires or in the countries which were semi-colonies. Such progress as was actually made was small in quantity and sporadic in character.

The halt in expansionism did not apply equally to all capitalist countries. In no period of capitalist development was the trend equal in all capitalist countries, and this was also true of the period between the two world wars.

But whilst European imperialist expansion ceased in this period, Japanese and United States expansion continued.

Specific Conditions of Japanese Imperialism

Modern Japan, like the major European industrial nations, developed from feudalism, but whereas the process of transition lasted for centuries in Europe, it was compressed into a few decades in Japan. It was only after the Meiji restoration in 1868 that Japan began to transform her feudal system and build up a modern political and social structure. The Japanese State itself laid the foundation for industrialization and continued to extend its control over it.* Japan never went through a period of liberal capitalism, and the Japanese State has exercised a direct and decisive controlling influence on the nation's economy from the beginning.

The dominance of the State was facilitated by the early emergence of large-scale monopolistic enterprises. Industrial organization in Japan had a strongly monopolistic character from the very beginning.

In Japan, and only in Japan, powerful monopolist concentration went hand in hand with the continued existence of an exceptionally strong feudal sector. The survival of feudal characteristics was particularly evident in the peculiar nature of Japanese land tenure. Japan is a country of small farms, the majority of which are managed by tenant or semi-tenant occupiers. Before the second world war

---

* The contrast between European and Japanese development in this respect has been clearly outlined by E. H. Norman in his book "Japan's Emergence as a Modern State", New York, 1940, p. 110.

"One might say that the mercantile system with its monopoly of trade and its reliance on the absolutist State (as in 16th and 17th century in France and England) was the crutch with which capitalism learned to walk. Grown to full strength European capitalism discarded the crutch, absolute State power, and, finding it a hindrance, turned against it and destroyed it. In Japan the immature capitalist class was unable to dispense with this crutch of absolutist power. . . ."

about 5·5 million [9] families were engaged in agriculture in Japan, and of these about 69 per cent, or nearly a third of the total population of the country, were either tenants who owned no land (27 per cent) or semi-tenant proprietors (42 per cent) who supplemented their own holdings by renting additional land. Only 31 per cent were really owner-cultivators. The base of the pyramid was made up of these tenants and semi-tenant proprietors. At the apex were the landowners who leased out their land to cultivators and did not work it themselves. This group consisted of nearly a million individuals. It has been calculated that about one half of all landowners own only about 9 per cent of the total area of cultivated land, and that about 8 per cent own about half the total area.[10]

The rents demanded of tenant cultivators are very high, often amounting to half the total value of the harvest, and the landlords provide no services whatever in return. Owing to these exorbitant rents and to the character of land tenure in general, with its parcelling of the land into small-holdings, little use can be made of modern agricultural techniques. In consequence the living standards of the agricultural population are very low.

The key position in this structure of Japanese society, with the domination of the State, a high degree of monopolistic concentration and the survival of feudalism in agriculture, was held by the army, whose leaders were drawn from the ruling industrial families and the descendants of the old feudal lords and *samurai*. Japan, like all the big industrial powers of continental Europe, had a system of compulsory military service even in peace-time.

Japan's military caste were well aware of the importance of rapid industrialization. They feared that unless Japan herself quickly became a major power she would be threatened with a fate similar to that of India and China—that, in other words, she might lose her political sovereignty and be reduced to the status of a colony or of a State with only nominal independence.

"The Meiji leaders thought somewhat as follows: 'What do we most need to save us from the fate of China? A modern army and navy. On what does the creation and maintenance of modern armed forces depend? Chiefly on heavy industries, engineering, mining, shipbuilding, in a word, strategic industries.' Thus, the first stage of industrialization in Japan was inextricably interwoven with military problems, and that fixed the pattern for its later evolution." [11]

Japan, with her triumvirate of industrial overlords, landlords and militarists, sought to overcome her industrial backwardness and to create a place for herself amongst the nations of the modern world as quickly as possible. In the intensive process of industrialization which now opened up she was able to skip many intermediate phases through which the older industrial countries had first groped their way.

In the sixties and seventies of the nineteenth century Japan was no more industrially developed than India, but by the beginning of the first world war she had laid a solid basis for industrial development, whilst British India still remained a colony—its industrial progress still subject to the needs of British imperialism. A comparison of Japan's foreign trade with that of India in the last year before the first world war is illuminating.

In 1913 almost two-thirds of Japan's imports consisted of raw materials (49 per cent) and half-finished goods (17 per cent), whilst imports of finished goods amounted to only 17 per cent of the total. In other words, even then Japan's industries were in a position to process the major part of the goods she imported. Indian imports of raw materials and half-finished goods, on the other hand, amounted to less than 6 per cent of the total in the fiscal year 1913–1914, whilst finished goods accounted for no less than 80 per cent of the total. Further, since Japan, as a politically independent State, was master of her own industrialization, half-finished goods amounted to 52 per cent of her exports as early as 1913, and finished goods amounted to 29 per cent, whilst raw materials represented only 8 per cent of the total. India's exports, on the other hand, were made up to nearly 50 per cent by raw materials in the fiscal year 1913–1914, whilst finished goods represented only 23 per cent of the total.

The difference between Japanese and Indian economic development increased steadily.* Even before the first world war the composition of Japan's foreign trade was becoming similar to that of the older industrial nations, and the further development of industrialization in Japan went hand in hand with imperialist expansion.

In this respect Japan was very favourably situated; Korea, Manchuria and China were, so to speak, on her own doorstep, whilst the colonial areas of the European imperialist powers were thousands of miles away from the metropolitan centres. Thus Japan's army had a much greater and more direct role to play in the process of imperialist expansion than the armies of the European imperialist powers.

Japan was much less industrially developed than the big imperialist countries of Europe when she began her imperialist expansion. Even as late as 1928 she accounted for only 2·35 per cent of

* "A governing group which understood its people and really cared for their welfare should make an effort to teach them better ways of earning a living, and this the Japanese Government tried to do, and as a result the Japanese are about two generations in advance of India. Whilst Indian craftsmen were literally starving, unemployed Japanese of the same group were learning to operate modern machinery. Often this was set up by the government itself for demonstration to both capitalists and labourers; and as soon as possible the home market was preserved for home producers." D. H. Buchanan, "The Development of Capitalist Enterprise in India", 1934, p. 471.

world production, as compared with 11·55 per cent for Germany, 9·26 per cent for Great Britain, and 7 per cent for France. This industrially weak position of Japan in relation to the other big imperialist States was one of the decisive reasons why Japanese imperialism set itself, had to set itself, other aims.

When Great Britain and France founded their empires they were both already leading industrial countries, and their empires were not built up with the express intention of strengthening their own industrial position. Japan was in a very different situation. The aim of Japanese capitalism, which developed much later than its European counterparts, was to speed up its rate of development as quickly as possible in order to reduce the gap between Japan and the other capitalist countries, and to become as strong as, if not stronger than, they were.

However, existing conditions were not too favourable for this aim, in particular because Japan lacked certain strategic raw materials, or possessed them only in inadequate quantities, such as coal and iron. Japan therefore turned to her empire for assistance in accelerating the speed of her own industrial development. In consequence, her imperialist economic policy was analogous to that of the other imperialist powers only in certain points, whilst in others it was fundamentally different.

Like the European States, Japan held the key economic and political positions in her empire, and both the Japanese and European imperialists deliberately retained agrarian feudalism in their colonial territories. Like their European counterparts, the Japanese imperialists allied themselves with the existing strata of rich landed proprietors in their empire. But despite all these similarities, the economic policy of Japanese imperialism was quite different to that of the European imperialist powers because Japan looked to her empire for support in her development into a world power.

Japan's economic policy can be seen very clearly in Manchuria. In the ten years which passed between her first penetration into Manchuria and her entry into the second world war, Japan pushed on rapidly with the industrialization of Manchuria and, though to a lesser extent, other parts of her empire. In those ten years from 1931 to 1941 Japanese imperialism worked to such purpose that although the population of Manchuria is only about one tenth that of India, just as much as, if not more, industry was built up there than Great Britain had built up in India in a century of imperialist rule.

Of course, the Japanese imperialists did not do this in the interests of the Chinese population of Manchuria. They developed the production of coal, iron and oil there because at home they could not produce enough of these essential things to meet their own needs. They also built factories in Manchuria for the production of tank and aeroplane parts, because the role they had in mind for Manchuria in the event of war was that of an armaments base for Japanese forces operating on the Asiatic mainland. In short, the given historical conditions in which Japanese imperialism developed caused it to encourage the development of industrialization in its colonial territories. The very different historical conditions in which European imperialism developed caused it to prevent, or retard where total prevention was impossible, industrial development in its colonial empires.

We have already pointed out that otherwise valuable investigations into imperialism have been vitiated by the fact that though they were restricted to specific conditions existing in a particular country in a particular period, they drew general conclusions concerning imperialism in other countries and in other periods. The very summary observations we have made here concerning Japanese imperialism, and the striking differences between it and European imperialism, sufficiently indicate the inadequacy of any such method of analysis.

For instance, British and Japanese imperialism differed fundamentally not only in the aims of their economic policies, but also in the methods they adopted to pursue them. This was due, above all, to the fact that in this period the influence of the State on the economic system in Japan was much greater than it was in Great Britain or, in fact, in any other European imperialist country.

Like all other European imperialist countries, Great Britain founded and extended her colonial empire in a period of liberal capitalism, and at that time there was no central State power which directed and controlled the economic system. The idea that the State should intervene to guide Indian economic development along planned lines would have seemed ridiculous to Victorian England.

In Japan the situation was quite different. The feudal State continued to exist well into the second half of the nineteenth century, and it remained a decisive factor even when modern capitalist development began. In Japan the first steps to encourage industry were taken by the State, and there was no long phase of liberal capitalism. The modern Japanese imperialist State developed straight from the old feudal State, and powerful monopolistic tendencies arose from the very beginning. Thus Japanese imperalism developed at a time when the State already played a dominant role in the direction and control of the economic system. State organs for economic planning had already been established, and thus it was a simple matter to translate this system of economic planning from the Japanese mainland to the colonial areas, and to harness the industrial development of the latter to the needs of the former.

The course of industrial development in Manchuria—or Manchukuo as it was later called—was deliberately planned from the beginning to fit in with the industrial development of Japan so that the two should go forward together as an integrated whole.

"At the beginning of 1937 Manchukuo announced a Five-Year Plan for industrial and agricultural development. In April 1938 its aims were revised upwards. In the meantime there were Five-Year Plans in Japan for iron and steel, pulp, salt, gold, aluminium and other commodities. Then these various plans were merged." [12]

Thus Japanese development added a new chapter to the history of imperialism. Up to the time of the second world war there was no planned economy in the imperialist countries of Europe, and therefore there was none in their colonial territories either. Japan was the only capitalist country which had a system of planned economy at home, and she translated this system to her colonial territories. This Japanese imperialist planned economy was supported by a rapidly growing volume of trade between Japan and those territories.

"Japan completely dominates the trade of her two major colonies. Nearly 90 per cent of the exports and more than 80 per cent of the imports of both Korea and Formosa arise from trade with Japan." [13]

After her invasion of Manchuria, Japan's share in Manchurian foreign trade rose from 25·5 per cent in 1908 to over 70 per cent in the thirties, when she was urgently pressing on with the industrialization of the country.

Over and above this growth of Japan's foreign trade with her own colonial territories, her share of the foreign trade of the Asiatic countries generally increased. That applied to China's foreign trade, and it also applied to the foreign trade of the colonial empires of Europe.

For example, China's imports [14] from Japan, which had been worth on an average 132·9 million standard dollars, or 17·8 per cent of the whole, in the years 1900–1913, rose to an average of 490·1 million standard dollars, or 28·4 per cent, in the years 1925–1929. In the same period China's imports from Great Britain declined from 16·7 per cent of the whole to 9·8 per cent, whilst China's imports from Hong-Kong declined from 33 per cent to 10·3 per cent.

In 1913 India obtained no less than 64·2 per cent of her total imports from Great Britain, or goods to the value of 1,176 million rupees. But during the twenties Great Britain was hardly able to maintain the rupee value of her exports to India at pre-war level. Indian imports from Great Britain amounted to 1,153 million rupees in 1925, 1,192 million rupees in 1927, and 1,031 million rupees in 1929. As the value of the rupee in the twenties was less than in 1913, this meant that imports from Great Britain had declined in volume, and, in fact, as percentages of the whole, Great Britain's share fell from 51 per cent in 1925 to 47·7 per cent in 1927, and to 42·8 per cent in 1929.

But the development of India's import trade with Japan was very different in trend, as the following figures indicate: in 1913 India imported from Japan goods to the value of 48 million rupees, or 2·6 per cent of the whole. The figures for 1925 were 182 million rupees or 28 per cent; for 1927, 179 million rupees or 7·2 per cent; and for 1929, 236 million rupees or 9·8 per cent.

In other words, in so far as there was any expansion in Asia, Japanese capitalism reaped the major benefit.

But even in this period, Japan, including her empire, was still a third-class power, and in so far as she directly increased the stagnation tendencies of European imperialist expansion her influence was not of any very great account.

THE EFFECT OF U.S. EXPANSION

In this period the United States, which was already by far the most powerful industrial country in the world, proceeded to win a new position for herself on the world markets, and in the process the position of European capitalism and imperialism was seriously affected.

The halt in the process of European expansion beyond the frontiers coincided approximately with the end of the conquest of America by U.S. capitalism. But the latter did not stop its expansion when it had reached the limit of territorial possibilities at home; it then proceeded to expand beyond its own frontiers. And it started this at a time when the capitalist and imperialist expansion of the big industrial countries of Europe into Eastern Europe and Asia had more or less come to a standstill and was even declining. Even at that time U.S. capitalism was already in a much stronger economic position than European capitalism.

Thus not only did the United States cease to be an area into which European capitalism could expand, thereby increasing the tendencies towards stagnation from which European capitalism was already suffering, but she also, like Japan, began an expansion into the pre-capitalist and semi-capitalist colonial areas on her own account, and this expansion became a factor of primary importance for subsequent developments, because the United States was not on a level with Japan, whose share in the total industrial production of the world amounted only to between 2 and 3 per cent, whereas America's share in the total industrial production of the world was no less than 30 per cent even in 1913.

Thus although it is more or less true of Europe that the period of imperialist expansion ended approximately with the first world war, it was certainly not true either of Japan or the United States.

When U.S. capitalism had finished its territorial expansion at home, it turned its attention outward, and a strong American drive started up into the pre-capitalist areas of the world, and as this new development coincided with the slowing down of European imperialist expansion, it naturally greatly reinforced the tendency. However, U.S. expansion beyond the frontiers into the outside world never played anything like the decisive role which had formerly been played by U.S. expansion within its own frontiers, or by European imperialist expansion abroad, and that, as we shall see, was a decisive factor not only for the United States, but for the rest of the world.

There were two spheres which had previously been more or less controlled by European imperialism into which the United States now penetrated more and more vigorously: the whole American continent, outside the United States, and Asia.

Quite apart from the fact that during the war, when Europe's industries declined, America's industries grew stronger, the United States was greatly favoured in its drive beyond its own frontiers by the fact that in the meantime it had become a creditor State instead of, as previously, a debtor State. In the period from the end of the first world war up to the outbreak of the world economic crisis in 1929, U.S. capital exports were greater than those of the rest of the capitalist world put together.

> "From 1919 to 1929 foreign loans floated in the United States provided some 7,500 million dollars worth of new capital to other countries, or more than the total of similar issues floated in the United Kingdom, France, the Netherlands and all other capital-lending countries combined." [15]

As at that time by far the major part of British capital exports went to the Dominions and other countries of the British Empire, this meant that U.S. expansion outside the British Empire was greatly strengthened because it was now vigorously reinforced by capital exports. This was true in particular of the American continent, outside the United States, and of China, whose foreign trade increased quite considerably in this period, though the major benefits no longer went to the European powers, but to the United States.

U.S. INFLUENCE IN SOUTH AMERICA

A few examples will illustrate our thesis. Let us begin with South America, and first of all the Argentine. Total Argentinian imports in millions of gold pesetas were as follows:

1913.	1923.	1925.	1927.	1929.
496·2	868·4	876·8	856·8	862

The following table shows us how these imports were divided according to country of origin and that country's percentage share of the whole:

	1913.	1923.	1925.	1927.	1929.
(in millions of gold pesetas)					
Great Britain .	154·1	206·6	191·6	166·5	152
Germany. .	83·9	118·2	100·8	97	99·1
France . .	44·8	58·5	59·8	59·2	52·8
United States .	73	181·4	206·3	217·8	227·2
(percentages of the whole)					
Great Britain .	31·1	23·8	21·9	19·4	17·6
Germany. .	16·9	13·6	11·5	11·3	11·5
France . .	9	6·7	6·8	6·9	6·1
United States .	14·7	20·9	23·5	25·4	26·4

Before the first world war more than half the total Argentinian imports came from the three leading industrial countries of Europe, and Great Britain provided about a third of the total. In the twenties, however, the total share of these three countries was only a third of the whole, and Great Britain's share was less than one-fifth of the whole. On the other hand, the share of the United States had increased to more than a quarter of the whole.

The situation in the other countries of South America was very much the same. In 1913 Brazilian imports totalled 67·2 million pounds; in 1927 79·6 million pounds, and in 1929 86·7 million pounds. Great Britain's share in 1913 amounted to 24·4 per cent, in 1927 to 21·2 per cent, and in 1929 to only 19·1 per cent. The respective percentages for Germany were 17·4, 10·7 and 12·7, and for France 9·8, 6·3 and 5·3. The percentages for the United States were 15·8, 28·6 and 30·1.

Total Chilean imports were worth 989 million gold pesos in 1913, 1,073 million in 1927, and 1,617 million in 1929. Great Britain's percentage shares in the three years in question were 29·9, 18·4 and 17·7. Germany's shares were 24·6, 12·6 and 15·5. France's shares were 5·5, 5·1 and 4·4. On the other hand, the share of the United States steadily rose, being 16·7, 29·6 and 32·2 per cent.

Before the first world war no less than 60 per cent of all Chilean imports came from the three leading European industrial countries, and only one-sixth from the United States. Towards the end of the twenties, however, the share of the United States was over 30 per cent, and almost as big as the combined shares of Great Britain, Germany and France.

In the first post-war period Canada's imports increased considerably. In 1913 their total value amounted to 619·2 million dollars; but in 1927 they were 1,109 million dollars, and in 1929 1,246·3 million dollars. Even before the first world war the United States was at the head of the list of countries exporting to Canada. In 1913 the U.S. share of Canada's imports amounted to 64 per cent; by 1927 it was 64·9, and in 1929 67·9, whilst in the same years Great Britain's percentage shares were 21·4, 16·7 and 15·2. Europe had hardly any share in the considerable growth of Canada's import trade, and Europe's percentage share of the total continued to fall.

In Mexico the situation was very similar. Here, too, the United States was in the lead even before the first world war, and after it she strengthened her position at the expense of the European powers. Total Mexican imports in 1913 were 192·3 million pesos, in 1927 346·4 million pesos, and in 1929 382·2 million pesos. The share of the United States in these imports amounted to 50·6 per cent in 1913, to 67·2 per cent in 1927 and to 69·1 per cent in 1929. Great Britain's share declined from 13·5 per cent in 1913 to 6·5 per cent in 1927, and rose slightly in 1929 to 6·7 per cent. Germany's share declined from 13·1 per cent in 1913 to 8·5 per cent in 1927 and 8 per cent in 1929. France's share declined from 9·5 per cent in 1913 to 4·9 per cent in 1927, and rose slightly in 1929 to 5 per cent.

These examples are sufficient to indicate the trend, which was general everywhere on the American continent. In the years following the first world war there was general economic improvement throughout the American continent, but European countries had very little share in it, and for them the days of pre-war expansion were over. With the United States the situation was very different; the general improvement offered considerable possibilities for expansion, and U.S. foreign trade with these countries greatly increased.

Central and South America were at one time important components of the general pre-capitalist and semi-capitalist periphery of the European capitalist imperialist States, and in some cases Central and South American countries were so dependent on them as to be practically semi-colonies. After the first world war the stagnation of European capitalist expansion in Europe and the colonial empires was accompanied by stagnation, as far as European capitalism was concerned, throughout the American continent.

The development of the situation in China was very similar. In so far as there was any improvement and any increased volume of foreign trade despite the civil war, the United States and Japan practically shared it between them, whereby the greater share went to the former. The share of the United States in China's foreign trade increased threefold, from 6 per cent in 1913 to 18 per cent in 1929. In the same period China's imports from Great Britain and Germany remained practically stationary.

We have now covered the whole world in order to obtain as complete a picture as possible of the essential factors which distinguished the period after the first world war from the period which ended with it. Let us summarize our conclusions.

One of the most important trends in capitalist development in the century before the first world war was that growing industrial concentration was accompanied by a tremendous volume of expansion, as a result of which a greater and greater area of the world, consisting in part of almost uninhabited districts and in part of pre-capitalist districts, was drawn into the operations of the capitalist system, so that the percentage of the population of the world living and working under capitalist methods of production rose from 10 per cent in 1850 to between 25 and 30 per cent in 1914.

But in the period which followed the first world war the process of capitalist expansion came to a halt for world capitalism as a whole, though the European capitalist States were far more deeply affected than the United States and Japan.

In addition, European imperialist capitalism, which had created an enormous pre-capitalist and semi-capitalist periphery around itself, now saw itself faced with a new and hostile principle in Russia, where the Bolshevist November Revolution had been successful and had broken away from the capitalist world and upset its former trading relations with Russia. Further, in Eastern Europe, in the countries between Russia and Germany, European capitalism found itself up against a political "Balkanization" which greatly diminished the rate of industrial development in those countries, and thus hampered its own expansion. And in the colonial empires European capitalism was faced—on account of its own parasitic policy towards the colonial countries—with industrial stagnation, and thus its expansion was halted in this direction too. At the same time there were no longer any unclaimed areas which would have made a quantitative strengthening of the colonial empires possible.

A halt to European capitalist expansion had also been called in countries like the United States and Japan, which before the war had contributed to its progress as markets for industrial products and machinery, as fields for the investment of its capital, and as areas to which its surplus man-power could emigrate. In other words, both the United States and Japan had ceased to be objects of European imperialist expansion. And further, these two countries, whose capitalist industrial development had been greatly accelerated by the first world war, now began to penetrate into backward, under-developed areas on their own account.

The expansion of European capitalism in China was also halted, although there, unlike in India, there was a certain upward trend after the first world war, which was, however, largely monopolized by the United States and Japan.

The same thing applied to the American continent, although here, too, there had been quite considerable economic improvement after

237

the first world war, but once again it was the United States which benefited from it, and not the European capitalist countries.

The halt in European capitalist imperialist expansion coincided more or less with the conclusion of the process in which U.S. capitalism had completely opened up its own territory—that is to say, at a time when European capitalist expansion beyond its own frontiers had come to an end, United States capitalism began to expand more and more vigorously beyond its own frontiers, whilst its influence on the American continent and in Asia grew rapidly. Thus in the early post-war period United States capitalism found a certain compensation for its inability to expand any farther within its own frontiers by expanding instead over the American continent and into Asia, quite apart from its capital exports to Europe in the same period, which were on a large scale.

However, we have already pointed out that any assumption that this U.S. capitalist expansion beyond its own frontiers must necessarily have similar effects in the United States to those brought about in the European industrial countries by their outward expansion, would be totally erroneous.

The United States entered this period of vigorous outward expansion at a time when its productive apparatus was very much stronger than that of any single European great power, and therefore, even with a large-scale drive of U.S. capitalism beyond its own frontiers, U.S. foreign-trade figures were still very much less important in relation to U.S. production as a whole than had previously been the case with European foreign-trade figures in relation to European production. U.S. foreign trade never amounted to even 10 per cent of U.S. production as a whole.

The situation with regard to Japan was different. For Japan, too, the period in which European capitalism's outward expansion came to a halt was a period of vigorous outward expansion for Japanese capitalism, and as Japan's productive apparatus was relatively small, Japanese imperialist expansion on the Asiatic continent—which was a contributory factor to European imperialist stagnation—had quite important effects at home, and that was one of the reasons why Japanese capitalist development up to the outbreak of the world economic crisis was different from European capitalist development, and why Japan was less affected by that crisis than the European countries, and managed to surmount it more rapidly and more thoroughly than they did.

Capitalist development on all fields was decisively affected by the tremendous process of expansion which took place in the nineteenth century and lasted approximately up to the outbreak of the first world war.

We must now discover just how the ending of this great period of expansion—which affected the United States very considerably and the European capitalist States to a very much greater extent, and which operated in the period before the world economic crisis, during the crisis itself and after the crisis up to the outbreak of the second world war—affected capitalist development as a whole in the period between the two world wars.*

CHAPTER TWO

BEFORE THE WORLD ECONOMIC CRISIS

THE MOST STRIKING feature of the development of world capitalism in the period up to the first world war was perhaps its general uniformity.

In the development of the world economic system—we are now compelled to use the term world economic system rather than world capitalism—after the first world war it was the lack of uniformity which was often most striking, though, of course, certain common tendencies still existed.

This lack of uniformity was primarily caused by three factors:

1. The United States, which had hardly been affected by the war, entered the post-war period with increased industrial and financial strength—unlike the European countries—and at first its progress continued.

2. As a result of the first world war the Soviet Union appeared on the scene as a unique social organism and a breakaway from capitalism, and its development followed its own laws, and was no longer in the least in accordance with the developments in capitalist countries.

3. The degree of social disturbance suffered by the European capitalist countries as a result of the first world war varied very considerably as between the victors and the vanquished.

* In the twenties, before the outbreak of the world economic crisis, the author was already dealing with this problem. Chapter III of his book on imperialism (Fritz Sternberg, "Der Imperialismus", Malik Verlag, Berlin 1926), entitled "The Economic Crisis of Imperialism", analyses the gradual slowing down of imperialist and capitalist expansion in much the same way as we have done here and then raises the question:

"Will the crisis cycle, which we must now expect, be of a character similar to that of the crises in the pre-war period, or have the quantitative changes already become so great that we are now entering into a new phase of the crisis cycle?"

And after investigating the question was answered:

"We are now living in an epoch in which the intensification of the economic crises goes parallel with the intensification of the political crises."

And further:

"The intensification of the economic crises increases the probability of war."

239

At first the United States seemed to continue its capitalist advance in the same way as it had done in the years before the first world war.

The United States had emerged from the war with increased production on almost all fields. The total national product in 1918 was 115 as compared with 100 in 1914, readjusted according to 1914 prices.[1]

The period of depression experienced in the United States in 1920–1921 was only temporary, and production did not fall very considerably. Even after the depression U.S. production was higher than the 1914 level, whereas in Europe after the war production was only two-thirds of the pre-war volume.

Now, although the level of U.S. production was already very high compared with Europe's production, the twenties saw a new tremendous rise both in production itself and in productive capacity. According to the index of the Federal Reserve Board (1935–1939 = 100), production in 1922 had already reached 74, as against 72 in 1919; it rose to 90 in 1925, to 99 in 1928, and reached its climax at 110 in 1929.

Whilst the industrial countries of Europe were struggling to reach the pre-war level of production, U.S. production, which was already above pre-war level in 1919, continued to rise so rapidly that immediately before the outbreak of the world economic crisis U.S. industrial production was almost twice as high as it had been in 1914.[2]

Even before the first world war industrial development in the U.S.A. had proceeded more rapidly than in Europe, and in the period from the first world war to the outbreak of the economic crisis this tendency was even more marked.

We can perhaps best illustrate this exceptionally rapid industrial development by a comparison of U.S. industrial production with that of Germany, which even before the first world war took second place in world production behind the United States.

German Industrial Production as a Percentage of U.S. Industrial Production [3]

Year.	Percentage.
1870	90 .
1900	48
1913 (old frontiers)	40
1913 (new frontiers)	36
1929	23·9

German industrial production, which had been almost as big as that of the U.S.A. in 1870, fell around 1900 to less than half, and was rather less than a quarter after the first world war.

The tremendous increase of U.S. production and the great growth of productive capacity were accompanied by a growing process of industrial concentration. Even during the first world war it was much greater in the United States than in any of the European industrial countries. As in Europe, the tendency towards industrial concentration was strengthened by the effects of war economy during the war years, and it continued beyond the war into the twenties.

Despite the exceptional importance of this process of industrial concentration, we need not describe it in any detail, because the facts are generally known. In the period before the outbreak of the world economic crisis the process of concentration in the United States had already gone so far that about 200 big industrial corporations exercised a decisive influence on the country's economic life.

"Nearly all these companies had assets of over one hundred million dollars, and fifteen of them had assets of over a milliard dollars. . . .

"When we compare the combined assets of the 200 largest non-banking corporations with the assets of all non-banking corporations, their dominant role is further emphasized. These companies, 42 railroads, 52 public utilities, and 106 industrials, each with assets over 90 million dollars, had combined assets at the beginning of 1930 of 81,074 million dollars. According to an estimate based on income-tax figures, the total assets of all non-banking corporations at the beginning of 1930 amounted to 165,000 million dollars. *Thus 200 big companies controlled 49·2 per cent, or nearly half, of all non-banking corporate wealth, while the remaining half was owned by more than 300,000 smaller companies. . . .* *

"The influence of the larger company on prices is often greatly increased by its mere size, even though it does not begin to approach a monopoly. Its political influence may be tremendous. Therefore, if roughly half of corporate wealth is controlled by 200 large corporations, and half by smaller companies, it is fair to assume that very much more than half of industry is dominated by these great units. This concentration is made even more significant when it is recalled that as a result of it, approximately 2,000 individuals out of a population of 125 millions are in a position to control and direct half of industry." [4]

For our purposes it is very important not only that the process of industrial concentration was much more advanced in the United States than in Europe, but also that it continued to advance swiftly in the years after the first world war.

* My italics.—F. S.

241

"In 1909 the assets of the 200 then largest non-banking corporations amounted to only 26,000 million dollars. By 1919 they had reached 43,700 million dollars, an increase of 68 per cent in ten years. In the next ten years, from 1919 to 1929, they had increased to 81,100 million dollars, or a further increase of 85 per cent. . . .

"Though the growth of the large corporation is rapid, it is truly significant only if it has been more rapid than the growth of all industrial wealth. . . .

"When the rates of growth of the wealth of all non-financial corporations and of the assets of the 200 largest corporations are thus compared, they show the large corporations as a group to be growing very much more rapidly than all corporations. For the period from 1909 to 1928 their annual rate of growth has been 5·4 per cent, whilst that of all corporations (assuming the estimates to be reliable) has amounted to only 3·6 per cent, and for corporations other than the largest 200 only 2 per cent. . . .

"From 1924 to 1928, a period of most rapid growth, the annual rates were respectively 7·7 per cent for the large, 4·9 for all, and only 2·6 for corporations other than the largest 200, indicating that the large corporations were growing more than half as fast again as all corporations, and three times as fast as the smaller corporations."

And if this process of concentration continues what is likely to be its effect on the future?

"Just what does this rapid growth of the big companies promise for the future? Let us project the trend of the growth of recent years. If the wealth of the large corporations and that of all corporations should each continue to increase for the next twenty years at its average annual rate for the twenty years from 1909 to 1929, 70 per cent of all corporate activity would be carried on by 200 corporations by 1950." [5]

Now, after the appearance of the book by Berle and Means from which all the above quotations have been drawn, the United States experienced the worst economic crisis in history, the New Deal and the second world war. But the process of industrial concentration still continued, and after the second world war the 200 corporations controlled a sector of the U.S. economic system which produced more than the whole U.S. economic system before the outbreak of that war.

The process of industrial concentration in the twenties in the United States was so great that despite the fact that there was a tremendous increase in industrial production from the end of the first world war until the peak prosperity point before the outbreak of the world economic crisis, there was no increase in the number of indus-

242

trial undertakings; in fact, there was a slight decline. In manufactures the number of undertakings in 1919 was 210,268, whilst in 1929 it had dropped slightly to 206,663. Sociologically more important, however, was the fact that in the same period the number of owners and partners dropped by almost half—namely, from 249,881 in 1919 to 132,686 in 1929.[6] Now, although the tendencies towards the destruction of the independent urban middle strata increased in this period, the living standards of the dependent middle strata, and also of the working class, increased, *though the increase in wages lagged behind the increase in the productivity of labour.*

We shall return to this last-mentioned point because it is of decisive importance.

As the tendency to rising wages continued, the attitude of the American workers remained much the same as it had been in the years before the war. The upper strata of the working class felt that they belonged to the middle class, and their general outlook was middle class. Thus the great degree of social stability with which the United States entered the first world war and emerged from it continued to exist throughout this period.

However, despite the high degree of social stability and the great industrial developments still taking place, decisive changes began to make themselves felt as compared with the half-century of development which ended with the first world war.

They were primarily due to the fact that U.S. capitalism had largely reached the limit of its possibilities of territorial expansion at home, i.e. had reached its inner frontier. Prior to the conclusion of this period of expansion at home an enormous volume of capital and an enormous mass of immigrant labour-power had come from Europe.

Before the limits of territorial expansion at home were reached, there had been a tremendous volume of industrial growth, so that despite the increase in the productivity of labour the number of workers engaged in industry had steadily increased.

At the same time, the number of agricultural undertakings and the number of people engaged in agriculture in the United States—unlike the situation in Europe—had also increased.

Before the limits of this expansion at home were reached, the fact that America's inner structure was still colonial had meant a possibility of more than "normal" investments. The railroads had to be built over vast territories, and investment possibilities grew by leaps and bounds, because living standards of workers and farmers and of the population in general rose.

But the situation changed when the limits of territorial expansion at home had finally been reached.

From 1900 up to the outbreak of the first world war the U.S. railway network had steadily increased by something like 60,000 miles.

243

It will give us some idea of the magnitude of this increase if we remember that the combined British and German railway networks were not bigger than this increase in the U.S. railway network.

After the first world war the building of further railway lines ceased almost entirely. Steam railways operated in 1919 had a total network of 258,525 miles; in 1929, or ten years later, the total was still only 260,570 miles. In other words, territory was now fully opened up. The limits of territorial expansion at home had been reached.

New U.S. immigration laws came into operation, and the result was a great fall in the number of immigrants, and that applied even to the period of prosperity before the outbreak of the world economic crisis.

Excess of Admissions over Departures [7]

Year.						Total.
1910–1914	.	.	.	.	.	3,316,146
1920–1924	.	.	.	.	.	1,968,884
1925–1929	.	.	.	.	.	1,238,893

In the whole decade from 1920 to 1929 the excess of immigration was not greater than formerly in half a decade, and in the years after 1929 the immigration figures dropped to record low levels.

The end of the period of inner expansion was also reflected in the situation on the labour market.

In the period of expanding capitalism before the first world war the working class in the big industrial countries increased in size both absolutely and relatively.

A change now came about. The increase in the productivity of labour in the twenties was so great that it resulted in a tremendous increase in industrial production *without any increase in the number of workers employed by comparison with* 1919.

Although industrial production increased from 72 in 1919 to 110 in 1929 (1935–1939 = 100), the number of wage-workers employed actually fell slightly in the same period; in 1919 it was 8,423,964, and in 1929 it was 8,369,705.

There are no exact statistics concerning unemployment in the United States in this period, but there are many signs to indicate that even in this period of prosperity there was a considerable amount of unemployment.

"During the late twenties the phenomenon of technological unemployment was beginning to manifest itself. Boom periods had ordinarily been accompanied by acute labour shortages, but this was not the case, generally speaking, in the twenties. A survey made by the Brookings Institution (Isador Lubin, 'The Absorption of the Unemployed by American Industry', 1929) during this period revealed that workers displaced by technological improvements in certain industries were finding serious difficulty in obtaining employment elsewhere." [8]

U.S. AGRICULTURE NOT PROSPEROUS

For the first time in its history, the United States experienced a tremendous period of prosperity without any increase in the number of industrial workers in employment, and further, for the first time in history, the United States experienced such a period of prosperity *and at the same time an absolute decline in the number of people engaged in agriculture*.

Previously the existence of further possibilities of inner expansion in the United States had permitted the number of people engaged in agriculture to rise steadily. That growth was very considerable up to 1900, and it continued to some extent in the years before the first world war.

A change now took place, and it applied to the whole period between the two world wars. The agricultural population declined not only relatively but absolutely, as the following figures [9] indicate:

Agricultural Population of the United States *

(in thousands)

	June 1st, 1900.	April 15th, 1910.	Jan. 1st, 1920.	April 1st, 1930.	April 1st, 1940.
Gainfully occupied, ten years and over .	10,912	11,592	11,449	10,472	9,163

Thus a new period in U.S. history began. In previous U.S. economic crises there was a migration from the towns into the countryside. With the absolute decline in agricultural population, which now became a permanent phenomenon, that migration practically ceased.

The agricultural section of U.S. economy, in which the number employed now decreased absolutely, did not share in the period of industrial prosperity in the twenties. In fact U.S. agriculture, which

* The total for 1930 may well be an underestimate because of the omission of workers employed on some small farms. Generally speaking, the methods by which these figures were obtained were not very reliable, and here and there they may be subject to correction, but nevertheless the general trend of development is beyond all question. Taking into account all the objections which can be made to the census, Barger and Landsberg [10] write:

"After 1900 numbers gainfully occupied appear to have increased for about a decade, and to have reached a maximum at a level some 5 or 10 per cent above that at the opening of the century. Thereafter this total declined fairly steadily: in 1930 it was about the same as, or slightly below, the figure for 1900."

245

had done very well during the war by exporting very large quantities of agricultural produce to Europe, began to show marked signs of stagnation and depression, and agricultural exports steadily declined.

U.S. farmers found no adequate compensation at home for the drop in agricultural exports; so even in the period of prosperity in the twenties U.S. agriculture was constantly faced with the problem of over-production. In the circumstances it was not surprising that agricultural prices dropped considerably, because U.S. agriculture had more than six million undertakings, and it was not sufficiently elastic to react to a decline in demand by throttling down production.

As the prices obtained for agricultural produce throughout this period were lower than those paid by farmers for the industrial products they needed, and unfavourable as compared with the pre-war period, the share of the farmers in the total national income declined, and it declined much farther than the general decline of the agricultural population compared with the population of the United States as a whole.

In 1919 the farmers' share in the national income was 16 per cent; in the period before the outbreak of the world economic crisis it had dropped to 8 per cent. The situation of numerous farmers in the United States was the same as that of many German peasants: they could no longer live on the income from their farms, and they fell more and more into debt. This burden of debt was not caused by any attempt to modernize farming, but largely by personal expenditure. Many farmers were even forced to give up their farms altogether.

"For the first time in the history of the United States, the acreage of land in crops decreased. Between 1910 and 1924, 13 million acres were allowed to go back to grass, brush and woodland." [11]

Whilst capitalism was still in its infancy the agricultural population had been bigger than the industrial population, even in the leading industrial countries, and a considerable part of the agricultural sector had not been entirely dependent on the capitalist market, or integrated with the mechanism of capitalism.

But subsequently agriculture in the leading industrial countries, and particularly in the United States, had been drawn more and more into the sphere of capitalist operations, and in the United States the overwhelming portion of agricultural production had gone to the markets, and only a comparatively small proportion had been held back for the farmers' own consumption.

This process of harnessing agriculture into the general capitalist system had at first been accompanied by a considerable increase of the agricultural sector, and both the number of farmers and the amount of land under cultivation had increased. But now this development came to an end. The number of persons engaged in agriculture declined, and, further, agriculture as a whole was no longer immune to the effects of capitalist crises.

The situation was somewhat similar to that which existed in Germany, though for different reasons: in a period of great prosperity, with growing industrial production and growing productive capacity, a whole sector of the economic system had hardly any share in the prosperity and clearly showed signs of stagnation and depression. Thus it did not reinforce this prosperity, and when the economic crisis finally broke out it was made worse by the situation in agriculture, because agriculture had already been badly shaken before the crisis began.

Thus the fact that the inner territorial expansion of U.S. capitalism had finally reached its limits was already making itself clearly felt in certain sectors of the U.S. economic system. At the same time there were fundamental changes in the position of the United States in the world economic system.

During the first world war the United States became a creditor country for the first time in history. It now had an excess of credits over debits abroad of about 3 milliard dollars,[12] and it is as well to note that this was quite apart from the war debts owed to the U.S. Government, which were, in fact, never met.

The world position of the United States as a creditor nation was consolidated and extended in the twenties. Before the world war the revenue from the export surplus had been used to pay the interest on foreign capital invested in the United States. In the post-war years, although America was already a creditor country, she used the revenue from this surplus to increase her investments abroad. In this period her capital exports were greater than those of the rest of the world put together.

This capital wealth was one of the main factors which facilitated the U.S. drive beyond the frontiers. Capital exports went not only to industrially backward countries, but also to European industrial countries, and, in fact, it was U.S. capital export which made the whole lunatic game of German reparations payments possible in the first place.

In the first world war and in the immediate post-war years U.S. export surpluses were tremendous, as the following annual average figures for U.S. foreign trade [13] show:

Year.	Exports.	Imports.
1911–1915 . . .	2,331,648	1,712,319
1915–1920 . . .	6,416,513	3,358,354

In the twenties U.S. export surpluses were naturally not so large as they had been during the war years, but they were still far above pre-war levels.

Year.	Exports.	Imports.
1921–1925 . . .	4,310,221	3,450,103
1926–1930 . . .	4,687,788	4,033,469

Unlike developments in Europe, U.S. foreign trade figures and U.S. production in general in this period were far above pre-war levels, and to this extent also U.S. capitalism demonstrated that it was still on an upward curve. However, even this considerable volume of foreign trade was not very great when compared with the volume of U.S. production as a whole. Its increase in absolute figures was not greater than the increase in U.S. production as a whole, so that, in fact, the proportions did not change at all.

The U.S. export surplus amounted to roughly 800 million dollars annually, or about 8 milliard dollars in ten years, and it represented about the same sum as American capital exports in this period. But what did 8 milliard dollars worth of capital exports mean for the U.S. economic system as a whole? It was less than the capital formerly invested to extend the U.S. railway network.

In other words, U.S. capitalist expansion beyond the frontiers was relatively small compared with U.S. production as a whole—too small to compensate for the fact that inner territorial expansion had come to an end.

In the whole period before the first world war it was inner territorial expansion, with all its direct and indirect effects, which had created a situation in which both production and productivity increased and living standards of all sections of the population rose.

U.S. capitalism was now faced with the task of balancing the growth of production and consumption without the aid of internal territorial expansion.

It did not succeed in resolving the problem.

The increase of production and productivity led to an increase in the national income, but this increase was not proportionally distributed amongst the various strata of the population. We have already mentioned that the share of the farmers in the total national income declined, but what was much more important was the fact that, owing to the unfavourable situation on the labour market, there was no longer any shortage of man-power, but technological unemployment, so that the rise in wages lagged far behind the rise in the productivity of labour. Thus the lion's share in the increase in the national income as the result of increased productivity went to the upper strata of society, whose economic power grew stronger and stronger as a result of the process of industrial concentration.

248

As a conservative economist, Harold G. Moulton, writes:

"The national income was becoming increasingly concentrated. During the prosperity period of the twenties there was a rapid increase in the total national income. The *per capita* income from current production activities increased between 1919 and 1929 by as much as 23 per cent. This increase was not, however, participated in equally by all portions of the population. The aggregate dollar income of the farm population showed a slight decline after 1925. *Wage income increased in absolute terms but did not quite keep pace with the increase in national income as a whole. The greatest increase occurred in the high-income grades,* including salaried officials and receivers of profits from business enterprise. Moreover, there was a rapid growth in the number of income recipients in the higher-income brackets." [14] *

As the rich thus became richer, the amount of accumulated savings capital looking for profitable investment increased enormously. However, the possibilities of internal territorial expansion were now more or less at an end, and outward expansion offered no such possibilities as had previously existed at home. Consumption was then artificially raised by the granting of many milliard dollars worth of so-called consumer credits, and further capital, which could find no field of investment in production, turned to stock-exchange speculation. Thus the gap between the development of production and productivity on the one hand and the lagging development of consumer markets on the other was temporarily closed, but the expedient adopted was a dangerous one.

However, as long as the period of prosperity continued, people did not bother their heads about the signs of stagnation and depression in agriculture, or about the significant fact that the number of workers employed in industry was no longer increasing, or about the growing difficulties of capitalist expansion in the world, or about the fact that the two biggest industrial countries in the world after the United States, Great Britain and Germany, were already—before the outbreak of the crisis—struggling grimly against the obstacles to their expansion. On the contrary, people in the United States assumed that the prosperity they were enjoying was a permanent phenomenon—for example, on December 4th, 1928, Calvin Coolidge, the President of the United States, declared in the annual presidential message to Congress "on the state of the nation":

"No Congress of the United States ever assembled, on surveying the state of the Union, has met with a more pleasing prospect than that which appears at the present time. . . . The great wealth created by our enterprise and industry, and saved by our economy,

* My italics.—F. S.

249

has had the widest distribution among our own people, and has gone out in a steady stream to serve the charity and the business of the world. The requirements of existence have passed beyond the standard of necessity into the region of luxury. Enlarging production is consumed by an increasing demand at home and an expanding commerce abroad. The country can regard the present with satisfaction and anticipate the future with optimism."

Many economists began to believe that capitalism had entered into a period in which economic crises would diminish in violence.

"In the last century and a half the capitalist manner of production has suffered from many 'infantile sicknesses', to use Spiethoff's phrase. The exploitation of vast new resources, revolutionary inventions and techniques, crop fluctuation in a world still largely dependent upon agriculture, and an uncontrolled credit economy —these are the major disturbing influences that have produced, in the last century and a half, feverish booms and depressions. These dynamic factors are being mitigated, and so the character of the business cycle is changing." [15]

It was quite true that the character of the business cycle was changing, but, as we have already seen from our analysis of the changes which have taken place in the historical environment of the capitalist mode of production, it was changing in a very different fashion from that supposed by Alvin Hansen, the author of the above passage.

The factors making for a great intensification of economic crises were incomparably stronger at that time than those factors which tended to mitigate their severity.

EUROPE FROM THE FIRST WORLD WAR TO THE WORLD ECONOMIC CRISIS IN 1929

As far as the United States was concerned, the first world war did not represent any decisive turning point, as it did for European capitalism. The turning point for U.S. capitalism came with the world economic crisis of 1929.

The first world war ended the similarity of European and U.S. development not only during the war itself, but also in the period which followed.

Although developments in the individual capitalist countries of Europe differed greatly from each other, they all had this in common, that they started from a very much lower level than in the United States.

The upward trend in the United States after the ending of the first world war began at a level of production which was already approximately 15 per cent above pre-war. The upward trend which began at the same time in Europe started off at a level which was more than a third less than pre-war. And whilst American capitalism experienced a new powerful upward drive, despite the fact that it was already well in advance, European capitalism had to make enormous efforts even to reach its pre-war level of production.

Thus the world economic crisis hit European capitalism at a time when it had hardly made good the direct damage done in the first world war, and as from the trough of the crisis up to the outbreak of the second world war the production of peace-time goods in Europe never again reached 1929 levels, we can say for the period as a whole that it was not a phase of progress for European capitalism, but on the whole one which was marked by stagnation, depression, economic crisis and preparations for war.

That was true not only of the vanquished European powers, but also of the victors. Let us deal with the victors first.

BRITISH EXPORTS BELOW PEACE-TIME LEVELS

Why was Britain only able, and that with great difficulty, to reach the pre-war level of production in the period between the first world war and the outbreak of the world economic crisis? Allowing for a certain over-simplification, the answer is: because her export industries were unable to extricate themselves from what was practically a chronic crisis, and because, in view of the specific structure of British society and British economy, the export industries represent an unusually strong sector, and a crisis in that sector is quite enough to wipe out all the advantages achieved elsewhere by the rise of new industries, whose production was nevertheless considerable.

Great Britain was the biggest foreign-trading country in the world, but throughout the period between the two world wars she never once succeeded in bringing her exports up to the level of 1913.

Even in the best years after the first world war and before the world economic crisis the volume of her exports, allowing for price differences, never reached more than four-fifths of peace-time levels; but, on the other hand, the volume of her imports in 1924 was more than the average of imports in pre-war years.

BRITISH FOREIGN TRADE AND BALANCE OF PAYMENTS

This very great worsening of Britain's position on the world markets had decisive results for the British economic system as a whole.

The exceptional strength of Britain's position as the biggest exporter of capital in the world, and as the financial centre of the world, had done much to compensate for the fact that she had not kept pace industrially with the more progressive countries. But the first world war shook this leading financial position, whilst at the same time her imports exceeded pre-war levels whilst her exports remained well below them. The result, even during the period of semi-prosperity which preceded the outbreak of the world economic crisis, was a very considerable deterioration of Great Britain's balance of payments as compared with pre-war, and, in consequence, a big decline in British capital exports.

After the first world war Great Britain remained the only European power which still exported capital to any extent, but these post-war capital exports were only about one quarter of the peace-time volume. In the years from 1907 to 1913 British capital exports amounted to about 160 million pounds annually, but in the period from 1920 to 1927 they were only about 45 million pounds annually, reckoned on the basis of pre-war values.[16]

The decline of Great Britain as the financier of the world did not begin with the first world war, however; it had started, less perceptibly, generations before. Whilst Great Britain still enjoyed a certain industrial monopoly in the world—that is to say until 1870—she increased her old foreign investments from her direct surpluses, because, thanks to her revenues from shipping, banking, etc., her balance of payments was already active, and also from the profits and interest on her capital already invested abroad.

Even when competition set in from the newly developing industrial States, Britain was still economically strong enough to let the greater part of the interests on her foreign investments stay abroad, and in this way she steadily increased the volume of capital standing to her credit in other countries.

However, as a result of the first world war she lost part of her foreign investments, and her position on the world market deteriorated considerably, so much so that she was now compelled to use the greater part of the interest on her foreign investments to finance her own imports, so that only a small part remained for further capital investment abroad. Then came the second world war, and liquidated the bulk of Britain's remaining investments abroad—a point we shall deal with in detail later—whilst her position on the world market deteriorated so seriously that she required American aid in order to bridge the gap between her exports and imports.

In the period after the first world war Britain enjoyed a certain advantage over Germany because a great part of her former capital investments abroad was still intact, and, because of her active balance of payments, she was able to undertake certain new investments. On the other hand, however, Britain's capital exports were now so small that outside her Empire there was not very much left for any big investments. The following diagram illustrates the decline of British capital exports abroad to countries other than the Empire:

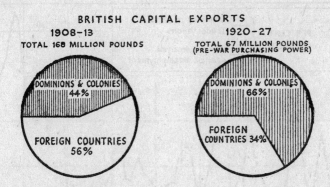

BRITISH CAPITAL EXPORTS

1908-13
TOTAL 168 MILLION POUNDS

DOMINIONS & COLONIES
44%

FOREIGN COUNTRIES
56%

1920-27
TOTAL 67 MILLION POUNDS
(PRE-WAR PURCHASING POWER)

DOMINIONS & COLONIES
66%

FOREIGN
COUNTRIES 34%

The decline of British capital exports also resulted in making the already precarious situation of numerous British industries still more difficult. Formerly Britain's capital exports had been a buffer to ease the pressure of her relative industrial backwardness, but now, in a period when European capitalism as a whole was experiencing increasing difficulties in its efforts to expand outwardly and when, naturally, competition was growing fiercer, Great Britain found herself deprived of her most important weapon in the struggle—namely, large exports of capital.

Great Britain's export industries, whose productive methods were often backward, lost numerous markets, and the result was an almost permanent crisis in these industries.

UNEMPLOYMENT IN BRITAIN BEFORE THE CRISIS

Further, in the whole period between the two world wars Great Britain suffered from chronic unemployment which amounted to millions, a phenomenon which up to that time had been unknown in the history of British or world capitalism.

There are no figures available for unemployment in general before the first world war, but only for unemployment amongst organized workers, where statistics have been kept by their unions. Great Britain is the only country in which we can follow the trend of unemployment amongst trade-union members from the fifties of the nineteenth century on. The British White Paper on Unemployment,[17] issued under the war-time coalition government, contains a very interesting chart concerning British unemployment from the sixties on.

253

The main features of this chart call for no lengthy comment. From the fifties of the nineteenth century up to the first world war unem-

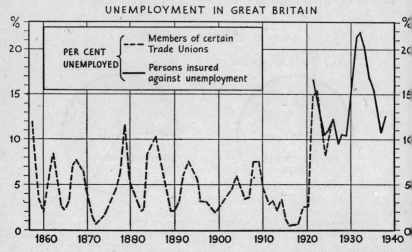

UNEMPLOYMENT IN GREAT BRITAIN

PER CENT UNEMPLOYED { --- Members of certain Trade Unions / ——— Persons insured against unemployment

[*From* Employment Policy, *courtesy The Macmillan Company*

ployment in Great Britain varied between 2 and 8 per cent. As Sir William Beveridge [18] points out:

> "The crests of the waves, apart from the exceptional boom of 1872, are at about 98, representing 2 per cent of unemployment. The troughs, apart from the exceptionally severe depression of 1897 with more than 10 per cent of unemployment, are usually at 92, representing 8 per cent of unemployment."

But in the period between the two world wars the level of unemployment in Great Britain varied between a minimum of 10 per cent and a maximum of 20 per cent. Thus unemployment in the period between the two world wars was greater than in the decade before the war, and greater than at any time during the second half of the nineteenth century.

Mass unemployment in Great Britain reaching into millions began as early as 1921, and it had not been liquidated either when the world economic crisis broke out in 1929 or when the second world war broke out in 1939.

Economic development in Great Britain in the years leading up to the first world war showed certain stagnation tendencies, but nevertheless the general trend was on the whole upward, and after the war and the defeat of her greatest capitalist and imperialist competitor, Great Britain hoped that the signs of stagnation would disappear and a new period of progress open up. Nothing of the sort occurred. The general difficulties of capitalist and imperialist expansion under which European capitalism as a whole suffered were particularly onerous for Great Britain, and the result was that in this period of semi-prosperity after the war up to the outbreak of the world economic crisis the signs of stagnation increased, instead of diminishing.

Production no longer increased steadily; all that happened was that it increased until the direct losses occasioned by the war had been made good. The volume of foreign trade no longer increased steadily (as it had done before, though more slowly than that of Britain's chief competitor); exports remained permanently below the pre-war level, and at the same time there was a chronic worsening of Britain's balance of payments and a weakening of her position as the financial centre of the world.

Thus the halt in external British capitalist expansion was a decisive blow for the British economic system as a whole, and at the same time it was a blow to Britain's social structure, because mass unemployment now became a permanent phenomenon throughout the whole period.

The Position of the British Middle Strata

Any analysis of Great Britain's social structure in this period must differentiate clearly between a comparison of developments in Great Britain with those on the continent, and a comparison of the situation in Great Britain with that which existed formerly.

The importance of this distinction becomes very clear when we regard the British middle strata. Compared with their fellows on the continent, their situation was in many respects much more stable, particularly because Great Britain had distributed the burden of paying for the war more equitably amongst the various strata of the population. The end of the first world war saw Great Britain saddled with an enormous burden of war debt, but, thanks chiefly to her taxation policy, there was very little inflation by comparison with continental Europe, and only a moderate depreciation of the pound sterling took place.

Great Britain made no attempt to shuffle off the burden of her internal war debt, and interest and amortization payments were made regularly. It can therefore be said that on the whole the costs of the war were distributed fairly equitably amongst all classes of the population. In so far as Great Britain became poorer as a result of the first world war, all classes of society became poorer. As the pound sterling depreciated only very little by comparison with the currencies of continental Europe, the British middle strata and the better-off workers retained the greater part of their property and/or savings. This is one of the main reasons why the process of disintegration proceeded much more slowly in the social structure of Great Britain in the years after the first world war than it did in the social structure of the continental countries, and particularly of Germany.

Nevertheless, the tendency was there, and one of its causes was the continued destruction of the independent middle strata, the independent small entrepreneurs.

This tendency existed, of course, even in the years before the first world war, but that was a period of tremendous capitalist expansion, together with a great increase in production as a whole, and this gave rise to counter-factors which opposed and largely cancelled out the tendency. Now those counter-factors were absent. The process of industrial concentration continued throughout British capitalism, but this time general production levels rose only slowly and with great difficulty to pre-war.

There was another factor which applied to Britain in particular. Concentration in the "older" industries was often backward, by comparison with the United States and Germany, as a result of the fact that, as the centre of a large empire, Great Britain enjoyed a position of advantage in the world market for the products of just these industries. The lag in the process of concentration here had now to be made up. At the same time Great Britain developed a number of new industries which were founded from the beginning with a high level of industrial concentration. Thus, in so far as there was any extension of production, it took place chiefly in industries which were controlled by a few undertakings.

But this meant that the process of industrial concentration as a whole destroyed the independent middle strata to a greater extent than before, and undermined their social basis without creating any material counter-factors. The extent of this process of industrial concentration in Great Britain was pointed out in a paper by H. Leak and A. Maizels entitled "The Structure of British Industry". Summing up the results of their investigations, the *Economist* wrote:

"The statistical evidence marshalled by Mr. Leak and Mr Maizels settles once and for all the argument whether or no British industry is still predominantly in the hands of small concerns. They draw the line between small and large business units—arbitrarily but with some justification—at 500 employees, that is to say, units employing between eleven and 499 persons are small ones, and units employing 500 persons or over are large ones. By this definition there were in 1935 some 1,959 large business units employing together 3,970,000 persons, equivalent to 55 per cent of the total of 7,203,000 persons employed by all establishments with a personnel of more than 10 persons (establishments employing less than 10 persons were responsible for less than a tenth of total output). The same number of business units were responsible in 1935 for £2,025 million, or 57 per cent of the total value of the gross output of all establishments, amounting to £3,535 million, and for £931 million, or 58 per cent of the value of their net output of £1,603 millions.

"If the dividing line between small and large units were drawn at 1,000 employees, the large ones would still have accounted for nearly half the total output and employment, that is for 48 per cent of the gross output, 49 per cent of the net output, and 45 per cent of the total number of persons employed. It can thus reasonably be said that British industry is no longer predominantly small in scale." [19]

Although it was late as compared with the United States and Germany, the process of industrial concentration in Great Britain developed strongly in this period without having any material vent in the shape of outward expansion, and the result was that industrial concentration and stagnation together intensified the polarization of British society, though by no means to such an extent as in Germany, the most powerful industrial country in Europe.

GERMANY BEFORE THE WORLD ECONOMIC CRISIS

As a result of her defeat in the first world war, Germany:

1. Lost the greater part of her foreign investments.
2. Lost her former colonies.
3. Lost Alsace-Lorraine, and thereby a quite considerable part of her industrial production.
4. Found her expansion towards the East halted by the break-up of the old Austro-Hungarian Empire and the formation of the Little Entente.
5. Had to pay reparations.

And all this coincided with a period in which the external expansion of world capitalism as a whole had come to a stop. Germany entered the first post-war period with a tremendous burden of debt. Her war expenditure had been met chiefly by the floating of loans, and not by taxation. By the end of the war Germany's indebtedness totalled approximately 150 milliard marks. Judged by the old value of the mark, this burden of debt was equal to Germany's total national income for a period of three years.

Thus Germany's task was not merely reconstruction, but an increase of production on her diminished territory until it reached the pre-war total production of her former territory, until, despite the great deterioration of Germany's position in the world in consequence of the loss of her foreign investments, her colonies and so on, part at least of her old position had been recaptured.

Up to a point German capitalism did solve this difficult problem, but it did so with methods which brought about an exceptional aggravation of social antagonisms, far greater than in any other capitalist industrial country.

THE INFLATION AND DESTRUCTION OF THE URBAN MIDDLE STRATA

A depreciation of the German mark had taken place even during the course of the war itself, and maximum prices had been introduced only at a rather late stage. Germany entered the post-war period with a depreciated mark, and the process of depreciation continued into the peace. Stabilization came only when the value of the dollar was 4,000 milliard marks and the whole population had already begun to reckon only in gold.

The effects of currency inflation on Germany's social structure must be gone into at some length because inflation was one of the main factors which facilitated the subsequent victory of the National Socialists.

I have already dealt with the process in some detail in a book entitled "Der Niedergang des deutschen Kapitalismus", or "The Decline of German Capitalism", first published in Berlin in 1932, and it is that book which I am following largely here.

German capitalism "solved" the problem of war debts by inflation, but the war losses and the general decline in the national wealth were not shared equitably amongst the various classes of society so that those who were best able to do so bore the main burden. Quite the contrary happened. Germany's losses were largely loaded on to the shoulders of the working people and the middle strata, and the means to this end was inflation. As a result of the inflation, war-loan holdings were made completely valueless. Now, if war loans had been taken up in proportion to income and wealth, then the expropriation would have been the same for all; but, in fact, war-loan stock had been largely taken up by the masses of the working people and the middle strata, and the authorities had always boasted of the great numbers of the purchasers of war-loan stock.

Savings banks and similar institutions which held the deposits of working people and the lower middle strata had been particularly encouraged to invest in war-loan stock. Of course, to some extent the well-to-do also bought war-loan stock, but by the end of the war they had already got rid of the greater part of it. The vast slump in war-loan stock as the result of inflation therefore had the effect of placing the cost of the war largely on shoulders least capable of bearing it— those of the working people and the middle strata.

That was something achieved, but German capitalism was not yet satisfied. There was more to be loaded on to the backs of the people than merely war debts; Germany's industrial apparatus had to be built up again as rapidly and efficiently as possible.

Two conditions were necessary if this process was to be carried through rapidly: an increased exploitation of the workers on the one hand, and a further expropriation of the middle strata on the other, so that enormous profits could be obtained to speed up the accumulation of capital to the utmost. In the years from 1919 to 1923 German capitalism increased the exploitation of the working class and further expropriated the middle strata on the widest possible scale by means of continued reckless inflation.

In many books the reader is informed that, thanks to their industry and ability, the German people reappeared on the world market with a modernized productive apparatus in a comparatively short space of time after the war, *despite war and inflation*. We propose to formulate the thing rather differently: *despite war, and by means of inflation*, German capitalism succeeded in building up a new productive apparatus rapidly. Investments were particularly heavy in the inflation period and immediately following it. And this tremendous rate of accumulation in the inflation period, and these very considerable investments, were made possible by a notable reduction in working-class living standards on the one hand and the almost complete expropriation of the middle strata on the other.

THE INFLATION AND THE FALL IN WAGES

We need not discuss here the various stages of the process of inflation; we are interested only in its results. For one thing, it brought about a great drop in German real wages. From 1919 to 1923 the German worker earned progressively less and less. Thus inflation was a very profitable business for the German capitalists—as long as the masses failed to grasp its real significance. Inflation is possible only if it embraces one definite sector either nationally or internationally.

Internationally, inflation must affect only one country, or one group of countries, because it is only then that certain effects result from the currency depreciation of this one country as compared with other countries, both for its foreign trade and its position on the international capital market.

Inflation can exist nationally only if it embraces one particular sector; if there is, for instance, only one particular stratum of society which reckons in gold.

That was the case in Germany from 1919 to the autumn of 1923. Germany's capitalists had long been reckoning in gold, whilst the German workers received their wages in paper money, so that, thanks to the inflation, they received, reckoned in gold, less and less. Professor Lederer [20] writes:

"The German economic system experienced a period of inflation which lasted, with short interruptions, for more than five years. In this whole period wages were much lower than pre-war levels. *Per capita* production also decreased it is true, but not to the same extent as wages. Let us assume only an average of 500 marks per worker and salaried employee as the reduction in real wages which took place, and let us assume it for a period of four years only, because the first year was greatly troubled with a psychological unwillingness to work, and let us take between 12 and 14 million workers and employees (industry and commerce only, not including agriculture) then we have a sum of between six and seven milliard marks annually, or between 24 and 28 milliard gold marks for the whole four-year period, which accumulated in industry as unpaid wages. This sum and the savings, which disappeared entirely and return to-day only in a fraction of their original volume thanks to re-valuation, which may be reckoned at about 50 milliard marks, together with unpaid taxes, represented the funds with which the astonishingly rapid reconstruction of Germany's economic system took place without the help of foreign loans."

These 28 milliard marks went into the pockets of Germany's capitalists as unpaid wages as a result of the inflation, and reinforced normal profits. It is hardly necessary to mention that, thanks to this increase in the rate of exploitation, the rate of accumulation of capital in Germany also greatly increased. By means of inflation German capitalism depressed working-class standards of living to the level they had occupied at the very beginnings of the working-class movement, and, in addition, it robbed the overwhelming majority of the urban middle strata of their savings and their property.

Except for those engaged in agriculture, the property and savings of the middle strata melted to nothing during the inflation. They lost the money they had invested before the war in the loan-stock of the Government, the German States and the municipalities, and they lost the greater part of their savings and their bank deposits. In order to exist at all they had to sell such shares as they possessed and such housing and landed property as they owned. In this way they also lost the income on their capital. Before the war many of them had lived on small pensions or small investments, now they had to return to the process of production to earn a living. Where they had any supplementary revenue, this now also ceased.

The great reduction of wage standards and the expropriation of the middle strata during the inflation were the sources of the tremendous investments to build up Germany's new productive apparatus. Thus even during and immediately after the inflation period there was a big boom in investments, whose immediate effect was a considerable increase in production leading to the so-called rationalization boom.

The great speed with which Germany's productive apparatus was rationalized and modernized on the one hand, and the deterioration of Germany's export position in Eastern Europe and the intensification of competition on the world market on the other, were thus closely related in this period of stagnation in world capitalist expansion. It was all the more important for German capitalism to open up new markets for itself beyond its frontiers because the possibilities of capitalist expansion at the expense of pre-capitalist forms in Germany were now more or less at an end.

"The still available 'pre-capitalist' strata within Germany are not, either numerically or from the point of view of their absorption capacity, important enough to result in any similar big increase of industrial production as a whole as took place in the pre-war period. . . . Capitalist large-scale industry cannot now squeeze out broad sections of handicraftsmen as it did around 1860. As industry's share in production as a whole already amounts to between 70 and 80 per cent, there is also little hope of expansion where agriculture is concerned by 'industrializing' agriculture. On the contrary, the agrarian protection policy makes it seem likely that there will be less industrialization in agriculture." [21]

GERMANY'S EXPORTS BELOW PRE-WAR LEVEL

As the outlook for German capitalist expansion at home at the expense of pre-capitalist forms was very narrow, and as the increase in the population was only very small (1·5 per cent annually before the war, and only 0·6 per cent from 1923 to 1929), German capitalism was under considerable pressure to open up new markets for itself outside the frontiers as a substitute for other investments. Therefore even after the end of inflation it began a particularly intensive export drive.

German Industrial Production and Exports [22]

(quantities 1913 = 100)

Year.	Industrial production.	Industrial exports.	Percentage of exports.
1913 * . . .	100	100	26·5
1925 . . .	83	66	21·3
1926 . . .	79	79	26·5
1927 . . .	100	82	21·6
1928 . . .	102	85	22
1929 . . .	102	95	24·7

* Former Reich's territory.

These figures show very clearly that there was a strong tendency to increase exports after the liquidation of the inflation, but that in no post-war year did German capitalism succeed in reaching the export figures for 1913. That was true not only in the years before the outbreak of the world economic crisis, but it was, of course, also true for the years of crisis and for the subsequent years of Nazi war economy in peace time, when the preparations for the second world war were in full swing. Like British capitalism, German capitalism did not succeed in reaching its pre-war export levels in any year in the period between the two world wars, whereas in the long period before 1913 there had been a tremendous increase in exports. Thus the stagnation in exports applied to the two leading industrial powers in Europe, but at the same time there were certain very important differences.

Great Britain had become poorer as a result of the first world war. She was no longer in a position to increase her wealth, as she had been before the war, but at least, though not so rich, she was still rich. She still increased her foreign investments, she still exported capital, and she still had her Empire, even though it was suffering to some extent from stagnation.

Germany, on the other hand, had lost most of her foreign investments as a result of the war, and she had also lost her privileged position in Eastern Europe. In the years before the outbreak of the world economic crisis Germany certainly built up a stronger position for herself abroad, but she could not do it by using any surplus in her balance of payments to back up her export industries, so she did it by borrowings; in other words, by taking a new great burden of debt on to her shoulders.

The Grotesque Game of German Reparations

We have already seen that the leading circles in all capitalist countries went into the first world war with totally erroneous conceptions about the period in which they were living. They may have been sadder men when they emerged from it, but they were certainly not much wiser. The Entente countries started off by demanding reparations amounting to milliards annually for an indeterminate period of years, all to be paid out of current German production. Now, as the Germans had already lost the greater part of their foreign investments, these reparations sums could only be paid, if at all, by tremendous export surpluses, and this could have come about only hand in hand with an enormous increase in the volume of world trade, big enough to ensure that Germany's great export surpluses would not damage the industries of the victorious powers.

But in Chapter One of Part III we have already seen that, owing to the halt in capitalist expansion in this period, any great increase in the volume of foreign trade was quite out of the question, and thus any increase of German export surpluses to a degree capable of meeting such vast reparations demands was equally out of the question. The result was that in reality from 1924 onwards Germany paid no reparations at all. But simple and true as this statement is, the process by which it came about was very complicated. Formally Germany continued to pay reparations after 1924, but at the same time she took up both short-term and long-term foreign credits to a sum several times greater than her reparations obligations. Between 1924 and 1929 Germany formally paid about 8 milliard marks in reparations. However, in that period she had no export surpluses, but a big passive trade balance.

So Germany performed a financial and economic miracle: she paid reparations, at the same time her balance of trade showed big import surpluses. But the miracle is easily explained: she borrowed money from abroad to pay both reparations and imports surpluses. Here are the figures:

Germany and the International Capital Market [23]
(in milliards of Reichsmarks)

	Dec. 31, 1934.	Dec. 31, 1925.	Dec. 31, 1926.	Dec. 31, 1927.	Dec. 31, 1928.	Dec. 31, 1929.
	Foreign investments in Germany.					
German short-term foreign indebtedness.	—	—	4·1	6·6	9	11·3 to 12·3
German long-term foreign indebtedness.	1	2·5	4·1	5·4	7	7·3
Other foreign investments in Germany.	—	—	3·5	4·5	5·5	6
Total foreign investments.	—	—	11·7	16·5	21·5	24·5 to 25·5
	German investments abroad.					
German short-term foreign investments.	—	—	3·6	3·9	4·5	5 to 6
German long-term foreign investments.	—	—	4 to 5	4 to 5	4 to 5	4 to 5
Total German foreign investments.	—	—	7·6 to 8·6	7·9 to 8·9	8·5 to 9·5	9 to 11

At the end of this period German foreign indebtedness amounted to approximately 25 milliard marks, whilst Germany on her part had about 10 milliard marks invested abroad. The balance of 15 milliard marks was used "to pay" reparations and to pay for Germany's import surpluses so that her balance of trade could be righted.

Observe that half of this total of 25 milliard marks borrowed from abroad consisted of short-term credits—i.e. they could be called in at short term notice. Observe further that Germany has supported her export industries with large exports of capital, but that these capital exports did not result from any activity of her balance of payments, but purely from borrowings.*

* Another point is noteworthy in this ridiculous game of "German Reparations". France received the greater part of the so-called reparations payments, whilst the greater part of Germany's foreign loans were taken up in the United States. Thus in reality the United States made a present of several milliard gold marks to France, because she never received anything back from Germany. The fact that France's industrial production rose considerably above pre-war level in this period was largely due to these indirect U.S. gifts, which bore legally the form of German reparations.

The rise in German industrial production in this period was fed from two sources. First of all from the increase in German exports brought about, in part at least, by Germany's enormous foreign indebtedness, and secondly from a German investment boom which rationalized and modernized Germany's industrial productive apparatus.

The process of rationalization in industry was so widespread and so intense that chronic unemployment developed as a result. In other words, it was technological unemployment, and not, as in Great Britain, the result of stagnating export industries.

There are no complete figures available for unemployment in Germany in the period before the first world war, but, as in Great Britain, there are figures for workers organized in trade unions. If we compare the last few years before the first world war with the post-war years we find:

"On an average in the years from 1907 to 1913 only 2·3 per cent of trade-union workmen were unemployed, but in the years 1927 to 1929 the percentage was between four and six times as great." [24]

Unemployment as a whole in the years 1924–1929 was as follows:

German Unemployment Figures [25]

(in 1,000's)

Year.							Annual average.
1924 .	.	.	.	.	.	.	911
1925 .	.	.	.	.	.	.	646
1926 .	.	.	.	.	.	.	2,011
1927 .	.	.	.	.	.	.	1,353
1928 .	.	.	.	.	.	.	1,353
1929 .	.	.	.	.	.	.	1,892

In the period after the liquidation of inflation there were thus on an average more than a million workers unemployed in Germany. In other words, unemployment in Germany in this period was already greater than it had been in periods of crisis before the first world war.

Thus there was chronic unemployment in Germany, whose level was well over the million mark, and in a period of prosperity there was a considerable section of the population which had no share whatever in it.

In addition, in this same period a quite considerable sector of the German economic system showed clear signs of crisis—that sector was, as in the United States, agriculture. Thanks to a policy of customs duties on agricultural produce, successive German Governments had prevented the ruin of German agriculture by overseas competition, and in this respect Germany's situation was different from Great Britain's. But even in the period before the first world war Germany's tariff policy was not clearly advantageous for German agriculture as a whole. It chiefly favoured the German junker feudal undertakings which produced grain and fodder, as against the peasants who produced primarily cattle and cattle products. The inevitable result of this protectionism was that agricultural technique remained rather backward, because, thanks to the tariffs, the junkers could make money easily owing to guaranteed prices.

The inflation of the first few years after the war relieved Germany's agricultural undertakings of the greater part of their indebtedness. In dealing with the fact that Germany's middle strata lost their savings and their property during the inflation, we were careful to point out that it was the urban middle strata. It did not apply to Germany's peasants, who actually profited by the inflation because they got rid of a considerable part of their indebtedness. They were thus the only middle stratum in Germany which retained more or less its old social basis: the farms which they ran themselves and a moderate income from the sale of their produce.

Thus the inflation period offered no incentive to modernize the technique of agricultural production, for German agriculture had no difficulty in selling its produce in the towns at good prices.

But after the inflation the burden of new debt which began to weigh on agriculture steadily increased. Short-term and middle-term loans rose from a total of 3,223·2 million marks in 1925 to a total of 7,342·7 million marks in 1929. This new volume of indebtedness would not have been too bad, because even at its peak in 1929 it was still below the figures for 1913, but two factors worsened the position. First of all, the rate of interest was quite generally much higher than it had been before the war, and the burden of interest obligations rose from 425 million marks in 1924–1925 to 920 million marks in 1928–1929, and was thus greater than the 1913 burden, which had amounted to between 750 and 800 million marks. The second factor was still more important.

What did the German peasant and farmer do with the credits he received? Did he use them to modernize his farm and to increase his production and his productive capacity? He did not. Investments in agriculture in the years 1924–1928 were less than the usual deductions for wear and tear.[26]

In other words, the new credits were used for current consumption, and this means that in the midst of prosperity the revenues of Germany's agricultural undertakings were not sufficient to guarantee the peasants their old middle-class standards of existence. That was not socially dangerous as long as Germany's farms could raise new credits and in this way obtain purchasing power in excess of their revenues, but when the economic crisis finally broke out, this circumstance greatly increased its severity.

Let us recall that, unlike the situation in former economic crises— for instance, those in the seventies—German agriculture, including both the junker and the peasant undertakings, was now closely integrated with the market system, and to this extent part and parcel of capitalism, so that any crisis suffered by capitalism necessarily fully involved agriculture.

To sum up: in the period of reconstruction German capitalism was prosperous. It had been able to make large new investments and bring production up to pre-war levels. So long as this investment boom went on the period generally was one of prosperity. But the capital invested was largely borrowed, and a part of the foreign credits used in this way were short-term credits. In this period Germany was a debtor country. Even before the war German capitalism had reached the limit of expansion at the expense of pre-capitalist forms at home. It still needed to expand, but after the war it never again attained pre-war foreign trade levels. And with its expansion greatly hampered, and its investment boom largely financed with borrowed capital, the process of polarization in German society went forward steadily.

The few years of prosperity after the inflation had not been sufficient to give the urban middle strata a comparatively stable social basis again, and even during this period of "prosperity" there were clear signs of stagnation and depression in the agricultural sector, and in the industrial sector chronic unemployment above the million mark. These were all clear enough signs of growing economic difficulties, but as long as the short period of prosperity lasted most people were unwilling to see them; and that was true not only of Germany, but also of the United States.

Werner Sombart [27] wrote:

> "When Marx developed his theory of crisis—at a time when England, and also the continent, was suffering from the worst 'crisis' ever—it was understandable for people to believe that the set-backs which followed on a boom period were becoming more and more serious. The general trend of the years 1825, 1836 and 1847 could be projected into the future and then the logical deduction was the catastrophe theory developed by Marx. . . .
>
> "The crisis of 1857 was the last really big-scale crisis England experienced. Germany and Austria suffered a severe crisis in 1873, but since then there is a clear tendency in European economic life for the contradictions to cancel each other out so that they finally disappear. This tendency lasted up to the world war, and it was not diminished, or turned into its opposite, either by war or by anything that followed."

It is typical that Sombart is thinking only of the war as a factor enhancing economic contradictions, but it was not primarily the war which did that; it was the fact that outward capitalist economic expansion had ceased, which led—rather less than a year after the appearance of Sombart's book—to the worst crisis in the history of capitalism in general and of German capitalism in particular.

RUSSIA FROM THE REVOLUTION TO THE FIRST FIVE-YEAR PLAN

During the first world war a considerable area of European Russia was the scene of hostilities. At the same time Russia's military losses —approximately four million dead alone—were about as high as those of Great Britain, France and Germany put together. Even before the November Revolution Russia's industrial production had fallen to 70 per cent of the 1913 volume.* After the revolution, in the years of the civil war, production fell to very low levels. According to the figures of the State Planning Commission (Gosplan), the production index was as follows:

Russia's Industrial Production

Year.	Large-scale industry.	Small-scale industry.	Total.
1913 . . .	100	100	100
1916 . . .	116·1	88·2	109·4
1917 . . .	74·8	78·4	75·7
1918 . . .	33·8	73·5	43·4
1919 . . .	14·9	49	23·1
1920 . . .	12·8	44·1	20·4

"The output of large-scale industries, the administration of which was extremely centralized, declined much more rapidly than did that of small industries. Particularly large declines occurred in the production of the following materials: iron ore (in 1920 only 1·6 per cent of the 1913 output was produced); pig iron (1920 2·4 per cent of 1913); steel (1920 4 per cent of 1913); cotton manufactures (1920 5 per cent of 1913); sugar (1920 5·8 per cent of 1913). In 1912 production of prime necessity goods amounted, per head of the population, to 18·2 gold roubles; in 1920 to only 2·4 gold roubles. In 1912 manufactured consumer goods sold to the population were valued at 2,099 million gold roubles, whilst the value of those sold in 1920 amounted to only 262 million gold roubles." [28]

No Western European power could have survived such a catastrophic fall in production. Soviet Russia was able to do so because she was a very backward industrial power. More than four-fifths of her population lived on agriculture, and as the living standards of the

* Prokopovitch, "War and the National Economy", p. 173, quoted by Alexander Baykov in his book "The Development of the Soviet Economic System", C.U.P., 1946. Where no particular sources are quoted the figures here are taken from Baykov's book.—F.S.

vast majority of the people were very low indeed, it proved possible
to maintain a primitive level of existence for them. That applied to
the villages, but before long it was not entirely true of the towns.
The State had large-scale industry, but it no longer produced very
much. However, industrial production with a supply of industrial
goods to the villages was absolutely necessary if the peasants were to
be persuaded to send the requisite supplies of foodstuffs into the towns
to keep the urban population alive. But there were tremendous
difficulties in the way.

THE FIRST STAGE OF RUSSIA'S AGRARIAN REVOLUTION

The November Revolution in Russia liquidated feudalism. The
feudal owners of land were expropriated without compensation.

The following figures, borrowed by Baykov from Lenin, for the
distribution of the land carried out by the November Revolution
give some idea of the tremendous transformation involved:

	No. of owners (millions).	Million desiatines.*	Average per owner.
Poorest peasantry	10·5	75	7
Middle peasantry	1	15	15
Rich peasantry and medium estates .	1·5	70	46·7
Big estates, appanage and Crown land, industrial and mercantile . .	0·03	70	2,333
Not divided in groups . . .	—	50	—
Total	13·03	280	21·4

* A desiatine is about 2·6 acres.

Thus a good quarter of the land of Russia formerly in feudal possession was distributed during the November Revolution. But this
distribution was not systematic. It took place largely by peasant
seizure. The new State was not strong enough to intervene and
regulate the process. At first, therefore, feudal ownership gave way
to individual peasant ownership. It should also be remembered that
this redistribution of the land took place whilst the civil war was still
raging.

War and civil war brought about a great decline in agricultural
production and in the area in crops. In the years 1909–1913 the
sown area in Russia amounted to 83·1 million desiatine, but in 1920
it was only 62·9 million desiatine, and by 1921 it had declined still
further to 58·3 million desiatine. The actual decline in agricultural
production itself was even greater. The gross yield of crops in 1909–
1913 was 3,850 poods.† In 1917 it was somewhat lower, and
reached 3,350 million poods, and after that it fell rapidly: in 1920 it
was 2,082 million poods, and in 1921 it was only 1,689 million poods.

† A Russian pood is 36 lb.

Thus during the years of the civil war agricultural production in Russia was less than half normal. It is true that this decline in agricultural production was very much less than that in industry, but it was big enough to threaten the urban areas with famine.

In addition to this great decline in agricultural production, another factor appeared which made the situation very much worse. The peasants of Russia were not like the farmers of America, and the small and medium peasants in particular were much less bound up with the ordinary capitalist market and with the town. In general, they consumed the greater part of their produce themselves. The following figures show from what strata of the agricultural population the towns in Russia were fed before the November Revolution:

Russian Agriculture and the Market [29]

Class of producer.	Gross production.		Marketable grain.		Percentage of marketable grain.
	Million poods	Per cent	Million poods	Per cent	
Landowners . . .	600	12	281·6	21·6	47
Kulaks or rich peasants .	1,900	38	650	50	34
Middle and poor peasants	2,500	50	369	28·4	14·7
Totals . .	5,000	100	1,300·6	100	26

These figures show that the former feudal landowners sold half their agricultural produce on the market, and that about one-quarter of the total supplies of agricultural produce for the towns came from their estates, whilst, on the other hand, poor and middle peasants sold only about a seventh of their total produce on the market. Thus the liquidation of feudalism hit that sector of Russian agriculture hardest which produced "marketable grain", or, in other words, was a big source of food supplies for the towns.

Further, the so-called Kulaks, or well-to-do peasants, were not prepared to continue sending their produce into the towns without receiving industrial products in return, and they wanted them at once, because the constant depreciation of the rouble made them unwilling to take payment in paper roubles.

LENIN INTRODUCES THE NEW ECONOMIC POLICY

Faced with the insuperable difficulties of keeping the towns supplied with foodstuffs in the ordinary way, the Bolshevist State began to organize the requisition of food. The natural result was that agricultural production declined still further. Lenin therefore decided on a fundamental change of tactics. He still believed that the upheavals brought about by the first world war would lead to a

269

revolution in one of the more industrially developed countries of the west—he had Germany in mind—and thus completely change the situation for Russia. What he needed above all at the moment—or so he thought—was time. He therefore introduced a new economic policy which became generally known by its initials (the same in Russian as in most other languages) N.E.P., or, shortly, the NEP.

Under this policy small private industrial undertakings and private retail trade were allowed to operate. The idea was to secure a quick increase in industrial production, particularly of consumer goods, and thus be able to supply the villages with industrial goods in return for food for the towns.

Lenin was well aware that the step he was taking was a dangerous one, but as the new Russian State occupied the commanding heights of the economic system, he believed that it would prove strong enough to overcome the dangers, and to those who pointed out the dangers of introducing State capitalism he replied:

> "State capitalism, such as we have it here, is not discussed in any theory or in any literature for the simple reason that all the normal implications of the word involve bourgeois government in a capitalist society. With us . . . it is not the bourgeoisie but the proletariat which rules the State. State capitalism in our case means capitalism which we shall keep restricted. . . . And it depends entirely on us what sort of State capitalism it will be. We have adequate political power at our disposal and we also have adequate economic reserves." [30]

Lenin realized that there would be a strengthening of private capitalism as a result of the NEP, but he believed that at the same time the power of the Soviet State would be strengthened much more, and that with a speedy increase of production the existing economic deadlock could be broken. Speaking to the Tenth Congress of the Russian Communist Party in March 1921 he declared:

> "We are living in such conditions of impoverishment and ruin, of overstrain and exhaustion of the principal productive forces of the peasants and the workers that for a time everything must be subordinate to one fundamental consideration: at all costs to increase the quantity of goods. . . . By the spring of 1921 we had suffered a more serious defeat on the economic front in our attempt to go over to communism than any defeat previously inflicted on us by Koltchak, Denikin or Pilsudsky. The compulsory seizure of grain in the villages and a direct communist approach to the problem of reconstruction in the towns interfered with the growth of the productive capacity of the country and proved to be the main cause of the profound economic and political crisis which faced us in the spring of 1921. . . The New Economic Policy means the

restoration of capitalism to a quite considerable extent. . . . From the strategic viewpoint the real question is: who will first succeed in taking advantage of the new situation? Who will win in the end? Will it be the capitalists, who are now being let in through a door we have opened, and who may be let in by other doors about which we now know nothing and which may open against our will? Or will it be the sovereign proletarian power?" [31]

On the whole, Lenin's experiment was successful. Production increased in both town and country, and by 1923–1924 agricultural production reached three-quarters of its pre-war volume. Although industrial production did not grow so rapidly, it grew nevertheless, and goods gradually began to flow into the villages in exchange for agricultural produce, with the result that the towns were better supplied. Thus the dangers of famine were averted for the time being, and the Bolshevist State was now faced with the famous problem? What next?

The Creation of a New Industrial Apparatus

Lenin died on January 21st, 1924. The German inflation had come to an end a few months before. The German mark was now stabilized, and bolshevist hopes that the intense aggravation of social antagonisms in Germany as a result of the inflation would lead to the long-delayed German Revolution, which Lenin had expected as a direct result of the first world war, were again disappointed.

But if there was no hope of a socialist revolution in Germany, then this obviously meant that in the foreseeable future there would be no socialist revolution in any of the big industrial countries of Europe. Even the bolshevists did not believe that there would be any social revolution in Great Britain or France; Germany had been their last hope.

The Soviet State, which had hardly succeeded in overcoming the difficulties and dangers of the famine and the NEP, now saw itself faced with a problem which Lenin had always declared insoluble. What were they to do with their victory in the industrially most backward country in Europe now that it was quite clear that the Russian Revolution was not the forerunner of socialist revolutions in the industrially developed countries of Europe?

The leadership of the Russian State was already in the hands of Stalin, and he answered the question in the famous slogan: the building up of socialism in one country alone. The economic consequences of this policy were clear. As Russia was very far from having reached that level of industrialism which socialists, including the bolshevists, had always declared to be necessary before any transition to a socialist society could be envisaged, then obviously the centralized control of the new State must be utilized to build up a productive

271

apparatus strong enough to permit this transition. But such a productive apparatus had taken generations and generations to build up in the more highly developed European countries within the framework of capitalism.

What was the equipment of the Russian State for this new task? It held the commanding heights in the economic system. It had full political power. It controlled the bigger, more centralized industries. It controlled the transport system. It controlled the banks. And it had established a State monopoly of foreign trade. But what it did not possess at this time was any powerful lever to control what was still by far the largest section of the Russian economic system, agriculture. There was little it could do to control the peasants or retail trade. However, any political dangers which threatened from this quarter were greatly diminished by the fact that these economic influences had no means of political expression, whereas the State possessed all the organs of political power. Therefore in this period when agriculture and retail trade were slowly growing, the bolshevists used the State apparatus to consolidate and extend the State sector.

Considerable successes were undoubtedly obtained, and in 1927–1928 industrial production more or less reached pre-war levels. However, there had been an important change in the composition of industrial production. All possible efforts had been made to press on with the development of large-scale industry and, in particular, with the production of capital goods. Even when Lenin introduced the NEP he had laid special stress on this point:

"Large-scale industry, its success and development, are the fundamental and primary conditions for the building up of communism. . . . It is the social force which is establishing the communist revolution of the industrial proletariat. Therefore our main task in our economic policy for the development of the productive forces is to strengthen large-scale industry." [32]

Whilst industry as a whole reached pre-war production levels in 1927–1928 this did not apply to the consumer-goods or manufacturing industries, which remained far below peace-time levels, and the result was that living standards did the same.

"Moreover, small-scale industry and, in particular, home handicrafts which manufactured mainly articles of general consumption, had not yet recovered to the same extent as big industry. This was due to the handicaps imposed on private industry and on craftsmen outside the co-operative associations, and in particular to difficulties in purchasing raw materials, which were bought up by the supply syndicates of big industry. The import of general consumption goods, compared with Russia's pre-revolu-

272

tion imports, was considerably less. As a result, the supply of manufactured general consumer goods on the market throughout the recovery period was below the level of pre-revolutionary Russia." [33]

The development of large-scale industry was encouraged by the State through its monopoly of foreign trade. As we have already seen, during the civil war Russian foreign trade sank practically to nothing, but in the twenties it again began to increase. Russia's imports rose from 28·7 million roubles in 1920 to 269·8 million roubles in 1922, to 723·5 million roubles in 1924–1925, and to 945·5 million roubles in 1927–1928. In the same period exports also rose as follows: 1·4 million roubles in 1920, 81·6 million roubles in 1922, 558·6 million roubles in 1924–1925, and 777·8 million roubles in 1927–1928.

Unlike the days of Tsarism, Russia's imports after the November Revolution did not consist largely of consumer goods, but of raw materials and machinery for the development of her own heavy industries. Another decisive difference was that no capital exports of any size were made to Soviet Russia. The November Revolution had expropriated all foreign capital investments in Russia without compensation, and, naturally, foreign capitalists had no inclination to throw good money after bad and make further investments. Certain foreign undertakings played a role in some industries, but their share in Russian industrial production as a whole in this period was less than half of 1 per cent.

To sum up, we can say that, like the European industrial countries, Soviet Russia had more or less reached pre-war production totals in both industry and agriculture a year or two before the outbreak of the world economic crisis, although as a result of the protracted civil war the process of recovery set in later and at a much lower level. Russia's economy reached pre-war levels under a system of extreme State centralism. Special efforts had been made to develop large-scale industry; the State monopoly of foreign commerce had been used to further this development, and no foreign loans of any size had been floated for the purpose. Feudalism had been liquidated and peace-time production levels had been reached on a basis of individual peasant farming. At that time agricultural collectivism played an almost negligible role. Peace-time levels had been reached chiefly by repairing and operating the old productive apparatus. Of course, there were already some new works, but they did not as yet play any very important role in the volume of production as a whole. There was also, as yet, no all-embracing planned economy guided by the State, but the latter had already begun to create the necessary organs for the introduction of such a planned economy.

Internal tension resulted in a further intensification of the dictatorship. The dictatorship had in the first place been a dictatorship of the Bolshevist Party, which had expropriated the owners of the means of industrial production and supported the peasant masses when they had proceeded to liquidate feudalism on their own initiative. After the civil war it was the dictatorship of the party which had won the war. Under the dictatorship the State had taken and held the commanding heights in the economic system. As the revolution had taken place in an industrially backward country, the dictatorship was the rule of a minority from the beginning, because, of course, the overwhelming majority of the peasants were not bolshevists. And in the subsequent period the dictatorship still remained that of a minority. Now that feudalism had been liquidated, the richer peasants were actively hostile to the regime, whilst the poorer peasants were, in the best case, benevolently neutral.

The social basis of the dictatorship thus grew narrower. During the revolution itself and in the subsequent civil war the dictatorship enjoyed the support of the majority of the workers, many of whom had ensured the victory of the revolution. A large proportion of these revolutionary workers had been absorbed into the new State apparatus, and the strong industrial development which now set in gave many more of them unexpected opportunities to rise from the ranks.

At the same time, even in this period, a tendency became visible which was subsequently to become of great importance for the whole future of the Soviet Union. This was the fact that heavy industry was developed out of all proportion to the consumer-goods industries, with the result that working-class living standards remained extremely low, and sometimes fell even lower. In other words, an exceptionally high percentage of production was used for new investments, in order to force production up still higher, and at the same time this increase in the total product was not used for the benefit of the workers, but in order to extend the productive apparatus still further and build up industries such as had been built up in capitalist countries generations before.

The opinion of the Russian workers on the point was never frankly canvassed, and there is little doubt that if they had been able to express their views through the usual machinery of democratic voting they would never have agreed to industrial construction on a scale and, above all, at a rate which imposed such terrible sacrifices on them.

The fact that the new economic programme had to be carried through against the will of large sections of the peasants, and, in the best case, with the rather hesitant approval of the working class, led to a further intensification of the dictatorship.

In the beginning the dictatorship was the will of a party; in this period it became the will of a part of a party, which proceeded more and more ruthlessly to suppress the opposition of the other part.

The time had not yet come when members of the opposition were physically liquidated, but things had already gone so far that Stalin and his State apparatus made it quite clear to all oppositional elements that in such a tense and uncertain economic and political situation they would not be tolerated much longer. It was at this time that the opposition was gagged and deprived of all legal means of expressing its opinions, and all fractional activity in the Communist Party was crushed by the weight of the State apparatus.

The Leninist form of dictatorship was gradually replaced by the dictatorship of Stalin.

In this period Soviet Russia was still far behind the European industrial countries. When she once again reached pre-war production levels in 1927–1928—in other words, when she at last produced as much as Tsarist Russia had once produced—her production was still only about half the total industrial production of France, and hardly a third of German production. Thus in the period between the two world wars the Soviet Union was not a world power; she became that only after the second world war. Apart from the drive of the Red Army which flung the Polish invader from Russian soil and reached the gates of Warsaw, there was not the slightest attempt at any time throughout this whole period to bring Russian military strength to bear outside the Russian frontiers.

RUSSIA AND THE COMMUNIST PARTIES

The Russian method of obtaining influence abroad was through the Communist Parties in the various countries. These Communist Parties rapidly became more and more dependent on Russian directions, until finally they were reduced to completely subservient tools of Russian foreign policy.

As a logical consequence of his erroneous views on European capitalist development and on the attitude of the European working class, Lenin founded the Communist International, and sought to detach the workers from their old socialist leaders; all he succeeded in doing was to split the working class from top to bottom. However, in his view the Communist International was to be the decisive instrument for the socialist revolution outside Russia.

The socialist revolution did not materialize outside Russia. There were not even any serious attempts to bring it about. After the war Communist Parties were formed in most European countries, very often in a vigorous struggle against the Right wings of the old social-democratic parties which had identified themselves completely with their own brand of capitalism during the war. Without organized Russian intervention the international working-class movement would probably have become unified again, but the interests of the new Russian State lay in the other direction. Although before long the sociological and economic reasons for the existence of separate Communist Parties had largely disappeared, the Russian State insisted on their retention as instruments to influence the European working-class movement in the interests of Russian foreign policy.

The narrowing down of the basis of the dictatorship in the Soviet Union now fundamentally changed the nature of the Communist Parties abroad. They became mere sounding-boards for the major fraction in Russia's internal party squabbles. The leadership of the Communist Parties did not develop out of the requirements of the working-class movement at home, but in relation to these internal party squabbles. Only those who supported Stalin unreservedly had any chance of becoming party leaders. Thus, owing to constant Russian intervention, the leadership of the Communist Parties and the parties themselves rapidly degenerated.

Because the Russian State maintained the Communist Parties, it perpetuated the disruption of the European working-class movement throughout the whole period between the two world wars, and undermined the effectiveness of all working-class action.

In the period of European capitalist stagnation the European working-class movement was also stagnant, and quite incapable of carrying out any effective action on a large scale, and the main reason for this was the political intervention of the Russian State, a point with which we shall deal again later.

The period in which the Soviet Union managed to reach Tsarist pre-war levels of production was essentially a period of reconstruction. When it was finally ended, the period of construction began and the first Five-Year Plan was launched. The Plan started at a time when there was still a phase of capitalist prosperity in Europe and the United States, but its decisive years coincided with the first years of the world economic crisis.

CHAPTER THREE

THE WORLD ECONOMIC CRISIS NEVER FULLY LIQUIDATED

THE PERIOD OF "prosperity" which preceded the world economic crisis of 1929 lacked many of the features which marked normal periods of prosperity in earlier phases of capitalism. For one thing, the prosperity did not affect all sectors of the economic system, and both in the United States and in Germany large parts of the agricultural system clearly showed signs of stagnation and depression even before the crisis broke out. For various reasons, a considerable volume of unemployment—in each case well over the million mark—existed in the United States, Great Britain and Germany. Many British export industries were unable to extricate themselves from a period of chronic depression. And the leading industrial countries of Europe were unable to reach pre-war foreign-trade levels.

The end of capitalist expansion was affecting developments even in the prosperity period, which was, in any case, a period of semi-prosperity only, although post-war reconstruction did much to conceal the real situation.

Now, just as this prosperity period before the world economic crisis differed from previous periods of prosperity, so the crisis, when it finally did break out, differed from previous crises.

It is not necessary for us to describe and analyse the various phases of the world economic crisis which broke out in 1929; the facts are well known and not in dispute; but what we must do is to recognize them in their order of importance both nationally and internationally, and to recognize why the crisis was fundamentally different from all previous crises which had shaken the capitalist system, why it shook the capitalist system to the core, and why it represented a turning point on the way to the ultimate transformation of the system as a whole.

WORLD TRADE AND INDUSTRIAL PRODUCTION DECLINE

The tremendous depth of the crisis when it did come can be readily seen from the great fall in industrial production in all the leading countries with the exception of the Soviet Union.

World Indices of Industrial Production [1]

(Average for 1929 = 100)

Year.	World including U.S.S.R.	World excluding U.S.S.R.	U.S.A.	Germany.	France.	United Kingdom.	Japan.	Italy.
1930	88·6	86·5	80·7	85·9	99·1	92·3	94·8	91·9
1931	79·1	74·8	68·1	67·6	86·1	83·8	91·6	77·6
1932	69·8	63·8	53·8	53·3	71·6	83·5	97·8	66·9

These figures show that world industrial production, not including the Soviet Union, declined between 1929 and 1932 to 63·8 per cent of its 1929 level, or by more than one-third. The decline was greatest in the two leading industrial countries, the United States and Germany, where production was almost halved. Industrial production in the United States fell to 53·8 per cent, and in Germany to 53·3 per cent. But in Britain and France the decline was also very great. In France it was almost 30 per cent. Great Britain came through the crisis rather more favourably than the other highly developed capitalist countries, and her production declined by "only" 16·5 per cent.

Never in the history of capitalism had there been any remotely comparable decline in production. The decline in world capitalist production during the crisis was not only greater than it had ever been in history before, but it was even considerably greater than the decline in world production during the course of the first world war. During the war European industrial production dropped by about a third, but non-European industrial production actually increased, and to such an extent that the actual world decline as a result of the war was only about 10 per cent. The fact that U.S. production during the war increased very considerably helped to accelerate the speed of European reconstruction after the war by supplying foodstuffs, raw materials and capital.

In other words, during the first world war the productive apparatus of the United States was immune to war damage and to any decline of production in consequence of the war. And as a large sector which is immune in a crisis usually greatly assists in the process of overcoming the crisis, so the strengthening and extension of the economic organism of the United States made it possible to overcome the effects of the war in Europe sooner than would otherwise have been the case.

But during the world economic crisis the United States was not an immune sector. On the contrary, it was affected particularly badly, and at a time when the share of the U.S.A. in world production had greatly increased.

The decline of world production as a whole as a result of the first world war was a good 10 per cent, but in the world economic crisis it was (outside the Soviet Union) no less than 36·2 per cent. *In other words, the decline of world capitalist production in the crisis was more than three times as great as the decline in production as a result of the first world war*, or about as great as the decline in production in the European belligerent countries after four and a half years of the first world war.

The fact alone that the decline of world capitalist production during the crisis was three times as great as it had been as a result of the first world war, ought to be sufficient to explode the contention that the 1929 world economic crisis was quantitatively not essentially different from the previous crises experienced by capitalism.

We have already seen in Part One of this book that the former crises experienced by capitalism were only temporary interruptions of an otherwise steady period of progress. The following diagram, although it refers only to Germany, graphically shows the decisive

278

difference between the economic crisis of 1929 and all the other crises which preceded it:

INDEX OF INDUSTRIAL PRODUCTION IN GERMANY (1913 = 100)*
The arrows indicate the years of depression

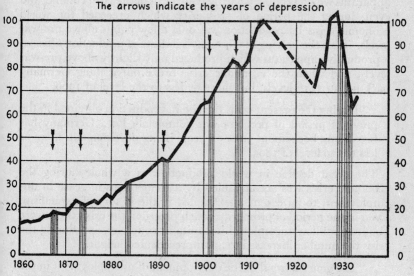

Both in the United States and in Germany, the period which preceded the crisis was marked by a particularly strong investments boom, by a modernization and rationalization of the productive apparatus and by resultant technological unemployment to a quite considerable degree even in that period of prosperity. In these two countries—the leading industrial countries in the world—both of which had shown particularly big rises in production in the period of prosperity which preceded the crisis, the decline of production in the crisis was much greater than elsewhere; for instance, approximately three times as great as in Britain.

Now, although both the United States and Germany suffered approximately equally in production losses during the economic crisis, there was one fundamental difference between them. The halving of industrial production which took place in the United

* This diagram is taken from "The Social Consequences of the Economic Depression" by Vladimir Voytinsky, who writes concerning the decline of production in Germany in earlier crises:

"From 1860 to 1913 the rise in German industry was interrupted six times (in 1867, 1872, 1883, 1891, 1900 and 1907) by economic depressions. But twice (in 1883 and 1900) the effect of the depression was only to slow down the expansion of industrial production. On the four other occasions there was an absolute shrinkage of production of 6 per cent from 1867 to 1874, of 3 per cent from 1891 to 1892, and of 6 per cent from 1906 to 1908. . . . A decline of about 5 per cent may thus be regarded as typical of pre-war periods of depression in Germany " (p. 51).

States affected a productive apparatus which had turned out more goods in 1919 than in 1913, and more goods in 1929 than in 1919, and approximately twice as much as in 1913. Germany emerged from the first world war, on the other hand, with a productive apparatus which produced hardly two-thirds of the 1913 volume, and even during the period of prosperity which preceded the world economic crisis its production was only a few points above pre-war levels. Thus the halving of Germany's industrial production affected a productive apparatus which produced only slightly above pre-war levels, and when the economic crisis broke out it flung Germany back not to 1913 levels, but more or less to the level of 1900.

"During the present crisis the rise in production obtained in the previous period of progress was completely lost. Germany has been flung back about 30 or 35 years in her development, more or less to the level of 1895." [2]

The great decline in world production as a whole during the economic crisis was accompanied by a tremendous increase in unemployment to an extent unexampled in the history of capitalism. Even in the period of prosperity which preceded the crisis there were about 10 million unemployed in capitalist countries, and during the crisis the number increased to an unprecedented height.

"The general trend in the development of unemployment in the world throughout the depression is shown by the general index of unemployment compiled by the International Labour Office. This index takes as a basis of comparison the average level of unemployment in 1929 (which it puts at 100), a period in which industrial production was booming, although there were a million unemployed workers in Great Britain, 2 millions in Germany, nearly 3 millions in the United States, 300,000 in Italy, about the same in Japan, 200,000 in Austria, etc. Allowing for the omissions from official estimates, the total volume of unemployment in the world in 1929 must have been about 10 millions in round figures. From 1929 to 1932 this total was tripled; in the countries covered by the statistics there were almost 30 million unemployed workers when the depression was at its worst. This figure does not include workers on short time, or 'invisible' unemployment. If these two items are added, the total would certainly exceed 40 millions." [3]

The volume of increased unemployment in the various countries was approximately in proportion to the decline in industrial production, and it was thus greatest in the United States and Germany. In Germany it was therefore bigger than anywhere else in Europe, several times greater than either in Britain or France.

Together with a tremendous decline in production and an equally tremendous increase in unemployment, there was also a catastrophic fall in world trade. The following table shows the total values of the imports and exports of the world throughout the crisis years:

(In milliard gold dollars)

	1929.	1930.	1931.	1932.	1933.[4]
Imports . .	35·6	29·1	20·8	14	12·5
Exports . .	33	26·5	18·9	12·9	11·7

World trade during the crisis decreased by over 60 per cent, but that was reckoned in gold dollars. In no previous crisis was there ever anything remotely approaching such a catastrophic decline. In the last thirty years before the outbreak of the first world war the volume of world trade did not decrease even by as much as 10 per cent in any crisis, and in some of the crises in this period the volume, as distinct from the value, of world trade even continued to expand slowly.

"From 1881 to 1913 the rising tendency of world trade was interrupted three times. The total value of imports and exports fell from 1883 to 1885 (by 9 per cent), from 1891 to 1894 (by 8 per cent), and from 1907 to 1908 (by 7 per cent). But during these same periods world prices (measured according to the wholesale-price index for the United Kingdom published by the *Economist*) contrasted even more (from 1883 to 1885 by 11 per cent, from 1889 to 1894 by 13 per cent, and from 1907 to 1908 by 9 per cent). The volume of international trade thus retained its rising tendency during these earlier periods of depression, very much in contrast to the experiences of the last few years." [5]

The diagram [6] on p. 282 clearly shows the contradictory tendencies of development.

In our analysis of the decline in world trade we must always remember that the situation in the leading industrial countries of Europe was very different from that in the United States. The first world war had brought about a tremendous increase of U.S. exports, and even in the twenties, when its total volume was less than that of the war years—which were, of course, quite exceptional—it was still far above pre-war levels. The fact that world trade as a whole in the period before the world crisis was greater in volume than before the first world war was primarily due to the growth of U.S. foreign trade.

The halt in European capitalist imperialist expansion had been reflected in the fact that neither of the two leading industrial countries of Europe, Great Britain and Germany, had succeeded in reaching the 1913 level of foreign trade in any post-war year up to the outbreak of the economic crisis. Thus as far as these two leading European industrial countries were concerned, when the world economic crisis broke out and brought a tremendous decline in world trade, their foreign trade was less than that of 1913. Thus it was thrown back approximately to the 1900 level, and sometimes even lower.

VALUE OF WORLD TRADE*(IMPORTS & EXPORTS)
In thousands of millions of gold dollars

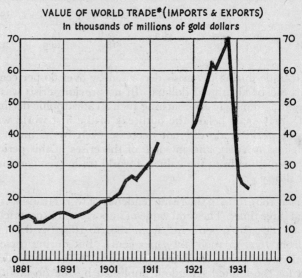

PARALLEL INDUSTRIAL AND AGRICULTURAL CRISES

Thus, as we have seen, the world economic crisis which broke out in 1929 was marked by a decline of production unexampled in the history of capitalism and by a similarly unexampled increase of unemployment. But another important feature of the crisis was that it was simultaneously an industrial and an agricultural crisis. This, too, was a specific characteristic of the 1929 crisis, and it was not present in most of the economic crises of the nineteenth century.

The process by which capitalism drew agriculture into its orbit was comparatively slow. Whilst pre-capitalist forms of production still dominated agriculture, whilst agricultural production was geared only in relatively small part to market requirements, and whilst peasants generally lived largely from their own produce, there were no agricultural crises on a scale commensurate with the industrial crises. The economic crises which broke out during the nineteenth century were noteworthy on the whole for the fact that the agricultural sector was often very little affected by them, and this immunity was of great assistance in the subsequent liquidation of the crises.

The big agricultural crisis which broke out in the second half of the

* Up to 1925, based on the calculations of the German *Statistisches Reichsamt*, from 1926 onwards from the Economic Intelligence Service of the League of Nations.

nineteenth century was not a true international crisis. Its effects were confined to European agriculture, and even then it did not affect European agriculture as a whole, but was restricted primarily to the production of grain.

It was of this crisis that Friedrich Engels [7] wrote:

"The transoceanic steamships, and the North and South American and Indian railways, brought quite unusual areas into a position to compete in the European corn markets. On the one hand there were the North American prairies and the Argentine pampas, great areas which nature herself had made ready for the plough; virgin soil which for years bore rich harvests even with primitive cultivation and without fertilisers. And on the other hand there were the great lands of the Russian and Indian communist communities, which were compelled to sell a part of their produce—an ever-increasing part—to obtain money to pay the taxes which the merciless despotism of the State extorted from them—often enough by torture. This produce was sold without relation to the costs of production, and at prices offered by the dealers, because the peasants just had to have the money to meet their payments on the appointed day. With the old rents the European lease-holders and peasants were unable to compete with the virgin soil of the new world and with the efforts of the Russian and Indian peasants under taxation pressure. A part of the land in Europe definitely ceased to be used for the production of corn for the market . . . and hence the agricultural misery from Scotland to Italy and from the South of France to East Prussia."

European agriculture answered that crisis by adopting intensive cultivation on an increasing scale, whilst the European Governments erected high tariff walls behind which home-grown corn was safe from the flood of transoceanic grain. As a result, prices for agricultural produce in continental Europe rose, but the urban working masses in the great industrial countries of Europe could afford to pay higher prices because the general increase of wages, which we observed earlier, was greater than the rise in food prices which resulted from the protective tariffs.

Compared with earlier crises, the 1929 crisis affected the United States as well as Europe and the colonial and semi-colonial countries, and it affected not only grain production but agricultural production as a whole, with the result that in the 1929 crisis there was no agricultural sector anywhere in the capitalist world which was immune to the crisis, and therefore this international agricultural crisis caused a further intensification of the industrial crisis.

The agricultural crisis of 1929 did not come upon the world like a bolt from the blue. On the contrary, it was already clearly visible at a time when the prosperity period in the towns had not yet ended.

In our analysis of the situation in the United States and in Germany we have already seen that the agricultural sector did not enjoy a share in the period of prosperity which preceded the world economic crisis of 1929, and that in both countries there were millions of farmers and peasants who could not make ends meet, and that therefore, although the burden of agricultural debt was growing, the credits taken up by agriculture were used to a very great extent not in order to modernize agriculture, but in order to meet the personal requirements of farmers and peasants. And then this agricultural sector, already in a precarious state, was hit by the worst crisis of all.

Over-production in industry, with millions of workers unemployed and millions of others poorly paid, unable to buy even all the necessities of life from their earnings or their unemployment pay, is a state of affairs which tends to undermine the whole social order. But over-production at the same time in agriculture, with millions of farmers and peasants facing ruin all over a world full of hungry people, was a state of affairs which necessarily and progressively furthered the destruction of confidence in the capitalist form of society altogether. Nowhere is the specific inherent feature of capitalist crisis more clearly visible than in an agricultural crisis.

Crises in pre-capitalist society came about in consequence of a deficit in production. As agricultural production was absolutely dominant in such social forms, this meant an absolute shortage of foodstuffs, with the result that masses of poor people went hungry or even starved. In those days the prayer "Give us this day our daily bread" was meant literally. But in the 1929 crisis far too much food was produced for the market to absorb, and as a result hundreds of thousands of farmers and peasants were threatened with eviction from their holdings; owing to the steep drop in agricultural prices, they could no longer meet their rent and interest payments. At the same time, however, masses of people in the towns badly needed their produce, but were unable to pay for it. The farmers and the peasants no longer prayed for good harvests; they hoped for the failure of the harvests. "Give us this day not anything like as much daily bread" became their heart-felt prayer.

Now, apart from the fact that the decline in production and foreign trade and the increase in unemployment were all much greater than ever before, there was a new factor which made the world crisis which broke out in 1929 much more profound and much more dangerous than any previous crisis—namely, the fact that nowhere within the framework of the capitalist system was there any sector which still enjoyed immunity from the effects of the crisis. In earlier crises the situation had been different. Very often some countries had not been affected by the crises at all, but, with the exception of the Soviet Union, the economic crisis which broke out in 1929 involved all countries: the older industrial countries and those countries in

284

which agriculture still predominated; the imperialist metropolitan centres and the colonial and semi-colonial countries.

THE CRISIS AND THE MIDDLE CLASS

The crisis not only affected all countries, but it affected all sectors of the capitalist economic system. Nothing and no one escaped. Former crises had often affected only employers and their workers. Farmers, peasants, officials and people living on fixed incomes were often unaffected, and therefore represented a sector which was more or less immune to the crisis. In fact, when, as often happened, the incomes of these strata in the currency of their own countries remained stable, the fall in prices increased their real income. And the existence of a sector within the framework of capitalist society which was immune to the effects of a crisis greatly assisted its subsequent liquidation.

There was no immune sector in the 1929 crisis, which was so profound that it affected all strata of society without exception. Production was almost halved and, as Joseph A. Schumpeter [8] writes: "Three-quarters of all businesses in the United States (including farms) had to face the necessity of an adaptation which threatened them with economic death". There was no escape from the effects of the crisis for any section of society.

In earlier crises the farmers and peasants had often not been directly affected, but the 1929 crisis was simultaneously an industrial and an agricultural one, and the profound disturbances brought about in agriculture aggravated the industrial crisis still further. In earlier crises people living on fixed incomes had often been unaffected, but in the crisis of 1929 all currencies were affected one after the other, and this, together with hundreds of thousands of bankruptcies, naturally greatly affected the position of this stratum of society.

In earlier crises the salaries of officials had often remained stable, but in the 1929 crisis their salaries were either cut down by direct measures or indirectly reduced by currency depreciation, or both. The State reacted to the decline of production, and therefore the decline of its tax revenues, by cutting down its expenditure, including the salaries of its officials.

"Never in the history of the past fifty years did the income of the people fall so much as it fell in this crisis. Never in any previous crisis was there such an all-round decrease in income as there has been in this crisis, which has not spared the salaries of officials, the incomes of independent persons or the income of agriculture, sources of income which were not touched, or hardly touched, in former periods of industrial crisis." [9]

This was written by the official German Institute for Economic

285

Research about the situation in Germany during the crisis, but it applied with equal force to the situation in all capitalist countries throughout the world.

Thus in the crisis of 1929 the middle strata who up to then had been the main basis for the social stability of capitalism were deeply affected. It applied to all the middle strata, both the old and the new. A big section of the newer middle strata was made up of commercial and other employees—the so-called white-collar proletariat. During the period of capitalist progress which had seen the particularly rapid increase of this stratum—that is to say, from the eighties of the nineteenth century on—capitalist crises had not been very severe, and therefore the total volume of unemployment had not been very great. But in the 1929 crises there was mass unemployment not only for workers, but also for clerical employees. Up to that time chronic unemployment had not been within the experience of this section of the middle strata, but in the two leading industrial countries—the United States and Germany—*unemployment figures for these employees alone were greater than the figures for unemployment as a whole in the crises of the late nineteenth century*. Thus during the 1929 economic crisis this stratum of the new middle classes lost its economic basis throughout the world.

Amongst the newer middle strata, together with employees and professional men, were many semi-independent owners of small businesses which had grown up with the increasing wealth of the industrial countries, particularly small businesses in the so-called tertiary industries. The condition of their existence was a smoothly operating, wealthy capitalist industrial system. It is therefore quite obvious that a decline of about 50 per cent in industrial production must have played havoc with these strata. Great masses of the population found it difficult to meet their minimum requirements during the crisis, and the production of the tertiary industries was often outside these minimum requirements. The result was a large-scale closing down of these particular undertakings, and unemployment for millions of members of these new middle strata, a particular form of unemployment which was not reflected in the normal unemployment figures because these people had not been statistically registered as workers.

The same was true of millions of members of the older middle strata. Where smaller businesses managed to survive the crisis which flung millions of industrial workers to the streets, their owners were often faced with the necessity of finding some sort of employment for their unemployed relatives, with the result that there were millions more unemployed concealed here and not included in the official unemployment statistics.

Thus the crisis of 1929 not only brought about the biggest fall in production and foreign trade ever known in capitalist history, and it

286

was not only a crisis in both industry and agriculture, but it was also, though to differing degrees, the first big world crisis for the middle strata, both the old and the new.

The fact that in the crisis of 1929 there was no sector immune from its effects anywhere in any of the big capitalist countries is of decisive importance. This is a point we must stress, because it is greatly neglected in most of the books which have been written about the crisis and about the history of what is called the business cycle in general. It is, of course, closely connected with the fact that in the period in which the 1929 crisis broke out the percentage of those people in the big capitalist countries who produced more or less outside the capitalist system had sunk practically to nil.

Numerous economists who do admit that the crisis of 1929 was particularly severe—much more severe than the crises of the latter part of the nineteenth century—often go on to say that the 1929 crisis touched the trough of a long wave, and that the crises in the seventies of the nineteenth century were almost as bad.

We have already seen that this claim is false, and that the world economic crisis which broke out in 1929 was much more profound in industry and foreign trade than any of the economic crises of the seventies.

Their contention also ignores the fact that in the seventies *the capitalist sector was by no means predominant* even in the big industrial countries. In the seventies in Germany, for example, the value of agricultural production was still higher than that of industrial production. The official German Institute for Business Research writes:

> "According to rough calculations the value of industrial production equalled the value of agricultural production for the first time between 1880 and 1890." [10]

And in the seventies the majority of the population of the United States (53 per cent) were still engaged in agriculture.

In the seventies in Germany there were very few undertakings employing more than a hundred workers:

> "Most factories employed between 30 and 100 workers." [11]

In 1870 the urban population in the United States totalled 9·9 millions, whereas the population of the rural areas still totalled 28·7 millions, and even in 1880 the figures were 14·13 millions to 36·03 millions respectively. In 1871 the urban population in Germany was still only 36·1 per cent of the whole.

Thus both in the United States and Germany in the seventies the agricultural population was still much greater than the urban population; small and medium undertakings still dominated in industry; and independent entrepreneurs represented the majority in both agriculture and industry.

287

In other words, although the purely capitalist sector in the big industrial countries had grown much stronger by comparison with the fifties, it was still not predominant, much less absolutely dominant.

Thus, even at home the sector which enjoyed a certain immunity from the effect of economic crisis was still very strong, and outside the leading industrial countries capitalism was still in its infancy. The fact that even in the big industrial countries the sector outside capitalism was so large meant that despite the economic crises, the social and political structure of the various capitalist countries were only superficially shaken.

To write a history of economic crises, of the so-called business cycles, without even mentioning the fact that the influence of the capitalist sectors, even in the industrial countries, was very different at different historical periods means to ignore one of the decisive factors of the whole problem and to overlook the thing which is of fundamental importance for any effective analysis of the 1929 crisis.

Why did the world economic crisis which broke out in 1929 shake capitalism to its foundations. If, as so many experts still insist, it was not much different from the economic crises which preceded it, why did it have such fundamentally different and so much more profound effects on the whole world?

The answer is that in the highly developed industrial areas of the world—in the United States, Germany and Western Europe in general—capitalism had not only become predominant, but almost absolutely dominant in the fifty years from the seventies up to 1929. In other words, *a crisis in the capitalist sector of the economic system was now identical with a crisis in the economic system as a whole.*

The development of capitalism had led in a strange and complicated fashion to a tremendous intensification of the phenomenon of economic crisis. After very severe economic crises in England, which was then the most highly developed capitalist country in the world, in the second quarter of the nineteenth century, the general picture changed, in so far as a tremendous period of capitalist expansion opened up which extended both home and foreign markets and diminished the severity of the economic crises.

However, whilst this development diminished the severity of the crises, it also increased the influence of the purely capitalist sector of the economic system in all the big industrial countries, until finally that sector represented not far short of the whole. In other words, *the vulnerability of the capitalist economic system as a whole and of capitalist society in general the phenomenon of economic crisis greatly increased.*

In the capitalist centres pre-capitalist methods of production had practically disappeared. Capitalism had become vulnerable to economic crisis as never before, and when the 1929 crisis came it was fundamentally shaken.

Further, the severity of the crisis when it did come made it much more difficult for the capitalist economic system to emerge from it in the traditional way by the operation of the automatic recovery factors within capitalism itself.

We have already pointed out that:

1. Formerly there were strong sectors in the capitalist countries which enjoyed a certain immunity to the effects of economic crisis. We now know that these, so to speak, invulnerable sectors have almost completely disappeared.

2. Apart from these almost immune sectors in the capitalist countries themselves, there were other countries which were often not affected by the crises, and therefore offered a possibility of further expansion. We have already seen that the outward expansion of capitalism had practically ceased before the outbreak of the 1929 crisis. We shall also see later on that during the crisis itself, and after capitalism had at least emerged from its trough, there was no further expansion of any moment beyond the frontiers.

3. Formerly neither the decline of production nor the increase of unemployment was very great; although wages fell in crisis periods, prices often fell even more, with the result that the real wages of those workers still employed often actually increased during crisis periods; and because unemployment was not very great as a result of crisis, the total real income of the working class did not decline very greatly. For this reason, too, it proved easier to liquidate a crisis.

But in the 1929 crisis the situation in the two leading industrial countries of the world—the United States and Germany—was much more difficult and dangerous. We shall deal later on with the specific situation in Great Britain.

Stanley Lebergott [12] has conducted a highly interesting investigation of the movement of wages in the United States during the 1929 crisis and since the nineties:

Money and Real Earnings of Average Non-Farm Employee

Year.	Full-time equivalent earnings.	Time lost by unemployment (percentage).	Money earnings.	Cost of living (1910–1914 = 100).	Real earnings in 1910–1914 dollars.
1890	559	6·2	524	81·4	644
1910	685	5	651	97·2	670
1929	1,535	4·9	1,460	174·9	835
1930	1,495	13·4	1,295	170·5	760
1933	1,170	36·5	743	131·9	563

What do these figures show? In the first years of the crisis the wages of a fully employed worker fell from 1,535 dollars in 1929 to 1,170 dollars in 1933. However, as in the same period the cost of living fell from 174·9 to 131·9, the real wages of fully employed workers remained more or less stable, but as, at the same time, unemployment increased enormously, average real earnings dropped from 835 dollars to 563 dollars, or to a level below that of 1890. Now, this enormous fall in total earnings in the United States was one of the reasons which made it so difficult for capitalism to overcome the crisis through the operation of its own inherent recovery factors.

Developments in Germany proceeded on somewhat similar lines. The real earnings of workers, employees and officials fell from 44,466 milliard marks before the crisis to 25,685 milliard marks in 1932, whilst the cost-of-living index fell from 153·8 in 1929 to 120·9 in 1932,[13] or to a far lesser extent.

In Germany, as in the United States, the real earnings of the working class sank considerably in the trough of the crisis as a result of mass unemployment, so that—unlike what happened in many of the nineteenth-century crises—the price fall did not set the automatic recovery mechanism into operation.

On the Causes of the 1929 Economic Crisis

Whole libraries of books have already been written about the decisive causes of the 1929 economic crisis. Most of the explanations offered are inadequate, and this is no accident. They are inadequate because their authors all start off by assuming that it is "normal" for the capitalist mode of production to operate smoothly, that "normally" profits and wages both increase, production and foreign trade likewise, and that although this development proceeds within the framework of the business cycle, depressions and disturbances are merely interruptions of the "normal" course of events, and therefore comparatively easily and quickly overcome.

Proceeding from these assumptions, they then asked themselves why the 1929 economic crisis was so exceptionally severe and why it did not fit into their hypotheses. And they offered a variety of explanations: the after-effects of the first world war, reparations, short-term international credits (with particular respect to the severity of the economic crisis in Germany) and so on.

We naturally do not propose to dispute the fact that these factors, and many others, played a role in bringing about the 1929 crisis, but *they were not the fundamental causes*. In Part One of this book we have already seen that there were a whole series of historical circumstances which led to the tremendous period of capitalist progress from the middle of the nineteenth century up to the outbreak of the first world war, a period of progress which was only temporarily interrupted by economic crises. Now, the truth is that this phase of steady capitalist progress was "normal" only so long as the specific historical conditions which actually brought it about continued to exist.

In Chapter One, Part III of our book we have seen that similar historical conditions for expansion did not exist in the period between the two world wars, and why, therefore, no such expansion took place. We have also seen that it was not primarily the war which was responsible for such a fundamental change in the historical conditions under which capitalism exists.

However, it is readily understandable that people in Europe should be inclined to attribute the particular violence of the 1929 crisis to the war, because, after all, Europe *was* tremendously affected by the war.

So far, so good; but it is certainly ridiculous to suggest that the first world war was primarily responsible for the severity of the 1929 crisis in the United States. It was not the first world war which put a stop to the expansion of U.S. capitalism within its own frontiers; that came about for quite other reasons, and would have come about even had there been no war. It was not the first world war which was responsible for the fact that, for the first time in U.S. history, the agricultural population decreased not only relatively but absolutely, and that for the first time in U.S. history the numbers of the industrial working class did not increase in a period of growing production and prosperity.

Further, it was not the war which was responsible for the fact that British industrial production was backward by comparison with U.S. and German production. That was already the case before the war. It was not the war which led to industrial stagnation and to the stagnation of foreign trade in the colonial and semi-colonial countries, but the policy of the imperialist powers, and that policy did not change in the period between the two world wars.

To put the problem in a different way; once its expansion, which was for the greater part of an imperialist nature, had more or less come to an end, European capitalism had to find a new equilibrium. In the same way, U.S. capitalism had to find a new equilibrium once its expansion within its own frontiers had more or less come to an end, and its possibilities of expansion beyond its own frontiers were relatively small.

That was the problem which faced capitalism both in Europe and in the United States. It was not solved. The acid test of synchronising the increase of the productive forces and of production with an increase of consumption on the basis of the capitalist profit-making system, but without any very great external expansion, found capitalism wanting.

The result was the world economic crisis of 1929.

It is quite impossible to understand its causes if the investigation is confined to one phase of the crisis—to the worst years of the depression. Any investigation which proceeds on this basis must necessarily only scratch the surface. The world economic crisis which broke out in 1929 must be analysed against a background of the decisive changes which had come about for the whole capitalist system. Only then shall we be able to grasp why the crisis was so severe and to understand the period from the trough of the crisis up to the outbreak of the second world war.

Now, the economic crisis itself was not only fundamentally different from all previous crises, but the period which followed it from 1933 to 1939 was also fundamentally different from all earlier periods of capitalist development. Most of the investigations which have been conducted into the 1929 crisis break down precisely because they limit themselves to the crisis itself, and thus all their explanations fail to tell us why the development of capitalism after the trough of the crisis had been passed—from 1933 up to 1939—had no parallel in history, and why it deviated so fundamentally from all previous trends of capitalism.

Incidentally, it is no accident that since the world economic crisis there has been a certain *rapprochement* between liberal reformers and socialist circles. Up to the outbreak of that crisis liberal economists had regarded it as a matter of course that capitalism functioned "automatically". After all, Ricardo and the classic economists had "proved" it, and economic history had confirmed their thesis, and for generations more goods had been produced, profits and wages had risen, living standards had improved and crisis severity had diminished. None of them grasped the prime importance of the functional relation between crisis, imperialism and capitalist expansion.

Before the first world war socialists found it difficult to refute their arguments, particularly because most socialists had adopted the Marxist viewpoint that the severity of the crises must progressively increase; and that was obviously—then—not the case.

The world economic crisis of 1929 shook the confidence of many liberal economists in the automatic recovery mechanism of capitalism, and in consequence the view became more and more widely held that the State must no longer play the role of passive spectator in times of crisis.

At the same time socialists found that their views about the nature of economic crises had received confirmation in practice. The liberal economists, following Keynes, and the socialists—without adopting the same theoretical attitude—now agreed that in times of crisis State intervention must take place on a much greater scale than before.

. . . . .

But to return to our main contention: the first world war proved a turning point in the history of European capitalism, and the economic crisis of 1929 was a turning point in the history of world capitalism. It ushered in a new phase of capitalist transformation.

Before we analyse the subsequent period it would be good to look back for a moment over the path we have travelled, so that we may better understand why such decisive factors now operated in the direction of this transformation.

Prior to the crisis of 1929 world capitalism as a whole had tremendous reserves at its disposal through its expansionist drive, and this expansion helped it to co-ordinate the growth of production and the growth of markets for that production.

It had also possessed powerful buffers which took the pressure in periods of depression, thus mitigating their effects and assisting their liquidation. These were in the form of strong sectors of the economic system which were immune, or largely immune, to the effects of economic crisis, and which therefore operated in all the phases of a crisis, in the period leading up to the crisis, in the trough of the crisis itself, and in the period immediately following the crisis.

Further, in this whole period of capitalist progress, both in the capitalist metropolitan centres in Europe and in the United States, the influence of the State on economic affairs was relatively small.

Where was the need for any intervention on the part of the State when the capitalist mode of production was quite well able, without any very great upheavals, to raise production, consumption, profits, wages, foreign trade, employment, the national income and living standards in general? As capitalism succeeded in doing precisely this for a very long time, even the experts began to believe that this was the "normal" state of affairs, and that capitalism would always be able to do it. Thus no attention was paid to the specific historical circumstances which favoured the advance of capitalism and at the same time ameliorated the severity of economic crises. The result was that when the world economic crisis of 1929 broke on the world with unprecedented violence, the capitalist economic system, and capitalist society in general, both in Europe and the United States, were completely unprepared for it and had no idea of how to ameliorate its effects and finally liquidate it.

THE NEW ROLE OF THE STATE

Capitalism was now faced with new problems.

Precisely because capitalism had become more and more the absolutely dominant mode of production, which meant that the whole economic system was now extremely susceptible to the effects of economic crisis, capitalism now sought to create a sector which should as far as possible enjoy immunity from the effects of the crisis, and continue to produce, crisis or no crisis. Further, this sector was not only to be immune to the effects of the crisis itself, but it was, by its very immunity and solidity, to help the rest of the capitalist economic system to overcome the crisis.

Such a sector could not, of course, be created within the framework of old-style liberal capitalism. The crisis had proved that clearly enough. In order to build up this new sector the State had to take up a new position within the framework of the capitalist economic system and capitalist society.

In other words, henceforth the State was to play more and more the role which had formerly been played by capitalist expansion and by those sectors within the framework of capitalism which had enjoyed a certain immunity to economic crisis. The State had first of all to create a new and big sector which should be immune to the effects of economic crisis, and secondly it had to bring the increase of production into better accord with consumption, or markets, than the automatically operating mechanism of capitalism was now in a position to do.

The world economic crisis of 1929 represented the transition from the old to the new phase of capitalist development. Expansion plus the automatically operating recovery mechanism of capitalism were no longer effective, whilst the State had not yet begun to carry out its new functions. It was only during the course of the crisis itself that the State gradually began to adapt itself to its new role. Now, in this process of transformation the State began to intervene in economic affairs, to a far greater extent than it had ever done in the nineteenth century, to perform its new task of closing the huge gap between production and consumption or, at least, if that should not prove altogether possible, to narrow it. To this end the State naturally had to intervene effectively to change the social structure as well.

From this it follows that although there were certain general similarities in the methods of the various capitalist States, there were also very great differences in detail, according to their social structure and the influence of the various social strata in them.

No Socialist Measures during the Crisis

There was no decisive turn towards socialism in any of the big industrial countries during the crisis, any more than there had been during the first world war, and no important steps in this direction were made in any of them.

As far as the U.S.A. was concerned, the reason for this was clear enough. U.S. capitalism had experienced an unprecedented phase of expansion not only up to the outbreak of the first world war, but even during the war and beyond it up to the outbreak of the world economic crisis. It is not surprising, therefore, that there was no very considerable support for any movement directed against capitalism. There seemed no need to oppose a system which had succeeded in raising general living standards to such an extent, even though there might be room for objection in minor matters.

Thus when the economic crisis struck the United States it had never known a socialist mass movement on the scale of the socialist movements in the industrial countries of Europe. This fact alone was sufficient to explain why there was no important move towards socialism and why, in fact, there could not possibly have been any such thing. There were no organized and trained socialist forces in the United States to launch any such move. Thus all the measures which were taken to combat the effects of the crisis were taken within the framework of the capitalist system.

In Europe the situation was different because in the leading industrial countries there were big working-class organizations whose final aim was a socialist transformation of society.

However, the violent disturbances suffered by European capitalism as a result of the first world war had also caused deep disturbances in the working-class movement; so much so that even progressive socialist elements did not enter the post-war period with the idea that a turning point had been reached in the development of capitalism and that now it was the task of the living socialist generation in this new period of capitalism to bring about a socialist transformation of society.

On the contrary, they entered the post-war period with the idea that the first world war had merely interrupted the progress of capitalism in Europe and that in the post-war years that progress would gradually be resumed.

In the first years after the war it was naturally an easy matter to ascribe all difficulties to the aftermath of war, and preliminary developments seemed to support this view, because from the middle twenties up to the outbreak of the crisis in 1929 very considerable progress was actually made.

Developments had not proceeded in the sense that after an almost uninterrupted period of capitalist progress lasting into the period of the first world war, an obvious decline had set in, subsequently to be dramatically accelerated by the crisis. If we represent pre-war production in the year 1913 at 100, then what happened was a heavy drop down to 60, followed after the war by a gradual rise up to 1929, by which time production levels had regained 1913 levels and were even a little higher here and there. It was then that the crisis broke out.

In the period which preceded the crisis, and during the crisis itself, developments in Europe were not uniform. Just as the victorious powers were not so seriously shaken by the war as Germany, so they were also not so seriously affected by the economic crisis when it came. Germany, which was worst hit by the crisis, was thus the only country in which big socialist actions would have been possible.

Instead of that, the counter-revolution was victorious.

The Crisis brought a Nazi Victory

Developments in Germany were very different from developments in the United States, in Great Britain and in Western Europe. Germany had that much in common with the United States, that she suffered far more heavily from the crisis than either Great Britain or France, and her industrial production dropped by approximately half. But whereas in the United States the answer to the crisis was Roosevelt and the so-called New Deal, Germany's answer was the victory of Hitler and "National Socialism". In short, the victory of the counter-revolution instead of the revolution.

Amongst the many factors which combined to bring about a Nazi victory was undoubtedly the circumstance that the bourgeoisie in Germany, which had so long been politically dominated by junkers and militarists, was not so mature as the bourgeoisie either in France or Great Britain, but that circumstance alone is far from sufficient to explain the victory of the Nazi counter-revolution.

We must delve deeper in our search for an explanation and examine all the economic and social factors which made Germany's development so very different from that of the United States even before the crisis. It would be totally inadequate and superficial to confine our analysis to the crisis itself and its direct effects. We must note the differences in the various social organisms which were affected by the crisis.

It is a matter of decisive importance whether the crisis struck an economically strong and socially stable organism, or whether it struck one which was already badly shaken, and therefore highly vulnerable.

The fact is, as I said in 1932: "Germany was the weakest link in the chain of highly-developed capitalist industrial countries." [14] German capitalism had been able to finance the few years of prosperity after the inflation only by taking up foreign credits on a big scale, and when the economic crisis broke out in the United States not only did all capital exports cease, but creditors began to press for the repayment of their credits, which were mostly short term. Thus German capitalism—which did not, like British and French capitalism, possess any big foreign investments, Germany being a debtor country—soon found the situation becoming catastrophic.

In our general analysis of the crisis we pointed out that, for the first time in the history of capitalism, the economic crisis embraced the whole economic system, and that affected all strata of the population. This was particularly true of the United States and Germany. There was hardly a sector immune from the effects of the crisis in either of these countries.

However, in the United States the crisis struck an economic organism which had just experienced a long and uninterrupted period of progress which had continued even during the first world war; in Germany it struck a social organism which had already been badly defeated and had suffered heavily in war, which had only recently gone through a terrible period of inflation, with devastating effects on the urban middle strata, and after a period of prosperity which had lasted only a few years. It is not surprising, therefore, that the situation in Germany was incomparably more serious than in the United States or in Great Britain and France.

In the United States the only question was how best to overcome the crisis, and no one doubted for one moment that it would be overcome without any radical transformation of the capitalist system. And although the capitalist system had been roughly shaken in Great Britain and France, by comparison with Germany it was much more stable, and normal democratic institutions still existed and functioned.

In Germany the crisis was much more severe than in any other European country, and it came after a lost war and after a terrible period of inflation, and it found a social organism which had only just got rid of its feudal-military rulers and introduced parliamentary democracy.

The more acute the economic crisis became the more it was obvious that, in view of the specific structure of Germany, it could hardly be overcome within the framework of the capitalist system and with the maintenance of the new democratic political institutions. Thus the alternatives for Germany were not the same as they were for the United States: whether to overcome the crisis by more conservative or more progressive methods; or for Great Britain and France: whether to overcome the crisis by more progressive or more reactionary measures, whilst leaving class relations more or less unchanged. In Germany the crisis was too deep, the upheaval too enormous, the dynamic of developments too rapid. The alternatives in Germany were: the maintenance of the capitalist system and at the same time the destruction of all the new democratic political institutions—in other words, the inauguration of a capitalist-fascist State—or decisive steps towards a radical social transformation of society.

Big Business was naturally in favour of the former solution. Germany's heavy industrialists had never been particularly democratic, and now, when they believed that the very basis of the capitalist system was threatened, they tolerated, and even supported, the rise of the Nazis. They adopted this attitude even during the economic crisis, and they did not change it materially after the Nazi seizure of power up to the outbreak of the second world war.

Germany's militarists were also in favour of the reactionary solution. After Germany's defeat in the first world war her army had not merely been reduced to its peace-time strength, as was the case in France, but officially, by the Versailles Treaty, to 100,000 men, or a mere fraction of its peace-time strength. The German army leaders had always stood well to the right in politics, as military men usually do in all countries. They were in favour of the counter-revolutionary solution because they hoped it would give Germany a stronger foreign-political position and lead to the building up of a big army again, and thus to a great increase in their own power.

The junkers—the remnants of the old German feudal structure— were naturally also in favour of the counter-revolutionary solution. They had managed to retain certain influential positions into the post-war years, despite the military defeat of their world, and they hoped that the victory of the counter-revolution would strengthen their hand.

All these social strata held influential positions, but, of course, their numbers were not very great.

The Middle Class was Fascism's Main Basis

The strata which were numerically decisive for the victory of the counter-revolutionary solution were the German middle strata in town and country. These strata represented a sector of German society which was numerically of approximately the same strength as the German working class, if not stronger. They represented about 50 per cent of the total population of the country.

The decisive factor which gave the Nazi movement a mass basis in Germany was that during the course of the economic crisis, and shaken by its effects, the German middle strata rallied to the Nazi slogans.

As this factor was not only decisive for the victory of the counter-revolution in Germany, but is also of great importance for coming developments, we propose to deal in some detail here with the rise of the Nazis during the period of economic crisis, and to show that it went hand in hand with the numerical decline of the four non-Catholic middle-class political parties in Germany, whilst the overwhelming majority of the German working class rejected all the blandishments of the Nazis and stood by their two political parties, the Social Democratic Party and the Communist Party, to the end.

Why did the great majority of the German middle strata go over to the Nazi counter-revolution during the economic crisis?

There were, of course, a variety of reasons, particularly as the German middle strata were made up of widely disparate elements, including the urban professional man and the peasant in a remote village. However, one or two points were common to them all.

The crisis was the first time in the history of German capitalism that the middle strata as a whole were severely affected. During the war, for example, this had not been the case. Then, and in the inflation period which followed it, the urban middle strata had been amongst the chief sufferers. On the other hand, the German peasants, like the farmers and peasants of all the belligerent countries, had done moderately well for themselves during the war, whilst even during the inflation their economic position had improved. However, the economic crisis was a great blow for both the urban middle

298

strata and the peasants, and both of them had to face it without any very great reserves to soften the blow. The urban middle strata had already lost most of their property and their savings during the war and inflation, and the peasants had lost a good deal of their substance in the years preceding the crisis, which had already been years of depression for them. The result was that the German middle strata were caught up in the crisis with the vague feeling that they were helpless pawns in an historical process which was cutting the social basis more and more from under their feet. In consequence they became very "radical" and demanded an alteration of the whole social and economic system. But they did not become socialists. Had they become socialists they would have realized that the historical process which was destroying their social basis was final and inevitable. They were, in fact, very far from any such realization, and that need not surprise us. It had taken generations before any very large sections of the European working class had answered the aggravation of social antagonisms in European capitalism by becoming socialists—i.e. by demanding a complete social transformation of capitalist society.

Almost a hundred years ago Marx wrote in the preface to his "Critique of Political Economy":

"The mode of production of material life determines the social, political and mental processes of life in general. It is not the consciousness of men which determine their being, but their social being which determines their consciousness. At a certain stage in their development the material productive forces of society come into conflict with existing productive relations, or with the property relations, which is merely a legal expression for the same thing, within which they have previously operated. From forms of development of the productive forces these relations become a drag on the productive forces. An epoch of social revolutions then opens up. As the economic basis changes so the whole tremendous superstructure changes more or less rapidly too." [15]

Many, many years passed between the time Karl Marx wrote his famous words and the time when the "superstructure" in the consciousness of the workers changed, and they began to realize that in order to achieve their aim they would need first to bring about a radical transformation in the whole capitalist system of society. But as far as the middle strata of society were concerned, the fundamental change in their economic and social basis was only just beginning to make itself felt to any extent. This process of change set in only with the first world war, and for some sections it did not noticeably begin until the outbreak of the world economic crisis. In consequence their outlook had not had sufficient time to change, and so, instead of reacting to their changing situation by throwing in their lot with the workers and seeking a progressive way out of the crisis, they longed at first for a return of the past—which was so near that a return seemed possible to them. In other words, their instinctive reaction was backward rather than forward, and they therefore turned to the party which was not compromised and discredited in their eyes because up to then it had had no part in the government of the country, particularly as this party promised them a return to the old comfortable social structure with a secure social basis for the middle strata. That was the so-called Nationalist Socialist Workers Party, better known as the Nazis.

The agricultural middle strata also went over to the Nazis almost in a body, with the exception of those who remained loyal to the Catholic parties for religious reasons. In this respect the situation in Germany was very different from that which had existed in Russia at the time of the November Revolution. The revolution in Russia had been preceded by long years of struggle for a radical agrarian reform and the abolition, or at least the reduction, of large-scale feudal landed-property relations. The revolution carried out this radical reform, and the landless labourers and poor peasants obtained the land. But Germany was already largely a peasant country; the peasants were not crying out for land; generally speaking, they already had it; what they wanted was a state of affairs which would allow them to live on the land they already possessed and at the same time maintain their old middle-class income. Their demands were therefore for higher prices, a lower rate of interest on mortgages, a moratorium for their debts, and so on. As these demands were not fulfilled by the Bruening Government or supported with sufficient vigour by the old middle parties, the peasants, who were anti-socialist just as all peasants are, went over to the Nazis.

At the same time a large section of the urban middle strata—the artisans, small business men, traders and even professional men—also flocked to the Nazis, because the crisis had so depressed their living standards that they were often no higher than those of the workers. They, too, did not react to this tremendous worsening of their standards under the capitalist system by demanding a radical transformation of the system; instead they still looked longingly back to the past and demanded a return of their former conditions. What they wanted was the re-establishment of their old social basis, which was, of course, an impossibility. The existing government could not give them what they wanted, and the socialists aimed at something very different, but the Nazis did promise it to them. The new Nazi State was to re-establish the old social stratification, and the middle strata in particular were to regain all their old comforts and dignities. The result was that many of these elements, although not themselves Nazis, gave their votes to the Nazis. After all, the Nazis did promise to protect their interests, so why not give them a chance

300

to carry out their promise? Things couldn't very well get much worse—or so they thought.

The greater part of the white-collar proletariat also joined the rural and urban middle strata in the general flow into the Nazi camp. This particular middle stratum suffered more than any other in the crisis, which was the first economic crisis in German history to produce mass unemployment amongst employees, commerical and otherwise. For example, unemployment amongst employees alone during the world economic crisis in Germany was almost as great as total unemployment had been in former crises. And the more the crisis developed the less grew the difference between the conditions of the employees and those of the workers. Neither before nor during the crisis, however, did the employees react to the worsening of their economic position by making common cause with the workers; on the contrary, they were still anxious to stress the social differences which, they imagined, separated them from ordinary working men. They wanted to be different from the workers; the majority of them were unwilling to believe that their interests demanded that they should make common cause with the workers, as witness the way in which they had always kept their own organizations distinct and separate from those of the workers.

Before the outbreak of the world crisis the great majority of these white-collar elements in Germany, almost three-quarters of them, had been organized in non-socialist, even anti-socialist, organizations (cf. table on p. 112). Unlike the workers, these elements had no socialist traditions; it was therefore understandable that under extreme pressure during the crisis they went over to the Nazis, and not to the organized socialist workers.

However, despite the anti-democratic attitude of German Big Business, despite the fact that the army and the old feudal junker elements supported, or at least tolerated, the Nazi counter-revolution, and despite the reactionary attitude of the great majority of the middle strata, the counter-revolution in Germany, which so fundamentally affected the fate of the whole world, could hardly have been victorious against a united socialist working class putting forward a programme of effective measures to combat the economic crisis and begin a process of socialist transformation.

Before the first world war such a united socialist working class had existed in Germany. The socialist movement there had been the strongest in the world. The first world war brought about a split. But for the victory of the Russian November Revolution and the founding of the Communist International by Lenin with the deliberate intention of disrupting socialist organizations, there is little doubt that sooner or later socialist unity in Germany would have been restored in the post-war period. Thanks to the prestige of the Russian Revolution and the backing of the Russian Government, the bolshevists always had the upper hand in the Communist International, and they effectively prevented any reunion of the German socialist working-class movement.

Although history clearly demonstrated that Lenin was wrong in his judgement of Western European capitalism and the position of the working classes in Western Europe, the bolshevists deliberately perpetuated the disruption of the German working class in order to have the German Communist Party as a subservient tool for the furthering of their foreign policy. Thus the disruption continued in Germany throughout the inflation and into the subsequent years of relative prosperity, and when the world economic crisis broke out it found the German working class still split and largely impotent.

During the course of the crisis the split had catastrophic results. A government of the middle parties under the leadership of Bruening was in power in Germany. The Social Democrats were not represented in this government, but they supported or "tolerated" it as "the lesser evil". During the economic crisis the policy of Bruening's Government was similar to that of the Hoover Government in the United States—i.e. it was largely passive. The State Budget was ruthlessly slashed during the crisis to bring expenditure into line with the greatly reduced revenues of the State. Thus the shrinkage in the capitalist economic sector was accompanied by a shrinkage in the State sector, always in the hope that sooner or later things would change for the better. The Bruening Government had no programme for dealing with the economic crisis because, in common with all other leading capitalist circles, it expected the crisis to develop like previous crises—i.e. it expected the automatic recovery mechanism of the capitalist economic system to operate effectively. But, for reasons which we have already analysed, the crisis did not take this "normal" course, and the result was that the cry for State intervention became louder and louder. The Bruening Government, however, could not be persuaded to intervene effectively, and in consequence it grew progressively weaker as the crisis developed.

Now, if the German socialist working class had been united it could have come forward at this juncture with a systematic programme for dealing with the crisis and combating its effects, and it is highly probable that it would have won the support not only of the workers, but also of considerable sections of the middle strata, many of whom somewhat reluctantly supported the Nazis because they could see no other way out.

The mere fact that there was no such united working-class movement was quite enough to prevent the carrying out of any such programme. Naturally, the middle strata had no confidence in a movement which was disrupted and broken up into two hostile parts, and which showed no signs of carrying out any effective action. Another result of the split in the working-class movement was that a considerable section of the young and enthusiastic working-class elements went over to the communists, and thus the policy of the Social Democratic Party tended to veer farther and farther to the Right of the average German working-class political mean.

The Social Democratic Party "tolerated" the Bruening Government, and in consequence it was unable, and unwilling, to launch any independent action of its own. In addition, its leaders concealed the real seriousness of the situation from the working class; they sought to create the impression that it was just an ordinary crisis which would disappear in the usual fashion: all the workers had to do was to pull in their belts a hole or two and wait patiently until things improved.

It was a tragi-comedy that German Social Democracy, which had long inscribed the socialist transformation on its banners, should, in a period in which capitalism was more shaken than ever before, and in which therefore the chances of this socialist transformation were particularly favourable, have sought to gloss over the seriousness of the situation. This was done, of course, in order to justify its toleration of the Bruening Government and its failure to undertake any effective action of its own in the crisis. Capitalist elements in Germany were much nearer the truth in their factual analysis of the situation.[16]

Thus, as a result of the disruption of the German working-class movement, Social Democracy was practically impotent in the crisis. But the communists were in no better pass, although they were much stronger in Germany than in Great Britain, France and any other European country. What possibilities of action they might have possessed in the crisis were ham-strung from the start by a catastrophically false policy. The Russians, whose tools they were, compelled them to regard their chief task not as the struggle against capitalism and the Nazis, but against the social democrats, who were denounced as "Social Fascists". The result was that the disruption of the German working class was made still worse and all chance of effective working-class action destroyed.

Because they concentrated their efforts on fighting against Social Democracy, the communists were compelled to adopt a totally false estimate of the strength of the Nazis. They had always under-estimated the strength of capitalism. With Lenin, they had expected that the first world war would bring a victory for the revolutionary forces in Germany. That belief had proved illusory, but they learned nothing from it, and now they made more or less the same mistake again, and under-estimated the strength of the counter-revolutionary forces.

At the September elections in 1930 the Nazi poll increased from approximately 800,000 to 6·4 millions, but the comment of the communist official organ, the *Rote Fahne*, on the day after the elections (September 15th, 1930) was:

"Yesterday was Herr Hitler's 'great day', but the so-called electoral victory of the Nazis is the beginning of their end."

Two months later the *Rote Fahne* had still learnt nothing, and on November 16th its leading article declared:

"September 14th was the peak point of the National-Socialist movement in Germany. What comes after that can only be a decline."

Although all the facts mercilessly castigated this folly, it was nevertheless obstinately maintained and developed into a systematic attitude. In a speech to the eleventh plenary session of the Executive Committee of the Communist International, the leader of the German Communist Party, Ernst Thälmann, declared: [17]

"After September 14th, which brought the Nazis a sensational success at the polls, all their supporters throughout Germany expected great things of them. On our part we were not misled by the feelings of panic which arose, even amongst some workers, and particularly amongst the supporters of the Social Democratic Party. We soberly and solemnly declared that September 14th was Hitler's best day, and that it would not be followed by still better days, but worse ones."

Having once stuck its head into the sand at the behest of its Russian masters, the German Communist Party kept it there firmly, and at a plenary session of the Central Committee of the German Communist Party on February 19th, 1932—or less than a year before the Nazi accession to power—Thälmann again declared:

"Nothing would be more fatal than an opportunistic over-estimate of the strength of Hitler fascism. If we were to allow ourselves to be overwhelmed by the tremendous growth of the Hitler movement so that we lost hold of our true class measure of events and fell into a panic . . . then this would inevitably lead to a false estimate of our practical policy not only towards the Nazis but also towards the Social Democratic Party."

In other words, the communist policy of belabouring the social democrats as "the chief social prop of the bourgeoisie" was to continue.

And on December 15th, 1932—six weeks before Hitler came to power—the "Communist International" wrote confidently:

"Of course Germany will not go fascist! The guarantee for this is the victories of the communists, beginning with the mass struggle against fascism and leading on to the struggle of the Berlin transport workers. The guarantee for this is the hundreds of thousands of working-class votes which were given to communism. The guarantee for this is the ceaseless advance of communism."

Many more such passages could be quoted, but these will suffice. Comment seems unnecessary.

Even after the Nazis had actually come to power the communists still grotesquely under-estimated the strength of the counter-revolution. They were quite confident that the Nazis would soon be discredited and that then their turn would come. It was an appalling error, and it cost the lives of hundreds of thousands of German anti-Nazis, and when Hitler decided to attack Russia the Russian masters of the German Communist Party had to pay for it with more than seven million Russian lives—and almost with their own.

Unfortunately there is still no indication that the Russians have learnt anything from their experiences.

During the world economic crisis the German communists concentrated all their efforts on combating Social Democracy, and all they succeeded in doing was to render the whole German working class impotent and incapable of opposing the Nazi threat effectively.

After the second world war the communists once again concentrated their attacks on the European democratic socialists. This time their policy threatens to cost even more. It may well cost the destruction of Europe *and* Russia and lead to an era of barbarism.

The Victory of the Counter-Revolution

Thanks to the Comintern policy pursued by Russia, the German working class was rendered helpless during the worst economic crisis the capitalist system had ever experienced. This meant not only that the counter-revolution, with the more or less direct support of German Big Business, the army and the feudal junker elements, and with a mass basis amongst the middle strata during the crisis, could capture one position after the other with comparative ease, but also that when the Nazis finally came to power there was little or no resistance. The political parties and the trade-union and other organizations of the German working class were destroyed almost without a blow. The counter-revolution was victorious in the biggest industrial country in Europe almost without a fight.

When the Nazis came to power in Germany a new era of world history began.

The victory of the Nazi counter-revolution in Germany greatly aggravated both social and foreign-political antagonisms in a period of European economic stagnation. The Nazis perpetuated the capitalist system and organized a war economy in peace-time for the first time in the history of capitalism. Thus the victory of the counter-revolution in Germany ushered in the period of the second world war.

The Rise of National Socialism

The matter is of such importance that it is worth while paying some attention to the developments which led to the Nazi victory.

The following figures show the progress of the Nazis as measured by the number of votes cast for them at the various German elections from 1924 to 1932: [18]

Nazi Poll and Percentages of the Total Poll at the German Reichstag Elections

	May 4th, 1924.	Dec. 7th, 1924.	May 20th, 1928.	Sept. 14th, 1930.	July 31st, 1932.
Nazi poll:					
(in 1,000's)	1,918	908	810	6,407	13,799
(in percentages)	6·6	3	2·6	18·3	37·3

In 1924, after the terrible experience of the German inflation and in consequence of widespread discontent, the Nazis polled 1,918,000 votes in the May Reichstag elections, or 6·6 per cent of the total poll. After that came the period of relative prosperity; the inflation was at an end; things improved, and the urban middle strata found their position improving, so that in the Reichstag elections which took place in December of the same year the Nazi poll fell to 908,000, or less than half, representing 3 per cent of the total poll. It is interesting and important to note that throughout the whole period of relative prosperity the Nazis remained a not very influential political sect rejected by the overwhelming majority of the German people of all classes, and by May 20th, 1928—almost ten years after the signing of the Versailles Treaty—the Nazis reached their lowest ebb, with 810,000 votes, or only 2·6 per cent of the total poll. Thus the popular explanation that it was the Versailles Treaty which caused it all is seen to receive no support from the facts.

When the world economic crisis broke out, however, the situation rapidly changed, and the Nazi poll increased by leaps and bounds until the word landslide became appropriate to describe what happened. The process is crystal clear: as the economic crisis grew worse, so the Nazi poll and Nazi influence increased.

In the early period of the crisis, in the Reichstag elections of September 14th, 1930, the Nazi poll rose with a great jump to 6,407,000, or 18·3 per cent of the total poll. In the Reichstag elections of July 31st, 1932—by which time the crisis effects had grown very much worse—it more than doubled, and rose to 13,799,000, or 37·3 per cent of the total poll.

It is interesting to discover just where the Nazis obtained their mass basis; from what sections of the population it came. There is very little doubt about the answer. The vast increase in their poll came primarily from the impoverished middle strata, the people who had formerly voted for the various middle-class parties. The final decisive increase came from the almost complete destruction of the three chief middle-class parties and from the very great weakening of a fourth, the so-called German National People's Party led by Hugenberg. The following table shows us the fate of these German middle-class parties in the Reichstag elections between 1924 and 1932:

Middle-Class Poll and Percentages in the Reichstag Elections
(in 1,000's)

	Dec. 7th, 1924.	July 31st, 1932.
German National People's Party .	6,209 or 20·5%	2,187 or 5·9%
German People's Party (Streseman) .	3,051 or 10·1%	436 or 1·2%
Economic Party	1,006 or 3·3%	147 or 0·4%
German State Party (Democrats) .	1,921 or 6·3%	373 or 1%

These four main German middle-class parties, which in ordinary times polled about 40·2 per cent of all votes in the Weimar Republic, polled only 8·5 per cent of the total votes between them towards the end of the acute crisis period. The 31·7 per cent of the poll which swung away from them was not much less than the increase in the Nazi poll during the same crisis period, which amounted to 34·3 per cent of the total poll. Thus the increase in the Nazi vote came overwhelmingly from these four middle-class parties. The German National People's Party led by Hugenberg kept its end up best, and the feudal junkers, heavy industry, higher officials and so on, who formed a big part of its voting strength, remained true to it even during the crisis.

Our conclusion as to the source from which the Nazi increase largely came is further confirmed by the fact that both the Catholic and the working-class parties in Germany materially retained the support of their followers even during the crisis period, and the difference in their poll before and during the crisis is not great. The two Catholic parties in particular—the Catholic Centre Party and its counterpart in Bavaria, the Bavarian People's Party—remained fairly stable, and their absolute poll even increased, though their percentage share in the total poll decreased slightly in 1932 as compared with 1924 because the total poll was larger, so that the Nazis had clearly made only small inroads into the solid Catholic poll.

As the following figures indicate, the situation was somewhat similar with regard to the two working-class parties:

Reichstag Elections Votes
(in 1,000's)

	May 4th, 1924.	Dec. 7th, 1924.	May 20th, 1928.	Sept. 14th, 1930.	July 31st, 1932.
Social Democrats	6,244	7,985	9,174	8,588	7,960
Communists .	3,693	2,712	3,265	4,590	5,370

Thus as between the social democrats and the communists the relation of strength varied considerably. Immediately after the inflation period, and before its effects had died away, the communists polled a little more than half the number of votes polled by the social democrats. During the period of relative prosperity the social-democratic poll rose and the communist poll declined; during the crisis the social-democratic poll declined both relatively and absolutely, whilst the communist poll increased both relatively and absolutely. But when the social-democratic and communist votes are combined as the total vote of the socialist working class, the picture is much more stable, as the following figures show:

Combined Social-Democratic and Communist Polls in the Reichstag Elections

May 4th, 1924.	Dec. 7th, 1924.	May 20th, 1928.	Sept. 14th, 1930.	July 31st, 1932.
		(in 1,000's)		
9,937	10,697	12,439	13,178	13,330
		(in percentages)		
33·9	35·3	40·5	37·6	35·9

Thus, generally speaking, we can say that the great mass of socialist working-class voters remained loyal, if not to one particular working-class party, then at least to the working-class political ideas. Of course, this does not mean that there were no important changes; for instance, during the crisis many liberals who had formerly voted democratic began to vote social-democratic when it was clear that the Democratic Party (subsequently merged into the German State Party) was dead. Many social-democratic workers voted communist during the crisis, and some social-democratic and communist workers even voted Nazi. The Nazis had a certain amount of influence amongst the working-class youth. However, the over-all picture remains: the great body of between 12 and 13 million German workers continued loyal to working-class political ideas before and during the crisis.

All in all, therefore, we can say that the Nazis drew their main voting strength from the four non-Catholic middle-class parties, most of which they practically wiped out; from amongst people who had been unaccustomed to go to the polls at all and who did so only under the pressure of the economic crisis; and from amongst young people who were voting for the first time. In short, it was the middle strata in town and country who provided the Nazis with the bulk of their mass support.

308

The following diagram [19] shows us the poll of the individual parties at the various Reichstag elections:

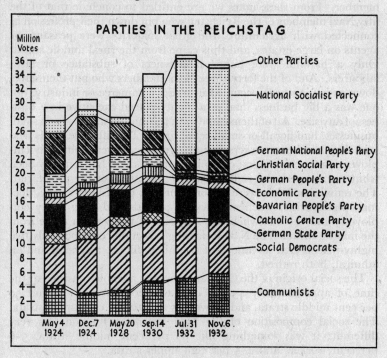

PARTIES IN THE REICHSTAG

The overwhelming majority of the Nazi electorate was made up of middle strata, and the social character of the Nazi leadership reflected this fact fairly accurately. Let us take, for example, the social composition of the Nazi Reichstag fraction after the elections of July 31st, 1932.

Professional Origin of Nazi Reichstag Members [20]

Agriculture	50
Trade, Commerce and Industry	43
Workers and Employees	55
Editors, Authors and Publishers	16
Clergy	1
Doctors and Pharmacists	5
Teachers	12
Lawyers	6
Civil Servants	20
Ex-Officers	9
Party Officials and Employees	13
	230

Thus, by social origin about 90 per cent of the Nazi members of the Reichstag were rural and urban middle strata.

The "Reichstag's Handbook", from which the above figures have been taken, also gives interesting biographical notes about each Nazi member. From these notes we are entitled to conclude that of the fifty Nazi members of the Reichstag who put down their profession as connected with agriculture, the great majority were peasants or agents on large estates, and thus came from the rural middle strata. Only a handful were either landowners of substance or farm labourers. And of the forty-three Nazi members who put themselves down as having been occupied in trade, commerce or industry, not one was a big business man or a highly-placed executive in a business of any size. All of them came from the middle strata—from small businesses, handicraft or small retail firms. The fifty-five Nazis who said they had been workers or employees were overwhelmingly employees, and not workers; only about ten of them had actually been what can properly be called workers—members of the proletariat. The remaining Nazis were editors, authors, publishers, clergy, doctors, pharmacists, teachers, lawyers, officials and Nazi Party employees, and the overwhelming majority of these again came from the middle strata. The Nazi Reichstag's fraction contained only two highly-placed civil servants and two high officers, a general and an admiral, both retired.

The social origin of the German people as a whole consisted at the time of approximately 45 per cent workers, between 45 and 50 per cent middle strata, and between 5 and 10 per cent upper strata. The social composition of the Nazi Reichstag fraction was very different; it was something like 90 per cent middle strata, 5–6 per cent workers and 4–5 per cent upper strata.

GREAT BRITAIN AND THE ECONOMIC CRISIS

The development of Great Britain in the period prior to the outbreak of the world economic crisis was not so dynamic as that of the United States and Germany, and therefore the crisis itself did not represent quite such a violent experience for Great Britain as it did for these other two countries.

Compared with the United States and Germany, the decline of production in Britain during the crisis was by no means so great. However, measured against the economic crises experienced by Great Britain from the middle of the nineteenth century onwards, the 1929 crisis was by far the biggest both with regard to the fall in production and the increase of unemployment, and this was true of Western Europe in general. In Great Britain, as in Western Europe, the process of decline which had made itself noticeably felt during the first world war continued and accelerated in the crisis, but it did not lead to the same fundamental innovations as did the "New Deal" in the United States and the Nazi victory in Germany.

One of the reasons for this was that during the course of the crisis itself there were certain trends which weakened its effects and made for stability, and they were connected primarily with the specific structure of British foreign trade and with the position of the British economic system and Empire within the general framework of the world economic system as a whole. Apart from the fact that industrial production in Great Britain during the crisis years was never less than four-fifths of what it had been in 1929, the decline in working-class standards of living was by no means so great as the decline in industrial production, and this fact naturally made for social stability. This is clearly shown in the following diagram.[21]

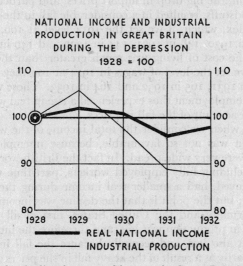

NATIONAL INCOME AND INDUSTRIAL
PRODUCTION IN GREAT BRITAIN
DURING THE DEPRESSION
1928 = 100

▬▬▬ REAL NATIONAL INCOME
――― INDUSTRIAL PRODUCTION

Why was the decline in general income in Great Britain during the crisis years so small? Primarily because the fall in prices for the goods Great Britain imported, chiefly foodstuffs and raw materials, was much greater than the fall in prices for the industrial goods she exported.

World industry reacted to the economic crisis by cutting down production; world agriculture reacted in the first place by a fall in the prices of agricultural produce.

During the crisis the value of British imports fell from £1,111 million in 1929 to £662 million in 1933, whilst the value of exports fell from £729 million in 1929 to £368 million in 1933, and thus the excess value of imports over exports fell from £382 million in 1929 to £258 million in 1933.

But when the volume of Great Britain's foreign trade, and not the value, is considered, the picture is very different. In volume British imports in any year of the crisis were never more than 10 per cent lower than they had been in the years before the crisis, whilst exports dropped by a third. Nevertheless, as we have seen, the excess of imports over exports declined as measured in pounds sterling. The reason for this was that if the price of British imports in 1930 is represented by 100, then they were 113 in 1929 and sank to 71 in 1933. British export prices, on the other hand, were 105 in 1929 and 82 in 1933. Thus during the crisis Great Britain was in a position to obtain in exchange for exports amounting to two-thirds the pre-crisis volume, imports amounting to nine-tenths the pre-crisis imports, whilst at the same time, reckoned in pounds sterling, reducing her excess of imports over exports.

In addition, the big drop in import prices, and particularly in the prices of foodstuffs, resulted in a considerable fall in the British cost-of-living index, which, if we set the 1914 level at 100, was 164 in 1929, 158 in 1930, 148 in 1931, 144 in 1932 and 140 in 1933. The decline in the cost of living was much greater than the decline in wages. If we set the level of wages in 1914 at 100 they were 172 in 1929, 168 in 1931, 165 in 1932 and 164 in 1933. Those workers who were in full employment thus experienced a rise in real wages during the crisis on account of the fall in prices.

However, when we consider the total income of the working class the situation was not so favourable, because unemployment and short-time were very widespread. In fact the British working class as a whole, including fully employed workers, part-time workers and the unemployed, had a smaller real income during the crisis years than before; but the point is that the decline was incomparably less than in Germany and the United States, first of all because the general fall in production was less, and therefore the increase in unemployment also less, and secondly because the fall in the cost of living, primarily as a result of the heavy fall in the prices of foodstuffs, was considerably greater than the fall in wages.

The combination and coincidence of the factors we have already enumerated, the lesser fall in industrial production as compared with the United States and Germany, the lesser fall in the national income, the rise of real wages for the employed workers even during the crisis, and the improvement of the balance of payments owing to the particularly heavy fall in the prices of the goods she primarily imported, meant that the effects of the crisis in Great Britain were not so profound as they were in either Germany or the United States.

In addition, Great Britain was also favourably placed by comparison with Germany because she was still a creditor country, and was therefore not so hard hit by the refusal of the United States to grant further foreign credits and by her insistence that those she had already granted should be repaid.

Great Britain found herself favoured by the difference in the price fall for various commodities, but the opposite was the case with countries which exported largely foodstuffs and raw materials, for instance, the Soviet Union and the objects of imperialist exploitation, the colonial and semi-colonial countries, particularly the Asiatic countries.

Thanks to imperialist expansion, part of the economy of these countries was linked up with the world economic system. During the period of prosperity the native populations enjoyed little of it, but, on the other hand, they were amongst the first victims of the crisis when it came, and it was their sufferings which made the situation of the capitalist metropolitan centres, and in particular Great Britain, easier.

JAPAN AND THE WORLD ECONOMIC CRISIS

But there was one Asiatic country which had retained its full political independence and had entered the path of imperialist expansion on its own account, and that was Japan, and *Japan suffered least of all from the world economic crisis*.

As we have already seen, Japan's development after the first world war up to the outbreak of the world economic crisis went its own way and bore no similarity to that of the United States and the European capitalist metropolitan centres.

If we take 100 to represent Japanese industrial production in 1929, then by 1931 it had sunk to 91·6. Thus the decline in Japanese industrial production in this period was only 8·4 per cent, whereas in the same period world capitalist production had already fallen by more than a quarter. From 1931 to 1932 world capitalist production continued to fall, until it was only 63 per cent of its original volume before the crisis, but Japanese industrial production increased in 1932 to 97·8 per cent, and in the following year it rose from 1929 levels, so that Japan was the only capitalist country which raised its industrial production in 1933 above 1929 prosperity levels.

Europe was profoundly shaken by the first world war, but the two big non-European powers, the United States and Japan, were not. The European powers and the United States were profoundly shaken by the world economic crisis, but Japan was not; she suffered very little and not for long. As far as she was concerned the 1929 crisis was no worse than the economic crises of the second half of the nineteenth century had been for the European powers and the United States. There were a number of reasons for this arising out of the specific position of Japan.

First of all, whereas in the European metropolitan centres and in the United States capitalism had become almost the only mode of production, with the result that a crisis in the capitalist sector was practically equivalent with a crisis in the economic system as a whole, the situation in Japan was very different. More than half the

313

total population of Japan was still engaged in agriculture, and a sector of industrial production still came from small undertakings; thus there was a very large sector of the Japanese economic system which was not closely integrated with capitalism.

Further, the crisis in the United States and in the European countries had been preceded by a period in which external capitalist expansion had slowed down almost to a standstill, whereas in Japan, thanks to the strengthening of her position during the first world war, imperialist expansion had continued, and this was true of the period which preceded the crisis.

This external expansion, and the existence of a military sector, had provided profitable markets for Japanese industry before the crisis, and these markets were not greatly affected by the crisis. It was the combination of these factors which made the decline of Japanese industrial production during the crisis so small and allowed it to recover so rapidly.

The army played a much greater role in Japanese expansion as a whole than it did where the European imperialist countries were concerned. Japan entered the crisis with a large army and a big military sector in comparison with her economic system as a whole. She went on strengthening this military sector at a time when world capitalist production was already declining.

In the United States, in Great Britain, in Germany and in Western Europe in general, the military sector played no important role during the crisis. In Germany, for example, it began to play a role only after the Nazis had come to power—i.e. after 1933. The situation in Japan was different. In 1931—that is to say, during the world economic crisis—Japan invaded Manchuria, and that invasion had naturally been carefully prepared by the Japanese army and by the Japanese armament industry. The developments in Germany from 1933, after the Nazis came to power, onwards, and in Great Britain and the United States with the outbreak of the second world war, began in Japan in the middle of the world economic crisis—i.e. the building up of a war economy. Even at that time war economy was a factor which prevented any great decline in Japanese industrial production, and soon permitted it to rise beyond the prosperity levels of 1929, and to a greater extent than in any other capitalist country.

SOVIET RUSSIA AND THE ECONOMIC CRISIS

During the world economic crisis developments in the Soviet Union continued to go largely their own way, and it was precisely during the crisis years that it became increasingly evident to what an extent the Soviet Union had emancipated itself from the laws of development which operated in the capitalist sector of the world economic system.

Shortly before the world economic crisis broke out Soviet Russia succeeded in reaching peace-time production levels. She did so as a State which, despite all tactical manœuvres, had never abandoned the commanding heights of the economic system, but which was still industrially the most backward of the European big powers, not only in *per capita* production, but also in absolute production figures. At the same time the vast majority of the population still lived and worked in the rural areas in individual family holdings, and were therefore economically more or less outside the control of the State.

From this basis the Soviet State now sought to attain two objectives. First of all it did its utmost to build up a new and powerful productive apparatus with a view to reducing the gap between itself and the more advanced industrial countries and finally to abolish it altogether. Secondly, it sought to bring about a radical reorganization of the economic and technical structure of Russian agriculture, and at the same time to extend its own power to the Russian village, thus bringing the whole population within its orbit.

The First Five-Year Plan

The first of the famous Five-Year Plans was the instrument with which it set out to accomplish these two aims. It was the first time in history that a State had deliberately set out in times of peace to control and re-organize the whole economic system. Before the first world war even the idea of such a thing would have been foreign to men's minds, but the unexpected length of that war and the resulting shortages in all branches of production had forced the belligerent governments to improvise a sort of planned economy, but their aims were comparatively limited; all they set out to do was to establish a scale of priorities for production because the productive apparatus was no longer able to produce as much as before, and now had to be concentrated on war production whilst producing only a bare minimum of consumer goods.

This type of planned war economy disappeared after the war, and when the Russians set out in peace time to prepare their first Five-Year Plan they were opening up new territory economically, sociologically and politically.

Outside Soviet Russia there was no system of planned economy anywhere in Europe, and not even the beginnings of anything of the kind. Indeed, nothing of the sort was possible, because for a planned economy a number of things are necessary: a sound knowledge of the total resources of the country concerned, organs to carry out the planning, and a State to do the planning and supervise its execution, and strong enough to enforce it against opposition if necessary. The sociological and political conditions for economic planning existed nowhere outside Soviet Russia.

These conditions had begun to develop in Soviet Russia for some time before the first Five-Year Plan was launched. For one thing, there was a centralized State power with a considerable knowledge of the economic conditions of the country. In the period of reconstruction a great fund of knowledge was gradually built up concerning the total economic resources of the country, and at the same time the necessary organs for a planned economy were developed as the various industries were reconstructed and extended. With the building up of heavy industry in particular, the State sector began to grow rapidly. Thus the first Five-Year Plan was from one point of view an attempt to co-ordinate the various plans for the development of the individual industries, of transport, of agriculture, and so on.

But this first attempt in history to co-ordinate a number of individual plans into an integrated whole was something more than that. It represented the first really comprehensive attempt on the part of a State not merely to intervene in an already existing and functioning economic system, but to build up anew and to transform an economic system, and with it the whole social structure.

This attempt was carried out in Soviet Russia under certain definite historical conditions. It was carried out in a country under a dictatorship, and the basis of that dictatorship had grown narrower. Thus it started as a dictatorial planned economy, and it became more and more so as it went on. However, despite the fact that this attempt was begun under certain specific historical conditions, its experiences—provided they were not transferred mechanically to other conditions—could prove of considerable value in the search for a solution of all the problems which the present and future generations will have to solve in the period of capitalist transformation.

The Russians were well aware from the beginning that, unlike all previous attempts at planning, their own Five-Year Plan meant that the State would not merely analyse the trends of economic development, but would exert its own power to enforce the carrying through of its plans, and Stalin [22] declared:

"These plans (in capitalist countries) are prognoses, guess plans which bind nobody, and it is impossible to direct the economy of any country on such a basis. Things are very different with us. Our plans are not prognoses, guess plans, but instructions which must be obeyed by all managements, and they determine the future course of economic development for our country as a whole. As you see, this implies a difference in principle."

The Russians were also well aware that because they were prospecting in new territory, and because therefore there could be, by the nature of the case, no systematic preparatory work, they would inevitably make many mistakes. For instance, the Chairman of the State Planning Commission (Gos-plan) [23] declared:

316

"We are convinced that planned economy is one of the commanding heights—in fact, potentially the most important one—of our economy. However, we are introducing this system of planned economy in one of the most technically backward countries and often in onerous conditions essentially connected with the period of transition from a private to a socialized economy. There are no fully-developed theories of how such a thing should be done, and by the nature of things there could not be because there are no precedents in history for what we are doing. In its early stages therefore socialism can proceed only by trial and error. It must grope its way forward. Wherever practice is in advance of theory perfection in execution is impossible."

One of the primary aims of the Five-Year Plan was to step up the development of industrialization in Soviet Russia, and in this respect the plan undoubtedly met with great successes and actually changed the position of Soviet Russia in world history and in the general relation of world forces.

Industrial production in Soviet Russia in all important branches of heavy industry rose far above the level of 1928, and thus above 1913 levels. The following table gives the figures for Russian industrial production before the first world war, at the beginning of the first Five-Year Plan and at the end of the plan:

Russian Production in the Main Branches of Industry [24]

	1913.	1929.	1939.
Steel (in million tons)	4·2	4·9	6·9
Rolled Steel (ditto)	3·5	3·9	5·1
Coal (ditto)	29·1	40·1	76·3
Oil (ditto)	9·2	13·8	22·5
Iron Ore (ditto)	9·2	8	14·4
Metallurgical and Engineering industries (in milliard roubles, 1926–1927 value)	1,466	3,054	10,822
Locomotives	418	602	941
Goods Trucks (in thousands) . .	14·8	15·9	18·2
Motor Cars (in thousands) . .	—	1·4	49·7
Electric Power (in milliard KWH) .	1·9	6·2	16·4
Pig Iron (in million tons) . . .	4·2	4	7·1
Copper (in thousand tons) . .	—	35·5	44·5
Aluminium (ditto)	—	—	7
Cement (in million tons) . .	1·5	2·2	2·7
Cotton textiles (in million metres) .	2,227	3,068	2,422
Woollen textiles (ditto) . .	95	100·6	86·1
Boots and Shoes (in million pairs) .		48·8	80·3
Raw sugar (in thousand tons) . .	1,290	1,283	995

This tremendous rise in industrial production as a whole above 1929 and 1913 levels—primarily in heavy industry and not consumer goods—took place at a time when the capitalist world was in the throes of economic crisis, at a time when world capitalist production

317

was declining more rapidly and farther than ever before in history. At the same time, whilst unemployment was reaching unprecedented heights in the capitalist world, it ceased to exist altogether in Soviet Russia during this period of swift industrial development. Russian unemployment figures were 1,741,000 in April 1929, 1,081,000 in April 1930, 236,000 in January 1931, and 18,000 in August 1931.[25]

With the construction of this new powerful productive apparatus a twofold change in the position of Soviet Russia in world production took place, first of all on account of its own increase in strength, and secondly because all other countries were at that time on the downward grade.

The following was the situation on the eve of the world economic crisis:

The Shares of Leading Countries in World Industrial Production [26]

Country.	1928.
United States	44·8
Germany	11·6
Great Britain	9·3
Soviet Russia	4·7

But by 1932, during the world economic crisis, the respective positions had changed considerably:

Country.	Middle of 1932.
United States	34·4
Soviet Russia	13·1
Great Britain	11·3
Germany	8·9

Russia, which before and after the first world war, had been the most backward country in Europe industrially, rose for a short period to second place in order of importance amongst the leading industrial countries of the world, ahead of both Great Britain and Germany.

Russia did not retain this position for long, because it was not entirely due to the increase in her own industrial production, but due in part to the decline in the industrial production of other countries during the world economic crisis. After the Nazis came to power in Germany there was a tremendous increase in German industrial production, and Germany rose once again to second place behind the United States, and it was not until after the second world war that Soviet Russia again displaced her.

However, the interesting and significant fact is that during the course of the world economic crisis developments in the capitalist world and in the Soviet Union took such a totally different direction.

318

The great increase in Russian industrial production was obtained by a tremendous accumulation of capital; it was enforced by an investment quota far above the level in capitalist countries—that is to say, consumer-goods industries developed only very slowly, and thus the increase in the productivity of labour was not even approximately matched by any increase in the manufacture of consumer goods, and thus a rise in living standards. Instead of that there was an increase of capital-goods production under forced draught, and in consequence an extension of the productive apparatus.

In so far as the Russian State had the means to control the carrying out of its plans, they met with very considerable success, but there were two sectors of the economic system which were largely outside its control, and here great difficulties arose. Setbacks were suffered which were not primarily due to the fact that new territory was being opened up. Their causes lay deeper.

THE ECONOMIC CRISIS AND RUSSIA'S FOREIGN TRADE

The first sector was the sphere of Soviet Russia's economic relations with other countries—in other words, primarily foreign trade. Soviet Russia was unable to obtain any long-term credits from other countries, and such credits as she was able to obtain were all for relatively short terms. On the whole, therefore, she had to pay for her imports with exports.

As we have already seen, Russia's foreign trade recovered somewhat in the middle twenties, and her imports helped to reconstruct her shattered industries. When the first Five-Year Plan was drawn up her foreign trade played an important part in it, but although they had done their best to take all eventualities into account, the Russians had not foreseen the outbreak of the world economic crisis, and the Plan had assumed that Russia's foreign trade, both imports and exports, would more than double itself in the years 1928–1933. This doubled volume of imports was to have included foreign machinery in particular, and the plan was based in part on the assumption that this machinery would be available to help build up industry.

As the following table shows, the world economic crisis upset these calculations:

Soviet Russian Foreign Trade

| Years. | Export. | | Import. | | Excess of exports, excess of imports (in million roubles). |
	Thousand tons.	Million roubles.	Thousand tons.	Million roubles.	
1929	14,145	4,045·8	1,936·7	3,857	+ 188·8
1930	21,486·4	4,593·3	2,855·9	4,637·5	− 98·2
1931	21,778·9	3,553·1	3,564·4	4,839·9	− 1,286·8
1932	17,967·9	2,518·2	2,322·1	3,083·5	− 565·3
1933	17,916·3	2,167·5	1,236·1	1,525·1	+ 642·4

Thus there was nothing like a doubling of Soviet Russian imports during the crisis years. In order to increase their imports above the 1929 level the Russians had to export far more than they had intended, and at the same time they had to sacrifice a considerable part of their not very big reserves of gold and foreign exchange. Whilst the British, as we have seen, benefited from the crisis because they were interested chiefly in the import of agricultural produce and raw materials, the Russians were the losers because they were chiefly interested in the import of machinery. The result was that in the years 1930–1932 they had a surplus of imports over exports which amounted to almost two milliard roubles, and when the drain on their reserves of gold and foreign exchange grew too great they had to cut down their imports, until by 1933 imports, not only in value but also in volume, were below 1929 levels.

It is obvious that the Russians could not possibly have made provision in their plans for all the effects of the world economic crisis; nevertheless they could have anticipated them to some considerable degree. But, in fact, the plan was based on the assumption that European and world capitalism would continue to advance as it had done during the twenties, with a consequent increase in world trade as a whole. It was only in such circumstances that Russian exports, with their comparatively high prices, could be expected to increase to an extent sufficient to pay for the volume of imports provided for in the Plan.

Thus the world economic crisis upset the Russian Five-Year Plan calculations. But as leaders and wire-pullers of the Communist International the Russians had anticipated the crisis, and whilst the Five-Year Plan was actually being carried out, the Communist International and the leaders of the German Communist Party constantly talked about the acute revolutionary situation which was supposed to exist. However, the men in the Kremlin did not even try to bring their views of the situation, as documented in the Five-Year Plan, with its assumption of further world capitalist progress, growing world trade and growing Russo-German trade, into line with the views of the Communist International and of the German Communist Party concerning the revolutionary situation to be expected as a result of the crisis.

THE COLLECTIVIZATION OF RUSSIAN AGRICULTURE

The second sector which was largely outside the effective control of the Russian State at the beginning of the Five-Year Plan was agriculture. The collectivization of agriculture had always been part of the bolshevist programme, but after the November Revolution and the run-away seizure of the land by the peasants it had been temporarily postponed. However, the Russian leaders were well aware that it would not be possible for a system of State industry to exist indefinitely side by side with millions of individual peasant farms, and speaking to a conference of "Marxist Students of the Agrarian Problem", Stalin [27] declared:

"The Marxist theory of reproduction teaches us that modern society cannot develop without accumulating from year to year. . . . Our large-scale, centralized socialist industry is developing according to the Marxist theory of expanded reproduction . . . but small-scale peasant farming still predominates in our national economy. Can it be said that our small-scale peasant farming is developing according to the principle of expanding reproduction? Not only is there no annual expanded reproduction in our small-scale peasant farming taken in the mass, but, on the contrary, it is not always possible to obtain even simple reproduction. Can we advance our socialized industry at an accelerated rate if we have to rely on such an agricultural basis? Can the Soviet Government and the work of socialist construction be based on two foundations for any length of time? On large-scale and concentrated socialist industry on the one hand, and on dispersed and backward small-scale peasant farming on the other? No, they cannot. Sooner or later a complete collapse of the whole national economy would result. What then is the solution? The solution lies in enlarging our agricultural units, in making agriculture capable of accumulation, of expanded reproduction, and thus changing the agricultural basis of our national economy. But how are our agricultural units to be enlarged? There is the capitalist way of doing this, which is to enlarge them by introducing capitalism into agriculture, a way which would lead to the impoverishment of the peasantry and to the development of capitalist enterprises in agriculture. That is a solution we reject as being incompatible with our Soviet economic system. But there is a second way, the socialist way, which is to set up collective and State farms; the way which leads to the amalgamation of small-scale peasant farms into large-scale collective farms technically and scientifically equipped, and to the squeezing out of capitalist elements from agriculture. We are in favour of this second way."

The original Five-Year Plan was to have taken the first decisive steps in the direction of agricultural collectivization. At the same time it was to bring about a tremendous development of industry. Measures for the achievement of these two aims were therefore co-ordinated and synchronized. Together with its efforts to step up industrialization, the Russian Soviet State launched its first attack on the individual peasant farms and took its first steps towards their collectivization. However, Soviet Russia's industrial backwardness in this period was also reflected in the fact that although she had begun the production of tractors and agricultural machinery, the output of these essential goods was very small indeed. The total number of tractors produced in Soviet Russia by 1930 was 72,000. By 1931 it had increased to 125,300, by 1932 it was 148,500 (483,500 in 1938). In the same years the total number of harvester machines available was 1,700, 6,400, 14,500 and (153,500) respectively.

In other words, the technical conditions for a modernization of Russian agriculture, for the creation of large-scale agriculture which would show higher yields than small-scale peasant farming, were not present in adequate measure. In consequence the Russian State had very little to offer the peasants when it sought first to persuade and then to compel them to abandon private individual peasant-farming in favour of collective farming. The result was that the collectivization of agriculture was vigorously resisted by large sections of the peasantry. The Kulaks, or well-to-do peasants, who employed paid labourers in the running of their farms, were particularly hostile to the scheme because naturally it meant their disappearance. But it was not only the Kulaks who resisted; they were joined by millions of peasant small-holders who were unwilling to give up their land and work in large-scale agricultural units. They were deeply attached to their own land and their own ways, and, in addition, the proposed collectivization offered them very little for the time being.

The Soviet State broke their resistance by force; riots and even risings were brutally suppressed and a civil-war atmosphere arose. At the same time agricultural production sank, because the peasants had no interest in exerting themselves for a collective farm whose produce did not belong to them and from whose yield they enjoyed very little advantage. The effect on cattle-farming was catastrophic, because the peasants said to themselves: "Very well, if the State forces us into its collective farms, then we'll eat our meat first and the State can provide for everything afterwards." The result was that in the first years of collectivization agricultural production in Soviet Russia sank below Tsarist level. The same applied to livestock, which remained below that level for a very long time afterwards.

Russian Grain Production [28]

(million quintals)

1913.	1930.	1931.	1932.
801	835·5	694·8	698·7

Russian Livestock

(in millions)

	1913.	1930.	1931.	1932.
Horses . . .	35·8	30·2	26·2	19·6
Cattle . . .	60·6	52·5	47·9	40·7
Pigs . . .	20·9	13·6	14·4	11·6

A decline in harvest yields together with a decline in livestock naturally meant a fall in living standards, and that applied to both town and country. The over-hurried and compulsory introduction of collectivization caused the living standards of the great masses of the Russian people to fall tremendously, often even to the level of famine, at a time when industrial production was rising steeply.

During the years of the world economic crisis both industry and agriculture suffered in the capitalist world. World industrial production (not including the Soviet Union) dropped steeply, but the agricultural crisis was a typically capitalist one, with a permanent latent volume of over-production because the prices of agricultural produce had fallen so low that farmers and peasants were no longer able to live from the produce of their soil and labour.

In Soviet Russia the situation was very different. On the one hand there was a tremendous increase in industrial production, whilst on the other there was a severe crisis in agriculture, but it was not a crisis of over-production as in the capitalist world, but a crisis of under-production brought about because at first the peasants were not prepared to work in the collective farms as they had worked on their own holdings. Famine, and conditions in many rural areas not far from civil war, greatly weakened Soviet Russia on the foreign-political field in this period.

Shortly before the Nazis came to power in Germany, Trotsky, then already long exiled, wrote a pamphlet in which he recommended that the Red Army should march against Germany to prevent the victory of the counter-revolution. The suggestion was impractical. The Soviet Government was far too preoccupied with its own difficulties at home to be able to use the Red Army anywhere outside its own frontiers.

CHAPTER FOUR

FROM THE CRISIS TO THE SECOND WORLD WAR

IN THE PERIOD between the two world wars world capitalist external expansion was almost at a standstill, and this was true also of the period from the trough of the world economic crisis up to the outbreak of the second world war. In addition, it applied not only to the European capitalist powers, but also to the United States. To some extent, however, both Germany and Japan were exceptions to this general rule, in that each of them experienced a certain outward expansion in this period.

Let us once again go over the individual factors which were responsible for this decline in world capitalist expansion and see how far they were operative in the period now under review.

1. The tendency towards autarky, or economic self-sufficiency, in the Soviet Union increased, and her foreign trade with the capitalist world declined considerably.

Throughout the whole period both before and during the world economic crisis Soviet Russia's trade with the rest of the world was below Tsarist levels. For this reason alone, Russia represented a declining market for European capitalism instead of an expanding market as she had been under Tsarism. In the period from the trough of the world crisis to the outbreak of the second world war the capitalist countries were unable even to maintain their markets in Russia, which shrank still further.

2. Capitalist development in the area between Germany and the Soviet Union, with its large population of approximately 100 million, was held up and hampered by the rise of a series of small independent States, and for this reason capitalist expansion into this area had slowed down very greatly even before the outbreak of the crisis. The period between the trough of the crisis and the outbreak of the second world war saw no appreciable change in this respect, and on the whole the stagnation continued. Just as in Western Europe, the utmost that was obtained was a return to the levels of production prevailing before the outbreak of the crisis. But in one respect there was a change.

When the Nazis came to power in Germany as the result of the economic crisis, a new form of German imperialist policy developed and was pursued with increasing vigour. Its effect in this period was that the slowly growing markets of Central Europe were monopolized more and more by the new German imperialism.

3. The stagnation in industrial development in the colonial empires of the European imperialist countries continued in this period. Thanks to the imperialist policy of the European metropolitan centres, many of the colonial and semi-colonial countries had suffered with particular severity from the world economic crisis, but there was no fundamental change in European imperialist colonial policy in this period. Thus industrialization in the colonial and semi-colonial countries still remained very limited, and the European metropolitan centres were unable to open up any new markets there in this period.

4. In so far as there was any considerable industrialization in the colonial and semi-colonial countries, the lion's share of the benefits went to Japanese imperialism.

The Japanese State continued its efforts to co-ordinate the industrialization of Japan with that of its colonial empire. Japanese State-planned economy and war economy, which practically monopolized

324

Japanese foreign trade, reduced the susceptibility of the Japanese economic system to the effects of economic crisis. It also brought about an increase in Japan's share of world trade at a time when the colonial empires of the European powers, which were particularly hard hit by the crisis, saw their own share declining.

5. Thus although the standstill in outward expansion continued for the European capitalist imperialist States, Japan experienced a certain degree of expansion even in this period, whilst the standstill for the United States was complete. Not only did this make it more difficult for the United States to overcome the crisis, but it made it more difficult for the rest of the world as well. For example, immigration from the European countries, which had already been greatly cut down by the adoption of new immigration laws even before the crisis, shrank still farther, and from 1929 up to the outbreak of the second world war immigration figures for the United States steadily declined. In 1930–1934 they totalled 426,953 and in 1935–1939 they were only 272,422.

Thus the total immigration for these ten years was less than in any single year between 1904 and 1914. The days when the United States relieved the pressure on the European labour markets by throwing open its gates to immigrants were past, and the reserve armies of labour in Europe increased to an unprecedented size.

At the same time by stopping capital exports the United States also weakened the factors which usually operated towards the overcoming of a crisis.

The biggest drop in world trade ever recorded took place during the world economic crisis. In the United States the fall in production was greater than in Europe and, in addition, she suffered a bigger decline in foreign trade than the rest of the world. U.S. capitalists also suffered greater losses with their capital exports, and the period after the 1929 crisis was not marked, like other post-crisis periods, by new capital exports. On the contrary, a section of the old capital exports was withdrawn, and in this way the economic difficulties of the world were aggravated.

"New long-term investment of American capital abroad was almost negligible . . . and was greatly outweighed by the withdrawal of capital previously placed abroad." [1]

In former crisis periods capital exports to industrially under-developed countries had helped to overcome the depression and bring recovery, but after the world economic crisis of 1929 the greatest exporter of capital in the world, the United States, practically stopped exporting capital and began to withdraw such capital investments as had already been placed abroad.

The fact that capitalist external expansion had practically ceased created a completely new situation for world capitalism as a whole, a situation which had no parallel in history.

The world economic crisis broke out in a period in which capitalist expansion abroad had either ceased altogether or proceeded only very slowly, and this was true not only of the crisis duration itself, but also of the years after the trough of the crisis had been passed.

For the first time in its history, capitalism had to overcome a crisis largely from its own resources, and it had to do so in a period in which, even before the outbreak of the crisis, there had been little or no opening up of new markets, in a period in which, even after the trough of the crisis had been passed, there was no large-scale extension of the capitalist mode of production. Capitalism entered the crisis without having previously opened up new markets to any considerable extent.

It now had to find its way out of the crisis without the assistance of new markets.

As a result of our whole previous investigations it is not difficult to understand why:

(1) The world economic crisis of 1929 was the most severe capitalism ever suffered.

(2) Capitalism found it impossible to liquidate it altogether.

We have already seen the figures which prove the first point to the hilt; let us now examine the facts which prove the second.

The following table shows the development of world industrial production from the trough of the crisis up to the year 1938, the last year of peace before the outbreak of the second world war:

Mining and Manufacturing Industries [2]
(1929 = 100)

Year.	World production, including the Soviet Union.
1934	85·8
1935	96·3
1936	110·5
1937	119·4
1938	111·5

Soviet industrial production in this period increased so tremendously that it began to influence world trends. When we speak of world industrial production in the period up to the outbreak of the economic crisis in 1929, it does not matter very much whether Soviet production is included or not, because it developed more or less along

326

the same lines as industrial production in other countries, and its share in world production, once the period of reconstruction after the war, revolution and civil war had been concluded, was only about 4 per cent.

But when we begin to discuss the development of world production from the trough of the economic crisis until the outbreak of the second world war, it makes a decisive difference whether we include Soviet production or not, because this was the period in which a tremendous increase took place in the Soviet Union in continuation of the trend which was already visible in the years from 1929 to 1932, in which its share of world production rose to 10 per cent.

Thus if we want to discuss the development of *capitalist* world production from the trough of the crisis on, then it is essential that Soviet industrial production should be excluded if we are to obtain an adequate picture. The same table as above, but without the Soviet Union, looks as follows:

Mining and Manufacturing Industries [3]

(1929 = 100)

Year.	World production, excluding the Soviet Union.
1934	77·7
1935	86
1936	96·4
1937	103·7
1938	93

This table shows that only in one year in that period, 1937, was capitalist world production a little over the pre-crisis level. On an average in the above years capitalist world production was approximately 8·6 per cent below the figures for 1929, and even this "average" represents the situation of world capitalist production in too favourable a light. If we examine capitalist world production in the period up to 1929 and then in the period until the trough of the crisis was reached, we shall observe, allowing for all differences as between one country and another, a certain uniform trend both in rise and fall, although the extent of the rise and fall varied considerably as from country to country.

That uniform trend was subsequently interrupted by the appearance of a new factor in the economic and productive developments of certain countries. That factor was the enormous increase of armament production in peace time, and it applied in particular to Germany and to a lesser degree to Japan and Italy. We shall deal with this point in some detail when we come to Germany. For the moment it is sufficient to point out that although in the period covered by the above tables capitalist world production was, on an average,

8·6 per cent below pre-crisis levels, it included the whole of Germany's armament production, Japanese and Italian armament production and the growing armament production of Great Britain, France, Czechoslovakia, and so on. If the above tables dealt only with the production of normal peace-time commodities, then capitalist world production would be very much more than 8·6 per cent below pre-crisis levels.

In no year between 1933 *and* 1938, *and in no year after* 1929 *and up to* 1933, *did the world capitalist production of peace-time commodities equal the* 1929 *figure.*

How greatly the former uniform trend of development was interfered with by armament production is made very clear if we compare U.S. and German production development in the years 1934–1938 inclusive: the last years of peace before the second world war. In both countries the volume of industrial production was practically halved during the crisis years, but subsequently developments were very different. Here are the respective figures:

Index of Industrial Production

Year.	Germany [4] (1929 = 100).	United States [5] (1935–1939 *average* = 100).
1929	100	110
1934	79·8	75
1935	94	87
1936	106·3	103
1937	117·2	113
1938	126·2	89

In Germany there was a steady increase in industrial production, but in the United States it was only in 1937 that the 1929 level of production was somewhat exceeded, and even then *per capita* production was lower than in 1929.

On an average in the years 1934–1938 U.S. industrial production stood at 93, or about 17 per cent below 1929 levels, and in 1938—the last year before the outbreak of the second world war—it was about one-fifth below 1929 levels.

This depression in world production was accompanied by an exceptionally high level of unemployment.

Even in the period before the outbreak of the world economic crisis, unemployment in the capitalist world was greater than at any previous time during a period of prosperity, and the volume of unemployment in the period from the trough of the crisis up to the outbreak of the second world war was far greater than in 1929.

Unemployment was greatest in the United States, and this is easy enough to understand if we do not forget that production was far

328

below 1929 figures whilst at the same time productivity per man-hour was still increasing.

Although the production levels of 1929 had been overtaken in Great Britain, there was still a permanent volume of unemployment, amounting to an average of about 1·5 million during the last five years before the second world war. The actual official figures of registered unemployed were:

United Kingdom Fully Unemployed Workers [6]

1934	.	.	.	.	.	1,801,913 or 13·9%
1935	.	.	.	.	.	1,714,844 or 13·1%
1936	.	.	.	.	.	1,497,587 or 11·2%
1937	.	.	.	.	.	1,277,928 or 9·4%
1938	.	.	.	.	.	1,423,662 or 10·3%

It is quite clear, in view of the smaller volume of industrial production, that in France, Czechoslovakia and in Western Europe in general, unemployment figures throughout this whole five years before the second world war were above the 1929 level.

WORLD TRADE BEFORE THE SECOND WORLD WAR

We have already seen that the standstill in external capitalist expansion applied not only to Europe, but also to the United States. When we now consider that Germany's developing system of war economy, or *Wehrwirtschaft* as it was called, strengthened the tendency towards economic self-sufficiency, or autarky, whilst the increasing danger of war had a similar effect elsewhere, it is not surprising that world foreign trade was heavily hit.

In 1929 world imports (reckoned in old U.S. gold dollars) amounted to 35,595 million dollars, whilst in the same year world exports amounted to 33,024 million dollars. In 1934 world imports (excluding Spain, which makes very little difference to the total) had sunk to 11,816 million dollars, and world exports to 11,215 million dollars. By 1937 world imports had improved to 16,247 million dollars and world exports to 15,347 million dollars. But the year 1938 saw a big drop in both world industrial production and world trade: world imports fell to 14,232 million dollars, and world exports to 13,356 million dollars.[7]

In one year only, 1937, did world production (excluding the Soviet Union) rise above the 1929 level, and that was primarily because of increased armament production. *In the same period there was not a single year in which world trade even reached, much less exceeded, the 1929 figures.*

For a century of capitalist history the sign that an economic crisis had been finally overcome was that the economic system succeeded in reaching and passing the peak production figures of the period of prosperity which preceded the crisis. Now in the ten years from the time the world economic crisis broke out in 1929 up to the second world war, world capitalism had not succeeded in doing this. *It is thus quite clear that when the second world war broke out world capitalism had not yet succeeded in completely liquidating the economic crisis of 1929.*

Such was the general picture of development, including industrial production, unemployment and world trade. Now let us see the developments in the most important countries within this general framework.

The U.S.A. from "The New Deal" up to the Outbreak of the Second World War

In order to understand the reaction of the United States to the world economic crisis we must first take into consideration the exclusive and specific characteristics of U.S. development.

The world economic crisis as it hit the United States was not only unexampled in U.S. history, but it affected a social body which was in many important respects fundamentally different from those of the other capitalist countries deeply involved in the crisis.

An analysis of these far-reaching differences (cf. the differences between the class stratification of Europe and the United States as set out in Part One) will help us to understand why the reaction of the United States to the crisis was so different from that of other countries.

1. The effects of the crisis in the United States, which halved industrial production and created a proportionately vast amount of unemployment, were greater than in the victorious European countries, Britain and France, and approximately as great as they were in the defeated country, Germany.

2. However, unlike the big European powers—Britain, France and Germany—the world crisis affected the United States as a country which had not been seriously affected by the first world war, as a country whose industrial production before the 1929 crisis was almost twice as great as it had been in 1919, the first year after the end of that war.

3. The crisis in the United States affected the richest capitalist country in the world, a country in which, even before the first world war, living standards had been considerably higher than in the European capitalist countries, and the gap between them had grown still larger in the period from 1919 to 1929.

4. The crisis in the United States affected a country in which, unlike the countries of Europe, such a thing as a socialist mass movement was unknown, a country which knew trade unionism, it is true, but to a much smaller extent than in Europe by reference to the working class as a whole.

5. The crisis in the United States affected a country in which the centralized apparatus of the State was only rudimentarily developed by comparison with Europe.

330

On the continent of Europe all the big powers had maintained large armies even in peace time, and the existence of compulsory general military service had led to the development of a strong centralized State apparatus in all these countries.

Before the first world war the United States had to all intents and purposes no standing army, and she had no army of any size during the period of the world economic crisis.

Although Great Britain had no standing army of any size comparable with those of the continental European powers, and although there was no conscription in peace time, there was nevertheless a relatively highly developed system of governmental social measures which had led to the rise of a centralized State apparatus.

This sort of thing was lacking in the United States, and it is therefore not surprising to discover that the proportion of U.S. Governmental expenditure in relation to the national income as a whole was incomparably smaller than the corresponding expenditure in any European country.

All the European countries, Great Britain included, entered the period of world economic crisis with an already highly developed and centralized State apparatus; in the United States it was still rudimentary, and it had to be developed during the crisis itself.

6. The crisis in the United States affected a country which was the only big capitalist industrial power in which agriculture was not only fully integrated in the capitalist system, but also produced enough to feed the whole population and then leave a surplus for export to other countries. In this respect the United States was very different from the industrial countries of Europe.

These six features which characterized the United States as distinct from other countries created a sociological framework fundamentally different from that existing elsewhere, and this framework inevitably influenced the reaction of the United States to the economic crisis.

The dangers of the economic crisis were regarded as quite as great as the dangers of war in former times. Roosevelt declared:

"This nation asks for action, and action now", and he went on to say that "if Congress failed", he would ask for "broad executive power to wage a war against the emergency, as great as would be given to me if we were, in fact, invaded by a foreign foe".

With Roosevelt's "New Deal" a new epoch opened up in United States history.

For the first time in history a U.S. government intervened in peace time on a wide scale in the various spheres of the economic system.

It continued to do so up to the outbreak of the second world war, in the war years in particular, and in the post-war period. Thus Roosevelt's "New Deal" opened up an era of greatly increased intervention on the part of the U.S. Government in economic affairs.

331

But although the "New Deal" opened up this new era in U.S. history, it certainly did not open up an era of planned economy. There was no systematic plan to combat the crisis, and no such plan developed during the "New Deal" period; various measures were taken to combat the effects of the crisis in various spheres of economic life, but those measures were not co-ordinated.

When private investments in Britain greatly declined during the crisis years the supporters of economic planning demanded that the Government should itself make big investments and that, in addition, it should "control" investments in the private sector. It is as well to make it quite clear from the beginning that when Roosevelt launched his "New Deal" he had no such far-reaching intentions and that at no time were any practical attempts made in this direction.

There was never any programme for the United States economic system as a whole, including both the sector under State influence and the sector completely in private hands, such as naturally developed later when America's entry into the second world war compelled her to adopt a system of war economy. Thus in peace time no attempt was made to create any organs for State intervention on such a scale. The "New Deal" consciously accepted the capitalist system, and although it envisaged State intervention on quite a large scale, it did not attempt to develop a system of planned capitalism in peace time.

It is also noteworthy that during the years of the "New Deal" no one even dreamed of using State intervention to develop an armament economy and thus narrowing the enormous gap which had opened up between productive capacity and consumption. In this connection the situation was very different from that which existed after the second world war, and it is a point which must be stressed if we are to understand the problems of that period.

Military expenditure played no material role in the United States in the period before the outbreak of the world crisis, during the crisis itself or in the period immediately following it. When the world economic crisis broke out, U.S. military expenditure amounted to half a milliard dollars annually, and represented less than 1 per cent of America's total national income. It did not increase during the crisis under Hoover's regime nor in the first years of the Roosevelt administration.

When the Nazis came to power in Germany and began to build up a German war economy, there was at first very little increase in the military expenditure of the Western European powers, and practically none at all in American military expenditure.

In fact, that military expenditure was so small that it can safely be left out of account altogether in any analysis of the crisis factors. In the years 1933–1938 it continued to remain negligible. Thus the increased intervention of the State in U.S. economic affairs was not a step in the direction of establishing a military sector large enough to count economically.

There was also no State intervention to encourage U.S. foreign trade, although it had been hard hit by the crisis, and had declined, relatively speaking, even more than world trade as a whole. It increased by comparison with the trough of the crisis, but not to any very great extent. From 5,240,995,000 dollars in 1929, U.S. exports declined to 1,611,016,000 dollars in 1932; they rose again in 1937 to 3,349,167,000 dollars, and were slightly less in 1938 at 3,094,440,000 dollars. Measured in dollars, therefore, the United States did not succeed in again reaching the 1929 figures in any of the years from the outbreak of the crisis up to the second world war. And the same was true of the volume of foreign trade:

Exports of United States Merchandise [8]

(1923–1925 average = 100)

Yearly average or year.	Total quantity.
1926–1930	122
1931–1935	76
1936	82
1937	105
1938	103
1939	110

We have already seen that U.S. production rose to a few points above the 1929 prosperity level in only one subsequent year—namely, 1937—but that then it fell again sharply in 1938. But U.S. exports did not recover in any single year, either measured in prices or in volume, not even in 1937. Even in the prosperity years before the world economic crisis U.S. foreign trade represented a very much smaller share of U.S. production than the foreign trade of the European countries did by comparison with their total production. No attempt was made under the "New Deal" even to ameliorate the effects of the crisis by carrying out new big capital exports, thereby encouraging the export trade, and thus stepping up production at home, and the sphere of U.S. Government intervention was largely restricted to production for the home market.

STATE INTERVENTION AND THE HOME MARKET

It is not our intention to analyse U.S. Government intervention in economic affairs in any detail; all we want to do here is to give a general picture of how that intervention affected U.S. society and the U.S. economic system on the one hand and the relation of the State to the economic system on the other.

The U.S. Government endeavoured to narrow the gap between production and consumption in three main ways.

1. The State accepted growing indebtedness in order to carry out a big programme of public works, but at the same time it avoided any extension of the State sector to industrial spheres regarded as the preserve of private enterprise.

2. The U.S. Government increased the mass purchasing power of the workers by:

(a) introducing collective working agreements with minimum wages and restricted working hours, and at the same time strengthening the position of the working-class organizations, the trade unions;

(b) introducing unemployment insurance and other socio-political measures to prevent any further decline in the living standards of the masses of the people.

3. The U.S. Government introduced a number of measures, including the restriction of agricultural production and the granting of agricultural subsidies, to maintain agricultural prices, and thereby to give the majority of farmers a middle-class standard of living once again.

The U.S. Government had no organization in being to carry out any great public works project, and therefore it was impossible to organize a big programme overnight, and the scheme came into operation only gradually.

At first there were illusions about the nature of the crisis, and hopes that it would soon be overcome, but the fact that production obstinately remained below 1929 levels, whilst unemployment remained exceptionally high, gradually destroyed both the illusions and the hopes. For the first time in history the United States had many millions of unemployed workers who wanted to work and were capable of working, but who were unable to find work in the private sector of the economic system—even after the trough of the crisis had been passed.

Roosevelt realized clearly that the country was faced with a new situation. In setting out his New Works Programme he pointed out that apart from workers on relief, who could find work only with great difficulty or not at all, there were approximately 3·5 million men who were employable.

"With them the problem is different, and the responsibility is different. This group is the victim of a nation-wide depression caused by conditions which were not local but national. The Federal Government is the only governmental agency with sufficient power and credit to meet this situation. We have assumed this task and we shall not shrink from it in the future." [9]

And thus the United States Government launched its Works Progress Administration, the famous W.P.A.

The W.P.A. programme began in 1935. It was not completed in

1939, when the second world war broke out, and it continued into 1940, in the period of Lend-Lease.

In the first five years of its existence the programme involved the expenditure of 11,365 milliard dollars, and it was estimated that W.P.A. projects gave employment to approximately 8 million workers and, if their dependants were included, the programme supported between 20 and 30 million people. The average volume of employment provided was, of course, much less, and amounted to about 2,100,000 annually.

The W.P.A. programme was not financed by taxation, but by government loans, and during the period of the "New Deal" the U.S. Government deliberately incurred a budgetary deficit.

The result was that, unlike earlier periods, in which the State Budget was balanced after the trough of the crisis had been passed, this time the U.S. national debt not only grew, but it grew more rapidly than in the years up to the trough of the crisis.

In the years of the crisis what is called the Gross Public Debt [10] of the United States rose from 18·2 milliard dollars in 1929 to 23·4 milliard dollars in 1932—that is to say, by about 5·2 milliard dollars —whilst the Net Public Debt grew from 15·7 milliard dollars in 1929 to 18·7 milliard dollars in 1932.

The following figures show the development of the U.S. Public Debt during the years of the Roosevelt administration:

Gross and Net Public Debt
(in milliards of dollars)

	1932.	1933.	1934.	1935.	1936.	1937.	1938.	1939.
Federal and Federal Agencies:								
Gross Public Debt	23·4	28·2	38	41·5	41·1	47·8	47·5	49·9
Net Public Debt.	18·7	21	23·1	26	29·5	31·3	32·6	34·8

In these years the Gross Public Debt increased by 26·5 milliard dollars, and the Net Public Debt by 16·1 milliard dollars. Thus the rate of increase was greater in the period after the trough of the crisis was passed than it was during the crisis itself.

Orthodox economists and the opponents of the "New Deal" used these figures to support their argument that it would lead to national bankruptcy, which was, of course, a gross exaggeration.

At the beginning of the economic crisis in 1929 the total U.S. public debt represented only a very small fraction of the annual national income of the American people, and the 16·1 milliard dollars which were added to the public debt under the Roosevelt Administration in the years 1933–1939 represented less than the military expenditure in three months during the second world war.

Of course, Roosevelt's deficitary budget policy did not remotely lead to national bankruptcy, and it is characteristic that the same people who had opposed Roosevelt's measures on behalf of the working people with the argument that the expenditure involved would lead to national bankruptcy, showed no qualms when the financing of America's part in the second world war involved public indebtedness vastly exceeding the "New Deal" expenditure.

Roosevelt's "New Deal" policy changed the position of the State in the crisis. In earlier crises, in which the fall in production was not so steep and the increase in unemployment not so great, in which the factor of external expansion and the existence of strata of the population which were practically immune from the effects of the crisis, assisted in overcoming the decline in State revenues in the crisis was answered by cuts in State expenditure. In other words, the State sector generally grew smaller, in sympathy with the decline in general economic activity. But in the 1929 crisis, which was exceptionally severe and which took place in a historical environment which hampered the operation of the automatic recovery mechanism of capitalism, any reduction of the State sector threatened to aggravate the crisis as a whole.

For this reason *Roosevelt's "New Deal" policy deliberately broke with the past.* In all previous crises the U.S. Government had on the whole played a passive role. It was able to do so with impunity because previous crises had not fundamentally shaken the economic system as the 1929 crisis did, and no important section of the American people expected the State to do anything else in those years of expansion and progress. But now things had fundamentally changed.

In the crisis, and on account of the crisis, an active role was forced on the State. Government revenues declined, but government expenditure increased, and the U.S. Government deliberately took the risks involved in a deficitary budgetary policy. It did so not only in order to provide work for at least a section of the unemployed, but also to break the economic deadlock by extending the State sector, and thus assisting the private sector of the economic system to overcome the trough of the crisis and raise production again.

When the automatic recovery mechanism of capitalism failed to operate effectively, the State had to intervene and help on the process of recovery, and this is just what Roosevelt and the "New Dealers" did, though they did not ask themselves why the automatic recovery mechanism was not operating effectively; the mere fact that it was not was sufficient.

The "New Deal" programme was never more than an attempt to encourage economic activity. It was merely something to fill the breach, and its aim was to assist the private sector to utilize its full capacity again. It tried to help the private sector to make its own investments, and thereby bring about a rise in production.

This extension of the State sector was never intended to be permanent. It was to disappear again as soon as the private sector had completely overcome the crisis.

The W.P.A. programme was not intended to remould the U.S. economic system and to lead to a permanent mixed economy with a State sector and a private sector. On the contrary, the intention was that the State sector should automatically liquidate itself once its aim —the recovery of America's economic activity—had been attained.

The decrease in unemployment as a result of the increased production brought about by the W.P.A. programme raised the purchasing power of the working peoole, and this process was accelerated by a rise in the wages of employed workers generally on account of the extraordinarily rapid growth of the trade unions.

The Growth of the Trade Unions

Before the first world war trade unionism in the United States played nothing like the role it played in Europe. In 1900 the number of U.S. workers organized in trade unions was only 791,000. By 1913 the number had grown to 2,661,000, of whom 1,996,000 or the overwhelming majority, were organized in unions affiliated to the American Federation of Labour.* During the first world war the trade unions greatly increased in strength because, just as in Europe, labour played a leading role in the production of armaments. The peak point of trade-union strength was reached in 1920, when the unions numbered 5,034,000 members, of whom 4,079,000, or approximately 80 per cent, were members of trade unions affiliated to the A.F. of L.

In the subsequent years up to the time of the economic crisis trade-union membership showed a falling off. As we have already seen, the total increase of production obtained in the United States in the twenties came about without any increase in the number of workers employed and solely as a result of an increase in the productivity of labour. So-called technological unemployment was on the increase even in the years before the outbreak of the crisis.

Thus even in the years of prosperity the situation on the labour market became less favourable for the workers and at the same time the strength of trade unionism declined, until in 1929, before the crisis, trade-union membership was only 3,625,000, of whom 2,934,000 were in A.F. of L. unions. In these years A.F. of L. unions alone lost more than a million members. It was estimated that "the percentage of workers deemed available for unionization who were organized, dropped by practically a half in the decade, from 17·5 per cent in 1920 to 9·3 per cent in 1930".[11]

Thus when the crisis broke out it found the American trade unions in a much-weakened condition, and during the crisis itself the decline

* All the figures in this section are taken from " Historical Statistics of the U.S. 1789–1945 ".

337

in trade unionism continued. By 1933 the number of workers organized in trade unions was only 2,857,000, of whom 2,127,000 were in A.F. of L. unions, and not much higher than in the years preceding the first world war.

But with the "New Deal" the situation changed, and this was one of the most important respects in which that policy changed the social structure of the United States. During the "New Deal" era the creation and development of trade unions were encouraged in every way. Section 7A of the National Industrial Recovery Act, for instance, declares:

"1. Employees shall have the right to organize and bargain collectively through representatives of their own choosing, and shall be free from interference, restraint or coercion of employers of labour, or their agents in the designation of such representatives, or in self-organization, or in other concerted activities for the purpose of collective bargaining, or other mutual aid or protection;

"2. No employee, and no one seeking employment, shall be required as a condition of employment to join any company union, or to refrain from joining, organizing, or assisting a labour organization of his own choosing."

Naturally, the trade unions took every possible advantage of this opportunity.

"Union organizers made skilful use of this declaration of policy. In the coal mines, for example, the news was carried from pit to pit that the United States guaranteed the right to join unions. Often the issue was further simplified. Taking advantage of Roosevelt's phenomenal popularity during the summer of 1933, great banners were prepared carrying the legend: 'President Roosevelt wants you to join a union'." [12]

The following table shows how trade unionism developed from 1933 to 1939:

Trade-Union Membership in the United States

Year.				All Unions.	American Federation of Labour.	Congress of Industrial Organization.
1933	.	.	.	.	2,857,000	2,127,000	—
1934	.	.	.	.	3,249,000	2,608,000	—
1935	.	.	.	.	3,728,000	3,045,000	—
1936	.	.	.	.	4,164,000	3,422,000	—
1937	.	.	.	.	7,218,000	2,861,000	3,710,000
1938	.	.	.	.	8,265,000	3,623,000	4,038,000
1939	.	.	.	.	8,980,000	4,006,000	4,000,000

As these figures show, within a comparatively short space of time, from 1933 to 1939, the membership of trade unions in the United

States more than trebled, and in 1939 it was more than twice as big as during the years of prosperity which preceded the crisis. In that year it was greater than at any other period in U.S. history.

At the same time U.S. production was approximately on the level of 1929. Whilst productive capacity could not be utilized to the full owing to the halt in external capitalist expansion, and whilst the number of unemployed was still many millions, there was nevertheless this enormous growth in trade unionism. The already existing unions grew stronger, and new unions arose for the organization of the masses of workers, most of them unskilled, engaged in the steel industry, the automobile industry, and so on.

Formerly the United States had always been behind Great Britain and the leading countries of continental Europe in the matter of trade unionism; now she began to make up for lost time very rapidly.

Parallel with the strengthening of trade unionism in the United States, which was supported and encouraged in every possible way by the U.S. Government in this period of the "New Deal" policy, went a more rapid development of social policy. For one thing, the nature of the economic crisis caused a break with the idea that unemployment assistance could be dealt with as usual on "welfare" lines, and unemployment insurance was introduced on a wide scale, though not all workers were included in the scheme. Side by side with unemployment insurance other forms of social policy were introduced and extended.

"No piece of legislation showed more clearly the break with the recent past than the Social Security Act, approved August 14th, 1935. . . .

"Framers and other friends of the Social Security Act did best in not proclaiming it as a solution but in defending it as a substantial beginning from which further progress would surely be made." [13]

The importance of such a combination of public works, the encouragement of trade unionism, the introduction of unemployment insurance, the development of social policy and the attempt to fix minimum wages and restrict working hours for a large section of the working class was very great. We have already seen that in the United States, as in Germany, the crisis was so profound that, despite the fall in prices, the total real income of the working class decreased considerably. This tremendous decline naturally destroyed all hope that the automatic recovery mechanism of capitalism would operate effectively as it had done in former crisis periods. Without State intervention, therefore, there would have been a very great danger of the crisis growing worse instead of better. State intervention helped to break the deadlock and start up the process of recovery.

State intervention prevented chronic mass unemployment from being used to depress wages still further, thus reducing purchasing

339

power even more, and at the same time its programme of public works, and the effects of that programme on production as a whole, increased the total purchasing power available.

In addition, the social position of labour was strengthened by socio-political legislation, which was introduced in the United States long after it had been introduced in Europe. It was strengthened by the growth of trade unionism, which became a mass phenomenon long after trade unionism in Europe. It was strengthened by the Wagner Act, which made labour an equal partner in collective bargaining. And the sum total of all this was that labour became a stronger force in the economic and political life of the American people than before.

It was, incidentally, no accident that the Wagner Act was introduced in this period—that is to say, in a period in which unemployment remained very high despite the fact that measures to reduce it had met with a certain amount of success.

In earlier years the bargaining power of labour had been quite considerable, despite the fact that trade unionism was not widespread and collective bargaining perhaps the exception rather than the rule. This was due to the internal colonial structure of the country, which involved a shortage of man-power over a protracted period.

But that period was gone for good, and unemployment was very heavy not only during the crisis itself but also in the years of the Roosevelt "New Deal" policy. In 1933 it represented no less than 25·2 per cent of the total available labour force, in 1934 it was 21·6 per cent, in 1935 19·9 per cent, in 1936 16·5 per cent, in 1937 13·8 per cent, and in 1938 18·7 per cent. In other words, in the period from 1933 to 1938 unemployment represented, on an average, 19 per cent of the total labour force available.

Thus in this period every fifth worker was unemployed, and he was unemployed not merely for a short period but often for years. It is quite obvious that with unemployment at that high level the bargaining power of the working class was not very great, and it was at this point that the U.S. Government intervened with the Wagner Act to strengthen the trade unions. Without the Wagner Act and all the other legislation introduced under the "New Deal" the position of the working class in the United States would have been very much less favourable. Thanks to the "New Deal", the position of labour was reinforced, and in this way the factors which would, without State intervention, have led to a deterioration of the position of labour were to some extent cancelled out.

In other words, the "New Deal" sought to compensate labour for some part of what had been lost during the crisis and in the years after the trough of the crisis owing to its exceptional severity and the fact that it was not fully liquidated. The "New Deal" strengthened trade unionism, but it did not strengthen the position of labour as a whole, because chronic mass unemployment and therefore, purely economically considered, the unfavourable bargaining situation of labour remained.

That was one of the chief reasons why Roosevelt succeeded in obtaining a majority in Congress for this part of the "New Deal": labour's position within the framework of the social forces of the United States in general was not strengthened; part of the deterioration as a result of the crisis was cancelled out—that was all.

We have already seen in our examination of the W.P.A. programme that it was kept deliberately within the framework of the capitalist system and that it never attempted to bring about any real social transformation. The same applies to all the labour legislation introduced by the "New Deal". The capitalist system was not attacked. The position of the ruling classes was changed to some extent, but not materially weakened, and at the same time there were tendencies which considerably strengthened their position—namely, the development of further economic, industrial and financial concentration.

America's Two Hundred Families

With the decline of American economic activity during the crisis the big corporations naturally suffered heavy losses, but, equally naturally, they were better able to stand losses than the smaller undertakings, with the result that, as the following table shows, during the years of the crisis they actually increased their share in the totality of all corporation assets:

Proportion of Assets of all Non-Financial Corporations held by the Two Hundred Largest Corporations [14]

(money figures in millions of dollars)

Total assets.	1929.	1930.	1933.
200 largest non-financial Corporations .	98,597	107,073	95,617
All other non-financial Corporations . .	100,832	91,258	72,104
Total non-financial Corporations . .	199,429	198,331	167,721
Concentration ratio: 200 largest to all non-financial Corporations (per cent) . .	49·4	54	57

With the increase of industrial production after the trough of the crisis, and with the recovery of heavy industry in particular, the strength of the big corporations, and especially that of the biggest amongst them, increased.

"A careful study of the inter-relationships between the large corporations disclosed eight more or less clearly-defined interest groups which so far overshadowed other groups as to justify the limitation of consideration to these groups. . . . Together they include 106 of the 250 larger corporations and nearly two-thirds of their combined assets." [15]

Eight Interest Groups and their Assets, 1935

(in millions of dollars)

	Morgan-First National.	Rocke-feller.	Kuhn-Loeb.	Mellon.	Du Pont.	Chicago.	Cleve-land.	Boston.	Total assets.
Industrials .	3,920	4,262	—	1,648	2,232	858	1,066	425	14,411
Rails .	9,678	—	9,963	153	—	—	—	—	19,794
Banks .	4,421	2,351	548	672	396	2,595	338	740	12,061
Utilities .	12,191	—	342	859	—	813	—	554	14,759
Total .	30,210	6,613	10,853	3,332	2,628	4,226	1,404	1,719	61,025

The following diagram gives a graphic picture of the degree of concentration:

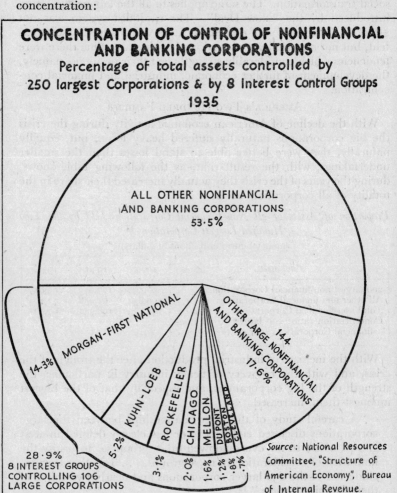

CONCENTRATION OF CONTROL OF NONFINANCIAL AND BANKING CORPORATIONS
Percentage of total assets controlled by 250 largest Corporations & by 8 Interest Control Groups 1935

ALL OTHER NONFINANCIAL AND BANKING CORPORATIONS 53·5%

MORGAN-FIRST NATIONAL 14·3%

OTHER LARGE NONFINANCIAL AND BANKING CORPORATIONS 144 17·6%

KUHN-LOEB 5·2%

ROCKEFELLER 3·1%

CHICAGO 2·0%

MELLON 1·6%

DUPONT 1·2%

BOSTON ·8%

CLEVELAND ·7%

28·9% 8 INTEREST GROUPS CONTROLLING 106 LARGE CORPORATIONS

Source: National Resources Committee, "Structure of American Economy", Bureau of Internal Revenue.

Nowhere in the world was the degree of industrial concentration as great as in the United States, and nowhere was the power of big business so enormous. It has been said of France that she is controlled by two hundred families; that is certainly true of the United States.

"Approximately two thousand men were directors of the 200 largest corporations in 1930. Since an important number of these are inactive, the ultimate control of nearly half of industry was actually in the hands of a few hundred men." [16]

The direct power of these "few hundred men" was not touched by Roosevelt's "New Deal" policy, and the social structure of the United States was affected under the "New Deal" only in so far as the position of the working class and its organizations was strengthened. How little the power of the big corporations was affected by the "New Deal" was seen very clearly when the second world war broke out and began to affect the U.S. economic system more and more. Roosevelt had to suspend Anti-Trust legislation in order to secure the co-operation of the giant corporations in his armament programme.

U.S. AGRICULTURE AND "THE NEW DEAL"

As we have already seen, the agricultural crisis in the United States was of longer standing than the general crisis. The crisis did not lead to a decline of agricultural production, which remained fairly stable, but it did bring about a steep drop in agricultural prices, and therefore in the incomes of America's farmers. Thus when the U.S. Government intervened in agriculture its aim was not to increase production, as it was in industry—that was not necessary—but to increase the income of farmers by raising price levels.

It should be pointed out here that, apart from one or two years during the war when agriculture was so prosperous that it needed no assistance, government intervention to stabilize farm incomes more or less on a middle-class basis had to become permanent. The only question for the American farmers, who are so proud of their "individualism", was in what form State assistance could best be granted. The main aim of government intervention at the time was to establish a reasonable relationship between agricultural and industrial prices such as had existed in the years before the first world war, thus increasing farm incomes accordingly.

The Agricultural Adjustment Act was passed on May 12th, 1933—i.e. at the beginning of the Roosevelt administration, at a time when the depression was at its lowest ebb, unemployment at its peak, and the purchasing power of the urban population very low. It is characteristic that it regarded the agricultural crisis not as a matter of under-consumption on the part of the urban masses, but as over-production by the farmers, and therefore the measures it introduced

343

to improve the situation were: (1) the restriction of agricultural output and the removal of surpluses from the market: and (2) direct payments to farmers in return for reducing their output.

Thus America's answer to the agricultural crisis was an attempt to reduce agricultural production. Let us recall that at the same time Soviet Russia was suffering from a severe agricultural crisis which was due to under-production. America's agricultural crisis was one of over-production, and yet there was mass unemployment and mass misery in the country.

> "In the summer of 1933 a Negro farmer from Georgia stood in the grounds of the White House to receive a medal from the President of the United States. He was honoured because he was the first to plough under his quota of cotton." [17]

Generally speaking, the appeal to cut down output was complied with. What else could farmers do? They had to sell their produce within the framework of capitalist market economy or go bankrupt.

The farm animals, it was reported, proved less amenable to the appeals to limit production.

> "It was reported at the time that a real obstacle to the cotton plough-up was the non-compliance of the Southern mule. For generations he had been taught with stick, trace and chain not to step on cotton, and now that he was urged to trample on it he refused. A policy which seemed good to the Secretary of Agriculture was rejected by the mule in the cotton row." [18]

Later on, however, Nature came to the assistance of the restriction policy, and there were severe droughts in 1934 and 1935 which greatly reduced crops.

> "The droughts increased prices of farm products, farm incomes and the purchasing power of the incomes. The effects of the droughts on agricultural prices continued beyond the immediate reduction of products, for carry-overs were diminished. As a consequence, in 1937, with bumper crops, and despite the drop in prices of farm products towards the end of the year, farm income had a buying power equal to that of the pre-depression period 1924–1929." [19]

Thanks to government subsidies and the policy of output restriction on the one hand, and the rise in industrial production, and in the purchasing power of the urban population on the other, a considerable increase in farm incomes resulted.

Gross farm income rose from 6,406 million dollars in 1932 to 7,055 in 1933, to 9,595 in 1935, to 11,265 in 1937, and even although there was a drop to 10,071 in 1938, the situation in agriculture remained much more favourable than it had been in the worst years of the depression.[20]

Thus all in all, the picture of U.S. economic and social developments in the period after the trough of the crisis had been passed was a very complex one.

Compared with 1932, industrial production had greatly increased; profits had increased and wages had risen; both industrial and agricultural incomes had increased. That was the credit side of the balance.

However, neither in industrial production nor in foreign trade had the figures of 1929 been reached again. Despite all the measures introduced in the "New Deal" period, a very large part of America's productive capacity remained unutilized. At the same time unemployment stayed very high: at approximately one-fifth of the total available labour force.

Even during the crisis the United States was still the richest country in the world with the highest standards of living, and no socialist movement of any consequence developed there. On the contrary, it is probably true to say that the "New Deal" reform programme caused socialism to lose adherents in the United States.

As the automatic recovery mechanism of capitalism, which had proved adequate in earlier crises, failed to operate effectively in this, the worst of all economic crises, the U.S. Government, whilst consciously approving of the capitalist system, intervened in economic affairs on a wide scale and extended the operations of the State sector into spheres which in Europe had long been recognized as appropriate for State intervention, as well as into new spheres. It was in this period that the U.S. Government laid the basis for a State unemployment insurance system and for other measures of a socio-political nature, most of which had been known in Europe even before the first world war. The U.S. Government also extended the State sector by adopting direct measures to combat the crisis, including a big programme of public works, just as was being done at the same time in numerous European countries.

It was in this period that the U.S. Government began to build up a big centralized State apparatus, to extend the State sector, and to increase the size of the State budget in relation to the national income as a whole.

State intervention under the "New Deal" regime chiefly benefited the U.S. working class, which had been harder hit by the crisis than any other stratum of U.S. society. Not only did wages rise as a result of this State intervention, but American trade unionism was strengthened to an unprecedented extent.

However, it must not be forgotten that this all took place against a background of mass unemployment, which continued to affect al-

most one-fifth of all employable adult workers, and of further industrial concentration which greatly strengthened the power of the giant
corporations. At the same time the State also intervened in agriculture, the only sector left in the economic system in which small independent undertakings still predominated, in order to guarantee a
certain middle-class standard of life to America's farmers.

GREAT BRITAIN AND FRANCE FROM THE TROUGH OF THE CRISIS TO THE SECOND WORLD WAR

At first glance it would seem that British and French developments
in this period had not much in common, although neither country
was so radically affected by the crisis as either the United States or
Germany. But once the trough of the crisis—which caused a decline
of French industrial production amounting to 28·6 per cent—had
been passed, developments in France and in Great Britain went
different ways.

In Great Britain the factors which had already considerably
ameliorated the effects of the crisis—Great Britain's position on the
world market and in her empire—enabled her to increase her production above 1929 levels as early as 1935. By 1937 British production was 20 per cent higher than in 1929, and although a certain set-
back was experienced in 1938, production in that year was still a
good 15 per cent above 1929 levels.

In France, on the other hand, there was no year after 1933 in
which the production level of 1929 was again reached. In 1937
French production was 18·3 per cent lower than in 1929, and after
the set-back in 1938 it was no less than 23·9 per cent lower.

And as economic development in Great Britain seemed to go in a
different direction from that in France, so also did political developments. In the 1931 elections, which took place during the economic
crisis, the Conservatives obtained a majority of votes and of seats,
and a Conservative Government remained in power from then on
up to the second world war.

In France, on the other hand, the right-wing government was
overthrown after the trough of the crisis had been passed, and in the
1936 elections both socialists and communists gained heavily without,
however, obtaining a majority with their combined polls, and Léon
Blum formed the first so-called Popular Front Government. It was
composed of socialists and left-wing capitalist politicians, and at first
it was "tolerated" by the communists. With this a definite move to
the Left began in France, and radical socio-political reforms were
introduced.

However, subsequent developments brought a shift to the Right
which lasted up to the outbreak of the second world war. At the time
of the notorious Munich meeting with the German dictator a purely
capitalist government was again in power in France.

346

Thus if we compare the development of production in Great Britain and in France on the one hand, and the political developments in the two countries on the other, it would seem that the general tendencies in these two leading European countries were very divergent. However, they had certain essential points in common.

It is true that British industrial production rose comparatively quickly over that of 1929, but, for all that, British production in 1929 was not very high. Unlike France and Germany, Britain had not at that time succeeded in again reaching the 1913 level of production although her total population was larger than in 1913. Further, neither in 1929 nor in any other subsequent year did Britain succeed in reaching 1913 export figures, and yet foreign trade played a much greater role in her economic and social structure than it did in that of France. The recovery period from 1932 onwards in Britain was based chiefly on a number of new industries (chemicals, electricity, motor-car production, etc.), whilst the old British export industries (coal, steel and textiles) remained in a chronic state of depression. Thus there was never really a period of prosperity in Great Britain which benefited the economic system as a whole, and important sections of it were always floundering in a chronic phase of crisis. It is true that unemployment decreased considerably by comparison with the worst years of the depression, but it still remained well above the million mark, and, in fact, in this period of relative prosperity it was greater than it had formerly been in periods of crisis.

In France, on the other hand, industrial production in 1929 was far above 1913 levels. France was the first of the big European industrial countries to exceed 1913 production levels in the post-war period. Thus the world economic crisis affected a productive apparatus in France which, like that in the United States and unlike that in Great Britain, had grown considerably by comparison with 1913. This is one of the facts which throws a somewhat different light on the apparent diversity of productive developments in the two countries, Great Britain and France. In addition, the agricultural population in France was relatively strong by comparison with all other big industrial countries. It was much greater than in either Germany or the United States, and immeasurably greater than in Britain, where the agricultural population was less than 10 per cent of the total population of the country.

However, French agriculture was not completely capitalist, not completely integrated with the capitalist market, and it still consumed a considerable part of its own production. Thus French agriculture enjoyed a certain degree of immunity from the effects of economic crisis, and this applied also to the small towns, which play a much greater role in French life than they do in British life. It should be remembered that, apart from Paris, France has only two towns with a population exceeding 500,000—namely Marseilles and Lyons.

To sum up, we can say that, generally speaking, despite the apparent diversity of industrial developments in the two countries in this period, neither Great Britain nor France was ever in a position to liquidate the 1929 crisis fully. Great Britain retained chronic unemployment above the million mark, and her old exporting industries continued to suffer from a chronic state of depression. In the period after the outbreak of the world economic crisis, France, on the other hand, never again succeeded in reaching 1929 production levels, and on an average her production in the years 1934–1938 was 22·5 per cent—or more than a fifth—below that of 1929. Thus, despite the fact that France's social structure was largely agricultural, and that small towns predominated, a considerable section of French economy suffered from chronic depression.

In neither Great Britain nor France were the upheavals brought about as a result of the first world war and of the world economic crisis of 1929 cancelled out by any subsequent period of prosperity embracing the whole economic system. On the contrary, both countries continued to suffer from a latent crisis, partial depression and chronic stagnation, with the result that there was social instability, an aggravation of social antagonisms and a state of social crisis which consciously affected all strata of society. In this respect developments in Britain and France were largely similar despite appearances to the contrary.

In both countries there had been a considerable degree of social stability in the period preceding the first world war. In both countries this social stability had been upset in the first world war and between the two world wars, though not by any means to the same extent as in Germany in the same period, and therefore there were no very strong fascist tendencies in either Great Britain or France. However, the antagonism between capital and labour intensified in both countries. It is true that in years immediately preceding the outbreak of the second world war Great Britain had a Conservative Government with a majority in parliament, but it was no longer faced merely with a Liberal Opposition which consciously approved of the capitalist basis of society, but with a Labour Opposition which was already beginning to question that basis and to make radical proposals for its reform. Despite the vacillations of the British electorate in the period between the two world wars, the characteristic feature of the period was that whereas before the first world war Labour was a weak third party and the Liberals were the official Opposition, the situation had changed so that Labour was now the official Opposition and the Liberals had become a weak third party.

In no election before the first world war had the Labour Party polled more than half a million votes, or more than 8 per cent of the total; in the period between the two world wars the situation was very different, as the following table shows:

Labour, Conservative and Liberal Voting Strength

Year.	Total Poll.	Labour Poll.	Percentages.		
			Labour.	Con-servative.	Liberal.
1918 . .	10,788,657	2,244,945	16	33	14
1922 . .	14,393,632	4,241,383	30	38	18
1923 . .	14,548,521	4,438,508	31	38	30
1924 . .	16,640,279	5,489,077	33	47	18
1929 . .	22,648,375	8,389,512	37	38	23
1931 . .	21,659,404	6,648,023	31	55	6
1935 . .	22,001,837	8,326,131	38	48	6

These figures clearly reveal the general trend towards increased labour support. The Conservatives now had to reckon permanently with a big Labour opposition in a country which was alone in the world in that its industrial workers represented the majority of the population.

The situation in France was somewhat similar in its general trend. Before the first world war, just as in Great Britain, it was a matter of course that a capitalist government should be in power, and the constant change of governments was really nothing but a change between various not very dissimilar cliques. After the first world war it was no longer a matter of course that a capitalist government should rule France, and the first Popular-Front Government was a clear indication of the changed situation. This government carried through a number of radical reforms, though it did not fundamentally change the social structure of the country. It was not long before it was overthrown, but social instability remained.

Whilst Hitler Germany was "liquidating" the economic crisis by means of a war economy built up in times of peace, a state of latent crisis continued to exist in the other European countries, including Great Britain, and in consequence social antagonisms continued to intensify, but without coming to a definite head. Thus a permanent crisis, together with the aggravation of social antagonism, became the normal state of affairs.

Not only did social unrest lead to economic unrest at home, but it also affected foreign policy.

Foreign policy now aimed, amongst other things, at preventing any further aggravation of social antagonisms not only at home, but abroad, and in this respect it differed radically from the period before the first world war, when such considerations played no role at all. Nazi Germany exploited this situation to obtain a tremendous advantage in armaments and military preparedness.

It was in this period that the Nazi Government rejected all the restrictions which had been imposed precisely in order to prevent a resurgence of German militarism, and Britain and France did not feel themselves in a position to answer adequately. To prevent Hitler's rearmament of Germany or, if this proved impossible, to answer it with a similar war economy in peace time, the social stratification of Great Britain and France would have had to be very different—different enough to make a real united national front against German Nazi aggression possible.

It was not so in either country; the aggravation of social antagonisms, which threatened the existence of capitalism without overthrowing it, made that quite impossible.

The European powers, including Great Britain, entered the second world war, like the United States, with an unresolved crisis in their economies, and at the same time their social antagonisms were much more acute than in the United States.

The Nazi State and its War Economy

Despite all national differences, the development of world capitalism in the period before the first world war was more or less uniform. As a result of that war Russia separated herself from this general trend and became Soviet Russia. During the world economic crisis her development went exactly contrary to that of the capitalist countries.

In the capitalist countries themselves there were certain uniform tendencies of development after the first world war, up to the outbreak of the world economic crisis in 1929 and until the trough of the crisis was reached. Subsequently that uniformity was broken up, particularly with regard to Germany, where the Nazis were now in power and German capitalism began to go its own way.

The difference in the trends in this subsequent period from the trough of the crisis up to the outbreak of the second world war can be seen very clearly from a comparison of the nature of State intervention in the United States and in Germany.

When the Nazis came to power the first thing they did was to destroy the working-class political parties, the Social Democratic Party and the Communist Party, and the German trade unions. However, they did not stop at that, but went on to destroy the capitalist political parties, the Catholic, Conservative and Liberal, as well, until only the Nazi Party was left. Henceforth Germany was a totalitarian State with one political party, and the capitalist system continued to exist.

In the United States, on the other hand, the period of the "New Deal" saw the extension of political democracy in many spheres and a strengthening of the tendencies towards social democracy. In Germany political democracy was utterly destroyed and all working-class organization broken up and suppressed.

350

In the United States an attempt was made to overcome the economic crisis by State intervention deliberately aiming at an improvement of working-class living standards, but no attempt whatever was made to draw up any plans for the economic system as a whole. In Nazi Germany State intervention went much farther and proceeded much more systematically. In fact, *for the first time in the history of capitalism, an integral planned economy was organized in times of peace.*

GERMAN WAR ECONOMY THE FIRST PLANNED WAR ECONOMY IN TIMES OF PEACE

Germany introduced a planned economy, but it was a planned economy of unusual character, and it was primarily based on the rapid development of a military economic sector on what was, in times of peace, an unprecedented scale.

With this war economy in peace time the Nazis introduced something entirely new into the history of capitalism. Unlike the United States, the big European countries (not including Great Britain) had had compulsory general military service in peace time for generations. They all maintained big standing armies supported by millions of trained reserves. This was a matter of course for France, Germany, Russia and Austria-Hungary.

However, as we have already seen in detail in Part Two, the first world war demonstrated very clearly that in the phase of modern capitalist industry purely military preparations for war were not sufficient. It demonstrated that, in addition to the purely military preparations for war, there must be an economic, an industrial armament, preparation as well, and that side by side with the military general staff there must be an economic general staff, not only during the war itself, but before the war, in times of peace.

It has often been said, with a good deal of justification, that generals always begin a new war with all the weapons and ideas of the war before, and this was true of both sides in the first world war.

The Germans lost that war, and precisely because they did lose it they were much more keen than the victors to learn from their experience and avoid making the same mistakes next time. Thus Germany's military men constantly stressed the lesson of the first world war, that a lack of economic and industrial preparations had been their chief handicap.

The situation when the Nazis came to power in Germany was one of economic crisis, a crisis more profound than any in the history of German capitalism, and they replaced a government which had reacted only negatively and passively to the crisis. Germany's ruling classes had no idea at all as to how the crisis was to be overcome; the German working class was hopelessly disunited and incapable of action; and the German people generally were in despair and crying out for some sort of action—they didn't much care what—which promised to extricate them from their difficulties.

Even before the Nazis came to power they had known more or less what they intended to do if they ever did come to power: above all, to strengthen Germany's foreign-political position and to resuscitate the imperialist policy which had been interrupted by defeat in the first world war. It was quite clear to them that any aggressive German foreign policy would require first of all a big and powerful German army.

When they did come to power they found a set of circumstances which greatly favoured their policy. They were prepared to start building up Germany's military strength again at once, and the German people expected them to do something radical to overcome the economic crisis and get economic life going again. The first world war had demonstrated that one of the reasons for Germany's defeat had been a lack of industrial armament preparations in peace time. Thus for them the conclusion was very simple: the building up of a powerful German army and, together with it, the organization in times of peace of industrial armament preparations adequate to a modern war of industries.

If the Nazis had happened to come to power at a time when the German economic system was functioning freely and busily producing peace-time consumer goods, then the building up of a strong German army together with the necessary industrial armament preparations would have meant a fall in living standards for the German people, and this would have undermined the political strength of the Nazis. But they were favoured by coming to power at a time when the trough of the world economic crisis had barely been passed, when living standards in Germany had sunk to an unusually low level, and when there was chronic mass unemployment affecting not only the working class but the middle strata as well.

In this situation they were able to build up a big and powerful army and simultaneously restore the activity of the German economic system and introduce full employment, so that, *despite the enormous expenditure on armaments, the living standards of the masses of the German people improved by comparison with the worst period of the economic crisis.*

In the United States during the war the military sector swallowed up about half the total production of the country, but the increase in U.S. production during the war, the liquidation of unemployment and the building of many new factories, meant that, although half of industrial output was being used for war purposes, the production of ordinary peace-time consumer goods did not decline, whilst the living standards of the worst-paid workers rose.

During the world economic crisis German industrial production dropped by approximately half, but by 1936, under the Nazis, it once again reached 1929 levels, and then rose higher and higher until

352

at the outbreak of the second world war it was more than 30 per cent above 1929 levels.

In those years German armaments production was naturally very much less than the half of total industrial production, and even if we include all the investments which were made directly or indirectly in connection with armaments production, and all the expenditure involved in making Germany as far as possible economically self-sufficient and more independent of foreign imports, all these costs were still far less than the half of her total production.

At the same time the production of armaments, the investments for the extension of already existing armament factories and the building of new ones for the production of cellulose wool, synthetic oil, synthetic rubber and so on, and for the furthering of autarkic tendencies, were so great that by 1936 the German economic system as a whole was fully occupied and unemployment had been reduced to a minimum. For this reason the building up of a powerful German army and the organization of an adequate system of industrial armaments could go hand in hand with an increase in the general production of consumer goods far above the levels of 1932, and an improvement of living standards for the masses of the German people by comparison with the worst years of the crisis.

Germany's war economy in peace time, unlike the "New Deal", was extensive enough to bring full employment to the whole economic system, to permit the full utilization of the productive apparatus, to increase the production of consumer goods and to liquidate unemployment almost completely, though, of course, this war economy in times of peace was considerably smaller than a military sector in times of war.

Judged from a purely economic standpoint, this German war economy in peace time often involved a considerable waste of economic resources, but this was not of very great importance by comparison with the vast amount of unutilized capacity, both in industry, and man-power, which had existed during the crisis itself.

Thus with their war economy in peace time the Nazis were able to comply with the demand of the German people for radical action—a demand which the government of the middle parties had never been able to satisfy—and "liquidate" the economic crisis. At the same time they made great play in their propaganda with their undoubted success in abolishing unemployment, whereas the democratic powers —the United States, Great Britain, France and Czechoslovakia— had not been able to do so.

The fact that the effects of the economic crisis were overcome by the Nazi war economy in peace time coupled with the building up of a powerful German army—and reinforced by the striking foreign-political successes won by the Nazis—had a great effect on the relationship of the various strata of the population to the Nazi State.

M

Even before the Nazis came to power in Germany, Big Business, the army and the junkers had either supported or at least tolerated them. They continued to do so in the period of Nazi war economy in peace time. The great increase in the production of armaments brought the German capitalist class big profits not only by comparison with the years of depression during the crisis, but also by comparison with the period of relative prosperity which had preceded the crisis. The Nazi State guaranteed the market not only for the old productive apparatus, but also for the new productive apparatus which had since been created. Like the United States in war time, the German Nazi State provided a ready-made market for production at a good profit to the German capitalists, and it did so in times of peace.

Most of Germany's big industrialists and business men had not been members of the Nazi Party before it came to power, and they did not join it even afterwards, but the great majority of them had been benevolently neutral towards the Nazis and they continued to be so after the establishment of the Nazi regime even though they disapproved of some of its methods, because, in their view, that regime offered the best protection for their interests and had destroyed the organizations of the German working class before they could become dangerous.

They also made their peace with the new regime because they had reason to hope—particularly in view of the striking foreign-political successes of the Nazis—that the existence of a powerful German army backed up by adequate armament production and the mere threat of war would open up a new period of external expansion for German capitalism and imperialism. They were supported in this belief by the fact that the Western Powers made far more concessions to Germany under Nazi rule than they had ever done under the Weimar Republic. In addition, under the Nazi regime Germany's position in Eastern Europe was greatly strengthened. Thus for a section of German large-scale capitalism the military and armament expenditure carried out by the Nazis was the price which had to be paid for improving Germany's position in the general framework of unfavourable conditions which existed for European capitalism as a whole, and, naturally, they were very willing to pay it. Thus opposition to the Nazis in these social circles was exceptional, and usually confined to a few individuals.

At the same time it was not surprising that most of the leaders and the higher ranks of the German army supported the Nazis, because the Nazis had restored the German army to its old eminence and built it up from a very low level to one even higher than that of Hohenzollern Germany in peace time.

Not only did the Nazis build up a big and powerful German army, but they also vigorously propagated an ideology which regarded the soldier as the most important member of society; they glorified war and the profession of arms, and they ruthlessly persecuted all pacifist elements. Thus all in all Germany's military leaders had every reason to be satisfied with the Nazis.

Although throughout this period there was considerable tension between certain military circles and the Nazis—partly because, as aristocrats, Germany's officers hated and despised the plebeian Nazis, and partly because they feared that the Nazis intended to obtain control of the army—the great majority of the upper strata of Germany's military caste either supported or tolerated the Nazis, and even those elements which had remained more or less neutral gradually abandoned their neutrality under the influence of the startling foreign-political successes obtained by the Nazis.

In this connection it should also be pointed out that the feudal junker estates, which had been undermined more and more in the last years of the crisis period, were not interfered with under the Hitler regime and that their general economic position even improved, which was one more reason for these capitalist feudal strata to support, or at least tolerate, the Nazis. On their part, the Nazis needed the military talents and traditions of these feudal aristocratic strata in the building up of Germany's new army, and because the junkers sent their sons into the officers' corps, the Nazis in return left them their estates. The result was that when the Nazi regime finally collapsed as the result of Germany's defeat in the second world war, her agricultural structure was not very different from what it had been after the first world war.

Before the Nazis came to power the great majority of the peasants had voted for them, and they remained their supporters throughout the period of war economy. Immediately after the Nazis came to power a moratorium for agricultural indebtedness had been proclaimed, so that the peasants no longer had to fear the loss of their land if they were unable to pay their debts. In the course of Nazi war economy the economic situation of the German peasants improved in very much the same way as the economic situation of the American farmers improved under the "New Deal". Just as in the United States, the growth of industrial production and the reduction of unemployment increased the purchasing power of the urban population, and, in addition, there were two special reasons why the situation of the German peasants in this period was even more favourable than that of the American farmers.

On the one hand, unemployment in Germany was practically abolished, and not merely reduced, as it was in the United States by the "New Deal", and at the same time German production rose steadily and without set-backs far above 1929 levels. Secondly, unlike the United States, Germany was a country which imported large quantities of agricultural produce because her own agricultural production was not sufficient to meet all her needs and never had been. The Nazi Government brought German foreign trade more and more under its control, and this made it very much easier to control the price of agricultural produce in such a way that the situation of the overwhelming majority of the German peasants greatly improved by comparison with the period of crisis.

This was the economic background for the almost complete absence of opposition to the Nazis in the rural areas. Although the Nazi Government intervened increasingly in agricultural production and agricultural marketing—something which, of course, the peasants resented—yet on balance this Nazi intervention held considerably more advantages than disadvantages for them.

Let us point out again here that the German peasants were the only middle stratum in Germany which survived two world wars, inflation, economic crisis and the Nazi regime without serious loss. Under the Nazis the peasants remained the owners of their farms, and, to that extent, they retained a firm economic basis, and when, thanks to rearmament prosperity, the whole German national income rose, their income rose with it, until they were once again enjoying a middle-class standard of life, and this continued throughout the period of war economy in peace time and on into the second world war.

The Situation of the Urban Middle Strata

The situation of the urban middle class in Germany was much more complicated. Let us deal first of all with the so-called independent existences. This stratum was particularly badly hit by the first world war and the subsequent inflation and then by the economic crisis. At first, after the Nazis came to power, they, too, profited from the armament boom and the general improvement of economic activity, but not for long.

What happened in this respect in Germany in the years from 1935 until the autumn of 1939, when the second world war broke out, we shall best be able to understand if we compare this phase of Germany's economy with German war economy during the first world war and with the war economy of the Anglo-Saxon powers during the course of the second world war. For a variety of reasons, war economy in a modern war of industry is not favourable to small-scale urban undertakings. However great the reserves of industrial production in any particular country may be, they are not inexhaustible, and therefore in war-time measures are sooner or later taken to concentrate production in the most productive undertakings—i.e. in those undertakings which require less man-power for the same quantity of production. Such undertakings are the large-scale factories, etc., not the smaller ones. During war-time the general tendency

356

towards a rationalization of production is intensified, and this once again favours the large-scale works. In addition, it is much simpler for a government bureaucracy which has to order gigantic quantities of war material, to have to deal with a comparatively few large-scale undertakings rather than with hundreds of thousands of small undertakings, and this is once again a factor which tells against the urban middle strata. And, finally, man-power difficulties grow worse and worse in war-time; there is a labour shortage everywhere, and the closing down of smaller undertakings and the transfer of their owners and their workers to the bigger undertakings become common.

It was characteristic for the war economy in peace time introduced by the Nazis, that all these difficulties arose years before the outbreak of the second world war, because, unlike the first world war, and unlike the Anglo-Saxon powers in the second world war, Nazi Germany began to organize her production of war material long before the war broke out. Thus a man-power shortage arose in Germany long before the war, whereas in Great Britain and the United States it arose only during the war itself. The Nazis therefore began to "comb out" the German independent middle strata in a determined effort to get new supplies of labour power into the big factories where they could be used to the best advantage.

It was only a few years after the coming of the Nazis to power that unemployment was liquidated, and it was only in those few years that the independent German urban middle strata had their share in the general rise in production and the general increase in national income. After that a process of social destruction began for them at a rate unprecedented in German history.

A German semi-official publication frankly admitted this mass destruction of the urban middle strata. In 1925 the number of proprietors in Germany amounted, together with their dependants, to 12,027,000 persons, or 20·9 per cent of the total population. By 1933 the figure had declined to 11,247,000, or 19·8 per cent of the population. But after that, in the first six years of Nazi rule—in the period of "Wehrwirtschaft", or war economy—the number declined still further to 9,612,000, or 16·2 per cent of the total population. The German publication in question, *Wirtschaft und Statistik* of 1940, p. 336, comments as follows on this phenomenon:

> "The decline in the number of proprietors together with their dependants (their total was reduced by 1·7 millions, or approximately 15 per cent, from 1933 onward) is in accordance with a long and steady trend of development. From 1895 onwards their numbers decreased from census to census, though the decline since 1933 is, of course, a *record* one." *

* Italics mine.—F. S.

Such was the economic fate of the German independent urban middle strata under the Nazis: an accelerated process of social destruction.

But this process of social destruction gives only one aspect of their fate. On the other hand, the Nazi State created more opportunities of employment for the dependent middle strata. The Nazi war economy in peace-time liquidated unemployment amongst commercial and other employees, who counted themselves amongst the middle strata, and unemployment amongst them had previously been greater than unemployment as a whole in earlier crises. Under the Nazi war economy all such commercial and other employees were fully employed, and not only them, but also all the "new" middle strata whose social basis had been threatened during the crisis.

At the same time the Nazis created certain substitute occupations for some sections of the old middle strata whose economic and social basis they had undermined by their war economy. Many of these formerly independent middle strata became officials of the State or employees of the huge Nazi Party machine, or officers and non-commissioned officers of the new German army.

Thus the fact that the Nazi State profoundly disappointed the hopes and aspirations, both economically and socially, of precisely those elements which, in their desperation, had returned them to power was concealed for the time being.

To sum up: the fact that the Nazis came to power in the crisis, and that very soon afterwards they began to build up a big and powerful German army and to organize the necessary armaments production for it, made it possible for them to offer something definite to those elements which had supported or tolerated them before they came to power: that applied to Big Business and to the army, to the junkers and to the peasants, and, with the exception of the independent middle strata, it applied to large numbers of the urban middle strata as well.

In the same period the Nazi State perfected and extended its terrorist apparatus and completed the destruction of all oppositional organizations. The work of the underground resistance movement was made more and more difficult. The Nazi State created a monopoly of the press, the wireless, the cinema—in short, of all the means of influencing the minds of the German people—and it used that monopoly ruthlessly.

However, it is important—particularly with regard to the possibility of a new fascist State—to note that the Nazis did not rule exclusively as a result of their terrorist apparatus, or their one-party monopoly of all the instruments of propaganda and public expression. In a period of rapidly developing war economy in peace time they were able to extend their social basis and materially assist the great majority of their former supporters and electors.

What about the opponents of the Nazi regime? Before the Nazis came to power they were opposed by the overwhelming majority of the German working class, and, as we have already seen, it was the only class in Germany of which this can be said, it is understandable therefore that the brunt of the Nazi terror should have fallen on the working people. Their organizations were destroyed and their newspapers suppressed. Tens of thousands of workers were killed, and the concentration camps were filled with the leaders and active members of the working class, and later with the members of its underground resistance movement.

The Nazis attempted with every means at their disposal to deprive the German working class of all political cohesion. Not only did they destroy all working-class organizations, but they concentrated their whole monopoly of the means of public propaganda on the task of preventing the working class from obtaining a true picture of the position in Germany and of their own situation under Nazi rule.

However, even here it was not the terror alone which operated in favour of the Nazis. The German workers had lost their organizations, and thus been deprived of their chief weapon in the fight to maintain and increase their living standards. If the Nazi war economy had been introduced in a period of prosperity, then, after the loss of their organizations, the German working class would hardly have been able to prevent the growing expenditure on armaments from adversely affecting their living standards. But, in fact, the Nazis developed their war economy at a time when half the German working class was unemployed in the crisis. Those workers who had been unemployed but were now employed under the Nazi war economy did not get the same real wages as they had received in the period of relative prosperity before the world economic crisis, but at least they were much better off than they had been during the crisis years, when they had received nothing but unemployment support of various kinds.

It is true to say of the years 1931 and 1932 that there was hardly a German working-class family which had not at least one or two members fully unemployed. Full employment, when it came to Germany under the Nazi war economy, meant not only that those workers who had been unemployed now lived better; it also meant that, even if those workers who had been employed during the crisis years received no higher wages, at least a working-class family as a whole earned more, and therefore enjoyed a higher standard of living. And in the final years of Nazi war economy the increasing shortage of labour resulted in wage increases for many sections of the working class, so that real wages were higher than in the crisis years.

The German workers, who were well aware how closely the Nazis were allied with Big Business, had feared that after the victory of the

Nazis, and after the break-up of their organizations and the reign of terror against their leaders and officials, they would suffer a further decline in their standards of living, but, as we have seen, this fear proved groundless. Germany re-armed, but at the same time there was an improvement, instead of a deterioration, in working-class standards of living, as compared with the years of the crisis—i.e. in the last years before the Nazis came to power.

The Nazis never succeeded in winning a majority of the workers, and the best proof of this was that when the military defeat of the regime restored organizational freedom, the workers flocked back to their own organizations at once. However, the Nazis certainly did succeed in neutralizing a considerable section of the workers.

The State and the Economic System under the Nazi War Economy

The terror regime and the domination of a single political party to the exclusion of all others naturally led to a very considerable growth in the power and influence of the State. In addition, it was not possible to develop a war economy without a system of planned economy under the control and guidance of the State. Germany had no capital investments abroad worth talking about; on the contrary, she was a debtor State. There were also many raw materials which she either did not possess at all, or possessed only in quantities which were not adequate for the creation of a big military sector; thus in order to maintain its armaments programme at a high level the Nazi State was compelled first of all to intervene ruthlessly in foreign trade. Lacking reserves of foreign exchange, Germany had to introduce a system of priorities favouring the importation of those raw materials, etc., which were of importance to her rearmament. The result was that, for the first time in the history of capitalism, practically a State monopoly of foreign trade was introduced in a capitalist country in times of peace. As Germany's imports had to be paid for, and as she was unable to obtain credits on any scale, she had to pay for them primarily with exports. This compelled the State to intervene in the production of certain industries in order to bring exports and imports into line.

Now the foreign-trade situation was very difficult, because, as a result of the crisis, world trade in general had suffered a catastrophic decline, and there was a great danger that Germany's exports would not prove sufficient to pay for all the imports she needed for her rearmament programme. In addition, the unfortunate experiences of the first world war had shown the necessity of, not abolishing altogether, because that was impossible, but at least greatly reducing Germany's dependence on imports.

Therefore, on the basis of its foreign-trade monopoly and its strongly centralized power, the Nazi State developed a number of new industries which were not in themselves profitable and had to be subsidized, but which did something to make Germany's economic system less susceptible to an economic blockade in the event of war.

In this way the Nazi State became directly responsible for a large sector of German industry. In addition, as we have seen, the State completely controlled foreign trade. It also controlled a considerable part of capital investments, and it guided the process of investment in numerous other industries. Now, in order to do this systematically and effectively, the State also had to control wages and prices. During the first world war capitalism had made the acquaintance of State planned economy on quite a big scale, and during the second world war it was to experience it on a bigger one. Thus the new feature of the Nazi war economy was not so much the thing itself, but the fact that it was introduced in peace time, and the fact that it was introduced and guided by a Nazi State—that is to say, by a capitalist anti-democratic totalitarian State.

It is interesting to note that long before the publication of Sir William Beveridge's book [21] declaring that the proper recipe for full employment in the present stage of capitalism was that the State should make big investments on its own account and also control and guide investments in the private sector, the Nazi State had already put his recipe into operation. But on the first occasion in world history when a capitalist State directed investments by its intervention in times of peace, it was done in order to organize a tremendous programme of armaments and to establish a great armament and military sector which grew and grew until finally the second world war broke out.

Hitler's Great Foreign-Political Victories

Germany's war economy and her re-armament policy were accompanied by an endless succession of foreign-political victories on the part of the Nazi State.

In Part One of this book we have seen that one of the main reasons for the outbreak of the first world war was that although Germany had become the leading industrial country in Europe she did not possess a colonial empire consonant with her industrial and economic strength, and that therefore in the epoch of imperialist colonialism her own attempts at expansion met with steadily growing difficulties because the colonial world was already largely divided between the older industrial powers.

In Part Two we saw that Germany's defeat in the first world war had the effect of intensifying this discrepancy between her industrial strength on the one hand and her possibilities of imperialist expansion on the other. The military provisions of the Treaty of Versailles were intended to maintain this state of affairs by force against all the logic of facts.

We have already seen why, economically speaking, the Versailles Treaty never functioned. It presupposed an economically flourishing Europe with a phase of ceaseless expansion such as existed in the years before the first world war. The end of external expansion throughout the world, which was particularly painful for European capitalism, made any such period of progress impossible. In consequence the whole scheme of reparations broke down at a very early date.

However, the military provisions of the Versailles Treaty had remained; but once the Nazis came to power they, too, were flung overboard. Germany introduced general compulsory military service, which was forbidden by the Versailles Treaty, and she re-occupied the Rhineland militarily, which was also forbidden. In short, she proceeded to ignore all the provisions of the treaty which were expressly directed to preventing any resurgence of her military strength.

There were a number of reasons why the western powers made no real attempt to call Nazi Germany to order when she proceeded to violate all the important military provisions of the Versailles Treaty in the first phase of her re-armament.

Apart from the fact that Great Britain and France were unable to agree on a united policy towards Nazi Germany, the real reason for their passivity was that powerful reactionary influences in both countries feared that if any effective steps were taken against Nazi Germany they might lead to the collapse of the Nazi regime altogether and its replacement by a left-wing regime determined to lead the country to social revolution.

In the first years after the Nazis came to power action against German re-armament would easily have been possible without involving war, because at that time the western powers, and France in particular, enjoyed a great military superiority. But once the Nazis had filled up the military vacuum and Germany had become militarily strong in accordance with her industrial strength, only war would have sufficed to prevent a further extension of her war economy, and when that stage had been reached the Nazis did not content themselves with maintaining their armaments, but proceeded to draw advantage from them by launching a policy of expansion once again.

NEO-FASCIST IMPERIALIST EXPANSION

This new policy of imperialist expansion took various forms. Without meeting with resistance, the troops of Nazi Germany marched into fascist Austria, whose government had some years before defeated the socialist working class in street-fighting and destroyed its organizations, and Austria became a province of Germany. Later on, after the Munich Agreement, Czechoslovakia was also annexed and turned into a Nazi satellite State.

These were the highlights of the openly carried out policy of annexation in the last few years before the outbreak of the second world war on the basis of Germany's military strength, but in an even earlier period there was another form of imperialist expansion indulged in by Nazi Germany, a form of economic imperialist conquest which is well worth analysis, because it shows once again that the forms of imperialist expansion can vary greatly, according to the structure of the imperialist metropolitan centre indulging in it and the aims bound up with it.

The Versailles Treaty deprived Germany of her small colonial empire and girdled her in the east with a ring of hostile States, so that for the time being German expansion in that direction was seriously hampered. With the victory of the Nazis in Germany a change came about here too. Under the Nazi regime Germany's industrial production again reached 1929 levels and then steadily rose above them. The State controlled and directed the economic system, and, thanks to its practical monopoly of foreign trade, it also closely controlled Germany's exports and imports. Germany had always played an important part in the foreign trade of Eastern and South-East Europe, and now her importance grew greater than ever.

Under the Weimar Republic her trade with the countries of Eastern and South-East Europe had taken the form of transactions between private firms on both sides, but under the Nazis what practically amounted to a State monopoly of foreign trade controlled all such transactions. With this, of course, Germany's position was greatly strengthened, quite apart from the fact that it was already very strong on account of Germany's immense industrial and economic superiority. When the German Nazi State set out to make purchases in any of these countries it bought in bulk, and was naturally able to throw the full weight of its centralized power into the scales. Under liberal capitalism no country was in such an advantageous position.

In addition, it should be remembered that the economic relations between Eastern and Western Europe were not the relations of equal partners, because Western Europe was, of course, much more strongly industrialized than Eastern Europe, and the former used its economic power to exploit the latter. No attempt was ever made to co-ordinate the industrial production of the small countries of Eastern and South-East Europe. We have already seen that as a result of the first world war, which broke up the Austro-Hungarian Empire and led to the establishment of a number of smaller States, there was a certain degree of economic stagnation in the whole area, so that when the world economic crisis broke out it hit States which were already suffering from economic stagnation. This was the situation in Eastern Europe when the Nazis set out to organize their war economy.

On the basis of Germany's industrial strength, reinforced by the

363

State monopoly of foreign trade, the Nazis proceeded to develop and extend the already close trading relationships with this part of the world on terms which were very profitable to Germany. At the same time they sought to harness these countries more and more to Germany's economic system, whilst leaving them, for the time being at least, their political independence. For instance, the Nazi State would propose that this or that country should concentrate on the production of this or that raw material required by Germany for her war economy, promising to guarantee a market for this increased production over a long period.

When Japan integrated her own Four-Year Plan of economic development with the Four-Year Plan for the industrial development of Manchuria, she was in a very favourable position, because her army occupied Manchuria, and Manchuria's industrial development was financed by Japanese capital. Germany's position in Eastern and South-East Europe was, of course, rather different, because the small States in this part of the world were all politically independent, and she could therefore not do exactly as she liked there; but she used her economic strength and her centralized trade apparatus to reinforce a policy of military-industrial expansion which turned these countries, economically at least, into satellites of Germany. Long before the war Nazi Germany succeeded in harnessing part of the production of these countries to her war economy. When the second world war broke out, and German troops flooded over these countries, they lost their political independence, and Germany found it much easier to incorporate them into her war economy proper, thanks to her experience with them in the years before the war.

All the foreign-political antagonisms in Europe which had led to the first world war reappeared with renewed force under Hitler. Germany was once again a powerful industrial country in the heart of Europe, with an army, more powerful than in 1913, backed up by an adequate production of armaments. Naturally, she sought to expand in every possible way; and her expansionist policy was now even more vigorous and aggressive than before. And whilst Germany's imperialist expansion was taking place in Europe in times of peace, Japan was expanding, though in a somewhat different fashion, in Asia.

JAPANESE EXPANSION BEFORE THE SECOND WORLD WAR

Japanese developments had not gone parallel with developments in the other capitalist countries during the world economic crisis, and the same was true of the period from the crisis to the outbreak of the second world war.

The development of Nazi Germany was marked by the establishment of a wide-scale armament economy in peace time; Japanese development in the same period was marked by a great extension of

364

the military sector and also by a powerful increase in imperialist expansion on the Asiatic mainland, including the launching of the war against China.

In Nazi Germany there was a dividing line between the period of armament economy and the outbreak of the second world war; in Japan the transition was much less noticeable. Military operations began for Japan in 1931 with the invasion of Manchuria, and in the years that followed, up to the outbreak of the second world war, Japan was all the time engaged in military operations on a fairly big scale in her war against China. However, it was a war against an industrially backward country, and it therefore required only a comparatively small part of the Japanese armed forces and of Japan's armament industry.

But although it was a war against a militarily inferior enemy, it nevertheless demanded the production of armaments, the replacement of equipment, etc. In consequence the military sector continued to extend, quite apart from the fact that Japan was engaged in preparations for a very much larger war, a totalitarian war. Not only did Japan conquer Manchuria militarily, but she also pushed forward the industrialization of the country and co-ordinated it with her own and with the economic system of the Japanese Empire as a whole. Thus the war against China, the development and extension of the military sector and the preparations for a much larger war, the industrialization of Manchuria, together with the development of Japan's own industries, all led to an increase of Japanese industrial production which was, relatively speaking, much greater than that of any other capitalist country, even including Nazi Germany. If we take Japanese industrial production in 1929 as being 100, then by 1934 it was already 128·7. It rose further to 151·1 in 1936 and to 173 in 1938.[22]

The United States and the Western Powers entered the second world war with productive organisms which were not fully utilized and with chronic mass unemployment which had lasted for many years. Germany entered the war with an already established system of war economy which had succeeded in liquidating unemployment in the years before the war. Japan entered the war with a productive apparatus which was being utilized to the full and after a long period of war on a smaller scale against China.

In the period before the second world war the Japanese imperialist drive on the Asiatic mainland had been limited to China and Manchuria, and in consequence it did not clash very seriously with the colonial interests of the European imperialist countries. This clash took place on a big scale only during the course of the war itself when Japan began to drive south. However, Japan's pre-war successes in China naturally limited the spheres of influence of the European imperialist countries.

365

In our analysis of the effects of the first world war we pointed out that one of them had been to weaken the position of the European capitalist imperialist metropolitan centres. That weakness subsequently became very apparent in the inability of the European imperialist powers to stop Japan's imperialist drive on the Asiatic mainland. Thus Japanese military and economic expansion accentuated the already existing stagnation tendencies from which the European imperialist countries were suffering. But it did more than that.

When Japan conquered Manchuria and North China she at first left the existing system of landlordism there intact, and sought to find some way of collaborating with the Chinese ruling classes. China's social organism had already been greatly shaken by long years of civil war; now came the Japanese invasion and the military and guerilla warfare against Japan. At times the war against Japanese imperialism embraced all sections of the population of China, including even those sections which were in favour of the maintenance of the old feudal order, though this participation was very often not altogether in accordance with their wishes or their interests.

The military defeat of China meant that where the Japanese military forces were successful and occupied the land, the old Chinese social order was undermined and the power of the ruling classes shaken. If Japan had been victorious in the end she might have been able to maintain the old feudal structure in China and in the territories of the old Chinese Empire. However, the first Japanese military successes actually strengthened the tendencies which made for social revolution in China and destroyed the old Chinese feudal structure and the social order it embodied.

Japan's first victories in China and her subsequent total military defeat in the second world war represented decisive factors in the development which led first to imperialist stagnation and then to imperialist decline, but they were not the only factors.

The Growth of the Anti-Imperialist Forces in Asia

From the standpoint of the European imperialist countries the period between the two world wars was a period of double imperialist stagnation (as we have already seen in Chapter One of this Part of our book); but from the standpoint of the colonial and semi-colonial countries which were the objects of imperialist exploitation it was by no means merely a period of stagnation, but a period in which anti-imperialist activity greatly increased, with the object of throwing off the imperialist yoke and creating independent native States.

The anti-imperialist struggles of the period between the two wars led to no concrete results, but they effectively prepared the ground for the period which was to come, when the second world war had still further weakened the imperialist colonial powers, accelerated the process of their own social transformation and opened up the process of imperialist decline. A whole series of factors strengthened the national-revolutionary movement in the colonial and semi-colonial countries, including the following:

1. The European colonial countries, including even the victorious countries, were greatly weakened as a result of the first world war. During the period between the two world wars Europe never regained the world position it had occupied in the second half of the nineteenth century and the first years of the twentieth century up to the outbreak of the war. Thus the national-revolutionary movements in the colonial and semi-colonial countries no longer had to contend with capitalist imperialist states which were still growng in strength and influence, but with countries which were already suffering from stagnation, with ruling strata which had already lost the spirit of conquerors.

2. Capitalism had certainly created a more or less co-ordinated economic and industrial development in the capitalist metropolitan centres, but it had done nothing of the sort in the colonial and semi-colonial countries. It had allied itself there with the old feudal ruling classes, but at the same time it had in many ways done a great deal to undermine the social basis on which feudalism rested. Although it had done its best to prevent any integrated industrial developments in the colonial and semi-colonial countries, it had nevertheless been unable to prevent the rise of a number of industries, although they were not satisfactorily co-ordinated with each other. It had supported the feudal order in agriculture, but at the same time it had radically changed the lives of tens of millions of peasants, because on the one hand it had robbed them of part of their means of life by exporting many articles to the colonial countries which had formerly been made on the spot by the peasants, and because on the other it had forced more and more of them to hire themselves for work on the big plantations whose products they could not use themselves and which were of no use to the colonial countries—products which were intended for sale on the world market and which were therefore subject to all the price vacillations of the capitalist market system.

Imperialism had also built railways and established a central administration. Generally speaking, only the upper reaches of the administration were occupied by Europeans, and natives were employed for the more subordinate tasks. But for this they had to be educated, and many of them were graduates of Oxford and Cambridge, London and Paris, Marseilles and the Hague. As undergraduates they learnt not only European administration, technics, medicine and so on, but they also made the acquaintance of European ideas of political democracy and political liberty, and they took back these ideas with them. It was these intellectuals who subsequently became the most vigorous enemies of European colonial imperialism, and they were very dangerous enemies, because their arguments were irrefutable. What, for instance, could the British administrators of India answer when these European-trained Indian intellectuals demanded liberty of development for their own country—the same liberty which their English universities had so glorified as the greatest heritage of human civilization? At the same time these intellectuals had the masses of the people behind them, because, with the exception of the feudal elements, the landlords and a thin stratum of socially corrupt elements, no section of colonial society supported European colonial imperialism.

Even the rich native industrialists were opposed to European imperialism because it hampered the development of their industries. And the native workers were certainly anti-imperialist, because they very often worked under conditions which were worse than European working-class conditions at the beginning of the industrial revolution. The native intellectuals as a whole, and not only those who had been educated abroad, were anti-imperialist because the national revolutionary movement alone held out hope of a tolerable future for them. And, above all, imperialism had to reckon with the enmity of the millions of peasants, who suffered more than any other section of native society from the exploitation of European imperialism because, although the imperialists undermined the old social order, they put nothing progressive in its place.

It was the fact that all important sections of native society were opposed to imperialism that made the Congress Movement in India at all possible, and it was a movement which embraced Indian conservatives, industrialists, socialists, intellectuals, workers and peasants. They were all convinced, if for various reasons, that only the overthrow of imperialist rule could open the way for a progressive development in their country.

During the first world war British imperialism was still able to rely on the assistance of the Indians in fighting its battles without even asking them first, because at that time the national-revolutionary movement was still in its infancy.

In the period between the two world wars the situation changed completely. The national-revolutionary movement in India developed so rapidly that the British were compelled to introduce reforms in the hope of taking off its edge, and they began to employ Indians in the administration on a bigger scale than before, though, of course, all the key positions were still kept safely in British hands. At the same time they undermined the effect of these reforms by proclaiming that the Indians were incapable of running their own affairs without British help.

Lord Birkenhead, Secretary of State for India, who was in charge of the Montagu-Chelmsford Reform, declared in the House of Lords in 1929:

> "What man in this House can say that he can see in a genera-
> tion, in two generations, in a hundred years, any prospect that the
> people of India will be in a position to assume control of the Army,
> the Navy, the Civil Service, and to have a Governor-General who
> will be responsible to the Indian Government and not to any
> authority in this country?"

That expressed the general views of leading British imperialists, and such talk not unnaturally strengthened the national-revolutionary movement to throw off the British yoke. The testing time came with the outbreak of the second world war. The British Conservatives insisted that the Indian National Congress had only a minority of the Indians behind it, but in the provincial elections of 1937 the Congress Party was supported by a majority of the voters in eight out of the eleven Provinces and represented strong minorities in the other three. This was proof enough that Congress had a majority of the Indian electorate behind it in its aim of making India independent of British rule. Thus a period which from the standpoint of Great Britain was one of stagnation was, politically at least, nothing of the sort for India, but one in which the national-revolutionary movement grew rapidly and embraced all sections of the population—the workers, industrialists and intellectuals in the towns, and the hundreds of millions of peasants in the countryside.

Thus the period between the two wars saw the end of India's passivity. The period of the second world war dramatically confirmed the changed situation.

Before the war actually broke out in September 1939, the British Government, under the premiership of Chamberlain, sent Indian troops, which were at that time still under the command of British officers, to the more threatened outposts of the British Empire—to Singapore, to Aden and to Egypt. Once again the Indians were not consulted, but they expressed their opinion by withdrawing their representatives from the All-India Legislative Assembly.

It was a significant gesture, but the British Government ignored it, and when Great Britain declared war on Germany the following month she declared war on India's behalf as well. Here, too, the British action met with bitter resistance from the Indian Congress. The Working Committee of the Congress published a manifesto in which it rejected fascism and the Nazi regime in the severest terms and condemned any "glorification of war" as a "violation of the recognized standards of civilized behaviour". With this manifesto Congress documented its willingness to go to war against Nazi aggression on the side of Great Britain, but as an ally, as an equal partner, not as a passive object of British decisions, and the manifesto stressed that: "Co-operation must be between equals by mutual consent for a cause which both consider to be worthy".

At the same time Congress was in doubt as to whether it would be possible for India and Great Britain under its then rulers to work out a common platform, in view of the continued policy of British imperialism. The manifesto therefore declared:

"If the war is to defend the *status quo* of imperialist privilege, then India can have nothing to do with it. If, however, the issue is democracy, and a world order based on democracy, then India is intensely interested in it."

But democracy at this stage for the Indian Congress meant the abolition of British rule in India; it meant complete Indian independence, and the manifesto therefore declared:

"The Indian people must have the right of self-determination to frame their own constitution through a Constituent Assembly without external interference, and must guide their own policy."

If Great Britain was prepared to give India political freedom and independence, then India was prepared to enter the war at her side as an ally against Nazi Germany. But if India was still to be treated as a passive object and fobbed off with promises for the future, without even having any guarantee that those promises would be honoured when the time came, the Indian Congress Committee refused to take any active part in the war.

Congress could obtain no satisfactory answer to the case set out in its manifesto, and so it took the only step open to it, and caused the ministers in the eight Provinces in which it had a majority to resign.

The struggle between Congress and British imperialism continued throughout the war. No agreement was obtained, and on a number of occasions the British authorities arrested and imprisoned various Congress leaders. Great Britain was still strong enough to do this, but it was not strong enough to keep India indefinitely in her old position as a helot State.

India was the biggest State in the British Empire. She was the great symbol not only of British imperialism, but of imperialism in general.

The strengthening of the national-revolutionary movement in India in the period between the two world wars—a period of imperialist stagnation—took place under historical conditions which were in many respects quite specifically and exclusively Indian. On the other hand, the process was typical of what was going on everywhere in all the European colonial territories in Asia, though perhaps the outward form was often different, and it applied to both French and Dutch colonial territory. Here too the period of imperialist stagnation was a period of growth for the national-revolutionary movements.

The European imperialist countries entered the first world war without having to bother their heads about the possible danger of intensified social antagonisms, and they did so with productive organisms which were occupied to the full with peace-time production. They entered the second world war with a foreign policy made hesitant and vacillating precisely because this time it was compelled to bother itself very much about the danger of intensified social antagonisms. Further, when the first world war broke out the European imperialist powers had full and complete control in their colonial empires, and there was no danger that the empires would become the scene of hostilities. At the time of the second world war the situation was very different. There were in their colonial empires nations which had at last awakened from a long period without independent history and were becoming nationally conscious and refusing to be treated any longer as the mere objects of imperialist policy. In addition, there was a very real danger that the territory of the European colonial empires would become the scene of hostilities, and in part it actually did.

Soviet Russia in the Period of the New Five-Year Plans

Whilst the United States was engaged with Roosevelt's "New Deal" policy, whilst Nazi Germany was organizing a war economy in peace time and developing an aggressive fascist and imperialist programme, whilst the Western European powers were still struggling to extricate themselves from the tail end of the crisis, to the accompaniment of intensifying political and economic antagonisms, and whilst world capitalism as a whole was unable to expand further and world trade stagnated, the Soviet Union was experiencing a tremendous increase in industrial production on the basis of its new Five-Year Plans.

This time the advance in Soviet industry was accompanied by an advance, though only a small one, in Soviet agriculture as well. But as a result of the tremendous increase in the military sector made necessary as an answer to the war economy of Nazi Germany, the dictatorship had become more onerous and its basis had grown still narrower.

The Growth in Industrial Production

Industrial production had increased tremendously in the period from 1929 to 1932, and that development now continued. The characteristics of the first Five-Year Plan were carried on into the subsequent Five-Year Plan periods—namely, the main weight was placed on the development of the basic industries at the expense of

371

the consumer-goods industries. Thanks to dictatorship and terror, the Soviet Government was able to maintain an unusually high rate of investment, and thus increase the speed of industrial development beyond that of capitalist countries and far beyond that of Tsarist Russia.

"Potentially, Russia possessed the same productive possibilities as the U.S.S.R.; the U.S.S.R., however, thanks to a planned utilization of existing potential productive resources in 12 years (1928–40) achieved results in the development of the national economy many times surpassing the results achieved by private enterprise in the course of the preceding fifty years, i.e. from the time of the abolition of serfdom and the elimination of formal obstacles to private enterprise in 1913." [23]

The following figures clearly show the industrial development of the Soviet Union from 1933 to 1938:

	1933.	1937.	1938.
Steel (million tons)	6·9	17·7	18
Rolled steel (million tons) . . .	5·1	13	13·3
Coal (million tons)	76·3	127·9	132·9
Oil (million tons) . . .	22·5	30·5	32·2
Iron ore (million tons)	14·4	27·7	26·5
Engineering and metallurgical industries (milliard roubles 1926–1927 value) .	10·8	27·5	33·6
Locomotives	941	1,581	1,626
Goods trucks (thousands) . . .	18·2	66·1	49·1
Motor cars (thousands) . . .	49·7	200	211·4
Electric power (milliard KWH) . .	16·4	36·4	39·6
Manganese ore (thousand tons) . .	1,021	2,275	2,273
Pig iron (million tons)	7·1	14·5	14·6
Copper (thousand tons) . . .	44·5	99·8	103·2
Aluminium (thousand tons) . .	7	37·7	56·8
Cement (million tons)	2·7	5·5	5·7
Cotton textiles (million metres) * . .	2,422	3,477	3,491
Woollen textiles (million metres) . .	86·1	108·3	114
Leather shoes (million pairs) . .	80·3	164·2	213
Raw sugar (thousand tons) . .	995	2,421	2,519

* It should be noted that the production of cotton textiles in 1933 was far below the 1929 level, which was 3,068 million metres.

What was the result of this tremendous increase of Soviet Russian production in the general relation of European and world forces? Even after this tremendous increase in her industrial production, Soviet Russia still remained a preponderantly agricultural country. Even after this period of forced industrial development, she still remained behind Germany and the Western Powers in *per capita* production. Nevertheless, as a result of this rapid and tremendous rise in industrial production in absolute figures the whole European relation of industrial forces was changed.

Under Tsarism both before and during the first world war Russia's industrial production in absolute figures had lagged behind the industrial production of Great Britain, France and Germany. But Soviet Russia had now passed British and French industrial production in absolute figures, and had greatly reduced the gap between her own industrial production and that of Germany, although in the same period Germany, thanks to her war economy in peace time, was utilizing her productive resources to the full. Under Tsarism Russia's share in world industrial production had been only 4 per cent. In Soviet Russia it had risen to approximately 12 per cent.

"So far as her share in the world production of important basic materials is concerned, the U.S.S.R. in many fields has moved into the front rank of great producers. . . . The industrial production of the U.S.S.R., which had to balance the heavy damage of the war and post-war years, increased considerably in the following years. Thus . . . a more rapid rate of growth of Soviet-Russian industrial production could be noted than would correspond to the 'world average'. . . . Simultaneously these Russian differences in growth effected a great rise in the share of the U.S.S.R. in industrial world production—according to our calculations—to 11·5 per cent in 1938 and 12 per cent in 1929." [24]

Germany still produced more *per capita* than Soviet Russia, but the difference had become very much smaller, and in absolute figures for heavy industrial production the relationship was now only 5 : 4 in Germany's favour. Much of the difference between the first and the second world wars is explained in these significant figures.

In the ten years from the world economic crisis up to the outbreak of the second world war, world capitalism had hardly been able to get back to the 1929 level in the production of peace-time commodities, but in the same period the Soviet Union had increased her 1929 production many times over.

The Decline of Soviet Foreign Trade

In the same period world capitalism never again succeeded in reaching 1929 levels for foreign trade, though compared with the very low levels of 1932 and 1933 there was a considerable degree of recovery. On the other hand, Soviet foreign trade developed on different lines from that of the capitalist countries. The first Five-Year Plan got into difficulties because, in drawing up their import plans, the Russians had reckoned with increased exports in a long period of world capitalist prosperity.

During the world economic crisis both Soviet Russia's exports and imports dropped considerably. The Russians drew their own conclusions from this, and in the subsequent Five-Year Plans their foreign trade played a much smaller and decreasing role.

373

The following table affords a comparison between Russia's foreign trade under Tsarism and from 1933 to 1938 under the Soviet regime:

Russia's Foreign Trade [25]

Years.	Exports.		Imports.	
	Thousand tons.	Million roubles.	Thousand tons.	Million roubles.
1909–1913 (annual average)	24,590·8	6,513·9	11,240·7	4,994·1
1933	17,916·3	2,167·5	1,236·1	1,525·1
1934	17,340·2	1,832·4	1,025·2	1,018
1935	17,190·4	1,609·3	1,259·1	1,057·2
1936	14,204	1,359·1	1,155·3	1,352·5
1937	12,969·4	1,728·6	1,285·8	1,341·3
1938	9,682·3	1,331·9	1,127·2	1,422·9

These figures show that through the whole period Soviet Russian foreign trade remained at an unusually low level—far below the figures of even the crisis years—and by comparison with the pre-war period under Tsarism it had dropped to about one-third.

During the course of the Five-Year Plans and after the great difficulties caused by the miscalculations at the beginning of the crisis, the development of industrial production and the development of foreign trade proceeded in opposite directions. The Soviet Government now made its economic system as far as possible independent of its foreign trade; in other words, it pursued an increasingly autarkic economic policy.

Before the first world war Russia's share of world industrial production was about 4 per cent and her share of world trade between 3 and 4 per cent. At the end of the period between the two world wars Soviet Russia's share of world industrial production had risen to more than 10 per cent, but her share of world trade had dropped to about 1 per cent. It was a matter of great importance for the further development of world history that on her way to becoming a first-class power the Soviet Union was so loosely connected with the world economic system that her share in world trade progressively declined, and that at the same time her foreign trade declined in comparison with her own industrial production.

The autarkic development of the Soviet Union in this period was facilitated by the upward development of her agriculture.

THE DEVELOPMENT OF SOVIET AGRICULTURE

In the course of the first Five-Year Plan the tremendous rise of Soviet Russian industrial production was accompanied by a decline in agricultural production as a result of the over-impetuous col-

374

lectivization. But gradually the picture began to change for the better.

The collectivization of agriculture was forced through against the resistance of millions of Russian peasants, but once it was achieved it proved permanent and developed still further. In addition, in the period under review the supply of agricultural equipment and machinery steadily increased. In 1932 there were 2,446 tractor and machinery stations. By 1935 the number had increased to 4,375, by 1938 it was 6,358 and by 1940 it was 6,980. At the same time the number of tractors available also greatly increased, from 148,500 in 1932 to 360,300 in 1935, to 483,500 in 1938 and to 523,000 in 1940. The corresponding figures for harvester combines were: 1932, 14,500; 1935, 50,300; 1938, 153,500, and 1940, 182,000.

The electrification of agriculture also increased very considerably, and the capacity of rural electrical generating plant increased threefold, from 53,000 KW in 1932 to 145,500 KW in 1937 and 162,500 KW in 1938. At the same time the output of electrical energy increased (in million KWH) from 74·4 in 1932 to 184·2 in 1937, and 237 in 1938.

Artificial fertilizers supplied to Soviet agriculture (in thousand tons) increased from 234·1 in 1928 to 922·8 in 1932 and to 3,216·3 in 1938.[26]

This great increase in industrial support for Soviet agriculture resulted in a quite considerable rise in agricultural production, despite the fact that there was still a great deal of unrest amongst wide sections of the peasantry.

The gross grain production of 1913 amounted to 801 million quintals. In 1932 it was only 698·7, but after that there was a very definite improvement (and bumper harvests in 1937 and 1939 particularly), as the following figures [27] show:

Soviet Grain Production
(in million quintals)

1933	898
1934	894
1935	901
1936	827·3
1937	1,202·9

	1928–1932.	1933–1937.	1938.	1939.
Average grain yield per hectare (quintals)	7·5	9·1	9·3	9·3
Average grain harvest (million quintals)	735·9	944·7	949·9	1,054·4

At the same time the number of farm animals (not including horses, which were increasingly and permanently replaced by tractors) rose. In 1913 there were 60·6 million head of cattle in Tsarist Russia. In 1929 the figure was 67·1. By 1932 it had dropped to 40·7, and by 1933 to 38·4. After that it increased as follows:

Head of Cattle in the Soviet Union [28]
(millions)

1934	.	.	.	42·4	1937	.	.	.	57
1935	.	.	.	49·2	1938	.	.	.	63·2
1936	.	.	.	56·7	1939	.	.	.	64·6

There was a similarly favourable development with regard to pigs.

As we can see from the above figures, the increase of agricultural production in the Soviet Union was not very great by comparison with Tsarist figures in 1913, particularly as in the meantime the population had considerably increased, but at least it was a hopeful sign that, by comparison with the famine period, which coincided with the last years of the first Five-Year Plan, the great increase in Soviet industrial production was now accompanied by a certain increase in agricultural production, and that the increase was steady in cattle as well as yields.

COLLECTIVIZATION STRENGTHENED THE POWER OF THE DICTATORSHIP

At the same time a decisive change came about in the relations of the Soviet State to agriculture, and we shall have to deal with this phenomenon in some detail because trends began to make themselves felt which were without parallel in modern history. They were of extreme importance for the structure of the Soviet State, and later, after the second world war, they decisively affected the relations of the Soviet Union to its satellite States.

Prior to the collectivization of agriculture in the Soviet Union there were millions of independent peasants families tilling the soil. They were divided roughly into three social groups: the so-called Kulaks, or richer peasants, who employed labourers in the working of their land; the peasants, who owned medium-sized farms and did not employ labour; and finally the poorer peasants, with very small holdings, who represented the overwhelming majority of the agricultural population. All these peasants were now compelled to join collective farms whether they liked it or not, until finally:

"Eighteen and a half million peasant families were united into 242,000 agricultural co-operatives comprising a total of 488,000,000 hectares (1,205,000 acres) of land." [29]

Naturally, these 242,000 collectives were not the same as 242,000 factories, and the 18·5 million peasant families were not like so many
376

factory workers. The situation was, and still is, much more complicated. For one thing, these 18·5 million peasant families organized in the collective farms all had the right to keep a small piece of land for themselves and to have a few cattle, and the yield of this remnant of property was their own to do as they liked with. However, this personal property was deliberately kept too small for its owners to live on, and the income they derived from it was only a supplement to their income as collective farmers.

Now, this income from the collective farms was not a fixed money income, and the collective farmers were not like workers who received a fixed sum in wages. Their income from the collective farms was closely related to the yield of the farms.

After deductions had been made from the total yield for the upkeep of tractors and other agricultural machinery, for the replacement of seed, for fodder, for administration expenses, and so on, the rest was divided amongst the members of the collective according to the number of working days, and according to the value set on the time of the various members, which differed very considerably. In fact, the tendency was for greater differentiation in payment rather than towards a uniform rate.

"Until 1947 the Kolkhoze member was remunerated for his work mostly on the basis of the number of annual workdays given to the Kolkhoze. The work-day is the standard unit for the recording and appraising of work done by each Kolkhoze member. It is designed to break down the Kolkhoze work into its components and to allow for higher remuneration to the members of the Kolkhoze whose specialized assignments require a greater degree of skill. Kolkhoze work has been divided into hundreds of specialized jobs grouped into seven categories. While category I includes unskilled farm hands, category VII is reserved for the most highly-skilled workers and for agronomists with academic training. Each specialized pursuit is placed in one of the seven categories on the basis of the degree of skill and the amount of labour it requires, taking into account also the importance and complexity of the job. The main feature of this system is that it entails different remuneration for each of the seven categories. For a day of satisfactory work a Kolkhoze member belonging to category I receives credit for 0·5 work-days, and each successively higher category receives credit for an additional 0·25 work-days. At the end of the year each member of the Kolkhoze receives remuneration in produce and cash equivalent to the total number of work-days he has given to the Kolkhoze. According to this scale of payment the highly-skilled workers belonging to category VII receive four times as much remuneration as an unskilled member of the Kolkhoze belonging to category I." [30]

Now, of course, industrial workers receive their wages independent of what happens to industrial production, whilst members of a collective farm receive their remuneration in accordance with the total size of the product of that farm and according to the conditions under which the product is sold. Thus although the relationship of the collective peasants to production is no longer as close as was that of the individual peasant family running its own little farm, it is still much closer than that of the ordinary industrial worker. Thus in this respect collective peasants stand between the former independent peasant farmers and ordinary industrial workers. The total product, its price and the proportion of it falling to their share are thus the decisive factors which determine the income of the collective peasants and their standard of living.

It is now interesting to inquire by what or whom the last two of these factors are determined. The answer is simple: it is the Soviet Government.

The overwhelming majority of the yield of the collective farms has to be sold to the Soviet State. In addition, it is the State which determines in the first place what proportion of the product of the collective farms shall go back for income distribution amongst their members, because the amount for the upkeep of the tractor and agricultural machinery stations is deducted from the price of the total product before any of it is distributed, and the proportion is once again decided by the State.

With this we have arrived at one of the sociologically and politically decisive points in our analysis of agricultural collectivization as carried out in the Soviet Union.

THE STATE SECTOR IN SOVIET AGRICULTURE

The Soviet State has given the collective farms the land they till for "eternal use", but it does not sell them the tractors and other agricultural machinery they need before they can operate, and it retains the property rights in this equipment itself. The State also decides under what conditions this equipment shall be made available to the individual collective farm. In this way the Soviet State wields direct and decisive influence on every collective farm, and thus in every village, even the most remote. And, what is more, the influence of the State is steadily growing.

The collectivization of Russian agriculture is based on its modernization and on the progressively increasing application of modern scientific techniques and modern agricultural machinery. We have already seen that the only aspect of agricultural production which never reached pre-war levels again was the number of horses, but that was because horses were, in any case, progressively replaced by tractors.

Now, the technical modernization of agriculture certainly in-

378

creases agricultural production, but at the same time it also increases the dependence of agriculture on machinery, which it cannot, by the nature of things, produce itself. The general tendency in Soviet agriculture is towards an increasing use of tractors and agricultural machinery, for more tractor and machinery stations, for a greater consumption of oil fuel, and so on. In other words, the general tendency is towards an increasing dependence of agriculture on industry and on its products. Thus to cut off Soviet agriculture from its industrial sources of machinery, etc., would inevitably lead to a catastrophic fall in agricultural production, and thus to a corresponding fall in rural living standards. This general tendency had set in clearly long before the outbreak of the second world war.

"In 1938 in socialist agriculture there were 440,000 tractor operators, 247,000 operators of combine harvesters, 214,000 truck drivers, 120,000 leaders of tractor brigades, 40,000 mechanics, etc. In 1940 there were 3,000,000 workers engaged in mechanized agricultural work." [31]

The Soviet State was the sole source of all the industrial requirements of Russian agriculture; it was the source of tractors, agricultural machinery and implements, fuel and lubricating oil, electricity and artificial fertilizers, and it owned the railways on which they had to be carried to their destinations.

The technical modernization of agriculture through collectivization is something which can never be reversed now, and it has caused agriculture to become completely dependent on the Soviet State. From the beginning of the process, which was interrupted for a while by the second world war, it has steadily increased. Such a complete dependence of agriculture has never existed to even remotely the same extent anywhere outside the Soviet Union. Naturally modern agricultural undertakings in capitalist countries also use tractors, agricultural machinery, fuel and lubricating oils, fertilizers and electricity, but at least they use them in a capitalist State—i.e. in a State in which such things are produced by individual manufacturers or individual associations of manufacturers. Certainly, there is often what amounts to monopolistic exploitation, but the decisive difference is nevertheless that nowhere outside the Soviet Union is everything which agriculture needs from industry concentrated into one single source of supply, and generally speaking in capitalist countries farmers have various ways and means of protecting themselves against excessive monopolistic exploitation. It is noteworthy for example, that in the country which has experienced greater monopolistic concentration than any other—the United States—the farmers, including the owners of smaller farms, are organized in strong associations which have often successfully opposed the making of monopolist surplus profits at their expense.

379

Whilst modern agriculture in all countries is to some extent dependent on industry, collectivized agriculture in the Soviet Union is absolutely dependent on the Soviet State. Thus, as we have already indicated, a state of affairs has been created in Soviet Russia for which there is no parallel in modern history. To find even a remote parallel we must go back to the history of certain oriental countries—Egypt, Babylon and various Asiatic territories, for example—in which agriculture was dependent on artificial irrigation, which, since this was in the hands of the State, meant that the government of the day dominated agriculture, and could dictate conditions to the peasants under threat of depriving them of water.

In Russia, of course, it is not a question of artificial irrigation, but of machinery and industrial auxiliary products. They may not play quite the same decisive role as water, but they are important enough and—a point which must be stressed—they are growing more and more important. Because the Soviet State has full and exclusive control of the machinery and other industrial products agriculture needs, it is all-powerful as against the peasants, and the situation is made still more unfavourable to the latter because the power of the Soviet State is centralized, whereas the 242,000 collective farms are not organized into one powerful association, as farmers in capitalist countries usually are, but represent merely so many dispersed units.

There is no independent association, or independent associations, of collective farms in the Soviet Union, and the Soviet Government would naturally never permit them to band themselves together in this way and thus obtain more say as to the conditions under which they are allowed the use of tractors, agricultural machinery and so on, and the conditions under which they sell their produce.

The power of the Soviet State over the collective farmers is thus very much what the power of a monopolist organization would be over workers not organized in trade unions. The Soviet Government holds all the trump cards. And that is precisely why the collectivization of agriculture has so increased the power of the dictatorship and made opposition so difficult, if not impossible.

It took the second world war and the German occupation of vast areas of Russia to weaken the hold of the Soviet State over the collective farms. At that period many peasants left the collective farms and went back to individual tilling. But the tremendous change which the previous collectivization had brought about could not be radically reversed even by the German occupation, and once the war was ended and the Germans expelled from Russian territory, the Soviet Government had little difficulty in restoring the former state of affairs.

"The promptness and efficiency with which these irregularities were eliminated during the first two years of the fourth Five-Year

Plan clearly indicate that the challenge to the increase of State participation in agricultural production was never serious." [32]

The full dependence of the collective farms on the Soviet State is not due entirely to the fact that the old individual peasant farms have been replaced by collective farms. Under different historical conditions agricultural collectives might well develop on entirely different lines. For instance, it is quite conceivable that, as the result of a social-democratic transformation in more developed industrial countries, agriculture would also be reorganized along collective lines. But in that case, arising in countries whose production was on a democratic-socialist basis and whose political system was democratic, the relationship of the collective farms to the State, to the industrial sector, to the towns, would naturally develop on that basis, and the agricultural collectives would consequently have an important say regarding the conditions under which they worked, bought or hired the equipment they needed, and sold their produce. In other words, in such circumstances the agricultural collectives would be just one more sector in a democratic socialist world.

In the Soviet Union collectivization was forced on the peasants at a time when even the Communist Party itself was under the dictatorship of one of its groups, with the result that the terror increased and the basis of the dictatorship grew still narrower. On the other hand, the resistance put up by millions of peasants to the process of forced collectivization led to an increase of the terror. Once collective farms had been set up on a large scale the new situation thereby created tremendously increased the dictatorial power of the Soviet State and extended its economic basis more than ever before.

The experience of agricultural collectivization in Russia, and the fact that it steadily undermined strong and determined opposition, persuaded the Soviet Government to push on with collectivization in all the Eastern European territory which subsequently came under its power.

SOVIET TRADE UNIONISM EMASCULATED

The totalitarian character of the Soviet regime was greatly enhanced by this fundamental transformation in Russian agriculture. It was increased still further by the fact that trade unionism in the Soviet Union was progressively deprived of its real function.

Before the first world war trade unionism was not very strong in Tsarist Russia, and that was natural enough, in view of the social structure of the Tsarist Empire: capitalism represented only a small sector, and the feudal elements were overwhelmingly preponderant.

After the November Revolution trade unionism grew tremendously in size, but not in strength, because in the course of the various Five-Year Plans it was deprived more and more of its real meaning.

The main function of trade unionism as understood in capitalist countries is to work, and if necessary fight, for the maintenance and improvement of the conditions of its members, to try to increase the share of wages in the total product, or, at least, to try to keep wages in line with the increased productivity of labour.

The situation in the Soviet Union was, and is, very different. The form of government is described as a dictatorship of the proletariat, but that is a mere phrase with no real content. On paper the Soviet Union is a socialist State already; but only on paper. In reality the Soviet Union is governed by the dictatorship of a party, and a part of a party at that. Although the Soviet State is not capitalist, it is certainly not socialist either.

The Soviet State is engaged in building up a new and powerful productive apparatus at the cost of the living generation, and the Soviet trade unions—or labour unions, as they are preferably called—are not in a position to do anything for their members except in very minor and unimportant matters, because the Soviet State has deprived them of all power to intervene in matters of importance. The reason for this attitude of the Soviet Government is quite simple.

If the Russian labour unions had fought for an increase in the real wages of their members, for an increase of the wage share in the total product, and for a proper relation between the increasing productivity of labour and working-class living standards, as real trade unions do, then the rate of Soviet industrial construction would have been impeded.

A rise in living standards for millions of workers coupled with the increased production of consumer goods for the benefit of the people could only have taken place at the price of a slowing down in the growth of heavy industry. In other words, any real trade-union struggle for the day-to-day interests of the workers would have made it impossible for the Soviet State to carry through its Five-Year Plans at the rate it desired. The Russian labour unions were therefore emasculated and turned into the equivalent of "company unions"; they became State organizations.

The ideological smoke-screen behind which this was carried out was deceptively simple. The Soviet State and the Russian workers are one, the latter were assured. The Soviet State defends the interests of the workers, and therefore in a Soviet State they need no organizations of their own to defend their class interests.

In many countries the trade unions have played a very important role in the democratic development and education of millions of working people; in the Soviet Union they have been gradually turned into organs of the State whose task is to carry out the instructions of the State just as all other State organs do. This was done in a State which was not a socialist State, which still lagged industrially

382

far behind the more progressive capitalist countries, which did everything possible to increase the productivity of labour (including a system of wage differentiation which tended to increase rather than diminish differences, so that finally the existing differences were at least as great, and often greater, than those prevailing in capitalist countries), which progressively abolished freedom of movement for labour and choice of the job, in order to carry out its programme, even introducing the labour pass, in order to shackle the workers still more effectively to their jobs.

The forced collectivization of agriculture carried the power of the Soviet State effectively even into the remotest village, and the transformation of the trade unions into State organs deprived of all the normal trade-union functions, and no longer independent, democratic organizations, still further increased the totalitarian character of the Soviet State. The Soviet Union rapidly became a police State, and the police apparatus grew in strength and size as its tasks increased. Under Tsarism and in the first ten years or so of Soviet power political opponents of the regime were banished to Siberia and other remote areas, but no great masses of people were involved in either case—perhaps not more than some tens of thousands all told. But in the second phase of the Soviet regime it was no longer a question of some thousands, or tens of thousands, or even hundreds of thousands; quite literally millions of people were regarded by the Soviet State as its political enemies. These people were not banished in the old sense, but sent to labour camps, where they had to work under conditions which were worse than the worst normally existing in Russia, conditions which were perhaps in the best case comparable with the worst conditions in the colonial and semi-colonial countries oppressed by imperialism.

This type of labour camp became an institution in the Soviet Union and affected general working and living conditions in innumerable ways.

At one time it had really seemed as though factors were at work to ease matters in the Soviet Union and bring about an improvement in general living standards. When not only industrial production, but also agricultural production increased, it had seemed as though a real improvement was about to take place in the general living standards of the Russian people. The most difficult years seemed already to belong to the past.

Soviet Russia had been compelled to face the fact that the November Revolution was isolated, and that no revolutions were going to take place in any of the more highly-developed capitalist countries. She therefore built up a powerful industrial apparatus of her own in a comparatively short space of time, though at the cost of great suffering for the masses of the Russian people. For the time being the bolshevists had to abandon their agrarian programme.

They returned to it about twelve years after the November Revolution. The forced collectivization was paid for by almost civil-war conditions and widespread famine, but in the end the State occupied the commanding heights in agriculture, thanks to its network of tractor and agricultural machinery stations, and agricultural production began to rise again.

The Russians knew, of course, that in future, too, the rate of investment would have to be unusually high, and that prime consideration would still have to be paid to the capital-goods industries; but nevertheless it seemed as though the day was not far ahead when, on the basis of a tremendously strengthened productive apparatus, it would be possible to increase production in the consumer-goods industries as well, so that living standards could rise—and perhaps even the dictatorship itself would become a little easier as compared with the days of enforced collectivization, when terrorism was at its height.

This was the period in which the Russians were promised a democratic constitution.

Soviet Russia's Answer to Nazi Germany's War Economy

All these hopes proved illusory. When the Soviet State had consolidated its position on the commanding heights of both industry and agriculture, thanks to its Five-Year Plans and its network of tractor and agricultural machinery stations, a new factor arose which decisively influenced Soviet-Russian development—namely, the system of war economy established in Nazi Germany.

Russian propaganda had always declared that the Soviet Union was "isolated" and surrounded by capitalist States, and that it must therefore constantly be prepared to meet the danger of war. In reality the Soviet Government had not taken such slogans very seriously and if any proof of that fact is needed it is provided in the structure of the first Five-Year Plan, in which military expenditure played a comparatively subordinate role.

With the rise of Nazi Germany the situation changed. For the first time since the days of the civil war and intervention, the Soviet Union really was threatened with war. On her western frontiers was the most powerful industrial country in Europe, and that country had now introduced a system of war economy in peace-time which made her militarily superior to the Soviet Union. The Soviet Union was now faced with a powerful industrial country which was already very rapidly turning its industrial strength into actual military strength even in peace time. The Soviet leaders anxiously followed German developments step by step, and at the same time they became more and more convinced that the Western powers had no intention of taking any serious measures to cope with Nazi Germany's military development. Such measures as they did take were hopelessly inadequate, and more and more signs seemed to indicate that the Western powers would not be averse to seeing Germany's expansionist drive turn towards the east. With this a new situation arose for the Soviet Union.

The Soviet Government answered it with a very great strengthening of her own military and armament sector. Even to-day it is impossible to obtain any accurate picture of Soviet Russia's military sector in this period. A Raymond W. Goldsmith points out: "Our ignorance of the details of Russia's war production may persist for a long period." [33] However, the general trend and the approximate relationships are clear enough, and the following table, which gives us the German, Russian, British and U.S. military expenditures from 1935 up to the German attack on Russia, provides us with a basis of comparison.

Munitions Production of the Major Belligerents
(in milliards of dollars at 1944 U.S. prices)

Country.	1935–1939.	1940.	1941.
Germany	12	6	6
Soviet Union	8	5	8·5
Great Britain	2·5	3·5	6·5
United States	1·5	1·5	4·5

Thus we observe that even in the period from 1935 to 1939 Soviet Russia's military expenditure had grown to two-thirds that of Germany, and that in 1940 it had grown to five-sixths. In the period from 1935 to 1939, when the Western reaction to Nazi Germany's rearmament was so feeble, Soviet Russia's military expenditure was more than 3·5 times as big as Great Britain's, and in 1940, when the British were already at war and the Russians not yet at war, Soviet Russia's military expenditure was still approximately 50 per cent higher.

Further, if the peak of armaments production in each country is represented as 100, we find that by 1938 the Russians had reached 12 per cent of theirs and the Germans 16 per cent, whilst the British had reached only 4 per cent. By 1939 the figure for Russia was 20 per cent, as compared with 20 per cent for Germany and only 10 per cent for Great Britain. And by the time Nazi Germany actually attacked Soviet Russia in 1941 the latter had reached approximately 50 per cent of her peak production.

As we have seen, in absolute figures Soviet military production was two-thirds of German military production in the years 1935–1939. When we consider that in this whole period Soviet Russia's heavy industrial production was less than Germany's, and that even at the end of the period it was still only four-fifths of the German, we can see that in relation to industrial production as a whole, Soviet

Russia's armaments sector was proportionate to Germany's even as early as 1935-1939.

In other words, the Soviet Union was the only country in the world which answered Nazi Germany's war economy in peace time with a comparable war economy of her own. This circumstance had decisive results for every sector of the Soviet economic system and for every phase of Soviet political and social life.

We have already seen that the rate of investment in the Soviet Union was unusually high, and that the consequent enormous capital investments had speeded up industrialization in order to reduce, and finally abolish, the gap between the Soviet Union and the more highly developed industrial countries. If it had been possible to expend these gigantic sums exclusively for the production of peace-time products, then it is very likely that there would have been an increase in the production of the consumer-goods industries even in this period. But now not only was an enormous percentage of the total product invested in the further development of the basic industries, but there was also a tremendous increase in the production of armaments, which are naturally not goods for normal consumption.

In addition, the Soviet Government had to adopt a policy of building up essential stocks on a big scale, so that millions of tons of grain and other foodstuffs would be available in the event of war. Further, the strength of the Red Army had to be increased, which meant taking millions of men away from industry and agriculture in the most productive years of their lives.

Another important point is that war economy in the Soviet Union began in very different circumstances. Hitler began to develop his war economy during the crisis period when there were millions of unemployed workers in Germany. Thus Nazi Germany could simultaneously increase both the production of armaments and the production of consumer goods, whereas in the Soviet Union the productive apparatus was already working to the full. There was no unutilized productive capacity and no reserve labour army of millions of unemployed workers. Thus the strengthening of the military sector, the tremendous increase of the armaments sector, took place in an economic system which was already fully employed. Even if the productivity of labour increased in this period, it did not mean that consumption increased and general living standards rose, because the whole increased productivity was devoted to the military and armaments sector.

Thus German Nazi imperialist expansion, coupled with the fact that the Western powers did nothing effective to check it, forced the Soviet Union to abandon all hope for an indefinite period of being able to improve the general living standards of the Russian people.

The Soviet third Five-Year Plan, which was drawn up in this

386

period of tremendously increased military and armament expenditure, set the target for the textile and woollen-goods industries for the end of the plan period—i.e. for 1942. It is significant to observe that these targets which were to have been achieved at the end of the plan period in 1942—naturally, the outbreak of the war interrupted everything—were below those which had already been fixed for the second Five-Year Plan, which ended in 1937.

In other words, the Soviet Government took the Nazi war threat so seriously that it found itself unable to hold out any hope of improvement in the economic situation of the masses of the Russian people in its plans for the next five years.

Nazi Germany's war economy in peace time and the Soviet Russian answer which it provoked resulted in a great intensification of the dictatorship in the Soviet Union. Let us consider the various stages in its development.

In the period of the November Revolution Lenin had hoped that the Russian Revolution would be followed by revolutions, or at least by a revolution, in highly industrialized Western Europe, and that after a time a socialist Europe would be able to dispense with the dictatorship of the proletariat, which was never envisaged as lasting beyond a certain transitional period.

The fact that the Russian Revolution remained isolated compelled the Soviet leaders to impose heavy sacrifices on the living generation in order to build up a great new productive apparatus which even before the outbreak of the second world war made Soviet Russia in absolute figures the third biggest industrial country in the world.

During the world economic crisis the situation in the Soviet Union became critical, because the enforced collectivization of agriculture resulted at first in a decline in agricultural production and a great slaughtering of cattle. Stalin answered with an intensification of the terror and a further strengthening of his terrorist apparatus.

Then, whilst industrial production continued to rise, and was at last accompanied by a growth in agricultural production, and there was some hope that the masses of the Russian people would at last obtain direct benefit in the shape of improved living standards, Nazi Germany introduced her peace-time war economy, and all hope of an improvement had to be abandoned, not for months, or even for years, but for an indefinite period. The deterioration of the living conditions of the Russian working masses intensified all the antagonisms in the political structure of the Soviet Union.

Once again Stalin answered, as he had answered every crisis, with an intensification of his dictatorship.

From the November Revolution up to the outbreak of the world economic crisis various fractions had been tolerated in the Russian Communist Party, even when they held divergent views on questions of decisive importance, but gradually Stalin eliminated successive oppositions, until by the end of the twenties no organized opposition of any sort was left. Although opposition had been crushed ruthlessly, up to that time there had been no resort to executions. Now, however, a new phase of the terror opened up in which real or suspected opponents of Stalin's dictatorship were slaughtered wholesale. *It is significant to note that this new and acute intensification of the terror coincided with the opening up of Soviet Russia's system of war economy in peace time.*

Of course, the relation was not as direct as that. It cannot be said that the new terror wave which physically exterminated almost all the surviving bolshevist leaders directly proceeded from the necessity to strengthen the military sector in the Soviet Union as a result of the Nazi threat, and from the destruction of all hopes of an improvement in the living standards of the workers and peasants. But Soviet Russian war economy certainly represented the background against which this tremendous intensification of the Stalinist terror took place.

When all signs began to indicate that the danger of war from Nazi Germany was growing more acute, Stalin may well have recalled Russia's experience in the first world war, the superiority of the German arms, the dictatorial Treaty of Brest-Litovsk and the dissensions amongst the leading bolshevists, which had weakened the Party and even threatened the continued existence of the young Soviet State.

Stalin knew perfectly well that although there was no organized opposition left, the leaders of the former oppositions were not in agreement with much of his policy, including in particular the enforced collectivization of agriculture, the failure to develop the consumer-goods industries sufficiently to improve general living standards, the growing suppression of all freedom of opinion in the Party, and the increasing power of the G.P.U. He also knew that the former leaders of the opposition were not alone in their views, and that they would receive vigorous support from large sections of the population if they were ever able to create any organized contacts with these discontented elements.

If war came and the German armies won any very considerable preliminary successes, it might well lead to a crisis in the regime with more than a possibility of a split headed by the leaders of the former oppositions.

Whatever the workings of his mind may have been, the fact is that, together with the development of Soviet Russia's war economy, Stalin unleashed a wave of terror which exceeded everything which had gone before and slaughtered the potential leaders of any future opposition wholesale.

Once the new wave of terror got under way there was no holding it. The G.P.U., having been given a free hand, made the most of it. It sought in the first place to prove that the overwhelming majority of the old bolshevists were traitors, but it did not stop at that, and everyone who had ever had any connection with them, even the remotest, was a potential—and often a very real—victim of the terror. These suspects included the majority of leading men and women in the State apparatus and the majority of those who had been entrusted with the carrying out of the Five-Year Plans.

In addition, the terror itself naturally had repercussions. Many of those whom Stalin threatened with death sought to defend themselves to the best of their ability. But in order to offer resistance to terrorism in a police State, power is necessary, and the only power outside the G.P.U. was in the Red Army; so the Red Army itself was involved in the terror and the possible counter-measures. Here, too, Stalin acted quickly, and carried out a mass slaughter in the upper reaches of the Soviet Russian military hierarchy.

Thus although in the period of the second world war the Soviet Union had a greatly strengthened industrial apparatus and an agriculture which, thanks to the enforced collectivization, was more dependent on the centralized State than ever before, it was weakened by a wave of terror and bloodshed that lasted until about 1939. That wave of terror affected all sections of the population and all spheres of public life, including the apparatus of the State itself, the economic organizations and the Red Army. The comparatively short time which remained between the end of the terror and the opening up of the Nazi attack on the Soviet Union was not sufficient to repair all the damage which had been done, or to replace the great number of skilled cadres in all spheres of Soviet life who had been exterminated. The fact that the Red Army suffered such terrible defeats in the first phases of the war was due in no small degree to the poor quality of Russian military leadership, and it was only slowly and to the accompaniment of still further defeats that this leadership was gradually improved.

World Capitalism on the Eve of the Second World War

Twenty-five years had passed between the outbreak of the first world war and the outbreak of the second. This quarter of a century had not proved sufficient to bring about any radical transformation of capitalist society, though it had shaken it very badly.

The epoch of tremendous progress, interrupted only from time to time, which preceded the first world war and was made possible by equally tremendous external capitalist expansion, had ended for good and all. The progress of European capitalism was definitely past history.

The period of European imperialist expansion which preceded the first world war had been followed by a period of stagnation, and this imperialist stagnation was accompanied by, and indeed was the cause of, a stagnation in the whole capitalist development of Europe.

Instead of capitalist progress in Europe there was stagnation, depression and crisis.

The United States, whose capitalist expansion had proceeded under quite different historical conditions, was not so hard hit either by the first world war or by the subsequent halt in the process of imperialist expansion as the European capitalist countries. U.S. capitalist progress lasted in an almost uninterrupted flow right up to the outbreak of the world economic crisis. In common with the European capitalist countries, the United States had not succeeded in extricating itself from this crisis when the second world war broke out. Thus world capitalism entered the war with an unresolved, a not completely liquidated crisis in its economic bones.

The characteristic feature of European capitalism in this period was stagnation, but not yet decline.

Mass unemployment, together with an increasing tendency towards social polarization, aggravated social antagonisms, and the capitalist monopoly of government in Europe was broken for the first time in history. However, the coalition governments which were formed on the continent with socialist participation, and the Labour Governments which were formed in Great Britain with only minority support in the House of Commons, did not lead to any progressive transformation of capitalist society.

The stagnation of capitalism as a whole in this period was accompanied by stagnation in the working-class movement as well.

But despite stagnation and crisis, democratic political institutions continued to exist and function adequately within the framework of the capitalist system, deeply shaken though it was, in Great Britain and in Western Europe. The same was not true of the most powerful industrial country in Europe—Germany.

The two great upheavals which had so shaken the capitalist system in Europe—the first world war and the world economic crisis—had hit Germany harder than any other of the leading European powers, including Great Britain. Germany was the weakest link in the capitalist chain. German capitalism had already been so shaken that its leading exponents were convinced that it would be unable to exist for long if democratic political institutions were left in being.

The result was the victory of the Nazi counter-revolution and the complete destruction of all working-class organizations, followed by a new phase of vigorous German imperialist expansion on a fascist basis, and this led in its turn to a new and rapid aggravation of all foreign-political antagonisms.

At least European capitalism did not have to cope with a Socialist

390

State able to demonstrate the superiority of socialist methods of production, but only with the Soviet Russian State, which, although it was capitalist no longer, was certainly not socialist.

Soviet power in Russia had managed to survive both civil war and intervention and the subsequent period in which it became clear that no effective socialist revolutionary action was to be expected anywhere in Europe and that the Russian Revolution would remain isolated. In this second phase of its existence the Soviet Union managed to build up a new and powerful industrial apparatus, but she did not succeed in improving the living standards of the Russian people, despite greatly increased industrial production, so that the working classes in Europe enjoyed a standard of living which was at least twice as high, and often more than twice as high, as the living standard of the working class in the Soviet Union. At the same time the isolation of the Russian Revolution, the necessity of pushing on with Russian industrialization by forced marches, and the further necessity of tremendously strengthening the Soviet Russian military sector in answer to the threat of Nazi war economy in peace time, led to a great intensification of the Soviet dictatorship and, at the same time, to a narrowing of its social basis.

Whilst not itself socialist, the Russian Soviet State was non-capitalist and anti-capitalist, and this fact was to play a great role in the foreign-political constellation in the period which led up to the second world war. The majority of European workers realized that the Soviet Union was not a socialist State, and in particular they strongly disapproved of the suppression of all political liberty and the lack of all democratic political institutions in the Soviet Union. Thus the Soviet State, with its low standards of living for the working people and its brutal system of political repression, was not a shining example for the European workers and offered them no encouragement whatever to take action to secure a social transformation of European capitalism.

As we have seen, European capitalist stagnation was brought about by the halt in capitalist imperialist expansion, and in this period of stagnation the forces were already at work which subsequently led to direct imperialist decline. With the imperialist successes of Japan on the Asiatic mainland, the position of European imperialism deteriorated still further, whilst they also undermined the social basis of China's ruling feudal clique. At the same time national-revolutionary movements in the European colonial empires grew in strength, not only in India, but also in the French and Dutch colonial empires.

In this period the relation of strength between the great powers changed both economically and politically all over the world.

From the end of the nineteenth century the list in order of importance had been: the United States, Germany, Great Britain and

391

France, and then, a long way behind, Austria-Hungary, Japan, Russia and Italy.

During the period between the two world wars the United States not only retained its position at the head of the list, but greatly increased the gap between itself and all the countries of Europe not only in industrial production, but also in living standards.

The United States entered the second world war not only as the socially most stable country in the world, but also as its industrial and, to an increasing extent, its financial centre.

Germany also maintained her position as second world power in this period, but at the same time the gap between her and the United States grew bigger, whilst the gap between her and the Soviet Union grew very much smaller.

It was at this point that important industrial and political changes took place. In 1914 Tsarist Russia had occupied a position of very minor importance amongst the industrially developed countries. At that time Russia was even behind a third-rate industrial power like Japan. But in the period between the two world wars the Soviet Union not only forged ahead of Japan, but of Great Britain and France as well, and occupied third place in the world list of powers.

In the period before the first world war there were many capitalist States in which long-established democratic political institutions flourished, for instance, the United States, Great Britain, France, the Scandinavian States and the smaller States of Western Europe. In addition, there were a number of States in which democratic political institutions were making progress, for instance, Germany and to some extent even Tsarist Russia, though the latter was still overwhelmingly feudal in make-up.

In this period world capitalism had no very great anxiety about social antagonisms or even about the situation in its colonial empires, and it was in this frame of mind that it entered the first world war.

On the eve of the second world war the situation was very different. In the period between the two world wars the development towards still broader democratic political institutions had not continued. Such institutions still existed in the United States, Great Britain, France and Western Europe generally, but all these countries were still suffering from an unresolved economic crisis. The economic crisis had actually been overcome in Germany, but only by destroying all democratic political institutions and organizing a vast peace-time programme of armaments. And in place of Tsarist Russia there was now the Soviet Union, a big power which was neither capitalist nor socialist. Thus though the capitalist system still dominated the greater part of the world, it had been considerably weakened, and its social antagonisms had grown to such an extent that they now represented a very important factor in foreign-political affairs and in the general relation of world forces.

392

In this general period of capitalist imperialist stagnation, German capitalism, which was now dominated by Nazi fascism, vigorously revived its old policy of imperialist expansion, whilst Japan continued her policy of expansion in the Far East.

Whereas the period before the first world war was characterized by the aggravation of foreign-political antagonisms on the one hand and the diminution of inner economic and social antagonisms on the other, the situation on the eve of the second world war was characterized not only by the aggravation of foreign-political antagonisms, but also by the aggravation of inner economic and social antagonisms as well.

PART FOUR

THE SECOND WORLD WAR

THE ALLIANCES OF THE SECOND WORLD WAR

A<small>LTHOUGH</small> <small>FOREIGN-POLITICAL</small> antagonisms steadily intensified in the period before the first world war, the war when it did break out was a complete surprise for hundreds of millions of people. After generations of peace people had not thought war possible.

It was very different when the second world war broke out. Unlike the period which led to the first world war, the period which led to the second was one of direct expectation of war, and people were not surprised when it finally came.

Once the Nazis had come to power in Germany they re-introduced general compulsory military service and began to build up a war economy in peace time. Hundreds of millions of people all over the world then no longer asked themselves: "Will there be another war?" but merely, "When will the war break out?" The fact that war would come was a certainty for them, and that was one of the things which distinguished the second from the first world war.

There were no more or less fixed alliances before the second world war, as there had been before the first world war, and right up to the last people were asking themselves how the nations would line up when war did come. It was a question which was not finally answered until the last few weeks before the outbreak of war.

Even in the spring of 1939, when Nazi Germany seized the whole of Czechoslovakia, it was still not clear, and people wondered whether the war would begin with an attack on Russia or an attack on the West, or perhaps both at once.

The reasons why people did not know, and could not know, how the nations would actually line up were not accidental; they lay very deep. They reflected the intensification of social antagonisms which marked the whole period between the two world wars.

G<small>ERMAN</small> I<small>MPERIALISM</small> T<small>HREATENED</small> <small>BOTH THE</small> W<small>ESTERN</small> P<small>OWERS</small> <small>AND THE</small> S<small>OVIET</small> U<small>NION</small>

Without these antagonisms it would have been practically a matter of course that Neo-German imperialism would wage a two-front war against Great Britain and France on the one side and the Soviet Union on the other, because German imperialist aggression threatened all three powers.

Germany had once again become the strongest industrial State in Europe, and in a period in which the expansion of world capitalism as a whole was meeting with more and more difficulties, she sought to organize an expansionist drive into the heart of Europe.

Neo-German imperialism under Hitler threatened Great Britain and France on the one hand, and the Soviet Union on the other, even more than Hohenzollern imperialism had threatened Great Britain, France and Tsarist Russia before the first world war. It endangered the Western Powers not only because Germany was the strongest industrial power in Europe, but because she grew ever stronger with her continuous expansion, which automatically weakened the power of the Western allies. It endangered the Soviet Union in particular because it sought to bring Poland, the Baltic States, Hungary and Czechoslovakia—Russia's western neighbours—into economic, and thus also political, dependence on Germany.

Germany endangered Great Britain, France and the Soviet Union still more because, unlike the period which led to the first world war, she now built up her armaments to an unprecedented extent in peace time. She prepared for war not only militarily but also industrially and economically, and extended her armament sector to a degree unparalleled in modern history.

If the western powers had answered the threat adequately they could have done so only at the expense of their living standards. In this way Neo-German imperialism threatened their way of life, because a deterioration of living standards would have meant an intensification of social antagonisms.

The same thing applied to the Soviet Union, but she did not hesitate to reply adequately, and the efforts to increase her living standards, which had already been interrupted on previous occasions, were now abandoned for an indefinite period.

In fact, as we have already seen, the Western Powers answered the German challenge reluctantly, very slowly and quite inadequately. A striking feature of the year 1938—the last year of peace—was that as a result of military requirements, Germany's production of steel rose from 19·3 million tons in 1937 to 24·9 million tons, whilst Great Britain's steel production fell in the same period from 14·5 million tons to 11·6 million tons, and French steel production fell from 8·7 million tons to 6·8 million tons, so that Germany produced almost a third more steel in 1938 than Great Britain and France combined.

Another interesting feature is that in 1938 British armament production amounted to only 4 per cent of its subsequent peak volume, and that in the five years which preceded the outbreak of the second world war British expenditure on armaments was only about one-fifth of German expenditure.

It was a Conservative Government under the premiership of Baldwin which refused to take the necessary steps to organize a war economy in peace time in answer to Germany's efforts. Baldwin feared that a big programme of armaments in peace time would undermine the political influence of his party. In reply to Winston Churchill he declared in the House of Commons: [1]

"The difference of opinion between Mr Churchill and myself is in the years 1933 onwards. . . . I have stated that a democracy is always two years behind the dictator. I believe that to be true. It has been true in this case. I put before the whole House my own views with an appalling frankness. You will remember at that time, the Disarmament Conference was sitting in Geneva. You will remember at that time there was probably a stronger pacifist feeling running through this country than at any time since the war. You will remember the election at Fulham in the autumn of 1933, when a seat which the National Government held was lost by about 7,000 votes on no issue but the pacifist. . . . My position as the leader of a great party was not altogether a comfortable one. I asked myself what chance was there—when the feeling that was given expression to in Fulham was common throughout the country—what chance was there within the next year or two of that feeling being so changed that the country would give a mandate for re-armament? Supposing I had gone to the country and said that Germany was re-arming, and that we must re-arm, does anybody think this pacific democracy would have rallied to that cry at that moment? I cannot think of anything that would have made the loss of the election from my point of view more certain."

The domestic political situation in Great Britain did not change much in the years up to Munich and the abandonment of Czechoslovakia to the Nazis, and thus the armament advantage of Nazi Germany and the gap between her armaments and those of the other countries remained for a further two years. In view of the existing aggravation of social antagonisms in Europe and the anti-war feeling in Great Britain, Baldwin and his party, in their own political interests, did not dare to organize a war economy which would have imposed great burdens on the people and depressed living standards. Thus the severe crisis from which the capitalist system was suffering, which shook it fundamentally but did not at the same time sufficiently strengthen the socialist forces to enable them to bring about a social transformation, prevented Great Britain from building up a military sector in peace time which would have been strong enough to answer the German challenge adequately.

What was true of Great Britain was in principle true also of France. The beginning of Nazi Germany's re-armament coincided with the existence of a reactionary government in France; it was continued under the first Popular-Front Government. As a result of re-armament, German industrial production reached 1929 levels in the winter of 1935–1936, and then rose considerably above it. French industrial production in 1935, on the other hand, was only 72·5 per cent of the 1929 volume. In 1936 it was 78 per cent; in 1937 81·7 per cent; in 1938 it fell to 76·1 per cent. The social unrest brought about by the economic crisis led to the formation of the first Popular-Front Government under Léon Blum, but although the French socialists led that Government, they never had a majority of the electorate behind them. They had taken office in a period of crisis, and the French workers expected them to raise wages, shorten working hours and introduce social legislation. The Popular-Front Government did its best to carry out its election promises, and in doing so it met with concentrated opposition from all the reactionary forces of France. If the Popular-Front Government had attempted to create a war economy in this period with a great strengthening of the military and armament sector, in accordance with the challenge of Nazi Germany, then it would have had to abandon its whole programme of internal reform and all hope of improving the living conditions of the French working people. With this the Popular-Front Government would have cut the ground from under its own feet. It refrained from doing so just as the Conservative, so-called National, Government in Great Britain had refrained from doing so. And when the first Popular-Front Government was overthrown in France and a shift towards the Centre took place with the Daladier Government, this Government answered only reluctantly and inadequately to the German threat, for fear of a new shift to the Left. So what Baldwin said was true also of France: "A democracy is always two years behind the dictator".

Precisely because their own answer to Hitler's threat was so feeble one might have thought that western powers would have turned towards the Soviet Union and sought an alliance against Nazi Germany, particularly as the Soviet Union had promptly answered the progressive increase in Germany's production of armaments with a tremendous increase of her own military sector.

Before the first world war France had invested a great deal of capital in Tsarist Russia in order, amongst other things, to increase the military effectiveness of the Russian Army in the event of war and thus diminish Germany's chances of victory in a two-front war. But without French or any other foreign capital, Russian military expenditure in the years before the second world war was greater than that of Great Britain and France put together.

The obvious move on the part of the western powers was thus to take steps long before the outbreak of war to establish an alliance, or at least a military entente, with the Soviet Union against Nazi Germany, so that if Nazi Germany did attack she would be compelled to fight on two fronts simultaneously.

No such alliance came about, and in view of its enormous importance there must have been some very profound reason for its absence.

400

There certainly was, and it was rooted primarily in the fact that the period between the two world wars was not one of capitalist progress. It was a period in which, although capitalism still prevailed in the big industrial centres outside the Soviet Union, and although the European capitalist countries were still in control in their colonial empires, the ruling classes felt themselves threatened both at home and in the colonial and semi-colonial countries.

It was not the fact that the political systems of France and Great Britain were so different from the political system of the Soviet Union which prevented the conclusion of an alliance before the outbreak of war. After all, the political systems of Great Britain and France had been very different from the political system of Tsarist Russia before the first world war, and nevertheless a firm alliance had been concluded. This alliance was made possible because neither Great Britain nor France felt her social structure threatened by the forces which ruled Tsarist Russia. Tsarism was very definitely not an export article, and it was even assumed that after the common victory in the first world war there would be a certain move towards democratic political institutions more or less along Western European lines.

In the period between the two world wars the situation was very different. This time the ruling classes both in Great Britain and France did feel their social structure threatened by the forces which ruled Russia, and although they did not greatly fear an actual bolshevist revolution at home, they did fear that the situation of their ruling classes might be made much more difficult.

And there was another important point: during the first world war they had not feared that a defeat of Hohenzollern Germany would lead to a socialist revolution there. They had assumed that after Germany's defeat certain feudal characteristics would disappear and that Germany would turn more readily to political democracy on the Western-European model. But this time the Nazis had abolished political democracy and set up a totalitarian State, and the ruling classes in Great Britain and France were not at all sure what might follow a defeat of Nazi Germany. They feared a social revolution in the heart of Europe which might not halt at the Rhine. It was this fear—a very lively one—which persuaded the western powers again and again to try appeasement towards Hitler, just as it was the fear of the national-revolutionary movements in their colonial empires which persuaded them to try appeasement in face of Japan's aggressive imperialist drive.

This retreat in the face of imperialist aggression motivated by fear of social upheavals and revolutions took place both in Europe and in Asia, and it took place not only in the years immediately before the outbreak of the second world war but for a whole decade before.

In fact, the year 1931 might well be described as the real beginning of the second world war. It was the year in which Japan invaded Manchuria and entered on the decisive stage of her plans to subjugate China. British imperialism was opposed to Japanese imperialism in so far as it feared the extension of Japan's sphere of influence on the Asiatic mainland, but at the same time the British Conservatives feared that a Japanese defeat would strengthen Chinese Nationalism too much and involve a strengthening of anti-imperialist activity throughout the whole of Asia, including Britain's own colonial empire. It was this fear of trouble in the Empire which at first persuaded the British Conservatives not to oppose Japanese imperialism. Their feelings were aptly expressed by Mr L. S. Amery, then Secretary of State for India, an office which he held right down to 1945, when the Labour Party came to office. Speaking in the House of Commons on February 27th, 1933, he declared:

"I confess that I see no reason whatever why, either in act or words, or in sympathy, we should go individually or intentionally against Japan in this matter. Japan has got a very powerful case based on fundamental realities. . . . Who is there among us to cast the first stone and to say that Japan ought not to have acted with the object of creating peace and order in Manchuria and defending herself against the continual aggression of vigorous Chinese nationalism? Our whole policy in India, our whole policy in Egypt, stands condemned if we condemn Japan."

So much for the situation in Asia at the time, and it was not much different in Europe. The Spanish civil war and the fascist intervention represented the preliminary skirmish before the general outbreak of hostilities in Europe. It began with a revolt of the Spanish generals, in alliance with the reactionary and feudal sections of Spanish society, against a Left-wing government elected on a democratic basis. Spanish fascism enjoyed the support of international fascism from the very beginning, and as the struggle proceeded, so international fascist intervention gradually became more powerful and more open. What was at stake was perfectly clear to the two fascist powers, Nazi Germany and Fascist Italy: a victory for fascism in Spain would mean a strengthening of the fascist forces throughout Europe and a corresponding weakening of the working class and its political positions in the Western-European democracies.

Further, a fascist Spain on the southern frontier of France would mean a weakening of the military position of the western powers and a corresponding strengthening of the military position of Germany and Italy.

Thus both the domestic and foreign-political aims of the fascist powers urged them to support Franco, and they did not hesitate to do so. The situation for Great Britain and France was very different and much more complicated. On the one hand their governments were well aware that a fascist victory in Spain assisted by Germany and Italy would weaken the political and military position of the two western powers in Europe, but, on the other hand, the British Conservatives and the French reactionaries were at that time in full cry against the Popular-Front Government of Léon Blum in France and against the danger of bolshevism which supposedly resulted from it, and they were horrified at the idea of strengthening the socialist-revolutionary movement in Spain by crushing the Franco revolt. The result was that the Left-wing forces in Spain received only very lukewarm support, and even that only in the beginning. In fact the Spanish civil war was an excellent object lesson of the extent to which the fear of social upheavals influenced the foreign-political actions of the leading world powers.

After the Spanish civil war and Hitler's annexation of Austria, Nazi Germany went a step farther and threatened the existence of the Czechoslovakian Republic. The only way to prevent the accomplishment of this act of aggression would have been joint intervention on the part of Great Britain, France and the Soviet Union, but the western powers fought shy of such a vigorous course of action; it appeared too dangerous to them. The British Conservatives were afraid that a defeat of Nazi Germany would strengthen the revolutionary forces throughout Europe. At the same time the French reactionaries feared the consequences of a victory over German National Socialism more than they feared the defeat of their own country.

The result was Munich.

Thierry Maulnier, a disciple of Maurras and a theorist of the monarcho-fascist movement in France, very clearly explained what he termed "the fundamental reasons" for the opposition of the French Right to any war against Nazi Germany:

"These parties (of the Right) felt that in the event of war not only would the disaster be immense, involving perhaps the defeat and devastation of France, but that a German defeat would mean the crumbling of the authoritarian systems which constitute the main obstacle to the communist revolution, and perhaps the immediate bolshevization of Europe. In other words, whilst a French defeat would most certainly be a defeat of France, a French victory would be less a victory of France than a victory for those principles which are rightly held to lead straight to her ruin and to the ruin of civilization itself." [2]

The Munich Agreement was a scrap of paper for Hitler from the beginning, and shortly afterwards German troops were set in motion against a defenceless Czechoslovakia and occupied the whole country. The next item on Hitler's agenda was Poland, and so he turned his attention towards the east. The danger of war grew rapidly, and

Britain introduced general compulsory military service in peace time for the first time in her history. Britain and France also gave Poland a formal guarantee that in the event of a German attack they would give her armed aid.

But one important thing was still missing in the preparations, now at last under way, to resist Nazi Germany's aggression. As the war preparedness of the western powers still lagged far behind that of Nazi Germany, it was more than ever necessary that they should seek a firm understanding, if not an alliance, with the Soviet Union. The first world war had started with a series of big German victories, but then their advance had bogged down on the Marne, partly because strong German forces had to be deployed in the east against the Russians and partly because Germany's armament preparations had not been adequate for such a tremendous war.

This time at least the Germans had no need to fear defeat on account of the latter factor; they were prepared. Thus it was all the more necessary that they should be compelled to deploy large forces in the east against the Soviet Union, and the only way to bring this about was by the conclusion of a treaty of alliance.

The Failure of the Franco-British Military Discussions in Moscow

The Soviet Government had not been invited to the Munich discussions, and the Soviet Union had had no share in the abandonment of Czechoslovakia to Nazi-German aggression. Munich had quite naturally made the Russians extremely mistrustful of the western powers. The thought which obviously sprang to their minds was that the latter were speculating on giving Hitler a free hand in the east in order that they might play the role of passive observers in a war between Germany and the Soviet Union, a war which, whatever its upshot, would greatly weaken both belligerents, and perhaps permit the western powers to slip into the role of compulsory arbitrators on the further fate of Europe.

This feeling of mistrust and suspicion was very natural in view of what had happened, and really serious efforts on the part of the British and French Governments would have been necessary to dissipate it. New discussions were then opened up in Moscow between the military representatives of Great Britain and France and those of the Soviet Union, but they came to nothing. The official reason given for their failure was that the Polish Government refused to give the Red Army the right to enter its territory and that the western powers felt themselves unable to exert sufficient pressure on the Poles to induce them to change their minds.

The real reason for the failure of the discussions lay deeper. If the question of an alliance between the western powers and the Soviet Union had been a purely foreign-political affair, and there had been no fear of social upheavals, as there had been none in 1914, Polish intransigence could have been overcome without much difficulty. War had not yet broken out. Hitler had won a series of striking foreign-political successes, but the time had now come to put a stop to Nazi Germany's expansion. This could be done only if Nazi Germany were shown clearly that in the event of further aggression she would have to reckon with war, and not only with war, but a war in which she would in all probability suffer defeat, because she would not hesitate to wage a war in which her prospects of success were good.

The only way to do this would have been to make it clear to Nazi Germany that from the very first day of a war she would have to fight on two fronts—against Great Britain and France in the West, and against the Soviet Union in the East. Thus a military alliance between Great Britain and France on the one hand and the Soviet Union on the other, whilst perhaps not being an absolute guarantee for the preservation of peace, was the only real hope.

This was certainly Winston Churchill's view, and he writes:

"There can, however, be no doubt, even in the after-light, that Britain and France should have accepted the Russian offer, proclaimed the Triple Alliance, and left the method by which it could be made effective in case of war to be adjusted between allies engaged against a common foe. . . . The alliance of Britain, France and Russia would have struck deep alarm into the heart of Germany in 1939, and no one can prove that war might not even then have been averted. The next step could have been taken with superior power on the side of the Allies. The initiative would have been regained by their diplomacy. Hitler could afford neither to embark upon the war on two fronts, which he himself had so deeply condemned, nor to sustain a check. It was a pity not to have placed him in this awkward position, which might well have cost him his life. . . . If, for instance, Mr Chamberlain on receipt of the Russian offer had replied: 'Yes. Let us three band together and break Hitler's neck', or words to that effect, Parliament would have approved. Stalin would have understood, and history might have taken a different course." [3]

But Chamberlain had no intention of doing anything of the kind, and neither had the French Government. Thus the negotiations dragged out without leading to a military alliance—the only thing which might have prevented war, or ensured at least that it would have been less protracted if it did come. In the meantime, and no doubt encouraged by the feeble attitude of the western powers, Nazi Germany adopted a more and more aggressive attitude towards Poland.

The "peaceable" conquest of Czechoslovakia had been prepared by separate negotiations with the western powers, but since Nazi Germany had torn up the Munich Agreement and seized Prague their attitude had stiffened, and there was now little prospect, Hitler realized, that a "peaceable" conquest of Poland could be obtained in the same way.

At the same time, when the Moscow military negotiations dragged on and led to nothing, the Russians feared that they might find themselves the victim of German aggression in a one-front war whilst the French and British looked on. That is the background against which they opened up negotiations with Nazi Germany whilst the Franco-British Military Mission was still engaged in talks in Moscow. Those negotiations led to the signing of the Nazi-Soviet Pact.

THE NAZI-SOVIET PACT

The successful conclusion of the Pact between Nazi Germany and the Soviet Union created the conditions Hitler required for the second world war. It guaranteed Nazi Germany against a war on two fronts, and therefore gave her what looked like an excellent chance of victory.

The Nazi-Soviet Pact demonstrated very clearly to the whole world what a tremendous change had taken place in Russia since the early years of the revolution. Russian and communist circles generally have often compared the Nazi-Soviet Pact with the peace treaty of Brest-Litovsk, which the Russians under Lenin were forced to sign during the first world war in order to obtain the peace the new Soviet State so desperately needed, but precisely this comparison with Brest-Litovsk reveals the great change which had taken place in Soviet Russia in the intervening years.

Lenin signed the treaty of Brest-Litovsk with Hohenzollern Germany, against strong opposition in his own party, because the state of the Russian army at the time rendered any further prosecution of the war impossible, and because any further attempt to fight would have endangered the political position of the bolshevists and perhaps have meant the victory of the reactionary, White-Guardist forces in Russia.

Unlike Russia at the time of the Brest-Litovsk Treaty, Stalin's Russia had not been engaged in war and brought to the verge of collapse. At the time of the Nazi-Soviet Pact the Soviet Union possessed great military strength, as she subsequently demonstrated, despite her initial defeats, when Nazi Germany did finally attack her. Thus at the time of the Nazi-Soviet Pact Stalin's Russia was not in the least in the desperate position of Lenin's Russia at the time of the Brest-Litovsk Treaty.

And further, the Brest-Litovsk Treaty was not a pact of friendship with Hohenzollern Germany. Lenin retained full freedom of political action, and in the period that followed he deliberately supported every possible move which promised to help the socialist-revolutionary movement in Germany.

For Lenin, the victory of the November Revolution was indissolubly connected with the socialist revolutionary movements in the more highly developed countries of capitalism. The situation when Stalin signed the Nazi-Soviet Pact was very different.

After the victory of the November Revolution the Communist International had been founded to further the cause of the world revolution. On paper it was an international association of independent Communist Parties; in actuality it had come completely under Russian dominance long before the signing of the Nazi-Soviet Pact. Stalin's Russia was no longer interested in Communist Parties as independent allies in the struggle for the world revolution, but only as obedient organs of Soviet foreign policy. The Nazi-Soviet Pact dramatically underlined the change which had taken place in Russia since the days of Lenin. The complete subservience of the Communist International to Russian orders was clearly demonstrated in this question, because the Communist Parties were now ordered to pursue a policy which was in diametrical opposition to the interests of the working classes they were supposed to represent.

The Communist Parties obeyed orders and became pawns of the Nazi-Soviet Pact. The German communists, for instance, were unable to offer any further resistance to Hitler's dictatorship as long as the Pact was in existence. The French communists had to attack their own government at a time when Nazi Germany was attacking France. And the slogan which was invented to cloak the treachery was that the war was an imperialist war on both sides.

Thus the fundamental change which had taken place in the Soviet Union under Stalin's leadership was very clearly reflected in its foreign policy in this period.

Under Lenin's leadership the Russian Revolution had been regarded as part and parcel of the world socialist revolution, and Lenin would have been prepared to impose the greatest sacrifices on the Russian people in the hope of furthering the socialist revolution in the more highly developed industrial countries of capitalist Europe. Under Stalin's leadership, on the other hand, the international communist movement was, and still is, only a weapon to be used in Russia's interests. For Stalin Russia's interests are decisive, and the interests of the international working class must be sacrificed to them ruthlessly at need.

This was, of course, not the first time they had been so sacrificed, and the disruption and weakening of the European working-class movement were very largely due to Russia's foreign policy under Stalin. This time, however, the interests of the international working class were sacrificed openly and shamelessly. The Soviet Union signed a pact of friendship with Nazi Germany, which persecuted

407

German communists, suppressed the German communist movement, and tortured and killed tens of thousands of active communists.

Stalin's policy had already turned the Communist Parties into servile instruments of Russia's foreign interests, and their leaders into uncritical time-servers and yes-men, but although many members left the Communist Parties as a result of the Nazi-Soviet Pact, the parties themselves were by that time so thoroughly enslaved that not one of them officially repudiated the treachery.

Thus, the Nazi-Soviet Pact also dramatically exposed the real nature of the change which had come about since the days of Lenin in the relationship of the Soviet Union to the Communist International, to the Communist Parties and to the international working-class movement.

But it revealed even more than that. Because Lenin regarded the November Revolution as part and parcel of the international socialist revolution, he had strictly opposed all forms of annexation. The progress of the socialist movement was bound up for him in the victory of the socialist movements in the industrially developed countries of the west.

With the Nazi-Soviet Pact Stalin's Russia not only documented the fact that the Communist International, the Communist Parties and the international working-class movement as a whole had been written off as independent political forces, but that the Russian State as such was now pursuing a policy of national expansion.

With the Nazi-Soviet Pact the Soviet Union took part in the destruction of independent Poland, receiving a part of the booty as a reward. Thus the Nazi-Soviet Pact was, so to speak, a forerunner of Soviet Russia's foreign-political expansionism after her victory in the second world war.

Of course, the Pact was not a real pact of friendship either for Hitler or for Stalin. Hitler signed it in order to have his hands free in the east for a one-front war in the west. Stalin signed it in order to gain time for further armament, and he made good use of the time, as we shall see in our next chapter, when we come to consider the great increase in Soviet-Russian military expenditure during the period of the pact. He also signed it in the hope that Soviet Russia's position would automatically be strengthened if Hitler Germany suffered heavy losses in a long and costly war with the western powers. Like many others, Stalin over-estimated the strength of the French army and the stability of France's social structure.

The Pact gave the Signal for War

The Nazi-Soviet Pact was the green light for war. It permitted Germany to wage the second world war on one front, at least in the beginning. It is true that there was fighting in both the west and the east, with Great Britain and France on the one hand and Poland on the other, but the campaign against Poland was short lived; it lasted only five weeks, and in that time the western powers did practically nothing to aid the Poles. Once they were defeated, Hitler was able to bring his troops back from the eastern front and prepare for the lightning war which was to roll up the allied front and crush France. The possibility of waging the war on one front only was the decisive condition of victory for Nazi Germany. The reason for this was clear enough. During the first world war, and with the support of the Austro-Hungarian Army, Germany had been unable to win a two-front war, despite the fact that Tsarist Russia's military strength was very much less than that of Soviet Russia.

Germany would have had little or no chance of victory from the outset if she had been compelled to fight straight away on two fronts in the second world war, because even the fact that she was now much better prepared for a big war, thanks to her huge armaments advantage over the western powers, was more than cancelled out by the further fact that her enemy in the east was now at least three times as strong as Tsarist Russia had been in 1914.

At the beginning of the second world war Germany was the second strongest industrial country in the world and the strongest in Europe, but she still accounted for only one sixth of the total world industrial production. Thus if she were to have any hope of victory, a necessary condition was disunion amongst her enemies. Now the facts that European capitalism had gone through a period of stagnation prior to the outbreak of the second world war—unlike the period which had preceded the first world war—that all social antagonisms had thereby been greatly aggravated, that capitalism had been shaken to the core by the world economic crisis, that the ruling classes in all capitalist countries now feared for their reign, that to the east was no longer Tsarist Russia, but a Soviet State with dynamic possibilities beyond its own frontiers—in short, the utter lack of social stability in Europe—gave Nazi Germany the opportunity of splitting the ranks of her enemies. With this she had a chance of victory which she would otherwise not have had.

After her lightning victories in the early stages of the war, Germany became master of the greater part of continental Europe. But Great Britain was still unconquered. Germany's air offensive against her brought no decision, and together with the British navy, the British air force proved so powerful that Germany did not even attempt an invasion.

Having failed to subdue Great Britain, Nazi Germany turned once again to the east, and in June 1941 she attacked the Soviet Union.

Nazi Germany was very anxious to wage this stage of the war as a one-front war also, but Great Britain rejected all her peace feelers. It is interesting to examine the reasons for such intransigence. Great Britain was no longer in danger. Nazi Germany was unable to defeat her even in the dark period following Dunkirk, and she was certainly still less able to do so a year later, when although there was still a gap between British and German armaments it had already noticeably diminished. The British air force had been greatly strengthened in the period following Dunkirk, and new infantry divisions had been organized and equipped. U.S. lend-lease had disposed of all financial difficulties where supply was concerned, with the result that as long as the war lasted Britain was able to import all the foodstuffs, raw materials and munitions and weapons of war she needed to continue the struggle. This great strengthening of Britain's position disposed once and for all of the danger of a Quisling regime which would have been prepared to treat with Nazi Germany—a danger which might well have grown acute after Dunkirk.

The strengthening of Britain's position allowed the British Government to examine Hitler's offers from a long-term world-political standpoint, and not under the urgent pressure of impending military disaster. From this point of view, Nazi Germany, which had already conquered practically the whole of continental Europe, was, for the moment at least, very much more dangerous to British interests than the Soviet Union. If in this phase of the war Great Britain had abandoned the Soviet Union to her fate, the Russians might well have been defeated by Nazi Germany, and then the latter would have been established as the one and only power in Europe without a single serious rival. Great Britain realized that if she once again succeeded in avoiding a two-front war Nazi Germany would be in a much stronger position to switch her attack against the island fortress and the British Empire generally and with much greater prospects of success. Thus the threat to the British Empire and to British interests generally from Nazi Germany was much greater and more immediate and direct than any future danger from the Soviet Union. At that time neither Great Britain nor the United States felt themselves directly threatened in any way by the Soviet Union.

The U.S., British, Russian Coalition

Therefore as soon as Nazi Germany attacked the Soviet Union, Winston Churchill, who by that time was Premier, declared that Great Britain would support the new victim of German aggression in every possible way. The fact that, like the Nazis, the British Conservatives greatly under-estimated the strength of the Soviet Union, and therefore under-estimated the very favourable position the Soviet Union would occupy in Europe and the world in the event of a Nazi defeat, may of course have played some role in the decision.

The military alliance between the Soviet Union and Great Britain under Churchill's leadership was created by Nazi Germany's attack. There was no formal alliance. All that happened was that when

Hitler attacked the Soviet Union, Great Britain remained in the field as a belligerent.

At first the United States remained outside the fighting war. She supported Great Britain powerfully, but she preferred not to become a belligerent herself. She was forced into the fighting war willy-nilly by the Japanese attack on Pearl Harbour, which was immediately followed by Germany's declaration of war. Thus Nazi Germany herself forged the coalition of the Anglo-Saxon Powers and the Soviet Union which finally led to her utter defeat.

How was such a coalition between States with totally different political and economic systems at all possible? We have seen that before Japan's attack on Pearl Harbour there was no such grand alliance, and that it came about only after the Axis attack. However, it rather over-simplifies matters to accept this as cause and effect, though it is true enough if we concern ourselves only with the immediate occasion of war. The real causes which made the coalition possible lay deeper.

It has been said that "Marxism" was refuted by the creation of this coalition, and that according to Marxist theories "capitalist" States could never ally themselves with a "socialist" State. For one thing, it is not true that the Soviet Union was, or is, a socialist State, and, for another, the argument is superficial and false. The main objection is that the November Revolution in Russia did not take place in an industrially highly developed country, did not take place in one of the big capitalist centres. If this had been the case, then it is quite possible, even probable, that a coalition of all capitalist countries against the country of the socialist revolution would have formed, because then the capitalist countries would have been directly threatened with the spread of the socialist revolution to their own territories.

But the revolution did not take place in a highly-developed industrial country, and the gap between living standards in the country in which it did take place, Russia, and living standards in the more highly developed capitalist industrial countries was therefore very great. It existed not only in the period of the November Revolution in 1917, but it still existed a quarter of a century later, in the period of the second world war.

Neither Great Britain nor the United States had any need to feel herself threatened because the Soviet Union had created a new social system which had clearly demonstrated itself as so superior to her own that decisive repercussions might be expected on her own system. Both countries certainly rejected the type of social system created in the Soviet Union, but that system represented no immediate danger to them.

Nazi Germany, on the other hand, was a very real and immediate danger. She had already conquered the greater part of Europe, and if she were now victorious over the Soviet Union the danger to

411

both Britain and the United States would become immeasurably greater.

What would happen once Nazi Germany was defeated and the Soviet Union thereby became the most powerful country on the Continent was an academic and largely speculative question by comparison with the immediate danger represented by Nazi Germany, and the Anglo-Saxon leaders consoled themselves with the thought that it would be possible to find some sort of solution once Nazi Germany was defeated. The pragmatic thought which is typical of the Anglo-Saxon peoples did not encourage them to worry their heads much about what the future might bring forth, and so an anti-Nazi coalition was established between Great Britain and the United States on the one hand and the Soviet Union on the other, which held fast even when the period of Hitler's defeats and set-backs began and the Soviet Union proved itself to be much stronger than most people in Great Britain and the United States had expected.

Social Stability Allowed the Coalition to Last

Before the outbreak of the second world war the Nazi State had presented itself to the world as a bulwark against bolshevism, and in consequence it had won the support of strong reactionary groups in Europe. Nazi Germany now began to put on this propaganda record again—and for the last time. It was quite clear by now that she no longer had any chance of victory and that, in fact, her one chance of bare survival lay in splitting the united front of her enemies in war as she had succeeded in splitting it before the outbreak of war and in its first phase, in repairing the fatal errors Hitler had made in attacking the Soviet Union and declaring war on the United States, and thus bringing about the terrible coalition which now threatened to crush her.

After Stalingrad Nazi Germany realized that unless she could split the coalition against her a German defeat was inevitable. The calculation was perfectly simple. Germany, with about a quarter of world industrial production at her disposal, could not possibly be victorious against countries which disposed of the other three-quarters if they remained united and transformed this enormous industrial preponderance into actual military strength. As the Anglo-Saxon powers had command of the sea and of the air, there was no possibility whatever of preventing them from closing the gap between their industrial strength and their actual military strength. And as the Russians were strong enough to mount their own military offensives, there was no hope of weakening them decisively by any further destruction of their industrial potential.

The only hope left for Nazi Germany was to separate her enemies in some way or the other, and the only way to do this was to prove to the Anglo-Saxon powers that the utter defeat of Germany meant a victory for the Soviet Union which would make her much more dangerous than if some sort of balance of power existed in Europe with Nazi Germany still counting as a factor in it.

It was certainly true that the total defeat of Nazi Germany did represent a very real danger to the Anglo-Saxon powers, and that was because the Soviet Union would thereby become not merely a great power in European affairs, but the only great power on the European continent, because the Red Army would then be not only a strong military factor in Europe, but the only really strong military factor. And then the capitalist system in Europe, which still existed despite all the heavy blows it had suffered, would be in greater danger than ever.

These are speculations which were subsequently to become very familiar when the differences between the United States and Soviet Russia came to a head after the war. They were plugged ceaselessly by Goebbels in his propaganda from about the middle of the war, in the summer of 1943, on, and increasingly so in 1944 and the beginning of 1945.

When we now ask how it came about that with such a good case Nazi Germany nevertheless failed to make any impression on the Anglo-Saxon powers and separate them from the Soviet Union, we find that a series of factors were involved. First of all, it is one thing to enter a military coalition for the purpose of waging war, and quite another merely to remain in it once it has been formed. Much greater energies have to be employed to break up a coalition once it has come into being than are required to form it in the first place.

A second factor is the relatively great degree of social stability which existed in the United States and the fact that the capitalist system there did not feel itself in the least threatened.

If strong radical socialist movements had existed in the Anglo-Saxon countries it is possible that the arguments of Goebbels would have had greater effect when he declared that a victory for the Soviet Union and her institutions in Europe would be much more dangerous than a Europe in which a Nazi Germany, greatly weakened by her war efforts, and a Soviet Union created a sort of balance of power, however unstable. But in fact there were hardly the beginnings of a political working-class movement in the United States, and although there was one in Western Europe it did not represent any very powerful centre of political force.

Stagnation in the European Working-class Movement

There were no strong working-class movements anywhere, and, in fact, the working-class movement generally was suffering from stagnation; nowhere was it capable of organizing its own country for a progressive domestic and foreign policy. This stagnation, which marked the whole period before the outbreak of the second world

413

war, must be dealt with in greater detail, in order to complete our analysis of the coalitions in which the war was fought.

The period before the first world war was marked by an increase of foreign-political and imperialist antagonisms and a decrease of social antagonisms, by rising standards of living for the working classes, by economic crises which were not particularly violent and by a relatively low level of unemployment.

That was the economic basis on which the working-class movement generally had become social reformist and abandoned all idea of a radical transformation of capitalist society, and why when the first world war broke out the overwhelming majority of the workers of all the countries involved rallied to their own governments, their representatives in parliament voting for the war credits. In short, in direct contradiction to Lenin's expectations, that is why the famous decisions of the Second International, and in particular its Basle Resolution, remained an empty form of words.

But after the war, in the period between the two wars, the situation had greatly changed. There was no longer any uninterrupted process of capitalist progress in Europe, and what post-war recovery there had been was soon submerged in the outbreak of the world economic crisis in 1929—by far the worst capitalism had ever experienced. Not only did unemployment rise to unprecedented heights during the worst years of the crisis, but even after its trough was passed unemployment figures still remained very high.

It was in this period between the two world wars that the trends in capitalism which Lenin and Rosa Luxemburg had erroneously assumed to exist in the period which preceded the first world war at last began to operate, and foreign-political antagonisms increased together with domestic social antagonisms.

As we have already seen, the ruling classes drew certain conclusions from this changed situation, but the working classes did not begin to play the role of a progressive force in domestic and foreign politics; they did not even begin to look like a force around which the majority of the nation might rally.

The Second Socialist International collapsed when the first world war broke out, and Karl Kautzky and his followers consoled themselves with the strange thought that a socialist international was something for peace and not for war-time. But that must have been a very poor consolation during the first world war and in the post-war period, when foreign politics became more and more important for the lives of all, a period in which the next world war was not an academic question but a very real one, so that very soon the only question that remained was not whether it would break out, but merely when.

Before the first world war the Second International was a very real international, in the minds of many workers if not in fact, but when it was resuscitated after the war there were few who believed in it as a power in international affairs.

In short, the stagnation from which capitalism was suffering was not accompanied by any advance of socialism or the Socialist International; on the contrary, it was accompanied by a profound crisis in the socialist movement and the socialist parties, which had lost all their old confidence in the inevitability of their victory.

There were a number of reasons for this. The first world war itself had already profoundly shaken the world of socialist ideas (cf. Part Two of this book), and it had already demonstrated that there was no foundation for the comforting idea that socialism must inevitably follow capitalism, and that, in fact, there were other possibilities, such as barbarism and a descent into an abyss without history. The perfect confidence that one day the socialist objective would be attained, even perhaps at great sacrifices, no longer existed.

That was a hard jolt for the European working-class movement and its leaders.

Further, during the course of the first world war a revolution had taken place in Russia. But in the intervening years Russia of the revolution had changed out of all recognition; she was now a dictatorial, terrorist, police State. Many millions of European workers enthusiastically welcomed the November Revolution, and they warmly sympathized with the Soviet Union for many years, but in the end they were compelled to recognize that the Soviet State and the form of society which was developing in Russia had very little in common with their own hopes of what would come about after a radical transformation of capitalist society.

Although the workers in the more highly developed industrial countries of Europe had not launched any powerful actions to transform their own capitalist societies into socialist societies, many of them had still hoped that the Soviet Union would give a practical demonstration to industrial Europe of the superiority of the socialist principle. In the end they were compelled to recognize that their hope had been vain, and that, in fact, in the course of development reactionary tendencies were more and more gaining the upper hand in Soviet Russia.

Thus on the one hand was European capitalism, no longer progressive, but already stagnant; and on the other hand there was not a socialist State to which socialists in Europe could point as a shining example of how things ought to be done. Instead, there was a dictatorial police State, and that all socialists rejected.

However, this State sought to gain a decisive influence on the European working-class movement through the Communist Parties. It did, in fact, succeed in exercising a decisive influence on that movement, though largely a negative one. Russian intervention through the Communist Parties led almost everywhere to a weaken-

415

ing of the working-class movement, and that weakening was in some cases decisive. It was, for instance, one of the main reasons for the victory of the Nazis in Germany (cf. Part Three of this book).

Thus although there were latent revolutionary possibilities as well as counter-revolutionary possibilities in the period between the two world wars, the European working class was no longer united and able to take advantage of them. It was split into two. On the one hand was the Communist International and its parties exploiting the great prestige of the November Revolution in Russia and mouthing revolutionary phrases, which actually succeeded in deceiving a large section of the socialist workers; on the other hand there was Social Democracy, whose leadership—thanks precisely to communist disruption—was farther to the Right than the general mass of the socialist workers.

But the working-class movement was not merely disunited; it was split into two hostile camps which fought each other fiercely, and the result of this was that many millions of workers, intellectuals and others who might have been attracted to a united socialist movement were repelled in something like disgust. In other words, in a period of capitalist stagnation when the objective situation favoured the socialist movement it was permanently split in two, and was thus unable to mobilize more than a fraction of its potential energies.

Such was the situation before the decisive swing to the Right took place in Germany. The Nazis won their victory without having to overcome any worth-while or determined resistance on the part of the German working class, which was perhaps more completely disrupted than any other. All the world knew that the Nazis had taken power without even having to sustain street-fighting such as took place, for instance, in February of the following year, 1934, in Vienna and other parts of Austria. This pitiful defeat of what had once been the most highly organized working class in Europe was a defeat for the whole European working-class movement, and a terribly heavy one.

The steady political degeneration of the Soviet Union was explained and excused first by the fact that the revolution had taken place in a backward country, and secondly by the fact that it had remained isolated and that no revolution had taken place anywhere in industrial Europe. The unspoken implication of this argument was obviously that if the socialist revolution took place in a more highly developed industrial country, then the transformation of society would be far more progressive. But when the crisis intensified in Germany it ended with the victory of the Nazi counter-revolution, and not with the victory of socialism, and Germany became not only an aggressive imperialist State, but the centre for all the reactionary forces of Europe.

The first world war had already disillusioned the European

416

socialist working-class movement and robbed it of its confident belief that development would always go forward and finally end in the socialist transformation of society; now the victory of the Nazi counter-revolution in Germany showed clearly how endangered the position of the working-class movement had become, and it also showed that barbarism threatened not only in war-time and as a result of war, but even in peace.

Whilst the counter-revolution was victorious in Germany, and Western-European capitalism was unable to overcome the effects of the 1929 crisis, the working classes of Western Europe and Great Britain were not strong enough to use the crisis as a starting point for a democratic socialist transformation of capitalist society.

There was no really profound transformation of society either in Great Britain or in France during the period between the two world wars. Neither the British nor the French working class was able to come forward with a systematic plan for the future of society, for the socialist transformation of capitalism without the moral degradation and degeneration which marked developments in the Soviet Union. Because there was no such practical plan, and because no practical steps were taken in this direction by the working class either in Great Britain or France, they were also impotent in foreign affairs and their influence was negligible. Their ruling classes pursued a policy of appeasement which made war certain, and they had nothing to offer as a practical alternative. In fact very often that fatal appeasement reflected the strongly pacifist and anti-military tendencies in the working-class movement.

So much for the situation which existed in the years which preceded the second world war. During the war there was no strong independent working-class action anywhere, and that is easy enough to explain. Before the first world war there was at least some show of international solidarity in the famous Basle Resolution of the Second International, which declared that the socialist movements in all countries would utilize the situation created by a war to launch revolutionary action. As we know, when the time came to put that resolution into effect the international working-class socialist movement was seen to be helpless on the foreign-political field, and the Second International collapsed.

But in the period which preceded the second world war there was not even a Basle Resolution. There was nothing. There was not even a collapse of the international, because there was no international to collapse.

The workers in those countries which were fighting against Nazi Germany entered the war behind their own capitalists. It would have been worse than useless, it would have been ridiculous, to call upon them to utilize the situation created by the war for revolutionary socialist action to transform society. The situation for that was unfavourable enough when the first world war broke out; it was out of the question when the second did.

Even at the conferences of the Second International which preceded the first world war, and which called upon the workers to answer the outbreak of war with revolutionary action and utilize the upheaval caused by the war to take decisive steps in the direction of a socialist revolution, there were voices which pointed out that if the workers of any particular country were actually to follow this advice they would weaken the military strength of their own country and improve the chances of victory for the enemy, who would then, after his victory, crush the revolution in the defeated country.

The answer to this and similar objections was that social conditions in Europe were very uniform, and that therefore a revolution in one country would easily spread to the others, and that the workers should therefore not wait until the revolutionary conditions for action were equally favourable in all countries before taking action.

Obviously, such arguments made no real impression on the masses of the workers, and when the first world war actually broke out there were no socialist revolutionary actions or movements to overthrow capitalism in any of the belligerent countries.

The situation in the second world war was even less favourable for such action. The German workers, for example, had been unable to offer any effective resistance to the Nazis to prevent their coming to power, and to expect that in war-time they would be able to do anything effective against the Nazi State was to indulge in unrealistic dreams.

And in the countries at war with Nazi Germany it was quite clear to the workers that any resistance to war on their part would only weaken the common front against the Nazi counter-revolution and increase the chances of a Nazi victory. Thus in so far as there were any tendencies amongst the workers of Europe to adopt a revolutionary attitude in the event of war—as a result of the aggravation of social antagonisms—those tendencies were more than counterbalanced by the fact that this time the war was not against Hohenzollern Germany—in which, after all, influential independent socialist elements had supported anti-war action, voted against the war credits, and so on—but against Nazi Germany, in which all working-class organizations had been utterly destroyed and in which all opposition had been suppressed years before by Gestapo terror.

Thus although the parallel strengthening of both foreign-political and domestic social antagonisms in the period which preceded the second world war frequently affected the foreign policy of the big powers, it did not produce any independent foreign-political action on the part of the socialist working class.

The result was that when the second world war did break out the working-class parties in the countries engaged in war with Nazi

418

Germany had no alternative but to support their own governments. They had to bide their time until the defeat of Nazi Germany, the centre of world reaction, should clear the way for their own action.

During the first world war big strikes took place in many belligerent countries. During the second world war none occurred. The workers stood solidly behind their own governments in the struggle against Nazi Germany, where of course strikes were out of the question.

The fact that the capitalist social system had been greatly shaken in the period between the two world wars and that it was more brittle than ever before, did not tempt the workers to take any action to overthrow capitalism during the war in the interests of a socialist transformation of society.

The fact that nowhere did the workers undertake, or even show any inclination to undertake, radical anti-capitalist actions during the war made it easier for the Anglo-Saxon countries to reject all the direct and indirect suggestions made by the Nazis that they should withdraw from their military alliance with the Soviet Union. In consequence, this military alliance lasted throughout the period of hostilities. Occasionally, it is true, its path was not smooth, and from time to time it experienced crises, but it survived them all and remained intact until the final defeat of Nazi Germany and Japan.

CHAPTER TWO

THE COURSE OF THE SECOND WORLD WAR

THE SECOND WORLD WAR did not begin as a world war, but as a European war, and even then not all of Europe was involved at first. Nazi Germany attacked Poland in the east, and when Great Britain and France stood by their pledge and declared war on Germany, hostilities began in the west.

It is interesting to note that the two powers which between them finally decided the upshot of the war, the United States and the Soviet Union, the two powers which stood out above all others in the general relation of world forces subsequently brought about by the war, were not actively involved in the war at all in its first phase.

The first world war became a war on one front for Germany only in its final phase, but by that time it was much too late to alter the outcome, because U.S. assistance both in men and materials was incomparably greater than any accession of strength to Germany on the Western Front as the result of the collapse of Russia and the transfer of German troops from east to west.

The one-front war was achieved by Germany after three years

hard fighting when she was already too exhausted to take full advantage of it. The German general staff and the Nazis had taken good note of this circumstance. They were well aware that Germany could hope to win a war only if it were a one-front war; a war on two fronts might once again prove fatal.

When Hitler had assured himself, by means of the Nazi-Soviet Pact, that the war would be to all intents and purposes a one-front war he launched his attack on Poland. Great Britain and France immediately declared war, but they took no effective military action to aid Poland, and within a few weeks she was utterly defeated.

After a comparatively short period of intensive preparations, often referred to foolishly as the period of the phoney war, Nazi Germany continued the struggle against Norway, Denmark, Holland, Belgium and France, and won a series of brilliant victories which ended the fighting in Europe for the time being. It was, despite the Polish preliminary, a one-front war, and Germany was successful.

THE CAUSES OF GERMANY'S LIGHTNING VICTORIES

Germany's swift victories may have appeared astounding, but there were very good reasons for them. First of all, the gap between Germany's preparedness and that of the western powers was very much larger than it was when the first world war broke out. This time Germany possessed not only a very great purely military advantage, but also a tremendous advantage in armament production. That was, of course, the whole significance of the Nazis' war economy in peace time. The western powers did not succeed in remotely closing this gap in the comparatively short period from the occupation of Prague—which destroyed the last hopeless illusions—to the actual outbreak of war, and although they then began to re-arm, it is questionable whether they even succeeded in reducing the gap, because in the present era of industrial warfare it takes years for a country, starting practically from scratch, to transform its industrial strength into military strength.

Winston Churchill deals with the point:[1]

"The question has been debated whether Hitler or the Allies gained the more in strength in the year that followed Munich. Many persons in Britain who knew our nakedness felt a sense of relief as each month our air force developed and the Hurricane and Spitfire types approached issue. The number of formed squadrons grew and the ack-ack guns multiplied. Also the general pressure of industrial preparation for war continued to quicken. But these improvements, invaluable though they seemed, were petty compared with the mighty advance in German armaments. As had been explained, munition production on a nation-wide plan is a four years' task. The first year yields nothing, the second

420

very little, the third a lot, and the fourth a flood. Hitler's Germany in this period was already in the third or fourth year of intensive preparations under conditions of grip and drive which were almost the same as those of war."

The second factor which made Germany's lightning victories possible was the Nazi-Soviet Pact. Even after the signing of that pact Germany was still compelled to station a part of her forces in the east, but at least there was no war there, and this meant that she did not have to organize and maintain a powerful supply system, as would otherwise have been the case. The result was that she was able to organize a powerful and uninterrupted concentration of her decisive forces on the Western Front.

The third factor which facilitated such striking and swift victories was the fact that the French social system was by no means so homogeneous and stable as when the first world war broke out. On the one hand the French Right feared a victory over Hitler Germany every bit as much as they feared the defeat of France, and on the other hand the French communists called for resistance and sabotage, obediently carrying out Russian instructions under the Nazi-Soviet Pact. It is quite obvious that in such circumstances French morale was low, and French troops went into action with a muddled idea of what they were really fighting about or fighting for.

It was the combination of these three factors which produced the series of German victories on the Western Front in the first phase of the second world war.

With these victories a situation was created which was fundamentally different from that which had existed in the first world war. After these victories Nazi Germany was the undisputed master of the greater part of continental Europe.

In the first world war only a comparatively small portion of French territory was occupied by the Germans, and the French Army remained intact as a fighting force to the end, and played an important part in the final military victory of the western powers. But in the second world war the French Army was utterly defeated and the Germans occupied about half of French territory; and French industrial production, like that of the smaller European countries, was harnessed to the German war effort.

This time the armies and the armament production of Great Britain could not be steadily built up behind a continental wall; its only sure shield was the English Channel.

During the first world war, before U.S. intervention turned the scale, the military forces of the Entente powers were approximately equal to those of Germany, but now the only power left in Western Europe was Great Britain, and her military strength was greatly inferior to that of Nazi Germany.

It should be stressed that Hitler and the German generals—and incidentally also the Russians and the Americans—had grossly over-estimated the military strength of the French Army and the stability and cohesion of France's social organism. Nazi Germany could have over-run France with a considerably smaller effort than she actually made.

This German over-estimation of French strength had one important consequence: it caused the Germans to make their preparations primarily with land warfare in view, and in consequence German naval and submarine preparations had been relatively neglected. The same applied also to an air force to support a possible invasion of Britain. The result was that once the victory had been gained on the continent there was little else the Germans could do. Great Britain could not be invaded, and therefore she could not be defeated, and so for the moment hostilities practically ceased.

The situation after the first year of the second world war was totally different from the situation at the end of the first year of the first world war. In the opening phases of the first world war the German armies had also won swift and striking successes, but at the end of the first year they were still engaged in a war on two fronts with armies which were intact and undefeated. This time however the one-front war had ended in complete victory on that one front. There was no French Army left, and there was none throughout the rest of the war.

Further, the complete defeat of the French army and the fact that there was no longer any front in the west gave Great Britain no time to build up her armies and her munitions and armaments production behind a continental wall of allied armies, as she had done in the first world war. This time she had to build up her armies at home, and, having done so, she was not in a position from her own resources to deploy them on the continent. The German armies which had won a complete victory over France within the space of a few weeks, and which were now supported by the industrial production of France and Western Europe generally, in addition to their own, could easily have dealt with any British attempt to make a landing on French soil.

Hitler was now at the zenith of his power. The adroit exploitation of the antagonism between the East and the West had borne ripe fruit. It had guaranteed Germany a one-front war, and Germany had won that one-front war, though, of course, only as far as continental Europe was concerned.

The question now arose of what she should do next. The air war against Great Britain had produced no decisive results, and therefore no invasion of Great Britain was attempted. In the winter of 1940–1941 the German armies were idle. Germany could have attempted to digest the fruits of her great victories. She could have proceeded first against the British Empire and then, when the time was considered ripe, against the British Isles. It would have been easy enough for her to have marched through Spain to the seizure of Gibraltar, and to have crossed to North Africa and driven on to Cairo and the Suez Canal.

If there is any doubt about her ability to have done this, it is sufficient to recall that in 1941–1942, at a time when Germany was already suffering very heavy losses in her war against the Soviet Union and the enormous majority of her resources were concentrated on the Eastern Front, she could still send a powerful army to North Africa and almost capture Cairo. Without the attack on the Soviet Union, a North-African campaign, with all that resulted from it, would have been a comparatively easy matter for Germany's vast military resources.

Or Hitler could have made really thorough preparations for an invasion of the British Isles, coupled with a gigantic air attack. An invasion would, of course, not have been an easy task; but if Germany's great reserves, now reinforced by the armament production of all the occupied territories, had been bent to that one aim, it is a daring man who would say that such an invasion would not have succeeded. In this connection we must not forget that U.S. aid for Britain was very small in 1940 and not much bigger even in 1941, and that therefore in 1941 Britain was still waging war without any very great assistance from the United States.

But Nazi Germany did not turn all her forces against the British Empire and against the British Isles; instead, after a short and victorious campaign in Yugoslavia, she threw her forces against the Soviet Union at a time when they were not fully prepared for such a campaign.

This was the fatal step which sealed Nazi Germany's ultimate doom.

Up to the time Hitler attacked the Soviet Union the second world war had been a one-front war for Nazi Germany, and it had been a one-front war which had ended with a lightning military victory. Nazi Germany had been able to concentrate such superior forces on whatever front she chose for an offensive that the fighting invariably lasted only a few weeks and ended with a German victory.

Hitler had also tried to wage the war against the Soviet Union as a one-front war, but Great Britain had rejected all his offers. However, he decided to attack the Soviet Union nevertheless, and in doing so he ended the one-front phase of the war for Germany. Not that he intended to; he believed that to all intents and purposes his war against the Soviet Union would be a one-front war. Of course, Germany was still at war with Great Britain, but it was a war in which neither of the combatants could really get at each other to deliver decisive blows. When Hitler launched his attack on the Soviet

Union there was not a single British unit on continental soil, and neither then nor at any time later was Britain in a position to mount a continental invasion with her own resources alone. Thus Nazi Germany was again in a position to concentrate by far the greater part of her forces on the front she had chosen—in this case the Soviet Union—whilst leaving only relatively small forces in the West to guard against the remote possibility of an invasion.

Hitler's strategic plan was undoubtedly to attack and overthrow the Soviet Union in a lightning campaign, a campaign which he no doubt reckoned would last rather longer than his campaign in the west, but which would nevertheless be of comparatively short duration. Having done that he would then be undisputed master of the whole of Europe, with all her potentialities at his disposal, and in a position to turn the full weight of his forces to the west to take up the real struggle again against Great Britain and the British Empire—if by that time whatever British Government might be in existence had any heart left to continue the struggle.

With such a strategy lightning campaigns ending in complete victory were more necessary to Germany than ever before, because in her rear was still an unsubdued Britain whose military strength came nearer and nearer to her industrial strength with every passing day, and who was now receiving increasing aid from the United States. In addition, it was more than ever necessary that Germany's preparations should be on such a scale that the war against the Soviet Union must rapidly lead to decisive success.

But the astounding fact is that in this situation Nazi Germany launched the war against the Soviet Union without any previous extension of her military and armament sector.

German Armaments Production did not Increase

The Nazi State had compelled the German people to build up a war economy without precedent in peace time, and in consequence the first phases of the war had brought Germany great victories. With this the previous enormous production of armaments in peace time seemed to have justified itself, and Hitler's apologists began to refer to it triumphantly as a very "productive" investment, because with it Nazi Germany had made herself mistress of the greater part of Europe.

However, Germany's armament production was by no means at its possible peak at that time. If we represent the peak possibility of German armaments production by 100, then in 1940, at the time of the Dunkirk evacuation, it was perhaps 35. Despite the growing weight of the Anglo-American bombing attacks on Germany, she succeeded in almost trebling her production of armaments in the period from 1941 to 1944, and that is some indication of the possibilities which were available to her.

424

The astonishing fact was, however, that after the crushing of the French armies and the evacuation of the British forces at Dunkirk, and up to the invasion of the Soviet Union on June 22nd, 1941, *Germany's production of armaments did not increase, but remained at approximately 35 per cent of the subsequent peak volume.*

In 1940 Germany expended 6 milliard dollars on her armaments production, and the same sum in 1941.[2]

It is understandable enough that Germany's armaments production was not increased immediately after Dunkirk, because at the time Hitler thought he had won the game. He had beaten France to her knees, and he thought that Great Britain would come to terms. Why therefore impose further unproductive—and, as he thought, unnecessary—sacrifices on the German people? Victory was already won.

However, Great Britain refused to admit that she was beaten and insisted on fighting on. At the same time, Germany's estimate of Britain's strength in defence and of her own unpreparedness for the type of warfare an invasion would involve dissuaded her from even attempting an invasion.

Thus, whatever he may have thought immediately after Dunkirk, Hitler knew in the winter of 1940–1941 that the war was not over, and that there was further hard fighting to do. From then on up to the invasion of the Soviet Union there was plenty of time to increase Germany's armaments production quite considerably. *Nothing was done, and her armaments production remained more or less at the same level.* There were no objective reasons why this was so; it was a matter of deliberate policy.

"That this deliberately slow expansion of munitions production, amounting to a virtual levelling during most of 1941, was the greatest blunder Germany made in the sphere of war economics, and the one that cost her every chance of victory, is now clear. What was responsible for it remains a matter of speculation. A complete misestimation of Soviet munitions production is certain to have been an important factor in this fateful decision."[3]

Germany's production of armaments could easily have been stepped up in that period. She had everything in her hands; all that was necessary was the decision to do so. That decision was not taken, and the personal responsibility rests on Hitler himself. Thus in this phase of the war a single individual exercised decisive influence on world history.

THE INDIVIDUAL AND WORLD HISTORY

It is a widespread and popular illusion that an individual must be a great man, a genius, before he can exercise any influence on the course of history. That is not in the least true; if the opposing forces are more or less evenly matched, then a mediocrity in power can most certainly exercise a decisive influence on the fate of the world. And this was a case in point.

It was not the only one. There had been precedents. Marx showed that it was so in the case of Napoleon III, and he demonstrated that the relation of forces which existed at that time permitted a French mediocrity to change the course of history by his personal intervention.

That was certainly true of Hitler. There was nothing to stop his preparing the German armies adequately for the task which faced them in Russia. He could have provided them with twice the armaments backing that they actually had when the campaign was launched. Had he done so, no one dare say that a Nazi victory over the Soviet Union would still have been impossible.

He did not do what was obviously required. Clearly, he grossly under-estimated the military strength of the Soviet Union. In his fanatical mind the bolshevist regime was a Jewish regime, and therefore just could not be very strong. It was one of those things which must not be, and therefore for him it was not.

It is wrong to believe that this gross under-estimate of the military strength of the Soviet Union by Hitler was based on ignorance. Even under Nazi rule a number of books and many articles had been published in Germany pointing out how very considerably the industrial strength, and therefore the military potential, of the Soviet Union had grown by comparison with Tsarist Russia, and stressing in particular the strength of Soviet military production in tanks and aeroplanes.

Major Karl Spalcke, a well-known German military expert, wrote in 1936:

"An investigation of what is, in the last resort, the material basis of any armaments industry—the production of coal, iron and steel —shows us that during the course of her Five-Year Plans Soviet Russia has created a heavy-industrial armaments basis which is already up to the level of that of a big modern military power. . . . Soviet Russia has sufficient food supplies and a thoroughly efficient raw-material basis for the development of her armaments industry. With regard to the production of such important raw materials as coal, iron ore, iron and steel, Soviet Russia has already moved up into the front ranks of the modern big powers." [4]

The following quotation is taken from a highly interesting book published in 1937 and written by an expert, Dr Erwin Haudann, on the motorization potential of the Soviet Union:

" As a result of experience gained during the world war the Soviet Union quickly recognized the possibilities and advantages of the use of the motor in various branches of national defence, and this recognition has been put into practice by motorizing the army intensively and on a wide scale. In a comparatively short space of time the Soviet Government has succeeded in motorizing the Red Army to such an extent that to-day it must be regarded as one of the best equipped armies in the world." [5]

Haudann also pointed out that the annual production of seventy-four Soviet-Russian factories, twenty-eight aeroplane factories proper and thirty-two factories for the production of aero-parts and accessories, had increased to 8,000 machines, and that the number of workers employed in the Soviet aero-industry was already 220,000.

He also pointed out that the Russians had based their production to a very considerable extent far away from their vulnerable western frontiers.

"The vital industries necessary for the maintenance and continued progress of Soviet Russia's motorization are all, with the exception of the older works in Leningrad, situated far away from the frontiers in Central Russia, on the Volga, and in the border districts of Europe and Asia. It is therefore hardly likely that the Soviet Union could be deprived of any of the industries necessary for the maintenance of her motorization potential by enemy attack. These industries are situated so far inland that even the loss of an area 500 kilometres in depth would represent no serious danger to the production of motors, tractors, tanks and aeroplanes." [6]

And in a book published in 1938 [7] the author of the present work pointed out, on the basis of material available in Germany, that the industrial and military strength of the Soviet Union had grown almost out of knowledge compared with Russia's industrial and military strength in the first world war, and he concluded:

"The decisive change which has taken place in the world political situation since the world war is the tremendous strengthening of Soviet Russia's war potential in comparison with that of Tsarist Russia. Naturally, it is not possible to give any exact quantitative estimate of the difference, but if we were to assume something like a twofold or threefold increase our estimate would more likely be too low than too high. . . . Germany's industrial strength is now faced for the first time with industrial strength on her eastern frontier. Modern warfare waged by Germany on the eastern front to-day would meet with an opponent who is also in a position to wage it. The industrial development of Soviet Russia is thus a decisive factor in the existing relation of forces, and it will make the coming war a protracted one."

It is quite true, of course, that at the same time German publications pointed out real or supposed weaknesses in the Soviet Union, and in particular the low level of *per capita* industrial production, the inadequacy of the Soviet railway system, the comparatively small number of highly-skilled workers, the damage done to the Soviet regime and its military leadership by the purges, and so on.

But it is a matter of principle for any general staff worth its salt that it should prepare itself for the most unfavourable variant when it is contemplating a war on a big scale, such as any war against the Soviet Union necessarily would be.

Hitler ignored this fundamental principle because his idea of the Soviet Union as a Bolshevist-Jewish State just would not permit Russia to be strong. Apparently therefore, he saw no reason to increase Germany's armaments production in the period from Dunkirk to the attack on the Soviet Union. He launched his armies against the Soviet Union in the belief that the whole campaign would end in a decisive German victory within a matter of weeks, or of months at the utmost.

And it is quite true that in a matter of months the final upshot of the war was decided—but not as Hitler had imagined. The Russian armies suffered big preliminary defeats, but nevertheless they remained intact and capable of fighting on. Not only that, but for the first time in the second world war the German armies had to retreat —in the winter of 1941–1942.

That was the first factor which led to a complete change in the situation in the second world war. The German armies were unable to take either Moscow or Leningrad. Between them and Moscow stood the Red Army, and the Red Army had to wage war on one front only.

It is, of course, true that the Russians had to keep strong military forces in the east for fear of an invasion by Japan, but that invasion did not take place, and although the threat occupied men, it did not use up materials. Thus because Nazi Germany had not succeeded— despite all her expectations—in obtaining a lightning decision on the Eastern Front, and because she was paying a terrible price in blood and destruction for her failure to prepare herself adequately for the gigantic task she had undertaken, she was now desperately anxious that Japan should enter the war and attack the Soviet Union in the rear.

Japan did, in fact, enter the second world war, but she followed her own interests, and not those of Nazi Germany; she attacked the United States, whereupon Nazi Germany, possibly still in the hope of a subsequent Japanese attack on the Soviet Union, immediately declared war on the United States as well.

With this Nazi Germany took the second decisive step which led to her subsequent defeat. Not only did she have to continue to wage a desperately bitter war against the Soviet Union—at whose hands she had already suffered her first defeats—not only did she have an un-

428

defeated and rapidly strengthening Britain in her rear, but she now had to deal with the armed forces of the most powerful industrial country in the world, the United States.

From the day Japan attacked Pearl Harbour and Germany declared war on the United States the war became a world war, and the question of a second front for Nazi Germany was no longer merely an academic one, but a very practical one. It was now only a question of time before on the other side of the English Channel and the other side of the Atlantic the slow but growing process of translating the industrial power of Great Britain, and the still greater industrial power of the United States, into real military strength would be sufficiently advanced to allow the blow to be struck. Great Britain and the United States had command of the seas and of the air, and there was not much either Germany or Japan, or the two together, could do to slow down the process materially.

However, although the opening of the second front in Europe was only a matter of time, because between them British and American military strength would inevitably grow big enough to enforce it, the war essentially remained a one-front war for Nazi Germany—a war against the Soviet Union—and it remained so for a very long time even after the United States was pushed into the shooting war.

This is not a military analysis of the Russo-German war, and we are therefore not particularly interested in the details of the struggle. What primarily interests us is why the German armies failed to defeat the Soviet Union even after the Germans had corrected their original miscalculation of Russia's military strength and had strained their own productive armament resources to the limit. In other words, why was the situation on the Eastern Front in the second world war so very different from what it was in the first world war?

The fundamental reason was the complete change which had taken place in the relation between German and Russian industrial strength. *Per capita* industrial production in Germany was still very much greater than in Russia, but by no means so overwhelmingly greater as it had been in 1914. It was now something like 3 : 1 instead of 10 : 1. In absolute figures Germany's industrial production was still greater than Russia's, but the difference was very much less than before. In the basic industries Russia's production amounted to about four-fifths of Germany's.

Stalin himself, in a speech which attracted a good deal of attention, gave us the figures of Russia's heavy industrial production for 1940—the last year of peace before the German attack. In that year Soviet Russia produced 18·3 million tons of steel, 15 million tons of pig iron and 166 million tons of coal. The corresponding figures for German production were 25 million tons, 18·5 million tons and 190 million tons. Thus Germany's heavy industrial advantage was now only in the order of 5 : 4.

The second reason was that long before the beginning of the second world war the Russians had built up a very powerful military sector in answer to Nazi Germany's introduction of a war economy in peace time. And when the threat to the Soviet Union grew more acute after the complete defeat of France in 1940, the Soviet Government stepped up her armament production very considerably, and continued to do so.

Whilst Germany, as we have already seen, did not materially increase her production of armaments in the period from Dunkirk to her attack on the Soviet Union, Soviet armaments production increased tremendously. Both the Germans and the Russians reached the peak point of their armaments production in and around 1944, but whereas at the time of her attack on the Soviet Union Germany had reached only about a third of her peak possibilities, the Soviet Union had already reached more than half of hers, or approximately 53 per cent.

> "As a result, the Soviet Union, at the time she was attacked, already turned out about half as many combat munitions as during 1944, and had accumulated a very substantial stock of reasonably modern weapons." [8]

As Soviet Russia's industrial strength had increased very considerably, as Soviet Russia—unlike the western powers—had immediately answered Nazi Germany's introduction of a war economy in peace time with a war economy of her own, as Soviet Russia had used the period of her neutrality for an enormous increase of her armaments production, so that, in fact, the relative strength of the military sector of Soviet Russia's total economy was far greater than the corresponding proportion of Nazi Germany's total economy, and as, in other words, "total" war had been organized far more thoroughly in the Soviet Union than in Germany, despite all the Nazi talk about it, the result was that in the first and decisive phase of the Nazi war against the Soviet Union, German armaments production in absolute figures was not much bigger than Soviet Russia's, and therefore the gap between the two belligerents on the Eastern Front was much less than it had been in 1940 on the Western Front.

> "At the time of Germany's attack on the Soviet Union, her accumulated munitions production, increased by the booty of her previous campaigns, may have been half as large again as that of the Soviet Union. However, Germany's material superiority on the Eastern Front must have been small, since a considerable part of the total had to be assigned to the West." [9]

It was this great reduction of the gap between the industrial and military production of Germany and that of the Soviet Union which

430

made it possible for the Soviet Union to offer successful resistance to the German attack.

However, even this important fact alone is not sufficient to explain entirely why the situation on the Eastern Front in the second world war was so totally different from what it had been in the first world war.

Although their superiority was no longer so very great, the German armies won tremendous victories in the summer of 1941. They were able to inflict terrible defeats on the Russian armies and to occupy vast areas of European Russia—i.e. that part of the Soviet Union which contained the major part of her industrial strength and in which therefore most of her armaments production was concentrated.

"The territory of the Soviet Union which was occupied by November 1941 included before the war about 40 per cent of the total population of the country, produced 63 per cent of the pre-war total of coal mined, 68 per cent of the total pig-iron output, 58 per cent of the steel output, and 60 per cent of the aluminium output. The territory temporarily occupied by Hitler Germany by November 1941 produced 38 per cent of the total pre-war gross grain harvest, 84 per cent of the total pre-war sugar production, and contained 38 per cent of the total number of cattle and 60 per cent of the total number of hogs. The length of railroad lines in the territory occupied by November 1941 constituted 41 per cent of the total length of railroad lines in the Soviet Union." [10]

Obviously, therefore, the question that immediately arises is how did it come about that, after such devastating defeats and industrial and territorial losses, the Soviet Union still managed to stay on its feet, keep its armies in the field and continue to supply them?

There were two factors which enabled the Soviet Union to avoid utter collapse. The first was that her social structure showed far greater cohesion and stability precisely in those dark days of defeat than Hitler had expected. He had confidently believed that after one or two heavy military defeats the Soviet system would collapse. Once again his calculations were wrong.

It was proved once again, as in the period of the Napoleonic Wars, that on the defensive Russia could stand far greater losses of man-power and territory than the western powers possibly could, and still retain her political unity and her social cohesion in face of the foreign invader.

Allowing for all the obvious differences, there is still a great similarity between the defeat of the Napoleonic invasion of Russia in the nineteenth century and the defeat of the Nazi invasion in the twentieth.

The similarity is particularly marked if we compare Tolstoy's description in "War and Peace" with observations made by Hitler's Chief-of-Staff, General Halder, concerning the first phase of the Russo-German War.

Here is Tolstoy on the Battle of Borodino in 1812:

"Napoleon's generals, Davout, Ney and Murat, who were near that region of fire and sometimes even entered it—repeatedly led into it huge masses of well-ordered troops. But contrary to what had always happened in their former battles, instead of the news they expected of the enemy's flight, these orderly masses returned thence as disorganized and terrified mobs. The generals re-formed them, but their numbers constantly decreased. . . . Napoleon was experiencing a feeling of depression like that of an ever-lucky gambler who, after recklessly flinging money about and always winning, suddenly, just when he has calculated all the chances of the game, finds that the more he considers his play the more surely he loses.

"His troops were the same, his generals the same, the same preparations had been made, the same dispositions, and the same proclamation *courte et énergique*, he himself was still the same: he knew that and he knew that he was now even more experienced and skilful than before. . . . All the old methods that had been unfailingly crowned with success: the concentration of batteries on one point, an attack by reserves to break the enemy's line, and a cavalry attack by 'the men of iron', all these methods had already been employed, yet not only was there no victory, but from all sides came the same news of generals killed and wounded, or reinforcements needed, of the impossibility of driving back the Russians, and of disorganization amongst his own troops. . . . It was not Napoleon alone who had experienced that nightmare feeling of the mighty arm being stricken powerless, but all the generals and soldiers of his army whether they had taken part in the battle or not, after all their experience of previous battles—when after one-tenth of such efforts the enemy had fled—experienced a similar feeling of terror before an enemy who, after losing half his men, stood as threateningly at the end as at the beginning of the battle. The moral forces of the attacking French army was exhausted. Not that sort of victory which is defined by the capture of pieces of material fastened to stick, called standards, and of the ground on which the troops had stood and were standing, but a moral victory that convinces the enemy of the moral superiority of his opponent and of his own impotence was gained by the Russians at Borodino." [11]

Even in the face of gigantic losses the Russians do not capitulate; that was true in 1812, and it was true again in 1941 and the subsequent years. Here is General Halder on Germany's experiences in the campaign against Soviet Russia:

"By July 8th, 1941, it appeared to the Germans that the Russians were no longer able to organize a continuous front. . . . The Russians cannot be beaten with operational successes, Hitler argued on July 26th, because they simply do not know when they are defeated. . . . By August 11th, 1941, Germany's last reserves were committed in a last desperate effort to keep the front line from becoming frozen in positional warfare.

"The whole situation makes it increasingly plain that we have underestimated the Russian colossus. . . . At the outset of the war we reckoned with about 200 enemy divisions. Now we have already counted 360. These divisions indeed are not armed and equipped according to our standards, and their tactical leadership is often poor, but they are still there. And if we smash up a dozen of them the Russians simply put another dozen in their place. The time factor favours them, as they are near their own resources, whilst we are moving farther and farther away from ours.

"And so our troops, sprawled over an immense front line, without any depth, are subjected to the incessant attacks of the enemy. Sometimes these are successful, because too many gaps must be left open in these enormous spaces.

"In the first three months Germany lost 15 per cent of an army of 3,400,000 men. By November the problem of supply determined German operations. On November 19th Hitler admitted that he could not annihilate the Russians. On November 27th the German supply chiefs reported that they were at the end of their resources in personnel and material, though confronted with the dangers of deep winter. By the 176th day of the campaign, on December 10th, 1941, a quarter of the army was gone." [12]

We have seen from Tolstoy's account that the preliminary victories won by Napoleon in his invasion of Russia were not of a nature to heighten the morale of his troops. What was true of Napoleon's preliminary victories in 1812 was equally true of Hitler's pyrrhic victories in 1941. In addition, the German armies which had to camp in the open steppes because they were unable to capture either Leningrad or Moscow, were unprepared for the bitter Russian winter, and they were no longer the same armies which had won lightning and decisive victories over Poland and France.

But even the tenacious inherent strength of Russia, which held her together socially and politically even in the darkest days of defeat, would not have been enough to stave off final disaster if the gap between the armament possibilities of the two belligerents had materially increased, as was to have been expected, after Russia had lost the greater part of her European provinces. But this gap did not

433

materially increase, and the question which now arises is how it came about that after the German armies had driven forward right up to Leningrad and Moscow, and thus deprived the Soviet Union of a great part of her armaments potential, Germany did not out-produce Russia to such an extent that she was able in the end to break down her resistance?

When the German armies decisively defeated the combined Franco-British armies and occupied a large part of the industrial areas of Western Europe, the industrial production of these areas was not only lost to the western allies, but Germany was able to harness a considerable part of it to her own economic war machine.

The situation in the east was very different. The German armies occupied vast areas of European Russia, but, despite enormous losses, the Russian armies remained in the field as fighting units. At the same time Germany found it practically impossible to harness any considerable sections of the industry left behind by the Russian troops to her own war effort, because the ruthless "scorched-earth" policy pursued by the Russians had put the major part of it out of commission for a very long time. In addition, Germany had to keep German armies supplied over very long lines of communication through hostile country in which there was a very great deal of harassing guerilla activity. The result was that quite a considerable part of her industrial strength was taken up in the organization and maintenance of this supply system. Further, after the preliminary defeats almost the whole of Russia's remaining industrial production was concentrated on armaments.

The Growth of Armament Production in Russia's Asiatic Provinces

In addition, Soviet Russia had succeeded in evacuating a considerable part of her industrial equipment from the lost provinces and setting it up again in areas far out of reach of military action, and even out of reach of Germany's bombers. And with her industrial equipment she also evacuated the able-bodied population, including the greater part of her industrial man-power, of the lost provinces. Thanks to the vast supplies of foodstuffs which had been deliberately accumulated in the days of the Nazi-Soviet Pact, and in particular after the record harvest of 1940, the Soviet Union was in a position to supply the evacuated millions with at least a basic minimum of foodstuffs.

And, as we have already seen, the Soviet Government had concentrated a growing part of her new industrial development during the Five-Year Plans in the Asiatic provinces, so that long before the outbreak of the second world war the proportion of Soviet Russia's total industrial production accounted for by these provinces was rapidly increasing. This is probably the most important of the factors which saved the Soviet Union from final defeat, because once the German offensive had bogged down before Leningrad and Moscow, the Soviet Government was in a position to increase production tremendously in the Asiatic provinces on the basis of the industries she had already built up there in peace time.

The following quotation gives us figures which enable us to form some idea of the magnitude of the evacuation and of Soviet-Russian industrial production during the war:

"Millions of people were on the move, hundreds of enterprises, tens of thousands of machine tools, rolling mills, presses, hammers, turbines and motors were being re-located in the course of some three months in 1941. 1,366 large-scale enterprises—mostly war enterprises—were evacuated to the eastern region of the Soviet Union. Of these, 455 enterprises were evacuated to the Urals, 210 enterprises to Western Siberia, and 250 enterprises to Central Asia and Kazakhstan. In the same period vast new construction was under way. The volume of capital construction in the regions of the Urals, Siberia, Kazakhstan and Central Asia had increased, in spite of war-time difficulties, from 3·1 milliard roubles during the peace-time half of 1941 to 5·1 milliard roubles during the second, war-time, half of that year." *

The result was a substantial increase in the production of Eastern Russia during the war.

"In 1943 the output of all industry in the regions of the Volga, the Urals, Western Siberia, Kazakhstan and Central Asia was 2·9 times as large as in 1940."

In many branches the production of Eastern Russia during the second world war was greater than that of all Russia during the first world war.

"In the eastern regions of the Soviet Union alone more was produced in 1943 than in the whole territory of Russia in 1915: coal 2·3 times as much, steel twice as much, rolled ferrous metals 1·7 times as much, copper 4·1 times as much, lead 59 times as much, and zinc 18·8 times as much."

This gigantic industrial development in Eastern Russia before and during the war made it possible for Russian military production to tower far above that of the first world war despite the loss of a number of important European provinces.

* These figures and those that follow in this connection are taken from Russian official sources, "The Economy of the U.S.S.R. during World War II" by Nikholai Voznessensky. Like all other official Russian statistics, they are hard to verify, but we may take it that at least they accurately represent the general trend, which is what matters.—F. S.

"Twenty-nine times as many pieces of artillery were produced in the Soviet Union during the 'Patriotic War' as were produced in all the State and private plants of pre-revolutionary Russia during the first world war. The output of mortars in the Soviet Union during the same period was 89 times greater than the output in pre-revolutionary Russia.

"In the Soviet Union during the Patriotic War, 78 times as many machine-guns were produced as in pre-revolutionary Russia during the first world war. The output of rifles in the Soviet Union during the Patriotic War was 6·4 times greater than that in pre-revolutionary Russia during the years of the first world war.

"The number of shells for artillery pieces produced in the Soviet Union during the years of the Patriotic War was 8·2 times greater than the number of shells delivered to the army in pre-revolutionary Russia during the first world war. In the Soviet Union during the years of the Patriotic War, 6·9 times more of all kinds of small-arms munitions was produced than in pre-revolutionary Russia during the first world war."

These figures are sufficient to show us the enormously important role played by industrial production in Eastern Russia, and particularly Asiatic Russia, in military output during the second world war.

We have already indicated that some of these official figures may not be very accurate, but at the same time the fact that Soviet Russia's armaments production was tremendous even after the loss of the European provinces is vouched for by American experts.

"What was much more ominous for Germany was her inability to out-produce the Soviet Union once the attempt at speedy victory had failed, largely due to inadequate reserves of material. In each of the years 1942, 1943 and 1944, the Soviet Union actually seems to have produced nearly as many munitions as Germany. Since Germany had to allocate a growing proportion of her output to the western theatre of war, whilst at the same time the Soviet Union received substantial aid from her western allies—*not, however, exceeding about one-tenth of her own munitions production*—the Soviets during most of the war had at their disposal not only more men, but also more weapons, and the gap widened as the war continued." [13] *

Thus it was the tremendous increase of Russia's industrial strength, and therefore of her military potential, which prevented a decisive German victory even when Germany was able to wage the war to all intents and purposes as a one-front war.

Only a decisive victory for Nazi Germany in the east could pre-

* Italics mine.—F. S.

vent her own ultimate defeat and lead in the best case to a stalemate, because whilst the terribly bloody battles were going on between Germany and Russia in the east, the United States was vigorously engaged in translating her gigantic industrial strength into actual military strength.

The United States entered the second world war under very different political and strategic conditions from those which prevailed when she entered the first world war.

THE POSITION OF THE U.S.A. IN THE FIRST WORLD WAR AND THE SECOND

The United States entered the first world war on her own initiative in 1917, only just a little over a year before its end. At that time there was still a solid Franco-British military front in France, a front which the Germans had not succeeded in breaking up in almost three years of gruelling warfare. Thus when the United States entered the war she was not faced with any difficult strategic questions, and military questions were certainly not affected by any socio-political considerations. After having supported the western powers in the first world war with finance, food, raw materials, weapons and munitions of war generally, she decided that the time had come for her to support them with her armies as well. As when she entered the war the Western Front was intact, and there was only a small German preponderance, if any, over the western powers, a comparatively small effort in relation to her industrial power was enough for U.S. intervention to turn the scale decisively.

During the preliminary phase of the second world war the United States had also supported the western powers with food and raw material supplies, weapons of war and munitions. In the first place she delivered only for cash, but when Great Britain's financial resources ebbed dangerously she introduced the system of lend-lease.

The assistance given to the western powers, and a certain increase in her own military expenditure, had led to a strengthening of the military sector in the United States, and in 1941, before she was pushed into the war, it was greater than it had ever been in her peace-time history.

The fact that the United States was more heavily armed than ever before was well known to both friends and foes, but in itself that did not mean a great deal. The size of the military sector of a country is not something absolute; its significance can be measured only against the military sectors of other countries, in this case against those of Germany and Japan and those of the western powers and the Soviet Union in the years 1940–1941. Compared with the military sectors of the other great powers the military sector of the United States from the outbreak of the war up to Pearl Harbour was very small indeed. No single power, without exception, found itself at war in such a state of unpreparedness as the United States when she was faced with the *fait accompli* of Pearl Harbour.

Let us compare the absolute figures of U.S. military expenditure in the years before the war and in the war years up to Pearl Harbour with the absolute figures of the military expenditure of the other powers, and let us also compare them with her own potential war effort.

Volume of Combat Production of the Major Belligerents [14] *

(in milliards of dollars at 1944 U.S. prices)

	1935–1939.	1940.	1941.
United States	1·5	1·5	4·5
Great Britain	2·5	3·5	6·5
Soviet Union	8	5	8·5
Germany	12	6	6
Japan	2	1	2

If we represent the peak possible production of munitions for each belligerent country by 100, then we get the following very interesting table:

Trend of Combat Munitions Production [15]

	1938.	1939.	1940.	1941.	1942.	1943.	1944.
United States .	2	2	5	11	47	91	100
Great Britain .	4	10	34	59	83	100	100
Soviet Union .	12	20	30	53	71	87	100
Germany. .	16	20	35	35	51	80	100
Japan . .	8	10	16	32	49	72	100

Thus the above figures bear out our contention that there was no single belligerent country which was less prepared for war when it broke out than the United States. On the other hand, this meant that no single country possessed the same tremendous possibilities of still further extending its military sector.

Like all the other capitalist countries which had not organized a war economy in peace time, the United States entered the period of the second world war with a latent and not completely resolved crisis in its economic bones, and this meant that there were large unused reserves of productive capacity and a great volume of unemployment. Two other factors added to American strength. The first was that at no time during the war did her territory experience any fighting, and she was even exempt from bombing. The second was that during the course of the war she was able to build up an enor-

---

* Combat production for the purpose of these statistics includes all aircraft, naval ships, guns, small arms, armoured vehicles, ammunition, electronic and communications equipment.

mous new productive apparatus without any interference from her enemies.

The result was that by 1944 the United States had so increased her munitions production that she was turning out 50 per cent more than Germany and Japan together.

"In 1944 the United States produced over two-fifths of the entire world's munitions output and about 50 per cent more than either all its allies or all its enemies combined." [16]

With the enormous war industrial achievement behind it, the United States intervened in the second world war to a vastly greater extent than in the first. The first world war ended about a year after America's entry into it; the second world war had approximately three and a half years of bitter fighting to go after she became involved.

In the first world war the United States was able to bring about a decision with relatively small forces.

The situation in the second world war was quite different, for three main reasons:

(1) The French army no longer existed and there was no longer a fighting front anywhere in Western Europe.

(2) The Soviet Union was incomparably stronger both industrially and militarily than Tsarist Russia.

(3) The United States had to wage war not only against Germany, but also against Japan.

The U.S.A. Fought a Two-Front War from the Start

In the first world war all the United States was called upon to do was to strengthen an already strong and existing fighting front in France. In the second world war she was faced from the very first day with all the strategic problems resulting from the necessity of waging it on two fronts—against Nazi Germany and against Japan. The United States had to win the war against Japan practically off her own bat, and she had to make an incomparably bigger contribution to the winning of the war in Europe than she had had to do in the first world war.

The logical result of this new world historical situation was that the United States had to develop her military sector to a vastly greater extent than she had been called upon to do during the first world war. The strength of her armies in the second world war was many times greater than in the first world war, and her losses were more than six times as high. It was the greatest military achievement in United States history. In consequence, there has been a lot of talk about America's having waged a "total" war.

Let us point out at once that she did nothing of the sort. Compared with the sacrifices the war imposed on the peoples of Europe and Asia, with the repercussions of the war on Europe and Asia, and with the efforts of both her friends and enemies, the United States did not wage a "total" war at all, but merely a colonial war—a colonial war on a big scale, it is true, but not one which fundamentally affected the lives of her people or her own social structure and political stability.

Being faced from the first day of her entry into the war with the necessity of waging it on two fronts, the United States had to decide which front should have priority, and she soon decided that it would have to be the struggle against Nazi Germany. This was a logical decision, because once Hitler was defeated, then the preponderance of the United States and her allies over Japan would be so enormous that the only question remaining would be the best way to crush Japan most surely and speedily.

If, on the other hand, the United States had decided to give priority to the war against Japan, that might well have called for an excessive concentration of her forces in the Far East, and in the meantime Nazi Germany might have defeated the Soviet Union and concentrated her forces against Great Britain. Thus a victory over Japan would not be decisive, whereas a victory over Nazi Germany certainly would be.

However, the theoretical settlement of this strategic question as to which front should have priority was one thing; it was quite another to decide when and where to set up the second front which would compel Nazi Germany to wage the fatal two-front war.

WHY WAS THE SECOND FRONT SO LONG DELAYED?

It was quite obvious that there could be no second front in the West in 1941; Great Britain alone was not strong enough to mount or sustain an invasion of the European continent. But the second front was not opened in 1942 either, by which time the United States was in the war. And even in 1943 there was no second front, although by that time the Battle of Stalingrad had been fought to the bitter end and lost by Germany, and the Russians were now in a position to mount a great offensive *in summer* which drove back the German armies.

The second front was opened only in 1944. In other words, the Russian had to bear the brunt of the war against Nazi Germany for almost three years, and only in the last year of the war did the Anglo-American forces stage an invasion of the continent and set up a second front which really represented an alleviation of the pressure on the Russian armies.

Before the invasion of the European mainland the Anglo-American forces had landed in North Africa and crossed the Mediterranean to invade Italy. But these operations engaged only small German forces compared with German strength on the eastern front.

Parallel with their landing in North Africa and their invasion of

Italy, the Anglo-American powers had opened up a steadily growing bombing campaign against Germany's big towns and industrial centres. The opinion has often been expressed that these devastating raids represented such an alleviation of the Russian burden that in itself the Anglo-American air offensive against Germany represented a second front. This opinion is not borne out by the facts.

We have already pointed out that at the beginning of the German invasion of the Soviet Union, German armaments production was by no means at its peak. If that peak point is represented by 100, then at the time of the invasion of Russia it was only at 35. Despite all the attacks of the Anglo-American bomber squadrons it rose to 51 in 1942, to 80 in 1943 and to 100 in 1944. In other words, Germany's armaments production almost trebled itself in the period from the first attack on Russia up to the Anglo-American cross-Channel invasion of the European mainland.

This increase was made possible in the first place by the fact that it was only in these years that general standards of living sharply declined in Germany in favour of armaments production and that Germany really began to wage "total" war. Another factor which contributed to the increase was that Germany put much of her armaments production underground, where it could not be affected by bombing. This process was greatly facilitated when Germany—particularly after Speer took over full control of all armaments production—developed a highly decentralized system of production which permitted her to react more elastically to the devastation of individual factories and centres of production.

Of course, all this does not mean that the Anglo-American bombing raids were ineffective and useless, and the undoubted fact is that but for these raids Germany's armaments production would have increased very much more than threefold. However, the equally undoubted fact remains that despite these heavy raids her armaments production increased from 35 to 100, and that in 1942 and 1943 the Russians had to fight against German armies whose armaments grew steadily stronger. Thus the Anglo-American bombing raids on Germany, as valuable as they were, did not represent an adequate substitute for the opening up of a second front on land. The raids were unable to prevent German tanks, artillery, machine-guns and rifles, with all the impedimenta to serve them, reaching the eastern front in steadily increasing numbers.

Thus the opening of the second front in the west did not begin with the Anglo-American air offensive on Germany's towns and industrial centres, and it did not even begin with the landing in North Africa, or the invasion of Sicily, or the subsequent invasion of Italy and the European mainland from the south. It began solely when the Anglo-American forces landed in Normandy.

That was in 1944. And the question which now arises is why did it happen only then and not earlier—or perhaps later?

THE ANGLO–AMERICAN–RUSSIAN COALITION SUBJECT TO QUALIFICATION

This question was the most important question of the second world war once it had become a world war. It was one of the most important questions for the situation in the post-war world, and for the development of the world political relation of forces we know to-day.

Even now it is still impossible to give a final and conclusive answer to it, because many of the details in the whole important complex of questions which it involves have not yet been satisfactorily cleared up. However, the decisive factors which brought about the opening of the second front in 1944 are already more or less clear, so that a preliminary answer to the main question is now possible.

First of all, the second world war was an Anglo–American–Russian coalition war only in a very qualified sense. It was certainly not a coalition war in a political sense, and it was so only conditionally even in a military sense. Long before the United States found herself willy-nilly involved in the war there had been close and friendly co-operation between her and Great Britain, and once the United States was in the shooting war there was a joint Anglo-American general staff. There were constant joint staff discussions on military operations and the closest possible exchange of military information and experiences. And finally, when the second front was launched there was one supreme commander, General Eisenhower, under whose orders both British and U.S. troops fought.

There was no comparable co-operation in the Anglo–American–Russian coalition. There was a Russian war arena, a North African, an Italian and later a French and German, and there were certain arrangements by which the allies kept each other informed about immediately pending operations. But that was about all. There were no joint staff discussions, and the Russians had no direct influence on where and when the Anglo-Americans opened up the second front in Europe. The Russian influence on this question was almost entirely confined to the indirect circumstance that the possibility of a Russian collapse played an important role in Anglo-American decisions, and, in fact, in the last resort it was the unexpected strength and tenacity of Russian resistance which to some extent delayed the opening of the second front.

There were many reasons why complete military co-operation between the Anglo-Americans on the one hand and the Russians on the other was impossible. Quite apart from the fact that the political regimes of the western and eastern allies were so totally different, and quite apart from the fact that geographically the Russian arena of war was so far removed from that of the Anglo-Americans that at no

442

phase of the war did Anglo-American and Russian armies fight side by side on the same front, there was the whole time an undercurrent of mistrust on both sides, and above all the suspicion that the other partner might after all make a separate peace with Germany.

The Anglo-Americans feared that what had happened once—the Nazi-Soviet Pact—could happen again. And their anxiety was particularly marked in the years 1942–1943, when the Russians had to fight alone and bear the brunt of the losses. Their suspicions were again roused when the Russians began to use General Paulus, whom they had captured at Stalingrad, as the mouthpiece of a so-called "Free-German Committee" to make propaganda in Germany for a speedy conclusion of the war. After all, they told themselves, it was quite possible that, following a long-established tradition, the Russians might join with the German generals and the German nationalists after the overthrow of Hitler.

On the other hand, the Russians had their reasons for mistrust and suspicion. They had not forgotten the years before Munich, or Munich itself, at which they had been deliberately cold-shouldered. They knew the attitude of influential Right-wing and Conservative circles in Great Britain, and they knew that there were influential elements in the United States which were opposed to any coalition with the Soviet Union. They knew, and the Anglo-Americans also knew, that long before July 1944 and the unsuccessful attempt on Hitler's life an influential Right-wing Conservative opposition to Hitler in Germany had several times attempted to establish contacts with the Anglo-Americans, and they feared that in the event of Hitler's removal and the overthrow of the Nazi regime in Germany these elements would come to power through the German Army and make a separate peace with the Anglo-American powers, opening Germany's western frontiers to the British and U.S. troops, leaving the Russian forces still fighting on their own territory.

It is quite obvious that with such profound mistrust, and so many reasons for it, there could be no full military coalition of the Anglo-Americans and the Russians.

And apart from these circumstances which hampered any really close and friendly co-operation between the Anglo-Americans and the Russians, there were the completely dissimilar preliminary conditions in this inadequately functioning coalition.

The British were the first to fight, but they were the weakest of the three powers in the coalition, and with the end of the so-called "Blitz" on London and other British towns in 1940–1941, which achieved no decisive results, Britain was safely out of the danger zone.

The Russians, on the other hand, had the enemy on their own soil. They had already lost the greater part of their European provinces, and they were now fighting literally for survival.

443

The United States was by far the most powerful industrial country in the world, but when she was precipitated into the shooting war she was the least prepared of all the belligerent countries to fight it. Thus for the time being, even after the United States had become a belligerent, there was no question of the opening up of any second land front. Once the Japanese offensive had come to a halt, the United States had to create the industrial armament and the purely military conditions for the opening of a second front before it could become a practical proposition.

Part of these conditions was created throughout the course of 1942, and in that year U.S. armaments production was very considerably increased. In 1942 the United States reached approximately the half of her peak potentialities. In other words, in 1942, in absolute figures, her armaments production was bigger than that of the Russians. However, part of this already large production had to be used against Japan, and another part had to be used to organize the complicated and costly transport operations which were necessary over vast distances. The Russians, on the other hand, had the enemy immediately before them on their own soil, so that frequently munitions and supplies had not to be transported very far before they were available for use at the front. Despite these extra difficulties the Americans had to cope with, the amount of armaments which were ready for immediate use at the front was very considerable.

But the Americans suffered at first under another very big disadvantage. In 1942 the German armies had already been fighting for three years, and in that bloody and costly fighting German troops had become seasoned and their leaders had gained practical and tremendously valuable experience in the co-ordinated use of all modern weapons. On the other hand, the vast majority of the American troops were untried and without any war experience, and even those older officers who had had some experience of fighting in the first world war needed some time before they learned to adjust their ideas to the new military conceptions of the second world war.

These were the chief reasons why even the most determined supporters of a second front in the United States realized that it was out of the question for 1942, whilst assuming that it would be feasible for the spring, or at the latest the summer, of 1943. But in this question there was a sharp difference of opinion between Britain and the United States.

Once Hitler had launched his attack on the Soviet Union, Britain was out of the immediate danger zone. It was absolutely out of the question that with the majority of her troops engaged against the Russians on the eastern front, Germany could even seriously consider mounting an overseas invasion of the British Isles. Britain then became an aircraft-carrier for the air offensive against Germany and a training-ground for an ever-increasing army of American soldiers.

Nazi Germany was not capable of defeating Britain as long as she had a war with the Soviet Union on her hands. In fact, until final victory was won in the east, Germany had no chance at all in the west. And even if Nazi Germany did win the final victory in the east and was able to bring back her troops to the west, her chances of staging a successful invasion now that Great Britain had largely succeeded in translating her industrial strength into military strength, and now that the United States was rapidly becoming stronger and had powerful forces already stationed in Great Britain, were slender indeed.

Thus although the British were still interested in prosecuting the war against Nazi Germany to a successful conclusion, they were no longer so desperately interested in doing it as quickly as possible. Of course, every day of the war meant military and economic losses for them, but they were not on the same scale as those suffered by the Russians, who were losing some 5,000 men a day, as compared with British losses of 200 a day. In addition, the British were not suffering gigantic material losses by the devastation of their territory as the Russians were. Thus although the British were interested in waging the coalition war to a successful conclusion they preferred to do so in a way which caused them least losses and offered them the most favourable conditions for the political rebuilding of Europe after the war.

At the same time it is only fair to say that they could see, perhaps better than anyone else, the terrible dangers involved in any miscalculation of the time for a cross-Channel invasion, the terrible dangers involved in a precipitate, over-hasty and inadequately prepared invasion attempt against seasoned German divisions waiting to repel it on the other side. The British were keenly aware that despite Anglo-American command of the sea and the air, there was a big danger that even if the landings were successful the invaders might still be hurled back into the sea. Churchill in particular had not forgotten the experiences of the first world war, in which France lost almost a million and a half dead on the western front and Great Britain not far short of a million. Churchill was therefore determined to avoid anything which might result in such a new and terrible blood-letting for the British people, with its resultant weakening of Great Britain's social organism.

The Russians, of course, were not slow to point out that their losses in man-power during the first world war were much heavier than the combined losses of the British and French, and that this time again, in the years 1941–1943, they had lost vastly more men in the struggle against Nazi Germany than the British. But the answer to that was simple enough: not only was Russia's population much bigger in the first place, but the Russian birth rate and the rate of increase in her population were incomparably greater than those of

Britain, and Russia was therefore in a much better position to stand such admittedly heavy losses.

Thus although Britain had every interest in waging the war against Nazi Germany to a successful conclusion, she was no longer so interested in forcing the pace. She was in favour of waiting until such time as the Anglo-American build-up became so strong that the chances in favour of a cross-channel invasion became practically a certainty, and it could then be carried out as swiftly as possible and with a minimum of losses.

Thus America's efforts to bring about a second land front in Europe had to overcome not only the military technical difficulties which arose out of the fact that she found herself engaged in war which as we have already seen she was ill-prepared to wage, but also the perhaps understandable reluctance of the British to take anything they considered to be an excessive risk, a reluctance whose highly ingenious and articulate mouthpiece was Mr Winston Churchill.

Henry L. Stimson,[17] who constantly urged the necessity of the opening of a second land front as quickly as possible, has given us interesting information concerning the various phases of its preparations.

ANGLO-AMERICAN DIFFERENCES ON THE QUESTION OF THE SECOND FRONT

"The plan for which Stimson * and Marshall were arguing went under the code name of 'Bolero'. It contemplated a maximum build-up of American strength in Great Britain, looking towards a full-scale invasion in the Spring of 1943, with 50 divisions, 60 per cent of them American, on the continent of Europe by the end of that summer. In the event of a desperate crisis on the Russian front in 1942, it also included the alternative possibility of a much smaller 'beach-head' invasion in the autumn of that year. . . . His objective was to secure a decision to invade Europe from the British base at the earliest practicable moment; only developing events could show whether that moment would be in 1942 or 1943."

In a letter dated June 19th, 1942, Stimson wrote:

"After the discussion with Mr Churchill's party here last December the need for a carefully-planned offensive became very evident. Russia has successfully fought off the entire German army for six months. Winter has begun, and the shaken and battered German army would be helpless to renew its offensive for nearly

---

* The book was actually written by McGeorge Bundy, hence the use of the third person in referring to Stimson.—F. S.

six months more. The one thing Hitler rightly dreaded was a second front. In establishing such a front lay our best hope of keeping the Russian army in the war and thus ultimately defeating Hitler. To apply the rapidly developing man-power and industrial strength of America promptly to the opening of such a front was manifestly the only way it could be accomplished."

Now, there was no desperate crisis on the Russian front in 1942, and so the necessity of organizing a "much smaller 'beach-head' invasion in the autumn of that year" did not arise. On the contrary, even without very great Anglo-American assistance the Russians showed themselves to be much stronger than the Americans at least had expected.

In the autumn of 1942 the fortunes of war changed at Stalingrad, and Stimson writes:

"The shift of the Russians from the defensive to a massive counter-attack in the following weeks finally banished the spectre of a German victory in Russia, which had haunted the council table of the western allies for a year and a half."

Thus the victory of the Russians at Stalingrad was the decisive reason why the Americans no longer pressed for at least a "beach-head" invasion of the European mainland in 1942.

But why, at least, was the second front not launched in 1943? The Americans knew very well that neither North Africa nor even Italy represented an effective second front.

"The great commitment in North Africa led inexorably to later operations in the Mediterranean theatre which were certainly a great contribution to victory; equally certainly those operations were unimportant in comparison with the land and air offensive finally launched from Great Britain. If Stimson or Marshall had been Commander-in-Chief the invasion of France would in all probability have been launched in 1943, one year earlier than it actually occurred."

The invasion was not launched in 1943 because the British, led by Winston Churchill, were opposed to it.

"At Casablanca in January 1943 the British again refused to go ahead with any cross-Channel operation in the coming year, and it was therefore agreed that the next great move should be to Sicily."

In the same year that the Anglo-American forces made their first landing in Italy proper, the Russians undertook, at the cost of immense sacrifices, their first successful big summer offensive. By this time there was obviously no further danger that Nazi Germany could defeat the Soviet Union. But the fact that the Germans had suf-

447

fered enormous losses on the eastern front under the hammer-blows of the Russian offensive, the fact that they were compelled to keep the great majority of their forces in the east to repel, if possible, further Russian offensives, and the obvious fact that this weakened their ability to oppose any cross-Channel invasion, were still not enough to dissipate all British objections to the attempt. Even in the summer of 1943 it was still not definitely settled that the invasion should take place in 1944, and in a highly interesting letter addressed to President Roosevelt, dated August 10th, 1943, Stimson writes:

"First, we cannot now rationally hope to be able to cross the Channel and come to grips with our German enemy under a British commander. His Prime Minister and the Chief of the Imperial General Staff are frankly at variance with such a proposal. The shadow of Passchendaele and Dunkirk still hangs too heavily over the imagination of these leaders of his government. Though they have rendered lip-service to the operation, their hearts are not in it and it will require more independence, more faith, and more vigour than it is reasonable to expect we can find in any British commander to overcome the natural difficulties of such an operation carried on in such an atmosphere of his government. There are too many natural obstacles to be overcome, too many possible side avenues of diversion which are capable of stalling and thus thwarting such an operation.

"Second, the difference between us is a vital difference of faith. The American staff believes that only by massing the immense vigour and power of the American and British nations under the overwhelming mastery of the air, which they already exercise far into Northern France, and which can be made to cover our subsequent advance in France just as it has in Tunis and Sicily, can Germany really be defeated and the war brought to a real victory.

"On the other side, the British theory (which cropped up again and again in unguarded sentences of the British leaders with whom I have just been talking) is that Germany can be beaten by a series of attritions in northern Italy, in the Eastern Mediterranean, in Greece, in the Balkans, in Roumania and other satellite countries. . . .

"To me, in the light of the post-war problems we shall face, that attitude . . . seems terribly dangerous. We are pledged quite as clearly as Great Britain to the opening of a real second front. None of these methods of pinprick warfare can be counted on by us to fool Stalin into the belief that we have kept our pledge."

The final decision was irrevocably taken at the conference in Teheran, and Stimson goes on:

"At Teheran the President was reinforced by the blunt firmness of Marshal Stalin, whose comments on the doubts and diversionary suggestions of Mr Churchill Stimson followed in the minutes of the meetings with great interest. 'Overlord' * became at last a settled commitment. . . . Marshal Stalin emphatically stated at Teheran that he could not consider the 'Overlord' promise definite until a supreme commander had been appointed, and under this spur the President reached his decision in a meeting with Marshall at Cairo."

Stimson was keenly aware of the danger to the coalition represented by the constant postponement of the second-front project in view of the tremendous losses the Russians were suffering.

"In 1943 and 1944 Stimson's concern for a proper second front led him to a certain sympathy with Russian suspicion of Western motives; not to open promptly a strong western front in France, he felt, would be to leave the real fighting to Russia. During the discussions at Washington in May 1943, Stimson told the President 'that the argument on the other side reminded me of the story of Lincoln with regard to General Franz Sigel, who, Lincoln said, was a pretty poor general, who, although he couldn't skin the deer, could at least hold a leg. Those who oppose invasion are trying to arrange this matter so that Britain and America hold the leg for Stalin to skin the deer, and I think that will be dangerous business for us at the end of the war. Stalin won't have much of an opinion of people who have done that, and we will not be able to share much of the post-war world with him'."

The Teheran decision was actually carried out in 1944. The second front in Western Europe was duly opened and the Anglo-American armaments preponderance proved so great, particularly as the German armies had been very considerably weakened by years of bloody fighting in the east, that after the successful landing and despite one or two set-backs, the issue was never in doubt.

Thus 1944–1945 was the year of the war on two fronts for Germany, the only year in which Germany had to fight such a war, and the year of Germany's complete military and political eclipse.

How were the armies equipped which brought about the total defeat of Germany in this one year of real coalition war? The gigantic armaments production of the United States was naturally showing itself very clearly in this year.

"The rapid success of the invasion of the continent in 1944 finds its counterpart among these figures in the massive preponderance of the accumulated and current production of munitions in the hands of the attacking forces. The United States, the United Kingdom and Canada in the eighteen months preceding the invasion, and during the six months after its start, produced over

* "Overlord" was the code name for the cross-channel invasion project.—F. S.

60 milliard dollars worth of munitions if it is assumed that slightly over one-half of the American and about four-fifths of British and Canadian armaments output was destined for the European theatre. Germany and her satellites, on the other hand, in that period only turned out less than 15 milliard dollars worth for use on the western front if total output be apportioned on the basis of estimated troops strength each year on the two fronts. *The Allies' advantage was thus of the order of* 5 : 1, a figure that may help to explain the relatively short duration of operations in the west." [18] *

What was the situation with regard to the Russian armies? Before the Anglo-Americans opened up the second front they had supported the Russians with war materials and weapons. In 1941–1942 that support was not of any very great volume, and that was due to the fact that it was only in 1942 that the United States really began to carry out her enormous programme of armaments, and at first, of course, after Pearl Harbour, her efforts had chiefly to be concentrated in the Pacific.

Thus up to the Battle of Stalingrad the Russians had to rely more or less on their own strength and resources. It was primarily their efforts which flung back the German armies and made their own offensive possible.

But even after Stalingrad the picture did not change very materially. U.S. aid for Russia certainly increased, but at no time did it amount to more than 10 per cent of Russia's own armaments production, though it must be said that its military significance was often far more than 10 per cent, because the Americans helped the Russians primarily at the points where they were weakest—for instance, a large supply of American lorries greatly strengthened the mobility of the Russian armies at the decisive moments.

American aid to the Soviet Union never rose to more than 10 per cent of Russia's total armaments production and so, as the following figures show, it was never greater than the total of Canadian armaments production.

Russian and Canadian Combat Munitions Production [19]

(in milliards of dollars)

	1942.	1943.	1944.
Russian production	11·5	14	16
Canadian production	1	1·5	1·5

As a result, and despite American aid, Russian armaments superiority on the eastern front was only very small.

* Italics mine.—F. S.

"On the eastern front the advantage always lay with the forces disposing of the larger quantities of material—up to 1942 the Germans, thereafter the Russians—even though the material superiority on neither side ever approached that prevailing in the west. For that reason the Russians' ability and willingness to expend military man-power on a lavish scale was of particular importance for the final outcome in the east." [20]

On the eastern front the Russians stood almost alone in the struggle against Nazi Germany for three years, and even in the last stages of the war their armaments were only slightly superior to those of Nazi Germany. In the west the Anglo-American forces, supported by an armaments production many times stronger than that of Germany, began the invasion in the last stage of the war with big armies and with an armaments preponderance of between 4 : 1 and 5 : 1 in their favour. That was the armaments situation in the coalition war, and it explains why the losses of the Russians and of the Anglo-American forces were so unequal. It explains why the Russians, with a population which was rather smaller than that of Great Britain and the United States together, suffered a death roll of 7·5 millions, or more than ten times as great as that of the Anglo-American forces combined. At the same time more Germans died on the eastern front than on all the other fronts combined.

When the German armies finally collapsed the Russians had not only driven through all the countries which lay between Russia and Germany, but they already occupied large tracts of German territory.

If the invasion and the opening of the second front in France had taken place in 1943, there is no doubt that the Anglo-American forces would have suffered very much heavier casualties than they actually did; but, as against that, the course of world history might have been different: there might have been no Soviet Russian Empire extending to the Elbe.

THE WAR IN ASIA

The main battlefield of the second world war was in Europe, and it was there that the decision was obtained. By comparison with the European conflict, the war in Asia was never more than a side-show, but—and in this respect the situation was very different from that which existed in the first world war—this war was an Asiatic war. It was an Asiatic war in a double sense: it was fought in Asia and it was fought about Asia.

It was a different kind of war to that which was being fought out in Europe, where well-equipped armies of millions of men wrestled with each other bitterly for years, and where at last, in a two-front war, the armies of Russia, Great Britain and the United States finally defeated and crushed the German army.

451

Throughout the war in Asia there was never any comparable struggle of millions of men with modern equipment, neither in the period which preceded the beginning of the war in Europe nor in the period after the United States was drawn into the war.

Not with Pearl Harbour, but approximately two years before, the Sino-Japanese war took on a certain static character. From that time on there were no large-scale operations in that conflict. There was guerilla warfare against the Japanese on a large scale, and from time to time there was fighting between the Chinese Nationalists under Chiang Kai-shek and the Chinese communists under Mao Tse-tung, and the hostility between these two Chinese groups was never fully buried even in face of the Japanese attack. In other words, the civil war in China did not disappear altogether even in the period of Japanese aggression; it was always at least latent.

In the other colonial and semi-colonial countries the national-revolutionary struggle for freedom overshadowed all other interests, so much so that social antagonisms were greatly diminished, and even the burning question of agrarian reform was largely shelved in the interests of the common national front. This was not the case in China.

The Civil War and the Sino-Japanese War

China was never so completely subjugated by foreign imperialist powers as India or the Dutch East Indies, and the main reason for this was that a number of foreign imperialist powers intrigued against each other and jockeyed each other to obtain the biggest share of the booty. Thus China enjoyed a greater degree of independence than the other Asiatic countries, and this was perhaps the main reason why the social struggles and the struggles for agrarian reform had produced an agrarian revolutionary movement even in this period.

However, despite great social tension, which had broken out again and again in civil war, the first years of the struggle against Japan's encroachments had led to the formation of a Chinese united front between the Chiang Kai-shek regime and the Chinese communists for the defence of China against foreign aggression. This united front was unable to prevent Japan from seizing China's coastal towns, but it certainly saved China from complete collapse in face of the Japanese invader.

Apart from the big towns and a strip of territory along the railways, Japan was unable to break the resistance of the Chinese guerillas. During the first years of the war of defence against Japan the Chiang Kai-shek regime had made certain social concessions to the masses of the people. If the Chinese people were to continue their persistent guerilla struggle in the rear of the Japanese, then at least they had to be given something to fight for. The prospect of remaining semi-slaves of the landlord clique allied with Chiang Kai-shek even after a victory over Japan was not sufficiently attractive to make any man want to risk his life in the guerilla war against Japan.

The united front which was formed against Japan was not maintained throughout the whole of the struggle, and one of the reasons for this—as odd as it may sound—was the entry of the United States into the war.

Once the United States, with all her enormous strength and resources, was in the war and determined to crush Japan, the Chiang Kai-shek Government realized that victory over the Japanese was only a question of time, and it was no longer particularly interested in a united front of the whole Chinese people in order to free China from the Japanese: the Americans were obviously going to do it in any case, and there was no need for any very violent Chinese exertions.

After the loss of China's towns and ports to Japan the feudal reactionary clique had become dominant in the Chiang Kai-shek Government, and because of its character it was deeply interested not so much in the liberation of China from Japanese imperialism as in just how that liberation was to be brought about. Or, to put it differently, it was interested primarily in the question of who would hold power in China when the Japanese had been ejected.

If the liberation of China and the defeat of Japanese imperialism were brought about in a fashion which strengthened the progressive social forces of the country, if a real people's war developed against Japan, then this involved the danger that the final defeat of Japan might also mean the victory of the masses of the Chinese people over the old feudal reactionary forces represented in the Chiang Kai-shek Government, and that, in its turn, meant a fundamental change in the whole structure of China. The feudal landlords and the reactionary clique who had the upper hand in Chiang Kai-shek's Government had no interest whatever in a victory obtained over Japan in such a fashion, and therefore as the United States exerted more and more strength in the struggle against Japan, so the military efforts of the Chiang Kai-shek Government declined in the strictest ratio.

General Stilwell, the Commander-in-Chief of the U.S. forces engaged in China, who was at the same time officially Chiang Kai-shek's Chief of Staff, was finally compelled to recognize that all his efforts to develop the Chinese Nationalist Army into an efficient fighting force were nullified by the corrupt feudal system which Chiang and his friends represented, and "The Stilwell Papers" declare:

"Chiang Kai-shek is the head of a one-party government supported by a Gestapo and a party secret service. . . . He will not make an effort to fight seriously. He wants to finish the war coasting, with a big supply of material so as to perpetuate his regime.

He has blocked us for three years and he will continue to do so. . . . A gang of thugs with the one idea of perpetuating themselves and their machine. Money, influence and position the only considerations of the leaders. Intrigue, double-crossing, lying reports. Hands out for anything they can get; their only idea to let someone else do the fighting; false propaganda on their 'heroic struggle'; indifference of 'leaders' to their men. Cowardice rampant, squeeze paramount, smuggling over duty, colossal ignorance and stupidity of staff; total inability to control factions and cliques; continued oppression of masses. . . . And we are manœuvred into the position of having to support this rotten regime and glorify its figurehead, the all-wise great patriot and soldier, Peanut *—my God!" [21]

Thus the Japanese controlled a great area of China for years without having to fight very hard either to conquer it in the first place or to maintain their occupation of it afterwards. In the territory occupied by the Japanese the old Chinese administration was largely abolished. Where the old ruling clique had not fled they now willingly became Japanese puppets, and only in very exceptional cases did they take an active part in the guerilla warfare of the people against the Japanese. When Japan was finally defeated and forced to withdraw her troops it was naturally not difficult for the Chinese communists to take control in these areas, because all the credit and authority of the old ruling classes had been hopelessly compromised in the period of Japanese occupation.

"From its tiny beginnings in 1921, the Chinese communist movement during World War II grew into a *de facto* government with an army and an administration which controlled the countryside of North China. This growth was mainly a war-time development. During the war the modernized upper-class government of the Kuomingtang, having been pushed out of the scene by the Japanese occupation of the modern centres and communication routes, was unable to maintain its former control over the North China countryside where it had never been as deeply entrenched as in the South. By their excesses the Japanese invaders antagonized the peasants and opened the way for a people's revolution under communist leadership and in the name of national resistance." [22]

JAPAN'S WAR AND THE EUROPEAN COLONIAL EMPIRES

Not only China, but also a considerable area of the colonial empires of the European imperialist powers, was turned into a battlefield, and the indissoluble unity of political, social and economic questions became clearly visible here too.

* Stilwell's favourite term of contempt for Chiang Kai-shek.—F. S.

The parasitic nature of the policy pursued by the European imperialist powers in their colonial empires, their alliance with the old feudal strata in the exploitation of the masses of the native population, and the extremely low level of general living standards for these people were now revealed to the whole world in all their stark reality.

Nowhere in any of the colonial empires were the native population prepared to join hands with the military forces of the European imperialist powers to defend their country against the Japanese invasion, and because the natives refused to fight for their oppressors against the Japanese—some of them even welcomed the Japanese with their slogan "Asia for the Asiatics!" and collaborated with them as the supposed liberators of the Asiatic peoples from generations, sometimes centuries, of oppression by the European imperialist powers—the Japanese did not meet with any very great military difficulties in their enormous conquests.

The number of Europeans in the colonial empires was small, and therefore relatively small Japanese contingents were sufficient to sweep them away. The millions of natives watched the struggle indifferently, and often their sympathies were with the Japanese.

But although they took no active part in the struggle, its lessons were not lost on them. The ease with which the Japanese won their victories showed them how weak the position of the white "master race" had become. Tens of millions of natives in the colonial countries of Asia have not forgotten this lesson of the second world war, although the war is now years past. In other words, the almost unresisting collapse of a considerable part of the structure of European imperialist domination in Asia under the blows—taps, one might almost say—of the Japanese invasion forces, and the conclusions drawn from it by the masses of the native population, were to represent an important factor in the subsequent political relation of forces in Asia after the second world war.

INDIA AND THE WAR IN ASIA

India was the biggest object of imperialist exploitation in Asia, and never at any time throughout the war was India the scene of hostilities.

We have already seen that even before Japan formally plunged into the second world war, the antagonism between the British Government and the Indian nationalist movement had become very acute. Whilst the war was on, the former found no means of satisfactorily resolving the conflict. Proposals for half a loaf instead of full independence carried to India by Sir Stafford Cripps during the war as the representative of the British war-time National Government, a coalition of the Conservative and Labour Parties, were rejected by the Indians. In the meantime the Indian national-revolutionary movement went from strength to strength, and it became so widespread that it even affected a considerable part of the Indian Army, both Hindus and Mohammedans.

Although India was not directly involved in the fighting, the leaders of the Indian national-revolutionary movement closely followed the successful Japanese drive in neighbouring areas of Asia, parts of which were European colonial territory. The Indians, too, were not slow in recognizing just how weak the European imperialist powers had become, and thus the almost unresisting collapse of European colonialism in the areas bordering on India was one of the factors which contributed to accelerating and strengthening the Indian national-revolutionary struggle for independence from British imperialism.

U.S. CONDUCT OF THE WAR IN ASIA

There is no need for us to go into any great detail concerning the purely military side of the war in Asia. Like Nazi Germany in Europe, Japan, as the aggressor, won important preliminary successes, including the destruction of important American naval units at Pearl Harbour, and successes in the Philippines, successes against the Dutch and French colonial empires, and against the British—for example, at Singapore.

But Japanese successes could only be lasting on two conditions: either if the Japanese could in some way prevent the United States from translating her mighty industrial strength into military power, or if the war in Europe took up the attention of the United States to such an extent that only very little of her strength remained for use in the Asiatic theatre of war.

In fact, Japan's leaders had reckoned with the fulfilment of both these conditions. It was not long before they were made to realize that they had miscalculated.

By 1942 Japan's drive in the Pacific had been brought to a standstill. The result was that Japan had no means of preventing the steady build-up of America's military power behind the impassable barrier of the Pacific, which, although it started later than the war efforts of all the other powers, was tremendously efficient and fairly rapid once it did start.

The following table shows the tremendous change which came over the relationship between American and Japanese armaments strength as the years passed:

Volume of Combat Munitions Production [23]

(in milliards of dollars at 1944 U.S. prices)

	1935–1939.	1940.	1941.
United States . . .	1·5	1·5	4·5
Japan	2	1	2

	1942.	1943.	1944.
United States . . .	20	38	42
Japan	3	4·5	6

Thus although during the war the Japanese were ablaze to increase their armaments production threefold, the Americans increased theirs almost tenfold in the same period, and in the years 1942 to 1944 America's armaments production was approximately seven times as great as that of Japan.

As the Russians had proved themselves much stronger than had been expected, a quite considerable part of this gigantic U.S. armaments production was made available for use in the war against Japan.

"At the time of Pearl Harbour, Japan's production of munitions may have been substantial compared to that available to her enemies for the Pacific war. Already in 1942, however, the United States produced about twice as many combat munitions for use in the Pacific as Japan, and increased that lead in 1943 and 1944." [24]

Of the sevenfold American superiority in armaments production approximately half was ear-marked for use in the Pacific.

"For the Pacific theatre of war the United Nations had available 70 milliard dollars worth of munitions, of which the United States contributed at least four-fifths. Total Japanese munitions production from 1935 through the middle of 1945 amounted to not much over 20 milliard dollars." [25]

In view of this tremendous American superiority in armaments production over Japan, and after the Japanese drive had been brought to a standstill in 1942, it was an easy matter for the Americans to take the offensive systematically in the Pacific, and that offensive brought them nearer and nearer to Japan herself.

The war against Japan was practically won by the United States alone. The Russians did not at first declare war on Japan because they needed all their military strength for the operations against Nazi Germany. But in this period they did hold down a certain section of the Japanese army in Manchuria. Only after the Anglo-American cross-Channel invasion had taken place and maintained its footing, thus making victory over Nazi Germany a certainty, did the Russians agree to declare war on Japan. At that time the atom bomb had not been successfully tested, and American military circles reckoned with the necessity of an invasion before Japan could be defeated, just as a cross-Channel invasion had been necessary to defeat

Nazi Germany. In this case, of course, an attack on the Japanese forces in Manchuria by the Russians would have accelerated victory. That was the basis on which, in the final negotiations with the Soviet Government, important concessions were made in return for Soviet agreement to take part in the war against Japan.

However, an invasion proved unnecessary. After the explosion of two atom bombs over Hiroshima and Nagasaki, Japan sued for peace.

As a result of the use of the atom bomb there was no clash of modern mass armies even in the final phase of the war in Asia. In the first phase of the war, when Japan invaded China, she needed no very large armies for the purpose, and the same applied to her conquest of the Philippines and the colonial territory of the European imperialist powers.

When the United States launched her counter-offensive the Japanese were driven out of numerous islands on the way across the Pacific, but in these operations also not very large armies were employed. The combat forces in action were never even of the order of 50,000 strong.

During the latter part of the war American superiority in the air proved to be so overwhelming that there was no need for any fighting in Japan proper. The Japanese land forces in Manchuria surrendered when Japan surrendered, and the Russians had no need to engage in any very difficult fighting. Thus Japan's armies, which had been built up over a long period of years, lost their share of the second world war without ever having been used on a mass scale— unlike the armies of all the other main belligerent powers. For this reason Japanese losses were incomparably smaller than those of the Russians and Germans, for example.

The use of the atom bomb made it unnecessary to invade Japan and brought the war in the Pacific to a sudden end. There was only a short period between the end of the war in Europe and the end of the war in the Pacific.

Japan lost the second world war in much the same circumstances as Germany lost the first world war: her own territory was not fought over and her own people were not direct witnesses of her defeat.

Another important point was that the old ruling caste was in power in Japan right up to the last day of the war, and this fact was of great significance for the subsequent relation of forces in Asia after the war.

QUANTITATIVE EFFECTS OF THE SECOND WORLD WAR

In order to understand the social and political relation of forces which is beginning to develop as a result of the second world war, we must first of all examine the basis from which this development started.

What were the direct and numerically calculable effects of the second world war? If we compare them in certain spheres with those of the first world war the difference will become clear.

The first world war was essentially a European war which was won by an Anglo–American–French coalition against Germany one year after the victory of the November Revolution in Russia. After over four years of war Great Britain and France together had lost rather more than two million dead, and Germany had lost about the same number. Thus the European industrial countries had suffered more or less equally, and at the same time their industrial decline was more or less of the same order. Russia, on the other hand, lost about four million dead, or as many as all the other combatants together, and a large area of her European territory had been fought over. The decline in her industrial production was also greater than that of the other powers.

The non-European countries which had taken part in the war had not been deeply involved. The United States had used only a relatively small part of her strength, and Japan had hardly been engaged at all. The United States suffered very few man-power losses and her industrial production actually increased. And at the end of the first world war there was no political vacuum in Asia, where very little fighting had taken place. And there was only a very temporary one in Europe, because Germany remained a political unit and was deprived of only a small part of her sovereignty, whilst the break-up of the old Austro-Hungarian Empire was soon followed by the establishment of a series of small independent succession States.

The second world war was won in Europe by an Anglo–American–Russian military coalition, and it was won in Asia practically by the United States alone.

Military Losses Unequal

The direct effects of the second world war on the chief belligerent powers were very varied. Let us begin with the question of military losses, the point about which we are, relatively speaking, fairly well informed.

George C. Marshall,[26] U. S. War Secretary, gives the following figures for dead and missing:

Soviet Union: 7·5 million dead, or one in every 22 of its 1940 population.

United States: 295,904 dead, or one in every 500 of the 1940 population.

United Kingdom: approximately 305,770 dead, or one in every 150 of the 1940 population.

The figures for the U.K. refer only to the British Isles; the total number of dead for Great Britain and the British Commonwealth was 452,570, or 0·08 per cent of the total population.

France: 200,000 dead, or 1 in every 200 of the 1940 population.

Germany: 2,850,000 dead, or one in every 25 of the 1940 population.

Italy: 300,000 dead, or one in every 150 of the 1940 population.

Japan: 1·5 million dead, or one in every 46 of the 1940 population.

China: 2·2 million dead, or one in every 200 of the 1940 population; excluding Manchuria and not including the six years of "undeclared" Sino-Japanese warfare that began in 1931.

"The total cost to the principal belligerents, both Allied and Axis, in military personnel killed and missing in battle exceeded 15,000,000. The very considerable costs to the smaller countries, particularly Poland and the nations in south-eastern Europe, added hundreds of thousands more to the total."

These figures are very illuminating. They throw light both on the prosecution of the war and on the situation which developed after the war.

The United States was one of the decisive victors. She fought the war with the employment of all her vast resources. She was longer at war this time than in the first world war, and she experienced very heavy fighting both in Europe and in Asia. In consequence, her losses were much greater than they were in the first world war. On the other hand—and in this respect there is a parallel to the first world war as far as the United States is concerned—her losses were still small in relation to those of the European powers, in particular Germany and Russia, and they were also small in relation to Japanese losses. In the second world war, as in the first, the United States was the country least affected.

Thus as far as military man-power losses was concerned the difference between the United States and the European big powers was much the same in the second world war as it had been in the first. The situation in the second world war as between the European powers was very different. In the first world war the combined losses of Great Britain and France were approximately the same as those of Germany. This time French military man-power losses were almost negligible by comparison, because, although France had mass armies in the field, she did not wage war with them for long. And although Great Britain waged the war from beginning to end, her losses this time were very much smaller than in the first world war, when she had fought for over four years with rapidly growing armies engaged in bitter fighting on the European mainland. This time she experienced hard fighting on a big scale only in the first phase of the war, which ended with Hitler's lightning victory, and in the final phase of the European war, when she invaded Europe together with the United States.

The result was that in the second world war *the combined British and French losses were hardly one quarter of those suffered by Germany.* On the other hand, Germany's losses this time, even allowing for the fact that they included the Austrian dead, were greater than in the first world war.

Once again the Russians suffered exceptionally heavy losses. Their losses were bad enough in the first world war, but up to the November Revolution she had waged war only for three years, and she had never had more than a relatively small part of the German army against her. In the second world war, however, Russia had to fight for about four years, and this time, at least during the first three years, she had to face by far the major part of Germany's military strength, and even in the final year of the war she had to cope with more than half the German Army.

As the Russians had to fight for a long time with inferior armaments, and as even in the final year they never enjoyed any very great superiority in this respect, their losses were very heavy. They were not only heavier than in the first world war, but they were as heavy as the combined losses of all the other belligerents.

Russia's losses in the second world war were almost twice as great as the combined American, British, French, German and Italian losses—i.e. the losses of those countries which together represented the capitalist centre of world industrial production. Russia's losses were more than eight times as great as the combined losses of all her allies, although their combined populations were much larger than hers.

Her victory over a country which was so superior in industrial production and which she had to fight practically on her own for the greater part of the war, cost her a tremendous price in blood and treasure.

Unlike the first world war, the second was also an Asiatic war in which both the Chinese and the Japanese suffered heavy casualties. But because Japan never had cause to engage in large-scale fighting either against the Russians or the Americans, her total losses, even including the casualties of the protracted war against China, did not approach, for example, those of the Russians.

As far as China's losses are concerned, it must be pointed out that the Chinese figures are not likely to be very accurate. In addition, owing to the nature of the Sino-Japanese war, which largely consisted of guerilla activity behind the Japanese lines and in the territories occupied by the Japanese, it is often not possible to draw any very clear dividing line between military and civilian casualties.

During the first world war there were no very great civilian losses in any of the belligerent countries. This was not the case in the second world war. The barbarity with which the Nazis waged war against the Soviet Union, and also the bombings of towns and indus-

461

trial centres carried out in varying degree by all the combatants, caused very heavy civilian losses. But here, too, the losses of the various belligerents were by no means on the same scale. Like military losses, civilian losses in the second world war were not heaviest in the defeated countries and lightest in the victorious countries. Roughly speaking, the order of magnitude was as follows: in the United States there were no civilian casualties at all; there were comparatively few in France and Western Europe generally; rather more in Great Britain and Japan; still more in Germany; and they were gigantic in Eastern Europe, the Soviet Union and China.

The inequality of military losses as between the various belligerent countries is thus reinforced by the inequality of civilian losses. Once again the United States was in the most favourable position. She had no civilian losses at all, and she never had to suffer air bombings. Great Britain and Western Europe suffered losses, but not heavy ones. Germany's losses were very much greater than in the first world war. Victorious Russia had more civilian losses than defeated Germany, Great Britain and Western Europe generally combined.

The Difference in Productive Developments Enormous

An analogous trend was visible in productive developments during the second world war. Both the similarities and the differences of the two wars are very clear. All countries entered the first world war after a period of long prosperity, and none of them had any very large reserves of unutilized productive capacity, or any very great degree of unemployment. In view of the fact that the various economies of the belligerent powers had been working more or less to capacity before the war, the war in Europe led to a big decline of industrial production, and its scale was more or less the same for the Entente powers and Germany—namely, approximately one third.

In Russia, become Soviet Russia, the civil war following immediately on the war in Europe caused a very much greater decline in industry.

On the other hand, industrial production in Japan, whose part in the war was negligible, and in the United States increased.

As in the first world war, so in the second, there was a great difference between productive developments in the United States and in Europe. U.S. production rose once again whilst European industrial production declined. However, this similarity should not blind us to the very great difference.

Like Western Europe, the United States entered the second world war with an unresolved crisis in her economic bones, with a great part of her industrial capacity unutilized and with unemployment totalling many millions. The full utilization of her productive capacity on the one hand, plus a big programme of new construction on the other, produced an increase in U.S. industrial production not of 15 per cent this time, but of more than 50 per cent. It was thus paradoxical that at no period in her history did the United States experience such a tremendous increase of industrial production as in the years of the second world war.

This enormous increase of U.S. industrial production took place at a time when the second world war was bringing about a great fall in industrial production in other countries. However, like the military losses, the production losses were far from being equally distributed amongst the European belligerent powers.

Like the United States, Great Britain and France entered the second world war suffering from an unresolved economic crisis, with a great deal of their productive capacity unutilized and with large armies of unemployed workers. The war abolished unemployment everywhere in Europe, just as it did in the United States. For the first time since 1921 Britain's economic system was working at full blast and without a reserve army of unemployed in the background.

When we consider that apart from the first phase of the war, which ended with Hitler's lightning victory over France, Great Britain had comparatively large military forces on the continent for only about a year, it is readily understandable that her industrial production did not drop so steeply in the second world war, and that after its conclusion she did not find it difficult to recover her pre-war level of production and even to exceed it. Much the same was true of France. If we recall (cf. Part Three of this book) that in 1938—the last year before the outbreak of war—the industrial production of France was more than a quarter below the level of her production in the last year of prosperity, 1929, it is clear that she possessed strong reserves of unutilized productive power when she entered the war. If her industrial productive capacity had been used to the full in 1938 she would have produced approximately 30 per cent more goods than she actually did in that year.

During the first world war France was an arena of hostilities for over four years. In the second world war that was true for only a few weeks whilst Hitler's armies rolled forward to crush her, and then again, but only for a comparatively small part of the country, when the cross-Channel invasion got under way. Once again, therefore, it is not surprising that France and Belgium, like Great Britain, did not take very long after the war to recover their pre-war productive levels, and by no means so long as it took them after the first world war.

That was the position for the victorious countries in the west. The situation in Germany, the defeated country, was very different. After the second world war there was no similarity in industrial developments in Great Britain and France on the one hand and Germany on the other, as there had been after the first world war. Whilst Great Britain and France suffered smaller productive losses in

463

the second world war than they had in the first, Germany suffered much heavier losses. Nazi Germany entered the second world war with a productive apparatus working at full blast and without any reserve armies of unemployed workers. But in the second world war it was not only her outlying districts which were fought over, but practically the whole country as the Russian armies advanced from the east and the Anglo-American armies from the west.

In addition, her towns and industrial centres had been targets for the Anglo-American bombers for years. Thus this time there was not only the "normal" decline in production as a result of the indirect effects of war, as in the first world war, but also a decline as a result of the direct destruction of factories and works and the devastation of towns.

For all these reasons there was a great difference between productive developments in the individual belligerent countries of Europe, and the inequality was reinforced by industrial developments in the Soviet Union. The end of the first world war found the new Soviet Russia still engaged in civil war, having already experienced a year of it. The end of the second world war saw the victorious armies of the Soviet Union in Berlin.

By the time the first world war came to an end, and after the November Revolution and a year of civil war, industrial production in Soviet Russia was at its lowest ebb. At the end of the second world war the industrial production of the Soviet Union was about three-fifths of its peace-time volume. By the following year, 1946, it had already risen to 70 per cent of the peace-time volume. Thus the decline in industrial production during the second world war was more or less of the same order as that of the capitalist countries of Europe in the first world war.

At the same time we should take into consideration in this connection the fact that the decline of industrial production in Russia's European provinces—which were bitterly fought over in both directions, taken by the Germans, recaptured by the Russians, often changing hands several times—was very much greater than the general average, and that the direct destruction in these provinces was often even greater than the destruction in Germany. The comparatively favourable overall situation was due primarily to a trend which had been operative for some time before the outbreak of war—namely, the concentration of new industrial production in the eastern provinces, and in particular the Asiatic provinces, of the Soviet Union beyond reach of the German armies and even of the German bombers.

The industrial productive position during the second world war was thus: tremendous increase in the United States, comparative stability, with perhaps minor decline, in Great Britain and Western Europe generally, big productive decreases in Germany, still bigger decreases in the European provinces of the Soviet Union, together with big increases in the Asiatic provinces.

Thus productive developments during the second world war were far from being uniform for all the belligerent countries. The increase of production in the United States was greater than the decline of production in the heart of Europe and the decline in Asia combined.

The result of all this was a phenomenon for which there is no parallel in world history—namely that *at the end of the second world war, which brought unexampled destruction to many countries, the world as a whole produced more than it did before that war.*

Incidentally, this is another example of the fallacy of talking in our time about *world* production, or attaching any importance to the average of world production, because this average is the result of a variety of factors, many of them contradictory.

We can certainly say with truth that the second world war was the most devastating in the history of mankind. But at the same time it is equally true to say that it produced little or no quantitative change in the total of world industrial production. It is an irony of history that the essential unity of the world should become manifest during a war whose effects on the big powers engaged in it were many degrees more variable than they were during the first world war.

The primarily European character of the first, so-called, world war, was demonstrated, amongst other things, by the fact that European production declined considerably, whilst non-European production increased. The Eurasian character of the second world war was demonstrated, amongst other things, by the fact that during the war Japanese production declined very considerably, partly because Japan was greatly dependent on imports from her empire and from other countries, and partly because of the direct effects of air warfare against her towns and industrial centres. The decline of Japanese industrial production to one-third of its peace-time volume was far greater—twice as great—than the decline of European industrial production during the first world war.

This short summary of the direct and quantitatively measurable effects of the second world war on the main belligerent countries, including their military and civilian losses and their productive developments, gives us a picture of the basis from which developments proceeded in the post-war period.

However, these limited factors are by no means sufficient to allow us to analyse adequately the relation of world forces which exists to-day as a result of the war.

Only on the assumption that the countries which waged the second world war had emerged from it as independent political powers, as they entered it, and that thus there had been no fundamental shifting of power relations; that, further, the relation of the imperialist countries to their colonial empires had remained more or less the same, and that the process of social transformation which was so decisive for the whole period between the two wars had not been materially affected, would our previous analysis more or less cover the essential tendencies of world developments.

But, as we have seen, these assumptions cannot be made.

As a result of the second world war there have been decisive changes in power relations as between the leading countries, together with limitations of, and threats to, the political sovereignty of countries which were formerly independent sovereign States. As a result of the second world war a new period of imperialist development has opened up. Further, the process of social transformation has not only continued, but in some places has greatly intensified.

Our analysis must therefore be continued with regard to these various points if we are to form the fullest possible picture of the world situation to-day.

However, before we go on to this we must turn our attention elsewhere for a while. We have already spoken a great deal about war and its direct and indirect effects on the world, and we have done so because in the first half of the twentieth century the character of war has changed to such an extent that any analysis of capitalism which failed to take this change, with all its consequences, into account would inevitably break down at decisive points.

Thus before we proceed to analyse the relation of forces which has come about in the world as a result of the second world war we must first systematically analyse the essential change which has taken place in the nature of war.

PART V

THE WORLD OF TO-DAY

THE CHANGE IN THE NATURE OF WAR

CAPITALISM IS POSSESSED of tremendous dynamic force. It has changed social life in the world at a more rapid rate than any previous method of production.

Side by side with this transformation has gone a change in the nature of war.

During the several thousand years of human history with which we are more or less acquainted there have been numerous wars. Those wars were as different from each other as the social systems within whose framework they took place.

> "Half-educated Tartars, the republics of the old world, feudal lords and trading towns of the middle ages, kings in the eighteenth century and, finally, rulers and peoples of the nineteenth century, all waged war in their own way, waged it differently and with different methods and different aims." [1]

Thus wrote Clausewitz in his famous book on war, published after his death. Clausewitz was born in 1780, the son of an officer who had served in Prussia under Frederick the Great. He lived in a period of transition from one form of warfare to another. He grew up in Prussia, whose army was organized according to the principles of a feudal State, and he lived to see the armies of Prussia and of the other European States suffer defeat after defeat at the hands of the French armies under Napoleon.

Napoleon won these victories not merely because he was a great general, but because he was also, up to a point, the heir of the French Revolution, and as such he had re-organized, modernized and, as far as it was possible at the time in a country still dominated by agricultural production, turned the French Army into a mass army, a people's army.

Living in the transition between two periods, a time which decisively changed the form of armies and the nature of war, Clausewitz was well aware of the various historical characters of warfare. He recognized the decisive influence of the process of social transformation which had opened up with the French Revolution on the art of warfare as practised by the French, and on the course of the wars in Europe.

In the hundred years approximately which separated the Napoleonic Wars from the beginning of the first world war, the nature of warfare changed decisively as a result of the capitalist industrial revolution, and in the second world war certain important tendencies which had already begun to show themselves in the first world war became more and more clearly visible.

The general trend of development can be summed up in a phrase: *war is becoming more and more total*.

This is true from three angles:

1. The number of countries which engage in it.
2. The extent of the sectors within the belligerent countries which they are willing and able to harness to the prosecution of the war.
3. The changes in the periods which precede and follow war, from a period of peace to an armistice period, to a period of armament economy.

WARS ARE BECOMING WORLD WARS

With regard to the first point, the general trend is for wars to involve *simultaneously* all the powers in the world.

In this respect there has been a decisive change in comparison with the days of Clausewitz and the whole of the nineteenth century, and that change is nothing but the military expression of the fact that we have entered into a new phase of history—into the period of world history proper, and thus into the period of world powers.

At the time of the French Revolution and the Napoleonic Wars, at the beginning of the European industrial revolution when capitalism was taking its first big strides, there was no *world* history properly so called, just as in earlier periods of the history of the world there was no world history.

History was confined essentially to the various continents. Even in earlier phases of history there were world powers—for instance, the Roman Empire was a world Power, and so was the Chinese Empire. In her own orbit Rome was a world Power, and she tolerated no independent States near her, only satellites. But the Roman Empire embraced only a small part of the world, and influenced only part of the world. The Chinese Empire existed at the same time, and it ruled a larger part of the world and for a longer period than the Roman Empire did. As Nehru rightly observes:

> "We read a great deal of the greatness of Rome during this period, and one is apt to think that Rome overshadowed the world. 'Mistress of the World' Rome has been called. But though Rome was great then, and growing greater, China was vaster, and a more powerful empire." [2]

It was characteristic of this period of human history that Rome and China existed quite separately and hardly came into contact with each other, that they could and did exist side by side without friction, that there was in reality no real world power which extended its sway throughout the world, and no real *world* history. In the days of the Roman Empire there were no world wars, only wars within the orbit of the Roman Empire.

Even in the days of Napoleon there were no world wars, and the wars that Clausewitz describes are essentially European wars, wars which affected only one part of the world, though an important part.

To that extent, therefore, such wars, by their essentially European character, were *isolated* wars.

Further, at the time of the Napoleonic Wars, though France was in a state of war for many years, she was not waging war against the whole of Europe at the same time. Her wars were almost exclusively fought against individual European countries. The 1813 period was exceptional, and it lasted only for a comparatively short time, though then almost all the nations of Europe were in coalition against France.

What was true of the Napoleonic Wars was true also of the succeeding hundred years up to the outbreak of the first world war: wars were usually wars between individual nations, fought out whilst the great majority of other peoples lived in peace. Thus to that extent wars were isolated happenings. And after the Franco-Prussian War for almost half a century up to the outbreak of the first world war, wars were generally fought in countries which lagged behind the main capitalist centres in industrial and capitalist development.

The first world war—perhaps the historian of the future will regard it as the real beginning of the twentieth century—brought about a decisive change. It was no longer a war fought out away from the centres of industrial production, like Japan's war against China or the Balkan wars in Europe which preceded the first world war; it was a war between the European great powers, fought out in the heart of Europe. All the big European powers in Europe were involved, including Britain, and this time her participation was not limited to economic subsidies and the sending of a small expeditionary force, as it was in the Napoleonic Wars; instead she exerted her full economic power and maintained large armies on the continent throughout the war. Not only were all the big powers involved, but they were simultaneously involved, not for a few months, but for several years.

Having regard to the number of nations which took part in it and the efforts they put forth, the first world war was already a total war for Europe; but it was not so for the whole world, and not even for the whole capitalist world, because the United States was not called upon to exert her full strength by any means, and Japan's war effort was negligible.

This tendency, which arose during the first world war, was continued and strengthened in the second, when, once again, all the big European nations and most of the smaller ones were involved, and the United States and Japan. This time, however, both the United States and Japan were deeply involved and, in addition, a great part of the Asiatic world, though the social organism of the United States was not affected to the same extent as the social organisms of the other belligerents, both European and Asiatic.

Thus with regard to the number of nations which took part and the magnitude of the efforts they made in the prosecution of the war, the second world war went a step farther on the way to totality in warfare.

There are very good reasons to suppose that this trend will continue and strengthen in the future.

The Epoch of World Powers

The second world war was really the first *world* war, not only because it involved every important country in the world, but also because of the war aims of at least one of the belligerents. The Nazis were frankly out for world domination.

The characteristic feature of the period in which the second world war took place (a period in which the war itself was only a milestone) was that the question of world domination was no longer merely a theoretical one for discussion in books and articles, but a very practical one. A single great power had worked out a plan for securing world domination, and that plan was carried a long way towards final achievement. A hair's breadth separated Germany from victory over Great Britain. It is quite possible that had Nazi Germany succeeded in defeating Great Britain she would also have been able to defeat the Soviet Union. A Nazi Germany which had defeated Great Britain and the Soviet Union would have been a big step nearer to world domination. Nazi Germany succeeded in defeating neither Great Britain nor the Soviet Union, but her very serious attempt to do so is an indication that we no longer live in a period of great powers but of world powers.

The fact that the plans of Nazi Germany went awry and she was utterly defeated does not mean that the general trend we have observed is now at an end.

It still exists because we have entered into a new phase of history—a phase in which the balance of power is no longer obtained in an interplay between a number of big, powerful, independent and politically sovereign States. It is a phase of world powers—world powers which are not confined to their own territories, but which expand vigorously from their own centres out into the rest of the world, world powers which to-day, unlike the days of ancient Rome and China, are in close contact and share wide surfaces of friction in a great variety of places, precisely because, sociologically speaking, our world has become much smaller.

The countries of the world are entering this new epoch with very disparate economic structures. There is nothing new in this fact; in earlier epochs of human history countries with very disparate economic and political systems lived side by side. But the new feature of the second world war and its post-war era is that highly developed capitalist States, States in which the capitalist system is seriously threatened, States like the Soviet Union, in which capitalism has ceased to exist, and territories in which pre-capitalist forms still prevail, exist side by side and are more closely bound up with each other than ever before.

The world powers meet each other in countries whose social structure is very different from their own, in countries which are themselves involved in a gigantic process of transformation.

Our final chapter will show why it is that when war is discussed today it means a war between the two world powers of our post-war era—war between the United States and the Soviet Union. These two powers together would be so strong that in no foreseeable future would it be possible for any coalition of forces to wage war against the two of them with any chance of success.

At the same time a war between these two world powers would be really a war on a world-wide scale, the first war which would embrace all continents, a war in which all the nations of the world would willy-nilly be involved either actively or passively. Such a war would thus be a total war, unlike all former wars, and, in particular, unlike those wars which Clausewitz took as the basis of his analysis of war.

But this is not the only reason; there is a second one—namely, the magnitude of the efforts which the nations of the world would be willing and capable of exerting in its prosecution.

This magnitude of effort, or, what is practically the same thing, the size of the military sector, has been decisively affected by the progress of industrialization.

The change which has come about was first demonstrated in the first world war; it was a change which completely altered the nature of war as compared with the wars of the previous thousand years, including the wars of the nineteenth century.

All the wars in world history before the twentieth century were wars between countries in which the agricultural population was absolutely predominant. That was true of all Asiatic wars, of Greece and Rome, of the wars of Frederick the Great, and even of the Napoleonic Wars which Clausewitz describes. It was also true of the nineteenth century, including the Franco-Prussian War and the Sino-Japanese War. It was also true of the Russo-Japanese War of 1904–1905 and of the Balkan Wars before the outbreak of the first world war.

In the first world war it was no longer true, for the first time in history. Here for the first time nations were at war whose social structure and populations were primarily industrial.

It was this fact which brought about the decisive change in the nature of war.

There were two consequences of the fact that in former times, agriculture was predominant and anything between four and ten men working on the land were necessary to feed one man living in the town. First of all the greater part of production, often the overwhelmingly greater part, went on just the same in war as it had done in peace. The whole agricultural sector remained much the same in war as it had been in peace. And in such circumstances the belligerent countries were not in a position to harness the major sector of their economic life to the prosecution of war, and when peace came again—leaving out the possibility of direct devastation as a result of the war—this major sector of the national economy was able to go on just as before.

Secondly, because a great number of people working on the land were necessary to feed a small number of people living in the towns, armies could not be very big in relation to the size of the total population, and, in fact, they were always very small indeed by comparison with the mass armies which took the field during the first world war.

The Napoleonic Wars are illuminating in this respect. *Neither Napoleon nor any of his enemies had at any time an army in the field which approached the million mark.* At the end of his book [3] Clausewitz reckoned out how big the armies of the European States, not including Russia, could be in the event of a new war with France:

> "The countries mentioned have, not including their non-European possessions, over 75 million inhabitants at their disposal, whereas France has only 30 millions, and the army they could put into the field in a serious war against France could, without exaggeration, be as follows:
>
> | | |
> |---|---|
> | Austria | 250,000 |
> | Prussia | 200,000 |
> | The Rest of Germany | 150,000 |
> | The Netherlands | 75,000 |
> | England | 50,000 |
>
> "If these forces are deployed effectively, i.e. at full strength, then they would very probably be superior to anything that France could put into the field against them, because under Bonaparte the country never had a fighting force of such a size."

Thus France, with 30 million inhabitants in the Napoleonic era, never had an army of even 725,000 men. But the France of the first world war, with a population only about 10 millions bigger (in 1910 the population of France was 39·2 millions), mobilized no less than five million men.

474

In other words, the armies of the industrial powers grew in size parallel with the progress of industrialization. At the same time that sector of the total economic system of a belligerent country which could be harnessed to the prosecution of war also grew in size, for the same reason.

This tendency was very evident for the first time in the 1914–1918 war—not at the beginning of that war, but during its course.

The European powers had to some extent prepared themselves for the first world war, but because they had lived in peace for so long, and because there had never been a war between countries in which industrial production predominated, they had not provided themselves with a previous armaments economy. During the course of the war they were compelled to do just that, and the result was the growth of a military sector harnessed to the prosecution of the war on a scale never previously experienced in known history.

Frederick the Great declared of the wars of the eighteeenth century: "The peaceable citizen should not even notice that his country is at war." And even during the Napoleonic Wars in the nineteenth century the greater part of the life of the belligerent nations went on more or less as usual. All that had changed for Europe with the first world war.

With the enormous growth in the size of armies on the one hand, and with the harnessing into the services of war of not merely a small sector of economic life, but of the major portion of it on the other, the nations now knew not only that their armies were fighting, but that they themselves were fully engaged in the struggle. Thus in the magnitude of the resources and man-power mobilized for war purposes the first world war became more and more a total war for the European belligerents. But that was not the case for the non-European countries, and in particular the United States. The non-European nations for the greater part did not even join in the first world war, and where the United States was concerned, although she joined in, she did so only with a comparatively small part of her man-power and economic resources.

In our analysis of the nations taking part in the war we have already seen that the total character of war intensified in the period between the two wars, and the same was true of the magnitude of that sector of their economic life harnessed to the prosecution of the second world war.

The changes referred in particular to the non-European belligerents. Japan formally declared war in the first world war, but she took no important part in it; for the second world war she mobilized all her man-power and all her economic resources. The United States took a greater part in the first world war than Japan, and she even tipped the scales in it, but she was engaged in military operations for little more than a year, and her military expenditure and her war production never amounted to more than a quarter of her total production. For the second world war, however, she mobilized an incomparably larger sector of her economic system, and at its peak it represented about 50 per cent of her total production. She kept it mobilized for a much longer period, and at the same time she created armies which were more than three times as big as her armies in the first world war.

By comparison with her military effort in the first world war, the second world war was thus much more of a total war even for the United States. But by comparison with the other belligerents, both European and Asiatic, the United States was the one country in which for the majority of the population civilian life went on during the war without any really decisive changes.

The Industrial Areas of the World More and More in the Firing Line

The second world war intensified the tendency towards total war not only by the fact that it involved an incomparably larger section of the life of nations in direct war production, but also because to a greater extent than ever before it exposed the industrially developed areas of the world to direct destruction as a result of military operations.

In this respect there was a fundamental difference between the first world war and the second.

It is true that in the first world war the big industrial nations—the nations in which the capitalist mode of production dominated—were involved for the first time, but in that war the towns and industrial centres of the belligerent countries were in the firing line only to a relatively limited extent.

In the period of the first world war the United States was the leading industrial power in the world, as she still is; Germany came second and Great Britain third. Neither the United States nor Great Britain were territorially involved in the fighting—the air bombing and isolated naval bombardment of British towns in the first world war were of negligible military importance. And German territory was involved only for a short time in the frontier districts. Thus during the first world war the productive apparatus of none of the three chief industrial powers was directly affected by war devastation.

During that war the arena of hostilities for years was made up of a part of European Russia, Serbia, a part of Austria-Hungary, the greater part of Belgium and a part of France. At that time France accounted for not more than 7 per cent of total world production, and Tsarist Russia, in which agriculture was still predominant, for only about 4 per cent. Thus we can say that although all the leading industrial nations of the world took part in the first world war, *only a sector which accounted for between 5 and 7 per cent of world production* was directly in the firing line.

In other words, although the European industrial powers waged the war with the mobilization of all their economic resources, only a comparatively small sector of their towns and productive apparatus was directly in the fighting and subject to direct devastation.

The situation in the second world war was already very different. The methods of warfare had changed because the process of industrialization had made great progress and war had become essentially a war of factories and industries, but the object of war was still to destroy the enemy forces, and the principle of Clausewitz still held good: "The forces of the enemy must be destroyed, i.e. they must be placed in a position in which they are no longer able to continue the struggle." [4] At the same time it was becoming more and more important to destroy the industrial apparatus which the enemy needed to equip and maintain his armies, to destroy or reduce his industrial potential.

When war was waged between primarily agricultural States, the object of warfare was to destroy the enemy army. But when subsequently war was waged between industrial nations the object of warfare was extended. It was not only to destroy the enemy's army, but also to destroy his war production or, if possible, to seize and harness it to one's own war production, as Nazi Germany did after Dunkirk with a very considerable part of Europe's industrial production.

The second world war also brought an incomparably greater part of the industrial and urban sector into the firing line all over the world.

It is true that in the second world war, as in the first, the largest industrial centre in the world—the United States—remained outside the sphere of direct military action both for land and air forces, but for the second and third powers on the list the situation was very different. Germany entered the second world war as second on the list, as she had been in the first world war. This time the greater part of her territory was in the firing line, not only as the result of air warfare on an unprecedented scale, but also in land operations by the Russians in the east and the Anglo-American forces in the west. Thus there was not only the normal reduction of industrial production as an indirect result of the war, but, in addition, a great measure of direct urban and industrial destruction, which also reduced production.

This was equally true of the Soviet Union, which was now the third industrial power in the world. In the second world war, as in the first, Russian territory was an arena of hostilities for years. But the Russia of the second world war, unlike Tsarist Russia in the first, was already a big industrial power, and the direct destruction caused on her territory was much greater than that suffered in the first world war, because both the Germans and the Russians were well aware of the importance of industrial production for war and they both waged war accordingly. The Soviet Union answered the Nazi advance with the famous "scorched-earth" policy, in order to leave in the hands of the enemy as little as possible which could be put to use and turned against her. And when the German armies were finally forced to retreat they "scientifically" destroyed everything they could in order to damage Soviet Russian productive capacity, and to some extent they were successful.

But apart from Germany and Soviet Russia, whose towns and industrial areas suffered most from the direct destruction of war, whose territories were fought over by millions of men and attacked by powerful air fleets, the towns and industrial areas of Great Britain and Japan were also subjected to direct war damage by air raids.

In the second world war French and Belgian territory was again fought over, as was also the territory of all the countries situated between Russia and Germany. All in all therefore during the second world war *almost a third of the total industrial sector of the world was drawn into the direct arena of military action.*

At the same time there are important indications which suggest that the general historical process is tending to increase the size of the industrial sector which will be involved in any new war.

U.S. industry was once again outside the direct sphere of military operations in the second world war. This was also largely true of Britain's productive apparatus for the greater part of the war. It was also true of Soviet Russia's productive apparatus in her Asiatic provinces. Thus a good two-thirds of the world's industrial sector went unscathed during the second world war, because it was outside the sphere of land operations, and difficult or impossible to attack by air.

It was primarily the fact that the productive apparatus of the United States not only maintained itself during the war but very considerably increased in size, that Russian production increased in the Asiatic provinces, and that British industrial production remained relatively stable, which made it possible once the war was over, for the world to recover so rapidly from the industrial damage caused by it, and for the recuperative forces to operate so speedily and effectively.

Just as in an economic crisis the fact that a large sector of the economic system is immune to its effects is of great assistance in overcoming the crisis, so the fact that during the second world war such a large sector of the world's industrial apparatus was immune from the direct destruction of war was decisive for the rapidity with which world productive losses were subsequently made good.

But in any future war there will be a danger that *the industrial sector*

478

exposed to direct destruction in the course of the war will be greater than the sector which is immune, that for the first time in history such a war will really be total, not only in that all industrial countries will be involved with the sum total of all their resources, but that precisely the most highly developed countries industrially will be the theatre of war. In other words, the war will not be fought almost entirely outside the towns and industrial centres, as the first world war was, or with two-thirds of the towns and industrial centres outside the battle area as in the second world war, but with the towns and industrial centres themselves as the primary area of battle.

A war of the world powers would in all probability involve not only the industrial apparatus of European Russia, but also that of her Asiatic provinces, or a great part of it. It would in all probability involve not only the whole of continental Europe once again, but the industrial apparatus of Great Britain as well, and to a much greater extent than ever before. Further, the development of air warfare and new bombs, including the atom bomb, will certainly bring the U.S. industrial apparatus into the danger zone for the first time in history.

Thus the twentieth century has progressively made towns and industrial centres the objects of warfare, and the development of modern weapons of war intensifies all the dangers in this direction.

In the second world war the use of the atom bomb as a weapon was confined to two attacks on Japan. All we can hazard with any probability about the use of the atom bomb in the next war, should there be one, is that the industrial apparatus of the whole world is likely to be its target.

It is true that Japan had no defence at all against the atom bomb, and it is also true that the whole history of war for the past thousand years and more has shown that when new weapons come into use, new methods of defence are sooner or later developed. But whether new methods of defence will be devised this time against the atom bomb, and if so to what extent, no one can say with any certainty.

Thus it is probable that in any future war not only will by far the greater part of the world's towns and industrial centres be directly involved in the fighting, but that they will be attacked with new weapons whose destructive powers may be very much greater than the recovery forces which still operated in the period of the second world war.

THE ARMISTICE ECONOMY

The change in the nature of war is making itself more and more felt in the fact that it is transforming the whole epoch, turning periods of "peace" into armistice periods, periods in which armament pro-

479

duction represents a great sector of the economic system—periods, in short, of armament economy.

The various phases of this process are fairly well defined to-day, and we have already dealt with them on a number of occasions previously. The earlier stages of human history, in which agricultural production largely predominated, knew no armament economy in peace time. In fact, such a thing was impossible, and the result was that even in the immediate pre-war period, when the final preparations for war were being made, agriculture, and thus by far the major part of the economic system, continued to produce as usual. This was true of Asia and of Ancient Greece and Rome, and it was also true of the early phase of capitalism's development, of the eighteenth century and of the Napoleonic Wars in the nineteenth. The astonishing fact that the economic and social system recovered so rapidly and so thoroughly after the many wars of that earlier epoch was due precisely to the circumstance that in the years of peace before and after wars there was no extensive armament economy in operation.

From the technical point of view the new departure with which we are now dealing could have come into operation before the first world war. Technically speaking, the industrial nations of Europe were in a position to draw the logical conclusions from the fundamental changes which had taken place in the nineteenth century, and thus to prepare for the first world war not only by raising, training and equipping great armies of millions of men, as they did, but also by turning a considerable part of their industrial resources to war purposes even in peace time.

However, as our analysis has shown (cf. Part One of this book), none of the European States actually did this before the first world war, neither Germany and the Central Powers nor the Entente.

Thus the first world war, which developed more and more into a total war for the European powers, was not preceded by any period of armament economy. In consequence, it is possible to analyse the development of capitalism up to the outbreak of that war without having to pay any considerable attention to war and the preparations for war, because they played no important role in that development.

But the situation changed greatly in the period which followed the first world war and led up to the second. This period is clearly divided into two by the taking of power in Germany by the Nazis. Immediately after the first world war there was a great demobilization of armies and dismantling of armament production in all countries, and even when the world economic crisis broke out in 1929 no attempts were made anywhere to answer it by strengthening the military sectors.

But after the Nazis came to power in Germany the world saw the creation of a powerful peace-time armaments industrial sector for the first time in history. The only big power to answer the threat by building up a strong armaments sector of its own was the Soviet Union. Britain, France and the United States made no effective answer, though for years before the war broke out industrial armament production played a bigger role in large parts of continental Europe than ever before in times of peace.

What was true before the second world war of large parts of continental Europe is now true of the whole world.

In the period after the second world war there is no such division as was created in the period after the first by the coming to power of the Nazis. Immediately after the defeat of Germany and Japan, immediately after the end of the second world war, the world had no peace; it merely entered into a period of armistice.

After the first world war Great Britain and the United States demobilized their armies, and the Russians did not then possess an army which was in a position to wage war against a big power. After the second world war the United States and Great Britain kept their armies in being, but on a very much reduced scale. The Soviet Union also kept its army in being.

After the first world war the world returned to a peace-time economy, and it was fifteen years before a war economy, an armament economy, was established in peace time. After the first world war this war economy, which applied in particular to the last five years before the outbreak of the second world war, was still largely a European affair, and America's military sector was a very small affair.

To-day, soon after the second world war, we have an armament economy throughout the world. It is no longer largely a European affair. It applies to the United States and to the Soviet Union; it applies to those powers who have signed the Atlantic Pact, and it applies to all the satellites of the Soviet Union. As we are now living in a period of world history, as in this era of the atom bomb we have to reckon with world powers, thus war economy, armament economy in peace time, has become a world-wide affair.

But this means that war, if it comes, will be more total than ever before, not only because it will involve all the big world powers with all their resources, not only because it threatens to involve an ever-growing section of the towns and industrial centres of the world as a direct battle area, but also because its shadow, the preparations which are being made for it, falls over the period of "peace" before its outbreak, turning it into little more than a truce, an armistice period.

The Danger of a Descent into Barbarism

Not from one day to the next but over a period of many years, the nature of war has changed with the rapid progress of industrialization throughout the world; it has affected different nations to different degrees, but the main trend and its basic elements are already becoming more and more clear: wars, which for a variety of reasons were of an isolated and localized character, are now becoming more and more total. On the one hand, they are developing more and more into industrial and laboratory wars, and, on the other, the world has entered into a phase of real *world* history with, for the first time, real *world* powers. And with this change in the nature of war its relations to the social organisms which wage it must also change.

The wars which took place in the early period of capitalism's development—the wars of the eighteenth century, the Napoleonic wars, the wars of the nineteenth century—had, with all their differences, one thing in common: they were means to an end.

The famous dictum of Clausewitz: "War is only a continuation of policy with other means", applied to all of them. And he goes on to say:

> "Thus war is not merely a political act; it is a real political instrument, a continuation of previous political relationships, a continuation of policy with other means."

Towards the end of his famous book Clausewitz [5] formulates the same idea in greater detail:

> "On the other hand we contend: war is nothing but a continuation of political relations with the intervention of other means. We say with the intervention of other means in order to stress at once that these political relations do not end with the war itself and are not changed into something else, but continue to exist in their essence no matter what may be the nature of the means they adopt, and that the main lines along which warlike events take place and to which they are attached, are only its guiding lines which proceed through the war into the subsequent peace. And how should anything else be conceivable? Do the political relations of various peoples and governments ever cease to exist with diplomatic notes? Is not war merely another form of writing and language to express their content. It is true that it has its own grammar, but not its own logic, i.e. not its own ways of proper thought."

CLAUSEWITZ OUT OF DATE

Under what conditions did these maxims of Clausewitz apply? On the assumption that war was not total, on the assumption that it did not include all great nations simultaneously, on the assumption that it involved only a small sector of the economic system and of the general life of a nation, and that the casualties and the destruction remained within certain bounds; in other words, on the assumption that its effects on the economic body as a whole were to a certain extent isolated and localized.

At the time they were formulated his maxims represented a real advance in man's knowledge of the nature of war; they showed that war itself was not isolated from general political developments, and they showed, in addition, that war was only a means to an end.

In other words, the maxims of Clausewitz were valid so long as wars, which may have damaged society, did not shake it to the core, *so long thus as the countries engaged in war were in a position to control not only the beginning of the war but also its further course right up to its end.*

Our ideas on the nature of war are still strongly under the influence of the maxims of Clausewitz, although the conditions under which they were valid are being more and more shattered.

The maxim that war was the continuation of policy with other means still applied to the whole of the nineteenth century; it no longer applied altogether even to the first half of the twentieth century. Even in the first world war the upheaval and the destruction in Europe were so great that they fundamentally affected the European countries involved. It was true even of the first world war that although the belligerent countries were in a position to control its beginning, their control over its subsequent course grew less and less.

This tendency to lose control has grown stronger since then, and it did not cease to grow with the second world war.

If all the big powers are engaged in a future war with all their resources, and if the industrial sector of the world is not only a battle area but even the primary battle area, then it may well come about that to speak of the war as the continuation of policy with other means will be meaningless. The process of destruction in the industrial sector of the world in particular—that is to say, in the total life of present-day great powers—may well be so great that the very life of nations will be threatened. It may well be possible that the result of the war will prove to be beyond the control of the nations which begin it, because the nations themselves and their social organisms will be paralysed by the extent of the consequent destruction. It may well be possible that war will grow out of its previous function as a means for the attainment of political ends, leaving that function behind, for the simple reason that it destroys the nations engaged in it and their social organisms, and after that destruction it will not be possible to speak of war as the continuation of policy with other means.

Any attempt to analyse the future course of development which does not take this change in the nature of war into consideration cannot be regarded seriously. Any policy which, in our present epoch of world powers and atom bombs, sees in warfare only the continuation of policy with other means is obsolete. It is more than that: it is horribly dangerous, because it can lead to barbarism and the destruction of civilization as we know it.

The dangers involved in this direction become very clear when we consider the strength, history and political structures of the two decisive world powers to-day.

First of all we must realize that an analysis of the respective strengths of the Soviet Union and of the United States—the only two world powers in existence to-day—leads to the conclusion that one side is not so superior to the other in strength that in the event of war any speedy victory may be expected. On the contrary, there are many important factors which suggest that a war between these two powers would be long and arduous, and that therefore the magnitude of the destruction it would involve would be far greater than anything suffered in Europe during the second world war. In addition, despite the horrible dangers a new war would involve, very little has been undertaken by and in either of the two potential belligerent world powers to prevent it.

The United States is the one big power left in the world which has not yet experienced to any material extent the change in the nature of war in the twentieth century, the development towards more and more total warfare.

As far as the United States was concerned, the two world wars were little more than gigantic colonial wars fought well outside its own territory, and after each of these wars the U.S.A. was even more powerful than before.

Precisely because she entered the second world war with a latent crisis in her economic life and mass unemployment amounting to almost 20 per cent of her total available labour force, and because U.S. standards of living increased considerably both during and after the war, the consciousness of the decisive change in the nature of war and the dangers of barbarism which any future war will involve, is less active in America than anywhere else. Peoples do not learn from books; they learn only from their own history. The previous history of the United States had done nothing to teach the American people the dangers of barbarism inherent in any new war.

The people of the Soviet Union experienced the second world war in a very different fashion. They knew what war really meant, and they suffered terribly. But the dictatorship in the Soviet Union had grown stronger and its basis still narrower even in the period before the war, and victory in the war still further strengthened the power of the totalitarian State, because all the terror of the pre-war period now seemed justified by the fact of victory. Thus the people of the Soviet Union entered the post-war period without any loosening of their totalitarian regime; in fact that regime became still more onerous. The result is that they have no means of expressing their

484

desire for peace, which must have been greatly strengthened precisely by their experiences in the second world war, and no means of influencing the foreign policy of their dictatorial government.

So in this second half of the twentieth century, in which a new war might well destroy civilization as we know it, on account of the increasingly total nature of war and the increasingly destructive character of the new weapons of war, the two principal actors in that drama, if it ever takes place, will be two world powers whose total military strengths are not greatly different.

The people of one of these world powers—unlike the peoples of Europe—still know very little at first hand about the dangers of barbarism involved in war, and the people of the other, although they know the dangers from their own experiences in the second world war, are, on account of the dictatorial regime under which they live, unable to express their desire for peace in any practical fashion.

Thus there is a very grave danger of war, and if war should come, then there is every likelihood that the barbarous tendencies which increasingly showed their ugly features in the second world war will develop and spread still further.

When the Nazis came to power in Germany it was not long before the peoples of Europe began to ask not whether there would be a war, but when the war would break out.

Unfortunately the years following the second world war have offered little encouragement to people to abandon that pessimistic outlook.

And to-day it is not only the people of Europe who ask that question, but the peoples of the whole world.

The anxious question: will there be another war? is one which exercises the minds and haunts the dreams of people all over the world to-day. It is a decisive factor not only for the relation of forces which has developed as a result of the second world war, but also for the actions which will influence its subsequent development.

The danger for our whole culture is based on the change in the nature of war and the possibility of destruction on a scale never previously experienced.

However, it is not weapons which lead to war. Modern weapons merely increase the possibility that barbarism will result from war. What threatens our world with war to-day is the aggravation of its social and political antagonisms.

485

THE WORLD RELATION OF FORCES

THE FINAL PERIOD before the outbreak of the second world war was marked by severe crises in the most important capitalist countries and by a parallel growth of foreign-political antagonisms.

Have there been any decisive changes in this respect since? We can hardly say there have, because the first post-war years were once again marked by severe economic and social crises in the leading industrial countries—for the time being with the exclusion of the United States—and by a parallel growth of foreign-political tension and the constant danger of a new war.

Thus the difference, if any, is not very great, and that is hardly surprising.

The first world war represented the close of an age. It ended a period of capitalist progress and capitalist expansions, and opened up a period of social transformation for the capitalist system.

The second world war opened up no new period in the world's history, and it was not the close of a period, as the first world war was. It was no more than a stage in a great process of transformation. The fundamental political and social problems which existed before it broke out exist to-day. But on the eve of the first two world wars it was Europe which occupied the foreground. It was European imperialist antagonisms which led to the first world war, which was, in fact, largely a European war. It was the aggressive imperialist policy of Nazi Germany which was the chief factor responsible for the outbreak of the second world war. It was Nazi Germany which was the dynamic centre of world politics in the period before the outbreak of that war.

One of the most important factors in the present situation after the second world war is that Europe no longer occupies this decisive position in world politics. Europe is, of course, still a factor of great importance in the relation of world forces, but often more as an object than an actor.

The world centre of gravity has moved away from Europe. It is now precariously balanced between the United States on the one hand and the Soviet Union on the other.

An analysis of the relation of forces after the second world war must therefore begin with the two world powers and then go to Europe and Asia.

THE WORLD POLITICAL BACKGROUND OF AMERICA'S POSITION

As a result of the second world war the United States has become the first world power in this new period of world history. In a very short space of time measured historically the United States has become a world power overtopping all others. At the same time it is a power whose influence extends beyond its own frontiers and profoundly affects the fate of Europe and Asia and the future history of the world.

The general tendency which has now been operative for generations is for the rate of U.S. industrial and economic development generally to be faster than that of the rest of the capitalist world. That tendency was interrupted for a while during the world economic crisis, but it came into operation again, and was greatly accentuated by the second world war. Whereas the production of the rest of the world at the end of the war was well below the levels of the pre-war period, U.S. production was already 50 per cent higher.

The following diagram graphically shows the difference between the U.S.A. and the rest of the world:

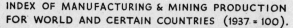

INDEX OF MANUFACTURING & MINING PRODUCTION FOR WORLD AND CERTAIN COUNTRIES (1937 = 100).

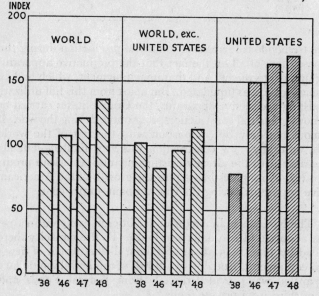

The history of modern capitalism knows no parallel to a situation in which approximately the half of world industrial production is concentrated in one country.

At the beginnings of large-scale industrial development around the middle of the nineteenth century, Great Britain was in a somewhat similar position, but that was only because industrial development

487

started there. She did not hold this favoured position for long once large-scale industrial development began in other countries.

Now, in the middle of the twentieth century, the United States holds this position as the leading world power.

The ten-year period from 1929 to 1939 was one of crisis and stagnation, but since then U.S. industrial development gives us the following picture:

Industrial Production Index 1929–1949

Monthly average.	Total industrial production [1] (1935–1939 = 100).
1929	110
1939	109
1942	199
1944	235
1945	203
1946	170
1947	187
1948	192
1949	175

The tremendous increase of industrial production during the war was based first of all on the fact that the productive apparatus was being utilized to the full and that unemployment, which had existed on a mass scale, was liquidated. But apart from this full utilization of the existing productive apparatus, the United States carried out an enormous industrial construction programme during the war. It was enormous not only by comparison with the rest of the world—in which, naturally, new construction was very limited—but also by comparison with the already existing gigantic American productive apparatus. A rough estimate puts the growth of the American productive apparatus during the war at about 50 per cent.

"The Nation's manufacturing facilities in existence in 1939 had cost about 40 billion dollars to build. To this capacity there was added by June 1945 about 26 billion dollars worth of new plant and equipment. Roughly two-thirds of this 26-billion dollar plant expansion was provided directly from Federal Funds and the other third from private funds." [2]

The military orders brought about by the war created the necessary market for the products of this old and new productive apparatus, and the war naturally brought a fundamental change in the trend of American employment. The following statistics give us the figures for the prosperity year 1929, for the year in which the second

488

world war broke out, 1939, and for the war and first post-war years:

Labour Force, Employment and Unemployment [3]
(thousands of persons, 14 years of age and over)

Period: monthly average.	Total labour force, including the armed forces.	The armed forces.	Civilian labour force.				
			Total civilian labour force.	Employment.			Unemployment.
				Total.	Non-Agricultural.	Agricultural.	
1929	49,440	260	49,180	47,630	37,180	10,450	1,550
1939	55,600	370	55,230	45,750	36,140	9,610	9,480
1940	56,030	390	55,640	47,520	37,980	9,540	8,120
1942	60,230	3,820	56,410	53,750	44,500	9,250	2,660
1944	65,890	11,260	54,630	53,960	45,010	8,950	,670
1945	65,140	11,280	53,860	52,820	44,240	8,580	1,040
1947	61,608	1,440	60,168	58,027	49,761	8,266	2,142
1949	63,571	1,466	62,105	58,710	50,684	8,026	3,395

Like the European countries, the United States completely liqui-dated unemployment during the war. But more than that, despite the enormous increase in the armed forces, the civilian labour force still increased because, apart from those workers who had formerly been unemployed, it was swollen by millions of women, youths and older men who came back to the factories, etc.

But this increase in the labour force did not include agriculture. On the contrary, there was not a single war year in which the number of workers employed in agriculture was not lower than in 1939, and the decline continued throughout the post-war years. Thus an enormous increase in agricultural production was obtained with a decreasing labour force, and the tendency which had been operative for many years continued.

The growth in the number of employed workers exclusively swelled the non-agricultural labour force.

MANUFACTURING EMPLOYMENT INCREASED FOR THE FIRST TIME SINCE 1919

Together with the tremendous increase in industrial production there was an increase in the number of workers employed in the manufacturing industries. In 1929 the number of workers employed in these industries was 10·5 millions, in 1938 it was 9·2 millions and in 1939 it was 10 millions. But during the war it rose to 15 millions in 1942, and reached its highest point in 1943, with 17·3 millions. But even in 1945 it was still 15·3 millions, and in 1949 14·1 millions.

With this the trend which had operated throughout the period between the two world wars was interrupted. In the years before the world economic crisis there had been a great increase in industrial production, but at the same time the rise in the productivity of

489

labour was so great that the increase in production was obtained without any increase in the number of workers employed. During the years of crisis industrial employment naturally declined very sharply, but then in the war and post-war years there was again a tremendous increase, and at the same time U.S. industry employed not only all those workers who had been unemployed previously, but new millions of workers in addition.

Industrial Concentration in the Second World War

With the tremendous increase in industrial production the trend to industrial concentration which had been so marked in the United States for many years continued, and its extent and speed increased very considerably.

During the war years there was a double process of concentration. First of all there was a concentration in the already existing productive apparatus as the workers were concentrated into the most productive factories and production centres (although, on the other hand, the tremendous expansion of production as a whole led to the opening up of a series of smaller undertakings). Secondly, the new construction which took place during the war years was carried out on a basis of concentration incomparably higher than anything in the already existing productive apparatus.

This was reflected, amongst other things, in the distribution of the labour force.

"In each of the war industries, with but one exception, firms with 10,000 or more employees grew in relative importance. In manufacturing as a whole, these few giants accounted for 13 per cent of total employment in 1939, and for fully 31 per cent of the total in 1944." [4]

These giants controlled the overwhelming majority of the new factories which were built during the war.

"Who, then, controls this vast productive plant? How much of it is held by big business and how much by the smaller firms? The answer to these questions may be obtained by examining the holdings of the nation's 250 largest manufacturing corporations—31 of which are controlled by five financial interest groups.

"These 250 largest manufacturing corporations are, for the most part, the traditional giants of American industry. . . . In total they owned, in 1939, 65 per cent of the nation's production facilities (gross capital assets); operated during the war 79 per cent of all new privately operated plant facilities built with Federal funds; and in September 1944 held 78 per cent of the active prime war-supply contracts." [5]

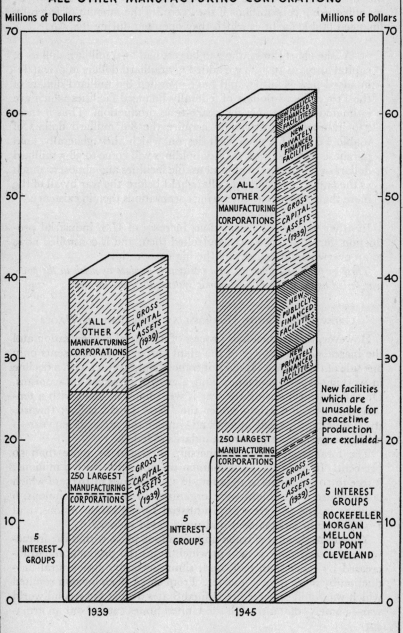

250 LARGEST MANUFACTURING CORPORATIONS AND ALL OTHER MANUFACTURING CORPORATIONS

Millions of Dollars

Millions of Dollars

70

70

60

60

NEW PUBLICLY FINANCED FACILITIES

NEW PRIVATELY FINANCED FACILITIES

ALL OTHER MANUFACTURING CORPORATIONS

GROSS CAPITAL ASSETS (1939)

50

50

ALL OTHER MANUFACTURING CORPORATIONS

GROSS CAPITAL ASSETS (1939)

40

40

NEW PUBLICLY FINANCED FACILITIES

NEW PRIVATELY FINANCED FACILITIES

30

30

New facilities which are unusable for peacetime production are excluded

ALL OTHER MANUFACTURING CORPORATIONS

GROSS CAPITAL ASSETS (1939)

20

250 LARGEST MANUFACTURING CORPORATIONS

GROSS CAPITAL ASSETS (1939)

20

250 LARGEST MANUFACTURING CORPORATIONS

GROSS CAPITAL ASSETS (1939)

5 INTEREST GROUPS

ROCKEFELLER
MORGAN
MELLON
DU PONT
CLEVELAND

10

5 INTEREST GROUPS

5 INTEREST GROUPS

10

5 INTEREST GROUPS

0

0

1939

1945

The diagram on page 491 shows graphically the tremendous war-time expansion of the nation's manufacturing facilities and the amount of these facilities which will be held by these 250 largest manufacturing corporations if they acquire the amount of federally financed usable facilities which they operated during the war.

"As the chart shows, the 250 largest had 25·9 milliard dollars of capital assets in 1939, have added 3·7 milliard dollars in privately-financed new facilities, and have operated 8·9 milliard dollars of the 11·5 milliard dollars of federally financed facilities which are estimated to be usable for peace-time production. Thus if these 250 industrial giants finally acquire the 8·9 milliard dollars of usable Federal-financed facilities on which they generally hold purchase options, their facility holdings will come to 38·5 milliard dollars or 66·5 per cent of total usable facilities and almost as much as the entire 39·6 milliard dollars held before the war by all of the more than 75,000 manufacturing corporations then in existence." [6]

In other words, the tremendous increase of U.S. industrial production during the war was controlled then, and is controlled now, to an overwhelming extent by the big corporations.

These corporations alone are in a position to produce as much in the post-war period as the whole U.S. economic system did before the war.

GROWTH OF TRADE UNIONISM AND THE RISE IN WAGES

However, this tremendous process of industrial concentration and the increase in the power of the giant corporations represents only one side of the picture. It did not come about together with a decline in working-class organization and a growth in social antagonisms. On the contrary, during the war it went hand in hand with a tendency, which had arisen under the "New Deal" policy, towards strengthening the trade unions and—unlike the previous ten years—raising wages and improving standards of living.

The total trade-union membership increased by more than 50 per cent. In 1940 total trade-union membership was 8·9 millions; it rose to 10·7 millions in 1942 and to 14·8 millions in 1945, of which latter figure 6·9 millions were organized in A. F. of L. unions, 6 millions in the Congress for Industrial Organization unions, and 1·9 millions in independent and unaffiliated unions.[7]

This strengthening of trade unionism took place within the framework of an economic system in which industrial production had increased by more than half, and, simultaneously, agricultural production by more than a quarter. From this a phenomenon resulted which was valid only for the United States during the second world war—namely, that although the United States carried out an armaments programme which was finally far bigger than the combined armaments programmes of Germany, Italy and Japan, and although this armament programme accounted for almost half of America's total production, the production of consumer goods during the war did not decrease, wages rose—and real wages at that—standards of living improved, savings increased, and the income of farmers as a whole increased.

During the first world war, when the increase of industrial production in the United States was "only" 15 per cent, the increase in wages was very little higher than the increase in prices, but in the second world war the increase in wages was very much more than the increase in prices, with the result that real wages and living standards rose.

Weekly earnings in manufacturing rose from an average of 23·86 dollars in 1939 to 46·08 dollars in 1944,[8] or an increase of almost 100 per cent, and at the same time hourly wages increased considerably from 0·633 dollars in 1939 to 1·019 dollars in 1944—i.e. an increase of more than 60 per cent. In the same period the "Consumer Index for Moderate-income Families in Large Cities" which stood at 100 in the years 1935–1939, rose from 99·4 in 1939 to 125·5 in 1944, or by a good 25 per cent. Even if we take into consideration the fact that the official index is not an absolutely accurate reflection of the real situation, because during rationing higher prices were often paid for many commodities, the fact still remains that wage increases for all workers were considerably higher than the increase in the cost of living during the second world war.

In particular, the increased earnings of those workers who were formerly unemployed, and of those workers who were formerly ill-paid, led to a direct rise in living standards. Above all, the workers ate better. Civilian food consumption *per capita*, which was 100 in the years 1935–1939, increased during the war to 112. Thus the millions of workers who were formerly unemployed and the millions who were formerly badly paid enjoyed a very much higher standard of nutrition during the war than they had ever had during the period of the unresolved crisis.

At the same time the real wages of the better-paid workers also increased. What did they do when they found that the rationing of many articles of general consumption made it difficult for them to turn their increased real income into increased consumption? They saved a part of their earnings. The result was that during the second world war the savings of the whole nation increased, including those of the working people, who to some extent had to save, and so the U.S. workers entered the post-war period with greater savings than ever before.

Naturally, whilst profits and wages were rising in the United States, the income of farmers generally also greatly increased, because with increased food consumption at home and increased food exports, the market for agricultural production, which had increased by about 30 per cent, was guaranteed at higher prices. The net income of "farm marketing of persons on farms" (*per capita*) which can be represented as 100 in the years 1935–1939 rose to 213 in 1944.

PLANNED WAR ECONOMY IN THE UNITED STATES

The planned-economy war sector of the United States was relatively smaller than that of the other belligerent countries, because first of all U.S. territory was never a battle area even for a single day, and secondly, as a result of the tremendous increase in production as a whole during the war it was possible to keep the U.S. rationing system restricted to certain particularly scarce commodities.

On the other hand, compared with America's own past, the planned economic intervention of the State was very great—greater than it had ever been before. During the first world war a military sector had to be created in a State which had never known a centralized apparatus on the lines familiar to Europe, but that military sector was always far outweighed by the sector which still continued to produce peace-time goods. Armaments production then, and with it State intervention in economic affairs, represented only a temporary interruption. After the war the U.S. Government dismantled it all as speedily as possible.

The situation during the second world war was different in every respect. First of all, when the war broke out the productive apparatus of the United States was not being utilized to the full. Secondly, thanks to the previous "New Deal" period, there was already a centralized State organization, and thus a ready-made basis for the administration during the war. Thirdly, this time the United States was not in the shooting war merely for a year, but for more than three years. Fourthly, this time the U.S. military sector represented, not a relatively small part of the whole economic system, but a very large part, and at its peak it was almost as great as the total production of the United States in the period before the outbreak of the war.

In the second world war the State had to intervene systematically in order to organize the whole economic system. First of all it had to guarantee production for the military sector and give it what was known as A1 priority. But the State not only controlled the armament sector of the national economy, which represented about half the total production of the country, it also had to intervene to control the production of consumer goods. The State decided what consumer goods should be produced, and—what was just as important —what consumer goods should no longer be produced; for example, the production of most of what was termed "durable" consumer goods was suspended for the duration of the war.

494

Essential characteristics of a planned war economy which had shown themselves in the European industrial countries during the first world war, now began to show themselves in the United States. It is not necessary for us to deal with them in any detail.

But it is necessary for us to realize why this tremendous system of planned war economy in the United States functioned so smoothly during the second world war, and why the economic and social antagonisms which had marked the years before the war were, relatively speaking, easily overcome.

The ten years before the second world war were marked by the violent upheavals of the world economic crisis, and by a stagnation of production, by an inability to find new markets for increased productive capacity. The result was that it was very difficult, if not impossible, to bring the interests of Big Business and those of the workers into some sort of harmony.

The second world war brought about a change in this respect too. During the war it was a comparatively easy matter for the State to harmonize the various interests of the different sections of the population.

The tremendous programme of new industrial construction which was carried out in the United States during the second world war was financed overwhelmingly by the State. Big Business refused to bear the costs. The memory of the 1929 crisis, which had not been wholly resolved even when the war broke out, and the memory of the great amount of productive capacity which it was found impossible to utilize, was still too fresh in the minds of America's business men. If Big Business invested its own capital in increased productive capacity during the war, who would guarantee that after the war, when production was switched to peace-time goods, the new factories would find a market for their products? The risk was too great; Big Business turned the idea down.

If the State considered such an enormous extension of productive capacity to be necessary for war purposes, then it should bear the main burden of financing it, and so take the risk out of the proposal for Big Business, went the argument. And this was done, but it must not be supposed that with this gigantic programme of new industrial building, financed for the first time in history by the State, a State industrial sector was created, as was, for instance, the case in Great Britain after the war with the various Nationalization Acts. The U.S. Government did not run the new factories itself, but left their running to private corporations, and primarily to the giant corporations. At the same time the private corporations were granted very favourable terms.

But the U.S. Government went even farther than this: it gave these private corporations the option of buying the factories after the war on very favourable terms once it was obvious that there would, after all, be a market for the increased productive capacity they represented.

The political power of Big Business in the United States was strong enough to get its way without taking the risk of financing this new programme of industrial construction in the first place. It took over the factories afterwards, and thus prevented any further State intervention on the basis of a productive apparatus, organized and controlled by the State.

Under such circumstances, therefore, Big Business, which represented a decisive section of the American social organism, was quite in agreement with the planned economy introduced during the war. But it was not only Big Business which approved, and it was not only profits which rose. Without endangering the power of Big Business, full employment came into being, and the wages of the working class, including the hourly rates, also increased.

The State had brought about full employment, and at the same time profits increased considerably. The State relieved Big Business of the risk attached to expansion. Simultaneously wages rose and trade unionism grew in strength. The State guaranteed the market for a tremendous increase of production by its armament orders.

And as the incomes of all sections of the population, including the farmers and the commercial and other employees, rose, everyone was satisfied, and quite prepared to accept the large-scale intervention of the State in the nation's economic affairs, if only as a necessary evil.

A State planned economy needs power behind it to enforce the carrying out of its plans against opposition if necessary. The U.S. Government was liberally supplied with such power during the war because the overwhelming majority of the American people were in agreement with the object of the war: the military defeat of the Axis powers. At the same time they realized the necessity of a gigantic increase of military production in order to bring this about, and the necessity of a great extension of the power of the State to intervene in the nation's economic affairs.

This general approval of the measures taken by the State which existed in America during the war resulted from a unique situation in which Big Business, workers, farmers—in fact all sections of the population—found their incomes, their profits, wages and farm revenues increasing. That was possible because U.S. war economy was organized in a country whose productive apparatus had previously been only about two-thirds utilized. The tremendous increase in utilization thus benefited everybody, and the increased strength of Big Business on the one hand was balanced by the rise in real wages and a growth in the power of trade unionism on the other. Finally, in this war economy, which could never fully satisfy all requirements,

496

the question of markets for the product of the whole productive apparatus was solved.

Thus with increasing profits and increasing wages, and with guaranteed markets, America's planned war economy was not a difficult matter to carry through, and the economic crisis which had broken out in 1929, and which had not been fully liquidated by the outbreak of war, was finally liquidated in the course of the war itself.

But although the war liquidated the crisis, it did not abolish the causes which had led to the crisis in the first place.

AMERICA'S POST-WAR ECONOMY

If we take the war period and the post-war years as a whole, we can say that the war "boom" and the direct economic effects of the war gave the United States a new economic equilibrium on a higher level. U.S. industrial production declined by comparison with the peak years of the war, but by comparison with the last pre-war years the level of industrial production and of production as a whole was very much higher indeed. Further, compared with these pre-war years, the volume of unemployment after the war was relatively small, and it remained relatively small even in the recession of 1949.

If we compare the years 1929 and 1949, the United States is seen to have continued her economic progress on much the same scale as in the preceding century. In those twenty years production approximately doubled. It increased so much more rapidly than the increase in population that, quite apart from the new industrial construction programme carried out during the war years, the general living standards of the whole population, including the specific living standards of the working people, rose considerably.

In these twenty years the general trend of U.S. development was thus once again very different from the trend in Europe. After the first world war the European industrial nations had to exert themselves to the utmost to regain their pre-war levels of production in the twenties, whereas the United States entered the period after the first world war with a higher level of production than pre-war. When the second world war came it once again threw the peoples of Europe back, whereas once again the United States entered the post-war period with a tremendously extended productive apparatus and a much higher level of production than before the war.

If we represent European production, excluding the Soviet Union, by 100, then U.S. production in 1937 was about 76 per cent of European production, but by 1947 it was 151 per cent, and even in 1948 it was still 135 per cent.[9]

Thus the United States enters the second half of the twentieth century with a productive apparatus which is in a position to produce

497

one-third more goods than all the industrial countries of Europe (not including the Soviet Union) put together.

However, to take the years 1929 and 1949 as standards of comparison is a little misleading. It shows us what the U.S. productive apparatus can do once it is used to full capacity, as was the case during the war, when the State, thanks to its military and armament expenditure, guaranteed markets for the total product. It remained the case during the first post-war years, when the indirect economic effects of the war created a market which permitted the almost complete utilization of U.S. productive capacity. For instance, as happens after every war, enormous investments were necessary to fill up the gaps caused by the war. After the second world war in particular the demand for consumer goods rose tremendously, because during the war it was not only the normally well-to-do sections of the population who had been in a position to save, but also the lower middle-class strata and the working people. Thus when these savings were released in the post-war period the demand for consumer goods increased very considerably.

In addition, there was America's contribution to European recovery and to foreign aid for Asia.

Thus immediately in the first post-war period the fall in military requirements was counter-balanced by the operation of a series of non-recurrent factors which helped to fill the enormous gap.

But these indirect economic effects of the war in the post-war period were, of course, of limited duration. They were able to postpone the operation of those factors which make for economic crisis, but they were not able to abolish them altogether. The decisive question is therefore: will the U.S. economic system be in a position to utilize its gigantic productive capacity to the full in the future, or will it once again find itself involved in market difficulties and economic crisis?

The United States enters the second half of the twentieth century in very different circumstances from those which prevailed in the twenties. Its productive apparatus is almost twice as large, its process of industrial concentration is very much farther advanced, and with it the power of the giant corporations has increased still further. On the other hand, the living standards of its working people are higher and the power of trade unionism is greater than in any previous period of U.S. history.

At the same time, although the influence of the American State is now much reduced by comparison with the planned economy of the war years, it still maintains a very much bigger and more powerful apparatus than it did in the twenties, whilst at the same time it controls a much larger part of the national income through taxation than it did in any previous period of U.S. history.

The following diagram shows us the increase which has taken

place in U.S. government revenue, particularly in the period of the second world war:

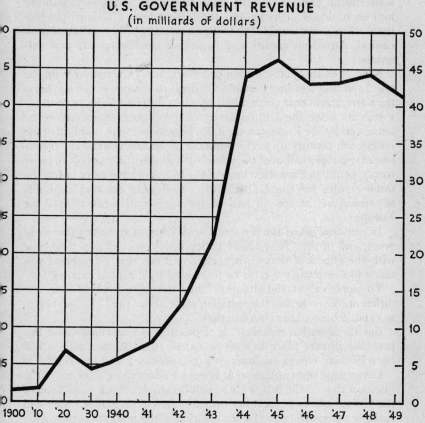

U.S. GOVERNMENT REVENUE
(in milliards of dollars)

The role of the United States in world economy and in world politics is changed, and the influence of the state is much stronger than before on both these fields.

U.S. External Expansion and the Opening-up of New Markets

We do not propose to deal as yet with the repercussions of American policy on the future of Europe and Asia, but to examine first of all the effects of this new situation on U.S. economic development. The first question which arises is whether we can now expect such a tremendous expansion of the United States beyond its own frontiers that, like the external expansion of the European capitalist powers in the second half of the nineteenth century, it will go far to obviate the dangers of economic crisis for a long period by bringing production into more harmonious accord with consumption?

After the second world war the United States was the only great power left in the world with the necessary resources for making large-scale capital exports. At the same time it is the country with the highest standard of living and the highest level of labour productivity. The world outside the United States urgently needs American capital, American credits and American machinery and raw materials.

Now, does this juxtaposition of tremendous U.S. resources on the one hand and a strong demand for them in the rest of the world on the other, mean that there might be—in a different form, of course—a repetition for the United States of the process of expansion experienced by the European capitalist powers in the second half of the nineteenth century up to the outbreak of the first world war? A process of expansion all over the world with analogous results? In other words, could an expansion beyond the frontiers have more or less the same results for the United States to-day as external capitalist expansion in the second half of the nineteenth century had for Europe?

In our analysis of the economic crisis of 1929 and the subsequent years, and of the "New Deal" policy which was developed to cope with the effects of that crisis, we pointed out that no attempt was made to overcome the crisis by increasing U.S. capital exports.

To some extent the situation after the second world war was different. Even before the recession came about the U.S. had begun to expand beyond her own frontiers.

But the question remains: Is it possible, is it probable that this process will take place to such an extent that its repercussions will have decisive effects on America's own economy and markets?

Let us state our conclusion at once: we may regard it as out of the question that in the future there will be any economic expansion of the United States beyond her own frontiers to an extent which will make it a decisive factor for the solution of the market problem.

Let us see why we are forced to this conclusion.

First of all, the industrial production of the United States is much greater than that of Europe, not including the Soviet Union. Now, when a social organism *which accounts for almost half the total production of the world* enters a phase of outward expansion, then that expansion must take on an incomparably greater scale if it is to obtain the same results as were obtained by European capitalist expansion in the second half of the nineteenth century. When we analysed the reasons which led to the stagnation of European imperialism between the two world wars we pointed out that when—as was the case when "The Manifesto of the Communist Party" was written—only 10 per cent of the world is embraced by the capitalist sector, the situation is very different from a period when—as was the case at the time of the first world war—between 25 and 30 per cent of the population of the world lives in countries in which the capitalist system is dominant.

The same thing now applies to the United States. A really gigantic volume of outward expansion would be necessary to obtain even approximately the effects which imperialist expansion had on Europe in the second half of the nineteenth century. And it must not be forgotten that this gigantic expansion would have to be carried out by an economic organism whose foreign trade in relation to its production as a whole was always much smaller than was the case with any of the European industrial powers.

There was no period in history when U.S. foreign trade amounted to more than 10 per cent of total production. We have seen the figures for the past, and we can already say confidently that all indications suggest that in the future, too, the export trade of the United States will not represent more than between 5 and 7 per cent of her total production. Thus foreign trade is never likely to be of the same importance to the United States as it was, and still is, for the European industrial powers.

It is interesting to compare developments immediately after the second world war with developments after the first. A report drawn up by the United Nations [10] provides us with illuminating figures:

United States Production and Foreign Trade

(in milliards of current dollars)

	After the First World War.		Inter-War Period, 1921–1939, annual average.	After the Second World War.	
	1919.	1920.		1946.	1947.
U.S. Gross National Production . .	81·6	94·7	84·3	203·7	228·2
U.S. Total Exports .	7·9	8·2	3·6	10	15·1
Ratio of Exports to Gross National Production (%) . .	9·7	8·7	4·3	4·9	6·6

What do these figures show? In the years immediately following the first world war American exports represented not much less than 10 per cent of the total product. After the second world war they rose substantially in absolute figures, but in spite of all the aid that the United States has given Europe and Asia in the past few years, in spite of the large American export surplus, exports amounted in 1946 to only 4·9 per cent of the total U.S. product, and in 1947 rather more—namely, 6·6 per cent—a percentage much smaller than in the years immediately after the first world war.

The Marshall Plan has brought about no fundamental change in this respect. Even in the first two years, when its costs were highest, when the U.S. financed the unusually large import surplus of Europe, U.S. exports did not even succeed in maintaining the 1947 level. Thus, although the Marshall Plan prevented any intensification of the European crisis which would have led to a considerable drop in U.S. exports and have endangered America's own prosperity, it did no more than that. The volume of U.S. exports as compared with the total U.S. product has not been fundamentally affected by the Marshall Plan.

Thus any analysis of future American developments and America's possible increasing extension beyond her own frontiers must take into consideration the fact that the conditions under which any such expansion would start are very different from the conditions which existed when Great Britain and the other big European states began their period of expansion, and that, in particular, the proportion of U.S. foreign trade compared with the total U.S. product is very small indeed.

Not only are these conditions totally different, but the general foreign-political situation also is totally different.

Europe's great expansion beyond the frontiers took place in a period when the big industrial powers were at peace with each other, a period in which wars, if they took place at all, were comparatively minor affairs fought away from the industrial centres, and therefore, compared with foreign capital investments, military expenditure was relatively low.

Before the outbreak of the first world war Britain's total foreign-capital investments were estimated to be around 3·5 milliard pounds sterling, or between 17 and 18 milliard dollars at the values then prevailing. The annual interest on foreign capital investment alone was greater than the total annual military expenditure before the first world war.

Before the first world war Germany's total capital investments abroad amounted to about 30 milliard marks at the values then prevailing. In 1913, at the pre-war peak point, Germany's military expenditure totalled about 2 milliard marks—in other words, Germany's capital investments abroad were about fifteen times as great as her annual military expenditure, and the additional new capital investments made abroad each year were not much less than the total of military expenditure. In short, peace time was the great period of European expansion.

The situation is very different to-day. After the second world war foreign-political antagonisms are so acute that America's military expenditure even before the Korean War amounted to about 15 milliard dollars annually—in other words, it was about as big in one year as the total sum of U.S. capital investments abroad.

New private U.S. capital exports amounted to 300 [11] million dollars in 1946, 700 million dollars in 1947, one milliard dollars in 1948, and 400 million dollars in 1949,* or an average of 600 million dollars a year in those four years. In other words, U.S. military expenditure amounted to about twenty-five times as much as private capital exports in a year.

As long as a world situation exists in which this relation continues, in which annual capital exports amount to between 4 and 6 per cent of military expenditure, it is unlikely that U.S. private capital will be willing to make investments on a large scale outside the country. But big capital exports above all are necessary if U.S. exports are to increase to such an extent that the relation between them and the total U.S. product is fundamentally changed. That is why we feel justified in concluding that U.S. exports will not solve the market question for U.S. economy in the appreciable future any more than they have done in the past.

America's "normal" exports plus economic aid given through the Marshall Plan, or through similar channels, can temporarily do something to seal off the U.S.A. from any violent economic upheavals outside and prevent them from reinforcing crisis tendencies in the United States. They can help to avoid threatening over-production in certain industries and, above all, in agriculture. Thus they can serve as a sort of buffer to take exceptional strains, but they cannot, as things stand, and in this stage of world history, solve the problem of markets for the United States.

U.S. EXTERNAL EXPANSION IN A PERIOD OF CAPITALIST DECLINE

Although America's expansion beyond her own frontiers and the economic repercussions which result from it are not, as we have seen, a decisive factor for the U.S. economic system itself, they are nevertheless of fundamental importance for numerous other countries into which this expansion extends. That is a point which can hardly be over-stressed.

The same figures which play a very subordinate role in the U.S. economic balance as a whole are of paramount importance for other countries.

The milliard dollars which represents the approximate aid for Great Britain annually under the Marshall Plan was less than 0·5 per cent of U.S. gross national income, but, nevertheless, in some years it represented a decisive factor for the whole course of Great Britain's economic and political development. Because the Marshall Plan, and U.S. expansion generally, is of such paramount importance for other countries, there has often been a tendency to overestimate its importance for the U.S. economic system. On the other hand, just because the Marshall Plan and U.S. expansion generally

* The 1949 estimate is based on incomplete data. Some sources give the total private capital exports from the U.S. in that year at a milliard dollars.

are of only minor importance for the U.S. economic system, U.S. circles have tended to under-estimate their importance for other countries.

In this connection we must now examine the question: what is the world historical situation in which U.S. expansion is taking place to-day? In doing so we shall have to anticipate some of our subsequent conclusions with regard to the Soviet Union, Europe and Asia.

The situation is once again quite different from that in which European capitalism carried out its victorious drive—in part an imperialist drive—over the world. Not only did that expansionist drive proceed from a much smaller industrial basis as compared with the United States to-day, but it took place in a general period of capitalist progress, in a period in which capitalism had nowhere to fight for its very existence, in a period in which economic crises were no more than temporary interruptions of a general rising trend, and, finally, in a period in which imperialism met with no very great resistance on the part of the objects of its exploitation.

In all these points there have been fundamental changes. U.S. expansion is not accompanied by capitalist expansion elsewhere. It is not taking place in a period of capitalist progress everywhere in the world. On the contrary, U.S. expansion is taking place in a period:

1. When after a phase of stagnation between the two world wars, European capitalism, the protagonist of former world capitalist expansion, is threatened with extinction as a social and economic system.

2. When a fundamental change has taken place in countries which were formerly, and in part still are, the objects of imperialist exploitation, when a period of stagnation for imperialism is being clearly followed by a period of decline in which some of the countries which were formerly the objects of imperialist exploitation have already won their independence, whilst others are still engaged in a vigorous struggle to attain the same end.

3. When U.S. expansion collides with Soviet Russian expansionist drives aimed at exploiting the difficulties of European capitalism and the decline of colonial imperialism in order to build up a powerful Russian empire.

The specific structure of U.S. economy and society, and the present changes in Europe, Asia and the Soviet Union already clearly indicate that there can be no very great U.S. expansion beyond the frontiers along the lines of European capitalist expansion from Waterloo to Sarajevo.

INDUSTRIAL EUROPE IS THE MAIN SPHERE FOR U.S. EXPANSION

The main sphere for European capitalist imperialist expansion from the middle of the nineteenth century on was that part of the world which had lagged greatly behind the capitalist metropolitan centres in industrial development.

But to-day the main sphere for U.S. expansion does not lie in such countries, and will not do so in any foreseeable future. The main sphere for U.S. expansion lies in industrial Europe, particularly in Western Europe—in areas, in short, which produced more industrially than the United States did in the period before the first world war, and which, with the full utilization of all their productive possibilities, could produce even to-day approximately as much as the United States.

With this we have come up against a new phenomenon in world history: the relations of a powerful highly-capitalist-producing State to other industrial capitalist-producing States which are, on the whole, on the same level as itself industrially, though in some respects, of course, the United States is industrially more advanced; but States which differ greatly from the United States in that their social structure is badly shaken.

Once again the time-tables of U.S. and European developments are not identical. Precisely because the social structure in the European industrial countries is so shaken that the very existence of capitalism in Europe is called into question, U.S. expansionism is faced with problems which European expansionism never had to face.

In Europe there was also capitalist expansion into big and powerful countries which retained their political sovereignty—for instance, for a long time Great Britain greatly accelerated capitalist and industrial developments in Germany. In addition, the more highly developed industrial countries of Europe did a great deal to accelerate capitalist and industrial developments in Russia and Japan. But that economic expansion into Germany and Japan took place without threatening the political independence of these countries or interfering with their social structures.

The situation to-day where the United States is concerned is very different. The European crisis is so profound and so protracted that four years of the Marshall Plan will not prove sufficient to make Europe economically independent, but America's power is so great that American expansion into Europe will affect the future development of the social structures of the European countries concerned. They will no longer be in a position to decide their future entirely on their own. That future will be affected to some extent by U.S. action—i.e. by the action of a social organism which is incomparably stronger than theirs, which is also militarily stronger, which possesses resources and reserves which can help to alleviate the European crisis, and whose social structure is in many respects different from theirs.

There is, of course, no question of any direct political domination of the United States over the industrial countries of Europe. The

United States represents only one factor in the future of Europe, but it is a factor of very great importance because of U.S. strength on the one hand and the depth of the European crisis on the other. At the same time, and despite all weaknesses and difficulties, the European industrial countries are still strong enough to play a role in their own future development.

The Main Instrument of U.S. Expansion is the State

Another difference whose significance will become more and more clear in the future is the new form of U.S. expansion in Europe. It is not primarily carried out by private capital, because there are no particularly high profits connected with the U.S. position in Europe. In fact, from the point of view of direct profit it is even possible that U.S. expansion may prove to be an unprofitable venture. Not only will it in all probability not provide the extra profits which are usually associated with imperialist expansion, but it may well not provide even the normal rate of profit prevailing in the United States; in fact, a considerable part of the capital invested may one day have to be written off as a loss.

Precisely because there is every likelihood that, considered from the purely economic point of view, the losses of this expansion may outweigh the gains, the share taken in it by private U.S. capital is relatively small. Thus the American State is, and is likely to remain, the chief instrument of this process of expansion.

When the European capitalist industrial states entered into their phase of imperialist expansion, it was essentially an economic imperialism, but the expansion of the United States into Europe in the present post-war period is essentially a political expansion. Its aim is to prevent Soviet Russia from exploiting the extraordinarily deep crisis in Europe, which threatens capitalism all over the continent, for her own ends. The United States is seeking to strengthen those forces which uphold the capitalist system. At the same time the U.S. Government is prepared to pay a big price for success in this venture. The Marshall Plan is a part of that price, but only a part. The expense is not being met by private U.S. capital, but by the American State.

It was also the American State which financed by far the major part of the great new industrial building programme which was carried out during the second world war. American Big Business was not prepared to take the risk involved, though it subsequently pocketed the profits.

Once again it is the American State which is putting up the money to meet the tremendous expenditure involved in this great strengthening of America's position in Europe. Big Business is prepared to invest capital only when there is a prospect of relatively high profits without too much risk.

The fact that the American State has used its resources to intervene in the course of the crisis outside the U.S.A., and particularly in Europe, is one of the factors which has increased the U.S. Budget, and thus the share of the State in the national income, so far above pre-war levels.

Thus this increase has taken place upon a foreign-policy basis, and not for any domestic or economic reasons. This is a point to which we shall return later.

U.S. EXPANSION IN UNDER-DEVELOPED AREAS

It is not only in U.S. relations with Europe—that is to say with highly-developed industrial countries—that the U.S. State is the chief instrument of American expansion. It is also beginning to play the same role with regard to the industrially backward countries of the world, the so-called "under-developed areas", including countries which are still parts of colonial empires and countries which have managed to retain a certain degree of political independence.

In this respect, too, American expansion will take on quite different forms from those of European colonial imperialism in the old days.

European countries seized colonial areas and made them completely subject both politically and economically. This phase of European colonial imperialism is approaching its end, and there is nothing to suggest that the United States has any intention of carving out a new colonial empire of this kind.

If the United States is to have any chance at all of gaining an influence over these countries, then the former objects of parasitic colonial imperialism must be offered some tangible advantage; they must be assisted in their efforts to abolish feudalism and develop industrialism. Any attempt to continue the old discredited imperialist policy along the lines of "classic" European colonial imperialism would not only undermine American influence, but it would at the same time strengthen Soviet Russian influence in these areas.

American expansion in these areas began approximately at a time when the European powers saw themselves compelled to change their relationship to the colonial areas which still remained to them. Thus American expansion is taking place in very different world political conditions to those which existed when European expansion began. It is taking place in a period of great agrarian revolutions, at a time when national-revolutionary movements are growing in strength, and when the relationship of the former colonial and semi-colonial areas to the European capitalist metropolitan centres is experiencing a fundamental change. This expansion is taking place at a time when the State sector exercises a great influence over America's own development. And, finally, it is faced with vigorous communist and Russian expansionist drives.

From this it follows that in this particular sphere of expansion, though for different reasons, the American State will again play the decisive role as the instrument of expansion, whilst the private sector of the American economic system will play only a minor role and is, in fact, not in a position to play anything else. Thus the specific forms of U.S. expansion in the present world historical era tend to strengthen the power and increase the importance of the State sector, and that not merely for a short time, but for a whole era.

However, this is not the only factor which works in this direction, and it is not even the most important.

Armaments Economy in Peace Time

There is a second factor operating to-day which is beginning to have powerful repercussions on the U.S. economic system and on U.S. society generally, and that is the existence of an armament economy in peace time.

The essential points of this development have been dealt with in the previous chapter. In the present era of world history and world powers, and in the present stage of war technique, which may well mean that U.S. territory will be directly in the firing line in any future war, the military position of the United States has completely changed.

The United States is the only great power on the American continent, but it is not the only great power in the world. In the present era of world history all the countries of the world have become next-door neighbours. If one power in the world has a big military sector, then all the others must, willy nilly, have one too.

The United States entered the present post-war period with a strong military sector. It is true that immediately after the war its strength was very greatly reduced, but to nothing like the same extent as it was after the first world war. The military sector remained strong even after the reductions, and an army remained in being which was stronger than any army the U.S. had ever before maintained in peace time. At the same time U.S. armament production also remained greater than ever before in peace time. There is, in fact, little to suggest that the U.S. military sector will ever again be fully dismantled, at least not in any foreseeable future. In addition to direct military expenditure, there is the heavy expenditure for the development of atomic energy, and the military expenditure to support the European signatories to the Atlantic Pact. In the years before the Korean War this expenditure totalled something like 15 milliard dollars. Thus it was not only twenty-five times as great as the sum of private capital export, but it was also many times greater than the sum of foreign aid. Marshall Aid never totalled more than 5 milliard dollars in any one year, in fact, the total expenditure envisaged in the four years of the Marshall Plan is little more than 15 milliard dollars.

Military expenditure alone accounted for about one-third of U.S. Government expenditure, and represented the most influential factor of the whole. It is such military expenditure that strengthens the influence of the State, and it will continue to do so in the foreseeable future.

When we analysed the economic crisis which broke out in 1929 and the subsequent "New Deal" policy devised to combat its effects, we could safely ignore military expenditure, because at the beginning of the crisis it was negligible, and it continued to be so throughout the period of the "New Deal".

To-day, *before* the danger of economic crisis has increased to any considerable extent, the U.S.A. has answered the acute intensification of foreign-political antagonisms with the establishment of an armament economy in peace time for the first time in the history of the country, and that represents a fundamental difference between that period and this.

The United States now wields far greater influence on the development of the rest of the world than ever before. But it is not a one-way affair. From now on, through U.S. expansion beyond the frontiers, and still more through the military sector, foreign policy will exercise a decisive influence on the U.S. economic system and on U.S. society.

Any discussion of U.S. social development which limited itself to the United States would be useless, because America's position in the present world relation of forces, with all its foreign-political, economic and military consequences, has become so important for the development of America's own economic system and her own social organism that it can be neglected only at the risk of creating a completely distorted picture.

From now on the military sector is an essential part of American life.

This military sector, and the whole foreign-political situation, now represent part and parcel of the general relation of world forces which will determine the further economic and social development of the United States.

ARMAMENT ECONOMY, CRISIS AND ANOTHER NEW DEAL

Even before the Korean War the armaments sector and the foreign-aid programme created markets for the U.S. economic system to the tune of over twenty milliard dollars. Before the outbreak of the world economic crisis in 1929, annual U.S. capital exports, together with the military sector, totalled approximately 1·5 milliard dollars. Taking into account the depreciation of the dollar, this sector was already eight or ten times as great in 1949 as it was in the twenties. This explains why military expenditure and the foreign-aid programme were important factors which helped to reinforce

U.S. prosperity in the first post-war years. But, if they had remained more or less at this level, even they would not have been able to do this for long. Between 20 and 25 milliard dollars annually is certainly a gigantic sum, and auxiliary markets of this magnitude would mean prosperity for a long period in any other industrial country today, but not so in the United States.

The economic organism of the United States is too big for that. It grew too much during the course of the second world war. In addition, the productivity of American labour and the size of the American labour force are continuing to grow.

If the productive forces available in the United States are utilized to the full, then in 1954 the country will be in a position "to achieve . . . an expansion of about 18 per cent in total output, and about 12·5 per cent in *per capita* output over that of 1949. At current price levels this would mean the attainment of a gross national product in excess of 300 milliard dollars",[12] as compared with 260 milliard dollars in 1949.

With a national income of 300 milliard dollars, a sector of twenty milliard dollars would certainly be considerable, but in the long run it would hardly be sufficient to obviate the danger of crisis altogether. The war in Korea, and its direct and indirect effects, have, for the moment, shelved the problem of finding markets for increased production. But how long this situation will last we cannot say with any degree of certainty. America's own military expenditure will more than double, and in addition her expenditure in support of the Atlantic Pact powers will also greatly increase. For the immediate future, therefore, U.S. capitalism will have no difficulties in finding markets even for an increased production and an increased productive capacity. As in time of war, the State creates markets, and, again as in time of war, the State abolishes unemployment or reduces it to a minimum. This period of armament economy can last for a long period. However, on the assumption that there is no world war, the time will come when the U.S. armaments sector stabilizes itself at a certain level, and perhaps even declines. When this comes about, the U.S. economic system and U.S. society will be faced with the question which Roosevelt tried and failed to answer in the "New Deal"—namely, how to close the gap between a gigantic volume of production and a volume of consumption which lags behind it, or, perhaps better, how to prevent the gap from opening up in an economic organism for which the process of external expansion has not, and cannot have, anything like the effect that it formerly had for Europe.

U.S. capitalism has pushed its expansion to the territorial limits at home. The process of doing so caused its development to be very different from that of Europe, but the process is now at an end.

The U.S. economic organism is already too big for any external expansion to help it to any great extent to solve the problem of its own inner contradictions.

U.S. capitalism will have to find an answer to the question which no capitalism anywhere in the world has yet succeeded in answering: how is the problem of the crisis to be solved when external expansion can no longer play a decisive part in the process?

On the answer to this question may depend not only the future of the United States, but the future of the whole human race.

U.S. capitalism will meet this great test with a social structure which is incomparably more stable than that of any European industrial country. Let us remember that, as far as the United States is concerned, development was never determined by external imperialist expansion, and that therefore the change which is taking place—has already taken place—in the relations of the capitalist industrial countries to the colonial and backward areas, and hits the European capitalist centres so hard, only indirectly affects the United States. Let us also remember that of the three great upheavals which shook the world in the first half of the twentieth century—the first world war, the world economic crisis which broke out in 1929 and the second world war—the United States was adversely affected socially only by the economic crisis because, unlike Europe and Russia, she was never engaged in total war.

Thus the United States will face this test with a social structure which is more or less stable, with a population whose outlook for the past hundred years has on the whole been determined by the fact that living standards have steadily risen, with a productive apparatus which, although temporarily shaken by economic crisis, has constantly extended, and with a society in which the increase in the productivity of labour—with the exception of the crisis period in 1929 and the subsequent years—was accompanied by an increase in both profits and wages.

On the other hand, however, we must not forget that precisely the U.S. economic organism has become extremely vulnerable to economic crisis—as the 1929 crisis clearly demonstrated—that the gigantic increase of production and industrial concentration has still further increased this vulnerability, and that no section of the population is immune from the effects of a crisis.

THE STRUGGLE FOR POWER IN THE STATE

Precisely this vulnerability to economic crisis of the U.S. economic system has brought about a change in the general social atmosphere. Before the outbreak of the world economic crisis in 1929 the belief in the efficacy of the automatic recovery forces of the capitalist mode of production was very strongly established in the United States. To-day that confident belief is no longer held by the majority of the population. To-day the demand that the State should intervene to prevent a crisis from becoming as severe as the last one, when production was halved and unemployment rose to over fifteen millions, is so strong that no government could possibly ignore it.

Before the world economic crisis there was no big centralized State apparatus in existence in the United States, and during the crisis, under the Roosevelt administration, such an apparatus had to be improvised in order to create an instrument to combat the effects of the crisis. To-day such an apparatus already exists.

The struggle which was waged around the "New Deal" policy, for and against the strengthening of the State sector—which at that time was clearly a sector which supported the working people and gave the "under-dog" a "New Deal"—was a struggle on a purely inner-economic battlefield.

The "New Deal" policy was developed in a country which did not seek to gain any particular influence on other countries, and whose army and military sector were very small.

To-day the situation is fundamentally different.

If the United States is ever again threatened by an economic crisis, then a State sector will already be in existence, and it will be a much more powerful State sector than anything which was improvised to carry out the "New Deal" policy. But this very much more powerful State sector has been created through an armament economy, on account of foreign politics, on account of the direct and indirect effects of the second world war. Without the second world war and the new military and world political position of the United States, the State budget in relation to the total national income would be very much smaller than it was at the time of the "New Deal".

Any increased State intervention to combat the effects of an economic crisis would have to take place in a State in which the military sector and foreign policy already earmark the greater part of the State budget for their own purposes.

Another "New Deal" policy would have to be carried out in a State in which the military sector is, by the nature of things, not a constant, but which can change considerably; it would therefore have to proceed in competition with this military sector. That is a point which can hardly be over-stressed.

Further, another "New Deal" policy would have to be much wider than the Roosevelt "New Deal" policy was, and it would have to go much deeper. In so far as Roosevelt's "New Deal" affected industrial production at all, it was primarily through a series of public works. The "New Deal" policy did succeed in ameliorating the effects of the crisis, but it did not succeed in overcoming the crisis itself. A "New Deal" on the old lines—in 1938–1939 whilst it was in operation there was unemployment numbering between eight and ten millions and the productive apparatus was by no means fully utilized—would, of course, provide no solution.

Another "New Deal"—if it were to have any chance of success—would have to intervene so radically in the running of the economic system that it could create full employment with a steady growth of production and labour productivity.

So far there has been no such radical "New Deal" anywhere in the world, neither in the United States nor in any other capitalist State. Where the State did proclaim it its duty to create "Full Employment"—as, for instance, in Great Britain—it was not carried out on the basis of any "New Deal" (i.e. on the basis of a policy which deliberately sets out to preserve the capitalist system as such), but quite deliberately as part and parcel of an attempt to transform the capitalist system radically.

But long years of stagnation between the two world wars were necessary before British public opinion sufficiently strengthened those forces which were seriously prepared to bring about a radical transformation in the economic system and in society. The people of the United States have not experienced any such period.

If the world situation to-day were not so very different from that which existed at the time of the world economic crisis, the American answer to a crisis could probably be summed up as State intervention in the form of another "New Deal" more extensive than the last, but still not radical enough to get to the roots of the matter.

But the world situation to-day is fundamentally different to what it was in the twenties. A crisis for U.S. society, or even a sharp recession, would no longer remain confined to the United States. In view of the present position of the United States in the world economic system and in world politics, it would be a happening of international importance. Any disturbance which affected the U.S. economic system would have much stronger repercussions on all the countries in receipt of American aid, because, unlike the United States, they have no big reserves to fall back on. Thus a U.S. crisis would mean not only a weakening of the United States, but a weakening of the whole foreign-political block of which the United States is the centre, and at the same time, quite automatically, a strengthening of the second world power, the Soviet Union, and of the foreign-political block of which it is the centre.

Economic crisis and inner economic instability can therefore easily become a factor which increases the danger of war, and, conversely, any action taken to obviate, or at least diminish, the danger of crisis would simultaneously be action to strengthen the cause of peace.

As the strongest power in the world, but at the same time one which is highly vulnerable to the danger of economic crisis, the United States has become a decisive factor for the whole world and in particular for Europe and Asia—that is to say, for States and nations which are themselves in a tremendous process of political, social and economic transformation.

The danger of war is very greatly increased by the fact that the Soviet Union is striving to exploit this process of transformation in Europe and Asia in the interests of its own expansion.

The Soviet Union and the Russian Empire

The United States became the leading power in the world in a long period of development. The trend was accelerated by the second world war, and one of the reasons for this is that U.S. territory was never a battle area even for a single day during the war.

The Soviet Union rose to third place in the order of industrial strength in the world in a comparatively short period, which extended from the November Revolution up to the beginning of the second world war. Now, although she suffered terrible losses in that war, its upshot was to raise her to second place, and she is now the second world power, and head and shoulders above all others, apart from the United States. Owing to her defeat in the war, Germany, which up to then had been the second world power, was temporarily excluded from the general reckoning as a decisive political factor, and she is, of course, still divided. With this the Soviet Union automatically takes second place in the world.

But there is more to it than merely that. Thanks to its geographical situation, the Soviet Union enjoys a unique position, because it is simultaneously a European and an Asiatic power. As a result of Germany's defeat it became the strongest power in Europe, and as a result of Japan's defeat it became the strongest power in Asia, because Japan was the only great power in Asia. In other words, as far as Europe and Asia are concerned, the Soviet Union is *the* world power.

By comparison with continental European countries and with Asiatic countries, she is so overwhelmingly strong that these countries are no longer in a position to repel her expansionist drive from their own strength and resources, and the result is that America's preparedness to intervene is necessary to prevent any further expansion of the Russian Empire.

Post-War Reconstruction was Quicker this Time

At the end of the second world war the Russians were in Berlin as one of the victorious powers, but behind the Red Army was something very much like a desert, on account of the vast amount of destruction which the war had brought to the European provinces of Russia. In the areas occupied by the Germans, production in 1945 was only a third of peace-time production, and in 1946 it rose only to 40 per cent.

The Russians were thus faced with a gigantic work of reconstruction, and although this time the decline in production was often due to the direct destruction of factories and industrial centres, the Soviet

514

Union achieved peace-time levels of production in a much shorter space of time than after the first world war, and then exceeded them. After the first world war it was 1926—about eight years after the end of the war for Russia and about five years after the end of the civil war—before the pre-war level of production was again reached. This time the process lasted only about three years, and in 1949 Soviet production as a whole was higher than the 1940, or pre-war level. How was this obtained so quickly?

1. First of all, unlike the situation after the first world war, the process of reconstruction did not have to begin under a completely new regime in a country devastated by war and civil war. This time it began under the regime which had been in power before the war, and had led the country to victory. It also began earlier—before the war had ended—because as soon as the Russian armies had recaptured a province the work of reconstruction was started at once.

2. After the first world war revolutionary Russia had to begin the reconstruction of her economic system as the most backward industrial country in Europe and without an adequate supply of experienced administrators, engineers and skilled workers, and without any experience either of their own or of others in the organization of a planned economy embracing the whole of the economic system. This time there was already a State apparatus in existence with great experience of running a planned economy, and at the same time, despite the very huge losses of man-power during the war, there were large numbers of experienced administrators and engineers, and large bodies of skilled and semi-skilled workers available.

3. The process of reconstruction was also accelerated by the fact that, unlike the situation after the first world war, a considerable part of Russian industrial production was located beyond the Urals,* where it was immune from all direct effects of enemy action and where it had been greatly developed even during the war years.

4. The rate of Russian post-war reconstruction was also acceler-

* The Russians are continuing this policy of concentrating on the development of industry in the Asiatic provinces with special reference to the dangers of a possible atomic war. When the current Five-Year Plan is ended the proportion of Russian industry located in the Asiatic provinces will have changed as follows:

	1940.	1950.
	%.	%.
Iron ore	29	44
Steel	34	51
Rolled steel . . .	33	51
Coal	36	47·5
Oil	12	36

These figures have reference to the share of the Asiatic provinces in Russia's total output of the above listed commodities.

ated by the fact that Russia, as a victorious power, forced the defeated countries to pay her reparations in various ways. Factories were dismantled and carted off to Russia from both Germany and Manchuria, and, in addition, millions of prisoners of war were used for years both during and after the war, working to rebuild Russia's devastated areas. The Red Army lived off the land in the territories it occupied, and, in addition, the countries concerned had to pay reparations from current production without any consideration in return.

Thanks to all these factors, Russian production developed as follows in the post-war years:

Index of Gross Industrial Output
(1940 = 100)

	1945.	1946.	1947.	1948.	1950. (planned)
Total Soviet production . .	58	70	92	114	148
Production of the Western Provinces which had been occupied by the Germans . .	—	40	53	73	115

Just as they did after the first world war, so this time the Russians carried out the reconstruction of their devastated industrial areas, etc., without the aid of foreign capital. Whereas considerable amounts of U.S. capital, in the form of grants, loans and credits, went to Europe, lend-lease to the Soviet Union stopped as soon as the war was at an end, and the stream of American commodities which had been going to Russia ceased almost entirely. Despite this, the rate of reconstruction in the Soviet Union did not lag behind that of the rest of Europe. Apart from the factors we have already mentioned, the pronounced autarky of the Soviet Union played an important role. No other economic organism was so closely bound up with the world as that of industrial Europe proper. Thus the tremendous transformations which had taken place in Europe and in Asia made big adaptations necessary in industrial Europe, and this slowed down the process of reconstruction.

On the other hand, no other economic organism was so little dependent on the rest of the world as that of the Soviet Union. The Five-Year Plans had brought about a tremendous increase in industrial production, but at the same time Soviet foreign trade declined so considerably that it represented approximately only one per cent of world trade. This very tenuous connection of the Soviet Union with the rest of the world through her foreign trade made her reconstruction almost entirely independent of the great process of transformation going on outside her frontiers.

In our analysis of the United States we have seen that the size of its foreign trade in relation to its production as a whole was almost incomparably smaller than the foreign trade of the European countries in relation to their total production, but this was exclusive of the Soviet Union, whose foreign trade percentage of its total production was even smaller.

In other words, the two powers whose foreign trade plays no noteworthy role in economic affairs, whose foreign trade is not a vital question at all, have become *the* two world powers.

Soviet-Russian Living Standards Very Low

For Soviet Russia the reaching of pre-war standards of production was by no means identical with reaching pre-war standards of living, as low as they were, precisely because, with the same volume of production, a considerably greater part was necessary than before the second world war to build a new productive apparatus. In addition, towns and houses had to be rebuilt and stocks of cattle replenished. Out of 2,567,000 dwelling-houses in towns occupied by the Germans, 1,209,000 were destroyed or very heavily damaged. In terms of dwelling space this represented over 50 per cent. The following live-stock was either killed or carried off by the occupying forces: 7 million horses out of a total of 11·6 millions; 17 million cattle out of a total of 31 millions; 20 million pigs out of a total of 23·6 millions; and 27 million sheep and goats out of a total of 43 millions.[13]

Molotov declared on one occasion that no less than 22 million people had been made homeless in European Russia as a result of the war, and were living in cellars and ruined houses. In order to build houses for these 22 million people, and so reach at least pre-war housing standards as far as they were concerned, Soviet Russia would need a volume of production far in excess of the peace-time volume, or she would have to devote a much higher percentage of her production to the building of houses than she did in the last years before the outbreak of the war. She is doing nothing of the sort.

Soviet Russia's Armament Economy after the Second World War

On the contrary, precisely because the Soviet Union launched a policy of ceaseless expansion immediately after the war, it had to maintain a large military sector in its economy and to mobilize its industries and its laboratories for its armament economy.

A very considerable part of the Red Army remained on a war footing. And in order to keep pace with the United States, the Soviet Union developed an armament economy, particularly with a view to catching up the United States in atom-bomb production. Its successes in this specific field are already well known.

But what was the effect of this on the living standards of the Russian people?

Even when Soviet Russia had to take up the armament race with Nazi Germany before the second world war, the burden on her war economy was so great (because *per capita* production was so low by comparison with Nazi Germany) that she had to abandon all hope of materially improving living standards for the masses of the people in this period.

But in an armament race with the United States her position is, of course, still more unfavourable. The relation of steel production as between Nazi Germany and the Soviet Union was 5 : 4 to the disadvantage of the latter. The relation as between the United States and the Soviet Union is approximately 4 : 1 to the disadvantage of the latter. Thus any attempt to keep pace with the United States means that the Soviet Union must devote a much greater percentage of production to the military sector.

How big is Soviet Russia's military sector? Official figures are 66 milliard roubles for 1947 and 79 milliard roubles for 1949. But these figures do not tell us a great deal because, first of all, the State fixes the prices for all commodities, including those of the military sector, and it can fix them higher or lower at will, and secondly, the Soviet State controls the whole of industry, and therefore all the expenditure involved in the maintenance and development of industry appears in the State budget. In 1949 this expenditure was 159 milliard roubles, or approximately twice as large as that of the military sector, with its 79 milliard roubles. But even then we do not know what percentage of this expenditure ostensibly for industrial purposes is really intended for direct or indirect military purposes.

Thirdly, in preparing for atomic warfare and their defence against it, the Russians are obviously keenly interested first of all in the greatest possible decentralization of their industry as far as its location is concerned, and secondly in putting their most important armament industries underground. When the Russian armies entered Germany in the second world war they were able to see for themselves to what extent the Germans had done just this. During the war the Russians realized from bitter experience how important to them, how absolutely vital for them if they were to survive at all, was the development of their industries in the Asiatic provinces.

It is more than doubtful whether the extra costs involved in building underground factories, in decentralizing the location of industry, and in rapidly developing industries in the Asiatic provinces, appear in the Russian military sector as expenditure. In all probability they are counted in with the general expenditure for economic development.

In other words, the specific economic structure of the Soviet State makes it possible for the Soviet Government to manipulate its budget in such a fashion that without direct falsification the military sector can be made to appear much smaller than it really is.

In the first years after the second world war the armament sector in the Soviet Union was very big indeed, and there is little doubt that it has remained so, because in view of the disturbed political, social and economic situation in both Europe and Asia, there are still very favourable chances for Russian imperialist expansion, and this expansion is largely based on Russia's military strength.

But so long as Russia's armament sector remains big, Russian living standards can rise only very slowly, if at all, and in the best case that means that for years to come they will be materially below those prevailing in industrial Europe.

This is a fact of very great importance in relation to Russia's policy of expansion and its chances of success in Europe.

SOVIET RUSSIA'S EXPANSION

Even after the first world war the Russian Red Army attempted to carry Russian expansion beyond the frontiers, and in the attempt it was defeated at the gates of Warsaw. But at the end of the second world war the Russian armies were already in Berlin, and they controlled and occupied the greater part of the territory between Russia and Germany. After the defeat of Nazi Germany there was, apart from the temporary presence of a large and powerful Anglo-American army, no other big army in Europe than the Red Army.

The victorious Red Army became the backing, and to a great extent the actual instrument, of a tremendous process of Russian expansion. The change which had come about in the structure of the Soviet Russian State was now clearly demonstrated, both in the methods and aims of Russian expansion and in the methods and aims of Russian foreign policy. When the Red Army advanced beyond the Russian frontiers after the November Revolution, it did so as the instrument of a social revolution which was still waging a struggle against its enemies at home. One of its slogans was self-determination for all nations. Lenin was well aware that Russia was a backward country. His great hope was for a socialist revolution in some highly-developed industrial country, preferably in Germany, so that on this basis there would be some chance of developing the revolution in Russia in a socialist sense.

But when the Russian armies poured over the frontiers towards the end of the second world war they were the armies of a State in which the dictatorship had grown steadily more onerous for many years. They were the armies of a State in which the dictatorship was no longer considered a temporary measure, but as a permanent institution.

By this time the Russian State was not in the least interested in any independent socialist movement in any of the countries outside Russia, and it was the task of the Red Army to create, not independent nations in the occupied territories, but completely subservient satellite States. The primary aim was the strengthening of the power of the Russian State, and the tremendous process of social transformation which was proceeding in Europe and Asia was made subordinate to it.

The Economic and Political Transformation of the European Satellite States

Although developments are to some extent still fluid, the main tendencies are already fairly clear.

In the political sphere the original "coalition" governments in the satellite States were turned, sooner or later, into purely communist governments. At the same time those elements in the Communist Parties which were prepared to accept Russian instructions uncritically and without question not only in foreign-political affairs, but also in their own economic affairs, were backed by an absolutely ruthless terror and given control to the exclusion of all other elements.

In the economic sphere all the satellite countries were compelled to nationalize their main industries without compensation to former owners. At the same time the former feudal landowners were deprived of their property, and steps were taken very early on towards agricultural collectivization. To that extent what is going on is analogous to what took place many years before in Soviet Russia after the November Revolution.

But two very important differences should be noted at once:

1. The Soviet Union was—and is—strongly autarkic, and she is not much interested in strengthening her economic relations and those of her empire with the rest of the world. Such a policy was possible in the Soviet Union because of the tremendous extent of her territory and because she produced most of the raw materials she needed within her own frontiers. It was, of course, not possible for the individual satellite States, which are all comparatively small, and are not able to provide themselves with the foodstuffs and raw materials they need and were all formerly dependent to a very great extent on foreign trade with countries outside the Russian orbit.

Russia's economic policy now aims at co-ordinating the Soviet Five-Year Plans with the plans of the satellite States and establishing a high degree of autarky for the whole Russian Empire within which the satellite States will become more and more economically dependent on the Soviet Union.

Soviet Russia aims at increased industrial development in the satellite States, but not, or not exclusively, in the interests of those States. Soviet Russia's own interests are paramount. As the satellite States are small, whilst the Soviet Union is big, as the satellite States are militarily very weak whilst the Soviet Union is militarily very strong, and as their governments are not independent but subject to the Soviet Union, it is quite clear that the latter holds all the trumps in the game and that the development of economic relations between Russia and her satellites will proceed according to the wishes of the former.

2. The collectivization of agriculture in the Soviet Union began about a dozen years or so after the November Revolution. The Russians were not prepared to wait so long in the satellite States, and quite generally the rate of progress there is not analogous to that in Russia. The Russians are well aware that the introduction of agricultural collectivization will greatly strengthen oppositional tendencies, and they have often forced it through against the resistance of the local Communist Parties, which are aware of it too. However, the Russians are willing to pay this price because they calculate that after the carrying out of agricultural collectivization the State will become so powerful that it will be a simple matter to deal with any opposition which may arise.

RUSSIAN EXPANSION AND IMPERIALISM

Imperialism has gone through many changes in accordance with the changes which have taken place in capitalism itself in its various phases, and in accordance with the various aims pursued by the capitalist countries in their imperialist expansion.

If imperialism is taken to mean that a State uses its economic and military power to influence the economic and political future of other countries, then present-day Soviet Russia is an imperialist country, because, for example, it is Soviet Russia—thanks precisely to her economic and military power—and not the peoples of Poland and Roumania which is determining the political and economic future of Poland and Roumania.

However, when people use the term "imperialism" in relation to Soviet Russia, they are apt to overlook the fact that there are fundamental differences between present-day Russian expansion and the capitalist imperialist expansion of the past. As the Russian State to-day is not identical with the capitalist States of the epoch of imperialist expansion, as the Russian State to-day is a State *sui generis*— a State which is neither capitalist nor socialist—it is clear that neither the significance nor the methods of Russian expansion can be identical with the significance and methods of the imperialist expansion of capitalist States in the past, and all analogies which ignore this fact must necessarily be misleading.

The concrete significance of Russian imperialist policy to-day cannot be deduced from comparisons with the imperialisms of the past. In order to understand it we must analyse the nature of the present Russian State, the situation of the objects of its exploitation, and the general world situation.

When communists mouth quotations from the days of the November Revolution, in an effort to persuade the peoples outside Russia that the Soviet Union still supports revolutionary-socialist movements abroad and represents their loyal ally, they are guilty of deliberate deception. The Soviet Union is not interested in such movements as allies or as independent forces, and if they cannot be persuaded or dragooned into abandoning their independence, then they are furiously attacked and vilified, as is the case to-day with Yugoslavia.

However, it is also misleading to talk about Russian imperialism without any closer analysis of the situation, because then it is too easy to identify Russian imperialism with former European or Japanese colonial imperialism, and to overlook the fact that Russian imperialism pursues a totally different economic policy, and therefore looks to very different elements for support, than did the European and Japanese imperialists in their colonies.

As a case in point to illustrate the difference: in all the history of capitalist imperialism there is not a single example of a capitalist metropolitan power introducing a radical agrarian reform in any of the countries of its empire. On the contrary, generally speaking, the imperialist powers sought allies precisely amongst the feudal landowing classes in the countries which they were exploiting.

On the other hand, there is no example either in Russian expansion in Europe or in Asia, where the Russians have not carried out a radical agrarian reform; they either enforce such a reform or they support it, or they support agrarian revolutions already in progress.

In this respect the Russian Soviet State, born of the November Revolution, which was the greatest agrarian revolution of all time, has remained more loyal to the forces which gave it being than in any other respect. Thus here we find that the social significance of Russian expansion is diametrically opposed to the social significance of all previous capitalist imperialist expansion, and as long as the Russian State has to fight directly or indirectly against the forces of feudalism, already dying and condemned to death by history, its dynamic vigour will be difficult to break, because as against feudalism it represents a progressive principle.

At the same time the Soviet Union supports, or enforces, a rapid process of industrialization in all the satellite States, together with the expropriation and liquidation of the former owners of the factories, etc., the nationalization of large-scale industries and the building up of new industries under State ownership and control.

With this policy of industrialization on a State basis in the satellite States, Russian expansion is once again in diametrical contradiction to former European capitalist imperialist expansion, which carried out only a very restricted industrialization in the countries it exploited, and for the most part prevented or hampered industrialization as far as it possibly could.

Again, the Soviet Union is not faced with the problem which formerly confronted the European capitalist imperialist States, of finding markets for their industrial products at the highest possible profit to themselves. Up to the present the Soviet economic system, as we have already seen, has always been an economy of shortages; it has never been able to produce enough, and therefore the question of markets has never arisen. So where Soviet Russia is concerned economic policy in her empire is directed to strengthening her own economic, political and military power, increasing the speed of her own industrialization, and helping to bridge the gap between herself and the more highly developed industrial countries of the world, in particular the United States.

With their policy of liquidating feudalism and expropriating the big landowners, and of seizing the factories and expropriating the capitalists and nationalizing the basic industries, the Russians have destroyed the social basis of all the former ruling classes in all the satellite countries. Capitalist imperialism, on the other hand, took these classes as their allies and helped to keep them in existence.

Now, as these elements and those who sympathize with them are naturally bitter enemies of the Soviet Union, the latter must search elsewhere for allies.

In the Soviet Union itself the supporters of Soviet policy were large sections of the working class and, before the enforced collectivization, the poor and small peasants.

In the satellite States the situation is different. Of course, there are workers there, and as such they are in favour of the nationalization of large-scale industry, but, unlike the workers in Russia at the time of the November Revolution, they did not seize power in a revolutionare situation, and they have never taken any independent action to change the social order. What happened in their case was that the victorious Red Army marched in and created the conditions in which they came to power.

There are, equally naturally, poor peasants and peasants with medium-sized farms, and there are agricultural labourers too, and they all welcome the liquidation of the rich landowners; but that is because they are interested in getting the land for themselves, just as were the poor peasants and agricultural labourers in Russia in the days of the November Revolution. Naturally, the overwhelming majority of these peasants and agricultural labourers are opposed to the collectivization of agriculture.

Those sections of the working class which follow the communists, and certain groups of intellectuals and professional men, are not strong enough on their own to set up a dictatorial communist State to carry out the instructions of the Russians. At the same time, precisely because the Russians insist that the collectivization of agriculture shall be forced through much sooner than it was in Russia, there is little likelihood that the communists will be able to extend their social basis in the near future.

This means that the Red Army, the threat of Russian military intervention, is the decisive factor in the satellite countries at the moment, and likely to remain so in the immediate future. The Russians have completely destroyed the old social order in their empire, but at the same time the elements which have to rule for them there are not strong enough on their own, have not sufficiently powerful social forces behind them, to maintain their rule without Russian support.

THE RUSSIAN EMPIRE IN EUROPE

The following figures show the size of the populations now living in the Russian Empire in Europe:

The Population of Countries under Soviet Influence [14]

Albania	1·154 millions
Bulgaria	7·048 „
Czechoslovakia	12·164 „
Hungary	9·093 „
Poland	23·781 „
Roumania	16·53 „
Grand Total	69·77 millions

The population of Europe, with Great Britain but not including the Soviet Union, was estimated at 384 millions in 1947. The population of the Soviet Union was estimated at 193 millions in the same year. Thus the combined population of the Soviet Union and her satellites was approximately 263 millions in 1947, and that of Europe without Russia's satellites 314 millions. In other words, the population of the Soviet Union and of the Soviet Empire in Europe is approximately 50 millions smaller than the population of the rest of Europe, including Great Britain, and about the same size as the population of continental Europe.

The satellite countries are at very different stages of industrial development. Czechoslovakia, for example, was more or less at the same stage of industrial development as the more highly developed countries of continental Europe, whilst the Balkan countries, for example, were industrially very backward. Before the world economic crisis broke out in 1929 these various countries had the following percentage shares in world industrial production: [15]

Czechoslovakia	1·6
Poland	0·75
Hungary	0·36
Roumania	0·3
Bulgaria	0·1
Grand Total	3·11

To the above total must be added the industrial production of those German territories which, since the second world war, have been included in Poland, some of which were very highly developed industrially—for instance, Upper Silesia—and also the production of Eastern Germany, now under Russian military administration.

All in all we can say that before the war the Soviet Union accounted for about 10 per cent of total world industrial production, whilst the countries which are now her satellites, including Eastern Germany, accounted for a good 6 per cent. This means that since the end of the war the Soviet Union has drawn into her orbit territories which produced about two-thirds as much as she herself produced before the outbreak of the second world war.

That represents an enormous increase in the industrial production at the disposal of the Soviet Union. The Russian Empire in Europe produces far more in relation to the industrial production of the Soviet Union than any previous empire ever produced in relation to the industrial production of whatever European capitalist imperialist State ruled over it. Never, for example, did the industrial production of the British Empire even approximately approach two-thirds of the industrial production of Great Britain, and the same is true of France's colonial empire.

Further, the Russian Empire has been created in a comparatively short space of time—since the end of the second world war. On account of its size alone, the Soviet Union will have to make tremendous efforts to control and direct it centrally.

Living Standards in the Russian Empire often Higher than in the Soviet Union

There is another point which will confront the Soviet Government with a very difficult problem: the difference between living standards in many of the countries of the Soviet Empire and living standards in the "mother" country. Such a problem never confronted either European or Japanese imperialism, whose expansion took place in industrially backward countries whose living standards were naturally lower than those of the "mother" countries. Living standards were, of course, very much higher in the capitalist metropolitan centres, and the ruthless system of exploitation which the imperialist countries, in alliance with the old feudal ruling classes, introduced into their colonies did everything possible to perpetuate the difference, and sometimes even to increase it.

The Russian Empire is, in this respect, also a fact *sui generis*. It is the first time in modern history that an industrially backward country with a low standard of living has been victorious in a war against countries with a more highly developed industrial production and higher standards of living. The Russians did not merely win the war, but on the basis of their military victory they organized an em-

525

pire which embraced, amongst other countries, Eastern Germany, Czechoslovakia and Poland—three countries in which the living standards of the people were, and still are, higher than those of the Russian people, and in which industrial production *per capita* is higher than in Russia.

As the Russian armament sector is so exceptionally large, there is no hope that this difference in living standards between Russia and her Empire will be lessened by any rise in Russian standards of living in the next few years. The gap will remain, though it may possibly be reduced to some extent by a reduction in the living standards of the satellite peoples. But one way or the other this will create difficulties for the Soviet State.

RUSSIA'S STRENGTH COMPARED WITH THE U.S.A.

Russian expansion in Europe has largely been into countries whose economic systems were dominated by agricultural production. Up to the present Russia has met with no success in the heart of Europe, in the leading capitalist metropolitan centres. Although the Soviet Union and its satellites embrace almost half the population of Europe, their production in the major spheres of industry still lags far behind that of the rest of Europe. Great Britain, France and Western Germany together have a much greater industrial production than the whole Russian Empire. As long as this situation continues to exist, the Russians will not be in a position to break down America's great industrial supremacy, and so long will America remain the undisputed World Power No. 1.

The United States to-day has a population greater than the populations of Great Britain, France and Western Germany combined, and at the same time the productivity of U.S. labour is much greater than that of European labour. America's industrial superiority over the Soviet Union is very much greater than that of Nazi Germany before the second world war.

The Russians, of course, have tremendous plans for the further development of their production. Let us take the most favourable variant, and assume that they will be 100 per cent successful. In a speech which attracted a great deal of attention, Stalin informed the world of certain aims which the Soviet Union hoped to achieve after the successful carrying out of three or four Five-Year Plans.

In Stalin's picture of the future the Soviet Union was to produce 60 million tons of steel, 50 million tons of pig-iron and 500 million tons of coal.

Now, even if we assume that these plans are completely successful, the Soviet Union will still lag behind America even with her present production, not taking into account any extension of that production in this same period of fifteen or twenty years.

If the Russians actually produce 60 million tons of steel somewhere in the period between 1965 and 1970, they will be producing about two-thirds of America's actual production of steel at the time of the second world war. And there is no doubt that in this period America will be in a position to increase her production very greatly.

In other words, unless the U.S. economic system falls into the grip of an economic crisis so severe that it will be condemned to stagnation, the Soviet Union cannot remotely hope to overtake U.S. industrial production in the next fifteen to twenty years. The gap between them may perhaps be reduced, but that is all. A great gap would still remain not only between U.S. and Soviet industrial production, but also between the former and the latter plus the industrial production of Russia's satellites.

However, this will be true only if Russia can be prevented from making any further expansion in Europe. The situation would change dramatically if the Russians could make further conquests in Europe—if, for example, they could get their hands on the whole of Germany. Let us do a little simple addition. Before the first world war the Soviet Union accounted for about one-eighth of world production and Germany accounted for about one-sixth. If Germany were to fall completely under Russian influence, Russian strength on the European continent would become irresistible. A Russian Europe which extended to the Atlantic would have a possibility not only of catching up with United States industrial production, but even of exceeding it. A Russian Empire which extended to the Atlantic would have a well-founded hope of eventually becoming *the* world power.

In other words, if the Soviet Union succeeds in driving forward into the heart of industrial Europe, if she succeeds in incorporating Europe into her Empire, then the decisive turning-point in the world relation of forces will have been reached.

This is the reason for persistent Russian expansionist efforts on Russia's European frontiers, and those efforts will be continued for the whole of the present world phase.

How far the Russians will meet with success in their efforts in this direction depends on a variety of factors; not only on her own military strength, but also on the policy pursued by the United States and on the situation in the European countries themselves, in particular on the situation in Germany.

THE MILITARY STRENGTH OF THE SOVIET UNION

Before we deal with the European situation we can say definitely that the military strength of the Soviet Union in comparison with the military strength of the United States is much greater than would be expected having regard to the great gap between their industrial strengths. It would be a fatal error, for example, to suppose that because the United States is greatly superior to the Soviet Union industrially, she is also militarily superior *to the same extent*.

There are three main reasons why this is not so. First of all, in relation to their total industrial production, the Russians have an incomparably stronger military sector than the United States. That was true in the first post-war years, and it is still true to-day, although as a consequence of the war in Korea the United States has greatly increased its military sector. Russia's armies were demobilized to a far less extent than the armies of the United States, and, in addition, Russia's armaments production remained much higher, whilst her research work and her production of new weapons were even considerably stepped up. The main reason why the Russians succeeded in producing atomic bombs much more quickly than the Americans had expected was that their military and armament sector continued to remain so strong.

Thus the peace-time military strength of the Soviet Union in relation to the peace-time strength of the United States is very much greater than any mechanical comparison of their respective industrial capacities would lead us to suppose. In consequence of this it would be very much easier for the Soviet Union to reach the peak of her armaments production in a new war than for the United States, because the level from which she would start would be so very much more advanced.

Then there is the geographical situation of the Soviet Union to be taken into consideration. The whole of Europe is not only within easy reach of Russian bombers, but is also in imminent danger, in the event of war, of being rapidly over-run by Russian armies. There is thus a very grave danger that in the event of war the greater part of Europe's industrial potential would be incorporated in Russia's own military sector.

Finally, industrial strength has to be translated into military strength. It is not enough that the United States can produce three or four times more steel than the Soviet Union. That steel must be turned into weapons which can be used on a battlefield. In addition, the armies to use those weapons, and all their supplies, must first be transported to the battle area.

The fact that after their great victories in the opening phases of the attack on the Soviet Union the German armies nevertheless soon found themselves bogged down, was largely due to the fact that Germany's industries were so far away from the fighting front, and therefore Germany's military supplies had such a long way to travel, whereas Soviet Russia's industries—at least some part of them—were quite near to the battle fronts and it was relatively easy for her to supply her armies.

The distances between America's industries and the probable battle areas in a new war will be very much greater, and they will swallow up a great deal of America's industrial effort, if war does come, with the result that her approximate industrial superiority of 3 : 1 will be greatly reduced. Of course, the argument is equally applicable the other way round. If the Russians have to conduct military operations far away from their industrial bases, then that will greatly reduce their military potential. Thus the Russians have not even the very faintest chance of winning a war which had to be carried to U.S. territory.

However, the combination of the three factors we have adduced—the tremendous existing military and armament sector of the Soviet Union; the highly favourable geographical situation of the Soviet Union in Europe and Asia; and the enormous distances the Americans would have to cope with in the event of a war fought out either in Europe or Asia—greatly reduces the industrial superiority of the United States in so far as it can be translated into terms of military strength for use against the Soviet Union.

Thus, as far as military strength in Europe or Asia is concerned, there will not be such a great gap between the two world powers. If, despite the rapid development of modern weapons of war, the war should last for any length of time, there would probably be a slight balance in favour of the United States, or rather of the block led by the United States, which would, of course, have the military and industrial strength of Great Britain and the British Commonwealth at its disposal.

EXPANSION NOT AN ABSOLUTE NECESSITY FOR THE RUSSIANS

As the difference in the military strength of the world powers is very much less than the difference in their industrial strength, this represents an encouragement for the Russians to attempt further expansion. But—and this is a point of such importance that it can hardly be over-stressed—although we must quite certainly expect further attempts at Russian expansion in the future, they do not and will not result inevitably and of necessity from the structure of the Soviet State, from the nature of its social and economic structure. Since the carrying out of the enforced collectivization at the beginning of the thirties, the Soviet State has experienced no further fundamental changes. It existed for long periods without any expansion and without feeling the need for it. And to-day there are still no inner-Russian necessities which peremptorily demand further expansion.

The Soviet State has gone through tremendous upheavals and experienced tremendous difficulties whose causes were very different from those which upset capitalist society everywhere during the world economic crisis. However, the Soviet State managed to overcome these troubles—for instance, those which resulted from the enforced collectivization and those which resulted from its own armament economy—without indulging in expansionism.

And now, in the period after the second world war, Russia is undoubtedly going through a very difficult period. Although she was victorious, the masses of her people must now go back to a standard of living which was for years, and still is, even below the very low standard they had before the war. Although the Russians were victorious, their standards of living are below those of the defeated. Although they live in the victorious "socialist" motherland, they—workers, peasants and minor officials—have a standard of living below that of the workers, peasants or farmers, and minor officials in the more highly developed capitalist countries.

Now, it is clear that the Russians would find it easier to tolerate these conditions if Soviet Russian expansionism continued successfully, if their rulers could say to them: "The socialist principle reigns here in Russia and in the Russian Empire, and amongst the nations of Asia directly or indirectly supported by Russia, and the socialist principle is on the march. Capitalism reigns in the rest of the world, and capitalism is in decline. A clear proof of this is the expansion of the Russian Empire, the continued victorious drives beyond our own frontiers. This is a period of transition, and if you have to pull in your belts to ensure our further expansion, you are at least laying the basis of our final victory."

It is clear that with such a line of argument—if it appears based on fact—it is easier to demand further sacrifices of the Russian people, just as it was when the argument went that it was necessary to live austerely in order to reply to Hitler's war economy in peace time—an argument which was certainly based on fact and has been since justified by Russia's victory.

However, although it is quite clear that a continuation of Russia's victorious expansionism would make it easier for her to overcome certain difficulties in her development, this does not mean that she is compelled to expand, that expansion is a vital historical necessity for her.

The Soviet Russian State in its present form is under no inevitable compulsion to expand. Soviet Russia is not in the position of having to expand or perish. The corollary of this is, of course, *that her existence is not in the least threatened if she does not expand.* She could easily survive the stopping of her expansion, and she could go about her affairs without expansion just as she did for many, many years before she was as strong as she is to-day.

Soviet Russia is in a position to survive such a necessity easily and to swallow setbacks here and there, particularly as her expansionism is not confined to one continent.

Soviet Russia's Asiatic Expansion

The Soviet Union is both a European and an Asiatic great power. She has become stronger in Europe because she has created a

Russian Empire there, and she has become stronger in Asia in the first place because in the past ten, perhaps fifteen, years she has developed industry in her Asiatic provinces at a more rapid rate than in her European provinces.

The Soviet Union lies between Europe and Asia in more senses than the merely geographical. In *per capita* production and in living standards the Soviet Union is far behind Western Europe, but in the same respects she is ahead of almost all the other nations of Asia.

Thus so far as further Russian expansion in Europe is concerned, the low level of living standards prevailing in Russia represents a very difficult obstacle; but for further Russian expansion in Asia her higher technical standards and relatively higher living standards naturally represent an advantage.

Another difficulty where Russian expansion in Europe is concerned is the fact that a terrorist dictatorship exists in Russia, and it is one which tends to become more rather than less intense. This difficulty does not exist for Russian expansion in Asia, because there the population has been enslaved by feudalism for centuries, and in many cases subsequently oppressed by an alliance of capitalist imperialism and native feudalism.

For the European worker, for the European farmer or peasant, and for the European middle strata, the word democracy has a living meaning. They know what political and personal liberty is. In some cases they have lost it for a while, and now that they have it back again it is more precious than before. But for hundreds of millions of people in Asia democracy is a word vaguely heard of, and in the European and American sense it has little or no meaning to them. These people never have known what personal and political liberty means, and they still do not know to-day. They are much in the position of the masses of the people of Europe in the Middle Ages, like the serfs under feudalism, like the slaves of Ancient Greece and Rome. Thus for them the fact that the Russian form of government is a terrorist dictatorship is not in the least objectionable; they have never been used to anything else. For the majority of Europeans, on the other hand, the thought is frightening and repulsive.

For the peoples of Europe the Soviet Union is also a country in which ordinary people have a very low standard of life, and, in view of the experiences of the satellite peoples, they fear that Russian expansion into Europe would mean a lowering of their living standards. But for the Asiatic peoples the Soviet Union is a country with a higher standard of living, and a country which created this higher standard of living without any assistance, without any loans, from the still more highly developed countries—and this is a fact of cardinal importance so far as Asia is concerned.

At the same time, the three radical economic changes the Russians introduce wherever they have any direct or indirect influence are

531

more or less in accordance with the general trend of the social-revolutionary movements which are now in the ascendant throughout Asia.

(a) The struggle against feudalism which the Russians support vigorously everywhere, and which they bring to a victorious conclusion wherever they have the chance, is one which is of paramount importance for the whole of Asia. For the moment this problem is not in the foreground in India, but that must not blind us to the fact that when the Indians, having won their freedom from British colonial imperialism, begin to get to grips with their own social and economic problems they will come up against this particular problem almost at once.

(b) The Russian policy of forced industrialization everywhere is one which meets the great need of the Asiatic peoples, many of whom have to begin their industrial development at an even lower level than that of Russia in the days of the Tsars and at the time of the November Revolution.

(c) Accelerated industrial development under the control and influence of the State is also in accordance with the general trend in Asia.

All indications suggest that the capitalist development of Europe from feudalism to manufacture, from smaller factories to larger factories, to big monopolist organizations and giant corporations during a long phase of liberal capitalism without any very great interference from the State in economic affairs, will not be repeated in Asia.

There are also many reasons for believing that in most Asiatic countries the alliance between capitalist imperialism and native feudalism will be replaced by an economic system which, although it may differ considerably as between country and country, will give the State from the very beginning a decisive say in the development of both industry and agriculture.

In the first phase of Russian expansion in Asia after the second world war it differed essentially in its form and methods from Russian expansion in Europe.

It was largely the victorious Russian armies which enforced the tremendous social transformation which has taken place in the countries which now form the Russian European Empire. The inhabitants played only a subordinate role in the process.

The situation in Asia was very different.

It was the largely independent Chinese Revolution—one of the greatest events in world history, and one fraught with tremendous possibilities for world developments in the second half of the twentieth century—which carried through the process of transformation in China, and here it was the Russians who played the subordinate role. It was Chinese, not Russian, armies which destroyed Chinese

532

feudalism. The Russian role is merely to exploit the agrarian revolution in China as elsewhere in Asia, and the national-revolutionary movement against the old colonial powers, to strengthen Russia's own position and extend her sphere of influence.

Whether, and to what extent, Russia will succeed in attaining her objects in Asia will depend on a variety of almost equally important factors: her own military strength, to what extent the power and influence of the Asiatic countries themselves will develop in this gigantic process of social transformation against feudalism and imperialism, and to what extent the old European colonial powers, themselves now in a process of transformation, and the United States can succeed in influencing developments in Asia.

Now, important as further expansion in Asia is for the Soviet Union, the fact is that *in the immediate future* Asia will, on the whole, play a subordinate role in Russia's plans, because at present Asia's industrial and military strength is very small. For instance, the industrial production of Western Germany is greater than that of all the Asiatic countries combined. That is not only true to-day, but it will remain true for a very long time to come.

The Transformation of Europe

We speak of Europe as though it were a single entity, but in fact it is not. The second world war, for example, obviously affected defeated Germany very differently from victorious Britain. However, despite all differences, the second world war had decisive repercussions on the whole of industrial Europe.

First of all, Europe's position as the capitalist and industrial centre of the world no longer exists. In the period of world history into which we are now entering Europe is in danger of becoming an object of history rather than, as in the past, an actor.

Secondly, the capitalist system in Europe is more shaken than ever before, and there is already a move to bring about its radical transformation.

When we speak of Europe from now on, we shall mean that part of Europe which is outside the Russian Empire—i.e. the industrial Europe which was, before the first world war, the heart of capitalist production, the Europe which before the second world war still produced more than the United States, the Europe which was the capitalist centre of the world. Apart from anything else, the relative importance of Europe in the general relation of world forces has declined owing to the rising power of the United States on the one hand and the Soviet Union on the other. But that is not all: the absolute strength of Europe has considerably decreased, and this makes its relative position still weaker.

The figures for industrial production do not give us a proper picture of the situation. As the decline in production in Britain and

533

in Western Europe generally was not very great during the war, both Britain and France fairly easily reached pre-war production levels (100) again, and in 1948 they had both surpassed them, Great Britain with 121 and France with 108. At the same time the production of Europe as a whole, not including Germany, was 113 in 1948, and even including Germany it was 96.[16]

Thus this time Europe recovered her pre-war production levels much more rapidly than after the first world war, but the historical environment in which Europe's productive apparatus now has to work has changed so fundamentally that Europe's position has been greatly shaken.

The Decline of European Influence in Eurasia

Unlike the United States, whose capitalism expanded within her own borders, Europe became the industrial and imperialist centre of the world by means of a gigantic external expansion beyond her own frontiers, and at the peak of this development Europe was the industrial centre of a great outer area with a population four or five times as big as that of industrial Europe proper.

Russia herself once belonged to this European periphery, together with all the other countries of Eastern Europe, the countries of Asia and Africa, and, in rivalry with the United States, a great part of South America.

Europe was the factory centre for the vast Eurasian area.

As a result of the first world war and the November Revolution, Russia broke away from this area, and in the period between the two world wars there had already been a certain stagnation in the countries, many of them formed as a result of the war, between Germany and Russia, and at the same time there was a stagnation of imperialism in Asia.

Now, after the second world war, not only is Soviet Russia outside this area, but also the countries between her and Germany. They are largely lost as markets for European industrialism and have become a part of the Russian Empire. In the first years after the second world war their share, together with that of Russia, was only between one-third and two-fifths of the not very high pre-war figures for their trade with Europe.

In short, Eastern Europe has ceased to be simply a foodstuffs and raw material Hinterland for Western Europe, which now has to deal with Russia's satellites there. And throughout Asia the process of transformation which began to make itself more and more obvious in the years between the two world wars has now, after the second world war, developed tremendously. First of all there was the period of European imperialist expansion, a period which lasted roughly up to the first world war; then came the period of imperialist stagnation, covering roughly the period between the two world wars; and now comes the period of decline for European colonial imperialism. During the war it received heavy blows from Japanese imperialism, and owing to Europe's own decline it is now weaker than ever. It is no longer strong enough to oppose the national-revolutionary movements in the colonial and semi-colonial countries with any hope of success.

India, once the symbol for a whole epoch of European colonial imperialism, is now a free and independent nation. It was the British Labour Government which—against strong Conservative resistance —voluntarily brought the rule of British imperialism in India to an end.

It has ended for ever, and it is perfectly obvious that the final victory of the Indian national-revolutionary movement must have had strong repercussions throughout Asia. Not only is British imperialism losing its decisive position, but every European colonial imperialist position is threatened. But although European colonial imperialism has lost a great deal, it has not yet lost all.

European Imperialism and the Remains of its Colonial Possessions

The course of history did not bring about a sudden decline in European imperialism. The long period of imperialist expansion was followed by a period of stagnation in which no further advance was made, and only after that did a rapid decline set in. The second world war did not represent the end of colonial imperialism. We are now experiencing the decline which will lead to that end. It is not merely a simple decline, but certain former imperialist countries are now striving to change their relationship to the territories in which they are still dominant, and also to numerous semi-colonial countries and areas.

To-day, in a process of Asiatic revolution, in a big process of transformation in Europe itself, and in a period of intensified antagonism between the two world powers, it is not possible to say whether this attempt to change the relationship between the European metropolitan centres and the territories in which they still wield a great influence will be fruitful for Europe and the remains of its colonial possessions and spheres of influence. But even in the best case, a more progressive relationship between the metropolitan centres and these areas would take time to develop, and it would still remain true that for the immediate future Europe's position in Asia is fundamentally weakened.

The industrial countries of Europe found markets for their products not only in Europe, but also, and to a considerable extent, in the areas outside Europe—in the colonial and semi-colonial countries. The vast change which has now come about in these areas demands that Europe should widely adapt her production to the new situation

535

which has arisen. But the tremendous crisis of this process of transformation has to be met and overcome by Europe without any very great reserves of capital.

Here, too, the second world war did no more than draw a line under a process of development which began many years earlier. Europe was the only world exporter of capital in the long period before the first world war, and in the period between the two world wars she was second only to the United States in capital exports. But now, after the second world war, Europe as a whole has become a debtor area, and that is not a temporary phenomenon of the first post-war years.

The relation of Britain to India is symbolic and symptomatic in this respect. The big supplies from India to Britain during the second world war were not paid for with British exports. The greater part was set down to India's account for subsequent settlement, and the other part was met by the liquidation of British assets in India. When the war ended Britain found herself indebted to India for the first time in history; her debts far outweighed her assets.

After the first world war, Britain, a victor country, was still a financial centre with great capital assets abroad. Defeated Germany lost all her capital assets abroad.

In this respect the second world war left both victors and vanquished in the same position: they were all debtor countries.

Even before the second world war Europe needed to pay for only two-thirds of its imports with exports, because the other one-third was paid for with the interest on its foreign assets and by other "invisible" exports. Now, however, this favourable position has been largely lost. The decisive difference between the present period, after the second world war, and the period after the first world war is thus very clear.

At that time industrial production throughout Europe had fallen much more heavily than after the second world war, but at least Europe had large capital assets abroad, and very profitable economic relations still existed between the capitalist metropolitan centres and the colonial and semi-colonial areas in Asia, Africa and in South and South-East Europe. Thus very soon after the first world war it was possible for Europe to resume the tremendous exchange of European industrial products with raw materials and foodstuffs from these areas. Thus Europe's position as an industrial centre and independent power was not endangered by the first world war.

To-day the situation is different.

As part of the Eurasian continent, Europe's political and social structure has been greatly shaken by Russia's expansion in Europe and by the creation of the Russian Empire, by the Asiatic revolutions and the decline of its own imperialist position in Asia; in other words, by the gigantic process of transformation which embraces the whole Eurasian continent. That is why, although the fall in indus-

536

trial production was much smaller than during the first world war, Europe is now, after the second world war, experiencing the worst crisis in its history.

Europe's Foreign Trade and the Marshall Plan

The political, economic and social changes which have taken place on the Eurasian continent represent one of the decisive factors which has changed the relationship between industrial Europe and the United States. If Europe is to adapt her productive apparatus to the changes which have taken place in the colonial and semi-colonial areas which represented its periphery, if it is to do this without reserves of capital and without any drastic cuts in its standards of living, if it is to reach the scale of its peace-time imports without being able to pay for them with exports, then somehow or other the gap in its balance of foreign trade must be closed.

That was one of the objects of the Marshall Plan, which was to extend over a period of four years, and cost the United States about 15 milliard dollars—i.e. about the same as one year's expenditure by the United States on military preparedness before the war in Korea.

The Marshall Plan was publicized in the United States in the first place as a temporary measure to assist war-scarred Europe to bind its wounds and to facilitate the transition to a peace-time economy, and it was assumed, in complete misunderstanding of the real situation,[*] that Europe's foreign trade with Russia and her satellites, and in particular with the countries of Asia, would rapidly resume its pre-war volume.

Gradually it was recognized that, apart from the direct effects of the second world war, Europe's whole position had been greatly weakened, not merely temporarily, but for a very long time. Before the outbreak of the war in Korea it was already quite clear that Europe's dollar gap would continue to exist even after 1952. The great strengthening of the military sector in the United States and in the Western European countries may, in the immediate future, facilitate the closing of this dollar gap, particularly as the United States will make a very considerable contribution to Western European armaments. But, of course, armaments alone cannot, in the long run, solve this problem. In any case, Europe will continue to remain dependent on American aid for many years after 1952.

This is a factor which is of decisive importance for America's position in the world and for the future development of the European crisis and of the European process of transformation.

The decision with regard to the future social structure of Europe no longer rests with the European alone, and this factor greatly in-

[*] For greater details on this point see the author's "Living with Crisis", John Day Co., New York 1949, and in particular the chapter "False Calculation in the Marshall Plan".

creases the danger inherent in the European crisis. Perhaps it will give a clearer picture of the enormous difficulties which bar the way to the creation of a progressive, democratic society in Europe if we sketch the general social and political relation of forces in which the struggle must be fought out; if we compare this real world with the expectations of Karl Marx and of the Social Democratic Parties which developed in Europe on the basis of his ideas.

Europe was the centre of the democratic socialist labour movement, which aimed at bringing about socialist economic and political principles step by step. Democratic socialism never became a mass movement anywhere outside Europe.

There was no chance for it in the United States, because up to the outbreak of the world economic crisis in 1929 U.S. industrial production and U.S. labour productivity expanded almost without interruption and the living standards of all sections of the population improved. In such circumstances there was, of course, no mass opposition to capitalism. It is characteristic that even to-day there is still no socialist daily newspaper in the English language published in the United States, whilst in Europe almost every big town has its own socialist daily newspaper, and sometimes more than one.

At the same time democratic socialism could not become a mass movement in Russia or in Eastern Europe generally because these were industrially backward areas ruled by Tsarism. The main struggle there was against Tsarism, feudalism and reaction, and not against modern industrial capitalism.

In China, India and the other colonial and semi-colonial countries it was also impossible for a democratic socialist movement to develop on any scale, because the fight there was for political independence against foreign oppression, and the struggle for national liberation outweighed all other considerations.

To-day, Europe, the centre and birth-place of the democratic socialist movement, the only part of the world in which there have ever been mass socialist parties, the area in which socialist thought and socialist ideas have developed for the past hundred years, is now, as a result of the long train of development which began with the first world war and culminated in the second, facing a situation such as that envisaged by Karl Marx over a hundred years ago when he wrote "The Manifesto of the Communist Party" and, approximately twenty years later, "Das Kapital". Industrial Europe is now entering a phase in which imperialism and external expansion are no longer possible, because the vast area which was formerly their dependent periphery is now rapidly becoming more and more independent.

Whilst conditions in industrial Europe are approaching nearer and nearer to the categories in which Karl Marx undertook to analyse capitalist development *as a whole*, and with it, and within it, European

538

development, the position of industrial Europe itself has changed decisively.

Throughout Marx's life Europe was the centre of world capitalism and world industry, and he assumed that if fundamental changes occurred in the centre they would spread out to the periphery. But now that changes such as Marx foresaw are actually taking place in industrial Europe, Europe's general position has been critically weakened. Europe is no longer the heart of world capitalism and world industry. First of all, it has lost its industrial leadership to the United States, and secondly a new State has arisen on the borders of industrial Europe, the Soviet Union, the strongest military power on the Eurasian continent, and this new State is doing its utmost to influence the development of Europe in its own favour.

Karl Marx believed that socialism would first be victorious in the industrial centre of the world, and that from there it would spread outwards, and as the world then was a socialist victory in Europe would have had little to fear from any outside intervention.

But to-day the situation is very different. Marx believed that the only power which stood between the workers of the industrial countries and socialism was the resistance of their own ruling class. But nowadays if democratic socialists should come to power as the result of the altered conditions in industrial Europe, and then attempt to remodel their countries along socialist lines, they would no longer have only the resistance of their own ruling class to contend with. There would be other factors.

1. They would have to overcome considerable opposition amongst the workers themselves, as a result of the fact that for the past hundred years they have benefited from the exploitation of Europe's colonies and of the industrially backward periphery generally. Though, historically speaking, the era of colonial imperialism is drawing to an end, it is not yet at an end; we are now in mid-process, and as long as it still goes on sections of the working class will continue to have a certain interest in upholding imperialist rule in the colonies and allying themselves with the capitalists.

2. Still more important than the difficulties likely to arise on account of the remnants of colonial imperialism, is the fact that in the present period of world powers it would be quite impossible to carry out a complete socialist transformation in one European industrial country alone. Such a thing would be possible only if the basis of operations were widened to include at least the greater part of industrial Europe. From this it results that in order to have any hope of success, the socialists of Europe must break down all national barriers, because they are utterly incompatible with a socialist Europe.

3. They would also have to overcome the opposition of powers outside industrial Europe—for instance the United States, whose influence on industrial Europe is greater to-day than ever before. The

United States has a vastly different social structure, one built up in and shaped by different historical conditions. There has never been a mass socialist Party in the United States at any time in history.

4. They would also have to cope with the opposition of the Soviet Union, which is the strongest power in Europe to-day. The Soviet Union is also a country which has never known a democratic socialist movement on a mass scale, and it would certainly feel that its present social system was indirectly threatened by a democratic socialist victory in industrial Europe.

A paradoxical situation has arisen in which conditions in Europe are beginning to show trends that Marx expected to arise at a much earlier date, but that the conclusions to be drawn from them now are by no means the same as he supposed, because in the meantime the position of Europe has been very greatly weakened.

It is an indication of Marx's genius that he did occasionally refer to such a possibility, but he never did so in any systematic detail: "The difficult question for us is this," he wrote on one occasion.[17] "On the continent the revolution is imminent and will immediately take on a socialist character. But will a revolution in this part of the world not necessarily be crushed, since in a much larger territory the movement of bourgeois society is still in the ascendant?"

Thus more than ninety years ago Marx foresaw that conditions for a social revolution might mature in industrial Europe, whilst in the United States bourgeois society and capitalist production were still in the ascendant. Even then Marx asked himself whether the socialist revolution, and with it the establishment of a new society, would be able to maintain themselves under such conditions.

The present situation differs from the one Marx envisaged in three important particulars:

1. Marx was thinking of a socialist revolution similar in many ways to the bourgeois revolution of 1848, which he had witnessed as a young man, a revolution with dramatic clashes. But in reality the revolution in industrial Europe is a long and difficult process of transformation and we are living in the midst of it to-day.

2. From this it follows that the danger of intervention does not arise only after the victory of socialism in industrial Europe, but at every step which is taken towards a socialist transformation.

3. Intervention threatening industrial Europe's efforts to create a new social order would come not only from the United States, but also, and simultaneously, from a State with a new social system, the Soviet Union. That was a possibility Marx did not foresee and could not have foreseen.

Europe has to contend with the intervention of these two world powers, the United States and the Soviet Union, in every phase of its post-war development.

We shall deal with this intervention further in our analysis of the

540

two biggest industrial powers in Europe, Germany and Great Britain.

The intervention of the two world powers in European affairs can be seen very clearly in Germany.

We have already dealt at some length with Soviet Russian intervention. A part of Germany to-day is already a Russian satellite State, and, of course, Russian expansionist efforts towards Western Germany are not by any means at an end. They can be pushed into the foreground again as soon as the state of Russo-American relations on the one hand, and the intensification of the political and social crisis in Germany on the other, seem to offer the Russians a favourable chance for new action.

The intervention of the United States is of a more complex character, and it is primarily an intervention in the process of social transformation which is going on in Germany.

THE EFFECTS OF THE SECOND WORLD WAR ON GERMANY

Germany lost the second world war and suffered military losses six times as great as those of Britain and France put together. At the same time the fall in German industrial production caused by the war was not only incomparably greater than the corresponding fall in British and French industrial production, but it was also very much greater than the analogous fall in production during the first world war, and it was caused in part by the devastation of Germany's towns and industrial centres.

We have already seen of Europe as a whole that it was profoundly affected by the great changes which occurred and which are still occurring in its one-time periphery in Eastern Europe and Asia, and that it entered the present post-war period acutely short of capital. All this applies in particular to Germany.

Germany lost that colonial periphery which she directly controlled as an imperialist power as the result of her defeat in the first world war—it was never very large.

To-day Europe has a powerful Russian Empire as its neighbour in the east, instead of a series of politically independent small States. For Germany the situation is much worse: the western frontier of the Russian Empire cuts right through the middle of her territory.

To-day Europe has no very large capital assets abroad and has become a debtor area. Germany was a debtor country even after the first world war, and she is even more impoverished than the rest of Europe, and even shorter of available capital.

After the second world war Europe as a whole had at least a strong and intact productive apparatus with which to answer the tremendous transformation process which was taking place in the former periphery, a productive apparatus which reached peace-time production levels very soon after the end of the war and then considerably exceeded them. But for years after the end of the war Germany's productive apparatus was producing at far below peacetime levels, and it needed years more before Germany finally reached them and found herself more or less in the position that Great Britain, for example, had occupied almost immediately after the war.

Whilst the whole of Europe is adversely affected by the fact that Eastern Europe is no longer simply an agricultural and raw material Hinterland, the situation is much accentuated for Germany, because she was the biggest industrial power in Europe before the war and had the biggest volume of foreign trade with Eastern Europe.

Because Western Germany has lost most of the districts which had a surplus of agricultural production over their own requirements, and because her population has been increased by between 8 and 10 million deportees and displaced persons from the Eastern provinces and from Czechoslovakia, etc., she has, with 45 million souls, a bigger population than before the war, whilst her agricultural import requirements have doubled. It was formerly said of Great Britain that she must export or perish; to-day this is truer than ever of Germany. It is not merely an oratorical flourish; it is a literal fact.

The utter military defeat of Nazi Germany and the destruction of the Nazi State and its terror apparatus, together with the tremendous intensification of all political and social antagonisms, could have cleared the way in Germany for a libertarian socialist transformation of society. That development was prevented by the direct intervention of the occupying powers.

And the famous phrase of Karl Marx has once again become true, though under different historical conditions: the Germans suffer the restoration periods of other peoples without experiencing their revolutions.

In fact, the present situation is even worse than that: the reactionary forces of other peoples are directly influencing Germany's future.

The Russians had their November Revolution, which included many progressive tendencies. However, it was not a revolutionary Russia which intervened in Germany, but the present-day Soviet Union, with its tremendous terror apparatus, which suppresses every independent socialist movement.

But it was not only from the east that reactionary forces intervened. It happened from the west, too, from the Anglo-American powers.

America Prevented the Socialization of the Ruhr

At a time when the Labour Party came to power in Great Britain, and when liberal-progressive tendencies were wrestling with the reactionary forces in the United States, these two countries combined to hamstring those forces in Germany which made for a progressive, libertarian, socialist transformation of society, and to encourage the reactionary forces.

Thus not only were the first years after the war years of privation and hunger for Germany, but for the most determined opponents of the Hitler terror they were years without hope, because every step in the direction of a socialist transformation of society was blocked by the occupation powers.

In Western Germany, immediately after the defeat, a decisive step towards a democratic socialist transformation of society would have been possible. With the collapse of the Nazi State the position of those elements—for instance German Big Business, and in particular the Ruhr industrialists—which had supported the Nazis even before they came to power, or had, at least, adopted a policy of benevolent toleration towards them, was greatly shaken.

For the moment there was no German Government. For the moment there was no fully producing and functioning German heavy industry. Western Germany, in which lies the greater part of Germany's heavy industry, is occupied by three powers, but the Ruhr lies in the British zone, and for the time being the decision was in the hands of the British Labour Government, which was thus in a position to facilitate socialist democratic development in Germany and therefore in Europe as a whole.

But the Labour Government made only a tentative hesitant move. In a speech to the House of Commons on October 22nd, 1946, a good year after the end of the war, the British Foreign Secretary, Ernest Bevin, announced that Great Britain had assumed control of coal and steel production in the Ruhr, that the engineering and chemical industries would be taken over next, and that these industries would never again pass into private ownership.

"Our intention is that these industries shall be owned and controlled in future by the public. . . . They should be owned and worked by the German people, but subject to such international controls that they cannot again become a threat to their neighbours. . . . The case for public ownership in these heavy industries was never stronger than it is in Germany to-day."

But the British Labour Government did very little to put this Bevin promise into action. To carry it into execution seriously would have demanded that, in its own zone at least, the British Government should look for support to those elements which had always been in favour of the socialization of heavy industry—i.e. the democratic socialist movement. But the British Military Administration in Germany, which was largely composed of reactionary elements sympathetic to the British Tories rather than to the British Labour Government, had not the slightest intention of implementing Bevin's words, and in the face of this sabotage the British Labour

Government showed itself too feeble to insist. Its leaders did not seem to realize how greatly their own position might be threatened by the fact that their policy at home was not accompanied and reinforced by a similar policy on the continent.

If the British Labour Government had possessed courage and energy enough to stand by the words of its own Foreign Secretary and to socialize the basic industries in its own zone, taking them out of the hands of those who had collaborated with the Hitler regime, it would have created a *fait accompli* that subsequently could hardly have been undone. It did not do so when it had the chance, and later on it was no longer in a position to do so.

In order to pay for her tremendous import surpluses, Great Britain accepted American aid even before the Marshall Plan was launched. She took a loan of almost 4 milliard dollars, and during the negotiations the U.S. Government insisted that no steps towards socialization should be taken in the Ruhr.

"During the conference, Mr Thorp (Assistant Secretary of State for Economic Affairs) put the United States on record as flatly opposed to the British plan for the socialization of the Ruhr mines and industries. . . . It was understood at the outset of the negotiations that British Foreign Secretary Bevin had agreed with Secretary Marshall that the question of socialization in the combined zone was to remain 'on ice' for from three to five years." [18]

As the British Labour Government put up only a very feeble resistance, the Americans won the day. The reconstruction of Germany's industries was carried out on a primarily capitalist basis, and the socialization plans of the British Labour Government were silently buried.

The Hitler regime in Germany was not overthrown by a German revolution. It collapsed as a result of the military victory of the Allies. The United States held the trumps in the west, and it used its power to see to it that the overthrow of the Hitler regime was not accompanied by any social transformation and the destruction of the economic and social power of those elements which had collaborated with Hitler both before and after his accession to power, and had helped him in the preparation and prosecution of the second world war.

It was thus America's intervention in the first years after the war which prevented any fundamental changes in the social structure of Germany.

THE GROWTH OF SOCIAL ANTAGONISMS IN GERMANY

At the time when the world economic crisis broke out the United States was the leading industrial power in the world, followed by Germany. America's answer to the worst crisis in the history of

544

capitalism was the "New Deal"; Germany's answer was the victory of the counter-revolution which brought the Nazis to power.

Twenty years ago and more, Big Business in Germany had come to the conclusion that social antagonisms were so acute that it would not be possible to preserve German capitalism and at the same time maintain democratic political institutions.

The United States emerged from the second world war with a very much stronger productive apparatus and with higher standards of living for the whole population, for working people and for the middle strata as well. Germany emerged from that war with a productive apparatus which had been very seriously damaged by the direct results of the war, and in consequence even five years after the end of the war her industrial production had not yet reached pre-war levels. At the same time social antagonisms in Germany were even more acute after the war than they had been in the period before the Nazis came to power.

The process of social polarization, which had been more marked in Germany than in any other capitalist industrial country, was intensified by the Nazi regime of war economy, by the war itself and by the consequences of the war. In so far as one can speak of any stability amongst the middle strata, it was the peasants in Germany who were less hit by the war and post-war periods. But because the agricultural sector in Western Germany to-day is much smaller in relation to the population as a whole than it was in pre-war Germany, there has been an important change in the social structure, in that Germany now stands in the same position as Great Britain, having a population in which the working class represents the majority of the population.

The urban middle strata, situated between the workers and the still numerous well-to-do strata, have seen their social basis undermined again and again in the last thirty years or so. After the first world war it was the inflation, and soon after that the world economic crisis, which hit Germany particularly hard. After the second world war these strata were once again impoverished, and in the inflation of the first post-war years most of them lost what little they had been able to save through the years of Nazi rule.

In addition to this long process, which had undermined the social basis of the German middle strata, already accelerated by the war, came a further factor to reinforce the process of social polarization.

A "Fifth Estate" of the Displaced and Bombed-Out

Germany's defeat in the second world war created a social stratum such as had not existed in industrial Europe for a century—a sort of "Fifth Estate" of people who possess absolutely nothing but what they stand up in: the displaced persons from the former German eastern provinces and from Czechoslovakia, Hungary and so on, and the bombed-out.

Before they were driven away from their homes, these displaced persons were robbed of everything they possessed. In the best case they were allowed to take a few hundred pounds of household goods with them, but the overwhelming majority of them arrived in Western Germany with only the clothes they wore and perhaps a small bundle. The number of these deported people now totals about a sixth of the population in Western Germany, and if we add the large number of bombed-out families, then together they probably amount to between a fifth and a quarter of the total population. In other words, numerically they are almost as strong as the former urban middle strata.

In short, social antagonisms in Germany are greater now, and they will remain so, at least in the immediate future, than they were in the period before the Nazis came to power, and certainly greater than they were in any previous period of modern German history. Without outside intervention, the continued existence of the capitalist system would probably be called into question before long.

About twenty years ago the last card of German capitalism was the counter-revolution, the Nazi State. That card has been played. At first the move seemed to be successful, but in the end it resulted in total defeat.

There are many indications that but for outside interference the answer of Western Germany to the gigantic destruction caused by the war, to the exceptionally intense social polarization of the German people, to the change in the position of Europe as a whole and Germany's position in it, would be a strong tendency towards a socialist democratic planned economy.

Any decisive transformation of Germany's social structure in the years immediately following the Nazi military collapse was prevented by the western powers, and in particular by the United States.

If developments in Germany were determined by German factors without interference from the two world powers, then even now there would still be a good chance that the trend towards socialism, though held up for the time being, would continue. It is a trend which operates not only in Germany, but also in many other European countries, though of course it varies a good deal in strength. This trend has already led to concrete results in Great Britain, the classic birthplace of modern industrial capitalism.

THE SOCIAL TRANSFORMATION IN GREAT BRITAIN

On two occasions the British Labour Party formed a government in the period between the two world wars, but as on neither occasion did it have a majority in the House of Commons, it could not even begin to re-organize the country on democratic socialist lines. But in the first post-war elections in 1945 it went to the people with a clear programme for the transformation of Britain's economic and social system, and it was returned to power with a big majority in the House of Commons for the first time.

This first decisive victory of the British Labour Party on the basis of a democratic socialist programme was an event of world historic importance. It was symptomatic of the development of European capitalism, and with it the European working class, since the outbreak of the first world war.

In the period before the first world war there were no socialist parties which had any very clear idea of how the transition from capitalism to socialism was to take place.

The famous Erfurt Programme (cf. Part Two of this book) of the German Social Democratic Party did not deal with the question of what a socialist party would do, if it found itself in power in a capitalist State, to bring about a socialist transformation of society with the means placed at its disposal in a democratic parliamentary State. The reason for this striking omission was that capitalism at that time was not yet shaky; there was no immediate hope that it was approaching its end. Thus a practical programme of socialist transition from capitalism had not become historically necessary.

The shattering impact on capitalism of the two world wars and of the world economic crisis between the wars created the basis and the necessity for such a programme of immediate democratic socialist action. The British Labour Party drew up such a programme. It provided for the nationalization of the main heavy industries, coal-mining, iron and steel, of the railways and of the Bank of England; all in all, the creation of a State sector which would directly embrace about 20 per cent of the total British product. But as that 20 per cent included the basic industries, and with them other commanding heights of the economic system, it meant that the influence of the State would be very much greater than the figure of 20 per cent suggests. With the direct control of such an important 20 per cent of British production, the State would naturally have tremendous influence on the remaining sector of the economic system not directly under its control, and still producing by capitalist methods. In other words, with the carrying out of this programme an important step was taken towards the socialist transformation of the British economic system and of British society. It is a step which will make further progress in the same direction easier.

The British Labour Party went into the 1945 elections with a clear and definite programme, and the British working people and the British people generally knew perfectly well what was at stake. And as a result of the elections, Great Britain—the only country in the world which had had a working-class majority in its population for a long period—became the first, and so far the only, big industrial

547

power in which a working-class party had been given a parliamentary majority, and was therefore able to govern without entering into a coalition with non-socialist parties.

As soon as it came to power in 1945, the British Labour Government began to carry out the socialist programme for which the British electorate had given it a mandate. With this a big step was taken for the first time in the direction of socialization and a radical transformation of a capitalist State, a capitalist economic system and a capitalist society, and it was taken on a completely democratic basis.

The Socialization of the Basic Industries

Bills for the nationalization of certain industries were brought before Parliament and passed into law against an opposition which had every possibility of making its views known to the British people. The former owners of the industries concerned were expropriated, but not without compensation, which was paid approximately in accordance with the value of their former holdings. In this way the State obtained control of the chief commanding heights in the British economic system.

There is no previous example in history of State intervention in the economic affairs of a capitalist nation in peace time on the scale carried out by the British Labour Government, without production being turned largely to armaments and with the maintenance of all decisive political and personal liberties. With the Labour Government Great Britain has penetrated into new territory.

When the British Labour Government began to put its programme into action it enjoyed the confidence and support of the overwhelming majority of the British working class, and it retained that confidence and support throughout the period of its first effective term of office. This was not merely because the Labour Government promptly carried out its pledge to nationalize the basic industries (the worker found that his position was very little changed by nationalization, and it will take a tremendous amount of effort to make him feel that at last he is an equal partner in industry*), but primarily because the

---

* As the evidence of Francis Williams shows, the problem of the worker in the nationalized industries is a very real one:

"More serious than organizational difficulties, which experience will put right, is the fact that in the whole field of public ownership there is not yet much evidence that nationalization has altered the attitude of the workers as radically as was hoped, or has created any definite feeling of partnership in a national enterprise. . . . The worker, if he is a socialist, may feel that as a citizen he will benefit from a planned instead of an unplanned economy, but as a worker he is not conscious of any radical change in his condition. . . . There is nothing much yet to make the millions of ordinary workers in factories and mines and workshops and offices feel that socialism has given them any bigger share than they had before in running things. . . . It is the problem of making socialism something more than an economic plan. The success of the British pattern of socialism largely depends on finding an answer to it." [19]

working people felt that, in addition, the Labour Government really was using its power to give the under-dog a fairer deal and to re-model society according to democratic socialist principles.

Labour's Wage and Taxation Policy

Taxation in Great Britain is very high, and the tax revenues of the State amount to approximately two-fifths of the total national income of the British people.

> "In the year 1947 the revenue of the State itself, of its local governments and of the social insurance funds, derived from taxes of all sorts and from the net profits of trading enterprises (which are barely distinguishable from taxes), amounted to 3,779 million pounds after eliminating all duplication. In 1948 the figure was 4,298 million pounds, and in 1949 the estimate contained in the 'Economic Survey', which assumes the continuance of the present rates of tax, is no less than 4,475 million pounds. . . . The total of private income—that is, the corpus of income from which all taxation must be levied—was 9,911 million pounds in 1947. In that year therefore, taxation took 38·2 per cent of the total of incomes, individual and corporate, subject to it." [20]

The *Economist*, from which the above quotation has been taken, estimates the proportion of State revenue at 39·1 and 39·4 per cent respectively for the subsequent years.

On the basis of this powerful position, the British Labour Government has reinforced and accelerated the trend of development towards a democratic socialist transformation throughout this whole period.

Production in Great Britain rose, whilst consumption for the British people as a whole remained below pre-war levels, but in consequence of the wage and taxation policy of the British Labour Government reflected in legislation, a considerable improvement was brought about in the living standards of the working people and a corresponding reduction in the living standards of the British upper classes.

> "When all adjustments are made, the average earner would appear to be receiving real wages at least 10 per cent . . . higher than before the war, and the lower-paid workers have benefited even more. . . . The real value of the total amount paid in interest and profit has probably fallen by around 25 per cent." [21]

Thus the wage share in the total product increased considerably under the British Labour Government.

> "The proportion of wages to the total of all gross incomes obtained from work and property . . . increased from 37 per cent in 1938 to 44 per cent in 1948." [22]

549

The tax legislation of the Labour Government reinforced this tendency.

"If the comparison is made on the more telling basis of income after the payment of direct taxes, the rise was from 39 per cent to 48 per cent. So, in 1948, wage earners received nearly half the total disposable money. Salaries and profits both declined in the same period." [23]

Thus, whilst the increase in the wage share of the total product reduced the income of the former ruling classes quite considerably, their income was still further reduced by tax discrimination.

"At one end of the scale, therefore, the low wages of the past have been ended; the number of those with net incomes above 150 pounds a year has more than doubled, and the number of those in the middle group between 5 pounds and 10 pounds a week net nearly trebled. But there are 25 per cent fewer people with net incomes above a thousand pounds a year than there were before the war, and very high incomes have practically disappeared. Only some 35,500 people have a net income above two thousand pounds a year, and there are only 45 people in the whole country with a net income of about six thousand pounds a year." [24]

The *Economist* confirms the above observations with regard to very large incomes in Great Britain:

"Taxation by 1947 had crippled the large income to such an extent that, by pre-war standards, the very large income had disappeared." [25]

It is not a matter of fundamental importance whether these figures remain absolutely unaltered during the coming years; the important thing is the general trend, and this went clearly in the direction of reducing the class differences in income which were particularly marked in British society.

When the British upper classes found their incomes declining, they began to live to some extent on their capital, but that obviously cannot go on indefinitely.

"Particularly in the higher-income groups there are still considerable—though diminishing—private fortunes that can be drawn upon as net income falls. Such drawings on capital may, for some time, mask the full extent of the egalitarian trend of income levels.

"But the estate duty on large inheritances has already been greatly increased and is likely to be increased further. It now amounts to 24 per cent of estates of 50,000 pounds, and rises to 60 per cent of those estates over 500,000 pounds, and to 75 per cent of those above two million pounds. The great inherited fortunes which in the past provided one of the major sources of inequality will therefore in time disappear. Britain is moving rapidly towards a social pattern which would have seemed inconceivable even ten or fifteen years ago." [26]

Apart from the fact that British tax legislation weighs particularly heavily on high incomes, whilst death duties do the same for big fortunes, that the wage share in the total national product is increasing, that the State has introduced a scheme of planned economy which has created full employment in Great Britain for the first time since 1921, the Labour Government has used the instrument of taxation to carry out a big socio-political programme which, once again, chiefly benefits the working people and the poorer sections of the population, including a socialist health scheme, a housing programme which favours building for letting purposes rather than for ownership, and therefore favours the lower-income groups, and a system of food subsidies.

Thus by means of democratic socialist legislation the British Labour Government had taken a decisive step towards the transformation of British society, and this process of transformation went so far in the first years of the British Labour Government's term of office that it began to have important domestic political effects.

We have already seen that even in the United States the argument is not for or against State intervention, but rather about just how big that State intervention shall be. In Great Britain the first term of office of a Labour Government with a parliamentary majority has so changed the political situation in the country that at the elections in 1950, which returned the Labour Government for a second term of office with a bare majority of seats in the House of Commons, the Conservative Party felt itself compelled to take over part of the Labour Party programme. In other words, an important part of the transformation of British society brought about by the Labour Government can never be undone.

This, of course, does not mean that if the Conservatives ever got to power again they would not do their best to turn back the historical trend. In the meantime, equally naturally, the Labour Party will continue its efforts to further that trend.

However, even assuming that the British Labour Government succeeds in retaining power, it is hardly likely that history will bring a steady development from the first decisive steps, to the second, and then to the third, and so on in an uninterrupted flow to the final transformation of British capitalism and British capitalist society.

THE DIFFICULTIES OF SOCIALISM IN GREAT BRITAIN

We have already dealt briefly with some of these difficulties in analysing the historical environment in which European democratic socialists must try to carry out their plans to-day, and here we need deal only with the specifically British conditions.

Great Britain, as the one-time leading colonial imperialist power, is now faced with the task of carrying out her process of social transformation at a time when she has largely lost her imperialist Hinterland and is seeking for a new relationship with the remains of her colonial possessions. This creates an extremely unstable situation, because at the same time Great Britain has lost her big reserves of capital which would otherwise have facilitated her adaptation to the changing situation.

In its first decisive victory at the polls in 1945, the British Labour Party won a big majority of the seats in the House of Commons, but that big majority did not accurately reflect its support in the poll, which was fairly equally divided between the Labour Party and its two opponents, the Conservative and Liberal Parties, the overwhelming majority of the Opposition poll being given to the former. Now, as the process of transformation in Great Britain proceeded on a democratic political basis, this oppositional half of the population had every opportunity of organizing its resistance, particularly because although the U.S. Government carefully avoided any direct intervention in British political affairs, it nevertheless let it be seen very clearly where the sympathy of America's ruling classes lay.

Thus even if the Labour Government succeeded in remaining in power, the further steps in the process of social transformation in Great Britain will meet with growing difficulties in the country itself, and the Labour Government will hardly find it possible to overcome them unless its own actions at home are reinforced by similar actions in other parts of the world.

Such support is not to be expected in the United States in the near future, because U.S. capitalism is very much more strongly rooted than British or continental capitalism. The best that can be hoped for, as far as the United States is concerned, is that those forces which are benevolently neutral towards Britain's transformation will increase their influence in American public life. But that is not enough.

Great Britain too Small for a Democratic Socialist Transformation

The first steps towards a democratic socialist transformation of British society have been taken in a period when such a transformation is impossible if it is confined to Great Britain alone. It is true that Great Britain is incomparably stronger industrially than Tsarist Russia was at the time of the November Revolution, and because that is so, and because the working class represents the majority of the population in Great Britain, it was possible for this process of transformation to begin in democratic forms.

But, on the other hand, British industrial production represents

552

less than 10 per cent of world industrial production, and in the present epoch of world powers and world history—that is to say at a time when developments in one country affect developments in all others, at a time of crisis, at a time of great European weakness— Great Britain alone represents too small a basis for a democratic socialist transformation.

Although Russia was a vastly bigger country with a much greater chance of standing on her own, it was nevertheless impossible for her to carry out a socialist transformation of society, and the fact that the November Revolution remained isolated was largely responsible for the subsequent development which more and more ruthlessly stifled the progressive tendencies of the early days of the revolution.

Now, Great Britain is much more closely bound up with the rest of the world in every way than Russia ever was, and therefore on her own she has no chance of fully carrying through her democratic socialist transformation. She was able to take the first steps towards it, and to that extent she did pioneering work, but before she can take any further decisive steps in the same direction there will have to be a broadening of the basis of action, and in the present world situation this means that the democratic socialist transformation of Great Britain must be linked up with a similar process on the continent outside the Russian Empire if it is to make any further real progress.

This is not altogether impossible. Capitalism in general is greatly threatened in Europe, and German capitalism in particular can hardly hope to survive for long without outside assistance.

Now, if future developments in Great Britain and Germany, both of which have had mass socialist parties for a long time and still have, were left to the internal play of forces in these countries, then there would be a reasonable hope that developments in Europe would proceed somewhat on the same lines as they have done in Great Britain; in other words, that an attempt would also be made on the continent to master the European crisis by democratic socialist means.

But there is U.S. intervention to be reckoned with.

In our analysis of Germany we have seen that U.S. policy prevented the transformation of Germany's social structure in a democratic socialist sense. We have also seen that a revival of German capitalism is impossible in the long run without constant outside support. But the fact that in the historical long run any such attempt at revival is doomed to failure does not mean that it will not be made. It will, in fact, be made, and U.S. foreign policy will encourage it.

That attempt will have important consequences. If Germany's heavy industry in the Ruhr is built up again on a capitalist basis with American help, probably in part at least under the same people who collaborated with Hitler—and there are many indications that this is

553

what is intended—then the repercussions will be felt far beyond Germany's frontiers.

As U.S. policy in the Ruhr will lead to a revival of capitalism in Germany, it will at the same time, despite all declarations to the contrary, operate against the United States of Europe.

Thus U.S. policy in Germany in general, and in the Ruhr in particular, has not only prevented a progressive solution in the past and is not only preventing it at present, but it will do the same thing in the future, and a tremendous effort will be necessary not only to overcome the natural difficulties in the way of any United States of Europe, but to overcome the additional difficulties created by American policy.

In addition, any strengthening of capitalism in Germany will weaken the forces in the British Labour Party which are working for the United States of Europe, because of the danger that Labour and socialism would not have a majority in such a body.

American policy to date in Europe, and in particular in Germany, has been one of the biggest difficulties in the way of any synchronization of a socialist Labour policy in Great Britain and a democratic socialist policy on the continent.

The second factor is that the Soviet Union uses such influence as she possesses in the same direction—i.e. to sabotage the development towards democratic socialism. The Russians have an interest in a weak and divided Europe shaken by permanent crisis, because as long as Europe is unable to extricate itself from its difficulties, the Russians have a chance of extending their influence, despite their own very low standards of living and despite their terrorist dictatorship. For this reason they are determined to block any progressive socialist solution in Europe, and they have numerous possibilities of translating their opposition into action. First of all, they can, and do, keep up a constant atmosphere of military tension without actually taking direct military action, thereby strengthening military and reactionary tendencies in Germany and in Europe as a whole. Secondly, through their foreign-political instruments, the Communist Parties, they perpetuate the disruption of the working-class movement on the continent, and thus weaken its powers of action.

Any American intervention in the social structure of Europe which runs counter to the general historical trend in Europe is a gift for the Communist Parties, which represent one of Soviet Russia's strongest weapons in her efforts to prevent a united Europe. Every American action which encourages and supports reactionary capitalist forces, as in Germany, or reactionary feudal forces, as in Italy, is immediately seized upon by Russia and the Communist Parties in order to discourage those elements which work for a democratic socialist transformation in Europe. "Your position is hopeless," they are assured, and, indeed, it must sometimes look very much like it.

"You are between the upper and nether millstones of history. The United States is against you and in favour of the reactionary capitalist and feudalist groups, whilst the Soviet Union supports the communists. Give up the hopeless struggle."

Thus the policy of the United States plays into the hands of the Russians, and both the United States and Russia tug at the same rope in a determined attempt to prevent the establishment of a strong and progressive Europe.

So there is a grave danger that Europe will remain weak and hopeless, militarily and economically more or less dependent on the United States, and that at the same time the great attempt to transform the British social and economic system as the beginning of a European social and economic transformation will not be completed successfully. Instead of a great and powerful Europe on Russia's western frontier, there would then be a group of enfeebled countries in which capitalism was on the verge of death and kept alive by outside help. And not one of these countries would be large enough to carry out a socialist transformation of society on its own. Their internal politics might then sink into a morass of fruitless bickering, because not one of them alone is strong enough to make world politics.

Let us realize clearly that such a Europe would not represent a counter-weight to Russia, and that, on the contrary, such a state of affairs would sooner or later provide Russia with favourable conditions for a new imperialist drive westward, with all the acute danger of a third world war that would involve.

However, if, despite all foreign-political antagonisms, peace is somehow maintained for, say, ten or a dozen years, then there is still a chance that the democratic socialist transformation of Great Britain will make further progress, accompanied by the rise of similar trends on the continent—provided always that in its foreign policy the British Labour Government remains conscious of how closely any action for the transformation of British society must be connected with similar action on the continent, and provided that America's Labour and Liberal elements grow strong enough to influence not only America's domestic policy but also her foreign policy.

The Revolution in Asia

Even when capitalism was in its heyday, it never embraced even half the population of the world. About half the population of the world lived, and live, in Asia alone, and thanks to the methods of capitalist colonial imperialism, this half of the world's population was exploited in such a fashion as to make any progressive liquidation of feudalism impossible.

After the tremendous changes brought about by the second world

555

war, it is not likely that the capitalist mode of production will develop in the Asiatic countries.

The title of this book is, "Capitalism and Socialism on Trial". Capitalism is, in fact, on trial in Europe and in the United States, but not in Asia.

Capitalism is not on trial in Asia because it never existed there to any great extent, and because it is extremely improbable that the Asiatic peoples will now go through the sort of development which the peoples of Europe and the United States experienced.

The first world war led to the November Revolution in Russia, but in industrial Europe proper the capitalist system, though greatly shaken, continued to exist. The second world war led to the opening up of attempts at a socialist transformation of society in Great Britain, to the revolution in China and to the establishment of Indian national independence.

The second world war led to the opening up of a new historical era in Asia, and at the same time to a new world historical era.

European and Japanese colonial imperialism suffered a decisive blow in that the greater part of the Asiatic nations were freed from their dominance. At the same time it would cause us to misread the full significance of the revolution in Asia if we looked at it solely from the standpoint of its effects on Europe and Japan. As long as imperialist dominance continued in Asia, so long as the Asiatic peoples were mere pawns in the historical process, this standpoint was sufficient, but to-day that is no longer true, and it will be less true than ever in the future.

The defeat of Japan in the second world war and the success of the Chinese Revolution ended the period in which China was a semi-colonial country in her relations with the colonial imperialist powers, and these events are therefore of great importance for the further economic development of these powers. But in addition—and, what is much more important, henceforth—China will be an actor in history, and not merely a pawn in the historical process.

The establishment of Indian national independence must have tremendous repercussions on Great Britain and on the British Empire, but over and above that, it may well be the beginning of a period in which the Indians will make their own history, and, like the Chinese, become actors instead of pawns in the historical process.

A new epoch of history is now opening up in Asia, and the previous history of the world offers us no analogy to the developments at present taking place there.

The agrarian revolution has already spread over large parts of Asia, and feudalism is steadily losing ground. Europe experienced the French Revolution and a process of development from feudalism to capitalism, but at the time of the French Revolution capitalism was only in its infancy, and a gradual process of transformation followed which lasted for generations. In addition, at the time of the French Revolution France was one of the most progressive countries in the world.

The Chinese agrarian revolution, on the other hand, falls in a period in which capitalism in China does not exist on any scale, whilst in Europe it has already a century and a half behind it since the days of the French Revolution, and is already in decline at many points.

The Chinese agrarian revolution is taking place in a country which is one of the most backward in the world, and it involves an economic system and a social organism which are not at all equivalent to those which existed in Europe at the time of the French Revolution.

And what is true of China is also true of India and of most of the other countries and nations of the Asiatic continent.

In other words, the agrarian revolutions and agrarian reforms in Asia are taking place in a different historical environment from those which took place so long ago in Europe. In Europe they took place at the beginning of a great period of capitalist industrial development, and it was the more highly developed countries, the countries with the highest standards of living, which destroyed or greatly restricted feudalism.

The agrarian revolutions which are now taking place in Asia are occurring in a period in which capitalism is already greatly undermined and in which it is having to fight hard to maintain itself at all. These agrarian revolutions are taking place in the most backward countries in the world, in countries which, on account of previous long years of alliance between feudalism and imperialism, have extremely low standards of living.

Feudalism is now being destroyed in Asia. In China this is being done by revolutionary means; in the other Asiatic countries it is being done to some extent by means of radical reforms. Feudalism is being destroyed in countries which are even less industrially developed than Tsarist Russia was at the time of the November Revolution, and whose living standards are even lower.

The result of the November Revolution was that the new Russia did not experience the classic capitalist form of development, and her industrialization did not take place along the same lines as in Great Britain, Western Europe generally and the United States. In Asia the line of development will also be different. At the same time it is also unlikely that developments in Asia will proceed along Russian lines.

At the time of the November Revolution the Western Powers and Central Powers were still at war with each other in Europe, and the result was that foreign intervention against the revolution was on a small scale and for a relatively short time only. In consequence,

557

Russia's reconstruction and the subsequent period of new construction was not interrupted by foreign intervention.

The Asiatic revolutions, however, are taking place in a different historical epoch—in an epoch of world history and world powers. The period in which they are taking place is primarily marked by the violent antagonism of the two world powers; and it is a period of armament economy both in the Soviet Union and the United States.

Thus there is a danger that the Asiatic countries, hardly freed from the old forms of colonial imperialism, and not yet very strong, may be drawn into the conflict between the two world powers, each of which will strive, with different methods, to draw them into its orbit.

The State a Decisive Factor

Whatever happens, it seems probable that the development of the Asiatic nations and peoples will go its own way. To deal with one point in brief, there are many indications that the role of the State will be much greater, and that it will intervene directly in economic and social life to a much greater extent than was the case in European and American development.

After the French Revolution, and particularly in the nineteenth century—the main period of capitalist development—there was a long spell in which the direct influence of the State on economic affairs even declined in Europe and the United States.

But the Asiatic revolutions and the destruction of feudalism are taking place at a time when the influence of the State outside Asia has grown tremendously in economic affairs. In the Soviet Union, for example, it is omnipotent; in Great Britain it is considerable, and in the United States the State sector has grown tremendously, and the great question which will determine future developments there is, How quickly will the growth of the State sector and of State influence on economic affairs develop?

The agrarian revolution in Asia and the beginnings of its industrialization on a really important scale, are thus taking place in a world historical environment which is totally different from that in which the European nations proceeded to destroy or transform their system of feudalism. In all probability the State will intervene decisively right at the beginning of this great process of industrialization to direct and control it, and not after a century of capitalist development, as was the case in the occident.

Asia can already show us one example of vigorous State intervention in the early stages of the process of industrialization—namely, in Japan. However, Japan was a State which, although it intervened to direct and accelerate the process of industrialization, permitted feudalism to continue on a big scale. It was a State which at the same time carved out an empire to serve as a market for its industries, and built up a strong military sector.

Thus Japan will also not provide us with any precedent for the future development of Asia, because the background of this development is precisely the agrarian revolution and big agrarian reforms and the preceding long struggle against imperialism. Thus States will be created in Asia in which the feudal classes will not be predominant. They will be States which will organize a co-ordinated economic development, and they will not build up industries whose markets will rely on imperialist expansion.

Political developments in Asia at the moment are exceptionally violent, owing to the tremendous revolutionary forces which are at present at work there.

At the same time we must remember how low, thanks to a century of imperialist exploitation and oppression, is the level from which the Asiatic countries are starting off on their own development. It will therefore take them a long time before they can rise even to the level of, say, Eastern Europe prior to the first world war.

For a long time the great majority of the people of Asia will continue to live largely from agriculture, although the percentage of the population going into the towns and working in industry will gradually increase.

In dealing with the changed nature of war, we pointed out that all wars preceding the first world war were between countries in which agriculture predominated. From the first world war onwards the situation changed. It changed for Europe and the United States and it changed for the Soviet Union. But it has not changed for the nations of Asia, and it will not change materially for a long time to come. Thus these countries are entering the new world historical epoch with social organisms in which agriculture greatly predominates, and should there be a new war, it will not affect the Asiatic countries as violently as it will the industrial countries because the former are primarily agricultural countries.

Japan's Social and Political Crisis

That applies to most of the nations of Asia, but it does not apply to Japan. In a future war Japan would be just as much endangered as Europe, the Soviet Union or the United States. In addition, the present armistice period is at the same time a period of great social and political instability for Japan.

The second world war ended in the total military defeat of Nazi Germany and Japan. But in Nazi Germany defeat came upon a country and a social organism which had been worse hit by the first world war and the world economic crisis than any other. The situation in Japan was materially different, because Japan profited by the first world war, and she suffered much less from the world economic crisis than any other capitalist industrial country.

For European imperialism the long period of progress and expansion which ended with the first world war was followed by a period of stagnation and depression in the period between the two world wars, which, however, did not affect Japan, which experienced an almost uninterrupted period of tremendous internal and external expansions from her victorious war over China in the nineties, to her victory over Tsarist Russia in 1904, to her profitable politico-economic neutrality in the first world war (her declaration of war on Germany was little more than a formality), to her invasion of Manchuria and her occupation of the economically most highly developed of China's coastal towns and ports. Japanese capitalism entered the second world war after fifty years of victory and success, and although at first her luck held and she continued her series of successes, she then suffered utter and complete defeat.

Japan entered the second world war with a much more stable social structure than most of the European States, but the ultimate result for her was that her period of progress and expansion was followed, not by a period of stagnation, as in Europe, but directly by a period of imperialist decline. With her defeat in the second world war Japan lost not only all the conquests which she had made during the war, but everything she had won for decades past, including Formosa, Korea, Manchuria and all the territory of China she had occupied.

Japan's empire played a much more important role for her than did the empires of the European imperialist countries for them. Japan herself was only a third-class—perhaps even fourth-class—industrial power. The role of the Japanese Empire was not merely to serve as a market for Japan's own industries, but to reinforce and strengthen the industrial development of the "Motherland".

By her military defeat in the second world war Japan lost her empire and her army, and, in view of the tremendous importance of both empire and army, powerful repercussions are inevitable.

The destruction of the empire and the dissolution of the army meant the disappearance of two important auxiliary markets which had previously helped Japanese capitalism to overcome the difficulties created by the narrowness of the home market owing to the maintenance of feudalism and the extremely low living standard of almost half the population.

The unique combination of monopolist industrial capitalism and powerful feudal remnants cannot be maintained in the long run without an empire and a strong military sector. In other words, with a peace-time economy, and deprived of the empire and the military sector, tremendous changes in the social structure of Japan become inevitable.

However, the decision on peace or war and the maintenance of a peace-time economy do not depend on Japan, and in this respect her position is very different from that of Germany after the first world

560

war. Germany had no empire after that war, but she was the strongest industrial country in Europe, and second only to the United States in the world, and thus she was in a position to plunge the world into war again.

Japan, even with her empire, was industrially weaker than either Great Britain or France, and without her empire she was a fourth-class industrial nation, and therefore in an epoch of world powers she is not strong enough to launch a war on her own. For the moment she is no longer an actor, but a pawn in the historical process. Her only significance now can be as a satellite of the United States in the event of an intensification of Russo-American antagonisms. She can be of importance, for example, as an air base for the U.S.A. And, if the necessity ever arises, she can be of service to the United States on the Asiatic mainland with her armies.

Thus the future development of Japan is dependent on the state of Russo-American relations. On this will depend whether her old social structure, which was hard hit by her military defeat in the second world war, will survive, or whether the effects of the second world war will lead to a radical transformation of Japanese society.

The Growth of Social and Political Antagonisms Increases the Danger of War

It is the existence of strong social and political antagonisms which threatens the world with a new war. That was our conclusion from our analysis of the change in the nature of war. We have already described the very serious crises—partly apparent and partly latent—and the danger spots which make the world situation so unstable to-day and greatly increase the danger of war.

First of all there is the fact that the two world powers, neither of which has a decisive military superiority over the other, represent two totally different political and economic systems, but this is by no means enough to account for the urgency and gravity of the war danger which threatens the world to-day. There have always been a variety of political and economic systems existing side by side in the world, and nevertheless the world has known generations of peace.

But to-day this fact of the disparity of social and political systems is reinforced by two others. The first is that, sociologically speaking, the world has grown very much smaller, with the result that the two systems find a dozen and one points of friction. In other words, they do not exist side by side in the world, as for instance the Roman and Chinese Empires did, but they exist together. The second fact is that the world outside these two powers has a population greater than theirs, and industrial production and resources greater than theirs, but is at the moment very weak both politically and militarily, and, in addition, is so shaken by tremendous revolutionary processes that frontiers are no longer stable. It is not at all certain to which camp some countries belong, and whether perhaps they have strength enough to keep outside both camps. The result is that, owing to the instability of these States and nations, and to the interference of the two world powers in their process of transformation, the relation of world forces itself has become unstable, and this is the case not merely for the first few years after the second world war, or even for the immediate future, but for the whole present historical epoch.

The disparity of the political and economic systems of the two world powers in the present period of world history, together with the revolutionary and evolutionary processes of transformation which are now going on in most of the States and nations of the world —processes in which both world powers interfere in their own interests—greatly increases the danger of war and, in view of the present character of war, the danger that a large part of the industrial apparatus of the world will be destroyed, the danger of the destruction of our present civilization, the danger of a long period without history, the danger of a decline into barbarism.

It is a paradox of contemporary development that on the one hand capitalism has made such great progress in the past century with regard to the productivity of labour that in the most advanced capitalist country—the United States—the complete abolition of poverty and the provision of a middle-class standard of living for the enormous majority of the population, including the working class, is not merely an academic question, but one which is directly within grasp; whilst on the other hand political and social antagonisms in the world have so intensified that the possibility of a new war leading to a descent into barbarism is no longer a theoretical possibility, but an immediate danger so great that it is quite impossible to take it too seriously.

Marx and Engels naturally did not foresee, and could not have foreseen, the antagonisms between the two world powers to-day, but for them, trained as they were in the analysis of history, it was by no means a foregone conclusion that subsequent developments must necessarily be progressive, and so in their famous "Manifesto of the Communist Party", written together in their youth, they wrote:

> "Freeman and slave, patrician and plebeian, lord and serf, master and journeyman, in a word, oppressor and oppressed, stood in constant opposition to each other, carried on an uninterrupted, now overt, now covert, fight, a fight that always ended either in a revolutionary transformation of society or in the common ruin of the contending classes."

To-day we are threatened with the common ruin of precisely the most highly developed and progressive industrial countries.

The danger of this common ruin is great. No attempt should be made to represent it as less threatening than it is, or its results as less terrible than they would be. That danger will exist for a long time. If it can ever be overcome, it will take the best part of the second half of the twentieth century to do it.

Let us make no mistake about it, we and our whole civilization are threatened with ruin. But if we clearly recognize the danger, and realize its causes, then its very magnitude may help to develop those forces which are capable of warding it off and banishing it for good.

No Arms Agreement or Neutral Zones can Avert the Threatened Danger

The danger which threatens us is that the two world powers will clash in arms. That would involve the whole world. The danger cannot be overcome by any agreement on the subject of permitted and prohibited weapons. Weapons themselves are not the cause of the clash, but it is their development in our modern age which will make the consequences of any such clash so devastating and terrible.

Similarly, the danger of war cannot be overcome by the creation of any neutral zone between the two world powers, when, as is the case to-day, the countries which lie between them are shaken to the core by violent political and social crises, and thus are weak and powerless by comparison with the two world powers.

The only thing which could be effective is not the creation of a neutral zone, but the creation of a *Third Force* which would, on its own, represent a considerable power in relation to either one of the world powers, and which would at the same time have a social structure progressive and powerful enough to exercise an influence on them and their internal developments. One of these world powers—the United States—is threatened by a latent economic crisis, and the other—the Soviet Union—is experiencing a process of degeneration under a dictatorship whose social basis is growing ever narrower and a terror which is growing more and more intense, so that the progressive tendencies which were let free by the November Revolution are being more and more overlaid.

Up to the present neither of the world powers has had any material influence directly on the development of the other, and what influence there was has been largely negative.

At the same time the world between them has not been sufficiently strong and sufficiently progressive in its own development to exercise much influence on either of them.

When Soviet Russia comes up against feudalism and colonial imperialism outside her frontiers or her sphere of influence, then there is no chance of such forces exercising any progressive influence on her own development; on the contrary, they merely open up new fields for further expansion. And when Soviet Russia comes up against a Europe labouring in constant social and political crises and striving to solve them with counter-revolutionary, semi-fascist or neo-fascist methods, then here, too, there is nothing to exercise a progressive influence on her own development; on the contrary, it means further chances for her expansionist policy.

Not only that, but if Europe continues to flounder in social and economic crises, if development continues to stagnate as it did between the two world wars, and if reactionary forces come to the top, then further Russian aggression and attempts at expansion will be the result. And this in its turn would in all probability greatly strengthen the already very strong elements in the United States which are bitterly opposed to any social transformation anywhere, either at home or abroad, give them the upper hand, and thus accelerate the development which is sweeping our world towards the abyss.

We have analysed the historical forces which enabled the capitalist metropolitan centres to alleviate their internal social antagonisms in the period of expanding imperialism, and which subsequently prevented any revolution in the industrially developed countries, thus leaving the Russian Revolution, isolated in the most backward industrial country in Europe, to degenerate more and more from its original ideals.

We have analysed the historical forces which governed the development of U.S. capitalism and allowed it to expand at home rather than abroad, at the same time postponing the growth of social antagonisms for generations.

We have also analysed those forces which brought European imperialist expansion to an end and made it imperative, whatever else happens, that a radical transformation of European society should take place.

But, as we have seen, this decline of European capitalism does not necessarily result in socialist progress. The United States may continue to interfere with the historical trend in Europe for a long time to come, and with U.S. assistance there may well be an attempt to revive capitalism. Simultaneously the Soviet Union will seek to exploit counter-revolutionary and reactionary tendencies in Europe to undermine the position of democratic socialism and extend her own influence.

This would lead quite automatically to an increase in the danger of war.

A Progressive, Socialist Europe an Important Factor for Peace

As far as the situation in Europe is concerned, the danger of war will decline only if Europe finds a progressive solution—and to-day that means a democratic socialist solution—to its crisis. This is the only way in which it will be possible to diminish social and political antagonisms. At present they are growing to such an extent that they greatly increase the danger of war.

564

In this chapter, and in particular in our observations concerning Europe, we have pointed again and again to the tremendous difficulties of any democratic socialist solution of Europe's crisis.

It should be obvious, therefore, that we are not inclined to indulge in facile optimism.

But if, despite all the difficulties, a progressive solution of Europe's crisis is attained—and there is still a chance that it will be—then the strong and powerful Europe which would arise in consequence would have a good chance of obtaining decisive world historic results.

A progressive democratic socialist solution of the crisis in Europe would be a decisive step forward to the goal of a United Europe, which can in any case come about only if there is a strong trend towards a *rapprochement* of the social structures of the leading European States.

A strong federation of European industrial States would represent a decisive power factor in the world situation because such a federation would be industrially very much stronger than Russia and her empire combined.

If such a federation came about, and were protected in its initial stages from Russian military attack, it could develop military strength at least equal to, if not greater than, that of Russia and her empire combined, and it would therefore no longer be in any danger of a Russian attack.

Further, if this United States of Europe were organized on democratic socialist lines, it would not be threatened ideologically by communism. Such a Europe would have two decisive weapons in its armoury against Russian penetration: first of all its higher living standards, which would remain higher certainly for many years to come, and secondly, a regime of political and personal liberty consonant with a democratic socialist planned economy.

Any real effort to carry democratic socialist principles into effect fatally undermines the whole strength of communism. This fact has already been strikingly demonstrated by the British Labour Government, and in the 1945 elections the Communist Party was not able to win a single seat, or come anywhere near to winning a single seat, up and down the country. A similar successful effort in Europe would result in a similar communist *débâcle*.

Then, and then only, will the emergence of democratic currents within the Russian dictatorship be a real possibility.

It is an over-simplification to speak of the Russian dictatorship and of the totalitarian State in Russia as though they were something given and unchangeable. There are various trends within both. The Russian dictatorship which existed in the twenties was a very different thing from the Russian dictatorship which existed during the second world war. Even a dictatorship is not absolutely rigid;

there are possibilities in one direction as in the other. That was demonstrated in Russia in the past; it is no less true to-day.

For one thing, we should not forget that although for more than twenty years the Russian dictatorship was confined to Russian territory, it has now been extended over a Russian empire which, in large part, has a higher standard of living than Russia herself. The Russian dictatorship to-day has to adapt itself to given circumstances, just as it did in the past.

Should a progressive United States of Europe come into being on Russia's western frontiers, it will not fail to exercise an influence on Russia and on the Russian Empire. It will affect Russia herself, and it will affect her satellites.

Again, people talk about the "Iron Curtain" as though it were something absolutely impenetrable. This is misleading. As far as the Soviet Union is concerned, this "Iron Curtain" has been punched full of a great many holes since the last years of the second world war.

Before that time only a few thousand highly placed and trustworthy officials had ever been allowed to pass through it into the outer world, but since then millions of Russians have been outside it into Eastern and Central Europe, and they have been there long enough to see a good many things they were previously unaware of. To-day it is not only a few thousand carefully screened officials who have had the opportunity of seeing the outside world, but millions of Red Army men.

And there is another interesting point: since the war the Germans in the Eastern Zone, and tens of millions of people in the satellite countries, have had ample opportunity to compare communist "theory" and propaganda with Russian reality, with the Russian police State, the Russian administration and the Russian terror.

Even in the Soviet Union, strictly isolated from the outside world, it took a long time before the dictatorship could develop the strength it showed in the second world war. Russia's satellites have just begun, perforce, to collectivize their agriculture, and they are now floundering in all the difficulties and disorganization we have seen in connection with Soviet Russia's own agricultural collectivization. If the other European peoples outside the Russian Empire enjoy higher standards of living, and at the same time political and personal liberty, then no "Iron Curtain" will be strong enough to prevent the facts leaking through and having their effect on the peoples of Russia's Empire.

In other words, a progressive democratic socialist Europe would become a very real, and dangerous, competitor of the Soviet Union in the struggle for the minds of men.

Only from such a Europe could we expect social and political repercussions on the structure of Soviet Russia—though, of course, not from one day to the next. Soviet Russia has over thirty years of dictatorship behind her, and that dictatorship has become even more onerous in recent years. It was established in the first place over a people who had never known real political and personal liberty and who had been gagged and oppressed by Tsarism and feudalism for centuries. A process of democratic transformation in Russia would therefore not be an easy matter. But there would be a very real chance of its coming about if a United Socialist Europe arose on Russia's western frontier, a Third World Power which, on its own, would be industrially and militarily stronger than Russia, and yet would have not the slightest reason or desire to attack her. Once a united Europe arose, too strong to be threatened by Russian military aggression—a Europe which combined economic progress with political and personal liberty—then there would be every likelihood that, in answer to the moral challenge such a Europe would represent, the Russian dictatorship would be compelled by force of circumstances to give way gradually to a more democratic regime.

At the same time, the influence of a united Europe, once a progressive democratic solution had been found to its troubles, would not be confined to the Russian dictatorship; it would exercise an important, and perhaps decisive influence on the other world power, the leading world power—the United States. The United States regime is no more unchangeable than the Russian regime. Reactionary and progressive forces are already engaged in a determined struggle for power and for control of the U.S. Government.

If and when the United States is again called upon to stand the test of an economic crisis, there will be both reactionary and progressive ways of meeting it. In a new period of economic crisis, which would be fraught with terrible danger not only for the United States but for the rest of the world as well, it could be of decisive importance if democratic socialist forces outside the United States had already demonstrated in action, and not merely in words, that a progressive solution of economic and political crisis is a real possibility, that a democratic socialist society can exist and maintain itself, that, in other words, the totalitarian Soviet State is not the inevitable alternative to the capitalist system, and that the alternative is practically demonstrated in countries like Great Britain and the industrial countries of Europe, which are not so very different in their social and political structure from the United States.

Thus a progressive democratic socialist solution of Europe's crisis could help to reduce the danger of war on many fields. It could do this first of all because it would make an end of the instability and impotence which now enfeeble the most important countries which lie between the two world powers, and therefore greatly reduce the opportunities for expansionist drives on the part of the Soviet Union. Secondly, it could do this because the existence of a strong federation of European States would have repercussions on the two world

567

powers and accelerate their progressive transformation. This is a factor whose significance for the diminution of the war danger can hardly be over-estimated.

There is still a chance that all this can come about. But it is no more than a chance.

From the middle of the nineteenth century until the middle of the twentieth century capitalism developed in two main streams.

In Europe it amalgamated more and more with imperialism. To-day, at the beginning of the second half of the twentieth century, imperialism has largely been destroyed, and its main instrument, European capitalism, has been so greatly shaken that it cannot hope to survive for long without outside help.

In the United States capitalist development was never very closely connected with imperialism. To-day U.S. capitalism is still very strong indeed, but it is strong in a period when outside the United States the decline of the capitalist system can perhaps be retarded, but not prevented altogether.

In such circumstances it is extremely unlikely that capitalism even in the United States will survive the twentieth century. What will come after it no one can say.

There is a chance for a democratic socialist development in the world.

On the other hand, it is possible that the world may plunge into barbarism.

Capitalism and socialism are on trial everywhere.

Capitalism will hardly survive the twentieth century.

As yet no man can say what will be its heir.

DEVELOPMENT TRENDS IN THE SECOND HALF OF THE TWENTIETH CENTURY

As these lines were written the war in Korea was still going on. It is, to date, a localised war, but it is one which places a real strain on the main resources of China, whilst involving the resources of the United States only to a relatively minor extent. Prophecy in such matters is outside our province, but at least we can say that it is quite possible that the war in Korea will remain a localised war and will not develop into the overture of the third world war. Hostilities may even cease in the form of an armistice.

However, the danger of a third world war remains, and it might break out at any time. Nevertheless, in view of the fact, appreciated by the leaders of both sides, that a new world war would result in a tremendous amount of devastation in the world, and in particular in Russia and the United States, it is quite possible that peace, or rather, the period of armistice in which we are now living, will be maintained for quite a long period, and that, in fact, it may never end in war.

The following observations have been written with this possibility in view. They aim at laying bare certain general trends operating behind the façade of everyday events, trends which are of decisive importance for the development of the leading world powers in the second half of the twentieth century.

First of all, it is improbable that the world will enjoy a real period of peace for a long time to come. In the present situation there is such a wide gap between the actual military strength of the United States and of the Western Powers in general and their potential military strength measured against their industrial resources, that their first task will be to increase their military sector very considerably. They need not do this to the same proportion of their national incomes as the Soviet Union and the Russian Empire in general has done, because their total industrial production is much greater. However, for the time being the proportion of their national incomes devoted to re-armament will become greater, and their armament sector will show a strongly rising tendency. This means that the dangers of economic crisis will be postponed for a while, perhaps for a very long while.

If we compare the leading States and nations which are making history to-day, at the beginning of the second half of the twentieth century, with those which made history at the beginning of the twentieth century, or, better, at the beginning of the first world war, then we find ourselves faced with one factor of almost incalculable importance. It is the circumstance that of all the leading powers to-day the United States is the only one which is entering the second half of the twentieth century with approximately the same ruling class in the saddle with which it left the nineteenth century to enter the twentieth.

Even at the beginning of the twentieth century the United States was the leading capitalist industrialist country in the world. It is so, and even more so, to-day, and its leading position has been further consolidated.

The United States entered the second world war with the same ruling class in the saddle as at the time it entered the first, and it emerged from it—without any very great convulsions—with the situation materially unchanged.

It is true that the United States was greatly shaken by the economic crisis which began in 1929, but it is still the most powerful industrial country in the world, and, unlike the big industrial countries of Europe, it has never known a socialist mass movement, and therefore it has never known any serious attempts at a socialist transformation of the economic system and of the basis of society in general. In recent years trade unionism in the United States has made tremendous progress, but it is still impossible even to hazard a guess at when the U.S. working class is likely to build itself a Labour Party with the specific aim of bringing about a fundamental reorganization of U.S. society.

Americans are often still unaware of this factor of social and political stability in their country by comparison with other countries because, seen against their own historical background, they certainly experienced quite considerable political and social changes in the first half of the twentieth century.

However, this political and social stability of the United States in the last forty or fifty years becomes very evident when we compare it with the fundamental changes which have taken place in the other States and nations which are actors on the stage of world history to-day.

Russia entered the first world war as a semi-feudal, industrially backward country under Tsarist rule. In 1917 the November Revolution overthrew the old ruling classes and established a new type of State in which, although capitalism has been ended, a growing terror has reduced political and human rights to an even lower level than under Tsarism. Russia entered the twentieth century as the most backward industrially of the big powers in Europe. She entered the second world war as the third industrial country in the world, and she emerged from it, and she enters the second half of the twentieth century, as the second industrial country and one of the two world powers with the United States.

570

In the last quarter of a century the rate of Russia's industrial development has been more rapid than that of any of the other big industrial powers. The primary reason for this is the fact that the Russian dictatorship compels the masses of the Russian people to contribute a much greater quantity of their annual labour power to the development of production and to the extension of the productive apparatus, and a much smaller quantity to the production of consumer goods for their own use than is usual elsewhere. Thus the present generation in Russia is compelled to make constant sacrifices to reduce the gap between Russia and the other industrial countries of the world.

In latter years a certain approximate relationship has established itself in the industrial countries of Europe and in the United States between the increase in the productivity of labour and the increase of real wages. At the same time the trade unions, which have become more and more powerful in the countries living under a system of political democracy, have made it their main business to see that the working people obtain a proportionate share of the growing national product created by the increase of labour productivity, in other words, that their living standards are proportionately raised. In Russia this more or less automatic relationship between the increase in the productivity of labour and the rise in the living standards of working people has been more or less put out of action by the dictatorship.

The Russian Five-Year Plans were based—even before the second world war—and are still based on the increasing exploitation of the working class and of the great masses of the Russian people in general, and as long as this enforced speed of industrial development is maintained there can be no question of socialism in Russia, and the dictatorship must persist and even become more intense.

Great Britain and Germany entered the twentieth century as the third and second industrial countries in the world respectively. Their social structures were relatively stable, and the Europe in which they existed was still the industrial and capitalist centre of the world. They entered the second half of the twentieth century in a Europe which had lost its leading position in the world, which was very much weakened, and which, for the first time in centuries, was in danger of losing its role as an actor on the world stage and of sinking into the role of a mere object of world history.

Germany entered the first world war as a monarchy; she emerged as a republic. As a result of the first world war, the world economic crisis, the victory of the National Socialist counter-revolution and the second world war she has been profoundly shaken, far more so than any other capitalist country. German capitalism has therefore been thoroughly undermined, so much so that, on its own and without assistance, it can hardly survive for long.

Unlike Germany, Great Britain experienced no big socialist mass movements in the second half of the nineteenth century, but since the beginning of the twentieth century the British Labour Party has developed tremendously. As early as the beginning of the twentieth century British capitalism showed certain signs of stagnation, and they became still more evident in the period between the two world wars. Parallel with this capitalist stagnation and the decline of colonial imperialism went the growth of the British Labour Party until, after the second world war, for the first time in Great Britain and for the first time in the history of any big power, the political party of the working people obtained an absolute majority of the seats in parliament and proceeded to carry out a programme which aimed at a socialist transformation of the British economic and social system on the basis of political democracy.

Both India and China entered the twentieth century as colonial and semi-colonial countries respectively, as the objects of imperialist exploitation, as feudal countries hampered by the imperialist metropolitan powers in their efforts to develop their industries even up to Eastern-European and Russian levels. At the same time they were extremely poor countries with living standards far below those which existed in Europe and the United States.

But both India and China are entering the second half of the twentieth century as independent States determined from now on to play the role of actors in the shaping of their own future, and thus as countries playing the role of subjects in the development of world history.

China, still a feudal State at the opening of twentieth century, has now, after many years of civil war, and as a result of the second world war, begun to carry out an agrarian revolution that later historians may well regard as one of the most important world-historical happenings of the second half of the twentieth century. China is thus entering a new epoch of her history with a complete change in her social structure.

In 1914 and again in 1939 Great Britain was in a position to declare war on behalf of India without consulting her. To-day India is an independent State, and the transformation of her social structure is a matter of the immediate future—in some respects it has already begun.

But both China and India enter the second half of the twentieth century as poor as they were at its beginning; in fact, the gap between their standards of living and those prevailing in the leading industrial countries of the world has grown greater rather than smaller. However, they are both facing the future with the firm determination not to suffer this humiliating poverty any longer, and refusing to believe that it represents a natural necessity of their lives. At the same time, with them, the whole of Asia is beginning to

572

realize that its poverty is intimately connected with its social structure, and with the parasitic alliance which has existed until comparatively recently between imperialism and feudalism, impoverishing hundreds of millions.

The Asiatic peoples will now do their utmost to raise their standards of living, and whoever helps them in this task—and only whoever helps them in this task—will have any hope of influencing them.

These few observations, which have, of course, necessarily been very sketchy, will have shown us that, during comparatively recent years, all the leading world powers, apart from the United States, have experienced a fundamental change in their social structure and in the composition of their ruling classes, and that in consequence they are entering the second half of the twentieth century with a very different social and political basis than the one with which they entered the first.

The fact that in the same period the world basis of capitalist production has become narrower, and that the general trend at the opening of the second half of the twentieth century is clearly working to make it still narrower, is only another expression of the same state of affairs. This trend is not a new phenomenon. It has been in existence now for decades, even although it looks, from world-historical perspectives, as though the period of decline or of the transformation of capitalism will not last so long as the period of its rise, which stretched over centuries.

From a world historical standpoint we can say that the rise of capitalism lasted into the period of the first world war. Up to that time production in the older countries of capitalism had steadily increased, and up to that time more and more countries were still being drawn into the capitalist orbit, some of them retaining their political independence, others becoming colonial or semi-colonial objects of imperialist exploitation.

As a result of the first world war, however, Russia was prised out of this capitalist world; capitalist development entered a period of stagnation in most European countries, and world capitalism found no substitute for the loss of Russia because at the same time the period of European colonial imperialism was also coming to an end. Imperialist expansion came more or less to a halt everywhere.

However, although the development of world imperialism thus came to a halt there was still capitalist progress in the United States, at least in the first period after the war up to 1929.

As a result of the second world war the countries of Eastern Europe which lie between Russia and Germany were also prised out of the capitalist orbit. In addition, capitalism in Great Britain and in Western Europe in general is being more and more profoundly undermined, and whilst a decisive transformation of its

573

social basis is taking place in its old strongholds there is little reason to suppose that, *as capitalism*, it will find a substitute in the industrially backward areas of the world that could be used as, so to speak, a new jumping-off ground for further development. All indications suggest that there will be no capitalist development in India, China and Asia in general in the second half of the twentieth century such as was typical of Europe in the nineteenth century.

Americans should therefore realize that in all probability the tendency towards a still further narrowing of the world capitalist basis, the general tendency to capitalist decline, will continue in the second half of the twentieth century. At the same time people in Europe, in Russia and in Asia should realize that during the past 150 years developments in the United States have never conformed with developments in the rest of the world, and that therefore the continued decline of capitalism outside the United States may well be temporarily paralleled by a continued progressive trend of capitalism in the United States.

However, the continued undermining of capitalism in Europe and the very slender chance of any extension of the basis of capitalism in Asia do not necessarily mean the inevitable extension of the Soviet Empire. At the moment that is an open question. It may, of course, happen that way, but with a systematically progressive policy it can be prevented. In this respect the problem in Europe is fundamentally different in one decisive point from the problem in Asia. In Great Britain, Western Europe and Germany living standards are incomparably higher than they are in Russia. Not only are they higher, but the gap between the former and the latter will remain very great for a very long time to come. The result is that hundreds of millions of people in Europe know what they would have to lose economically, socially and culturally in the event of an extension of the Soviet Empire sufficient to engulf them, and their readiness to defend themselves against such an extension is readily understandable. All that is necessary as far as they are concerned is to show them, to prove to them, that there is still time to build up sufficient military strength to make a successful defence against Russian aggression feasible. Once Russian military preponderance on the European mainland is countered, and if this is achieved without war in the present period of armed peace, then the Russians will, for the time being at least, have no very great chance of becoming the heirs of European capitalism.

In Asia the situation is very different. In Asia Russia has not only military chances, but also economic and social chances, and the reason for this is very simple: although she is very backward by comparison with Europe and the United States, she is economically progressive by comparison with India, China and the rest of Asia,

574

as the following figures, based on tables compiled by the U.S. State Department,* show:

Country.	Per capita *income* (*U.S. dollars per annum*).	Per capita *daily intake of all foods* (*in calories*).	Per capita *net consumption of cotton, wool and rayon* (*in lb.*).
United States .	554	3,098	29·01
United Kingdom .	468	3,095	21·80
Soviet Union . .	158	2,827	6·70
India . . .	34	1,976	4·37
China . . .	29	2,234	3·51

Country.	Energy consumed per day (*H.P. hours* per capita).	Annual freight carried (*tons-miles* per capita).	Expectation of life at birth (*in years*).		Date.
			Male.	Female.	
United States .	37·6	2,977	62	66	1939–41
United Kingdom .	27·1	424	60	64	1937
Soviet Union .	6·8	1,134	47	50	1940
India . . .	0·5	60	27	27	1931
China . . .	0·5	17	—	—	—

Country.	Percentage of the population aged 10 and over (*about* 1930).
United States . . .	Below 5
United Kingdom . . .	Below 5
Soviet Union . . .	19
India	91
China	85

Thus although Russia is far behind the United States and Europe, she is in many respects far ahead of the Asiatic nations. The latter have therefore no higher standard of living to defend against Russian encroachments; on the contrary, they can hope to learn from the Russians how to raise their own living standards. In consequence the problem of Russian expansion is not a purely military one in Asia, as it is in Europe. In fact, it is primarily an

* "Point Four", The Department of State, January 1950. The figures apply to the last year before the outbreak of the second world war, but the relative position of the Soviet Union towards the United States and Europe on the one hand and towards Asia on the other has not materially changed since then.—F. S.

economic and social one. Always on the assumption that we do not find ourselves plunged into a third world war, we can say that a great part of the second half of the twentieth century will be marked by the efforts of the Asiatic countries to raise their present ignoble standards of living. Now the all-important question in that long period will be to what extent these countries will find it possible to obtain support from the various other powers, and on what social systems they will be able to rely for assistance.

If, on the other hand, there should be a third world war, then the tendencies which have arisen in recent decades and greatly strengthened the position of the Asiatic peoples, transforming them from passive objects of world history into active subjects in the shaping of world history, will in all probability make themselves felt even more vigorously because by comparison with the United States, Europe, Russia and Japan the Asiatic countries are much less vulnerable to an atomic war. The recuperation forces which would begin to operate after such a war would then in all probability arise more strongly amongst the Asiatic half of the world's population.

Fritz Sternberg.

London, May 1951.

SOURCES

PART ONE

CHAPTER I

[1] Vierteljahrshefte zur Konjunkturforschung, Sonderheft 31. "Entwicklungstendenzen der deutschen und internationalen Industrieproduktion 1860–1932", Berlin, 1933, p. 18.
[2] "Historical Statistics of the United States, 1789–1945", United States Department of Commerce, 1949, p. 25.
[3] Clark, Colin, "The Conditions of Economic Progress", Macmillan, London, 1940, pp. 83, 95, 107.
[4] "Löhne und Lebenskosten in West-Europa im 19. Jahrhundert", Schriften des Vereins für Sozialpolitik, Munich, 1914, No. 145, Part 3. p. 99, "Die Bewegungen des Arbeitslohn in Gross-Britannien im Laufe des 19 Jahrhunderts". Also "Wages in the United Kingdom in the Nineteenth Century", by Arthur L. Bowley, C.U.P., 1900, p. 126.
[5] "Deutsche Wirtschaftskunde", Statistisches Reichsamt, Reimer Hobbing, Berlin, 1930, p. 104.
[6] Clark, Colin, "The Conditions of Economic Progress", pp. 449–50.
[7] Ibid., p. 461.
[8] Buchanan, D. H., "The Development of Capitalist Enterprise in India", Harvard Pubs., Cam., Mass., 1934, p. 450.

CHAPTER II

[1] Supan, Professor Alexander, "Die Territoriale Entwicklung der Europäischen Kolonien", Gotha, 1906.
[2] Marx, Karl, "Ausgewählten Schriften", Vol. II, Zurich, 1934, pp. 627–8.
[3] Robequain, Charles, "The Economic Development of French Indo-China", O.U.P., London, 1944, p. 269.
[4] Keith, A. B., "Speeches and Documents on Indian Policy, 1750–1921", World's Classics, London, 1922, Vol. I, p. 215.
[5] Robequain, Charles, "The Economic Development of French Indo-China", pp. 82–3.
[6] Lenin, Vladimir I., "Imperialism, the Highest Stage of Capitalism", Foreign Languages Publ. Hse., Moscow, 1947. Hilferding, Rudolf, "Das Finanzkapital", Vienna, 1910.

CHAPTER III

[1] Sombart, Werner, "Sozialismus und soziale Bewegung", Jena, 1919, pp. 97–8.
[2] Marx, Karl, "Das Kapital", Hamburg, 1894, Vol. III, p. 226.
[3] Marx, Karl, "Ausgewählte Schriften", Zurich, 1934, Vol. II, p. 449.
[4] Pinner, Felix, "Die grossen Weltkrisen", Max Niehans Verlag, Zurich, 1937, pp. 38–49.
[5] "Statistical Tables and Reports on Trade Unions", Fourth Report, 1891, p. 523.
[6] Marx, Karl, "Das Kapital", Vol. I, pp. 477–9.
[7] Tugan-Baranovsky, "Studien zur Theorie und Geschichte der Handelskrisen in England", Jena, 1901, pp. 258–60.

T

[8] Ibid., p. 282.
[9] Engels, Friedrich, "Die Lage der arbeitenden Klasse in England", Dietz Verlag, Stuttgart, 1913, p. 18. Engl. ed., Allen & Unwin, Ltd., London.
[10] Tugan-Baranovsky, "Studien zur Theorie und Geschichte der Handelskrisen in England", pp. 41–2.
[11] Ibid., pp. 40–1.
[12] Ibid., pp. 43–4.
[13] Marx, Karl, "Das Kapital", p. 454.
[14] Nehru, Jawahar-Lal, "The Discovery of India", Meridian Books, London, 1946, pp. 279–99.
[15] Ibid., pp. 299–300.
[16] Interim Report of the European Recovery Programme, Vol. I, Paris, 1948.
[17] Ibid., Part III, p. 2.
[18] Schumpeter, Joseph, "Business Cycles", McGraw-Hill, London, New York, 1939, Vol. II, p. 494.
[19] Hobson, J. A., "Imperialism", Allen & Unwin, London, 1948.
[20] Ibid., pp. 51–3.
[21] Ibid., pp. 80–1.
[22] Ibid., p. 85.
[23] Ibid., p. 47.

CHAPTER IV

[1] Dewhurst, Frederick J., and Associates, "America's Needs and Resources", The Twentieth Century Fund, New York, 1947, p. 32.
[2] "Historical Statistics of the United States 1789–1945", Bureau of the Census, 1949, p. 21.
[3] Marx, Karl, "Das Kapital", Vol. I, pp. 813–14.
[4] Slichter, Sumner H., "The American Tariff and World Trade", *Atlantic Monthly*, December, 1945, p. 61.

CHAPTER V

[1] Marx, Karl, "Ausgewählte Schriften", Moscow, 1934, Vol. I, pp. 203–11.
[2] Marx, Karl, "Das Kapital".
[3] "Deutsche Wirtschaftskunde", Berlin, 1933.
[4] "Statistical Abstract of the United States", U.S. Department of Commerce, 1948, p. 190.
[5] "Internationale Pressekorrespondenz", August 28th, 1928, p. 1713.
[6] Marx, Karl, "Das Kapital", Hamburg, 1921, Vol. III, Part 2, pp. 153–4.
[7] Sternberg, Fritz, "Der Imperialismus", Malik Verlag, Berlin, 1926, p. 501.
[8] "Statistical Abstract of the United States", p. 603.
[9] Barger and Landsberg, "American Agriculture", National Bureau of Economic Research, New York, 1942, p. 4.
[10] Clark, Colin, "The Conditions of Economic Progress", p. 182.
[11] Ibid., p. 185.

CHAPTER VI

[1] Zweig, Konrad, "Strukturwandlungen und Konjunkturschwingungen im englischen Aussenhandel der Vorkriegszeit", *Weltwirtschaftliches Archiv*, Vol. 30, July 1929, No. 1, pp. 102–3.
[2] Ibid., p. 103.
[3] Ibid., p. 103.
[4] Ibid., p. 102.

[5] Ibid., p. 59.
[6] Vierteljahrshefte zur Konjunkturforschung, Sonderheft 31, "Die Indus-triewirtschaft", Berlin, 1933, p. 12.
[7] Ibid., p. 17.
[8] Beveridge, W. H., "Population and Unemployment", *Economic Journal*, Vol. 33, 1932, p. 462.
[9] Reichstagsdenkschrift, No. 564, 1906–1907.

PART TWO

CHAPTER I

[1] Marx, Karl, "Ausgewählten Schriften", Zurich, 1934, Vol. II, pp. 476–7.
[2] Helfferich, Carl, "Der Weltkrieg", Vol. II. "Vom Kriegsausbruch bis zum uneingeschränkten U-Bootskrieg", Berlin, 1919, pp. 41–2.
[3] Reichsarchiv, "Der Weltkrieg 1914–1918", Vol. I, "Kriegsrüstung und Kriegswirtschaft", Berlin, 1930, pp. 341–2.
[4] Delbrück, Clemens von, "Die wirtschaftliche Mobilmachung in Deutschland 1914", *Verlag für Kulturpolitik*, Munich, 1924, pp. 101–2.
[5] Bethmann-Hollweg, Theobald von, "Betrachtungen zum Weltkrieg", Berlin, 1919.
[6] Delbrück, Clemens von, "Die wirtschaftliche Mobilmachung in Deutschland 1914", pp. 101–2.
[7] Engels, Friedrich, "Sozialismus in Deutschland", *Die Neue Zeit*, Year 1891–1892, Vol. I, p. 580.
[8] Ibid., p. 586.
[9] Ibid., pp. 585–6.

CHAPTER II

[1] Friedensberg, Ferdinand, "Kohle und Eisen im Weltkrieg und in den Friedensschlüssen", Oldenburg, Munich and Berlin, 1934, p. 62.
[2] Ibid.

CHAPTER III

[1] Luxemburg, Rosa, "Die Akkumulation des Kapitals", Berlin, 1921, pp. 117–18.
[2] Lenin, Vladimir I., "Sämtliche Werke", Vol. XX, p. 181.
[3] Baykov, Alexander, "The Development of the Soviet Economic System", C.M.P., 1946, p. 29.
[4] "Deutsche Wirtschaftskunde", Berlin, 1940, p. 109.

CHAPTER IV

[1] Schub, David, "Lenin—A Biography", Doubleday & Co., New York, 1948, p. 366.
[2] Lenin, Vladimir I., "Ausgewählte Werke", Vol. VII, p. 283.
[3] Ibid., p. 298.
[4] Ibid., pp. 406–7.
[5] Ibid., p. 4.
[6] Schub, David, "Lenin—A Biography", p. 130.
[7] Lenin, Vladimir I., "Ausgewählte Werke", Vol. V, pp. 179, 201.
[8] Ibid., p. 9.
[9] Marx, Karl, "Ausgewählte Schriften", Vol. II, p. 682.

PART THREE

Chapter I

[1] Organization for European Economic Co-operation, Interim Report on the European Recovery Programme, Vol. I, Paris, 1948.
[2] Hertz, Frederick, "The Economic Problem of the Danubian States", Gollancz, London, 1947, p. 194.
[3] Ibid., p. 194.
[4] Farley, Miriam S., "The Problem of Japanese Trade Expansion in the Post-War Situation", Institute of Pacific Relations, New York, 1939, p. 81.
[5] League of Nations, "Network of World Trade", Geneva, 1942, p. 29.
[6] Ibid.
[7] Mitchell, Kate L., "Industrialization of the Western Pacific", 1942, p. 102.
[8] "Die Wirtschaft des Auslandes 1900–1927", Einzelschriften zur Statistik des Deutschen Reiches, No. 5, Berlin, 1928, p. 697.
[9] "Japan-Manchukuo Year Book", 1940.
[10] Pelzer, Karl J., "Population and Land Utilization", Institute of Pacific Relations, New York, 1941, p. 118.
[11] Norman, E. H., "Japan's Emergence as a Modern State", N.Y., 1940, p. 118.
[12] Schumpeter, E. B., "The Industrialization of Japan and Manchukuo, 1930–1940", Macmillan, New York, 1940, p. 273.
[13] Greene, Katrine R. C., and Phillips, Joseph D., "Transportation and Foreign Trade", Economic Survey of the Pacific Area, Part II, Institute of Pacific Relations, New York, 1942, p. 161.
[14] Economic Survey of the Pacific Area, p. 181.
[15] "The United States in World Economy", Economic Series, No. 23, United States Department of Commerce, Washington, 1943, p. 31.

Chapter II

[1] Kusnetz, Simon, "National Product in Wartime", National Bureau of Economic Research, N.Y., 1945, p. 148.
[2] "Historical Statistics of the United States", p. 180.
[3] Vierteljahrshefte zur Konjunkturforschung, Sonderheft 31, Berlin, 1933, pp. 20 & 39.
[4] Berle, Adolf, and Means, Gardiner C., "The Modern Corporation and Private Property", Macmillan, New York, 1939, pp. 19, 28 & 32.
[5] Ibid., pp. 33–5, 40–1.
[6] "Historical Statistics of the United States", p. 179.
[7] "Statistical Abstract of the United States, 1942", U.S. Government Printing Office, Washington, 1943, p. 479.
[8] Moulton, Harold G., "Controlling Factors in Economic Development", The Brookings Institute, Washington, 1949, pp. 69–70.
[9] Barger, Harold, and Landsberg, Hans H., "American Agriculture 1899–1939", National Bureau of Economic Research Inc., New York, 1942, p. 231, and U.S. Bureau of the Census, "Trends in the Proportion of the Nation's Labor Force engaged in Agriculture 1820–1940", Press Release, March 28th, 1942.
[10] Barger, Harold, and Landsberg, Hans H., Ibid., p. 245.
[11] "Yearbook of Agriculture", 1928, pp. 8–9.
[12] Lewis, Cleona, "America's State in International Investments", The Brookings Institute, Washington, 1938, pp. 447, 450.
[13] "Statistical Abstract of the United States, 1942", pp. 552–3.

580

[14] Moulton, Harold G., "Controlling Factors in Economic Development", p. 70.
[15] Hansen, Alvin H., "Business-Cycle Theory", University of Minnesota, 1927.
[16] Zweig, Konrad, "Die internationale Kapitalwanderung vor und nach dem Kriege", *Weltwirtschaftliches Archiv*, Vol. 27, April 1928, No. 2, pp. 249–50.
[17] "Employment Policy", H.M. Stationery Office & Macmillan, New York, 1945, p. 42.
[18] Beveridge, Sir William, "Full Employment in a Free Society", W. W. Norton & Co., New York, 1945, p. 42.
[19] *Economist*, February 24th, 1945, p. 250.
[20] Lederer, Professor, "Strukturwandlungen der deutschen Volkswirtschaft", Vol. I, p. 51.
[21] Vierteljahrshefte zur Konjunturforschung, Sonderheft 31, "Die Industriewirtschaft", Berlin, 1933, pp. 30–2.
[22] Ibid., p. 33.
[23] *Wirtschaft und Statistik*, 1930, p. 894.
[24] "Deutsche Wirtschaftskunde", Reich's Statistical Office, Berlin, 1933, p. 297.
[25] "Konjunkturstatistisches Handbuch 1933", Institut für Konjunkturforschung, Berlin, 1933, p. 15.
[26] "Kapitalbildung und Investitionen in der deutschen Volkswirtschaft 1924–1928", Institut für Konjunkturforschung, Berlin, p. 112.
[27] Sombart, Werner, "Das Wirtschaftsleben im Zeitalter des Hochkapitalismus", Munich and Leipzig, 1928, Vol. III, Part 2, p. 702.
[28] Baykov, Alexander, "The Development of the Soviet Economic System", pp. 8, 13.
[29] Ibid., p. 15.
[30] Lenin, "Collected Works", Vol. XVIII, Part 2, pp. 31–2.
[31] Ibid., pp. 67, 343–4.
[32] Ibid., Vol. XVII, p. 348.
[33] Baykov, Alexander, "The Development of the Soviet Economic System", p. 122.

CHAPTER III

[1] League of Nations, "Statistical Year Book 1938–1939", pp. 180–1.
[2] Institut für Konjunkturforschung, Sonderheft, Berlin, p. 43.
[3] Voytinsky, Vladimir, "The Social Consequences of the Economic Depression", Geneva, 1936, pp. 142–3.
[4] League of Nations, "Statistical Year Book 1933–1934", p. 195.
[5] Voytinsky, Vladimir, "The Social Consequences of the Economic Depression", pp. 66–7.
[6] Ibid., p. 66.
[7] Marx, Karl, "Das Kapital", Hamburg, 1894, Vol. III, Part 2, "An Interpolation of Engels", pp. 259–60.
[8] Schumpeter, Joseph, "Business Cycles", p. 908.
[9] Vierteljahrshefte zur Konjunkturforschung, Sixth Year, Vol. B, p. 42.
[10] Institut für Konjunkturforschung, Sonderheft, Berlin, p. 7.
[11] Ibid., p. 7.
[12] Lebergott, Stanley, *Journal of the American Statistical Association*, March 1948, Vol. 43, No. 241.
[13] "Konjunkturstatistisches Jahrbuch 1933", Berlin, pp. 80, 124.
[14] Sternberg, Fritz, "Der Niedergang des deutschen Kapitalismus", Berlin, 1932.
[15] Marx, Karl, "Kritik der politischen Oekonomie".

[16] Sternberg, Fritz, "Der Niedergang des deutschen Kapitalismus", pp. 330–5.
[17] "Kommunistische Internationale", 1931, Vol. 17–18, p. 799.
[18] "Reichstagshandbuch", 1924, 1928, 1930 and 1932.
[19] "Deutsche Wirtschaftskunde", 1933, p. 397.
[20] "Reichstagshandbuch", Sixth Election Period, 1932.
[21] Voytinsky, Vladimir, "The Social Consequences of the Economic Depression", p. 77.
[22] Stalin, Joseph, Speech at the 15th Party Congress, Verbatim Report, p. 67.
[23] "Control Figures of the National Economy of the U.S.S.R. for 1928–1929", p. 2.
[24] Baykov, Alexander, "The Development of the Soviet Economic System", p. 307.
[25] Ibid., p. 213.
[26] Vierteljahrsheft zur Konjunkturforschung, Sonderheft No. 31, Berlin, p. 42.
[27] Stalin, Joseph, "Leninism", Lawrence & Wishart, London, 1940, pp. 277–8.
[28] Baykov, Alexander, "The Development of the Soviet Economic System", p. 325.

CHAPTER IV

[1] "The United States in World Economy", Economic Series No. 23. U.S. Department of Commerce, Washington, 1943, p. 188.
[2] League of Nations , "Statistical Year Book 1938–1939", pp. 180–1.
[3] Ibid.
[4] Ibid., p. 180.
[5] Federal Reserve Board.
[6] League of Nations, "Statistical Year Book 1938–1939", p. 65.
[7] Ibid., p. 219.
[8] "Statistical Abstract of the United States, 1942", p. 550.
[9] Address of the President, Jan. 4th, 1935, House Document No. 1, 75 Con., 1. Sess.
[10] U.S. Department of Commerce, Bureau of Foreign and Domestic Commerce, Survey of Current Business (July 1944).
[11] Mitchell, Broadus, "Depression Decade", Rinehart & Co., New York, 1947, p. 268.
[12] Barck, Oscar T., and Blake, Nelson M., "Since 1900", New York, 1947, pp. 543–4.
[13] Mitchell, Broadus, "Depression Decade", pp. 306, 308.
[14] "The Structure of American Economy", Washington, 1939, p. 107.
[15] Ibid., p. 161.
[16] Berle, Adolf, and Means, Gardiner C., "The Modern Corporation and Private Property", p. 46.
[17] Mitchell, Broadus, "Depression Decade", p. 179.
[18] Ibid., pp. 180–1.
[19] Ibid., p. 202.
[20] "Historical Statistics of the United States 1789–1945", p. 99.
[21] Beveridge, Sir William, "Full Employment in a Free Society".
[22] League of Nations, "Statistical Year Book 1938–1939", p. 181.
[23] Baykov, Alexander, "The Development of the Soviet Economic System", p. 303.
[24] Wochenbericht des Deutschen Instituts für Konjunkturforschung, April 30th, 1940.
[25] Baykov, Alexander, "The Development of the Soviet Economic System", pp. 274–5.

26 Ibid., p. 331.
27 Ibid., p. 325.
28 Ibid., p. 325.
29 Vucinich, Alexander, "The Kolkhoz", *American Slavic and East European Review*, Vol. VIII, No. 1, February 1949, p. 10.
30 Ibid., pp. 15–6.
31 Ibid., p. 17.
32 Ibid., p. 12.
33 Goldsmith, Raymond W., "The Power of Victory", Munitions Output in World War II, Military Affairs, Spring 1946.

PART FOUR

CHAPTER I

1 Churchill, Winston S., "The Gathering Storm", Houghton Mifflin Co., Boston, 1948, p. 216.
2 "Combat", November 1938, quoted by Charles A. Micaud in "The French Right and Nazi Germany", Duke University Press, 1943.
3 Churchill, Winston S., "The Gathering Storm," pp. 362–3 & 365.

CHAPTER II

1 Churchill, Winston S., "The Gathering Storm", p. 336.
2 Goldsmith, Raymond W., "The Power of Victory", p. 75.
3 Ibid., pp. 73–4.
4 Spalcke, Major Karl, "Kriegswirtschaftliche Jahresberichte 1936", Hanseatische Verlagsanstalt, 1936, pp. 165, 172.
5 Haudann, Dr Ervin, "Das Motorisierungspotential der Sowjet-union", Hanseatische Verlagsanstalt, Hamburg, 1937, p. 40.
6 Ibid., p. 114.
7 Sternberg, Fritz, "Germany and a Lightning War", Faber & Faber, London, 1938, pp. 97–8.
8 Goldsmith, Raymond W., "The Power of Victory", p. 73.
9 Ibid., p. 75.
10 Voznessensky, Nikolai A., "The Economy of the U.S.S.R. during World War II", Public Affairs Press, Washington, 1948, p. 22.
11 Tolstoy, Count Leo Nikolaevitch, "War and Peace", quoted from the New York edition 1932, pp. 894, 896 & 913–14.
12 Halder, General, quoted from *New York Times*, December 14th, 1948.
13 Goldsmith, Raymond W., "The Power of Victory", p. 75.
14 Ibid., p. 75.
15 Ibid., p. 72.
16 Ibid., p. 70.
17 Stimson, Henry L., and McGeorge Bundy, "On Active Service in Peace and War", Harper Bros., N.Y., 1947.
18 Goldsmith, Raymond W., "The Power of Victory", pp. 75–6.
19 Ibid., p. 75.
20 Ibid., p. 77.
21 Stillwell, General Joseph W., "The Stillwell Papers", New York, 1948, pp. 190–1 & 340.
22 Fairbank, John King, "The United States and China", Harvard U.P., Cambridge, Mass., 1948, pp. 199–200.
23 Goldsmith, Raymond W., "The Power of Victory", p. 75.

[24] Ibid., p. 76.
[25] Ibid., p. 78.
[26] Marshall, G. C., "Ten Eventful Years", World War II, pp. 768–9.

PART FIVE

CHAPTER I

[1] Clausewitz, General Carl von, "Vom Kriege", Vier Falken Verlag, Berlin, p. 553.
[2] Nehru, Jawahar-Lal, "Glimpses of World History", Lindsay Drummond, London, 1939, pp. 69–70.
[3] Clausewitz, General Carl von, "Vom Kriege", p. 36.
[4] Ibid.
[5] Ibid., p. 32.

CHAPTER II

[1] The Economic Report of the President, Washington, 1950, p. 163.
[2] "Economic Concentration and World War II", U.S. Government Printing Office, Washington, 1946, p. 37.
[3] The Economic Report of the President, Washington, 1950.
[4] Ibid., pp. 37, 39 and 40.
[5] Ibid., pp. 40 and 42.
[6] Ibid., pp. 40 and 42.
[7] "Historical Statistics of the United States", 1949, p. 72.
[8] The Economic Report of the President, Washington, January 1948.
[9] United Nations Economic Survey of Europe in 1948, Geneva 1949, p. 23.
[10] Ibid.
[11] The Economic Report of the President, 1950, p. 55.
[12] Ibid., p. 78.
[13] Voznessensky, Nikolai A., "The Economy of the U.S.S.R. during World War II", pp. 86–7.
[14] "Statistical Year Book", United Nations 1948, New York, 1949.
[15] Vierteljahrshefte zur Konjunkturforschung, Sonderheft No. 31, Berlin, 1933, p. 38.
[16] United Nations Economic Survey of Europe in 1948, p. 4.
[17] "Briefwechsel zwischen Engels und Marx, Bebel und Bernstein", Vol. II, p. 293.
[18] *New York Times*, September 11th, 1947.
[19] Williams, Francis, "Socialist Britain", Viking Press, New York, 1949, pp. 101–3.
[20] *Economist*, March 19th, 1949, p. 503.
[21] Williams, Francis, "Socialist Britain", p. 112.
[22] *Economist*, January 21st, 1950, pp. 120–1.
[23] Ibid.
[24] Williams, Francis, "Socialist Britain", p. 113.
[25] *Economist*, January 21st, 1950, p. 120.
[26] Williams, Francis, "Socialist Britain", p. 115.

INDEX

German Society, 354–6; German peasants, 355–6; German urban middle strata, 356–8; German working class, 359–60; social stability and coalition between U.S.A., Great Britain, and Russia, 412–3; stagnation in working-class movement, 413–9

"Classic" capitalist development, 35

Clausewitz, Karl von (1780–1831), 469–71, 473, 474, 482–3.

Clerks employed in U.S.A. (1900), 94

Cleveland Corporation, interests and assets, 342

Clothing industry: wages in Germany and U.S.A., 1900, 85

Coal: late development of, 23; production, 1855–1913 (tables), 23, 123, 126; role in first world war, 165–7; in Manchuria, 230; in Russia, 317

Collectivization of agriculture, 375–6

Colonies: under capitalism, 30–1; population and income, 31–2; growth of in Africa and Asia, 1876–1900 (table), 37; markets in, 38–9; changing social structure in, 39–40; Marx on industrial development in, 40–2; Imperialism and feudalism join hands, 42–4; backwardness of industrial development, 43–4; markets opened with imperialist expansion, 44–6; raw materials produced in, 46–7; standards of living, 46–7; "a vast system of outdoor relief for upper classes", 74; essential to European capitalist expansion, 88; standard of living, 101; "free" trade and "free" workers, 115; class stratification in, 119–21; feudalism and agriculture maintained, 120; intercolonial trade restricted, 120; industrial working class not created, 120; Europe's position undermined, 179–80; post-war trade stagnation, 221; industrial development artificially hampered, 223; imperialism allied to feudalism, 225–7; national-revolutionary movements, 225; Japanese developments, 230–2; during economic crises, 313; stagnation in, 324; anti-imperialism in Asia, 366–71; Japan's war and European colonial empires, 454–5, 456; U.S.A. expansion in underdeveloped areas, 507–8; European imperialism and remains of colonial possessions, 535–7

Combination Laws, repeal of, 54

Communications: percentage of U.S. working population engaged in, 1850–1910 (table), 109

Communist International, 275, 301–2; policy of, and German Socialism, 303–5; and "acute revolutionary situation", 320; subservience to Russia, 407

Communist Manifesto, 19, 27, 30, 51, 78–9, 91, 93–4, 102, 104

Communist Parties: all subservient to Russian dictation, 275–6; pawns of Nazi-Soviet Pact, 407; weakened by Russian intervention, 415–6

Communist Party, Chinese, 452–4

Communists, German: and Nazi movement, 298, 303; and disruption of Socialist Party, 302; on the 1930 elections, 303–5; poll in Reichstag elections, 1924–32 (tables), 307–8; and "acute revolutionary situation", 320

Communist Unions: German worker and employee members (table), 112

Concentration, industrial, in U.S.A., 1939–45 (diagram), 490–2

Confiscations by Bolshevists, 205

Congress Movement, India, 368 *et seq.*

Congress of Industrial Organization, U.S.A., 338, 492–4

Consumer-goods, increased production of, 23; shortage in Russia, 272–3

Consuming power, maldistribution of, 76

Consumption and production related to economic crisis, 48 *et seq.*

Coolidge, Calvin, 249

Copper, production in Russia, 1913–39, 317

Corn Laws, repeal of, 55

Cornwallis, 1st Marquess of: Permanent Land Settlement in India, 42

Corporations, industrial, 93, 95 *n.*; assets of, in U.S.A., 241

Cost of living: U.S.A., 1890–1933 (table), 289–90; Germany, 290; Great Britain, 1929–33, 312

Cotton industry: Marx on the development of, 54–5; exports and tariffs, 59 *n.*; number of spindles, 1875–1913 (table), 123, 124; British consumption, 1855–1913 (table), 126; controlled in China, 224–5

Craftsmen, hand, displaced by capitalist development, 57, 58

Cripps, Sir Stafford, 455

Crises, economic: during rise of capitalism, 47–77; over-production, 48–9; in pre-capitalist societies, 48; capitalist and socialist explanations of crises, 49–52; during domestic capitalist development, 52–60; not solved by increased exports, 59–60; reasons for severity of crises, 60; in period of imperialist expansion, 60–70; less violent crises, 70–7; irregular intervals between, 72–3; imperialism and economic crisis, 73–7; in the period of progress in U.S.A., 87–8; new

social structure of agriculture in industrial Europe, 183–5; post-war impoverishment, 184–5; inflation and urban middle strata, 185–6; post-war standards of living, 187–8; investments in Russia repudiated, 217; capitalist expansion halted, 217–8; trade with Japan, 219; decline of American markets, 220–1; hampering of colonial industry, 223; effect of U.S. expansion, 233–4; U.S. loans, 234; trade with S. America, Canada, Mexico, 235–6; trade with China, 235–6; from 1918–1929, 250–76; the 1929 world crisis, 283 *et seq.*; situation compared with U.S.A., 295; compulsory military service in, 351; the threat of Nazi Germany, 398 *et seq.*; stagnation in working-class movement, 413–9; colonial empires and Japanese war, 454–5; civilian losses in second world war, 461–2; no longer decisive in world politics, 486; production, 1937–47, 497; sphere for U.S. expansion, 504–6; the satellite States, 520–5; transformation of, 533–4; declining influence in Eurasia, 534–5; imperialism and remains of colonial possessions, 535–7; foreign trade and the Marshall Plan, 537–41; a debtor area, 541; dependence on the United States, 553–5; an important factor for peace, 564–8

Europe, Eastern, 101

Expansion, capitalist, 34; halted between the two wars, 216–8; halted outside Europe, 219–21; reasons for decline, 324–5

Exports: Increased exports not a solution to economic crises, 59–60; and the labour market, 63, 66

Exports, British: growth and decline, 123–4; endangered by Germany, 124–6; dependence on, 125; 1913, 1918–39, 251; 1929–33, 311–2

Exports, capital, 39, 181–2

Exports, Chinese, 1913–29 (table), 225

Exports: Cotton, 54

Exports: European and non-European countries, 1851 (table), 29

Exports, German: 1913–29 (table), 261; and reparations, 262–7

Exports, Indian, 222–3, 229

Exports, invisible, 69

Exports, Japanese, 229

Exports, Netherlands, 223

Exports, Russian: 1913–20 (table), 180; 1920–8, 273; 1929–33 (table), 319–20; 1909–38 (table), 374

Exports, U.S.A., 84; 1871–5 and 1910–4, 88; agricultural, 1911–30 (tables), 246 *et seq.*; 1929–38 (table), 333; 1919–20 and 1946–7, 501–3

Exports, world, 1929–33 (table), 281; 1929–38, 329

Expropriation, by Bolshevists, 204

Factories, confiscated in Russia, 205

Fairbank, John King, 33 *n.*, 224 *n.*

Feudalism: joins hands with imperialism, 42–4, 115–6, 225–6; remnants in Germany and England, 116–9; maintained in Colonies, 120; destruction of, in Asia, 557

Fishing, a "primary" industry, 109 *n.*; percentage of U.S. working population engaged in, 1850–1910 (table), 109

Foodstuffs: capitalist development of, 23; imports in U.S.A., 88; U.K. consumption, 1855–1913 (table), 126; controlled by State in war, 169

Foreign-political tensions before 1914, 142

Forestry, a "primary" industry, 109 *n.*; percentage of U.S. population engaged in, 1850–1910 (table), 109

Formosa: trade with Japan, 232

"Fourth Estate" in Europe = working class of metropolitan centres, 118

France: rise of industrial production, 1860–1913 (table), 21–2; pig iron, steel, and coal production, 1855–1913, 23; national and individual incomes, 1850–1913 (table), 26–7, 32; real wages, 1850–1900, 27; exports and imports, 1851, 29; colonial possessions, 1876–1900 (table), 37; colonial industrial development, 41; dominant capitalism, 46; English exports to, 1840–50, 59 *n.*; holdings of U.S. securities, 84; rise in real wages, 100; working-class percentage of population, 103; industrial development compared with Great Britain, Germany, and U.S.A., 122 *et seq.*; iron, cotton, coal, and steel production, 1875–1913 (tables), 122–4; independent of food imports, 125; colonial possessions safe, 129; the Entente Cordiale, 137–8, 143; war of revenge for 1870, 138; increased military expenditure, 140; standard of living on eve of first war, 141; fears of social revolution and defeatism, 143; alliance with Russia, 143; army in 1914, 155; reorganization for total war, 159; casualties, 165; coal and steel areas in German occupation, 166–7; decline of production, 178–9; the 1929 crisis, 178–9; war loans, 185; inflation, 186, 187; paying for the war, 186; foreign investments lost, 187; post-war military situation, 192; colonial trade, 223; in China, 223–4; percentage of

589

world production, 230; U.S. loans, 234; trade with S. America, 1913–29, (table), 235–6; and reparations, 263 *n.*; no "hope" of social revolution, 271; index of industrial production, 1930–2 (table), 277, 278; 1929 crisis and Germany, 296–9; from crisis to world war, 346–50; industrial production, 1929–38, 346 *et seq.*; elections, 346; "Popular Front", 346, 349; agriculture, 347–8; eve of war, 391 *et seq.*; industrial production, 399–400; Popular Front Government, 400 *et seq.*; failure of discussions in Moscow, 404–6; stagnation of working-class movement, 417; instability of Social system and Hitler's initial victories, 421; complete defeat of, 422; casualties, 460; productive developments, 463 *et seq.*; growth of army, 474

Franco, General, 402 *et seq.*

Franco-Prussian war, 122–3, 133, 137, 188, 473; compared with First World War, 144–5; supplies of armaments for, 157–8

Franco-Russian alliance, 143

Frederick II, the Great, King of Prussia, 158, 165, 469, 473, 475

Freedom, in Russia, after March and November Revolutions, 207

Free trade, 115

French Revolution, 469, 470

French Second Empire, 188

Friedensberg, Ferdinand, 166

Gas production, a "secondary" industry, 109 *n.*

General Elections: United Kingdom, 1929, 127

German Business Research Institute, reports of, 21

German Empire, under Peace Treaties, 192

German High Command, 189

Germany: development of capitalism in 19–20, 35; rise of industrial production, 1860–1913 (table), 21–2; pig-iron, steel, and coal production, 1855–1913, 23; capital and consumer goods, 1855–1913, 24; urban and rural population, 1875–1900, 25; national and individual incomes, 1860–1913 (table), 26–7, 32; number of workers, 1875–1907 (table), 28; exports and imports, 1851, 29; extension of English capitalism to, 36; colonial possessions, 1876–1900 (table), 37; dominant capitalism, 46; foreign trade, 63; production curves, 71; struggle for new markets, 75; holding of U.S. Securities, 84; wages compared with U.S. levels, 1900 (table), 85; the "Erfurter Programme", 93;

agriculture and independent industries, 1875, 94; occupational census (1925), 94–5; rise in real wages, 100; social stratification, 1882–1925 (diagram), 103; number and extent of agricultural holdings, 1822, 1895, and 1907 (table), 105–6; independent operators in agriculture and industry, 1925, 108; undertakings engaged in trade and in industry, 1875–1907, 111; associations and political groupings of employees (table), 112–3; influence of feudal remnants, 116–9; industrial developments compared with Great Britain, U.S.A., and France, 122 *et seq.*; foreign political antagonisms, 122 *et seq.*; iron, coal, cotton, and steel production, 1870–1913 (tables), 122–4; growing exports and British foreign trade, 124–6; independent of food imports, 125; export of capital and consumer goods, 1880–1913 (table), 125; exports of iron and steel, 125; without an Empire, 127–9; capital investments abroad, 127; colonial trade negligible, 128; geographical situation unfavourable to imperialism, 129–31; building a navy, 129–30; alternatives for imperialist drive, 129–30; leader of hostile block against U.K., 131; Berlin–Bagdad Railway and Pan-Slavism, 139; increased military expenditure, 140; national income and military expenditure, 141; no fears of social revolutions, 143; alliance with Austria-Hungary, 143; Franco-German war and German hegemony, 144; war on two fronts, 145, 160, 162; no expenditure on armaments, 145; prepared only for short war, 145–6; no economic general staff, no food stores, and no industrial mobilization, 146–8; Social Democracy, 151; Engels on duty of German Socialists, 152; outbreak of war, 156; lightning decision needed, 156–7; French and Russian fronts, 157; failure to make economic and industrial preparation led to defeat, 157–9; defeat at the Marne decisive, 158–9; population under arms, 159; the turn to the East, 159–61; effect of British naval blockade, 161; effect of U.S. exports to western Allies, 161; errors of the High Command, 162–3; the last offensive, 163; cleavage between High Command and Parliament, 163; reasons for defeat, 163–4; power of State increased, 168; Nazi war-preparation economy, 170 *n.*; decline of production, 198; H.P. capacity used in industry, 1875–1907,

596

German Navy 129.

Engels of W War 151-3